JOHN ADAMS

John Adams

REVOLUTIONARY WRITINGS
1775–1783

Gordon Wood, editor

THE LIBRARY OF AMERICA

The paper used in this publication meets the
minimum requirements of the American National Standard for
Information Sciences—Permanence of Paper for Printed
Library Materials, ANSI z39.48—1984.

Distributed to the trade in the United States
by Penguin Group (USA) Inc.
and in Canada by Penguin Books Canada Ltd.

Library of Congress Catalog Card Number: 2010930473
ISBN: 978–1–59853–090–2

First Printing
The Library of America—214

Manufactured in the United States of America

John Adams: Revolutionary Writings 1775–1783
is published with support from

THE ANDREW W. MELLON FOUNDATION

and

THE BODMAN FOUNDATION

Contents

COMMISSIONER TO FRANCE AND FRAMER OF THE
MASSACHUSETTS CONSTITUTION, 1778–1779

PEACE NEGOTIATOR WITH BRITAIN AND MINISTER TO THE NETHERLANDS, 1779–1783

THE CONTINENTAL CONGRESS
1775–1777

To Abigail Adams

My Dear   Hartford May 2d. 1775
Mr. Eliot of Fairfield, is this Moment arrived in his Way
to Boston. He read us a Letter from the Dr. his Father dated
Yesterday Sennight being Sunday. The Drs. Description of
the Melancholly of the Town, is enough to melt a Stone. The
Tryals of that unhappy and devoted People are likely to
be severe indeed. God grant that the Furnace of Affliction may
refine them. God grant that they may be relieved from their
present Distress.

It is Arrogance and Presumption in human Sagacity to pretend to penetrate far into the Designs of Heaven. The most
perfect Reverence and Resignation becomes us. But, I cant
help depending upon this, that the present dreadfull Calamity
of that beloved Town is intended to bind the Colonies together in more indissoluble Bands, and to animate their Exertions, at this great Crisis in the Affairs of Mankind. It has this
Effect, in a most remarkable Degree, as far as I have yet seen or
heard. It will plead, with all America, with more irresistable
Perswasion, than Angells trumpet tongued.

In a Cause which interests the whole Globe, at a Time,
when my Friends and Country are in such keen Distress, I am
scarcely ever interrupted, in the least Degree, by Apprehensions for my Personal Safety. I am often concerned for you and
our dear Babes, surrounded as you are by People who are too
timorous and too much susceptible of allarms. Many Fears and
Jealousies and imaginary Dangers, will be suggested to you,
but I hope you will not be impressed by them.

In Case of real Danger, of which you cannot fail to have
previous Intimations, fly to the Woods with our Children.
Give my tenderest Love to them, and to all.

"OH THAT I WAS A SOLDIER!"

To Abigail Adams

My Dear   Phyladelphia May 29. 1775

Our amiable Friend Hancock, who by the Way is our President, is to send his Servant, tomorrow for Cambridge. I am to send a few Lines by him. If his Man should come to you to deliver this Letter, treat him very kindly, because he is a kind, humane, clever Fellow.

My Friend Joseph Bass, very cleverly caught the Small Pox, in two days after we arrived here, by Inoculation and has walked about the streets, every day since, and has got quite over it and quite well. He had about a Dozen Pimples upon the whole. Let his Father and Friends know this.

We are distressed here for Want of Intelligence and Information from you and from Boston, Cambridge &c. &c. &c. We have no regular Advices. I received one kind Letter from you, in one from Coll. Warren. An excellent Letter, I had from him. It has done him great Honour, and me much good.

My Duty and Love to all. I have had miserable Health and blind Eyes almost ever since I left you, but, I found Dr. Young here, who after scolding at me, quantum sufficit for not taking his Advice, has pill'd and electuary'd me into pretty good Order. My Eyes are better, my Head is better, and so are my Spirits.

Private. The Congress will support the Massachusetts. There is a good Spirit here. But We have an amazing Field of Business, before us. When I shall have the Joy of Meeting you and our little ones, I know not.

The military Spirit which runs through the Continent is truly amazing. This City turns out 2000 Men every day. Mr. Dickinson is a Coll.—Mr. Reed a Lt. Coll.—Mr. Mifflin a Major. He ought to have been a Genl. for he has been the animating Soul of the whole.

Coll. Washington appears at Congress in his Uniform and, by his great Experience and Abilities in military Matters, is of much service to Us.

Oh that I was a Soldier!—I will be.—I am reading military Books.—Every Body must and will, and shall be a soldier.

John Adams

To Moses Gill

Dr Sir   Phyladelphia June 10. 1775

It would be a Relief to my Mind, if I could write freely to you concerning the Sentiments Principles, Facts and Arguments which are laid before us, in Congress: But Injunctions, and Engagements of Honour render this impossible. What I learn out of Doors among Citizens, Gentlemen, and Persons of all Denominations is not so sacred. I find that the general Sense abroad is to prepare for a vigorous defensive War, but at the Same Time to keep open the Door of Reconciliation—to hold the sword in one Hand and the Olive Branch in the other —to proceed with Warlike Measures, and conciliatory Measures Pari Passu.

I am myself as fond of Reconciliation, if We could reasonably entertain Hopes of it upon a constitutional Basis, as any Man. But, I think, if We consider the Education of the Sovereign, and that the Lords the Commons, the Electors, the Army, the Navy, the officers of Excise, Customs &c., &c., have been now for many years gradually trained and disciplined by Corruption to the System of the Court, We shall be convinced that the Cancer is too deeply rooted, and too far spread to be cured by any thing short of cutting it out entire.

We have ever found by Experience that Petitions, Negociation every Thing which holds out to the People Hopes of a Reconciliation without Bloodshed is greedily grasped at and relyed on—and they cannot be perswaded to think that it is so necessary to prepare for War as it really is. Hence our present Scarcity of Powder &c.

However, this Continent is a vast, unweildy Machine. We cannot force Events. We must Suffer People to take their own

Way in many Cases, when We think it leads wrong—hoping
however and believing, that our Liberty and Felicity will be
preserved in the End, tho not in the Speedyest and Surest
Manner.

In my opinion Powder and Artillery are the most efficacious, Sure, and infallibly conciliatory Measures We can adopt.

Pray write me, by every opportunity—and beseech my
Friends to write. Every Letter I receive does great good. The
Gentleman to whom most Letters from our Province is ad-
dressed, has not Leisure to make the best use of them.

There are three Powder Mills in this Province—two in New
York but no Nitre—cant the Mass. begin to prepare both?
Pray write me, minutely the State of the People of Boston, and
our Army &c. Pray let me know if Mrs. Gill and Mr. Boylstone
are out of Prison. I have never heard and have sufferd much
Anxiety on their Account. My best Respects to them if they are
to be seen by you.

"AMERICA IS A GREAT, UNWIELDY BODY"

To Abigail Adams

June 17

I can now inform you that the Congress have made Choice
of the modest and virtuous, the amiable, generous and brave
George Washington Esqr., to be the General of the American
Army, and that he is to repair as soon as possible to the Camp
before Boston. This Appointment will have a great Effect, in
cementing and securing the Union of these Colonies.—The
Continent is really in earnest in defending the Country. They
have voted Ten Companies of Rifle Men to be sent from Pensylvania, Maryland and Virginia, to join the Army before
Boston. These are an excellent Species of Light Infantry. They
use a peculiar Kind of [   ] call'd a Rifle—it has circular or
[   ] Grooves within the Barrell, and carries a Ball, with
great Exactness to great Distances. They are the most accurate
Marksmen in the World.

I begin to hope We shall not sit all Summer.

I hope the People of our Province, will treat the General with all that Confidence and Affection, that Politeness and Respect, which is due to one of the most important Characters in the World. The Liberties of America, depend upon him, in a great Degree.

I have never been able to obtain from our Province, any regular and particular Intelligence since I left it. Kent, Swift, Tudor, Dr. Cooper, Dr. Winthrop, and others wrote me often, last Fall—not a Line from them this Time.

I have found this Congress like the last. When We first came together, I found a strong Jealousy of Us, from New England, and the Massachusetts in Particular. Suspicions were entertained of Designs of Independency—an American Republic—Presbyterian Principles—and twenty other Things. Our Sentiments were heard in Congress, with great Caution—and seemed to make but little Impression: but the longer We sat, the more clearly they saw the Necessity of pursuing vigorous Measures. It has been so now. Every Day We sit, the more We are convinced that the Designs against Us, are hostile and sanguinary, and that nothing but Fortitude, Vigour, and Perseverance can save Us.

But America is a great, unwieldy Body. Its Progress must be slow. It is like a large Fleet sailing under Convoy. The fleetest Sailors must wait for the dullest and slowest. Like a Coach and six—the swiftest Horses must be slackened and the slowest quickened, that all may keep an even Pace.

It is long since I heard from you. I fear you have been kept in continual Alarms. My Duty and Love to all. My dear Nabby, Johnny, Charly and Tommy come here and kiss me.

We have appointed a continental Fast. Millions will be upon their Knees at once before their great Creator, imploring his Forgiveness and Blessing, his Smiles on American Councils and Arms.

My Duty to your Uncle Quincy—your Papa, Mama and mine—my Brothers and sisters and yours.

Adieu.

WASHINGTON'S APPOINTMENT

To Elbridge Gerry

Dear Sir　　　　　　　　　　　Philadelphia, 18 June, 1775

I have at last obtained liberty, by a vote of Congress, to acquaint my friends with a few of the things that have been done.

The Congress have voted, or rather a committee of the whole house have unanimously agreed, that the sum of two million dollars be issued in bills of credit, for the redemption of which, in a certain number of years, twelve colonies have unanimously pledged themselves.

The Congress has likewise resolved that fifteen thousand men shall be supported at the expense of the continent; ten thousand at Massachusetts, and five thousand at New York; and that ten companies of riflemen be sent immediately; six from Pennsylvania, two from Maryland, and two from Virginia, consisting of sixty-eight privates in each company, to join our army at Boston. These are said to be all exquisite marksmen, and by means of the excellence of their firelocks, as well as their skill in the use of them, to send sure destruction to great distances.

General Washington is chosen commander-in-chief, General Ward the first major-general, and General Lee the second, (the last has not yet accepted,) and Major Gates adjutant-general. Lee and Gates are experienced officers. We have proceeded no further as yet.

I have never, in all my lifetime, suffered more anxiety than in the conduct of this business. The choice of officers, and their pay, have given me great distress. Lee and Gates are officers of such great experience and confessed abilities, that I thought their advice, in a council of officers, might be of great advantage to us; but the natural prejudices, and virtuous attachment of our countrymen to their own officers, made me apprehensive of difficulties. But considering the earnest desire of General Washington to have the assistance of these officers, the extreme attachment of many of our best friends in the southern colonies to them, the reputation they would give to our arms in Europe, and especially with the ministerial generals and army in Boston, as well as the real American merit of them both, I could not withhold my vote from either.

The pay which has been voted to all the officers, which the Continental Congress intends to choose, is so large, that I fear our people will think it extravagant, and be uneasy. Mr. Adams, Mr. Paine, and myself, used our utmost endeavors to reduce it, but in vain.

Those ideas of equality, which are so agreeable to us natives of New England, are very disagreeable to many gentlemen in the other colonies. They had a great opinion of the high importance of a continental general, and were determined to place him in an elevated point of light. They think the Massachusetts establishment too high for the privates, and too low for the officers, and they would have their own way.

I hope the utmost politeness and respect will be shown to these officers on their arrival. The whole army, I think, should be drawn up upon the occasion, and all the pride, pomp, and circumstance of glorious war displayed;—*no powder burned, however.*

There is something charming to me in the conduct of Washington. A gentleman of one of the first fortunes upon the continent, leaving his delicious retirement, his family and friends, sacrificing his ease, and hazarding all in the cause of his country! His views are noble and disinterested. He declared, when he accepted the mighty trust, that he would lay before us an exact account of his expenses, and not accept a shilling for pay. The express waits.

MILITARY POMP

To Abigail Adams

My Dear   Philadelphia June 23. 1775
I have this Morning been out of Town to accompany our Generals Washington, Lee, and Schuyler, a little Way, on their Journey to the American Camp before Boston.

The Three Generals were all mounted, on Horse back, accompanied by Major Mifflin who is gone in the Character of

Aid de Camp. All the Delegates from the Massachusetts with their Servants, and Carriages attended. Many others of the Delegates, from the Congress—a large Troop of Light Horse, in their Uniforms. Many Officers of Militia besides in theirs. Musick playing &c. &c. Such is the Pride and Pomp of War. I, poor Creature, worn out with scribbling, for my Bread and my Liberty, low in Spirits and weak in Health, must leave others to wear the Lawrells which I have sown; others, to eat the Bread which I have earned.—A Common Case.

We had Yesterday, by the Way of N. York and N. London, a Report, which distresses us, almost as much as that We had last fall, of the Cannonade of Boston. A Battle at Bunkers Hill and Dorchester Point—three Colonels wounded, Gardiner mortally. We wait to hear more particulars. Our Hopes and our Fears are alternately very strong. If there is any Truth in this Account, you must be in great Confusion. God Almightys Providence preserve, sustain, and comfort you.

June 27

This Moment received two Letters from you. Courage, my dear! We shall be supported in Life, or comforted in Death. I rejoice that my Countrymen behaved so bravely, tho not so skillfully conducted as I could wish. I hope this defect will be remedied by the new modelling of the Army.

My Love every where.

FALSE HOPES IN CONGRESS

To James Warren

Dear Sir   Phyladelphia June 6th. 1775
Every Line I receive from you, gives me great Pleasure, and is of vast Use to me in the public Cause. Your Letters were very usefull to me last Fall. Your Character became then known, and much esteemed. The few Letters I have received from you this Time, have increased the Desire of more, and some other Gentlemen who happened to know you, particularly Governor Hopkins and Ward of Rhode Island have con-

firmed, every Good opinion which had been formed. I must intreat you to omit no Opportunity of Writing and to be as particular as possible.

Want of frequent Communication and particular Intelligence led us into the unfortunate Arrangement of General Officers, which is likely to do so much Hurt. We never received the most distant Intimation of any Design to new model your Army; and indeed Some of Us, were obliged to give up our own Judgments merely from Respect to What We took to be the Arrangement of our provincial Congress. I have made it my Business ever Since I heard of this Error, to wait upon Gentlemen of the Congress at their Lodgings, and else where to let them into the secret and contrive a Way to get out of the Difficulty, which I hope We shall effect.

I rejoice to hear of the great military Virtues and Abilities of General Thomas.

Alass poor Warren! Dulce et decorum est pro Patria mori. Yet I regret his Appointment to such a Command. For God Sake my Friend let us be upon our Guard, against too much Admiration of our greatest Friends. President of the Congress Chairman of the Committee of safety, Major General and Chief surgeon of the Army, was too much for Mortal, and This Accumulation of Admiration upon one Gentleman, which among the Hebrews was called Idolatry, has deprived us forever of the Services of one of our best and ablest Men. We have not a sufficient Number of such Men left to be prodigal of their Lives in future.

Every Brain is at Work to get Powder and salt Petre. I hope We shall succeed: but We must be very Œconomical of that Article. We must not use large Cannon, if We can possibly avoid it.

This Letter will go by two fighting Quakers. Mr. Stephen Collins and Mr. John Kaighn. The first is the most hospitable benevolent man alive. He is a Native of Lynn—a Brother of Ezra Collins of Boston,—is rich, and usefull here. The last has been the Instrument of raising a Quaker Company in this City, who behave well, and look beautifully in their Uniforms. My Love, Duty, Respects &c where due, Adieu,   John Adams

Secret and confidential, as the Saying is,

The Congress, is not yet So much alarmed as it ought to be. There are Still hopes, that Ministry and Parliament, will immediately receed, as Soon as they hear of the Battle of Lexington, the Spirit of New York and Phyladelphia, the Permanency of the Union of the Colonies &c. I think they are much deceived and that We shall have nothing but Deceit and Hostility, Fire, Famine, Pestilence and Sword, from Administration and Parliament. Yet the Colonies like all Bodies of Men must and have their Way and their Honour, and even their Whims.

These Opinions of Some Colonies which are founded I think in their Wishes and Passions, their Hopes and Fears, rather than in Reason and Evidence will give a whimsical Cast to the Proceedings of this Congress. You will see a Strange Oscilation between Love and Hatred, between War and Peace. Preparations for War, and Negociations for Peace. We must have a Petition to the King, and a delicate Proposal of Negociation &c. This Negociation I dread like Death. But it must be proposed. We cant avoid it. Discord and total Disunion would be the certain Effect of a resolute Refusal to petition and negociate. My Hopes are that Ministry will be afraid of Negociation as well as We, and therefore refuse it. If they agree to it, We shall have occasion for all our Wit, Vigilence and Virtue to avoid being deceived, wheedled, threatned or bribed out of our Freedom.

If We Strenuously insist upon our Liberties, as I hope and are pretty sure We shall, however, a Negotiation, if agreed to, will terminate in Nothing. It will effect nothing. We may possibly gain Time and Powder and Arms.

You will see an Address to the People of G. Britain another to those of Ireland, and another to Jamaica.

You will also see a Spirited Manifesto. We ought immediately to dissolve all Ministerial Tyrannies, and Custom houses, set up Governments of our own, like that of Connecticutt in all the Colonies, confederate together like an indissoluble Band, for mutual defence and open our Ports to all Nations immediately. This is the system that your Friend has aimed at promoting from first to last; But the Colonies are not yet ripe for it. A Bill of Attainder, &c may soon ripen them.

July 6, 1775

BENJAMIN FRANKLIN

To Abigail Adams

My Dear   July 23 1775
    You have more than once in your Letters mentioned Dr.
Franklin, and in one intimated a Desire that I should write you
something concerning him.

    Dr. Franklin has been very constant in his Attendance on
Congress from the Beginning. His Conduct has been composed and grave and in the Opinion of many Gentlemen very
reserved. He has not assumed any Thing, nor affected to take
the lead; but has seemed to choose that the Congress should
pursue their own Principles and sentiments and adopt their
own Plans: Yet he has not been backward: has been very usefull, on many occasions, and discovered a Disposition entirely
American. He does not hesitate at our boldest Measures, but
rather seems to think us, too irresolute, and backward. He
thinks us at present in an odd State, neither in Peace nor War,
neither dependent nor independent. But he thinks that We
shall soon assume a Character more decisive.

    He thinks, that We have the Power of preserving ourselves,
and that even if We should be driven to the disagreable Necessity of assuming a total Independency, and set up a separate
state, We could maintain it. The People of England, have
thought that the Opposition in America, was wholly owing to
Dr. Franklin: and I suppose their scribblers will attribute the
Temper, and Proceedings of this Congress to him: but there
cannot be a greater Mistake. He has had but little share farther
than to co operate and assist. He is however a great and good
Man. I wish his Colleagues from this City were All like him,
particularly one, whose Abilities and Virtues, formerly trumpeted so much in America, have been found wanting.

    There is a young Gentleman from Pensylvania whose Name
is Wilson, whose Fortitude, Rectitude, and Abilities too,
greatly outshine his Masters. Mr. Biddle, the Speaker, has been
taken off, by Sickness. Mr. Mifflin is gone to the Camp, Mr.
Morton is ill too, so that this Province has suffered by the Timidity of two overgrown Fortunes. The Dread of Confiscation,

or Caprice, I know not what has influenced them too much: Yet they were for taking Arms and pretended to be very valiant.—This Letter must be secret my dear—at least communicated with great Discretion. Yours,   John Adams

FRUSTRATION WITH A "PIDDLING GENIUS"

To James Warren

Dear Sir   Philadelphia, July 24th, 1775
    In Confidence,—I am determined to write freely to you this Time.—A certain great Fortune and piddling Genius whose Fame has been trumpeted so loudly, has given a silly Cast to our whole Doings—We are between Hawk and Buzzard—We ought to have had in our Hands a Month ago, the whole Legislative, Executive and Judicial of the whole Continent, and have compleatly moddelled a Constitution, to have raised a Naval Power and opened all our Ports wide, to have arrested every Friend to Government on the Continent and held them as Hostages for the poor Victims in Boston. And then opened the Door as wide as possible for Peace and Reconcilliation: After this they might have petitioned and negotiated and addressed, &c. if they would.—Is all this extravagant?—Is it wild?—Is it not the soundest Policy?
    One Piece of News—Seven Thousand Weight of Powder arrived here last Night—We shall send along some as soon as we can—But you must be patient and frugal.
    We are lost in the extensiveness of our Field of Business—We have a Continental Treasury to establish, a Paymaster to choose, and a Committee of Correspondence, or Safety, or Accounts, or something, I know not what that has confounded us all Day.
    Shall I *hail* you Speaker of the House, Counsellor or what—What Kind of an Election had you? What Sort of Magistrates do you intend to make?
    Will your new Legislative and Executive feel bold, or irresolute? Will your Judicial hang and whip, and fine and im-

prison, without Scruples? I want to see our distressed Country once more—yet I dread the Sight of Devastation.

You observe in your Letter the Oddity of a great Man—He is a queer Creature—But you must love his Dogs if you love him, and forgive a Thousand Whims for the Sake of the Soldier and the Scholar.

Addressed, To the Hon. JAMES WARREN, Watertown. Favor'd by Mr. Hitchborne.

"THE GREAT AMERICAN CAUSE"

To Josiah Quincy

Dear Sir   Philadelphia. July 29th. 1775

I had yesterday the honour of your letter of July the eleventh, and I feel myself much obliged, by your kind attention to me and my family, but much more by your care of the public safety, and the judicious and important observations you have made. Your letters Sir, so far from being "a burden," I consider as an honour to me, besides the pleasure and instruction they afford me. Believe me, Sir, nothing is of more importance to me, in my present most arduous, and laborious employment, than a constant correspondence, with gentlemen of figure and experience, whose characters are known. The minutest fact, the most trivial event, that is connected with the great American Cause, becomes important, in the present critical situation of affairs, when a Revolution seems to be in the designs of Providence, as important, as any that ever happened in the affairs of mankind.

We jointly lament the loss of a Quincy, and a Warren; two characters, as great in proportion to their age, as any that I have ever known in America. Our country mourns the loss of both, and sincerely sympathises with the feelings of the mother of the one, and the father of the other. They were both my intimate friends, with whom I lived and conversed, with pleasure and advantage. I was animated by them, in the painful, dangerous course, of opposition to the oppressions brought upon our Country; and the loss of them, has wounded me too deeply, to be easily healed. "Dulce, et decorum est pro Patria mori."

The ways of Heaven are dark and intricate; but you may remember the words, which many years ago you and I, fondly admired, and which upon many occasions I have found advantage in recollecting.

> Why should I grieve,—when grieving I must bear.
> And take with guilt,—what guiltless I might share?

I have a great opinion of your knowledge, and judgment, from long experience, concerning the channels and islands in Boston harbour; but I must confess your opinion that the harbour might be blocked up, and seamen and soldiers made prisoners, at discretion, was too bold and enterprising for me, who am not apt to startle at a daring proposal; but I believe I may safely promise you powder enough, in a little time for any purpose whatever. We are assured in the strongest manner, of saltpetre, and powder, in sufficient plenty another year of our own make. That both are made in this city, you may report with confidence, for I have seen both, and I have seen a set of very large powder works, and another of saltpetre.

I hope Sir, we shall never see a total stagnation of commerce, for any length of time. Necessity will force open our ports. Trade if I mistake not will be more free than usual. Your friend Dr. Franklin, to whom I read your letter, and who desires his compliments to you; has been employed in directing the construction of row gallies for this city. The Committee of safety for this province have ordered twenty of them to be built, some of them are finished. I have seen one of them, it has twelve oars on each side. They rowed up the river the first time, four miles in an hour, against a tide which ran down four miles an hour. The Congress have recommended to the Colonies, to make provision for the defence of their navigation, in their harbours, rivers, and on their sea coasts. Of a floating Battery I have no idea—am glad you are contriving one. You tell me Sir, that General Lee complained that "he did not find things, as the Massachusetts Delegates had represented them." What General Lee could mean by this Sir, I know not. What particulars he found different from the representation, I do not know—nor do I know which delegate from the Massachusetts, he received a mistaken representation from. I think he should have been particular, that he might not have ran the risque of doing an injury. If General Lee should do injustice, to two of the Massachusetts delegates, he would commit ingratitude at the same time, for to two of them, he certainly owes his promotion in the American army, how great a hazard soever, they ran in agreeing to it. I know him very thoroughly I think, and that he will do great service in our army, at the beginning of things, by forming it to order, skill, and discipline. But we shall soon have officers enough. Your friend, and humble servant,

TEACHING SAMUEL ADAMS TO RIDE

To James Warren

Dr sir   Philadelphia Septr. 17. 1775
    I have nothing in particular to write. Our most gracious K– – – has given a fresh Proof of his Clemency, in his Answer to the City. But no more of Politicks, at present—if this Scratch of a Pen should fall into the Hands of the wiseacre Gage, as long as I confine myself, to Matrimony, and Horsemanship, there will be no Danger.
    Be it known to you then that two of the most unlikely Things, within the whole Compass of Possibility, have really, and actually happened. The first is the suden Marriage of our President, whose agreable Lady honours us with her Presence and contributes much to our good Humour, as well as to the Happiness of the President. So much for that.
    The next Thing is more wonderfull still.
    You know the Aversion, which your Secretary, has ever entertained to riding, on Horseback. He never would be perswaded to mount a Horse. The last time we were here, I often laboured to perswade him, for the Sake of his Health, but in vain.
    Soon after We sat out, on the last Journey, I reflected that some Degree of Skill and Dexterity in Horsemanship, was

necessary to the Character of a Statesman. It would take more Time and Paper than I have to Spare, to shew the Utility of Horsemanship to a Politician; so I shall take this for granted. But I pointed out the particulars to him, and likewise shewed him that Sociability would be greatly promoted, by his mounting one of my Horses.

On Saturday the second day of September 1775, in the Town of Grafton He was prevailed on to put my servant with his, into Harrisons Chaise and to mount upon my Horse, a very genteel, and easy little Creature.

We were all disappointed and Surprized, instead of the Taylor riding to Brentford We beheld, an easy, genteel Figure, upon the Horse, and a good deal of Spirit and facility, in the Management of the Horse, insomuch that We soon found our Servants were making Some disagreable Comparisons, and Since our Arrival here I am told that Fessenden (impudent Scoundrel!) reports that the Secretary rides fifty per Cent better than your Correspondent.

In this manner, We rode to Woodstock, where we put up for the Sabbath. It was Soon observed that the Secretary, could not Sit So erect in his Chair as he had Sat upon his Horse, but Seemed to be neither sensible of the Disease or the Remedy. I Soon perceived and apprised him of both. On Sunday Evening, at Mr. Dexters, where we drank Coffee and Spent an agreable Evening I perswaded him to purchase, two yards of flannell which we carried to our Landlady, who, with the assistance of a Taylor Woman in the House, made up a Pair of Drawers, which the next Morning were put on, and not only defended the Secretary from any further Injury, but entirely healed the little Breach which had been begun.

Still an Imperfection, remained. Our Secretary had not yet learned to mount and dismount—two Servants were necessary to attend upon these occasions, one to hold the Bridle and Stirrup, the other to boost the Secretary. This was rather a ridiculous Circumstance Still. At last, I undertook to instruct him the necessary Art of mounting. I had my Education to this Art, under Bates, the celebrated Equerry, and therefore might be Supposed to be a Master of it. I taught him, to grasp the Bridle, with his Right Hand over the Pummell of his Saddle, to place his left Foot firm in the Stirrup; to twist his left

Hand into the Horses Main, about half Way between his Ears and his Shoulders, and then a vigorous Exertion of his Strength would carry him very gracefully into the Seat, without the least Danger of falling over on the other Side. The Experiment was tryed and Succeeded to Admiration.

Thus equipped and instructed, our Horseman rode all the Way from Woodstock to Philadelphia, sometimes upon one of my Horses, Sometimes on the other. And Acquired fresh Strength, Courage, Activity and Spirit every day. His Health is much improved by it, and I value myself, very much upon the Merit of having probably added Several years, to a Life So important to his Country, by the little Pains I took to perswade him to mount and teach him to ride.

Sully and Cecil were both Horsemen, and you know I would not have our American, inferiour to them in the Smallest Accomplishment.

Pray Mrs. Warren to write to me. I would to her, if I had half so much Time.

From the Diary: September 24, 1775

1775. SEPTR. 24. SUNDAY.

Dyer is very sanguine that the 2 De Witts, one of Windham, the other of Norwich, will make Salt Petre in large Quantities. He produces a Sample, which is very good.

Harrison is confident that Virginia alone will do great Things from Tobacco Houses. But my faith is not strong, as yet.

Ld. North is at his old Work again. Sending over his Anodynes to America—deceiving one credulous American after another, into a Belief that he means Conciliation, when in Truth he means nothing but Revenge. He rocks the cradle, and sings Lullaby, and the innocent Children go to Sleep, while he prepares the Birch to whip the poor Babes. One Letter after another comes that the People are uneasy and the Ministry are sick of their Systems. But nothing can be more fallacious. Next Spring We shall be jockied by Negociation, or have hot Work in War. Besides I expect a Reinforcement to Gage and to Carlton, this fall or Winter.

Heard Mr. Smith of Pequay, at about 40 Miles towards Lancaster, a Scotch Clergyman, of great Piety as Coll. Roberdeau says: The Text was Luke 14:18. And they all with one Consent began to make excuse.—This was at Duffills Meeting. In the afternoon, heard our Mr. Gordon, in Arch Street. The Lord is nigh unto all that call upon him.

Call'd upon Stephen Collins who has just returned.

Stephen has a Thousand Things to say to Us, he says. A Thousand observations to make.

One Thing he told me, for my Wife, who will be peeping here, sometime or other, and come across it. He says when he call'd at my House, an English Gentleman was with him, a Man of Penetration, tho of few Words. And this silent, penetrating Gentleman was pleased with Mrs. Adams, and thought her, the most accomplished Lady he had seen since he came out of England.—Down Vanity, for you dont know who this Englishman is.

Dr. Rush came in. He is an elegant, ingenious Body. Sprightly, pretty fellow. He is a Republican. He has been much in London. Acquainted with Sawbridge, McCaulay, Burgh, and others of that Stamp. Dilly sends him Books and Pamphletts, and Sawbridge and McCaulay correspond with him. He complains of D. Says the Committee of Safety are not the Representatives of the People, and therefore not their Legislators; yet they have been making Laws, a whole Code for a Navy. This Committee was chosen by the House, but half of them are not Members and therefore not the Choice of the People. All this is just. He mentions many Particular Instances, in which Dickenson has blundered. He thinks him warped by the Quaker Interest and the Church Interest too. Thinks his Reputation past the Meridian, and that Avarice is growing upon him. Says that Henry and Mifflin both complained to him very much about him. But Rush I think, is too much of a Talker to be a deep Thinker. Elegant not great.

In the Evening Mr. Bullock and Mr. Houstoun, two Gentlemen from Georgia, came into our Room and smoked and chatted, the whole Evening. Houstoun and Adams disputed the whole Time in good Humour. They are both Dabbs at

Disputation I think. H. a Lawyer by Trade is one of Course, and Adams is not a Whit less addicted to it than the Lawyers. The Q. was whether all America was not in a State of War, and whether We ought to confine ourselves to act upon the defensive only. He was for acting offensively next Spring or this fall if the Petition was rejected or neglected. If it was not answered, and favourably answered, he would be for acting vs. Britain and Britains as in open War vs. French and frenchmen. Fit Privateers and take their Ships, any where.

These Gentlemen give a melancholly Account of the State of Georgia and S. Carolina. They say that if 1000 regular Troops should land in Georgia and their commander be provided with Arms and Cloaths enough, and proclaim Freedom to all the Negroes who would join his Camp, 20,000 Negroes would join it from the two Provinces in a fortnight. The Negroes have a wonderfull Art of communicating Intelligence among themselves. It will run severall hundreds of Miles in a Week or Fortnight.

They say, their only Security is this, that all the Kings Friends and Tools of Government have large Plantations and Property in Negroes. So that the Slaves of the Tories would be lost as well as those of the Whiggs.

I had nearly forgot a Conversation with Dr. Coombe concerning assassination, Henry 4., Sully, Buckingham &c. &c. Coombe has read Sullys Memoirs with great Attention.

HOPING TO LEAVE CONGRESS

To James Warren

Dr Sir   Philadelphia Septr. 26. 1775

This Afternoon, and not before I received a Line from the excellent Marcia, which is the first and only Letter I have received from the Family to which She belongs Since I left Watertown. Be pleased to thank her for this Favour, and to let her know that She must certainly have misinterpretted Some Passage in my Letter Since I never thought either Politicks or War, or any other Art or Science beyond the Line of her Sex:

on the contrary I have ever been convinced that Politicks and War, have in every age, been influenced, and in many, guided and controuled by her Sex. Sometimes it is to be feared by the unworthy Part of it: but at others, it must be confessed by the amiable and the good. But, if I were of opinion that it was best for a general Rule that the fair should be excused from the arduous Cares of War and State; I should certainly think that Marcia and Portia, ought to be Exceptions, because I have ever ascribed to those Ladies, a Share and no small one neither, in the Conduct of our American Affairs.

I have nothing new to communicate. Every Thing, has been done, and is now doing, to procure the *Unum Necessarium*: I wish I could give you a more agreable account of the Salt Petre Works in this City. I fear they have chosen injudiciously a Place for their Vatts, Vaults and Buildings, a low marshy Place which was lately overflowed by the Storm. Still We have Sanguine Accounts of the Skill and Success of some operators.

Coll. Dyer produces a Sample of excellent Salt Petre, made by two De Witts, one of Norwich the other of Windham, and he is confident that they can and will make large Quantities. Coll. Harrison of Virginia, whose Taste in Madeira, I know, and in Girls I believe, and in Salt Petre I hope to be much Superiour to his Judgment in Men, is very confident that they are making large Quantities from Tobacco House Earth, in his Colony.

We are hourly expecting Intelligence from Canada, as well as Massachusetts, and from London.

My dear sir, Let me intreat you to do every Thing in your Power to get ready the Accounts of all that our Province has done and expended in the Common Cause, for which they expect or hope to be reimbursed by the United Colonies. It has ever appeared to me a Thing of much Importance, that We should be furnished with these Accounts as soon as possible. From present appearances, our session will not be long, and if We should not be furnished with the Necessary Papers, very soon, We shall not be able to obtain any Reimbursement this Fall: and the next Spring We may be involved in so many Dangers, as well as new Expences as to render our Chance for obtaining Justice, more precarious. You know that your Delegates have been here, almost the whole Time since the Commencement of Hostilities, and therefore can say nothing of their own Knowledge concerning your Exertions or Expences, but must depend altogether upon Information from the General Court.

This is really a Strong Reason for a Change in the Delegation. We have been absent so long from our native Country as to be a Kind of Aliens and strangers there. If it is good Policy to reelect one of the old Delegates, because he is personally knowing to what has passed here; it is equally good Policy to elect Some new ones, because they are Witnesses of what has passed with you. For my own Part, as my political Existence terminates with the Year, I Sincerely wish to be excused in the next Election. I long to be a little with you in the General Court, that I may see and hear, and feel with my Countrymen. And I ardently wish to be a little with my Family, and to attend a little to my private Affairs. To be frank and candid to a Friend, I begin to feel for my Family, to leave all the Burthen of my private Cares, at a Time when my affairs are in so much Perplexity, to an excellent Partner, gives me Pain for her. To leave the Education of a young Family, entirely to her, altho I know not where it could be better lodged, gives me much Concern for her and them.

I have very little Property, you very well know, which I have not earned myself, by an obstinate Industry, in opposition to the Malice of a very infirm Constitution, in Conjunction with the more pernicious Malice of Ministerial and gubernatorial Enemies. Of the little Acquisition's I have made, five hundred Pounds sterling is sunk in Boston in a Real Estate, four hundred sterling more is compleatly annihilated in a Library that is now wholly useless to me and mine, and at least four hundred sterling more, is wholly lost to me, in Notes and Bonds not one farthing of the Principal or Interest of which, can I obtain, and the Signers are dying, breaking, flying every day.

It is now compleatly two years since my Business has been totally ruined by the public Confusions. I might modestly estimate the Profit of my Business before this Period at three hundred sterling a Year, perhaps more. I think therefore I may fairly estimate myself a sufferer immediately, to the amount of two Thousand Pounds sterling. I have purchased Lands, which these Causes have prevented me from paying for, and the

Interest is running on without a Possibility of my paying it, and I am obliged to hire Labour yearly upon my Farm to no Small amount.

In the mean Time, all that has been granted me by the general Court for the sessions of this Congress last Fall and this Spring has not defreyed my necessary Expences, however strange it may appear.

The Conclusion from all this is, that I am rushing rapidly into Perplexities and Distresses in my private Affairs from which I can never extricate myself. By retreating from public Life, in some Measure I might, preserve myself and Family from a Ruin, which without it will be inevitable. I am willing to sink with my Country, but it ought not to be insisted on that I Should Sink myself without any Prospect of contributing by that Means to make it Swim. I have taken my Trick at Helm, when it was not easy to get Navigators who would run the Risque of the storm. At present the Course is plain whatever the Weather may be, and the prospect of that is much better than it was when I was called to assist in steering the ship.

"THE TRADE OF AMERICA"

To James Warren

Dr sir   Philadelphia Octr. 7th. 1775

The Debates, and Deliberations in Congress are impenetrable Secrets: but the Conversations in the City, and the Chatt of the Coffee house, are free, and open. Indeed I wish We were at Liberty to write freely and Speak openly upon every Subject, for their is frequently as much Knowledge derived from Conversation and Correspondence, as from Solemn public Debates.

A more intricate and complicated Subject never came into any Mans thoughts, than the Trade of America. The Questions that arise, when one thinks of it, are very numerous.

If The Thirteen united Colonies, Should immediately Surcease all Trade with every Part of the World, what would be the Consequence? In what manner, and to what degree, and how soon, would it affect, the other Parts of the World? How would it affect G. B. Ireland, the English West India Islands, the French, the Dutch the Danish, the Spanish West India Islands? How would it affect the Spanish Empire on the Continent? How would it affect the Brazills and the Portuguese Settlements in America? If it is certain that it would distress Multitudes in these Countries, does it therefore follow that it would induce any foreign Court to offer Us Assistance, and to ask us for our Trade or any Part of it? If it is questionable Whether foreign States would venture upon Such Steps, which, would perhaps be Violations of Treatises of Peace, and certainly would light up a War in Europe is it certain that Smugglers, by whom I mean private Adventurers belonging to foreign Nations, would come here, through all the Hazards they must run. Could they be suffered to clear out for America in their own Custom houses? Would they not run the risque of Seizure from their own Custom house officers, or of Capture from their own Men of War? Would they not be liable to be visited by British Men of War, in any Part of the ocean, and if found to have no Clearances be seized? When they arrived on any Part of the Coast of N. America, would they not be seized by Brittish Cutters, Cruizers, Tenders, Frigates without Number: But if their good Fortune should escape all these Risques, have We harbours or Rivers, sufficiently fortified, to insure them Security while here? In their Return to their own Country would they not have the Same Gauntlett to run.

In Short, if We Stop our own ships, have We even a Probability that the ships of foreign Nations, will run the Venture to come here, either with or without the Countenance and Encouragement of their severall Courts or States public or private open or secret? It is not easy for any Man precisely and certainly to answer this Question. We must then say all this is uncertain.

Suppose then We assume an intrepid Countenance, and send Ambassadors at once to foreign Courts. What Nation shall We court? Shall We go to the Court of France, or the Court of Spain, to the States General of the United Provinces? To the Court of Lisbon, to the Court of Prussia, or Russia, or Turkey or Denmark, or Where, to any, one, more, or all of these? If We should is there a Probability, that Our Ambassadors would be received, or so much as heard or seen by any Man or Woman in Power at any of those Courts. He might possibly, if well skilled in intrigue, his Pocketts well filled with Money and his Person Robust and elegant enough, get introduced to some of the Misses, and Courtezans in Keeping of the statesmen in France, but would not that be all.

An offer of the Sovereignty of this Country to France or Spain would be listened to no doubt by Either of those Courts, but We should suffer any Thing before We should offer this. What then can We offer? An Alliance, a Treaty of Commerce? What Security could they have that We should keep it. Would they not reason thus, these People intend to make Use of Us to establish an Independency but the Moment they have done it: Britain will make Peace with them, and leave Us in the Lurch And We have more to dread from an Alliance between Britain and the United Colonies as an independent state, than We have now they are under one corrupted Administration. Would not Spain reason in the same manner, and say further our Dominions in South America be soon a Prey to these Enterprizing and warlike Americans, the Moment they are an independent State. Would not our proposals and Agents be treated with Contempt! And if our Proposals were made and rejected, would not this sink the Spirits of our own People, Elevate our Enemies and disgrace Us in Europe.

If then, it not be Safe to Stop our own Ships entirely, and trust to foreign Vessells coming here either with or without Convoy of Men of War, belonging to foreign States, what is to be done? Can our own People bear a total Cessation of Commerce? Will not Such Numbers be thrown out of Employment, and deprived of their Bread, as to make a large discontented Party? Will not the Burthen of supporting these Numbers, be too heavy upon the other Part of the Community? Shall We be able to maintain the War, wholly without Trade? Can We support the Credit of our Currency, without it?

If We must have Trade how shall We obtain it? There is one Plan, which alone, as it has ever appeared to me, will answer the End in some Degree, at first. But this is attended with So many Dangers to all Vessells, certain Loss to many, and So much Uncertainty upon the whole, that it is enough to make any Man, thoughtfull. Indeed it is looked upon So wild, extravagant and romantic, that a Man must have a great deal of Courage, and much Indifference to common Censure, who should dare to propose it.

"God helps those who help themselves," and it has ever appeared to me since this unhappy Dispute began, that We had no Friend upon Earth to depend on but the Resources of our own Country, and the good sense and great Virtues of our People. We shall finally be obliged to depend upon ourselves.

Our Country furnishes a vast abundance of materials for Commerce. Foreign Nations, have great Demands for them. If We should publish an Invitation to any one Nation or more, or to all Nations, to send their ships here, and let our Merchants inform theirs that We have Harbours where the Vessells can lie in Safety, I conjecture that many private foreign Adventurers would find Ways to send Cargoes here thro all the Risques without Convoys. At the Same Time our own Merchants, would venture out with their Vessells and Cargoes, especially in Winter, and would run thro many Dangers, and in both these Ways together, I should hope We might be supplied with Necessaries.

All this however Supposes that We fortify and defend our own Harbours and Rivers. We may begin to do this. We may build Row Gallies, flatt bottomed Boats, floating Batteries, Whale Boats, Vesseaux de Frize, nay Ships of War, how many, and how large I cant say. To talk of coping Suddenly with G. B. at sea would be Quixotish indeed. But the only Question with me is can We defend our Harbours and Rivers? If We can We can trade.

TRADE AND VIRTUE

To James Warren

Dr sir   Octr. 19. 1775

I want to be with you, Tete a Tete, to canvass, and discuss the complicated subject of Trade. I Say nothing of private Consultations or public Debates, upon this important Head.

When I write you Letters you must expect nothing from me but unconnected Scraps and broken Hints. Continual Successions of Company allow me Time only to Scrawl a Page of Paper, without Thought.

Shall We hush the Trade of the whole Continent and not permit a Vessell to go out of our Harbours except from one Colony to another? How long will or can our People bear this? I Say they can bear it forever—if Parliament Should build a Wall of Brass, at low Water Mark, We might live and be happy. We must change our Habits, our Prejudices our Palates, our Taste in Dress, Furniture, Equipage, Architecture &c. But We can live and be happy. But the Question is whether our People have Virtue enough to be mere Husbandmen, Mechaniks and Soldiers? That they have not Virtue enough to bear it always, I take for granted. How long then will their Virtue last? Till next Spring?

If We Stop all Trade, Great Britain, Ireland and West Indies will not be furnished with any Thing.

Shall We then give Permission for our Vessells to go to foreign Nations, if they can escape the Men of War? Can they escape the Men of War? How many will escape in Proportion? If any Escape, will they not venture to Britain, Ireland, and W.I. in defyance of our Association? If they do not, will not the British Dominions furnish themselves with our Produce from foreign Ports, and thereby avoid that Distress, which We expect will overtake them? Will not the W.I. Islands especially, who cannot exist without our Provisions for 6. Months, unless G[   ] Walker were ignorant.

If We should invite other maritime Powers, or private Adventurers from foreign Nations to come here, Will they venture? They run the risque of escaping Men of War, and the Dangers of an unknown Coast. Maps and Charts may give Strangers a confused Idea of the Geography of our Country, and of the Principal Inlets of Harbours, Rivers, Creeks, Coves, Islands &c. but without skillfull Pilots, the danger of Shipwreck will be 10 to one.

This vast object is never out of my Mind. Help me to grapple it. The W.I. Barbadoes particularly begin We are told here, by a late Vessell to be terrified out of their Wits.

"UNRAVELLING MENS THOUGHT"

To James Warren

Dear Sir   Octr. 24. 1775

When it is Said that it is the Prerogative of omniscience to Search Hearts, I Suppose it is meant that no human sagacity, can penetrate at all Times into Mens Bosoms and discover with precise Certainty the secrets there: and in this Sense it is certainly true.

But there is a sense in which Men may be said to be possessed of a Faculty of Searching Hearts too. There is a Discernment competent to Mortals by which they can penetrate into the Minds of Men and discover their Secret Passions, Prejudices, Habits, Hopes, Fears, Wishes and Designs, and by this Means judge what Part they will act in given Circumstances for the future, and see what Principles and Motives have actuated them to the Conduct they have held, in certain Conjunctures of Circumstances which are passed.

A Dexterity and Facility of thus unravelling Mens Thought and a Faculty of governing them by Means of the Knowledge We have of them, constitutes the principal Part of the Art of a Politician.

In a Provincial Assembly, where We know a Mans Pedigree and Biography, his Education, Profession and Connections, as well as his Fortune, it is easy to see what it is that governs a Man and determines him to this Party in Preference to that, to this system of Politicks rather than another &c.

But here it is quite otherwise. We frequently see Phonomena which puzzle Us.

It requires Time to enquire and learn the Characters and Connections, the Interests and Views of a Multitude of Strangers.

It would be an exquisite Amusement, and high Gratification of Curiosity, this Same Mystery of Politicks, if the Magnitude of the Interests and Consequences did not interest us sometimes too much.

From the Diary: October 25, 1775

OCTR. 25TH. 1775. WEDNESDAY.

Mr. Duane told me at the Funeral of our late virtuous and able President that he, Mr. Duane, had accustomed him self to read the Year Books. Mr. De Lancey who was C J of N. York he said advised him to it, as the best Method of imbibing the Spirit of the Law. De Lancey told him that he had translated a Pile of Cases from the Year Books, altho he was a very lazy Man.

Duane says that Jefferson is the greatest Rubber off of Dust that he has met with, that he has learned French, Italian, Spanish and wants to learn German.

Duane says, he has no Curiosity at all—not the least Inclination to see a City or a Building &c.

That his Memory fails, is very averse to be burthened. That in his Youth he could remember any Thing. Nothing but what he could learn, but it is very different now.

Last Evening Mr. Hewes of N. Carolina, introduced to my Namesake and me, a Mr. Hog from that Colony, one of the Proprietors of Transylvania, a late Purchase from the Cherokees upon the Ohio. He is an associate with Henderson who was lately one of the Associate Judges of N. Carolina, who is President of the Convention in Transylvania.

These Proprietors have no Grant from the Crown nor from any Colony, are within the Limits of Virginia and North Carolina, by their Charters which bound those Colonies on the South Sea. They are charged with Republican Notions—and Utopian Schemes.

EDUCATING THEIR CHILDREN

To Abigail Adams

29 October, 1775

Human nature with all its infirmities and depravation is still capable of great things. It is capable of attaining to degrees of wisdom and of goodness, which, we have reason to believe, appear respectable in the estimation of superior intelligences. Education makes a greater difference between man and man, than nature has made between man and brute. The virtues and powers to which men may be trained, by early education and constant discipline, are truly sublime and astonishing. Newton and Locke are examples of the deep sagacity which may be acquired by long habits of thinking and study. Nay, your common mechanics and artisans are proofs of the wonderful dexterity acquired by use; a watchmaker, in finishing his wheels and springs, a pin or needlemaker, &c. I think there is a particular occupation in Europe, which is called a paper-stainer or linen-stainer. A man who has been long habituated to it, shall sit for a whole day, and draw upon paper fresh figures to be imprinted upon the papers for rooms, as fast as his eye can roll, and his fingers move, and no two of his draughts shall be alike. The Saracens, the Knights of Malta, the army and navy in the service of the English republic, among many others, are instances to show, to what an exalted height valor or bravery or courage may be raised, by artificial means.

It should be your care, therefore, and mine, to elevate the minds of our children and exalt their courage; to accelerate and animate their industry and activity; to excite in them an habitual contempt of meanness, abhorrence of injustice and inhumanity, and an ambition to excel in every capacity, faculty, and virtue. If we suffer their minds to grovel and creep in infancy, they will grovel all their lives.

But their bodies must be hardened, as well as their souls exalted. Without strength and activity and vigor of body, the brightest mental excellencies will be eclipsed and obscured.

A NORTH AMERICAN MONARCHY

To James Warren

Dr Sir   Octr. 1775
What think you of a North American Monarchy? Suppose We should appoint a Continental King, and a Continental

House of Lords, and a Continental House of Commons, to be annually, or triennially or Septennially elected? And in this Way make a Supreme American Legislature? This is easily done you know by an omnipotent Continental Congress, and When once effected, His American Majesty may appoint a Governor for every Province, as his Britannic Majesty used to do, and Lt. Governor and secretary and judge of Admiralty—Nay his Continental Majesty may appoint the Judges of the Supream Courts &c. too—or if his American Majesty should condescend to permit the provincial Legislatures, or Assemblies to nominate two three or four Persons out of whom he should select a Governor, and 3 or 4 Men for Chief Justice &c. out of whom he should choose one, would not this do, nicely?

To his Continental Majesty, in his Continental Privy Council, Appeals might lie, from all Admiralty Cases, and from all civil Causes personal at least, of a certain Value and all Disputes about Land, that is about Boundaries of Colonies should be settled by the Continental King and Council, as they used to be by the British K. and Council. What a magnificent System?

I assure you this is no Chimæra of my own. It is whispered about in Coffee Houses, &c. and there are those who wish it.

I am inclined to think it is done, as one Artifice more to divide the Colonies. But in vain. It would be very curious to give you an History of the out a Door Tricks for this important End of dividing the Colonies. Last Fall the Quakers and Antipœdobaptists were conjured up to pick a Quarrell with Massachusetts. Last Spring the Land Jobbers were stimulated to pick a Quarrell with Connecticutt for the same End. The Quakers and Anabaptists were hushed and abashed, or rather the reasonable conscientious Part of them were convinced in one Evening. The Land Jobbers will meet no better success.

VIRTUE AND "OUR NEW GOVERNMENTS"

To William Tudor

Dear Sir   Novr. 14. 1775
    I received your kind Letter of the 28th. of Octr.—but yester-

day. It was such a Letter as I wish all my Friends would write me, as often as possible—that is it was long, full of Intelligence, well written and very entertaining.

I lament the Dishonour which falls upon the Colony by the mean, mercenary Conduct of some of her Servants. But in all Events I hope no Instance of Fraud or Peculation will be overlooked, but Strictly and impartially punished, untill every Rascall is banished from the Army, whatever Colony may have given him Existence.

It behoves the Congress, it behoves the Army to Shew that nothing but a rigid inflexible Virtue, and a Spotless Purity of Character, can preserve or acquire any Employment.

Virtue, my young Friend, Virtue alone is or can be the Foundation of our new Governments, and it must be encouraged by Rewards, in every Department civil and military.

Your Account of the Doctors Defence at the Bar of the House is every entertaining. I should have formed no Idea of that Hearing if you had not obliged me, with an Account. I think with the Candid, that Contempt is due to him for his Timidity and Duplicity. But I cannot wholly acquit him of something worse. He mentions in his Letter his having in a former Letter given his Correspondent a Hint of the Design against Bunkers Hill. Now I never can be clearly freed from Jealousy, untill I see that Letter. The *Hint* he mentions might have occasioned our Loss of that Post, and of all the Lives which were destroyed on the 17th of June. However I have hitherto kept my Mind in suspense.

I wish you would let me know who Bellidore is. What Country man, and in what Language he wrote—what was his Station Employment and Character.

We must make our young Genius's perfect Masters of the Art of War, in every Branch. I hope America will not long lie under the Reproach of not producing her own officers and Generals, as England has done a long Time.

Wearing an Uniform, and receiving Pay is not all. I want to see an Emulation among our young Gentlemen, which shall be the most perfect Master of all the Languages and Arts which are subservient to Politicks and War. Politicks are the Science of human Happiness and War the Art of Securing it. I would fain therefore have both perfectly understood.

RANK AND CEREMONY

To Samuel Osgood Jr.

Novr. 15. 1775

Your first Letter to me is now before me.

The true Cause why General Frie, has not received from me, any particular Intelligence, is that the Matter has been hitherto Suspended, and that I am under Such Engagements of Secrecy, that I could not in Honour acquaint him with any Thing that has pass'd in Congress.

As Soon as I arrived in Philadelphia, I made it my Business to introduce General Fries Name and Character into Conversation in every private Company where it could be done with Propriety, and to make his long services and Experience known. But I found an Interest making in private Circles in Favour of Coll. Armstrong of Pensilvania, a Gentleman of Character, and Experience in War, a Presbyterian in Religion, whose Name runs high for Piety, Virtue and Valour. What has been done in Congress I must be excused from Saying, but nothing in my Power has been omitted, to promote the Wishes of our Colony or the Honour and Interest of General Frie. It is Sufficient to say, that nothing has as yet been determined. But it will be settled soon. And let it be decided as it may, every good American, will acquiesce in the Decision.

New England, as you justly observe is the Nursery of brave and hardy Men, and has hitherto Stemmed the Torrent of Tyranny, and must continue to do it, but the other Colonies are making rapid Advances in the military Art, and We must be cautious that we dont hold our own Heads too high, and hold up invidious Distinctions. The other Colonies are capable of furnishing good Soldiers, and they Spare no Pains to emulate New England herself.

You observe that no Tory Province has been So contemned as ours. There may be Some ground of Complaint, but have not our People aimed at more Respect than was their due? No other Colony I am fully sensible could have born the shock as ours has done and it is possible that this Circumstance may have made our people expect more than their due.

It is certainly true that some of our Southern Brethren have not annexed the Same Ideas to the Words Liberty, Honour and Politeness that we have: But I have the Pleasure to observe every day that We learn to think and feel alike more and more.

I am Sorry that the Committee did not dine with General Ward, but am convinced there was no unfriendly Design. The Gentlemen politely told me that the only disagreable Circumstance in their Journey was that they had not Time to cultivate an Acquaintance, with Gentlemen in Camp and at Watertown, as they earnestly wished.

Am very Sorry for General Wards ill State of Health, and that this has made him entertain Thoughts of resigning. I cannot think that the Acceptance of the Invitation from the Connecticutt officers, was pointed, or intended as a Slight to General Wards. Perhaps the Connecticutt Gentlemen might send a Card, which General Ward might omit, or it might be mere Inadvertence or Accident. *A Card is an Engine of vast Importance in this World.* But even if it was designed it is not worth regarding. These Little things are below the Dignity of our glorious Cause, which is the best and greatest that ever engaged the human Mind.

It has been an inexpresible Mortification to me, to observe in So many Instances, the Attention of Gentlemen in high Departments both civil and military, to the little Circumstances of Rank and Ceremony, when their Minds and Hearts ought to have been occupied, by the greatest objects on this side of Heaven.

I have been sufficiently plagued with these Frivolisms myself, but I despise them all, and I dont much revere any Man who regards them.

I wish you to write me often and with Freedom. But you must not be too punctilious in waiting for my Answers for I assure you I have more things to do than I am fit for, if I had three Hours where I have one. I am &c.,   John Adams

NEW ENGLAND AND THE SOUTH

To Joseph Hawley

My dear sir   Philadelphia Novr. 25. 1775

This afternoon at five o Clock, I received your kind Letter of November the 14. dated at Brookfield—which was the more agreable because such Favours from you short as this is are very rare.

You tell me, Sir, "that We Shall have no Winter Army, if our Congress dont give better Encouragement to the Privates than at present is held forth to them"—and that "there must be Some Small Bounty given them, on the Inlistment."

What Encouragement is held forth, or at least has been, I know not, but before this Time no doubt they have been informed of the Ultimatum of the Congress. No Bounty is offered. 40 shillings lawfull Money Per Month, after much altercation, is allowed. It is undoubtedly true, that an opinion prevails among the Gentlemen of the Army from the Southward, and indeed throughout all the Colonies, excepting New England, that the Pay of the Privates is too high and that of the officers too low. So that you may easily conceive the Difficulties We have had to surmount. You may depend upon it, that this has cost many an anxious Day and Night. And the utmost that could be done has been. We cannot Suddenly alter the Temper, Principles, opinions or Prejudices of Men. The Characters of Gentlemen in the four New England Colonies, differ as much from those in the others, as that of the Common People differs, that is as much as several distinct Natures almost. Gentlemen, Men of sense, or any Kind of Education in the other Colonies are much fewer in Proportion than in N. England. Gentlemen in the other Colonies, have large Plantations of slaves, and the common People among them are very ignorant and very poor. These Gentlemen are accustomed, habituated to higher Notions of themselves and the Distinction between them and the common People, than We are, and an instantaneous alteration of the Character of a Colony, and that Temper and those sentiments which, its Inhabitants imbibed with their Mothers Milk, and which have grown with their

Growth and strengthnd with their Strength, cannot be made without a Miracle. I dread the Consequences of this Dissimilitude of Character, and without the Utmost Caution on both sides, and the most considerate Forbearance with one another and prudent Condescention on both sides, they will certainly be fatal. An alteration of the Southern Constitutions, which must certainly take Place if this War continues will gradually, bring all the Continent nearer and nearer to each other in all Respects. But this is the Most Critical Moment, We have yet seen. This Winter will cast the Die. For Gods sake therefore, reconcile our People to what has been done, for you may depend upon it, that nothing more can be done here—and I should shudder at the Thought of proposing a Bounty. A burnt Child dreads the fire. The Pay of the officers is raised that of a Captain to 26 dollars and one third per Month Lieutenants and Ensigns in Proportion. Regimental officers not raised. You then hint, "that if Congress should repeal or explain away the Resolution of 18 July respecting the appointment of military officers, and vest the Council with the sole Power, it would throw the Colony into Confusion and end in the Destruction of the Council."

The Day before Yesterday I wrote a Letter to the Honourable Board in answer from one from their President by order to us upon that Subject, which Letter Revere carried from this City yesterday Morning. Therein I candidly gave my opinion to their Honours that our Resolution was clear and plain, that the Colony might Use their own Discretion, and therefore that they might yield this Point to the House— and that the Point was So plain that I did not see the least occasion for laying the Controversy before Congress. But my dear Friend I must, take the Freedom to tell you that the same has happened upon this occasion which has happened on a thousand others, after taking a great deal of Pains with my Colleague your Friend Mr. Cushing, I could not get him to agree with the rest of us in Writing a joint Letter, nor could I get him to say what opinion he would give if it was moved in Congress. What he has written I know not. But it is very hard to be linked and yoked eternally, with People who have either no opinions, or opposite opinions, and to be plagued with the opposition of our own Colony to the most necessary Measures,

at the same Time that you have all the Monarchical super-
stitions and the Aristocratical Domination, of Nine other
Colonies to contend with.

GOVERNMENT AND MANNERS

To Mercy Otis Warren

Dear Madam   Braintree Jany. 8. 1776
   Your Friend insists upon my Writing to you, and altho I am
conscious it is my Duty, being deeply in Debt for a number
of very agreable Favours in the Epistolary Way, yet I doubt
whether a sense of this Duty would have overcome, my Inclination to Indolence and Relaxation, with which my own Fire
Side always inspires me, if it had not been Stimulated and
quickened by her.
   I was charmed with three Characters drawn by a most
masterly Pen, which I received at the southward. Copeleys
Pencil could not touched off, with more exquisite Finishings,
the Faces of those Gentlemen. Whether I ever answered that
Letter I know not. But I hope Posterity will see it, if they do I
am sure they will admire it. I think I will make a Bargain with
you, to draw the Character of every new Personage I have an
opportunity of knowing, on Condition you will do the same.
My View will be to learn the Art of penetrating into Mens Bosoms, and then the more difficult Art of painting what I shall
see there. You Ladies are the most infallible judges of Characters, I think.
   Pray Madam, are you for an American Monarchy or Republic? Monarchy is the genteelest and most fashionable Government, and I dont know why the Ladies ought not to consult
Elegance and the Fashion as well in Government as Gowns,
Bureaus or Chariots.
   For my own Part, I am so tasteless as to prefer a Republic, if
We must erect an independent Government in America, which
you know is utterly against my Inclination. But a Republic,
altho it will infallibly beggar me and my Children, will produce
Strength, Hardiness Activity Courage Fortitude and Enter-

price; the manly, noble and Sublime Qualities in human Nature, in Abundance.

A Monarchy would probably, somehow or other make me rich, but it would produce So much Taste and Politeness, So much Elegance in Dress, Furniture, Equipage, So much Musick and Dancing, So much Fencing and Skaiting; So much Cards and Backgammon; so much Horse Racing and Cock fighting; so many Balls and Assemblies, so many Plays and Concerts that the very Imagination of them makes me feel vain, light, frivolous and insignificant.

It is the Form of Government, which gives the decisive Colour to the Manners of the People, more than any other Thing. Under a well regulated Commonwealth, the People must be wise virtuous and cannot be otherwise. Under a Monarchy they may be as vicious and foolish as they please, nay they cannot but be vicious and foolish. As Politicks therefore is the Science of human Happiness, and human Happiness is clearly best promoted by Virtue, what thorough Politician can hesitate, who has a new Government to build whether to prefer a Commonwealth or a Monarchy? But Madam there is one Difficulty, which I know not how to get over.

Virtue and Simplicity of Manners, are indispensably necessary in a Republic, among all orders and Degrees of Men. But there is So much Rascallity, so much Venality and Corruption, so much Avarice and Ambition, such a Rage for Profit and Commerce among all Ranks and Degrees of Men even in America, that I sometimes doubt whether there is public Virtue enough to support a Republic. There are two Vices most detestably predominant in every Part of America that I have yet seen, which are as incompatible with the Spirit of a Commonwealth as Light is with Darkness, I mean Servility and Flattery. A genuine Republican can no more fawn and cringe than he can domineer. Shew me the American who can not do all. I know two or Three I think, and very few more.

However, it is the Part of a great Politician to make the Character of his People; to extinguish among them, the Follies and Vices that he sees, and to create in them the Virtues and Abilities which he sees wanting. I wish I was sure that America has one such Politician, but I fear she has not.

[   ] Letter begun in Gaiety, is likely to have [   ]

conclusion while I was writing the last Word [   ] Paragraph; my Attention was called off [   ] and most melodious sounds my Ears [   ] Cannon Mortars and Musquettes.

A very hot Fire both of Artillery and small Arms has continued for half an Hour, and has been succeded by a luminous Phoenomenon, over Braintree North Common occasioned by Burning Buildings I suppose.

Whether our People have attacked or defended, been victorious or vanquished, is to me totally uncertain. But in Either Case I rejoice, for a Defeat appears to me preferable to total Inaction.

May the Supreme Ruler of Events, overrule in our Favour! But if the Event of this Evening is unfortunated I think We ought at all Hazards, and at any Loss to retrieve it tomorrow. I hope the Militia will be ready and our Honour be retrieved by making Boston our own. I shall be in suspense this Night, but very willing to take my Place with my Neighbours tomorrow, and crush the Power of the Enemies or suffer under it.

I hope Coll. Warren sleeps at Cushings this night and that I shall see him in the Morning. Mean Time I think I shall sleep as soundly as ever. I am, Madam, your most humble servant, and sincere Friend,

Mrs. Adams desires to be remembered to Mrs. Warren.

From the Diary: January 24, 1776

1776. JANUARY 24. WEDNESDAY.

Began my Journey to Philadelphia, dined at C Mifflins at Cambridge with G. Washington, and Gates and their Ladies, and half a Dozen Sachems and Warriours of the french Cocknowaga Tribe, with their Wives and Children. Williams is one, who was captivated in his Infancy, and adopted. There is a Mixture of White Blood french or English in most of them. Louis, their Principal, speaks English and french as well as Indian. It was a Savage feast, carnivorous Animals devouring their Pray. Yet they were wondrous polite. The General introduced me to them as one of the Grand Council Fire at

Philadelphia, upon which they made me many Bows, and a cordial Reception.

Memorandum on Agenda for Congress

Mem.

The Confederation to be taken up in Paragraphs.

An Alliance to be formed with France and Spain.

Embassadors to be sent to both Courts.

Government to be assumed in every Colony.

Coin and Currencies to be regulated.

Forces to be raised and maintained in Canada and New York. St. Lawrence and Hudsons Rivers to be secured.

Hemp to be encouraged and the Manufacture of Duck.

Powder Mills to be built in every Colony, and fresh Efforts to make Salt Petre.

An Address to the Inhabitants of the Colonies.

The Committee for Lead and Salt to be fill'd up, and Sulphur added to their Commission.

Money to be sent to the Paymaster, to pay our Debts, and fullfill our Engagements.

Taxes to be laid, and levied, Funds established. New Notes to be given on Interest, for Bills borrowed.

Treaties of Commerce with F. S. H. D. &c.

Declaration of Independency, Declaration of War with the Nation, Cruising on the british Trade, their East India Ships and Sugar Ships.

Prevent the Exportation of Silver and Gold.

c. February 1776

OVERTURES TO CANADA

To Abigail Adams

My dearest Friend   February 18. 1776
    I sent you from New York a Pamphlet intituled Common
Sense, written in Vindication of Doctrines which there is Reason to expect that the further Encroachments of Tyranny and
Depredations of Oppression, will soon make the common
Faith: unless the cunning Ministry, by proposing Negociations
and Terms of Reconciliation, should divert the present Current from its Channell.
    Reconciliation if practicable and Peace if attainable, you very
well know would be as agreable to my Inclinations and as advantageous to my Interest, as to any Man's. But I see no Prospect, no Probability, no Possibility. And I cannot but despise
the Understanding, which sincerely expects an honourable
Peace, for its Credulity, and detest the hypocritical Heart,
which pretends to expect it, when in Truth it does not. The
News Papers here are full of free Speculations, the Tendency of
which you will easily discover. The Writers reason from Topicks which have been long in Contemplation, and fully understood by the People at large in New England, but have been
attended to in the southern Colonies only by Gentlemen of
free Spirits and liberal Minds, who are very few. I shall endeavour to inclose to you as many of the Papers and Pamphlets as I can, as long as I stay here. Some will go by this
Conveyance.
    Dr. Franklin, Mr. Chase, and Mr. Charles Carroll of Carroll-
ton in Maryland, are chosen a Committee to go into Canada.
The Characters of the two first you know. The last is not a
Member of Congress, but a Gentleman of independant Fortune, perhaps the largest in America, 150 or 200, thousand
Pounds sterling, educated in some University in France, tho a
Native of America, of great Abilities and Learning, compleat
Master of French Language and a Professor of the Roman
catholic Religion, yet a warm, a firm, a zealous Supporter of
the Rights of America, in whose Cause he has hazarded his all.
    Mr. John Carroll of Maryland, a Roman Catholic Priest and

a Jesuit, is to go with the Committee. The Priests in Canada having refused Baptism and Absolution to our Friends there.

General Lee is to command in that Country, whose Address, Experience, and Abilities added to his Fluency in the French Language, will give him great Advantages.

The Events of War are uncertain: We cannot insure Success, but We can deserve it. I am happy in this Provision for that important Department, because I think it the best that could be made in our Circumstances. Your Prudence will direct you to communicate the Circumstances of the Priest, the Jesuit and the Romish Religion only to such Persons as can judge of the Measure upon large and generous Principles, and will not indiscreetly divulge it. The Step was necessary, for the Anathema's of the Church are very terrible to our Friends in Canada.

I wish I understood French as well as you. I would have gone to Canada, if I had. I feel the Want of Education every Day—particularly of that Language. I pray My dear, that you would not suffer your Sons or your Daughter, ever to feel a similar Pain. It is in your Power to teach them French, and I every day see more and more that it will become a necessary Accomplishment of an American Gentleman and Lady. Pray write me in your next the Name of the Author of your thin French Grammar, which gives you the Pronunciation of the French Words in English Letters, i.e. which shews you, how the same Sounds would be signified by English Vowells and Consonants.

Write me as often as you can—tell me all the News. Desire the Children to write to me, and believe me to be theirs and yours.

From the Diary: March 1, 1776

1776 MARCH 1.

How is the Interest of France and Spain affected, by the dispute between B. and the C? Is it the Interest of France to stand neuter, to join with B. or to join with the C. Is it not her Interest, to dismember the B. Empire? Will her Dominions be safe, if B. and A remain connected? Can she preserve her Possessions in the W.I. She has in the W.I. Martinico, Guadaloupe, and one half of Hispaniola. In Case a Reconciliation should take Place, between B. and A. and a War should break out between B. and France, would not all her Islands be taken from her in 6 Months?

The Colonies are now much more warlike and powerfull than they were, during the last War. A martial Spirit has seized all the Colonies. They are much improved in Skill and Discipline. They have now a large standing Army. They have many good officers. They abound in Provisions. They are in the Neighbourhood of the W.I. A British Fleet and Army united with an American Fleet and Army and supplied with Provisions and other Necessaries from America, might conquer all the french Islands in the W.I. in six Months, and a little more Time than that would be required, to destroy all their Marine and Commerce.

PAINE'S "COMMON SENSE"

To Abigail Adams

March 19. 1776

Yesterday I had the long expected and much wish'd Pleasure of a Letter from you, of various Dates from the 2d. to the 10 March. This is the first Line I have received since I left you. I wrote you from Watertown I believe, relating my Feast at the Quarter Master General with the Coghnawaga Indians, and from Framingham, an Account of the ordnance there, and from New York I sent you a Pamphlet—hope you received these.

Since my arrival here, I have written to you as often as I could.

I am much pleased with your Caution, in your Letter, in avoiding Names both of Persons and Places, or any other Circumstances, which might designate to Strangers, the Writer, or the Person written to, or the Persons mentioned. Characters and Descriptions will do as well.

The Lye, which you say occasioned such Disputes at the

Tavern, was curious enough.—Who could make and spread it? Am much obliged to an Unkle, for his Friendship: my worthy fellow Citizens may be easy about me. I never can forsake what I take to be their Interests. My own have never been considered by me, in Competition with theirs. My Ease, my domestic Happiness, my rural Pleasures, my Little Property, my personal Liberty, my Reputation, my Life, have little Weight and ever had, in my own Estimation, in Comparison of the great Object of my Country. I can say of it with great Sincerity, as Horace says of Virtue—to America only and her Friends a Friend.

You ask, what is thought of Common sense. Sensible Men think there are some Whims, some Sophisms, some artfull Addresses to superstitious Notions, some keen attempts upon the Passions, in this Pamphlet. But all agree there is a great deal of good sense, delivered in a clear, simple, concise and nervous Style.

His Sentiments of the Abilities of America, and of the Difficulty of a Reconciliation with G.B. are generally approved. But his Notions, and Plans of Continental Government are not much applauded. Indeed this Writer has a better Hand at pulling down than building.

It has been very generally propagated through the Continent that I wrote this Pamphlet. But altho I could not have written any Thing in so manly and striking a style, I flatter myself I should have made a more respectable Figure as an Architect, if I had undertaken such a Work. This Writer seems to have very inadequate Ideas of what is proper and necessary to be done, in order to form Constitutions for single Colonies, as well as a great Model of Union for the whole.

Your Distresses which you have painted in such lively Colours, I feel in every Line as I read. I dare not write all that I think upon this Occasion. I wish our People had taken Possession of Nook Hill, at the same Time when they got the other Heights, and before the Militia were dismissed.

Poor Cousin!—I pitty him. How much soever he may lament certain Letters I dont lament. I never repent of what was no sin. Misfortunes may be born without Whining. But if I can believe Mr. Dana, those Letters were much admired in England. I cant help laughing when I write it, because they were really such hasty crude Scraps. If I could have foreseen their Fate, they should have been fit to be seen and worth all the Noise they have made. Mr. Dana says they were considered in England as containing a comprehensive Idea of what was necessary to be done, and as shewing Resolution enough to do it. Wretched Stuff as they really were, (according to him) they have contributed somewhat towards making certain Persons' to be thought the greatest Statesmen in the World.—So much for Vanity.

My Love, Duty, Respects, and Compliments, wherever they belong.

Virginia will be well defended, so will N.Y., so will S. Car. America will eer long, raise her Voice aloud, and assume a bolder Air.

REPUBLICAN GOVERNMENT AND THE SOUTH

To Horatio Gates

Dear Sir   Philadelphia March 23. 1776
    I had the Pleasure, a few days ago, of your Favour of 8th. Instant, for which I esteem myself under great obligations to you.

We rejoice here at the Prospect there is of your driving the Enemy from Boston. If you should Succeed in this I hope effectual Measures will be taken to fortify the Harbour, that the Navy may never enter it again. I think the Narrows may be So obstructed that large Ships will not be able to pass, and the Channell between Long Island and the Moon may be commanded by Batteries upon each of those Islands in such a manner that Boston may be Safe from Men of War. I hope my Countrymen will hesitate at no Expence to attain this End, if in order to accomplish it, they should be obliged to remove the rocky Mountains of my Town of Braintree into the Harbour.

But I cannot yet clearly Satisfy myself that they will leave Boston. It will be a greater Disgrace to the British Arms than to be taken Prisoners in the Town in a Body. If they should abandon the Persons and Property of their dear Friends the

Tories in Boston, will any other Tories in any other Part of the
Continent ever trust to their Protection? It will be considered
as such Impotence, or such Infidelity that I am inclined to
think, few Professors of Toryism would ever afterwards be
found any where.

I agree with you, that in Politicks the Middle Way is none at
all. If We finally fail in this great and glorious Contest, it will
be by bewildering ourselves in groping after this middle Way.
We have hither to conducted half a War, acted upon the Line
of Defence &c. &c. But you will See by tomorrows Paper, that
for the future We are likely to wage three Quarters of a War.
The Continental ships of War, and Provincial ships of War, and
Letters of Mark and Privateers are permitted to cruise upon
British Property, whenever found on the ocean. This is not Independency you know, nothing like it.

If a Post or two more, should bring you unlimited Latitude
of Trade to all Nations, and a polite Invitation to all Nations to
trade with you, take care that you dont call it, or think it Independency. No such Matter. Independency is an Hobgoblin, of
So frightful Mein, that it would throw a delicate Person into
Fits to look it in the Face.

I know not whether you have seen the Act of Parliament
call'd the restraining Act, or prohibitory Act, or piratical Act,
or plundering Act, or Act of Independency, for by all these
Titles is it call'd. I think the most apposite is the Act of Independency, for King Lords and Commons have united in Sun-
dering this Country and that I think forever. It is a compleat
Dismemberment of the British Empire. It throws thirteen
Colonies out of the Royal Protection, levels all Distinctions
and makes us independent in Spight of all our supplications
and Entreaties.

It may be fortunate that the Act of Independency should
come from the British Parliament, rather than the American
Congress: But it is very odd that Americans should hesitate at
accepting Such a Gift from them.

However, my dear Friend Gates, all our Misfortunes arise
from a Single Source, the Reluctance of the Southern Colonies
to Republican Government. The success of this War depends
upon a Skillfull Steerage of the political Vessell. The Difficulty
lies in forming Constitutions for particular Colonies, and a

Continental Constitution for the whole, each Colony should establish its own Government, and then a League should be formed, between them all. This can be done only on popular Principles and Maxims which are so abhorrent to the Inclinations of the Barons of the south, and the Proprietary Interests in the Middle Colonies, as well as to that Avarice of Land, which has made upon this Continent so many Votaries to Mammon that I Sometimes dread the Consequences. However Patience, Fortitude and Perseverance, with the Help of Time will get us over these obstructions.

Thirteen Colonies under such a Form of Government as that of Connecticutt, or one, not quite so popular leagued together in a faithfull Confederacy might bid Defyance to all the Potentates of Europe if united against them.

Pray continue to make me happy with your Favours, accept of my most cordial Wishes for your safety, Happiness and Honour, make my most respectfull Compliments to the General and the Ladies, and the whole Family, and believe me to be with great Respect your affectionate Friend and servant

John Adams

Notes on Relations with France

Is any Assistance attainable from F.?

What Connection may We safely form with her?

1st. No Political Connection. Submit to none of her Authority—receive no Governors, or officers from her.

2d. No military Connection. Receive no Troops from her.

3d. Only a Commercial Connection, i.e. make a Treaty, to receive her Ships into our Ports. Let her engage to receive our Ships into her Ports—furnish Us with Arms, Cannon, Salt Petre, Powder, Duck, Steel.

March–April 1776

Thoughts on Government, Applicable to the Present State of the American Colonies

My dear Sir,

If I was equal to the task of forming a plan for the government of a colony, I should be flattered with your request, and very happy to comply with it; because as the divine science of politicks is the science of social happiness, and the blessings of society depend entirely on the constitutions of government, which are generally institutions that last for many generations, there can be no employment more agreeable to a benevolent mind, than a research after the best.

> Pope flattered tyrants too much when he said,
> "For forms of government let fools contest,
> That which is best administered is best."

Nothing can be more fallacious than this: But poets read history to collect flowers not fruits—they attend to fanciful images, not the effects of social institutions. Nothing is more certain from the history of nations, and the nature of man, than that some forms of government are better fitted for being well administered than others.

We ought to consider, what is the end of government, before we determine which is the best form. Upon this point all speculative politicians will agree, that the happiness of society is the end of government, as Divines and moral Philosophers agree that the happiness of the individual is the end of man. From this principle it will follow, that the form of government, which communicates ease, comfort, security, or in one word happiness to the greatest number of persons, and in the greatest degree, is the best.

All sober enquiries after truth, ancient and modern, Pagan and Christian, have declared that the happiness of man, as well as his dignity consists in virtue. Confucius, Zoroaster, Socrates, Mahomet, not to mention authorities really sacred, have agreed in this.

If there is a form of government then, whose principle and foundation is virtue, will not every sober man acknowledge it better calculated to promote the general happiness than any other form?

FEAR is the foundation of most governments; but is so sordid and brutal a passion, and renders men, in whose breasts it predominates, so stupid, and miserable, that Americans will not be likely to approve of any political institution which is founded on it.

HONOR is truly sacred, but holds a lower rank in the scale of moral excellence than virtue. Indeed the former is but a part of the latter, and consequently has not equal pretensions to support a frame of government productive of human happiness.

THE foundation of every government is some principle or passion in the minds of the people. The noblest principles and most generous affections in our nature then, have the fairest chance to support the noblest and most generous models of government.

A MAN must be indifferent to the sneers of modern Englishmen to mention in their company the names of Sidney, Harrington, Locke, Milton, Nedham, Neville, Burnet, and Hoadley. No small fortitude is necessary to confess that one has read them. The wretched condition of this country, however, for ten or fifteen years past, has frequently reminded me of their principles and reasonings. They will convince any candid mind, that there is no good government but what is Republican. That the only valuable part of British constitution is so; because the very definition of a Republic, is "an Empire of Laws, and not of men." That, as a Republic is the best of governments, so that particular arrangement of the powers of society, or in other words that form of government, which is best contrived to secure an impartial and exact execution of the laws, is the best of Republics.

OF Republics, there is an inexhaustable variety, because the possible combinations of the powers of society, are capable of innumerable variations.

As good government, is an empire of laws, how shall your laws be made? In a large society, inhabiting an extensive country, it is impossible that the whole should assemble, to make laws: The first necessary step then, is, to depute power from the many, to a few of the most wise and good. But by what rules shall you chuse your Representatives? Agree upon the number and qualifications of persons, who shall have the benefit of choosing, or annex this priviledge to the inhabitants of a certain extent of ground.

THE principal difficulty lies, and the greatest care should be employed in constituting this Representative Assembly. It should be in miniature, an exact portrait of the people at large. It should think feel, reason, and act like them. That it may be the interest of this Assembly to do strict justice at all times, it should be an equal representation, or in other words equal interest among the people should have equal interest in it. Great care should be taken to effect this, and to prevent unfair, partial, and corrupt elections. Such regulations, however, may be better made in times of greater tranquility than the present, and they will spring up of themselves naturally, when all the powers of government come to be in the hands of the people's friends. At present it will be safest to proceed in all established modes to which the people have been familiarised by habit.

A REPRESENTATION of the people in one assembly being obtained, a question arises whether all the powers of government, legislative, executive, and judicial, shall be left in this body? I think a people cannot be long free, nor ever happy, whose government is in one Assembly. My reasons for this opinion are as follow.

1. A SINGLE Assembly is liable to all the vices, follies and frailties of an individual. Subject to fits of humour, starts of passion, flights of enthusiasm, partialities of prejudice, and consequently productive of hasty results and absurd judgments: And all these errors ought to be corrected and defects supplied by some controuling power.

2. A SINGLE Assembly is apt to be avaricious, and in time will not scruple to exempt itself from burthens which it will lay, without compunction, on its constituents.

3. A SINGLE Assembly is apt to grow ambitious, and after a time will not hesitate to vote itself perpetual. This was one fault of the long parliament, but more remarkably of Holland, whose Assembly first voted themselves from annual to septennial, then for life, and after a course of years, that all vacancies happening by death, or otherwise, should be filled by themselves, without any application to constituents at all.

4. A REPRESENTATIVE Assembly, altho' extremely well

qualified, and absolutely necessary as a branch of the legislature, is unfit to exercise the executive power, for want of two essential properties, secrecy and dispatch.

5. A REPRESENTATIVE Assembly is still less qualified for the judicial power; because it is too numerous, too slow, and too little skilled in the laws.

6. BECAUSE a single Assembly, possessed of all the powers of government, would make arbitrary laws for their own interest, execute all laws arbitrarily for their own interest, and adjudge all controversies in their own favour.

BUT shall the whole power of legislation rest in one Assembly? Most of the foregoing reasons apply equally to prove that the legislative power ought to be more complex—to which we may add, that if the legislative power is wholly in one Assembly, and the executive in another, or in a single person, these two powers will oppose and enervate upon each other, until the contest shall end in war, and the whole power, legislative and executive, be usurped by the strongest.

THE judicial power, in such case, could not mediate, or hold the balance between the two contending powers, because the legislative would undermine it. And this shews the necessity too, of giving the executive power a negative upon the legislative, otherwise this will be continually encroaching upon that.

To avoid these dangers let a distant Assembly be constituted, as a mediator between the two extreme branches of the legislature, that which represents the people and that which is vested with the executive power.

LET the Representative Assembly then elect by ballot, from among themselves or their constituents, or both, a distinct Assembly, which for the sake of perspicuity we will call a Council. It may consist of any number you please, say twenty or thirty, and should have a free and independent exercise of its judgment, and consequently a negative voice in the legislature.

THESE two bodies thus constituted, and made integral parts of the legislature, let them unite, and by joint ballot choose a Governor, who, after being stripped of most of those badges of domination called prerogatives, should have a free and independent exercise of his judgment, and be made also an integral part of the legislature. This I know is liable to objections, and if you please you may make him only President of the Council, as in Connecticut: But as the Governor is to be invested with the executive power, with consent of Council, I think he ought to have a negative upon the legislative. If he is annually elective, as he ought to be, he will always have so much reverence and affection for the People, their Representatives and Councillors, that although you give him an independent exercise of his judgment, he will seldom use it in opposition to the two Houses, except in cases the public utility of which would be conspicuous, and some such cases would happen.

IN the present exigency of American affairs, when by an act of Parliament we are put out of the royal protection, and consequently discharged from our allegiance; and it has become necessary to assume government for our immediate security, the Governor, Lieutenant-Governor, Secretary, Treasurer, Commissary, Attorney-General, should be chosen by joint Ballot, of both Houses. And these and all other elections, especially of Representatives, and Councillors, should be annual, there not being in the whole circle of the sciences, a maxim more infallible than this, "Where annual elections end, there slavery begins."

THESE great men, in this respect, should be, once a year

> "Like bubbles on the sea of matter borne,
> They rise, they break, and to that sea return."

This will teach them the great political virtues of humility, patience, and moderation, without which every man in power becomes a ravenous beast of prey.

THIS mode of constituting the great offices of state will answer very well for the present, but if, by experiment, it should be found inconvenient, the legislature may at its leisure devise other methods of creating them, by elections of the people at large, as in Connecticut, or it may enlarge the term for which they shall be chosen to seven years, or three years, or for life, or make any other alterations which the society shall find productive of its ease, its safety, its freedom, or in one word, its happiness.

A ROTATION of all offices, as well as of Representatives and Councillors, has many advocates, and is contended for with many plausible arguments. It would be attended no doubt with many advantages, and if the society has a sufficient number of suitable characters to supply the great number of vacancies which would be made by such a rotation, I can see no objection to it. These persons may be allowed to serve for three years, and then excluded three years, or for any longer or shorter term.

ANY seven or nine of the legislative Council may be made a Quorum, for doing business as a Privy Council, to advise the Governor in the exercise of the executive branch of power, and in all acts of state.

THE Governor should have the command of the militia, and of all your armies. The power of pardons should be with the Governor and Council.

JUDGES, Justices and all other officers, civil and military, should be nominated and appointed by the Governor, with the advice and consent of Council, unless you choose to have a government more popular; if you do, all officers, civil and military, may be chosen by joint ballot of both Houses, or in order to preserve the independence and importance of each House, by ballot of one House, concurred by the other. Sheriffs should be chosen by the freeholders of counties—so should Registers of Deeds and Clerks of Counties.

ALL officers should have commissions, under the hand of the Governor and seal of the Colony.

THE dignity and stability of government in all its branches, the morals of the people and every blessing of society, depends so much upon an upright and skillful administration of justice, that the judicial power ought to be distinct from both the legislative and executive, and independent upon both, that so it may be a check upon both, as both should be checks upon that. The Judges therefore should always be men of learning and experience in the laws, of exemplary morals, great patience, calmness, coolness and attention. Their minds should not be distracted with jarring interests; they should not be dependant upon any man or body of men. To these ends they should hold estates for life in their offices, or in other words their commissions should be during good behaviour, and their salaries ascertained and established by law. For misbehaviour the grand inquest of the Colony, the House of Representatives, should impeach them before the Governor and Council, where they should have time and opportunity to make their defence, but if convicted should be removed from their offices, and subjected to such other punishment as shall be thought proper.

A MILITIA LAW requiring all men, or with very few exceptions, besides cases of conscience, to be provided with arms and ammunition, to be trained at certain seasons, and requiring counties, towns, or other small districts to be provided with public stocks of ammunition and entrenching utensils, and with some settled plans for transporting provisions after the militia, when marched to defend their country against sudden invasions, and requiring certain districts to be provided with field-pieces, companies of matrosses and perhaps some regiments of light horse, is always a wise institution, and in the present circumstances of our country indispensible.

LAWS for the liberal education of youth, especially of the lower class of people, are so extremely wise and useful, that to a humane and generous mind, no expence for this purpose would be thought extravagant.

THE very mention of sumptuary laws will excite a smile. Whether our countrymen have wisdom and virtue enough to submit to them I know not. But the happiness of the people might be greatly promoted by them, and a revenue saved sufficient to carry on this war forever. Frugality is a great revenue, besides curing us of vanities, levities and fopperies which are real antidotes to all great, manly and warlike virtues.

BUT must not all commissions run in the name of a king? No. Why may they not as well run thus, "The Colony of to A. B. greeting," and be tested by the Governor?

WHY may not writs, instead of running in the name of a King, run thus, "The Colony of   to the Sheriff, &c." and be tested by the Chief Justice.

WHY may not indictments conclude, "against the peace of the Colony of   and the dignity of the same?"

A CONSTITUTION, founded on these principles, introduces knowledge among the People, and inspires them with a conscious dignity, becoming Freemen. A general emulation takes place, which causes good humour, sociability, good manners, and good morals to be general. That elevation of sentiment, inspired by such a government, makes the common people brave and enterprizing. That ambition which is inspired by it makes them sober, industrious and frugal. You find among them some elegance, perhaps, but more solidity; a little pleasure, but a great deal of business—some politeness, but more civility. If you compare such a country with the regions of domination, whether Monarchial or Aristocratical, you will fancy yourself in Arcadia or Elisium.

IF the Colonies should assume governments separately, they should be left entirely to their own choice of the forms, and if a Continental Constitution should be formed, it should be a Congress, containing a fair and adequate Representation of the Colonies, and its authority should sacredly be confined to these cases, viz. war, trade, disputes between Colony and Colony, the Post-Office, and the unappropriated lands of the Crown, as they used to be called.

THESE Colonies, under such forms of government, and in such a union, would be unconquerable by all the Monarchies of Europe.

YOU and I, my dear Friend, have been sent into life, at a time when the greatest law-givers of antiquity would have wished to have lived. How few of the human race have ever enjoyed an opportunity of making an election of government more than of air, soil, or climate, for themselves or their children. When! Before the present epocha, had three millions of people full power and a fair opportunity to form and establish the wisest and happiest government that human wisdom can contrive? I hope you will avail yourself and your country of that extensive learning and indefatigable industry which you possess, to assist her in the formations of the happiest governments, and the best character of a great People. For myself, I must beg you to keep my name out of sight, for this feeble attempt, if it should be known to be mine, would oblige me to apply to myself those lines of the immortal John Milton, in one of his sonnets,

> "I did but teach the age to quit their cloggs
>   By the plain rules of ancient Liberty,
>   When lo! a barbarous noise surrounded me,
>   Of owls and cuckoos, asses, apes and dogs."

April 1776

RESPONDING TO A REQUEST
TO "REMEMBER THE LADIES"

To Abigail Adams

Ap. 14. 1776

You justly complain of my short Letters, but the critical
State of Things and the Multiplicity of Avocations must plead
my Excuse.—You ask where the Fleet is. The inclosed Papers
will inform you. You ask what Sort of Defence Virginia can
make. I believe they will make an able Defence. Their Militia
and minute Men have been some time employed in training
them selves, and they have Nine Battallions of regulars as they
call them, maintained among them, under good Officers, at
the Continental Expence. They have set up a Number of Man-
ufactories of Fire Arms, which are busily employed. They are
tolerably supplied with Powder, and are successfull and assidu-
ous, in making Salt Petre. Their neighbouring Sister or rather
Daughter Colony of North Carolina, which is a warlike Colony, and has several Battallions at the Continental Expence, as
well as a pretty good Militia, are ready to assist them, and they
are in very good Spirits, and seem determined to make a brave
Resistance.—The Gentry are very rich, and the common
People very poor. This Inequality of Property, gives an Aristocratical Turn to all their Proceedings, and occasions a strong
Aversion in their Patricians, to Common Sense. But the Spirit
of these Barons, is coming down, and it must submit.

It is very true, as you observe they have been duped by
Dunmore. But this is a Common Case. All the Colonies are
duped, more or less, at one Time and another. A more egre-
gious Bubble was never blown up, than the Story of Commis-
sioners coming to treat with the Congress. Yet it has gained
Credit like a Charm, not only without but against the clearest
Evidence. I never shall forget the Delusion, which seized our
best and most sagacious Friends the dear Inhabitants of
Boston, the Winter before last. Credulity and the Want of
Foresight, are Imperfections in the human Character, that no
Politician can sufficiently guard against.

You have given me some Pleasure, by your Account of a

certain House in Queen Street. I had burned it, long ago, in Imagination. It rises now to my View like a Phœnix.—What shall I say of the Solicitor General? I pity his pretty Children, I pity his Father, and his sisters. I wish I could be clear that it is no moral Evil to pity him and his Lady. Upon Repentance they will certainly have a large Share in the Compassions of many. But let Us take Warning and give it to our Children. Whenever Vanity, and Gaiety, a Love of Pomp and Dress, Furniture, Equipage, Buildings, great Company, expensive Diversions, and elegant Entertainments get the better of the Principles and Judgments of Men or Women there is no knowing where they will stop, nor into what Evils, natural, moral, or political, they lead us.

Your Description of your own Gaiety de Coeur, charms me. Thanks be to God you have just Cause to rejoice—and may the bright Prospect be obscured by no Cloud.

As to Declarations of Independency, be patient. Read our Privateering Laws, and our Commercial Laws. What signifies a Word.

As to your extraordinary Code of Laws, I cannot but laugh. We have been told that our Struggle has loosened the bands of Government every where. That Children and Apprentices were disobedient—that schools and Colledges were grown turbulent—that Indians slighted their Guardians and Negroes grew insolent to their Masters. But your Letter was the first Intimation that another Tribe more numerous and powerfull than all the rest were grown discontented.—This is rather too coarse a Compliment but you are so saucy, I wont blot it out.

Depend upon it, We know better than to repeal our Masculine systems. Altho they are in full Force, you know they are little more than Theory. We dare not exert our Power in its full Latitude. We are obliged to go fair, and softly, and in Practice you know We are the subjects. We have only the Name of Masters, and rather than give up this, which would compleatly subject Us to the Despotism of the Peticoat, I hope General Washington, and all our brave Heroes would fight. I am sure every good Politician would plot, as long as he would against Despotism, Empire, Monarchy, Aristocracy, Oligarchy, or Ochlocracy.—A fine Story indeed. I begin to think the Ministry as deep as they are wicked. After stirring up Tories, Land-jobbers, Trimmers, Bigots, Canadians, Indians, Negroes, Hanoverians, Hessians, Russians, Irish Roman Catholicks, Scotch Renegadoes, at last they have stimulated the   to demand new Priviledges and threaten to rebell.

HOPES FOR THEIR CHILDREN

To Abigail Adams

April 15. 1776

I send you every News Paper, that comes out, and I send you now and then a few sheets of Paper but this Article is as scarce here, as with you. I would send a Quire, if I could get a Conveyance. I write you, now and then a Line, as often as I can, but I can tell you no News, but what I send in the public Papers.

We are Waiting it is said for Commissioners, a Messiah that will never come.—This Story of Commissioners is as arrant an Illusion as ever was hatched in the Brain of an Enthusiast, a Politician, or a Maniac. I have laugh'd at it—scolded at it—griev'd at it—and I dont know but I may at an unguarded Moment have rip'd at it—but it is vain to Reason against such Delusions. I was very sorry to see in a Letter from the General that he had been bubbled with it, and still more to see in a Letter from my sagacious Friend W at Plymouth, that he was taken in too.

My Opinion is that the Commissioners and the Commission have been here (I mean in America) these two Months. The Governors, Mandamus Councillors, Collectors and Comptrollers, and Commanders of the Army and Navy, I conjecture compose the List and their Power is to receive Submissions. But We are not in a very submissive Mood. They will get no Advantage of Us.

We shall go on, to Perfection I believe. I have been very busy for some time—have written about Ten sheets of Paper with my own Hand, about some trifling Affairs, which I may mention some time or other—not now for fear of Accidents.

What will come of this Labour Time will discover. I shall get nothing by it, I believe, because I never get any Thing by any Thing that I do. I am sure the Public or Posterity ought to get Something. I believe my Children will think I might as well have thought and laboured, a little, night and Day for their Benefit. . . . But I will not bear the Reproaches of my Children. I will tell them that I studied and laboured to procure a free Constitution of Government for them to solace themselves under, and if they do not prefer this to ample Fortune, to Ease and Elegance, they are not my Children, and I care not what becomes of them. They shall live upon thin Diet, wear mean Cloaths, and work hard, with Chearfull Hearts and free Spirits or they may be the Children of the Earth or of no one, for me.

John has Genius and so has Charles. Take Care that they dont go astray. Cultivate their Minds, inspire their little Hearts, raise their Wishes. Fix their Attention upon great and glorious Objects, root out every little Thing, weed out every Meanness, make them great and manly. Teach them to scorn Injustice, Ingratitude, Cowardice, and Falshood. Let them revere nothing but Religion, Morality and Liberty.

Nabby and Tommy are not forgotten by me altho I did not mention them before. The first by Reason of her sex, requires a Different Education from the two I have mentioned. Of this you are the only judge. I want to send each of my little pretty flock, some present or other. I have walked over this City twenty Times and gaped at every shop like a Countryman to find something, but could not. Ask every one of them what they would choose to have and write it to me in your next Letter. From this I shall judge of their Taste and Fancy and Discretion.

PUBLIC VIRTUE AND PRIVATE PASSIONS

To Mercy Otis Warren

Madam   April 16. 1776
Not untill Yesterdays Post, did your agreable Favour of March the Tenth, come to my Hands. It gave me great Plea-

sure and altho in the distracted Kind of Life, I am obliged to lead, I cannot promise to deserve a Continuance of So excellent a Correspondence yet I am determined by Scribbling Something or other, be it what it may, to provoke it.

The Ladies I think are the greatest Politicians, that I have the Honour to be acquainted with, not only because they act upon the Sublimest of all the Principles of Policy, vizt. the Honesty is the best Policy but because they consider Questions more coolly than those who are heated with Party Zeal, and inflamed with the bitter Contentions of active, public Life.

I know of no Researches in any of the sciences more ingenious than those which have been made after the best Forms of Government nor can there be a more agreable Employment to a benevolent Heart. The Time is now approaching, when the Colonies, will find themselves under a Necessity, of engaging in Earnest in this great and indispensible Work. I have ever Thought it the most difficult and dangerous Part of the Business, Americans have to do, in this mighty Contest, to contrive some Method for the Colonies to glide insensibly, from under the old Government, into a peaceable and contented Submission to new ones. It is a long Time since this opinion was conceived, and it has never been out of my Mind. My constant Endeavour has been to convince, Gentlemen of the Necessity of turning their Thoughts to those subjects. At present, the sense of this Necessity seems to be general, and Measures are taking which must terminate in a compleat Revolution. There is a Danger of Convulsions. But I hope, not great ones.

The Form of Government, which you admire, when its Principles are pure, is admirable indeed. It is productive of every Thing, which is great and excellent among Men. But its Principles are as easily destroyed, as human Nature is corrupted. Such a Government is only to be supported by pure Religion, or Austere Morals. Public Virtue cannot exist in a Nation without private, and public Virtue is the only Foundation of Republics. There must be a possitive Passion for the public good, the public Interest, Honour, Power, and Glory, established in the Minds of the People, or there can be no Republican Government, nor any real Liberty. And this public Passion must be Superiour to all private Passions. Men must be ready, they must pride themselves, and be happy to sacrifice their private Pleasures, Passions, and Interests, nay their private Friendships and dearest Connections, when they Stand in Competition with the Rights of society.

Is there in the World a Nation, which deserves this Character. There have been several, but they are no more. Our dear Americans perhaps have as much of it as any Nation now existing, and New England perhaps has more than the rest of America. But I have seen all along my Life, Such Selfishness, and Littleness even in New England, that I sometimes tremble to think that, altho We are engaged in the best Cause that ever employed the Human Heart, yet the Prospect of success is doubtfull not for Want of Power or of Wisdom, but of Virtue.

The Spirit of Commerce, Madam, which even insinuates itself into Families, and influences holy Matrimony, and thereby corrupts the Morals of Families as well as destroys their Happiness, it is much to be feared is incompatible with that purity of Heart, and Greatness of soul which is necessary for an happy Republic. This Same Spirit of Commerce is as rampant in New England as in any Part of the World. Trade is as well understood and as passionately loved there as any where. Even the Farmers, and Tradesmen are addicted to Commerce, and it is too true, that Property is generally the standard of Respect there as much as any where. While this is the Case, there is great Danger that a Republican Government, would be very factious and turbulent there. Divisions in Elections are much to be dreaded. Every Man must seriously set himself to root out his Passions, Prejudices and Attachments, and to get the better of his private Interest. The only reputable Principle and Doctrine must be that all Things must give Way to the public.

This is very grave and solemn Discourse to a Lady. True, and I thank God, that his Providence has made me Acquainted with two Ladies at least, who can bear it.

I think Madam, that the Union of the Colonies, will continue and be more firmly cemented, But We must move slowly. Patience, Patience, Patience! I am obliged to invoke thee every Morning of my Life, every Noon, and every Evening.

It is Surprising to me that any among you should flatter themselves with an Accommodation. Every Appearance is against it, to an Attentive observer. The Story of Commissioners is a Bubble. Their real Errand is an Insult. But popular Passions and Fancies will have their Course, you may as well reason down a Gale of Wind.

You expect, if a certain Bargain Should be complied with, to be made acquainted with noble and Royal Characters. But in this you will be disappointed. Your Correspondent, has neither Principles, nor Address, nor Abilities, for such Scenes, and others are as sensible of it, I assure you as he is. They must be Persons of more Complaisance and Ductility of Temper as well as better Accomplishments for such great Things.

He wishes for nothing less. He wishes for nothing more than to retire from all public stages, and public Characters, great and small, to his Farm and his Attorneys office. And to both these he must return.

ADVANCING TOWARD INDEPENDENCE

To James Warren

April 22. 1776

The Management of so complicated and mighty a Machine, as the United Colonies, requires the Meekness of Moses, the Patience of Job and the Wisdom of Solomon, added to the Valour of Daniel.

They are advancing by slow but sure steps, to that mighty Revolution, which You and I have expected for Some Time. Forced Attempts to accellerate their Motions, would have been attended with Discontent and perhaps Convulsions.

The News from South Carolina, has aroused and animated all the Continent. It has Spread a visible Joy, and if North Carolina and Virginia should follow the Example, it will Spread through all the rest of the Colonies like Electric Fire.

The Royal Proclamation, and the late Act of Parliament, have convinced the doubting and confirmed the timorous and wavering. The two Proprietary Colonies only, are still cool. But I hope a few Weeks will alter their Temper.

I think it is now the precise Point of Time for our Council and House of Representatives, either to proceed to make such Alterations in our Constitution as they may judge proper, or to

Send a Petition to Philadelphia for the Consent of Congress to do it. It will be considered as fresh evidence of our Spirit and Vigour, and will give Life and Activity and Energy to all the other Colonies. Four Months ago, or indeed at any Time Since you assumed a Government, it might have been disagreable and perhaps dangerous. But it is quite otherwise now.

Another Thing, if you are so unanimous, in the Measure of Independency and wish for a Declaration of it, now is the proper Time for you to instruct your Delegates to that Effect. It would have been productive of Jealousies perhaps and Animosities, a few Months ago, but would have a contrary Tendency now. The Colonies are all at this Moment turning their Eyes, that Way. Vast Majorities in all the Colonies now see the Propriety and Necessity of taking the decisive Steps, and those who are averse to it are afraid to Say much against it. And therefore Such an Instruction at this Time would comfort and cheer the Spirits of your Friends, and would discourage and dishearten your Enemies.

Coll. Whipples Letters from New Hampshire, are nearly in the Same Strain with yours to me, vizt. that all are now united in the great Question. His Letters inform him that even of the Protesters there is now but one left, who is not zealous for Independency.

I lament the Loss of Governor Ward, exceedingly because he had many Correspondents in Rhode Island, whose Letters were of service to Us, an Advantage which is now entirely lost.

After all, my Friend, I do not att all Wonder, that so much Reluctance has been Shewn to the Measure of Independency. All great Changes, are irksome to the human Mind, especially those which are attended with great Dangers, and uncertain Effects. No Man living can foresee the Consequences of such a Measure. And therefore I think it ought not to have been undertaken, untill the Design of Providence, by a series of great Events had so plainly marked out the Necessity of it that he that runs might read.

We may feel Sanguine Confidence of our Strength: yet in a few years it may be put to the Tryal.

We may please ourselves with the prospect of free and popular Governments. But there is great Danger, that those Governments will not make us happy. God grant they may. But I fear, that in every assembly, Members will obtain an Influence, by Noise not sense. By Meanness, not Greatness. By Ignorance not Learning. By contracted Hearts not large souls. I fear too, that it will be impossible to convince and perswade People to establish wise Regulations.

There is one Thing, my dear sir, that must be attempted and most Sacredly observed or We are all undone. There must be a Decency, and Respect, and Veneration introduced for Persons in Authority, of every Rank, or We are undone. In a popular Government, this is the only Way of Supporting order—and in our Circumstances, as our People have been so long without any Government att all, it is more necessary than, in any other. The United Provinces, were So sensible of this that they carried it to a burlesque Extream.

I hope your Election in May will be the most solemn, and joyfull that ever took Place in the Province. I hope every Body will attend. Clergy and Laity should go to Boston. Every Body should be gratefully pious and happy. It should be conducted with a solemnity that may make an Impression on the whole People.

"TO RIDE IN THIS WHIRLWIND"

To Abigail Adams

April 28. 1776

Yesterday, I received two Letters from you from the 7th. to the 14. of April. I believe I have received all your Letters, and I am not certain I wrote one from Framingham. The one I mean contains an Account of my dining with the Indians at Mr. Mifflins.

It gives me Concern to think of the many Cares you must have upon your Mind. Am glad you have taken   into Pay, and that Isaac is well before now I hope.

Your Reputation, as a Farmer, or any Thing else you undertake I dare answer for. . . . Your Partners Character as a Statesman is much more problematical.

As to my Return, I have not a Thought of it. Journeys of

such a Length are tedious, and expensive both of Time and Money neither of which are my own. I hope to spend the next Christmas, where I did the last, and after that I hope to be relieved for by that Time I shall have taken a pretty good Trick att Helm whether the Vessell has been well steer'd or not. But if My Countrymen should insist upon my serving them another Year, they must let me bring my whole Family with me. Indeed I could keep House here, with my Partner, four children and two servants, as cheap as I maintain my self here with two Horses and a servant at Lodgings.

Instead of domestic Felicity, I am destined to public Contentions. Instead of rural Felicity, I must reconcile myself to the Smoke and Noise of a city. In the Place of private Peace, I must be distracted with the Vexation of developing the deep Intrigues of Politicians and must assist in conducting the arduous Operations of War. And think myself, well rewarded, if my private Pleasure and Interest are sacrificed as they ever have been and will be, to the Happiness of others.

You tell me, our Jurors refuse to serve, because the Writs are issued in the Kings Name. I am very glad to hear, that they discover so much Sense and Spirit. I learn from another Letter that the General Court have left out of their Bills the Year of his Reign, and that they are making a Law, that the same Name shall be left out of all Writs, Commissions, and all Law Proscesses. This is good News too. The same will be the Case in all the Colonies, very soon.

You ask me how I have done the Winter past. I have not enjoyed so good Health as last Fall. But I have done complaining of any Thing. Of ill Health I have no Right to complain because it is given me by Heaven. Of Meanness, of Envy, of Littleness, of—of—of—of—I have Reason and Right to complain, but I have too much Contempt, to use that Right.

There is such a Mixture of Folly, Littleness, and Knavery in this World that, I am weary of it, and altho I behold it with unutterable Contempt and Indignation, yet the public Good requires that I should take no Notice of it, by Word or by Letter. And to this public Good I will conform.

You will see an Account of the Fleet in some of the Papers I have sent you. Give you Joy of the Admirals Success. I have Vanity enough to take to myself, a share in the Merit of the

American Navy. It was always a Measure that my Heart was much engaged in, and I pursued it, for a long Time, against the Wind and Tide. But at last obtained it.

Is there no Way for two friendly Souls, to converse together, altho the Bodies are 400 Miles off?—Yes by Letter.—But I want a better Communication. I want to hear you think, or to see your Thoughts.

The Conclusion of your Letter makes my Heart throb, more than a Cannonade would. You bid me burn your Letters. But I must forget you first.

In yours of April 14. you say you miss our Friend in the Conveyance of your Letters. Dont hesitate to write by the Post. Seal well. Dont miss a single Post.

You take it for granted that I have particular Intelligence of every Thing from others. But I have not. If any one wants a Vote for a Commission, he vouchsafes me a Letter, but tells me very little News. I have more particulars from you than any one else. Pray keep me constantly informed, what ships are in the Harbour and what Fortifications are going on.

I am quite impatient to hear of more vigorous Measures for fortifying Boston Harbour. Not a Moment should be neglected. Every Man ought to go down as they did after the Battle of Lexington and work untill it is done. I would willingly pay half a Dozen Hands my self, and subsist them, rather than it should not be done immediately. It is of more importance than to raise Corn.

You say inclosed is a Prologue and a Parody, but neither was inclosed. If you did not forget it, the letter has been opened and the Inclosures taken out.

If the Small Pox spreads, run me in debt. I received a Post or two past a Letter from your Unkle at Salem, containing a most friendly and obliging Invitation to you and yours to go, and have the Distemper at his House if it should spread. He has one or two in family to have it.

The Writer of Common Sense, and the Forrester, is the same Person. His Name is Payne, a Gentleman, about two Years ago from England, a Man who G Lee says has Genius in his Eyes. The Writer of Cassandra is said to be Mr. James Cannon a Tutor, in the Philadelphia Colledge. Cato is reported here to be Dr. Smith—a Match for Brattle. The oration was an insolent Performance. . . . A Motion was made to Thank the orator and ask a Copy—But opposed with great Spirit, and Vivacity from every Part of the Room, and at last withdrawn, lest it should be rejected as it certainly would have been with Indignation. The orator then printed it himself, after leaving out or altering some offensive Passages.

This is one of the many irregular, and extravagant Characters of the Age. I never heard one single person speak well of any Thing about him but his Abilities, which are generally allowed to be good. The Appointment of him to make the oration, was a great oversight, and Mistake.

The late Act of Parliament, has made so deep an Impression upon Peoples Minds throughout the Colonies, it is looked upon as the last Stretch of Oppression, that We are hastening rapidly to great Events. Governments will be up every where before Midsummer, and an End to Royal style, Titles and Authority. Such mighty Revolutions make a deep Impression on the Minds of Men and sett many violent Passions at Work. Hope, Fear, Joy, Sorrow, Love, Hatred, Malice, Envy, Revenge, Jealousy, Ambition, Avarice, Resentment, Gratitude, and every other Passion, Feeling, Sentiment, Principle and Imagination, were never in more lively Exercise than they are now, from Florida to Canada inclusively. May God in his Providence overrule the whole, for the good of Mankind. It requires more Serenity of Temper, a deeper Understanding and more Courage than fell to the Lott of Marlborough, to ride in this Whirlwind.

Resolution in Congress on Establishing New Governments

IN CONGRESS, MAY 15, 1776.

WHEREAS his Britannic Majesty, in conjunction with the Lords and Commons of Great-Britain, has, by a late Act of Parliament, excluded the inhabitants of these United Colonies from the protection of his crown: And whereas no answer whatever to the humble petitions of the Colonies for redress of grievances, and reconciliation with Great-Britain has been or is likely to be given; but the whole force of that kingdom, aided by foreign mercenaries, is to be exerted for the destruction of the good people of these Colonies: And whereas it appears absolutely irreconcileable to reason and good conscience, for the people of these Colonies now to take the oaths and affirmations necessary for the support of any government under the Crown of Great-Britain; and it is necessary that the exercise of every kind of authority under the said Crown should be totally suppressed, and all the powers of government exerted under the authority of the people of the Colonies for the preservation of internal peace, virtue and good order, as well as for the defence of their lives, liberties and properties, against the hostile invasions and cruel depredations of their enemies: Therefore

RESOLVED, That it be recommended to the respective Assemblies and Conventions of the United Colonies, where no Government sufficient to the exigencies of their affairs has been hitherto established, to adopt such Government as shall in the opinion of the Representatives of the People best conduce to the happiness and safety of their Constituents in particular, and America in general.   *Extract from the Minutes,*
CHARLES THOMSON, SECRETARY.

EXTINGUISHING BRITISH AUTHORITY

To Abigail Adams

May 17. 1776

I have this Morning heard Mr. Duffil upon the Signs of the Times. He run a Parrallell between the Case of Israel and that of America, and between the Conduct of Pharaoh and that of George.

Jealousy that the Israelites would throw off the Government of Egypt made him issue his Edict that the Midwives should cast the Children into the River, and the other Edict that the Men should make a large Revenue of Brick without Straw. He concluded that the Course of Events, indicated strongly the Design of Providence that We should be seperated from G. Britain, &c.

Is it not a Saying of Moses, who am I, that I should go in and out before this great People? When I consider the great Events which are passed, and those greater which are rapidly advancing, and that I may have been instrumental of touching some Springs, and turning some small Wheels, which have had and have such Effects, I feel an Awe upon my Mind, which is not easily described.

G B has at last driven America, to the last Step, a compleat Seperation from her, a total absolute Independence, not only of her Parliament but of her Crown, for such is the Amount of the Resolve of the 15th.

Confederation among ourselves, or Alliances with foreign Nations are not necessary, to a perfect Seperation from Britain. That is effected by extinguishing all Authority, under the Crown, Parliament and Nation as the Resolution for instituting Governments, has done, to all Intents and Purposes. Confederation be necessary for our internal Concord, and Alliances may be so for our external Defence.

I have Reasons to believe that no Colony, which shall assume a Government under the People, will give it up. There is something very unnatural and odious in a Government 1000 Leagues off. An whole Government of our own Choice, managed by Persons whom We love, revere, and can confide in, has charms in it for which Men will fight. Two young Gentlemen from South Carolina, now in this City, who were in Charlestown when their new Constitution was promulgated, and when their new Governor and Council and Assembly walked out in Procession, attended by the Guards, Company of Cadetts, Light Horse &c., told me, that they were beheld by the People with Transports and Tears of Joy. The People gazed at them, with a Kind of Rapture. They both told me, that the Reflection that these were Gentlemen whom they all loved, esteemed and revered, Gentlemen of their own Choice, whom they could trust, and whom they could displace if any of them should behave amiss, affected them so that they could not help crying.

They say their People will never give up this Government.

One of these Gentlemen is a Relation of yours, a Mr. Smith, son of Mr. Thomas Smith. I shall give him this Letter or another to you.

A Privateer fitted out here by Coll. Reberdeau and Major Bayard, since our Resolves for Privateering, I am this Moment informed, has taken a valuable Prize. This is Encouragement, at the Beginning.

In one or two of your Letters you remind me to think of you as I ought. Be assured there is not an Hour in the Day, in which I do not think of you as I ought, that is with every Sentiment of Tenderness, Esteem, and Admiration.

THE CONSENT OF THE PEOPLE

To James Sullivan

Dear Sir   Philadelphia May. 26. 1776

Your Favours of May 9th. and 17th. are now before me; and I consider them as the Commencement of a Correspondence, which will not only give me Pleasure, but may be of Service to the public, as, in my present Station I Stand in need of the best Intelligence, and the Advice of every Gentleman of Abilities and public Principles, in the Colony which has seen fit to place me here.

Our worthy Friend, Mr. Gerry has put into my Hand, a Letter from you, of the Sixth of May, in which you consider the Principles of Representation and Legislation, and give us Hints of Some Alterations, which you Seem to think necessary, in the Qualification of Voters.

I wish, Sir, I could possibly find Time, to accompany you, in your Investigation of the Principles upon which a Representative assembly Stands and ought to Stand, and in your Examination whether the Practice of our Colony, has been conformable to those Principles. But alass! Sir, my Time is So incessantly engrossed by the Business before me that I cannot Spare enough, to go through So large a Field: and as to Books, it is not easy to obtain them here, nor could I find a Moment to look into them, if I had them.

It is certain in Theory, that the only moral Foundation of Government is the Consent of the People. But to what an Extent Shall We carry this Principle? Shall We Say, that every Individual of the Community, old and young, male and female, as well as rich and poor, must consent, expressly to every Act of Legislation? No, you will Say. This is impossible. How then does the Right arise in the Majority to govern the Minority, against their Will? Whence arises the Right of the Men to govern Women, without their Consent? Whence the Right of the old to bind the Young, without theirs.

But let us first Suppose, that the whole Community of every Age, Rank, Sex, and Condition, has a Right to vote. This Community, is assembled—a Motion is made and carried by a Majority of one Voice. The Minority will not agree to this. Whence arises the Right of the Majority to govern, and the Obligation of the Minority to obey? from Necessity, you will Say, because there can be no other Rule. But why exclude Women? You will Say, because their Delicacy renders them unfit for Practice and Experience, in the great Business of Life, and the hardy Enterprizes of War, as well as the arduous Cares of State. Besides, their attention is So much engaged with the necessary Nurture of their Children, that Nature has made them fittest for domestic Cares. And Children have not Judgment or Will of their own. True. But will not these Reasons apply to others? Is it not equally true, that Men in general in every Society, who are wholly destitute of Property, are also too little acquainted with public Affairs to form a Right Judgment, and too dependent upon other Men to have a Will of their own? If this is a Fact, if you give to every Man, who has no Property, a Vote, will you not make a fine encouraging Provision for Corruption by your fundamental Law? Such is the Frailty of the human Heart, that very few Men, who have no Property, have any Judgment of their own. They talk and vote as they are directed by Some Man of Property, who has attached their Minds to his Interest.

Upon my Word, sir, I have long thought an Army, a Piece of

Clock Work and to be governed only by Principles and Maxims, as fixed as any in Mechanicks, and by all that I have read in the history of Mankind, and in Authors, who have Speculated upon Society and Government, I am much inclined to think, a Government must manage a Society in the Same manner; and that this is Machinery too.

Harrington has Shewn that Power always follows Property. This I believe to be as infallible a Maxim, in Politicks, as, that Action and Re-action are equal, is in Mechanicks. Nay I believe We may advance one Step farther and affirm that the Ballance of Power in a Society, accompanies the Ballance of Property in Land. The only possible Way then of preserving the Ballance of Power on the side of equal Liberty and public Virtue, is to make the Acquisition of Land easy to every Member of Society: to make a Division of the Land into Small Quantities, So that the Multitude may be possessed of landed Estates. If the Multitude is possessed of the Ballance of real Estate, the Multitude will have the Ballance of Power, and in that Case the Multitude will take Care of the Liberty, Virtue, and Interest of the Multitude in all Acts of Government.

I believe these Principles have been felt, if not understood in the Massachusetts Bay, from the Beginning: And therefore I Should think that Wisdom and Policy would dictate in these Times, to be very cautious of making Alterations. Our people have never been very rigid in Scrutinizing into the Qualifications of Voters, and I presume they will not now begin to be so. But I would not advise them to make any alteration in the Laws, at present, respecting the Qualifications of Voters.

Your Idea, that those Laws, which affect the Lives and personal Liberty of all, or which inflict corporal Punishment, affect those, who are not qualified to vote, as well as those who are, is just. But, So they do Women, as well as Men, Children as well as Adults. What Reason Should there be, for excluding a Man of Twenty years, Eleven Months and twenty-seven days old, from a Vote when you admit one, who is twenty one? The Reason is, you must fix upon Some Period in Life, when the Understanding and Will of Men in general is fit to be trusted by the Public. Will not the Same Reason justify the State in fixing upon Some certain Quantity of Property, as a Qualification.

The Same Reasoning, which will induce you to admit all

Men, who have no Property, to vote, with those who have, for those Laws, which affect the Person will prove that you ought to admit Women and Children: for generally Speaking, Women and Children, have as good Judgment, and as independent Minds as those Men who are wholly destitute of Property: these last being to all Intents and Purposes as much dependent upon others, who will please to feed, cloath, and employ them, as Women are upon their Husbands, or Children on their Parents.

As to your Idea, of proportioning the Votes of Men in Money Matters, to the Property they hold, it is utterly impracticable. There is no possible Way of Ascertaining, at any one Time, how much every Man in a Community, is worth; and if there was, So fluctuating is Trade and Property, that this State of it, would change in half an Hour. The Property of the whole Community, is Shifting every Hour, and no Record can be kept of the Changes.

Society can be governed only by general Rules. Government cannot accommodate itself to every particular Case, as it happens, nor to the Circumstances of particular Persons. It must establish general, comprehensive Regulations for Cases and Persons. The only Question is, which general Rule, will accommodate most Cases and most Persons.

Depend upon it, sir, it is dangerous to open So fruitfull a Source of Controversy and Altercation, as would be opened by attempting to alter the Qualifications of Voters. There will be no End of it. New Claims will arise. Women will demand a Vote. Lads from 12 to 21 will think their Rights not enough attended to, and every Man, who has not a Farthing, will demand an equal Voice with any other in all Acts of State. It tends to confound and destroy all Distinctions, and prostrate all Ranks, to one common Levell. I am &c.

THE NEED FOR MILITARY SKILL

To Henry Knox

Dear sir   Philadelphia June 2. 1776
    Your esteemed Favour of the 16 of May, came to my Hand a few Days ago.

    You have laid me under obligations, by your ingenious Observations upon those Books, upon military Science, which are necessary, to be procured, in the present Circumstances of this Country. I have been a long Time convinced of the Utility of publishing american Editions of those Writers, and that it is an object of sufficient Importance, to induce the public to be at the Expence of it. But greater objects press in such Numbers, upon those who think for the public, as Lord Drummond expressed it that this has been hitherto neglected. I could wish that the Public would be at the Expence not only of new Editions of these Authors, but of establishing Academies, for the Education of young Gentlemen in every Branch of the military Art: because I am fully of your sentiment, that We ought to lay Foundations, and begin Institutions, in the present Circumstances of this Country, for promoting every Art, Manufacture and Science which is necessary for the Support of an independent State. We must for the future Stand upon our own Leggs or fall. The Alienation of Affection, between the two Countries, is at length, so great, that if the Morals of the British Nation and their political Principles were made purer than they are, it would be scarcely possible to accomplish a cordial Re-Union with them.

    The Votes of the Congress and the Proceedings of the Colonies seperately must before this Time have convinced you, that this is the sense of America, with infinitely greater Unanimity, than could have been credited by many People a few Months ago. Those few Persons indeed, who have attended closely to the Proceedings of the several Colonies, for a Number of Years past, and reflected deeply upon the Causes of this mighty Contest, have foreseen, that Such an Unanimity would take Place, as soon as a Seperation should become necessary.

These are not at all surprised while many others really are and some affect to be astonished at the Phenominon.

The Policy of Rome, in carrying their Arms to Carthage, while Hannibal was at the Gates of their Capital, was wise and justified by the Event, and would deserve Imitation if We could march into the Country of our Enemies. But possessed as they are of the Dominion of the Sea, it is not easy for Us to reach them. Yet it is possible that a bold attempt might succeed. But We have not yet sufficient Confidence in our own Power or skill, to encourage Enterprizes of the daring, hardy Kind. Such often prosper and are always glorious. But shall I give offence if I Say, that our Arms, have kept an even Pace with our Councils? that both have been rather slow and irresolute? Have either our officers or Men, by sea or Land, as yet discovered that exalted Courage, and mature Judgment, both of which are necessary for great and Splendid Actions? Our Forces have done very well, considering their poor Appointments and our Infancy. But I may Say to you that I wish I could see less Attention to Trifles, and more to the great Essentials of the service, both in the civil and military Departments.

I am no Prophet, if We are not compelled by Necessity, before the War is over, to become more Men of Business and less Men of Pleasure. I have formed great Expectations from a Number of Gentlemen of Genius, Sentiment, and Education, of the younger sort, whom I know to be in the Army, and wish that Additions might be made to the Number. We have had Some Examples of Magnanimity and Bravery, it is true, which would have done Honour to any Age or Country. But those have been accompanied with a Want of Skill and Experience, which intitles the Hero to Compassion, at the Same Time that he has our Admiration. For my own Part I never think of Warren or Montgomery, without lamenting at the same Time that I admire, lamenting that Inexperience to which, perhaps they both owed their Glory.

ESTABLISHING "A MORE EQUAL LIBERTY"

To Patrick Henry

My dear Sir   Philadelphia June 3. 1776
    I had this Morning the Pleasure of yours of 20 May. The
little Pamphlet you mention is nullius Filius, and if I should be
obliged to maintain it, the World will not expect that I should
own it. My Motive for inclosing it to you, was not the Value of
the Present, but as a Token of Friendship—and more for the
Sake of inviting your Attention to the Subject, than because
there was any Thing in it worthy your Perusal. The Subject is
of infinite Moment, and perhaps more than Adequate to the
Abilities of any Men, in America. I know of none So competent, to the Task as the Author of the first Virginia Resolutions
against the Stamp Act, who will have the Glory with Posterity,
of beginning and concluding this great Revolution. Happy
Virginia, whose Constitution is to be framed by So masterly a
Builder. Whether the Plan of the Pamphlet, is not too popular,
whether the Elections are not too frequent, for your Colony I
know not. The Usages and Genius and Manners of the People,
must be consulted. And if Annual Elections of the Representatives of the People, are Sacredly preserved, those Elections
by Ballott, and none permitted to be chosen but Inhabitants,
Residents, as well as qualified Freeholders of the City, County,
Parish, Town, or Burrough for which they are to serve, three
essential Prerequisites of a free Government; the Council or
middle Branch of the Legislature may be triennial, or even
Septennial, without much Inconvenience.
    I, esteam it an Honour and an Happiness, that my opinion
So often co-incides with yours. It has ever appeared to me, that
the natural Course and order of Things, was this—for every
Colony to institute a Government—for all the Colonies to confederate, and define the Limits of the Continental Constitution
—then to declare the Colonies a sovereign State, or a Number
of confederated Sovereign States—and last of all to form Treaties with foreign Powers. But I fear We cannot proceed systematically, and that We Shall be obliged to declare ourselves

independant States before We confederate, and indeed before all the Colonies have established their Governments.

It is now pretty clear, that all these Measures will follow one another in a rapid Succession, and it may not perhaps be of much Importance, which is done first.

The Importance of an immediate Application to the French Court is clear, and I am very much obliged to you for your Hint of the Rout by the Mississippi.

Your Intimation that the session of your Representative Body would be long gave me great Pleasure, because We all look up to Virginia for Examples and in the present Perplexities, Dangers and Distresses of our Country it is necessary that the Supream Councils of the Colonies should be almost constantly Sitting. Some Colonies are not sensible of this and they will certainly Suffer for their Indiscretion. Events of such Magnitude as those which present themselves now in such quick Succession, require constant Attention and mature Deliberation.

The little Pamphlet, you mention which was published here as an Antidote to the Thoughts on Government, and which is whispered to have been the joint Production of one Native of Virginia and two Natives of New York, I know not how truly, will make no Fortune in the World. It is too absurd to be considered twice. It is contrived to involve a Colony in eternal War.

The Dons, the Bashaws, the Grandees, the Patricians, the Sachems, the Nabobs, call them by what Name you please, Sigh, and groan, and frett, and Sometimes Stamp, and foam, and curse—but all in vain. The Decree is gone forth, and it cannot be recalled, that a more equal Liberty, than has prevail'd in other Parts of the Earth, must be established in America. That Exuberance of Pride, which has produced an insolent Domination, in a few, a very few oppulent, monopolizing Families, will be brought down nearer to the Confines of Reason and Moderation, than they have been used. This is all the Evil, which they themselves will endure. It will do them good in this World and every other. For Pride was not made for Man only as a Tormentor.

I shall ever be happy in receiving your Advice, by Letter, untill I can be more compleatly so in seeing you here in Person, which I hope will be soon. I am with Sincere Affection and Esteem, dear sir, your Friend and very humble servant.

"THE VERY MIDST OF A REVOLUTION"

To William Cushing

Dear Sir   Philadelphia June 9. 1776
I had, yesterday, the Honour of your Letter of the 20th. of May, and I read it, with all that Pleasure, which We feel on the Revival of an old Friendship when We meet a Friend, whom, for a long Time We have not Seen.

You do me great Honour, sir, in expressing a Pleasure at my Appointment to the Bench; but be assured that no Circumstance relating to that Appointment has given me So much concern, as my being placed at the Head of it, in Preference to another, who in my opinion was so much better qualified for it, and intituled to it. I did all in my Power to have it otherwise but was told that our Sovereign Lords the People must have it so.

When, or Where, or how, the Secret Imagination Seized you, as you Say it did, heretofore, that I was destined to that Place, I cant conjecture: nothing, I am Sure, was further from my Thoughts, or Wishes.

I am not a little chagrined that Sargeant has declined, having entertained great Hopes, from his Solid Judgment and extensive Knowledge. Paine has acted in his own Character, tho scarcely consistent with the public Character, which he has been made to wear. At this, however, I am not much mortified, for the Bench will not be the less respectable, for having a little less Wit, Humour, Drollery, or Fun upon it—very different Qualities being requisite in that Department.

Warren has an excellent Head and Heart, and since the Province cannot be favoured and honoured with the Judgment of regularly educated Lawyers I know not where a better Man could have been found. I hope he will not decline. If he should, I hope that Lowell or Dana will be thought of.

Your appointment of Mr. Winthrop, whose Experience will be usefull in that Station and whose Conduct and Principles have deserved it, was undoubtedly very right and cannot fail to give universal satisfaction.

You shall have my hearty Concurrence in telling the Jury, the Nullity of Acts of Parliament, whether We can prove it by the Jus Gladii or not. I am determined to live and die of that Opinion, let the Jus Gladii, Say what it will. The System and Rules of the Common Law, must be adopted, I Suppose, untill the Legislature Shall make Alterations in Either, and how much Soever, I may, heretofore have found fault with the Powers that were, I suppose, I shall now be well pleased to hear Submission inculcated to the Powers that be—because they are ordained for good.

It would give me great Pleasure to ride this Eastern Circuit with you, and prate before you at the Bar, as I used to do. But I am destined to another Fate, to Drudgery of the most wasting, exhausting, consuming Kind, that I ever went through in my whole Life. Objects of the most Stupendous Magnitude, Measures in which the Lives and Liberties of Millions, born and unborn are most essentially interested, are now before Us. We are in the very midst of a Revolution, the most compleat, unexpected, and remarkable of any in the History of Nations. A few Matters must be dispatched before I can return. Every Colony must be induced to institute a perfect Government. All the Colonies must confederate together, in some solemn Compact. The Colonies must be declared free and independent states, and Embassadors, must be Sent abroad to foreign Courts, to solicit their Acknowledgment of Us, as Sovereign States, and to form with them, at least with some of them commercial Treaties of Friendship and Alliance. When these Things shall be once well finished, or in a Way of being so, I shall think that I have answered the End of my Creation, and sing with Pleasure my Nunc Dimittes, or if it should be the Will of Heaven that I should live a little longer, return to my Farm and Family, ride Circuits, plead Law, or judge Causes, just as you please.

The Rumours you heard of a Reinforcement in Canada, and those you must have heard before now of many Disasters there, are but too true. Canada has been neglected too much, to my infinite Grief and Regret, and against all the Remonstrances and Entreaties, which could be made. This has been owing to Causes, which it would tire you to read, if I was at Liberty to explain them. However nothing on the Part of your Delegates will be wanting, to secure with the Blessing of Heaven, a Reverse of Fortune, there. Dunmore is fled to an Island, having left behind him in their Graves most of his Negroes, and abandoned his Entrenchments on the Main. Our little fleet has had a shocking sickness, which had disabled So many Men, that the Commodore has sent out, on a Cruise two of his ships only. The Difficulty of defending So extended a sea Coast is prodigious, but the Spirit of the People is very willing, and they exert themselves nobly in most Places. The British Men of War are distressed for Provisions and even for Water, almost every where. They have no Comfort in any Part of America.

My good Genius whispers me very often that I shall enjoy many agreeable Hours with you, but Fortune often disappoints the Hopes which this Genius inspires. Be this as it may, while at a distance I shall ever be happy to receive a Line from you. Should be much obliged to you, for some Account of Occurences in your Eastern Circuit. Remember me, with every sentiment of Respect to the Bench, the Bar, and all other Friends. I have the Honour to be with very great Respect, your Affectionate Friend, and very humble servant

John Adams

RAISING AND SUPPLYING TROOPS

To Nathanael Greene

Dear sir   Philadelphia June 22. 1776
   Your Favour of the second Instant has lain by me, I suppose these Eighteen days, but I fear I shall often have occasion to make Apologies for Such omissions, which will never happen from Want of Respect, but I fear very often for Want of Time.
   Your Reasoning, to prove the Equity, and the Policy of making Provision for the Unfortunate Officer, or soldier, is extreamly just, and cannot be answered, and I hope that when

We get a little over the Confusions arising from the Revolutions which are now taking Place in the Colonies, and get an American Constitution formed, Something will be done. I should be much obliged to you for your Thoughts upon the subject. What Pensions should be allowed or what other Provision made? Whether it would be expedient to establish an Hospital &c. It is a Matter of Importance, and the Plan should be well digested.

I think with you that every Colony should furnish its Proportion of Men, and I hope it will come to this. But at present, Some Colonies have such Bodies of Quakers, and Menonists, and Moravians, who are principled against War, and others have such Bodies of Tories, or Cowards, or unprincipled People who will not wage War, that it is, as yet impossible.

The Dispute, is, as you justly observe, in all human Probability, but in its Infancy; We ought therefore to Study, to bring every Thing, in the military Department into the best order—Fighting, is not the greatest Branch of the Science of War. Men must be furnished with good and wholesome Provisions in Sufficient Plenty. They must be well paid—they must be well cloathed and well covered, with Barracks and Tents— they must be kept Warm with Suitable Fuel. In these Respects, We have not been able to do So well as We wished. But, Why the Regiments have not been furnished with proper Agents, I dont know. Congress, is ever ready to hearken to the Advice of the General, and if he had recommended such Officers, they would have been appointed. Collonells should neither be Agents, nor suttlers. Congress have lately voted that there shall be regimental Paymasters, who shall keep the Accounts of the Regiments. If any other Agent is necessary let me know it. Good Officers, are no doubt the Soul of an Army, but our Difficulty is to get Men. Officers, present themselves, in Supernumerary Abundance.

As to Pay there is no End to the Desire and Demand of it. Is there not too much Extravagance, and too little Œconomy, among the officers?

I am much at a Loss, whether it would not be the best Policy, to leave every Colony to raise their own Troops, to cloath them, to Pay them, to furnish them with Tents, and indeed every Thing but Provisions, fuel and Forage. The Project of abolishing Provincial Distinctions, was introduced, with a good Intention, I believe, at first but I think it will do no good upon the whole. However, if Congress, is to manage the whole, I am in hopes they will get into a better Train. They have established a War Office, and a Board of War and ordinance, by means of which I hope they will get their affairs into better order. They will be better informed of the State of the Army and of all its Wants.

That the Promotion of extraordinary Merit, may give disgust to those officers is true, over whom the Advancement is made—but I think it ought not. That this Power may be abused, or misapplied, is also true. That Interest, Favour, private Friendship, Prejudice, may operate more or less in the purest Assembly, is true. But where will you lodge this Power? To place it in the General would be more dangerous to the public Liberty, and not less liable to abuse from sinister and unworthy Motives. Will it do, is it consistent with common Prudence to lay it down, as an invariable Rule, that all Officers, in all Cases shall rise in succession?

I am obliged to you for your Caution not to be too confident. The Fate of War is uncertain—So are all Sublunary Things. But, We must form our Conjectures of Effects from the Knowledge We have of Causes, and in Circumstances like ours must not attempt to penetrate too far into Futurity. There are as many Evils, and more, which arise in human Life, from an Excess of Diffidence, as from an Excess of Confidence. Proud as Mankind is, their is more superiority in this World yielded than assumed. I learned, long ago, from one of the greatest Statesmen, this World ever produced, Sully, neither to adventure upon rash Attempts from too much Confidence, nor to despair of success in a great Design from the appearance of Difficulties. "Without attempting to judge of the future which depends upon too many Accidents, much less to subject it to our Precipitation in bold and difficult Enterprises, We should endeavour to subdue one Obstacle at a Time, nor Suffer ourselves to be depress'd by their Greatness, and their Number. *We ought never to despair of what has been once accomplish'd.* How many Things have the Idea of impossible been annexed to, that have become easy to those who knew how to take Advantage of Time, Opportunity, lucky Moments, the Faults of others, different Dispositions, and an infinite Number of other Circumstances."

I will inclose to you, a Copy of the Resolution establishing, a Board of War and Ordinance; and as you may well imagine, We are all, inexperienced in this Business. I Should be extreamly obliged to you for, any Hints for the Improvement of the Plan, which may occur to you, and for any Assistance or Advice you may give me, as a private Correspondent in the Execution of it. It is a great Mortification to me I confess, and I fear it will too often be a Misfortune to our Country, that I am called to the Discharge of Trusts to which I feel myself So unequal, and in the Execution of which I can derive no Assistance from my Education, or former Course of Life. But my Country must command me, and wherever she shall order me, there I will go, without Dismay. I am, dear Sir, with the greatest Esteem, your humble Servant.

RELIGIOUS TOLERATION

To Benjamin Kent

Sir   Philadelphia June 22. 1776
Your Letters of April 24. and May 26 are before me, both dated at Boston, a Circumstance which alone would have given Pleasure to a Man who has such an Attachment to that Town, and who has suffered So much Anxiety for his Friends, in their Exile from it.

We have not many of the fearfull, and Still less of the Unbelieving among Us, how Slowly soever, you may think We proceed. Is it not a Want of Faith, or a Predominance of Fear, which makes some of you So impatient for Declarations in Words of What is every day manifested in Deeds of the most determined Nature, and unequivocal signification?

That We are divorced, a Vinculo as well as from Bed and Board, is to me, very clear. The only Question is, concerning the proper Time for making an explicit Declaration in Words.

Some People must have Time to look around them, before, behind, on the right hand, and on the left, then to think, and after all this to resolve. Others see, at one intuitive Glance into the past and the future, and judge with Precision at once. But remember you cant make thirteen Clocks, Strike precisely alike, at the Same Second.

I am for the most liberal Toleration of all Denominations of Religionists but I hope that Congress will never meddle with Religion, further than to Say their own Prayers, and to fast and give Thanks, once a Year. Let every Colony, have its own Religion, without Molestation.

The Congress, ordered Church to the Massachusetts Council to be let out upon Bail. It was represented to them that his Health was in a dangerous Way and it was thought, he would not now have it in his Power to do any Mischief. No Body knows what to do with him. There is no Law to try him upon, and no Court to try him. I am afraid he deserves more Punishment, than he will ever meet. I am, your humble sert.

ARMY APPOINTMENTS

To Samuel Holden Parsons

Dear sir   Philadelphia June 22. 1776

Your obliging Favour of the third of June, has been too long unanswered. I acknowledge the Difficulty of ascertaining, the comparative Merit of Officers, and the danger of advancing Friends, where there is no uncommon Merit. This danger cannot be avoided, by any other Means, than making it an invariable Rule, to promote officers in succession. For if you make a King the Judge of uncommon Merit, he will advance favorites, without Merit, under Colour or Pretence of Merit. If you make a Minister of State the Judge, he will naturally promote his Relations, Connections and Friends. If you place the Power of judging of extraordinary Merit, in an Assembly, you dont mend the Matter much. For by all the Experience I have had, I find that Assemblies, have Favourites as well as Kings and Ministers. The Favorites of Assemblies, or the leading Members, are not always the most worthy. I dont know whether they ever are. These leading Members have Sons, Brothers and Cousins, Acquaintances, Friends, and Connections of one sort or other, near or remote: and I have ever found, these Leading Members of Assemblies, as much under the Influence of Nature, and her Passions and Prejudices, as Kings, and Ministers. The principal Advantage and Difference lies in this, that in an Assembly, there are more Guards and Checks, upon the Infirmities of leading Members, than there are upon Kings and Ministers.

What then shall We Say? Shall We leave it to the General and the Army? Is there not as much Favoritism, as much of Nature, Passion, Prejudice, and Partiality, in the Army, as in an Assembly? As much in a General as a King or Minister?

Upon the whole I believe it wisest to depart from the Line of Succession, as seldom as possible. But I cannot but think that the Power of departing from it at all, tho liable to Abuses every where, yet safest in the Hands of an Assembly.

But, in our American Army, as that is circumstanced, it is as difficult to Settle a Rule of Succession, as a Criterion of Merit. We have Troops in every Province, from Georgia to New Hampshire. A Colonel is kill'd in New Hampshire. The next Colonel in the American Army, to him, is in Georgia. Must We send, the Colonel from Georgia, to command the Regiment in New Hampshire. Upon his Journey, he is seized with a Fever and dies. The next Colonel is in Canada. We must then send to Canada, for a Colonel to go to Portsmouth, and as the next Colonel to him is in South Carolina We must send a Colonel from S. Carolina to Canada, to command that Regiment. These Marches, and Countermarches, must run through all the Corps of Officers, and will occasion such inextricable Perplexities, delays, and Uncertainties, that We need not hesitate to pronounce it, impracticable and ruinous. Shall We Say then that Succession shall take Place, among the Officers of every distinct Army, or in every distinct Department?

My own private Opinion is, that We shall never be quite right, untill every Colony is permitted to raise their own Troops, and the Rule of succession is established among the Officers of the Colony. This, where there are Troops of Several Colonies, Serving in the Same Camp, may be liable to some

Inconveniences. But these will be fewer, than upon any other Plan you can adopt.

It is right I believe, to make the Rule of Promotion among Captains and Subalterns, regimental only. And that among Field Officers, more general. But the Question is how general, it shall be? Shall it extend to the whole American Army? or only to the whole District, or Department? or Only to the Army, serving at a particular Place?

That it is necessary to inlist an Army to serve during the War, or at least for a longer Period than one Year, and to offer some handsome Encouragement for that End, I have been convinced, a long Time. I would make this Temptation to consist partly in Money, and partly in Land, and considerable in both. It has been too long delayed But I think it will now be soon done.

What is the Reason that New York must continue to embarrass the Continent? Must it be so forever? What is the Cause of it? Have they no Politicians, capable of instructing and forming the sentiments of their People? or are their People incapable of seeing and feeling like other Men. One would think that their Proximity to New England, would assimilate their Opinions, and Principles. One would think too that the Army would have some Enfluence upon them. But it Seems to have none. N. York is likely to have the Honour of being the very last of all in imbibing the genuine Principles and the true system of American Policy. Perhaps she will never, entertain them at all. I am, with much Respect, your Friend and servant.

ADVANTAGES OF DECLARING INDEPENDENCE

To John Winthrop

Dear sir   Philadelphia June 23. 1776
Your Favour of June the first is now before me. It is now universally acknowledged that we are, and must be independant states. But Still Objections are made to a Declaration of it. It is said, that such a Declaration, will arouse and unite Great Britain. But are they not already aroused and united, as

much as they will be? Will not such a Declaration, arouse and unite the Friends of Liberty, the few who are left, in opposition to the present system? It is also Said that such a Declaration will put us in the Power of foreign States. That France will take Advantage of Us, when they see We cant recede, and demand severe Terms of Us. That she and Spain too, will rejoice to see Britain and America, wasting each other. But this Reasoning, has no Weight with me, because I am not for soliciting any political Connection, or military Assistance, or indeed naval, from France. I wish for nothing but Commerce, a mere Marine Treaty with them. And this they will never grant, until We make the Declaration, and this I think they cannot refuse, after We have made it.

The Advantages, which will result from Such a Declaration, are in my opinion very numerous, and very great. After that Event, the Colonies will hesitate no longer to compleat their Governments. They will establish Tests and ascertain the Criminality of Toryism. The Presses will produce no more, Seditious, or traitorous Speculations. Slanders, upon public Men and Measures, will be lessened. The Legislatures of the Colonies will exert themselves, to manufacture, Salt Petre, Sulphur, Powder, Arms, Cannon, Mortars, Cloathing, and every Thing, necessary for the Support of Life. Our civil Governments will feel a Vigour, hitherto unknown. Our military Operations by Sea and Land, will be conducted with greater Spirit. Privateers will Swarm in great Numbers. Foreigners will then exert themselves to Supply Us with what we want. Foreign Courts will not disdain to treat with Us, upon equal Terms. Nay further in my opinion, such a Declaration, instead of uniting the People of Great Britain against Us, will raise Such a Storm against the Measures of Administration as will obstruct the War, and throw the Kingdom into Confusion.

A Committee is appointed to prepare a Confederation of the Colonies, ascertaining the Terms and Ends of the Compact, and the Limits of the Continental Constitution, and another Committee is appointed for Purposes as important. These Committees will report in a Week or two, and then the last finishing Stroke will be given to the Politicks of this Revolution. Nothing after that will remain, but War. I think I may then, petition my Constituents for Leave to return to my Family, and leave the War to be conducted by others, who understand it better. I am weary, thoroughly weary, and ought to have a little Rest.

I am grieved to hear, as I do from various Quarters of that Rage for Innovation, which appears, in So many wild Shapes, in our Province. Are not these ridiculous Projects, prompted, excited, and encouraged by disaffected Persons, in order to divide, dissipate, and distract, the Attention of the People, at a Time, when every Thought Should be employed, and every Sinew exerted, for the Defence of the Country? Many of the Projects that I have heard of, are not repairing, but pulling down, the Building, when it is on Fire, instead of labouring to extinguish the Flames. The Projects of County Assemblies, Town Registers, and Town Probates of Wills, are founded in narrow, Notions, Sordid Stingyness and profound Ignorance, and tend directly to Barbarism. I am not Solicitous who takes Offence at this Language. I blush to see such Stuff in our public Papers, which used to breath a Spirit much more liberal.

I rejoice to see, in the Lists of both Houses, So many Names, respectable for Parts and Learning. I hope their Fortitude and Zeal will be in Proportion: and then, I am Sure their Country will have great Cause to bless them. I am, sir, with every sentiment of Friendship and Veneration, your affectionate and humble servant

John Adams

CONGRESS VOTES FOR INDEPENDENCE

To Abigail Adams

Philadelphia July 3. 1776

Your Favour of June 17. dated at Plymouth, was handed me, by Yesterdays Post. I was much pleased to find that you had taken a Journey to Plymouth, to see your Friends in the long Absence of one whom you may wish to see. The Excursion will be an Amusement, and will serve your Health. How happy would it have made me to have taken this Journey with you?

I was informed, a day or two before the Receipt of your

Letter, that you was gone to Plymouth, by Mrs. Polly Palmer, who was obliging enough in your Absence, to inform me, of the Particulars of the Expedition to the lower Harbour against the Men of War. Her Narration is executed, with a Precision and Perspicuity, which would have become the Pen of an accomplished Historian.

I am very glad you had so good an opportunity of seeing one of our little American Men of War. Many Ideas, new to you, must have presented themselves in such a Scene; and you will in future, better understand the Relations of Sea Engagements.

I rejoice extreamly at Dr. Bulfinches Petition to open an Hospital. But I hope, the Business will be done upon a larger Scale. I hope, that one Hospital will be licensed in every County, if not in every Town. I am happy to find you resolved, to be with the Children, in the first Class. Mr. Whitney and Mrs. Katy Quincy, are cleverly through Innoculation, in this City.

I have one favour to ask, and that is, that in your future Letters, you would acknowledge the Receipt of all those you may receive from me, and mention their Dates. By this Means I shall know if any of mine miscarry.

The Information you give me of our Friends refusing his Appointment, has given me much Pain, Grief and Anxiety. I believe I shall be obliged to follow his Example. I have not Fortune enough to support my Family, and what is of more Importance, to support the Dignity of that exalted Station. It is too high and lifted up, for me; who delight in nothing so much as Retreat, Solitude, Silence, and Obscurity. In private Life, no one has a Right to censure me for following my own Inclinations, in Retirement, Simplicity, and Frugality: in public Life, every Man has a Right to remark as he pleases, at least he thinks so.

Yesterday the greatest Question was decided, which ever was debated in America, and a greater perhaps, never was or will be decided among Men. A Resolution was passed without one dissenting Colony "that these united Colonies, are, and of right ought to be free and independent States, and as such, they have, and of Right ought to have full Power to make War, conclude Peace, establish Commerce, and to do all the other Acts and Things, which other States may rightfully do." You will see in a few days a Declaration setting forth the Causes, which have impell'd Us to this mighty Revolution, and the Reasons which will justify it, in the Sight of God and Man. A Plan of Confederation will be taken up in a few days.

When I look back to the Year 1761, and recollect the Argument concerning Writs of Assistance, in the Superiour Court, which I have hitherto considered as the Commencement of the Controversy, between Great Britain and America, and run through the whole Period from that Time to this, and recollect the series of political Events, the Chain of Causes and Effects, I am surprized at the Suddenness, as well as Greatness of this Revolution. Britain has been fill'd with Folly, and America with Wisdom, at least this is my Judgment.—Time must determine. It is the Will of Heaven, that the two Countries should be sundered forever. It may be the Will of Heaven that America shall suffer Calamities still more wasting and Distresses yet more dreadfull. If this is to be the Case, it will have this good Effect, at least: it will inspire Us with many Virtues, which We have not, and correct many Errors, Follies, and Vices, which threaten to disturb, dishonour, and destroy Us.—The Furnace of Affliction produces Refinement, in States as well as Individuals. And the new Governments we are assuming, in every Part, will require a Purification from our Vices, and an Augmentation of our Virtues or they will be no Blessings. The People will have unbounded Power. And the People are extreamly addicted to Corruption and Venality, as well as the Great.—I am not without Apprehensions from this Quarter. But I must submit all my Hopes and Fears, to an overruling Providence, in which, unfashionable as the Faith may be, I firmly believe.

"THE MOST MEMORABLE EPOCHA"

To Abigail Adams

Philadelphia July 3d. 1776

Had a Declaration of Independency been made seven Months ago, it would have been attended with many great and glorious Effects. . . . We might before this Hour, have formed Alliances with foreign States.—We should have mastered Quebec and been in Possession of Canada. . . . You will perhaps wonder, how such a Declaration would have influenced our Affairs, in Canada, but if I could write with Freedom I could easily convince you, that it would, and explain to you the manner how.—Many Gentlemen in high Stations and of great Influence have been duped, by the ministerial Bubble of Commissioners to treat. . . . And in real, sincere Expectation of this Event, which they so fondly wished, they have been slow and languid, in promoting Measures for the Reduction of that Province. Others there are in the Colonies who really wished that our Enterprise in Canada would be defeated, that the Colonies might be brought into Danger and Distress between two Fires, and be thus induced to submit. Others really wished to defeat the Expedition to Canada, lest the Conquest of it, should elevate the Minds of the People too much to hearken to those Terms of Reconciliation which they believed would be offered Us. These jarring Views, Wishes and Designs, occasioned an opposition to many salutary Measures, which were proposed for the Support of that Expedition, and caused Obstructions, Embarrassments and studied Delays, which have finally, lost Us the Province.

All these Causes however in Conjunction would not have disappointed Us, if it had not been for a Misfortune, which could not be foreseen, and perhaps could not have been prevented, I mean the Prevalence of the small Pox among our Troops. . . . This fatal Pestilence compleated our Destruction.—It is a Frown of Providence upon Us, which We ought to lay to heart.

But on the other Hand, the Delay of this Declaration to this Time, has many great Advantages attending it.—The Hopes of Reconciliation, which were fondly entertained by Multitudes of honest and well meaning tho weak and mistaken People, have been gradually and at last totally extinguished.—Time has been given for the whole People, maturely to consider the great Question of Independence and to ripen their Judgments, dissipate their Fears, and allure their Hopes, by discussing it in News Papers and Pamphletts, by debating it, in Assemblies, Conventions, Committees of Safety and Inspection, in Town and County Meetings, as well as in private Conversations, so that the whole People in every Colony of the 13, have now adopted it, as their own Act.—This will cement the Union, and avoid those Heats and perhaps Convulsions which might have been occasioned, by such a Declaration Six Months ago.

But the Day is past. The Second Day of July 1776, will be the most memorable Epocha, in the History of America.—I am apt to believe that it will be celebrated, by succeeding Generations, as the great anniversary Festival. It ought to be commemorated, as the Day of Deliverance by solemn Acts of Devotion to God Almighty. It ought to be solemnized with Pomp and Parade, with Shews, Games, Sports, Guns, Bells, Bonfires and Illuminations from one End of this Continent to the other from this Time forward forever more.

You will think me transported with Enthusiasm but I am not.—I am well aware of the Toil and Blood and Treasure, that it will cost Us to maintain this Declaration, and support and defend these States.—Yet through all the Gloom I can see the Rays of ravishing Light and Glory. I can see that the End is more than worth all the Means. And that Posterity will tryumph in that Days Transaction, even altho We should rue it, which I trust in God We shall not.

STYLES OF WRITING

To Abigail Adams

Philadelphia July 7. 1776

It is worth the while of a Person, obliged to write as much as I do, to consider the Varieties of Style. . . . The Epistolary, is essentially different from the oratorical, and the Historical Style. . . . Oratory abounds with Figures. History is simple, but grave, majestic and formal. Letters, like Conversation, should be free, easy, and familiar.

Simplicity and Familiarity, are the Characteristicks of this Kind of Writing. Affectation is as disagreable, in a Letter, as in Conversation, and therefore, studied Language, premeditated Method, and sublime Sentiments are not expected in a Letter.

Notwithstanding which, the Sublime, as well as the beautifull, and the Novel, may naturally enough, appear, in familiar Letters among Friends.—Among the ancients there are two illustrious Examples of the Epistolary Style, Cicero and Pliny, whose Letters present you with Modells of fine Writing, which has borne the Criticism of almost two thousand Years. In these, you see the Sublime, the beautilfull, the Novell, and the Pathetick, conveyed in as much Simplicity, Ease, Freedom, and Familiarity, as Language is capable of.

Let me request you, to turn over the Leaves of the Præceptor, to a Letter of Pliny the Younger, in which he has transmitted, to these days, the History of his Uncles Philosophical Curiosity, his Heroic Courage and his melancholly Catastrophe. Read it, and say, whether it is possible to write a Narrative of Facts, in a better Manner. It is copious and particular, in selecting the Circumstances, most natural, remarkable and affecting. There is not an incident omitted, which ought to have been remembered, nor one inserted that is not worth Remembrance.

It gives you, an Idea of the Scæne, as distinct and perfect, as if a Painter had drawn it to the Life, before your Eyes. It interests your Passions, as much as if you had been an Eye Witness of the whole Transaction. Yet there are no Figures, or Art used. All is as simple, natural, easy, and familiar, as if the Story had been told in Conversation, without a Moments Premeditation.

Pope and Swift have given the World a Collection of their Letters; but I think in general, they fall short, in the Epistolary Way, of their own Emminence in Poetry and other Branches of Literature. Very few of their Letters, have ever engaged much of my Attention. Gays Letter, concerning the Pair of Lovers kill'd by Lightning, is worth more than the whole Collection, in Point of Simplicity, and Elegance of Composition, and as a genuine Model of the epistolary Style.—There is a Book, which I wish you owned, I mean Rollins Belles Letters, in which the Variations of Style are explained.

Early Youth is the Time, to learn the Arts and Sciences, and especially to correct the Ear, and the Imagination, by forming a Style. I wish you would think of forming the Taste, and Judgment of your Children, now, before any unchaste Sounds have fastened on their Ears, and before any Affectation, or Vanity, is settled on their Minds, upon the pure Principles of Nature. . . . Musick is a great Advantage, for Style depends in Part upon a delicate Ear.

The Faculty of Writing is attainable, by Art, Practice, and Habit only. The sooner, therefore the Practice begins, the more likely it will be to succeed. Have no Mercy upon an affected Phrase, any more than an affected Air, Gate, Dress, or Manners.

Your Children have Capacities equal to any Thing. There is a Vigour in the Understanding, and a Spirit and Fire in the Temper of every one of them, which is capable of ascending the Heights of Art, Science, Trade, War, or Politicks.

They should be set to compose Descriptions of Scænes and Objects, and Narrations of Facts and Events, Declamations upon Topicks, and other Exercises of various sorts, should be prescribed to them.

Set a Child to form a Description of a Battle, a Storm, a seige, a Cloud, a Mountain, a Lake, a City, an Harbour, a Country seat, a Meadow, a Forrest, or almost any Thing, that may occur to your Thoughts.

Set him to compose a Narration of all the little Incidents and Events of a Day, a Journey, a Ride, or a Walk. In this Way, a Taste will be formed, and a Facility of Writing acquired.

For myself, as I never had a regular Tutor, I never studied any Thing methodically, and consequently never was compleatly accomplished in any Thing. But as I am conscious of my own Deficiency, in these Respects, I should be the less pardonable, if I neglected the Education of my Children.

In Grammar, Rhetoric, Logic, my Education was imperfect, because unmethodical. Yet I have perhaps read more upon these Arts, and considered them in a more extensive View than some others.

Notes on Debates in Congress on the Articles of Confederation, July 30–August 2, 1776

JULY 30. 1776.

Dr. Franklin. Let the smaller Colonies give equal Money and Men, and then have an equal Vote. But if they have an equal Vote, without bearing equal Burthens, a Confederation upon such iniquitous Principles, will never last long.

Dr. Witherspoon. We all agree that there must and shall be a Confederation, for this War. It will diminish the Glory of our Object, and depreciate our Hope. It will damp the Ardor of the People. The greatest danger We have is of Disunion among ourselves. Is it not plausible, that the small States will be oppressed by the great ones. The Spartans and Helotes—the Romans and their Dependents.

Every Colony is a distinct Person. States of Holland.

Clark. We must apply for Pardons, if We dont confederate. . . .

Wilson. . . . We should settle upon some Plan of Representation.

Chase. Moves that the Word, White, should be inserted in the II. Article. The Negroes are wealth. Numbers are not a certain Rule of wealth. It is the best Rule We can lay down. Negroes a Species of Property—personal Estate. If Negroes are taken into the Computation of Numbers to ascertain Wealth, they ought to be in settling the Representation. The Massachusetts Fisheries, and Navigation ought to be taken into Consideration. The young and old Negroes are a Burthen to their owners. The Eastern Colonies have a great Advantage, in Trade. This will give them a Superiority. We shall be governed by our Interests, and ought to be. If I am satisfied, in the Rule of levying and appropriating Money, I am willing the small Colonies may have a Vote.

Wilson. If the War continues 2 Years, each Soul will have 40 dollars to pay of the public debt. It will be the greatest Encouragement to continue Slave keeping, and to increase them, that can be to exempt them from the Numbers which are to vote and pay. . . . Slaves are Taxables in the Southern Colonies. It will be partial and unequal. Some Colonies have as many black as white. . . . These will not pay more than half what they ought. Slaves prevent freemen cultivating a Country. It is attended with many Inconveniences.

Lynch. If it is debated, whether their Slaves are their Property, there is an End of the Confederation. Our Slaves being our Property, why should they be taxed more than the Land, Sheep, Cattle, Horses, &c. Freemen cannot be got, to work in our Colonies. It is not in the Ability, or Inclination of freemen to do the Work that the Negroes do. Carolina has taxed their Negroes. So have other Colonies, their Lands.

Dr. Franklin. Slaves rather weaken than strengthen the State, and there is therefore some difference between them and Sheep. Sheep will never make any Insurrections.

Rutledge. . . . I shall be happy to get rid of the idea of Slavery. The Slaves do not signify Property. The old and young cannot work. The Property of some Colonies are to be taxed, in others not. The Eastern Colonies will become the Carriers for the Southern. They will obtain Wealth for which they will not be taxed.

AUG. I. 1776.

Hooper. N.C. is a striking Exception to the general Rule that was laid down Yesterday, that the Riches of a Country are in Proportion to the Numbers of Inhabitants. A Gentleman of 3 or 400 Negroes, dont raise more corn than feeds them. A Labourer cant be hired for less than £24 a Year in Mass. Bay. The neat profit of a Negro is not more than 5 or 6£ pr. An. I wish to see the day that Slaves are not necessary. Whites and Negroes cannot work together. Negroes are Goods and Chattells, are Property. A Negro works under the Impulse of fear— has no Care of his Masters Interest.

17. Art.

Dr. Franklin moves that Votes should be in Proportion to Numbers.

Mr. Middleton moves that the Vote should be according to what they pay.

Sherman thinks We ought not to vote according to Numbers.

We are Reps of States not Individuals. States of Holland. The Consent of every one is necessary. 3 Colonies would govern the whole but would not have a Majority of Strength to carry those Votes into Execution.

The Vote should be taken two Ways. Call the Colonies and call the Individuals, and have a Majority of both.

Dr. Rush. Abbe Reynauld has attributed the Ruin of the united Provinces to 3 Causes. The principal one is that the Consent of every State is necessary. The other that the Members are obliged to consult their Constituents upon all Occasions.

We loose an equal Representation. We represent the People. It will tend to keep up colonial Distinctions. We are now a new Nation. Our Trade, Language, Customs, Manners dont differ more than they do in G. Britain.

The more a Man aims at serving America the more he serves his Colony.

It will promote Factions in Congress and in the States.

It will prevent the Growth of Freedom in America. We shall be loth to admit new Colonies into the Confederation. If We vote by Numbers Liberty will be always safe. Mass. is contiguous to 2 small Colonies, R.I. and N.H. Pen. is near N.Y. and D. Virginia is between Maryland and N. Carolina.

We have been too free with the Word Independence. We are dependent on each other—not totally independent States.

Montesquieu pronounced the Confederation of Licea the best that ever was made. The Cities had different Weights in the Scale.

China is not larger than one of our Colonies. How populous.

It is said that the small Colonies deposit their all. This is deceiving Us with a Word.

I would not have it understood, that I am pleading the Cause of Pensilvania. When I entered that door, I considered myself a Citizen of America.

Dr. Witherspoon. Repn in England is unequal. Must I have 3 Votes in a County because I have 3 times as much Money as my Neighbour. Congress are to determine the Limits of Colonies.

G Hopkins. A momentous Question. Many difficulties on each

Side. 4 larger, 5 lesser, 4 stand indifferent. V. M. P. M. make more than half the People. 4 may alw

C., N.Y., 2 Carolinas, not concerned at all. The dissinterested Coolness of these Colonies ought to determine. I can easily feel the Reasoning of the larger Colonies. Pleasing Theories always gave Way to the Prejudices, Passions, and Interests of Mankind.

The Germanic Confederation. The K. of Prussia has an equal Vote. The Helvetic Confederacy. It cant be expected that 9 Colonies will give Way to be governed by 4. The Safety of the whole depends upon the distinctions of Colonies.

Dr. Franklin. I hear many ingenious Arguments to perswade Us that an unequal Representation is a very good Thing. If We had been born and bred under an unequal Representation We might bear it. But to sett out with an unequal Representation is unreasonable.

It is said the great Colonies will swallow up the less. Scotland said the same Thing at the Union.

Dr. Witherspoon. Rises to explain a few Circumstances relating to Scotland. That was an incorporating Union, not a federal. The Nobility and Gentry resort to England.

In determining all Questions, each State shall have a Weight in Proportion to what it contributes to the public Expences of the united States.

AUG. 2d.

Limiting the Bounds of States which by Charter &c. extend to the South Sea.

Sherman thinks the Bounds ought to be settled. A Majority of States have no Claim to the South Sea. Moves this Amendment, to be substituted in Place of this Clause and also instead of the 15th Article—

No Lands to be seperated from any State, which are already settled, or become private Property.

Chase denys that any Colony has a Right, to go to the South Sea. . . .

Harrison. How came Maryland by its Land? but by its Charter: By its Charter Virginia owns to the South Sea. Gentlemen shall not pare away the Colony of Virginia. R. Island has more

Generosity, than to wish the Massachusetts pared away. Delaware does not wish to pare away Pensilvania.

Huntington. Admit there is danger, from Virginia, does it follow that Congress has a Right to limit her Bounds? The Consequence is not to enter into Confederation. But as to the Question of Right, We all unite against mutilating Charters. I cant agree to the Principle. We are a Spectacle to all Europe. I am not so much alarmed at the Danger, from Virginia, as some are. My fears are not alarmed. They have acted as noble a Part as any. I doubt not the Wisdom of Virginia will limit themselves. A Mans Right does not cease to be a Right because it is large. The Q of Right must be determined by the Principles of the common Law.

Stone. This Argument is taken up upon very wrong Ground. It is considered as if We were voting away the Territory of particular Colonies, and Gentlemen work themselves up into Warmth, upon that Supposition. Suppose Virginia should. The small Colonies have a Right to Happiness and Security. They would have no Safety if the great Colonies were not limited. We shall grant Lands in small Quantities, without Rent, or Tribute, or purchase Money. It is said that Virginia is attacked on every Side. Is it meant that Virginia shall sell the Lands for their own Emolument?

All the Colonies have defended these Lands vs. the K. of G.B., and at the Expence of all. Does Virginia intend to establish Quitrents?

I dont mean that the united States shall sell them to get Money by them.

Jefferson. I protest vs. the Right of Congress to decide, upon the Right of Virginia. Virginia has released all Claims to the Lands settled by Maryland &c.

Remarks in Congress on the Articles of Confederation

Recorded by Thomas Jefferson

John Adams advocated the voting in proportion to numbers. he said that we stand here as the representatives of the people. that in some states the people are many, in others they are few; that therefore their vote here should be proportioned to the numbers from whom it comes. reason, justice, & equity never had weight enough on the face of the earth to govern the councils of men. it is interest alone which does it, and it is interest alone which can be trusted. that therefore the interests within doors should be the mathematical representatives of the interests without doors. that the individuality of the colonies is a mere sound. does the individuality of a colony increase it's wealth or numbers? if it does; pay equally. if it does not add weight in the scale of the confederacy, it cannot add to their rights, nor weight in argument. A. has £50. B. £500. C. £1000 in partnership. is it just they should equally dispose of the monies of the partnership? it has been said we are independant individuals making a bargain together. the question is not what we are now, but what we ought to be when our bargain shall be made. the confederacy is to make us one individual only; it is to form us, like separate parcels of metal, into one common mass. we shall no longer retain our separate individuality, but become a single individual as to all questions submitted to the Confederacy. therefore all those reasons which prove the justice & expediency of equal representation in other assemblies, hold good here. it has been objected that a proportional vote will endanger the smaller states. we answer that an equal vote will endanger the larger. Virginia, Pennsylvania, & Massachusets are the three greater colonies. consider their distance, their difference of produce, of interests, & of manners, & it is apparent they can never have an interest or inclination to combine for the oppression of the smaller. that the smaller will naturally divide on all questions with the larger. Rhodeisld. from it's relation, similarity & intercourse will generally pursue the same objects with Massachusets; Jersey, Delaware & Maryland with Pennsylvania.

Mr. John Adams observed that the numbers of people were taken by this article as an index of the wealth of the state & not as subjects of taxation. that as to this matter it was of no consequence by what name you called your people, whether by that of freemen or of slaves. that in some countries the labouring poor were called freemen, in others they were called slaves; but that the difference as to the state was imaginary only. what matters it whether a landlord employing ten labourers in his farm, gives them annually as much money as will buy them the necessaries of life, or gives them those necessaries at short hand. the ten labourers add as much wealth annually to the state, increase it's exports as much in the one case as the other. certainly 500 freemen produce no more profits, no greater surplus for the paiment of taxes than 500 slaves. therefore the state in which are the labourers called freemen should be taxed no more than that in which are those called slaves. suppose by any extraordinary operation of nature or of law one half the labourers of a state could in the course of one night be transformed into slaves: would the state be made the poorer or the less able to pay taxes? that the condition of the labouring poor in most countries, that of the fishermen particularly of the Northern states is as abject as that of slaves. it is the number of labourers which produce the surplus for taxation, and numbers therefore indiscriminately are the fair index of wealth. that it is the use of the word 'property' here, & it's application to some of the people of the state, which produces the fallacy. how does the Southern farmer procure slaves? either by importation or by purchase from his neighbor. if he imports a slave, he adds one to the number of labourers in his country, and proportionably to it's profits & abilities to pay taxes. if he buys from his neighbor, it is only a transfer of a labourer from one farm to another, which does not change the annual produce of the state, & therefore should not change it's tax. that if a Northern farmer works ten labourers on his farm, he can, it is true, invest the surplus of ten men's labour in cattle: but so may the Southern farmer working ten slaves. that a state of 100,000 freemen can maintain no more cattle than one of 100,000 slaves. therefore they have no more of that kind of property. that a slave may indeed from the custom of speech be more properly called the wealth of his master, than the free labourer might be called the wealth of his employer: but as to the state both were equally it's wealth, and should therefore equally add to the quota of it's tax.

July 30, 1776

EXPECTATIONS FOR NEW ENGLAND

To Abigail Adams

Aug. 3. 1776

The Post was later than usual to day, so that I had not yours of July 24 till this Evening. You have made me very happy, by the particular and favourable Account you give me of all the Family. But I dont understand how there are so many who have no Eruptions, and no Symptoms. The Inflammation in the Arm might do, but without these, there is no small Pox.

I will lay a Wager, that your whole Hospital have not had so much small Pox, as Mrs. Katy Quincy. Upon my Word she has had an Abundance of it, but is finely recovered, looks as fresh as a Rose, but pitted all over, as thick as ever you saw any one. I this Evening presented your Compliments and Thanks to Mr. Hancock for his polite offer of his House, and likewise your Compliments to his Lady and Mrs. Katy.

Aug. 4

Went this Morning to the Baptist Meeting, in Hopes of hearing Mr. Stillman, but was dissappointed. He was there, but another Gentleman preached. His Action was violent to a degree bordering on fury. His Gestures, unnatural, and distorted. Not the least Idea of Grace in his Motions, or Elegance in his Style. His Voice was vociferous and boisterous, and his Composition almost wholly destitute of Ingenuity. I wonder extreamly at the Fondness of our People for schollars educated at the Southward and for southern Preachers. There is no one Thing, in which We excell them more, than in our University, our schollars, and Preachers. Particular Gentlemen here, who have improved upon their Education by Travel, shine. But in general, old Massachusetts outshines her younger sisters, still. In several Particulars, they have more Wit, than We. They have Societies; the philosophical Society particularly, which excites a scientific Emulation, and propagates their Fame. If ever I get through this Scene of Politicks and War, I will spend the Remainder of my days, in endeavouring to instruct my Countrymen in the Art of making the most of their Abilities and Virtues, an Art, which they have hitherto, too much neglected. A philosophical society shall be established at Boston, if I have Wit and Address enough to accomplish it, sometime or other.—Pray set Brother Cranch's Philosophical Head to plodding upon this Project. Many of his Lucubrations would have been published and preserved, for the Benefit of Mankind, and for his Honour, if such a Clubb had existed.

My Countrymen want Art and Address. They want Knowledge of the World. They want the exteriour and superficial Accomplishments of Gentlemen, upon which the World has foolishly set so high a Value. In solid Abilities and real Virtues, they vastly excell in general, any People upon this Continent. Our N. England People are Aukward and bashfull; yet they are pert, ostentatious and vain, a Mixture which excites Ridicule and gives Disgust. They have not the faculty of shewing themselves to the best Advantage, nor the Art of concealing this faculty. An Art and Faculty which some People possess in the highest degree. Our Deficiencies in these Respects, are owing wholly to the little Intercourse We have had with strangers, and to our Inexperience in the World. These Imperfections must be remedied, for New England must produce the Heroes, the statesmen, the Philosophers, or America will make no great Figure for some Time.

Our Army is rather sickly at N. York, and We live in daily Expectation of hearing of some great Event. May God almighty grant it may be prosperous for America.—Hope is an Anchor and a Cordial. Disappointment however will not disconcert me.

If you will come to Philadelphia in September, I will stay, as long as you please. I should be as proud and happy as a Bridegroom. Yours.

DESIGNING A GREAT SEAL

To Abigail Adams

Philadelphia 14. August 1776

This is the Anniversary of a memorable day, in the History of America: a day when the Principle of American Resistance and Independence, was first asserted, and carried into Action. The Stamp Office fell before the rising Spirit of our Countrymen.—It is not impossible that the two *gratefull* Brothers may make their grand Attack this very day: if they should, it is possible it may be more glorious for this Country, than ever: it is certain it will become more memorable.

Your Favours of August 1. and 5. came by Yesterdays Post. I congratulate you all upon your agreable Prospects. Even my pathetic little Hero Charles, I hope will have the Distemper finely. It is very odd that the Dr. cant put Infection enough into his Veigns, nay it is unaccountable to me that he has not taken it, in the natural Way before now. I am under little Apprehension, prepared as he is, if he should. I am concerned about you, much more. So many Persons about you, sick. The Children troublesome—your Mind perplexed—yourself weak and relaxed. The Situation must be disagreable. The Country Air, and Exercise however, will refresh you.

I am put upon a Committee to prepare a Device for a Golden Medal to commemorate the Surrender of Boston to the American Arms, and upon another to prepare Devices for a Great Seal for the confederated States. There is a Gentleman here of French Extraction, whose Name is Du simitiere, a Painter by Profession whose Designs are very ingenious, and his Drawings well executed. He has been applied to for his Advice. I waited on him yesterday, and saw his Sketches. For the Medal he proposes Liberty with her Spear and Pileus, leaning on General Washington. The British Fleet in Boston Harbour, with all their Sterns towards the Town, the American Troops, marching in. For the Seal he proposes. The Arms of the several Nations from whence America has been peopled, as English, Scotch, Irish, Dutch, German &c. each in a Shield. On one side of them Liberty, with her Pileus, on the other a Rifler, in his Uniform, with his Rifled Gun in one Hand, and his Toma-hauk, in the other. This Dress and these Troops with this Kind of Armour, being peculiar to America—unless the Dress was known to the Romans. Dr. F shewed me, yesterday, a Book, containing an Account of the Dresses of all the Roman Sol-diers, one of which, appeared exactly like it.

This Mr. Du simitiere is a very curious Man. He has begun a Collection of Materials for an History of this Revolution. He begins with the first Advices of the Tea Ships. He cutts out of the Newspapers, every Scrap of Intelligence, and every Piece of Speculation, and pastes it upon clean Paper, arranging them under the Head of the State to which they belong and intends to bind them up in Volumes. He has a List of every Specula-tion and Pamphlet concerning Independence, and another of those concerning Forms of Government.

Dr. F. proposes a Device for a Seal. Moses lifting up his Wand, and dividing the Red Sea, and Pharaoh, in his Chariot overwhelmed with the Waters.—This Motto. Rebellion to Tyrants is Obedience to God.

Mr. Jefferson proposed. The Children of Israel in the Wilderness, led by a Cloud by day, and a Pillar of Fire by night, and on the other Side Hengist and Horsa, the Saxon Chiefs, from whom We claim the Honour of being descended and whose Political Principles and Form of Government We have assumed.

I proposed the Choice of Hercules, as engraved by Gri-beline in some Editions of Lord Shaftsburys Works. The Hero resting on his Clubb. Virtue pointing to her rugged Moun-tain, on one Hand, and perswading him to ascend. Sloth, glancing at her flowery Paths of Pleasure, wantonly reclining on the Ground, displaying the Charms both of her Eloquence and Person, to seduce him into Vice. But this is too compli-cated a Group for a Seal or Medal, and it is not original.

I shall conclude by repeating my Request for Horses and a servant. Let the Horses be good ones. I cant ride a bad Horse, so many hundred Miles. If our Affairs had not been in so criti-cal a state at N. York, I should have run away before now. But I am determined now to stay, untill some Gentleman is sent here in my Room, and untill my Horses come. But the Time will be very tedious.

The whole Force is arrived at Staten Island.

REQUIREMENTS FOR OFFICERS

To William Tudor

Dear Sir   Philadelphia August 24. 1776

Your Favours of 18 and 19 of August are before me. I am much obliged to you for them, and am determined to pursue this Correspondence, untill I can obtain a perfect Knowledge of the Characters of our Field Officers.

If the Colonell quits the Regiment Austin will certainly be promoted, unless Some Stain can be fixed upon his Character, Since he has been in the Army. His Genius is equal to any one of his Age. His Education is not inferiour. So far I can Say of my own Knowledge. If his Morals, his Honour, and his Discretion, are equal there is not a Superiour Character of his Age in the Army. If I could Speak with as much Confidence of these as of those, I should not hesitate one Moment to propose him for the Command of a Regiment.

You mention a Major Lee in Glovers Regiment. I wish you had given me more of his Biography and Character. Captn. Jos. Lee the Son of Coll. Jer. Lee, has so much Merit, that I think he ought to be promoted. I never heard of these two Gentlemen before. I mean of their being in the Army. Are they Men of Reflection? That is the Question. Honour, Spirit, and Reflection, are Sufficient to make very respectable Officers, without extensive Genius, or deep Science, or great Literature. Yet all these are necessary to form the great Commander. You Say there are Several other young Officers of Parts and Spirit in that Regiment, I wish you had mentioned their Names and Characters. You Say they will never "basely cringe." I hope not: but I also hope, that they will distinguish between Adulation and Politeness: between Servility and Complaisance: between Idolatry and Obedience: A manly, firm attachment to the General, as far as his Character and Conduct are good, is a Characteristic of a good Officer, and absolutely necessary to establish Discipline in an Army.

I have a great Character of Lt. Coll. Shepherd and Major Brooks. I wish you would write me a History of their Lives. I know nothing of them. If Brooks is my old Friend Ned of Mistick, as Mr. Hancock this Evening gave me some Reasons to suspect, and if he deserves the Character I have received of him, as I doubt not he does, if he is not promoted before long, it shall be because I have no Brains nor Resolution. I never, untill this Evening Suspected that he was in the Army. Pray tell me what Regiment he is in.

The Articles of War, are all passed but one—that remains to be considered. But I fear, they will not be made to take Place, yet. Gentlemen are afraid, the Militia, now in such Numbers in the Army, will be disquieted and terrified with them. The General must quicken this Business, or I am afraid it will be very slow. Every Body seems convinced of the Necessity of them, yet many are afraid to venture the Experiment. I must intreat you to write me, by every Post.

Let me intreat you, Mr. Tudor, to exert yourself, among the young Gentlemen of your Acquaintance in the Army, to excite in them, an Ambition to excell: to inspire them, with that Sense of Honour, and Elevation of sentiment without which they must, and ought to remain undistinguished. Draw their Attention to those Sciences, and those Branches of Literature, which are more immediately Subservient to the Art of War. Cant you excite in them a Thirst for military Knowledge? Make them inquisitive after the best Writers, curious to know, and ambitious to imitate the Lives and Actions of great Captains, ancient and modern. An Officer, high in Rank, should be possessed of very extensive Knowledge of Science, and Literature, Men and Things. A Citizen of a free Government, he Should be Master of the Laws and Constitution, least he injure fundamentally those Rights which he professes to defend. He Should have a keen Penetration and a deep Discernment of the Tempers, Natures, and Characters of Men. He Should have an Activity, and Diligence, Superiour to all Fatigue. He should have a Patience and Self Government, Superiour to all Flights and Transports of Passion. He Should have a Candour and

Moderation, above all Prejudices, and Partialities. His Views should be large enough to comprehend the whole System of the Government and the Army, that he may accommodate his Plans and Measures to the best good, and the essential Movements of those great Machines. His Benevolence and Humanity, his Decency, Politeness and Civility, Should ever predominate in his Breast. He should be possessed of a certain masterly, order, Method, and Decision, Superiour to all Perplexity, and Confusion in Business. There is in Such a Character, whenever and wherever it appears, a decisive Energy, which hurries away before it, all Difficulties, and leaves to the World of Mankind no Leisure, or opportunity to do any Thing towards it, but Admire, it.

There is nothing perhaps upon which the Character of a General So much depends, as the Talent of Writing Letters. The Duty of a constant Correspondence with the Sovereign, whether King or Congress, is inseparable from a Commander in any Department, and the Faculty of placing every Thing, in the happiest Point of Light is as usefull as any, he can possess. I fear this is too much neglected by our young Gentlemen. I know it is by you, who can write but will not.

Geography is of great Importance to a General. Our Officers should be perfect Masters of American Geography. Nothing is less understood. Sensible of this, Since I have belonged to the Board of War I have endeavoured to perswade my Colleagues of its Importance and We are making a Collection of all the Maps, extant, whether of all America or any Part of it, to be hung up in the office, So that Gentlemen may know of one Place in America where they may Satisfy their Curiosity, or resolve any doubt. I should be obliged to you, if you would inquire at every Print sellers shop in New York, and of every Gentleman, curious in this Way concerning American Maps, in the whole or Part and send me an Account of them. Mr. Hazard is as likely to know as any Man, in New York. I should never find an End of Scribbling to you, if I had nothing else to do. I am, yours &c.,

John Adams

DISAPPOINTMENT WITH MASSACHUSETTS

To Joseph Hawley

Dear Sir   Philadelphia Aug. 25. 1776

It is So long Since I had the Pleasure of Writing to you, or the Honour of receiving a Letter from You, that I have forgotten, on which side the Ballance of the Account lies, at least which wrote the last letter. But Ceremonies of this Kind ought not to interrupt a free Communication of sentiments, in Times So critical and important as these.

We have been apt to flatter ourselves, with gay Prospects of Happiness to the People Prosperity to the State, and Glory to our Arms, from those free Kinds of Governments, which are to be erected in America.

And it is very true that no People ever had a finer opportunity to settle Things upon the best Foundations. But yet I fear that human Nature will be found to be the Same in America as it has been in Europe, and that the true Principles of Liberty will not be Sufficiently attended to.

Knowledge is among the most essential Foundations of Liberty. But is there not a Jealousy or an Envy taking Place among the Multitude of Men of Learning, and, a Wish to exclude them from the public Councils and from military Command? I could mention many Phenomena, in various Parts of these States, which indicate such a growing Disposition. To what Cause Shall I attribute the Surprizing Conduct of the Massachusetts Bay? How has it happened that such an illiterate Group of General and Field Officers, have been thrust into public View, by that Commonwealth which as it has an indisputable Superiority of Power to every other, in America as well as of Experience and Skill in War, ought to have set an Example to her sisters, by sending into the Field her best Men. Men of the most Genius Learning, Reflection, and Address. Instead of this, every Man you send into the Army as a General or a Collonell exhibits a Character, which nobody ever heard of before, or an aukward, illiterate, ill bred Man. Who is General Fellows? and who is General Brickett? Who is Coll. Holman, Cary, Smith?

This Conduct is Sinking the Character of the Province, into the lowest Contempt, and is injuring the service beyond description. Able Officers are the Soul of an Army. Good Officers will make good Soldiers, if you give them human Nature as a Material to work upon. But ignorant, unambitious, unfeeling unprincipled Officers, will make bad soldiers of the best Men in the World.

I am ashamed and grieved to my inmost Soul, for the disgrace brought upon the Massachusetts, in not having half its Proportion of General Officers. But there is not a Single Man among all our Collonells that I dare to recommend for a General Officer, except Knox and Porter, and these are So low down in the List, that it is dangerous promoting them over the Heads of so many. If this is the Effect of popular Elections it is but a poor Pangyrick, upon such Elections. I fear We shall find that popular Elections are not oftener determined, upon pure Principles of Merit, Virtue, and public Spirit, than the Nominations of a Court, if We dont take Care. I fear there is an infinity of Corruption in our Elections already crept in. All Kinds of Favour, Intrigue and Partiality in Elections are as real, Corruption in my Mind, as Treats and Bribes. A popular Government is the worse Curse, to which human Nature can be devoted when it is thoroughly corrupted. Despotism is better. A Sober, conscientious Habit, of electing for the public good alone must be introduced, and every Appearance of Interest, Favour, and Partiality, reprobated, or you will very soon make wise and honest Men wish for Monarchy again, nay you will make them introduce it into America.

There is another Particular, in which it is manifest that the Principles of Liberty have not sufficient Weight in Mens Minds, or are not well understood.

Equality of Representation in the Legislature, is a first Principle of Liberty, and the Moment, the least departure from such Equality takes Place, that Moment an Inroad is made upon Liberty. Yet this essential Principle is disregarded, in many Places, in several of these Republicks. Every County is to have an equal Voice altho some Counties are six times more numerous, and twelve times more wealthy. The Same Iniquity will be established in Congress. R.I. will have an equal Weight with the Mass. The Delaware Government with Pensilvania and Georgia with Virginia. Thus We are sowing the Seeds of Ignorance Corruption, and Injustice, in the fairest Field of Liberty, that ever appeared upon Earth, even in the first Attempts to cultivate it. You and I have very little to hope or expect for ourselves. But it is a poor Consolation, under the Cares of a whole Life Spent in the Vindication of the Principles of Liberty, to See them violated, in the first formation of Governments, erected by the People themselves on their own Authority, without the poisonous Interposition of Kings or Priests. I am with great Affection your Friend & Sert.

Plan of Treaties

There shall be a firm inviolable and universal peace and a true and sincere friendship between the most serene and mighty prince Lewis the Sixteenth, the most Christian King, his heirs and successors and the United States of America; and the subjects of the most Christian King and of the said states; and between the countries, islands, cities and towns situate under the jurisdiction of the most Christian King, and of the said United States and the people and inhabitants thereof of every degree, without exception of persons or places; and the terms herein mentioned shall be perpetual between the most Christian King, his heirs and successors and the said United States.

Art. I. The Subjects of the most Christian King shall pay no other duties or imposts in the ports, havens, roads, countries, islands, cities or towns of the said United States or any of them than the natives thereof, or any commercial companies established by them or any of them shall pay; but shall enjoy all other the rights liberties, privileges, immunities and exemptions in trade, navigation and commerce, in passing from one part thereof to another, and in going to and from the same from and to any part of the world, which the said natives or companies enjoy.

Art. II. The Subjects, people and inhabitants of the Said United States and every of them shall pay no other duties or imposts in the ports, havens, roads, countries, islands, cities or towns of the most Christian King than the natives of such countries, islands, cities, or towns of France or any commercial companies established by the most Christian King shall pay but shall enjoy all other the rights, liberties, privileges, immunities and exemptions in trade, navigation and commerce in passing from one port thereof to another and in going to and from the same from and to any part of the world, which the said natives or companies enjoy.

Art. III. His most Christian Majesty shall retain the same rights of Fishery on the banks of Newfoundland and all other rights relating to any of the said islands, which he is entitled to by virtue of the treaty of Paris.

Art. IV. The most Christian King shall endeavour by all the means in his power to protect and defend all vessels and the effects belonging to the subjects people or inhabitants of the said United States or any of them, being in his ports, havens, or roads or on the seas near to his countries, islands cities or towns, and to recover and to restore to the right owners, their agents or attornies all such vessels and effects, which shall be taken within his jurisdiction; and his ships of war or any convoys sailing under his authority shall upon all occasions take under their protection all vessels belonging to the subjects people or inhabitants of the said United States or any of them and holding the same course or going the same way and shall defend such vessels as long as they hold the same course or go the same way against all attacks, force and violence in the same manner as they ought to protect and defend vessels belonging to the subjects of the most Christian King.

Art. V. In like manner the said United States and their ships of war and convoys sailing under their authority shall protect and defend all vessels and effects belonging to the subjects of the most Christian King and endeavour to recover and restore them if taken within the jurisdiction of the said United States or any of them.

Art. VI. The most Christian King and the said United States shall not receive nor suffer to be received into any of their ports, havens, roads, countries, islands, cities or towns any pirates or sea robbers or afford or suffer any entertainment, assistance or provision to be afforded to them, but shall endeavour by all means that all pirates and sea robbers and their partners, sharers and abettors be found out, apprehended and suffer condign punishment: and all the vessels and effects piratically taken and brought into the ports and havens of the most Christian King or the said United States, which can be found, although they be sold shall be restored or satisfaction given therefor, the right owners, their agents or attornies demanding the same and making the right of property to appear by due proof.

Art. VII. The most Christian King shall protect defend and secure, as far as in his power, the subjects, people and inhabitants of the said United States and every of them and their vessels and effects of every Kind, against all attacks, assaults, violences, injuries, depredations or plunderings by or from the king or emperor of Morocco, or Fez and the States of Algiers, Tunis, and Tripoli and any of them and every other prince state and power on the coast of Barbary in Africa and the subjects of the said kings, emperors, states and powers and of every of them in the same manner and as effectually and fully, and as much to the benefit advantage, ease and safety of the Said United States and every of them and of the subjects, people and inhabitants thereof, to all intents and purposes as the King and Kingdom of Great Britain before the commencement of the present war protected, defended and secured the people and inhabitants of the said United States then called British colonies in North America, their vessels and effects against all such attacks, assaults, violences, injuries, depredations and plunderings.

Art. VIII. If in consequence of this treaty the King of Great Britain should declare war against the most Christian King, the said United States shall not assist Great Britain in such war with men, money, ships or any of the articles in this treaty denominated contraband goods.

Art. IX. The most Christian King shall never invade, nor under any pretence attempt to possess himself of Labradore, New Britain, Nova Scotia, Acadia, Canada, Florida nor any of the countries, cities or towns on the Continent of North America nor of the islands of Newfoundland, Cape Breton, St. Johns, Anticosti nor of any other island lying near to the said continent in the seas or in any gulph, bay or river, it being the true intent and meaning of this treaty, that the said United States shall have the sole exclusive, undivided and perpetual possession of all the countries, cities and towns on the said continent and of all islands near to it, which now are or lately were under the jurisdiction of or subject to the king or crown of Great Britain, whenever they shall be united or confederated with the said United States.

Art. X. The subjects, inhabitants, merchants, commanders of ships, masters and mariners of the states provinces and dominions of each party respectively shall abstain and forbear to fish in all places possessed or which shall be possessed by the other party. The most Christian King's subjects shall not fish in the havens, bays, creeks, roads, coasts or places which the said United States hold or shall hereafter hold. And in like manner the subjects, people and inhabitants of the said United States shall not fish in the havens, bays, creeks, roads, coasts or places which the most Christian king possesses or shall hereafter possess. And if any ship or vessel shall be found fishing contrary to the tenor of this treaty, the said ship or vessel with its lading, proof being made thereof, shall be confiscated.

Art. XI. If in any war the most Christian king shall conquer or get possession of the islands in the West Indies now under the jurisdiction of the king or crown of Great Britain or any of them, or any dominions of the said king or crown in any other parts of the world, the subjects, people and inhabitants of the said united states and every of them shall enjoy the same rights, liberties, privileges, immunities and exemptions in trade, commerce and navigation to and from the said islands and dominions that are mentioned in the second article of this treaty.

Art. XII. It is the true intent and meaning of this treaty that no higher or other duties shall be imposed on the exportation of any thing of the growth, production or manufacture of the islands in the West Indies now belonging or which may hereafter belong to the most Christian King to the said United States or any of them than the lowest that are or shall be imposed on the exportation thereof to France or to any other part of the world.

Art. XIII. It is agreed by and between the said parties that no duties whatever shall ever hereafter be imposed on the exportation of Molasses from any of the islands and dominions of the most Christian king in the West Indies, to any of these United States.

Art. XIV. The subjects, people and inhabitants of the said United States or any of them being merchants and residing in France and their property and effects of every kind shall be exempt from the Droit d'Aubeine.

Art. XV. The merchant ship of either of the parties which shall be making into a port belonging to the enemy of the other ally and concerning whose voyage and the species of goods on board her there shall be just grounds of suspicion, shall be obliged to exhibit as well upon the high seas as in the ports and havens not only her passports but likewise certificates expressly shewing that her goods are not of the number of those which have been prohibited as contraband.

Art. XVI. If by the exhibiting of the above certificates the other party discover there are any of those sorts of goods which are prohibited and declared contraband and consigned for a port under the obedience of his enemies, it shall not be lawful to break up the hatches of such ship or to open any chest, coffers, packs, casks or any other vessels found therein or to remove the smallest parcels of her goods, whether such ship belong to the subjects of France or the inhabitants of the said United States unless the lading be brought on shore in the presence of the Officers of the court of admiralty and an inventory thereof made; but there shall be no allowance to sell, exchange or alienate the same in any manner, untill after that due and lawful process shall have been had against such prohibited goods and the courts of admiralty shall by a sentence pronounced have confiscated the same saving always as well the ship itself as any other goods found therein, which by this treaty are to be esteemed free; neither may they be detained on pretence of their being as it were infected by the prohibited goods, much less shall they be confiscated as lawfull prize; but if not the whole cargo, but only part thereof shall consist of prohibited or contraband goods and the commander of the ship shall be ready and willing to deliver them to the captor who has discovered them, in such case the captor having received those goods shall forthwith discharge the ship and not hinder her by any means freely to prosecute the voyage on which she was bound.

Art. XVII. On the contrary it is agreed that whatever shall be found to be laden by the subjects and inhabitants of either party on any ship belonging to the enemy of the other or to his subjects although it be not of the sort of prohibited goods may be confiscated in the same manner as if it belonged to the enemy himself; except such goods and merchandize as were put on board such ship before the declaration of war or even after such declaration, if so be it were done without the knowledge of such declaration. So that the goods of the subjects and people of either party whether they be of the nature of such as are prohibited or otherwise, which as is afore said, were put on board any ship belonging to an enemy before the war or after the declaration of it without the Knowledge of it, shall no wise be liable to confiscation but shall well and truly be restored without delay to the proprietors demanding the same; but so as that if the said merchandizes be contraband it shall not be any ways lawful to carry them afterwards to any ports belonging to the enemy.

Art. XVIII. And that more effectual care may be taken for the security of the subjects and inhabitants of both parties, that they suffer no injury by the men of war or privateers of the other party, all the commanders of the ships of the Most Christian King and of the said United States and all their subjects and inhabitants shall be forbid doing any injury, or damage to the other side, and if they act to the contrary they shall be punished and shall moreover be bound to make satisfaction for all matter of damage and the interest thereof by reparation under the penalty and obligation of their persons and goods.

Art. XIX. All ships and merchandizes of what nature soever, which shall be rescued out of the hands of any pirates or robbers on the high seas shall be brought into some port of either state and shall be delivered to the custody of the Officers of that port, in order to be restored entire to the true proprietor as soon as due and sufficient proof shall be made concerning the property thereof.

Art. XX. It shall be lawful for the ships of war of either party and privateers freely to carry whithersoever they please the ships and goods taken from their enemies without being obliged to pay any duty to the Officers of the admiralty or any other judges, nor shall such prizes be arrested or seized when they come to enter the ports of either Party; nor shall the searchers or other Officers of those places search the same or make examination concerning the lawfulness of such prizes, but they may hoist sail at any time and depart and carry their prizes to the place expressed in their commissions, which the commanders of such ships of war shall be obliged to shew: On the contrary no shelter or refuge shall be given in their ports to such as shall have made prize of the subjects, people or property of either of the parties, but if such should come in, being forced by stress of weather or the danger of the sea, all proper means shall be vigorously used that they go out and retire from thence as soon as possible.

Art. XXI. If any ships belonging to either of the parties, their subjects or people shall within the coasts or dominions of the other stick upon the sands or be wrecked or suffer any other damage all friendly assistance and relief shall be given to the persons shipwrecked or such as shall be in danger thereof, and letters of safe conduct shall likewise be given to them for their free and quiet passage from thence and the return of every one to his own country.

Art. XXII. In case the subjects and people of either party with their shipping, whether public and of war or private and of merchants be forced through stress of weather, pursuit of pirates or enemies or any other urgent necessity for seeking of shelter and harbor to retreat and enter into any of the rivers, creeks, bays, havens, roads, ports or shores belonging to the other party, they shall be received and treated with all humanity and kindness and enjoy all friendly protection and help; and they shall be permitted to refresh and provide themselves at reasonable rates with victuals and all things needful for the sustenance of their persons or reparation of their ships and conveniency of their voyage; and they shall no ways be detained or hindered from returning out of the said ports or roads, but may remove and depart when and whither they please without any let or hindrance.

Art. XXIII. For the better promoting of commerce on both sides, it is agreed that if a war shall break out between the said two nations, six months after the proclamation of war shall be allowed to the merchants in the cities and towns where they live for settling and transporting their goods and merchandizes; and if any thing be taken from them, or any injury be done them within that term by either party or the people or subjects of either, full satisfaction shall be made for the same.

Art. XXIV. No subjects of the most Christian king shall apply for or take any commission or letters of marque for arming any ship or ships to act as privateers against the said United States or any of them or against the subjects, people or inhabitants of the said United States or any of them or against the property of any of the inhabitants of any of them from any prince or state with which the said United States shall be at war. Nor shall any citizen, subject or inhabitant of the said United States or any of them apply for or take any commission or letters of marque for arming any ship or ships to act as privateers against the subjects of the most Christian king or any of them or the property of any of them from any prince or state, with which the said King shall be at War; and if any person of either Nation shall take such commissions or letters of marque he shall be punished as a pirate.

Art. XXV. It shall not be lawful for any foreign privateers not belonging to subjects of the most Christian King nor citizens of the said United States, who have commissions from any other prince or state in enmity with either nation to fit their ships in the ports of either the one or the other of the aforesaid parties to sell what they have taken or in any other manner whatsoever to exchange either ships, merchandizes or any other lading; neither shall they be allowed even to purchase victuals except such as shall be necessary for their going to the next port of that prince or state from which they have commissions.

Art. XXVI. It shall be lawful for all and singular the subjects of the most Christian King and the citizens people and inhabitants of the said states to sail with their ships with all manner of liberty and security, no distinction being made, who are the proprietors of the merchandizes laden thereon from any port to the places of those who now are or hereafter shall be at enmity with the most Christian King or the United States. It shall likewise be lawful for the subjects and inhabitants aforesaid to sail with the ships and merchandizes aforementioned, and to trade with the same liberty and security from the places ports and havens of those who are enemies of both or either party without any opposition or disturbance whatsoever not only directly from the places of the enemy aforementioned to neutral places, but also from one place belonging to an enemy to another place belonging to an enemy, whether they be under the jurisdiction of the same prince or under several. And it is hereby stipulated that free ships shall also give a freedom to goods and that every thing shall be deemed to be free and exempt, which shall be found on board the ships belonging to the subjects of either of the Confederates, although the whole lading or any part thereof should appertain to the enemies of either, Contraband goods being always excepted. It is also agreed in like manner that the same liberty, be extended to persons who are on board a free ship with this effect that although they be enemies to both or either party, they are not to be taken out of that free ship, unless they are Soldiers, and in actual service of the enemies.

Art. XXVII. This liberty of navigation and commerce shall extend to all Kinds of Merchandizes excepting those only which are distinguished by the name of contraband: And under this name of Contraband or prohibited goods shall be comprehended Arms, great guns, bombs with their fuzes and other things belonging to them, fire balls, gunpowder, match, cannon ball, pikes, swords, lances, spears, halbards, mortars, petards, granadoes, saltpetre, musquets, musket balls, helmets, head-pieces, breastplates, coats of mail, and the like kind of arms proper for arming Soldiers, musket rests, belts, horses with their furniture and all other warlike instruments whatever. These merchandizes which follow shall not be reckoned among contraband or prohibited goods, that is to say, all sorts of cloths and all other manufactures woven of any wool, flax, silk, cotton or any other materials whatever, all kinds of wearing apparel together with the species whereof they are used to be made, gold and silver as well coined as uncoined, tin, iron, lead copper, brass, coals, as also wheat and barley and any other kind of corn and pulse, tobacco and likewise all manner of spices, salted and smoked flesh, salted fish, cheese and butter, beer, oils, wines, sugars and all sorts of salt, and in general all provisions which serve for the nourishment of mankind and the sustenance of life. Furthermore all kinds of cotton, hemp, flax, tar, pitch, ropes, cables, sails, sail-cloth, anchors and any parts of anchors, also ships masts, planks, boards, and beams of what trees soever, and all other things proper either for building or repairing ships and all other goods whatever, which have not been worked into the form of any instrument or thing prepared for war by land or by sea shall not be reputed contraband, much less such as have been already wrought and made up for any other use, all which shall be wholly reckoned among free goods; as likewise all other merchandizes and things which are not comprehended and particularly mentioned in the foregoing enumeration of contraband goods; so that they may be transported and carried in, the freest manner by the subjects of both confederates even to places belonging to an enemy, such towns and places being only excepted as are at that time besieged blocked up or invested.

Art. XXVIII. To the end that all manner of dissentions and quarrels may be avoided and prevented on one side and the other, it is agreed that in case either of the parties hereto should be engaged in a war, the ships and vessels belonging to the subjects or people of the other ally must be furnished with sea letters or passports expressing the name, property and bulk of the ship as also the name and place of habitation of the master or commander of the said ship, that it may appear thereby that the ship really and truely belongs to the subjects of one of the parties, which passports shall be made out and granted according to the form annexed to this treaty. They shall likewise be recalled every year, that is, if the ship happens to return home within the space of a year. It is likewise agreed that such ships being laden are to be provided not only with passports as abovementioned, but also with certificates containing the several particulars of the cargo, the place whence the ship sailed and whither she is bound, that so it may be known, whether any forbidden or contraband goods be on board the same, which certificates shall be made out by the officers of the place, whence the ship set sail, in the accustomed form; and if any one shall think it fit or adviseable to express in the said certificates the persons to whom the goods on board belong, he may freely do it.

Art. XXIX. The ships of the subjects and inhabitants of either of the parties coming upon any coast belonging to either of the said allies, but not willing to enter into port, or being entered into port and not willing to unload their cargoes or break bulk shall not be obliged to give an account of their lading, unless they should be suspected, upon some manifest tokens, of carrying to the enemy of the other ally any prohibited goods called Contraband. And in case of such manifest suspicion the parties shall be obliged to exhibit in the ports their passports and certificates in the manner before specified.

Art. XXX. If the ships of the said subjects, people or inhabitants of either of the parties shall be met with either sailing along the coast or on the high seas by any ship of war of the other or by any privateers, the said ships of war or privateers for the avoiding of any disorder shall remain out of cannon shot and may send their boats on board the merchant ship which they shall so meet with and may enter her to the number of two or three men only to whom the master or commander of such ship or vessel shall exhibit his passport concerning the property of the ship, made out according to the form inserted in this present treaty and the ship when she shall have shewed such passport shall be free and at liberty to pursue her voyage so as it shall not be lawful to molest or search her in any manner or to give her chase or force her to quit her intended course. It is also agreed that all goods when once put on board the ships or vessels of either parties shall be subject to no farther visitation, but all visitation or search shall be made before hand and all prohibited goods shall be stopped on the spot, before the same be put on board the ships or vessels of the respective State. Nor shall either the persons or goods of the subjects of his most Christian Majesty or the United States be put under any arrest or molested by any other kind of embargo for that cause, and only the subject of that state to whom the said goods have been or shall be prohibited and shall presume to sell or alienate such sort of goods shall be duely punished for the Offence.

The form of the Sea letters and passports to be given to ships and vessels according to the 28 Article

To all who shall see these presents Greeting. It is hereby made known that leave and permission has been given to——master and commander of the ship called——of the town of——burthen——tons or thereabouts lying at present in the port and haven of——and bound for——and laden with—— after that his ship has been visited and before sailing he shall make oath before the Officers who have the jurisdiction of maritime affairs that the said ship belongs to one or more of the subjects of——the act whereof shall be put at the end of these presents; as likewise that he will keep and cause to be kept by his crew on board the marine Ordinances and regulations and enter in the proper office a list signed and witnessed of the crew of his ship and of all who shall embark on board her, whom he shall not take on board without the knowledge and permission of the Officers of the marine and in every port and Haven where he shall enter with his ship he shall shew this present leave to the Officers and judges of the marine and shall give a faithful account to them of what passed and was done during his voyage and he shall carry the colours, arms and ensign of——during his voyage. In witness whereof we have signed these presents and put the seal of our arms thereunto and caused the same to be countersigned by——at——the—Day of—A.D.—.

The form of the act containing the Oath

We——of the admiralty of——do certify that——master of the ship named in the above passport hath taken the oath mentioned therein. Done at——the—Day of—A.D.—.

The form of the certificate to be required of and to be given by the Magistrates or Officers of the customs of the town and port in their respective towns and ports to the ships and vessels which sail from thence, according to the directions of the 28 Article of this present treaty

We——Magistrates (or officers of the customs) of the town and port of——do certify and attest that on the—day of the month of—in the year of our Lord—personally appeared before us——of——and declared by a solemn oath that the ship or vessel called——of about—tons, whereof——of—— his usual place of habitation is master or commander does rightfully and properly belong to him and other subjects of——and to them alone, that she is now bound from the port of——to the port of——laden with the goods and merchandizes hereunder particularly described and enumerated that is to say——.

In witness whereof we have signed this certificate and sealed it with the seal of our office. Given the—day of the month of—in the year of our Lord—.

September 17, 1776

GOVERNMENT AND DISCIPLINE

To James Warren

Dear Sir   Baltimore Feb. 3. 1777

It may not be a Mispence of Time to make a few Observations upon the Situation of Some of the States at this Time.

That Part of New York which is yet in our Possession is pretty well united, and pretty firm. The Jerseys have recovered from their Surprize, and are lending as much Assistance as can well be expected from them. Their Assembly is now Sitting, and are Said to be well disposed to do what they can. The Assembly of Pensilvania, is also Sitting. They have abolished the oath which gave so much Discontent to the People, and are gradually acquiring the Confidence of the People, and opposition has Subsided. The Delaware Government, have formed their Constitution, and the Assembly is now Sitting. Maryland has formed its Constitution—and their Assembly now sitting in Consequence of it, are filling it up. There is a Difficulty in two of the Counties, but this will last but a little while. In Virginia Governor Henry, has recovered his Health has returned to Williamsbourg, and is proceeding in his Government with great Industry. N. Carolina have compleated their Government, and Mr. Caswell is Governor. In Virginia and North Carolina, they have made an Effort, for the Destruction of Bigotry which is very remarkable. They have abolished their Establishments of Episcopacy so far as to give compleat Liberty of Conscience to Dissenters, an Acquisition in favour of the Rights of Mankind, which is worth all the Blood and Treasure, which has been and will be Spent in this War. S. Carolina and Georgia, compleated their Governments, a long time ago. Thus I think there are but three States remaining which have not erected their Governments, Massachusetts, N. York and New Hampshire.

These are good Steps towards Government in the States which must be introduced and established before We can expect Discipline in our Armies, the Unum necessarium to our Salvation.

I will be instant and incessant, in season and out of Season, in inculcating these important Truths, that nothing can Save Us but Government in the State and Discipline in the Army. There are So many Persons among my worthy Constituents who love Liberty, better than they understand it that I expect to become unpopular by my Preaching. But Woe is me if I preach it not. Woe will be to them, if they do not hear.

I am terrified with the Prospect of Expence, to our State, which I find no Possibility of avoiding. I cannot get an Horse kept in this Town under a Guinea a Week. One hundred and four Guineas a Year for the Keeping of two Horses, is intolerable, but cannot be avoided. Simple Board is fifty shilling a Week here, and Seven Dollars generally. I cannot get boarded, under forty shillings, i.e. five dollars and a third a Week for myself and fifteen for my servant—besides finding for myself all my Wood Candles, Liquors and Washing. I would send home my servant and Horses, but Congress is now a moveable Body, and it is impossible to travell and carry great Loads of Baggage without a servant and Horses, besides the Meanness of it, in the Eyes of the World.

CONGRESS AND FINANCE

To James Warren

Dear sir   Baltimore Feb. 12. 1777

The Certificates and Cheque Books for the Loan Office, I hope and presume, are arrived in Boston, before this Time, and notwithstanding the discouraging Accounts, which were given me, when I was there, I still hope that a considerable sum of Money, will be obtained by their Means.

It is my private opinion, however, that the interest of four per Cent, is not an equitable Allowance. I mean, that four per Cent, is not so much, as the Use of the Money is honestly worth, in the ordinary Course of Business, upon an Average, for a Year. And I have accordingly, exerted all the little faculties I had, in endeavouring on Monday last, to raise the Interest to six per Cent. But after two days debate, the Question was lost by an equal Division of the States present, five against five.

New Hampshire Massachusetts Bay, New Jersey, Pensilvania and Virginia on one side, and Rhode Island Connecticutt, North Carolina, South Carolina and Georgia, on the other. Here was an Example of the Inconvenience and Injustice of voting by States. Nine Gentlemen, representing about Eight hundred thousand People, against Eighteen Gentlemen representing, a Million and an Half nearly, determined this Point. Yet We must not be Startled at this.

I think it my duty to mention this to you, because it must be astonishing to most People in our State, that the Interest is so low. I know they are at a Loss to account for it upon any Principles of Equity, or Policy, and consequently may be disposed to blame their Delegates, but you may depend upon it, they are not in fault.

I tremble for the Consequences of this Determination:—if the Loan Offices should not procure Us Money, We must emit more, which will depreciate all which is already abroad; and So raise the Prices of Provisions and all the Necessaries of Life, that the additional Expence to the Continent, for Supplying their Army and Navy, will be vastly more than the two per Cent in dispute: besides all the Injustice, Chicanery, Extortion Oppression, and Discontent, which is allways, occasioned every where, by a depreciating Medium of Trade. I am much afraid of another Mischief. I fear that for Want of Wisdom to raise the Interest in Season, We shall be necessitated within a few Months to give Eight or Ten Per Cent, and not obtain the Money We want after all.

I have been So often a Witness of the Miseries of this after Wisdom, that I am wearied to death of it.

Had a Bounty of Twenty dollars a Man been offered Soldiers last Time, it would have procured more than the enormous Bounties that are now offered will procure. Had Government been assumed in the States, Twelve Months Sooner than it was it might have been assumed with, Spirit, Vigour and Decision, and would have obtained an habitual Authority, before the critical Time came on when the Strongest Nerves of Government, are necessary. Whereas, now, every new Government, is as weak as Water and as brittle as Glass.

Had We agreed upon a Non Exportation, to commence when the Non importation commenced, what an immense

Sum Should We have Saved? Nay very probably We Should have occasioned a very different House of Commons to be chosen the Ministry to have been changed and this War avoided. Thus it is. You who will make no ill Use of these Observations may read them. But the Times are too delicate and critical to indulge freely, in such Speculations. It is best I believe that no mention Should be made, that the Rate of Interest has been again debated, lest Some Saving Men Should withold their Money, in hopes of compelling the Public to raise the Interest. If the Interest Should never be raised, those who lend in our State, will fare as well as others: if it Should, the Interest of all will be raised, that which is borrowed now, as well as that which Shall be borrowed hereafter. I Sincerely wish that our People would lend their Money, freely. They will repent of it, if they do not. We shall be compelled to emit Such Quantities, that every Man except a few Villains will loose more by Depreciation, than the two Per Cent. Not to mention again the Scene of Anarchy and Horror, that a Continuation of Emissions will infallibly bring upon Us.

The Design of Loan Offices, was to prevent the further Depreciation of the Bills, by avoiding further Emissions. We might have emitted more Bills promising an Interest but if those had been made a legal Tender, like the other Bills, and consequently mixed in the Circulations with them, they would instantly have depreciated all the other Bills four Per Cent, if the Interest was four, and more than that too, by increasing the Quantity of circulating Cash. In order to prevent these Certificates from Circulation and consequently from depreciating the Bills, We Should give them such Attributes as will induce Men of Fortune and others, who usually lend Money, to hoard them up. The Persons who usually lend Money are 1. Men of Fortune, who live upon their Income, and these generally chose to have a Surplusage to lay up every Year, to increase their Capitals 2. opulent, Merchants, who have more Money than they choose to risque, or can conveniently employ in Trade. 3. Widows, whose Dower is often converted into Money, and placed out at Interest, that they may receive an annual Income to live upon, without the Care and Skill, which is necessary to employ Money, advantageously in Business. 4. orphans, whose Guardians seldom incline to hazard the Property of their

Wards, in Business. 5. a few Divines, Phisicians, and Lawyers, who are able to lay by, a little of their annual Earnings. 6. here and there a Farmer and a Tradesman, who is forehanded and frugal enough to make more Money, than he has occasion to spend. Add to these 7. Schools Colledges, Towns, Parishes and other Societies, which sometimes let Money. All these Persons are much attached to their Interest and so anxious to make the most of it that they compute and calculate it, even to farthings and single days.

These Persons can get Six Per Cent, generally, of private Borrowers, on good security of Mortgages or sureties.

Now, is it reasonable in the State to expect, that monied Men, will lend to the Public, at a less Interest, than they can get from private Persons? I answer Yes, when the Safety of the State is not in doubt: and when the Medium of Exchange has a stable Value. Because larger Sums may be put together, and there is less trouble in collecting and receiving the Interest and the Security is better. But the Case is otherwise, when Men are doubtfull of the Existence of the State, and it is worse still, when they see a Prospect of Depreciation in the Medium of Trade. All Governments in Distress are obliged to live an higher Interest for Money, than when they are prosperous.

The Interest of Money, always bears Some Proportion to the Profits of Trade. When the Commerce of a Country is small, in few Hands, and very profitable, the Interest of Money is very high. Charles the fifth was necessitated to give twenty four Per Cent. Afterwards it fell in Europe to Twelve, and since to six, Five, Four, and Three.

I think I never Shall consent to go higher than Six Per Cent, as much as I am an Advocate for raising it to that, and in this I have been constant for full Nine Months. The Burthen of Six per Cent, upon the Community, will very Soon be heavy enough. We must fall upon Some other Methods of ascertaining the Capitals We borrow. A depreciating Currency, We must not have. It will ruin Us. The Medium of Trade ought to be as unchangeable as Truth; as immutable as Morality. The least Variation in its Value, does Injustice to Multitudes, and in Proportion it injures the Morals of the People, a Point of the last Importance in a Republican Government.

March 15

Thus far I had written a long time ago, Since which, after many days Deliberation and Debate, a Vote passed for raising the Interest to six Per Cent. If this Measure should not procure Us Money, I know not what Resources We shall explore.

To read this will be Punishment enough for your omission to write to me all this While. I have received nothing from you since I left Boston. Yours,

From the Diary: February 23, 1777

1777. FEB. 23.

Took a Walk with Mr. Gerry, down to a Place called Ferry Branch, a Point of Land which is formed by a Branch of the Patapsco on one Side and the Basin before the Town of Baltimore on the other. At the Point is a Ferry, over to the Road which goes to Anapolis. This is a very pretty Walk. At the Point you have a full view of the elegant, splendid Seat of Mr. Carroll Barrister. It is a large and elegant House. It stands fronting looking down the River, into the Harbour. It is one Mile from the Water. There is a most beautifull Walk from the House down to the Water. There is a descent, not far from the House. You have a fine Garden—then you descend a few Steps and have another fine Garden—you go down a few more and have another. It is now the dead of Winter, no Verdure, or Bloom to be seen, but in the Spring, Summer, and fall this Scæne must be very pretty.

Returned and dined with Mr. William Smith a new Member of Congress. Dr. Lyon, Mr. Merriman, Mr. Gerry, a son of Mr. Smith, and two other Gentlemen made the Company. The Conversation turned, among other Things, upon removing the Obstructions and opening the Navigation of Susquehannah River. The Company thought it might easily be done, and would open an amazing Scæne of Business. Philadelphia will oppose it, but it be the Interest of a Majority of Pensilvania to effect it.

This Mr. Smith is a grave, solid Gentleman, a Presbyterian

by Profession—a very different Man from the most of those We have heretofore had from Maryland.

The Manners of Maryland are somewhat peculiar. They have but few Merchants. They are chiefly Planters and Farmers. The Planters are those who raise Tobacco and the Farmers such as raise Wheat &c. The Lands are cultivated, and all Sorts of Trades are exercised by Negroes, or by transported Convicts, which has occasioned the Planters and Farmers to assume the Title of Gentlemen, and they hold their Negroes and Convicts, that is all labouring People and Tradesmen, in such Contempt, that they think themselves a distinct order of Beings. Hence they never will suffer their Sons to labour or learn any Trade, but they bring them up in Idleness or what is worse in Horse Racing, Cock fighting, and Card Playing.

RENOUNCING MONARCHICAL CORRUPTIONS

To William Tudor

dear sir   Baltimore Feb. 25. 1777

I had last Evening yours of the 12 Instant. Am much obliged to you for it. Why did not the Court martial find Buckner guilty of Cowardice? Why did they only cashier him? When shall We have any Discipline? When shall We be decisive? When shall We punish, the worst Crimes, with the last Punishment?

I shall very soon become as clamorous an Advocate for Order, Subordination, Government, and Discipline, as ever Philanthrop was, indeed I am already.

I am extreamly mortified that those worthy Men, who Staid for Six Weeks, from the 1. of Jany, were obliged to go home unpaid. If I could explain to those honest Men the true Causes of this, they would acquiesce but I cannot. But they will be paid.

Am glad to hear, that the Army in Brunswick, are in a good Way. I hope We shall demolish them. We must. We will. Twenty thousand Men, are not necessary for this. But I hope nevertheless, you will have that number and more by the Time you mention.

I wish I could learn what Forces you have, at Morristown Chatham, Elizabeth Town, Princeton &c. &c. &c.

What has Heath done? How many Men has he? What has Spencer done?

I hope there will be Enquiries, Sometime or other, into the Conduct of our Armies from Long Island to this Moment.

I hope We shall e'er long renounce some of our Monarchichal Corruptions, and become Republicans in Principle in Sentiment, in feeling and in Practice, and among other Republican Institutions I hope We shall annually elect all our General officers. This would purge the Stream of Some Impurities. At least I hope so.

In Republican Governments the Majesty is all in the Laws. They only are to be adored. They must be obeyed.

But at present We are not sensible of this. Citizens must be made to feel, the force of civil Laws, and soldiers those of military ones.

Have you many Symptoms of Austere Republicanism in your Army? Is Virtue, or Rank? is Glory or Pay, your object.

Pray write me often, and let me know every Thing.

MILITARY DISAPPOINTMENT

To Nathanael Greene

Dear Sir   Philadelphia March 9. 1777

I had, last Evening the Pleasure of yours of March 3. by your Brother, to whom in his Business to this Place I shall give all the Assistance in my Power. In whose favour the Ballance of Letters lies, I cant Say: but if I am in debt, in Point of Numbers it must be because Some of my Remittances have miscarried.

I am not yet entirely convinced, that We are playing a desperate Game, tho I must confess that my feelings are somewhat less Sanguine than they were last June. This diminution of Confidence is owing to Disappointment. I then expected that the Enemy would have Seen two or three Bunker Hills, between the Point of Long Island and the Banks of the Delaware River. Two or three Such Actions would have answered my Purpose, perhaps one alone.

I have derived Consolation however, from these Disappointments; because the People have discovered a Patience under them, greater than might have been expected. It was not very surprising to me that our Troops Should fly in certain situations, and abandon Lines of such extent, at the sudden Appearance of a formidable Enemy in unexpected Places, because I had learn'd from Marshall Saxe, and from others that Such Behaviour was not only common but almost constant among the best regular Troops. But there was Reason to apprehend, that the People would be Seized with Such a Panick, upon Such a Series of ill success, that in the fright and Confusion whole States would have revolted, instead of a few paltry Individuals. Whereas every State has stood firm, and even the most confused and wavering of them, have gained Strength and improved in order, under all this Adversity. I therefore do not yet despair.

You Say you "are sensible I have not the most exalted Opinion of our Generals." From this Expression I Suspect, that Some busy Body has been endeavouring to do Mischief, by Misrepresentation. Be this as it may, I am generally So well Satisfied in my own Opinions, as to avow them.

I dont expect to see Characters, either among the Statesmen or the Soldiers of a young and tender State like ours equal to Some, who were bred to the Contemplation of great Objects from their Childhood in older, and more powerfull Nations. Our Education, our Travel, our Experience has not been equal to the Production of such Characters, whatever our Genius may be which I have no Reason to Suspect to be less than that of any Nation under the sun.

I dont expect to see an Epaminondas, to be sure, because in the opinion of Dr. Swift all the Ages of the World have produced but Six such Characters, which makes the Chances much against our seeing any such. When such shall appear I shall certainly have an exalted opinion.—

Notwithstanding this I have a sincere Esteem of our General Officers taken together as a Body, and believe them upon the whole the best Men for the Purpose that America affords. I think them Gentlemen of as good Sense, Education, Morals,

Taste and Spirit as any we can find, and if this Opinion of them is not exalted enough I am Sorry for it but cannot help it. I hope however that my Opinion as well as that of the World in general, will be Somewhat more sublimated, before next Winter. I do assure you that two or three Bunker Hill Battles, altho they might be as unsuccessfull as that was would do it. I lament the Inexperience of all of them and I am Sure they have all Reason to lament mine. But not to disguise my sentiments at all, there are Some of them, particularly from New England that I begin to think quite unequal to the high Command they hold.

It is very true that Success generally marks the Man of Wisdom, and in Some Instances Injustice is done to unsuccessfull Merit: But Still it is generally true that Success is a Mark of Wisdom, and that Misfortunes are owing to Misconduct. The sense of Mankind has uniformly Supported this Opinion and therefore I cannot but think it just. The Same Sense, has uniformly attributed the ill Success of Armies to the Incapacity or other Imperfections of the General Officers, a Truth which I have Sometimes presumed to Hint to some of our General Officers, with whom I could make So free. There Seems to be Justice in this because the Glory of Successfull Wars is as uniformly attributed to them.

I shall join with you, very chearfully, in burying past Errors, and in wishing to concert and execute the most effectual Measures to free America, from her cruel oppressors.

You ask why G. Lee is denied his Requests? You ask, can any Injury arise? Will it reflect any Dishonour upon Congress. I dont know that it would reflect any dishonour, nor was it refused upon that Principle. But Congress was of Opinion that great Injuries would arise. It would take up too much Time to recapitulate all the Arguments which were used upon occassion of his Letter. But Congress was never more unanimous, than upon that Question. Nobody I believe would have objected against a Conference, concerning his private Affairs or his particular Case. But it was inconceivable that a Conference should be necessary upon Such Subjects. Any Thing relative to those might have been conveyed by Letter. But it appears to be an Artfull Stratagem of the two gratefull Brothers to hold up to the public View the Phantom of a Negotiation, in order to give Spirit and Courage to the Tories, to distract and divide the Whiggs, at a critical Moment, when the Utmost Exertions are necessary to draw together an Army.

The Words of the Count La Tour, upon a similar Occasion, ought to be adopted by Us. "Remember that now there is room neither for Repentance, nor for Pardon. We must no longer reason, nor deliberate. We only want Concord and Steadiness.—The Lot is cast. If We prove victorious, We shall be a just free and Sovereign People; if We are conquered, We shall be Traitors, perjured Persons, and Rebels."

But further. We see what use G. and the two Houses make of the former Conference with Lord How. What a Storm in England they are endeavouring to raise against Us from that Circumstance.

But another Thing. We have undoubted Intelligence from Europe, that the Embassadors and other Instruments of the B. Ministry at foreign Courts made the worst Use of the former Conference. That Conference did Us a great and essential Injury at the french Court you may depend Upon it. Ld How knows it—and wishes to repeat it.

"The Princes of the Union were not diligent enough in preparing for War: they Sufferd themselves to be amused with Proposals of Accommodation, they gave the League time to bring together great Forces, and after that, they could no longer brave it. They committed the fault which is very common in civil Wars viz that People endeavour to Save Appearances. If a Party would Save Appearances, they must lie quiet, but if they will not lie quiet, they must push Things to an Extremity, without keeping any Measures. It rarely happens, but that otherwise they are at once both criminal and unfortunate." Bailes Life of Gustavus Adolphus.

They meant farther to amuse Opposition in England, and to amuse foreign Nations by this Maneuvre, as well as Whiggs in America, and I confess it is not without Indignation, that I See Such a Man as Lee Suffer himself to be duped by their Policy So far as to become the Instrument of it, as Sullivan was upon a former occasion. Congress is under no concern about any Use that the disaffected can make of this Refusal. They would have made the worst Use of a Conference. As to any Terms of Peace—look into the Speech to both Houses—the Answers of both Houses—look into the Proclamations.—it is useless to enumerate Particulars which prove that the Howes have no Power but to murder or disgrace Us.

The Retaliation that is to be practiced, on Lees Account, was determined on, when I was absent, So that I can give no Account of the Reasons for that Measure. Yet I have no doubt of the Right. And as to the disagreable Consequences you mention these I hope and presume will not take Place—if they do, they will be wholly chargeable on the Enemy. The End of Retaliation is to prevent a Repetition of the Injury. A Threat of Retaliation is to prevent an Injury, and it seldom fails of its design. In Lees Case, I am confident, it will Secure him good Treatment. If Lees Confinement is not Strict, that of Campbell and the Hessians ought not to be. The Intention was that they should be treated exactly as Lee is.

Our late Promotions may possibly give Disgust: But that cannot be avoided. This delicate Point of Honour, which is really one of the most putrid Corruptions of absolute Monarchy, I mean the Honour of maintaining a Rank Superiour to abler Men, I mean the Honour of preferring a single Step of Promotion to the Service of the Public, must be bridled. It is incompatible with republican Principles. I hope for my own Part that Congress will elect annually all the general officers— if in Consequence of this Some great Men should be obliged at the Years End to go home, and serve their Country in some other Capacity, not less necessary and better adapted to their Genius *I dont think the public would be ruined*. Perhaps it would be no Harm.

The Officers of the Army, ought to consider that the Rank, the Dignity, and the Rights of whole States, are of more Importance, than this Point of Honour, more indeed than the Solid Glory of any particular officer. The States insist with great Justice and Sound Policy, on having a Share of the General Officers, in Some Proportion to the Quotas of Troops they are to raise. This Principle has occasioned many of our late Promotions, and it ought to Satisfy Gentlemen. But if it does not, they as well as the Public must abide the Consequences of their Discontent. I shall at all Times think myself happy to hear from you, my dear sir, and to give the Utmost

Attention to whatever you may suggest. I hope I shall not often trouble you to Read So Long a Lurry of small Talk.

"THE SELFISH PRINCIPLES OF MONARCHY"

To an Unknown Correspondent

Philadelphia April 27th. 1777 Sunday

I think it is Montesqueiu, who, Somewhere observes, that the English of Charles's days were perpetually bewildered in their Pursuit of a Republic, for being themselves extreamly corrupt, they Sought, in vain for that pure and disinterested Principle upon which, alone, a Commonwealth can Stand.

The Principle of Republican Government, is as little understood in America, as its Spirit is felt. Ambition in a Republic, is a great Virtue, for it is nothing more than a Desire, to Serve the Public, to promote the Happiness of the People, to increase the Wealth, the Grandeur, and Prosperity of the Community. This, Ambition is but another Name for public Virtue, and public Spirit. But the Ambition which has Power for its object, which desires to increase the Wealth, the Grandeur, and the Glory of an Individual, at the Expence of the Community, is a very heinous Vice.

What Shall We Say of Oliver Cromwell? What Shall We Say of others, his Coadjutors? Can We Say, that they were actuated by a Love of the Public? Were they not governed by Selfish Motives? I make no Scruple to confess that I think Oliver, totally destitute of the Republican Principle of public Virtue. He thought himself honest, and Sincere. So did Balaam, when he asked Leave to curse Israel. There never was a greater self deceiver than Oliver Cromwell. The Man after Gods own Heart, to whom Nathan Said Thou art the Man, deceived himself, in the Same manner. How sincere was he, when he felt such honest Indignation against the Man, who had taken his poor Neighbours Lambs.

We, in America, are So contaminated, with the Selfish Principles of Monarchy, and with that bastard, corrupted Honour, that Monarchy inspires, that We have no Idea, no Conception, no Imagination, no Dream, of the Passions and Principles, which Support Republics. What will become of Us? God knows.

The Commissary General, this Evening related me an Anecdote, which gave me great Spirits as it seemed an Evidence that Integrity was not lost out of the World.

He Said that in comparing his Accounts he missed Seventy Pounds, and puzzled himself a long Time, to no Purpose to discover, where it could be gone. For several Months he had given it up, as lost and unaccountable. At last Coll Cary of Bridgwater, came to him and told him, that after he went home from Cambridge where he had commanded a Regiment of Militia, he paid off, every Bill, and had Seventy Pounds left. He recollected that he had received no Money but from the Commissary General, and therefore that he must have received too much. This accounted for the Commissarys Loss. Here was Integrity. If all Americans, were Carys, We should be fit for a Republic. But, how many Carys have We? I am afraid to Say how few I think We have.

BRITISH CRUELTY

To Abigail Adams

Ap. 27. 1777

Your Favours of Ap. 2 and Ap. 7. I have received.

The inclosed Evening Post, will give you, some Idea, of the Humanity of the present Race of Brittons.—My Barber, whom I quote as often as ever I did any Authority, says "he has read Histories of Cruelty; and he has read Romances of Cruelty: But the Cruelty of the British exceeds all that he ever read."

For my own Part, I think We cannot dwell too much, on this Part of their Character, and Conduct. It is full of important Lessons. If the Facts only were known, in the Utmost Simplicity of Narration, they would strike every pious, and humane Bosom, in Great Britain with Horror. . . . Every

Conscience in that Country is not callous nor every Heart hardened.

The plainest Relation of Facts, would interest the Sympathy, and Compassion of all Europe in our Favour. And it would convince every American that a Nation, so great a Part of which is thus deeply depraved, can never be again trusted with Power over Us.

I think that not only History should perform her Office, but Painting, Sculpture, Statuary, and Poetry ought to assist in publishing to the World, and perpetuating to Posterity, the horrid deeds of our Enemies. It will shew the Persecution, We suffer, in defence of our Rights—it will shew the Fortitude, Patience, Perseverance and Magnanimity of Americans, in as strong a Light, as the Barbarity and Impiety of Britons, in this persecuting War. Surely, Impiety consists, in destroying with such hellish Barbarity, the rational Works of the Deity, as much as in blaspheming and defying his Majesty.

If there is a moral Law: if there is a divine Law—and that there is every intelligent Creature is conscious—to trample on these Laws, to hold them in Contempt and Defyance; is the highest Exertion of Wickedness, and Impiety, that Mortals can be guilty of. The Author of human Nature, who gave it its Rights, will not see it ruined, and suffer its destroyers to escape with Impunity. Divine Vengeance will sometime or other, over-take the Alberts, the Phillips, and Georges—the Alvas, the Grislers and Howes, and vindicate the Wrongs of oppressed human Nature.

I think that Medals in Gold, Silver and Copper ought to be struck in Commemoration of the shocking Cruelties, the bru-tal Barbarities and the diabolical Impieties of this War, and these should be contrasted with the Kindness, Tenderness, Humanity and Philanthropy, which have marked the Conduct of Americans towards their Prisoners.

It is remarkable, that the Officers and Soldiers of our Ene-mies, are so totally depraved, so compleatly destitute of the Sentiments of Philanthropy in their own Hearts, that they can-not believe that such delicate Feelings can exist in any other, and therefore have constantly ascribed that Milk and Honey with which We have treated them to Fear, Cowardice, and conscious Weakness.—But in this they are mistaken, and will discover their Mistake too late to answer any good Purpose for them.

"VANITY, IS THE STRONGEST PASSION"

To Nathanael Greene

Dear Sir   Philadelphia May 9. 1777

Yours of the 2d Instant, came duly to hand. The Indifference of the People about recruiting the Army, is a Circumstance, which ought to make Us, consider what are the Causes of it. It is not, merely the Melancholly, arising from the unfortunate Events of the last Campaign, but the Small Pox, and above all the unhappy State of our Finances, which occasion this Evil. There are other Circumstances, which are little attended to, which contribute, much more than is imagined, to this unfavourable Temper in the People. The Prevalence of Dissipation, Debauchery, Gaming, Prophaneness and Blasphemy, terrifies the best People upon the Continent, from trusting their Sons and other Relations among so many dangerous snares and Temptations. Multitudes of People, who would with chearfull Resignation Submit their Families to the Dangers of the sword, shudder at the Thought of exposing them, to what appears to them, the more destructive Effects of Vice and Impiety. These Ideas would be received by many with Scorn. But there is not the less Solidity in them for that. It is Discipline alone that can Stem the Torrent. Chaplains are of great Use, I believe, and I wish Mr. Leonard might be in the Army, upon such Terms as would be agreable to him, for there is no Man of whom I have a better opinion. But there is So much difficulty in accomplishing any Thing of the Kind, that I wish G. Washington would either appoint him, or recommend him to Congress.

The Utility of Medals, has ever been impressed Strongly upon my Mind. Pride, Ambition, and indeed what a Philosopher would call Vanity, is the Strongest Passion in human Nature, and next to Religion, the most operative Motive to great

Actions. Religion, or if the fine Gentlemen please, Superstition and Enthusiasm, is the greatest Incentive, and wherever it has prevailed, has never failed to produce Heroism. If our N. Englandmen were alone, and could have their own Way, a great deal of this would appear. But in their present Situation, I fear We have little to expect from this Principle, more than the Perseverance of the People in the Cause. We ought to avail ourselves then of even the Vanity of Men. For my own Part I wish We could make a Beginning, by Striking a Medal, with a Platoon firing at General Arnold, on Horseback, His Horse falling dead under him, and He deliberately disentangling his Feet from the Stirrups and taking his Pistolls out of his Holsters, before his Retreat. On the Reverse, He should be mounted on a Fresh Horse, receiving another Discharge of Musquetry, with a Wound in the Neck of his Horse. This Picture alone, which as I am informed is true History, if Arnold did not unfortunately belong to Connecticutt, would be sufficient to make his Fortune for Life. I believe there have been few such Scenes in the World.

We have not Artists at present, for such Works, and many other Difficulties would attend an Attempt to introduce Medals.

Taxation is begun in N.E. The Mass. raises 100,000 this Year. The Regulation of Prices and the Embargo, are Measures, of which I could never see the Justice or Policy.

The Intimation in your Letter, that the Enemy lost in kill'd, wounded and Prisoners 600 Men, Surprizes me, much; because it exceeds, by at least two Thirds, the largest Account that has come from any other Authority. I wish our N. England Men would practice a little honest Policy for their own Interest and Honour, by transmitting to Congress and publishing in the Newspapers, true states of the Actions in which they are concerned. The Truth alone would be sufficient for them, and surely they may be allowed, to avail themselves of this shield of Defence, when So many Arts of dishonest Policy, are practiced against them.

Congress were too anxious for Ti. I wish our Army was encamped upon some Hill, twenty Miles from the Waters of the Lake, or at least Ten.

We are alarmed here with frequent Accounts of numerous Desertions from our Army. Is there no Remedy for this Evil.

Howe is trying his Hand at Bribery. He is sending his Emmis-saries, all about, and scattering ministerial Gold. They despair of the Effects of Force, and are now attempting Bribery and Insinuation which are more provoking than all their Cruelties. What Effect would these have in N. England!

Strechy the Secretary, is an old Partisan at Electioneering, long hackneyd in the Ways of Corruption, long a ministerial Agent, in that dirty Work and the greatest Master of it, in the Nation, selected for that very Purpose to be sent here. Pray dont You Generals sometimes, practice Methods of holding up Such Characters among your Enemies, to the Contempt and Hatred of the Soldiery?

I find I have written a long Story. Excuse me, and believe me to be, with great Truth and Regard, your most obedient servant.

STUDYING THUCYDIDES

To John Quincy Adams

My dear Son   Philadelphia August 11. 1777

As the War in which your Country is engaged will probably hereafter attract your Attention, more than it does at this Time, and as the future Circumstances of your Country, may require other Wars, as well as Councils and Negotiations, sim-ilar to those which are now in Agitation, I wish to turn your Thoughts early to such Studies, as will afford you the most solid Instruction and Improvement for the Part which may be allotted you to act on the Stage of Life.

There is no History, perhaps, better adapted to this usefull Purpose than that of Thucidides, an Author, of whom I hope you will make yourself perfect Master, in original Language, which is Greek, the most perfect of all human Languages. In order to understand him fully in his own Tongue, you must however take Advantage, of every Help you can procure and particularly of Translations of him into your own Mother Tongue.

You will find in your Fathers Library, the Works of Mr.

Hobbes, in which among a great deal of mischievous Philosophy, you will find a learned and exact Translation of Thucidides, which will be usefull to you.

But there is another Translation of him, much more elegant, intituled "The History of the Peloponnesian War, translated from the Greek of Thucidides in two Volumes Quarto, by William Smith A.M. Rector of the Parish of the holy Trinity in Chester, and Chaplain to the Right Honourable the Earl of Derby."

If you preserve this Letter, it may hereafter remind you, to procure the Book.

You will find it full of Instruction to the Orator, the Statesman, the General, as well as to the Historian and the Philosopher. You may find Something of the Peloponnesian War, in Rollin.

I am with much Affection your Father, John Adams

HOWE AND WASHINGTON

To Abigail Adams

My dear   Philadelphia September 1. 1777. Monday
We have now run through the Summer, and altho the Weather is still warm, the fiercest of the Heats is over. And altho the extream Intemperance of the late Season has weakened and exhausted me, much, yet I think upon the whole I have got thro it, as well as upon any former Occasion.

A Letter from General Washington, dated Saturday, informs that our light Parties have brought in four and twenty Prisoners, more. So that the Prisoners and Deserters, since Mr. Howe landed is near an hundred.

The Question now is, whether there will be a general Engagement? In the first Place I think, after all that has past it is not good Policy for Us to attack them unless We can get a favourable Advantage of them, in the Situation of the Ground, or an Opportunity to attack a Detachment of their Army, with superiour Numbers. It would be imprudent, perhaps for Us, with our whole Force to attack them with all theirs.

But another Question arises, whether Mr. Howe will not be able to compell Us to a General Engagement?—Perhaps he may: but I make a Question of it: Washington will maneuvre it with him, a good deal to avoid it. A General Engagement, in which Howe should be defeated, would be ruin to him. If We should be defeated, his Army would be crippled, and perhaps, We might suddenly reinforce our Army which he could not. However all that he could gain by a Victory would be the Possession of this Town which would be the worst Situation he could be in, because it would employ his whole Force by Sea and Land to keep it, and the Command of the River.

Their principal Dependence is not upon their Arms, I believe so much, as upon the Failure of our Revenue. They think, they have taken such Measures, by circulating Counterfeit Bills, to depreciate the Currency, that it cannot hold its Credit longer than this Campaign. But they are mistaken.

We however must disappoint them, by renouncing all Luxuries, and by a severe Œconomy. General Washington setts a fine Example. He has banished Wine from his Table and entertains his Friends with Rum and Water. This is much to the Honour of his Wisdom, his Policy, and his Patriotism, and the Example must be followed, by banishing sugar, and all imported Articles, from all our Families. If Necessity should reduce Us to a Simplicity of Dress, and Diet, becoming Republicans, it would be an happy and a glorious Necessity.

Yours—Yours—Yours.

From the Diary: September 15–21, 1777

SEPTR. 15. 1777. MONDAY.

Fryday the 12, I removed from Captn. Duncans in Walnutt Street to the Revd. Mr. Sprouts in Third Street, a few doors from his Meeting House. Mr. Merchant from Rhode Island boards here, with me. Mr. Sprout is sick of a Fever. Mrs. Sprout, and the four young Ladies her Daughters, are in great Distress on Account of his Sickness, and the Approach of Mr.

Howes Army. But they bear their Affliction with christian Patience and philosophic Fortitude. The young Ladies are Miss Hannah, Olive, Sally and Nancy. The only Son is an Officer in the Army. He was the first Clerk in the American War office.

We live in critical Moments! Mr. Howes Army is at Middleton and Concord. Mr. Washingtons, upon the Western Banks of Schuylkill, a few Miles from him. I saw this Morning an excellent Chart of the Schuylkill, Chester River, the Brandywine, and this whole Country, among the Pensilvania Files. This City is the Stake, for which the Game is playd. I think, there is a Chance for saving it, although the Probability is against Us. Mr. Howe I conjecture is waiting for his Ships to come into the Delaware. Will W. attack him? I hope so—and God grant him Success.

1777. SEPT. 16. TUESDAY.

No Newspaper this Morning. Mr. Dunlap has moved or packed up his Types. A Note from G. Dickinson that the Enemy in N. Jersey are 4000 strong. How is about 15 miles from Us, the other Way. The City seems to be asleep, or dead, and the whole State scarce alive. Maryland and Delaware the same.

The Prospect is chilling, on every Side. Gloomy, dark, mel-ancholly, and dispiriting. When and where will the light spring up?

Shall We have good News from Europe? Shall We hear of a Blow struck by Gates? Is there a Possibility that Washington should beat How? Is there a Prospect that McDougal and Dickinson should destroy the Detachment in the Jersies?

From whence is our Deliverance to come? Or is it not to come? Is Philadelphia to be lost? If lost, is the Cause lost? No—the Cause is not lost—but it may be hurt.

I seldom regard Reports, but it is said that How has marked his Course, from Elke, with Depredation. His Troops have plunderd Henroosts, dairy Rooms, the furniture of Houses and all the Cattle of the Country. The Inhabitants, most of whom are Quakers, are angry and disappointed, because they were promised the Security of their Property.

It is reported too that Mr. How lost great Numbers in the Battle of the Brandywine.

1777. SEPTR. 18. THURSDAY.

The violent N.E. Storm which began the Day before Yesterday continues. We are yet in Philadelphia, that Mass of Cowardice and Toryism. Yesterday was buryed Monsr. Du Coudray, a French Officer of Artillery, who was lately made an Inspector General of Artillery and military Manufactures with the Rank of Major General. He was drowned in the Schuylkill, in a strange manner. He rode into the Ferry Boat, and road out at the other End, into the River, and was drowned. His Horse took fright. He was reputed the most learned and promising Officer in France. He was carried into the Romish Chappell, and buried in the Yard of that Church.

This Dispensation will save Us much Altercation.

1777. SEPTR. 19. FRYDAY.

At 3 this Morning was waked by Mr. Lovell, and told that the Members of Congress were gone, some of them, a little after Midnight. That there was a Letter from Mr. Hamilton Aid de Camp to the General, informing that the Enemy were in Possession of the Ford and the Boats, and had it in their Power to be in Philadelphia, before Morning, and that if Congress was not removed they had not a Moment to loose.

Mr. Merchant and myself arose, sent for our Horses, and, after collecting our Things, rode off after the others. Breakfasted at Bristol, where were many Members, determined to go the Newtown Road to Reading. We rode to Trenton where We dined. Coll. Harrison, Dr. Witherspoon, all the Delegates from N.Y. and N.E. except Gerry and Lovell. Drank Tea at Mr. Spencers, lodged at Mr. S. Tuckers, at his kind Invitation.

SEPTR. 20. SATURDAY.

Breakfasted at Mrs. J. B. Smiths. The old Gentleman, his Son Thomas the Loan Officer, were here, and Mrs. Smith's little Son and two Daughters. An elegant Break fast We had of fine Hyson, loaf Sugar, and Coffee &c.

Dined at Williams's, the Sign of the Green Tree. Drank Tea, with Mr. Thompson and his Lady at Mrs. Jacksons. Walked with Mr. Duane to General Dickinsons House, and took a Look at his Farm and Gardens, and his Greenhouse, which is a Scæne of Desolation. The floor of the Greenhouse is dug up by the Hessians, in Search for Money. The Orange, Lemon and Lime Trees are all dead, with the Leaves on. There is a spacious Ball Room, above stairs a drawing Room and a whispering Room. In another Apartment, a huge Crash of Glass Bottles, which the Hessians had broke I suppose.—These are thy Tryumphs, mighty Britain.—Mr. Law, Mr. Hancock, Mr. Thompson, Mr.   were here. Spent the Evening at Williams's and slept again at Tuckers.

Mrs. Tucker has about 1600£ st. in some of the Funds in England, which she is in fear of loosing. She is accordingly, passionately wishing for Peace, and that the Battle was fought once for all &c. Says that, private Property will be plundered, where there is an Army whether of Friends or Enemies. That if the two opposite Armys were to come here alternately ten times, she would stand by her Property untill she should be kill'd. If she must be a Beggar, it should be where she was known &c. This kind of Conversation shews plainly enough, how well she is pleased, with the State of Things.

1777 SEPTR. 21. SUNDAY.

It was a false alarm which occasioned our Flight from Phila- delphia. Not a Soldier of Howes has crossed the Schuylkill. Washington has again crossed it, which I think is a very injudi- cious Maneuvre. I think, his Army would have been best dis- posed on the West Side of the Schuylkill. If he had sent one Brigade of his regular Troops to have heald the Militia it would have been enough. With such a Disposition, he might have cutt to Pieces, Hows Army, in attempting to cross any of the Fords. How will not attempt it. He will wait for his Fleet in Delaware River. He will keep open his Line of Communica- tion with Brunswick, and at last, by some Deception or other will slip unhurt into the City.

Burgoine has crossed Hudsons River, by which Gen. Gates thinks, he is determined at all Hazards to push for Albany, which G. Gates says he will do all in his Power to prevent him from reaching. But I confess I am anxious for the Event, for I fear he will deceive Gates, who seems to be acting the same timorous, defensive Part, which has involved us in so many Disasters.—Oh, Heaven! grant Us one great Soul! One leading Mind would extricate the best Cause, from that Ruin which seems to await it, for the Want of it.

We have as good a Cause, as ever was fought for. We have great Resources. The People are well tempered. One active masterly Capacity would bring order out of this Confusion and save this Country.

INFLATION AND TAXES

To Elbridge Gerry

My dear Sir   Braintree Decr. 6. 1777

You must expect for the Future, to find in me, Situated as I am by a blissfull Fireside, surrounded by a Wife and a Parcell of chattering Boys and Girls, only a Dealer in Small Politicks.

I find the Same Perplexities here, that We felt at York Town—a general Inclination among the People to barter, and as general an Aversion to dealing in Paper Money of any Denomination. Guineas half Jo's and milled Dollars, in as high Estimation as in Pensylvania.

The Monied Men, I am informed, generally decline receiving Paper for their Debts—many refuse—and it is said, all will, very soon. There is a Whispering about among the richer sort, that an Act is necessary for allowing a Depreciation, or an Appreciation, as the Case may be, upon Specialties. And the poorer Sort, look cunning, and give Hints, that the rich are aiming at a Depreciation.

I mention these Facts and leave you to draw your own Inferences. I know and feel the Delicacy of the subject, and am restrained from certain prudential Considerations, from writing my own sentiments freely. Two Things I will venture to Say,—one is that I am sick of Attempts to work Impossibilities, and to alter the Course of Nature. Another is Fiat Justitia ruat Cœlum. The rapid Translation of Property from Hand to Hand, the robbing of Peter to pay Paul distresses me, beyond

Measure. The Man who lent another an 100 £ in gold four years ago, and is paid now in Paper, cannot purchase with it, a Quarter Part, in Pork, Beef, or Land, of what he could when he lent the Gold. This is Fact and Facts are Stubborn Things, in opposition to Speculation. You have the nimblest Spirit for climbing over Difficulties, and for dispersing Mists and seeing fair Weather, when it is foggy, of any Man I know. But this will be a serious Perplexity even to you before it is over.

I am not out of my Wits about it—it will not ruin our Cause great as the Evil is, or if it was much greater. But it torments me to see Injustice, both to the public and to Individuals so frequent.

Every Mans Liberty and Life, is equally dear to him. Every Man therefore ought to be taxed equally for the Defence of his Life and Liberty. That is the Poll tax should be equal.

Every Mans Property is equally dear both to himself, and to the Public. Every Mans Property therefore ought to be taxed for the Defence of the Public, in Proportion to the Quantity of it. These are fundamental Maxims of sound Policy. But instead of this, every Man, who had Money due to him at the Commencement of this War has been already taxed three fourth Parts of that Money, besides his Tax on his Poll and Estate in Proportion to other People. And every Man who owed Money, at the beginning of the War, has put 3/4 of it in his Pockett as clear gain. The War therefore is immoderately gainfull to some, and ruinous to others. This will never do. I, am, with great Truth, your Friend,   John Adams

ACCEPTING A DIPLOMATIC COMMISSION

To James Lovell

My dear Friend   Braintree Decr 24. 1777

I cannot omit this opportunity of acknowledging the Receipt of your kind Favours of 27 or 28 Novr. I Say one or the other of those days, because although the Letter has no date yet it Says it was written on the Day when a certain Commission was voted me, and both the Commissions are dated the 27, altho the Copy of the Resolution of Congress by which I was appointed is dated the 28.

I should have wanted no Motives nor Arguments to induce me to accept of this momentous Trust, if I could be sure that the Public would be benifited by it. But when I see, my Brothers at the Bar, here, so easily making Fortunes for themselves and their Families, and when I recollect that for four years I have abandoned myself and mine, and when I see my own Children growing up, in something very like real Want, because I have taken no Care of them, it requires as much Philosophy as I am Master of, to determine to persevere in public Life, and to engage in a new scæne, for which I fear I am, very ill qualified.

However, by the Innuendoes in your Letter, if I cannot do much Good in this new Department, I may possibly do less Harm, than some others.

The Want of a Language for Conversation and Business, is however all the Objection that lies with much Weight upon my Mind: altho I have been not ignorant of the Grammar and Construction of the French Tongue from my Youth, yet I have never aimed at maintaining or even understanding Conversation in it: and this Talent I suppose I am too old to acquire, in any Degree of Perfection. However, I will try and do my best. I will take Books and my whole Time shall be devoted to it. Let me intreat the Benefit of your constant Correspondence, and believe me to be with much Affection your Friend.

COMMISSIONER TO FRANCE AND FRAMER OF THE MASSACHUSETTS CONSTITUTION

1778–1779

From the Diary: February 27–April 11, 1778

A Calm. As soft and warm as Summer. A Species of black Fish, which our officers call Beneaters, appeared about the Ship.

One Source of the Disorders in this Ship, is the Irregularity of Meals. There ought to be a well digested System, for Eating, Drinking and sleeping. At Six, all Hands should be called up. At Eight, all Hands should breakfast. At one all Hands should dine. At Eight again all Hands should sup. It ought to be penal for the Cook to fail of having his Victuals ready punctually.— This would be for the Health, Comfort and Spirits of the Men, and would greatly promote the Business of the Ship.

I am constantly giving Hints to the Captain concerning Order, Œconomy and Regularity, and he seems to be sensible of the Necessity of them, and exerts himself to introduce them.— He has cleared out the Tween Decks, ordered up the Hammocks to be aired, and ordered up the sick, such as could bear it, upon Deck for sweet Air. This Ship would have bred the Plague or the Goal Fever, if there had not been great Exertions, since the storm, to wash, sweep, Air and purify, Cloaths, Cots, Cabins, Hammocks and all other Things, Places and Persons.

The Captn. Yesterday went down into the Cock Pit, and ordered up every Body from that Sink of Devastation and Putrefaction—ordered up the Hamocks &c. This was in Pursuance of the Advice I gave him in the Morning, "if you intend to have any Reputation for Œconomy, Discipline or any Thing that is good, look to your Cock Pit."

Yesterday the Captn. brought in a Curiosity which he had drawn up over the Side in a Buckett of Water, which the Sailors call a Portuguese Man of War, and to day I have seen many of them sailing by the Ship. They have some Appearances of Life and Sensibility. They spread a curious Sail and are wafted along very briskly. They have something like Gutts, hanging down, which are said to be in a degree poisonous to human Flesh. The Hulk is like blue Glass. I pierced it with the sharp Point of my Pen Knife and found it empty. The Air came out, and the Thing shrunk up almost to nothing.

SATURDAY. MARCH 14.

I have omitted inserting the Occurrences of this Week, on Account of the Hurry and Confusion, We have been in. Tuesday We spied a Sail, and gave her Chase. We soon came up with her, but as We had bore directly down upon her, she had not seen our broadside, and knew not her Force. She was a Letter of Mark with 14 Guns, 8 Nines and 6 sixes. She fired upon Us, and one of her shot went thro our Mizen Yard. I happened to be upon the Quarter deck, and in the Direction from the Ship to the Yard so that the Ball went directly over my Head. We, upon this, turned our broadside which the instant she saw she struck. Captn. Tucker very prudently, ordered his officers not to fire.

The Prize is the Ship Martha, Captn. McIntosh from London to New York, loaded with a Cargo of great Value. The Captn. told me that Seventy thousand Pounds sterling was insured upon her at Lloyds, and that She was worth 80 thousands.

The Captain is very much of a Gentleman. There are two Gentlemen with him. Passengers, the one Mr. R. Gault, the other Mr. Wallace of N. York. Two young Jews were on board.

That and the next day was spent in dispatching the Prize, under the Command of the 3d Lt. Mr. Welch to Boston.

After that We fell in Chase of another Vessell, and overtaking her, found her to be a french Snow, from Bourdeaux to Miquelon.

We then saw another Vessell, chased and came up with her which proved to be a French Brig from Marseilles to Nantes. This last cost Us very dear. Mr. Barrons our 1st. Lt. attempting to fire a Gun, as a signal to the Brig, the Gun burst, and tore the right Leg of this excellent Officer, in Pieces, so that the Dr. was obliged to amputate it, just below the Knee.

I was present at this affecting Scæne and held Mr. Barron in my Arms while the Doctor put on the Turnequett and cutt off the Limb.

Mr. Barrons bore it with great Fortitude and Magnanimity—thought he should die, and frequently intreated me, to take Care of his Family. He had an helpless Family he said, and begged that I would take Care of his Children. I promised him, that by the first Letters I should write to America, I would earnestly recommend his Children to the Care of the Public, as well as of Individuals. I cannot but think the Fall of this Officer, a great Loss to the united States. . . . His Prudence, his Moderation, his Attention, his Zeal, were Qualities much wanted in our Navy. He is by Birth a Virginian.

MARCH 30. MONDAY.

This Morning at 5, the Officer came down and told the Captain that a lofty Ship was close by Us, and had fired two heavy Guns. All Hands called. She proved to be an heavy loaded Snow.

The Weather cloudy, but no Wind. Still—except a small Swell.

The Tour of Cordovan, or in other Words Bourdeaux Lighthouse in Sight, over our larbord Bow.

The Captn. is now cleaning Ship and removing his Warlike Appearances.

This Day has been hitherto fortunate and happy.—Our Pilot has brought us safely into the River, and We have run up, with Wind and Tide as far as Pouliac, where We have anchored for the Night, and have taken in another Pilot.

This forenoon a Fisherman came along Side, with Hakes, Skates, and Gennetts. We bought a few, and had an high Regale.

This River is very beautifull—on both Sides the Plantations are very pleasant. On the South Side especially, We saw all along Horses, Oxen, Cowes, and great Flocks of Sheep grazing, the Husbandmen ploughing &c. and the Women, half a Dozen in a Drove with their Hoes. The Churches, Convents, Gentlemens seats, and the Villages appear very magnificent.

This River seldom Swells with Freshes, for the rural Improvements and even the Fishermens Houses, are brought quite down to the Waters Edge. The Water in the River is very foul to all Appearance, looking all the Way like a Mud Puddle. The Tide setts in 5 Knots. We outrun every Thing in sailing up the River.

The Buildings public and private, are of Stone, and a great

Number of beautifull Groves, appear between the grand Seats, and best Plantations. A great Number of Vessells lay in the River. . . .

The Pleasure resulting from the Sight of Land, Cattle, Houses, &c. after so long, so tedious, and dangerous a Voyage, is very great: It gives me a pleasing Melancholly to see this Country, an Honour which a few Months ago I never expected to arrive at.—Europe thou great Theatre of Arts, Sciences, Commerce, War, am I at last permitted to visit thy Territories.—May the Design of my Voyage be answered.

MARCH 31. TUESDAY.

Lying in the River of Bourdeaux, near Pouliac. A 24 Gun Ship close by Us, under French Colours, bound to St. Domingue.—A dark, misty Morning.

My first Enquiry should be, who is Agent for the united States of America at Bourdeaux, at Blaye, &c.—who are the principal Merchants on this River concerned in the American Trade? What Vessells French or American, have sailed or are about sailing for America, what their Cargoes, and for what Ports? Whether on Account of the united States, of any particular State, or of private Merchants french or American?

This Morning the Captain and a Passenger came on board the Boston, from the Julie, a large Ship bound to St. Domingue, to make Us a Visit. They invited Us on Board to dine. Captn. Palmes, Mrs Jesse and Johnny and myself, went. We found half a Dozen genteel Persons on Board, and found a pretty ship, an elegant Cabin, and every Accommodation. The white Stone Plates were laid, and a clean Napkin placed in each, and a Cut of fine Bread. The Cloth, Plates, Servants, every Thing was as clean, as in any Gentlemans House. The first Dish was a fine french Soup, which I confess I liked very much.—Then a Dish of boiled Meat.—Then the Lights of a Calf, dressed one Way and the Liver another.—Then roasted Mutton then fricaseed Mutton. A fine Sallad and something very like Asparagus, but not it.—The Bread was very fine, and it was baked on board.—We had then Prunes, Almonds, and the most delicate Raisins I ever saw.—Dutch Cheese—then a Dish of Coffee—then a french Cordial—and Wine and Water, excellent Claret with our Dinner.—None of us understood French—none of them English: so that Dr. Noel stood Interpreter. While at Dinner We saw a Pinnace go on board the Boston with several, half a Dozen, genteel People on board.

On the Quarter Deck, I was struck with the Hens, Capons, and Cocks in their Coops—the largest I ever saw.

After a genteel Entertainment, Mr. Griffin, one of our petty Officers, came with the Pinnace, and C. Tuckers Compliments desiring to see me. We took Leave and returned where We found very genteel Company consisting of the Captn. of another Ship bound to Martinique and several Kings Officers, bound out. One was the Commandant.

C. Palmes was sent forward to Blaye, in the Pinnace to the Officer at the Castle in order to produce our Commission and procure an Entry, and pass to Bourdeaux. Palmes came back full of the Compliments of the Broker to the Captn. and to me. I shall not repeat the Compliments sent to me, but he earnestly requested that C. Tucker would salute the Fort with 13 Guns, &c.—which the Captn. did.

All the Gentlemen We have seen to day agree that Dr. Franklin has been received by the K in great Pomp and that a Treaty is concluded, and they all expect War, every Moment. . . .

This is a most beautifull River, the Villages, and Country Seats appear upon each Side all the Way. We have got up this Afternoon within 3 Leagues of the Town.

APRIL 11. SATURDAY.

Went to Versailles, with Dr. Franklin and Mr. Lee—waited on the Count De Vergennes, the Secretary of foreign Affairs —was politely received.—He hoped I should stay long enough to learn French perfectly—assured me, that every Thing should be done to make France agreable to me—hoped the Treaty would be agreable, and the Alliance lasting.—I told him I thought the Treaty liberal, and generous—and doubted not of its speedy Ratification. I communicated to him the Resolutions of Congress respecting the Suspension of Burgoines Embarkation, which he read through, and pronounced Fort bon.

I was then conducted to the Count Maurepas, the Prime Minister, was introduced by Dr. F. as his new Colleague and politely received.

I was then shewn the Palace of Versailles, and happened to be present when the King passed through, to Council. His Majesty seeing my Colleagues, graciously smiled, and passed on. I was then shewn the Galleries, and Royal Apartments, and the K's Bedchamber. The Magnificence of these Scænes, is immense. The Statues, the Paintings, the every Thing is sublime.

We then returned, went into the City, and dined with the Count   where was the Count De Noailles, his Secretary, and 20 or 30 others, of the Grandees of France. After Dinner, We went in the Coach, to see the Royal Hospital of Invalids, the Chappell of which is immensely grand, in Marble and Paintings and Statuary.

After this We went to the Ecole militaire, went into the Chapell and into the Hall of Council &c. Here We saw the Statues of the great Conde, Turenne, Luxembourg, and Saxe. Returned and drank Tea, at Mm. Brillons, who lent me Voyage picturesque de Paris, and entertained Us, again, with her Music, and her agreable Conversation.

FRENCH LUXURY

To Abigail Adams

My dearest Friend   Passy April 12. 1778

I am so sensible of the Difficulty of conveying Letters safe, to you, that I am afraid to write, any Thing more than to tell you that after all the Fatigues and Dangers of my Voyage, and Journey, I am here in Health. . . .

The Reception I have met, in this Kingdom, has been as friendly, as polite, and as respectfull as was possible. It is the universal Opinion of the People here, of all Ranks, that a Friendship between France and America, is the Interest of both Countries, and the late Alliance, so happily formed, is universally popular: so much so that I have been told by Persons of good Judgment, that the Government here, would have been under a Sort of Necessity of agreeing to it even if it had not been agreable to themselves.

The Delights of France are innumerable. The Politeness, the Elegance, the Softness, the Delicacy, is extreme.

In short stern and hauty Republican as I am, I cannot help loving these People, for their earnest Desire, and Assiduity to please.

It would be futile to attempt Descriptions of this Country especially of Paris and Versailles. The public Buildings and Gardens, the Paintings, Sculpture, Architecture, Musick, &c. of these Cities have already filled many Volumes. The Richness, the Magnificence, and Splendor, is beyond all Description.

This Magnificence is not confined to public Buildings such as Churches, Hospitals, Schools &c., but extends to private Houses, to Furniture, Equipage, Dress, and especially to Entertainments.—But what is all this to me? I receive but little Pleasure in beholding all these Things, because I cannot but consider them as Bagatelles, introduced, by Time and Luxury in Exchange for the great Qualities and hardy manly Virtues of the human Heart. I cannot help suspecting that the more Elegance, the less Virtue in all Times and Countries.—Yet I fear that even my own dear Country wants the Power and Opportunity more than the Inclination, to be elegant, soft, and luxurious.

All the Luxury I desire in this World is the Company of my dearest Friend, and my Children, and such Friends as they delight in, which I have sanguine Hopes, I shall, after a few Years enjoy in Peace.—I am with inexpressible Affection Yours, yours,   John Adams

From the Diary: April 16–May 8, 1778

APRIL 16. JEUDI.

Dr. F. is reported to speak French very well, but I find upon attending to him that he does not speak it Grammatically, and indeed upon enquiring, he confesses that he is wholly inattentive to the Grammar. His Pronunciation too, upon which the

French Gentlemen and Ladies compliment him, and which he seems to think is pretty well, I am sure is very far from being exact.

Indeed Dr. Franklin's Knowledge of French, at least his Faculty of speaking it, may be said to have begun with his Embassy to this Court. . . . He told me that when he was in France before, Sir John Pringle was with him, and did all his Conversation for him as Interpreter, and that he understood and spoke French with great Difficulty, untill he came here last, altho he read it.

Dined, at Mr. La Freté's. The Magnificence of the House, Garden and Furniture is astonishing. Saw here an History of the Revolution in Russia in the Year 1762.

This Family are fond of Paintings. They have a Variety of exquisite Pieces, particularly a Storm and a Calm.

1778 APRIL 21. MARDI.

Dined, this Day, at Mr. Chaumonts, with the largest Collection of great Company that I have yet seen. The Marquis D Argenson, the Count De Noailles, the Marshall de Maillebois, the Brother of the Count de Vergennes, and a great many others, Mr. Foucault and Mm., Mr. Chaumonts Son in Law and Daughter, who has a Fortune of 4 or 5000£ st. in St. Domingo, Mr. Chaumonts own Son and Miss Chaumont. Mr.   the first officer under Mr. Sartine.

It is with much Grief and Concern that I have learned from my first landing in France, the Disputes between the Americans, in this Kingdom. The Animosities between Mr. D and Mr. L—between Dr. F and Mr. L.—between Mr. Iz and Dr. F.—between Dr. B and Mr. L.—between Mr. C. and all. It is a Rope of Sand. . . .

I am at present wholly untainted with these Prejudices, and will endeavour to keep myself so. Parties and Divisions among the Americans here, must have disagreable if not pernicious Effects.

Mr. D. seems to have made himself agreable here to Persons of Importance and Influence, and is gone home in such Splendor, that I fear, there will be Altercations, in America about him. Dr. F., Mr. D. and Dr. Bancroft, are Friends. The L's and

Mr. Iz. are Friends. Sir J J insinuated that Mr. D. had been at least as attentive to his own Interest, in dabbling in the English Funds, and in Trade, and fitting out Privateers, as to the Public, and said he would give Mr. D. fifty thousand Pounds for his Fortune, and said that Dr. B. too had made a Fortune. Mr. McC insinuated to me, that the L's were selfish, and that this was a Family Misfortune. What shall I say? What shall I think?

It is said that Mr. L. has not the Confidence of the Ministry, nor of the Persons of Influence here—that he is suspected of too much Affection for England, and of too much Intimacy with Ld. Shel—that he has given offence, by an unhappy disposition, and by indiferent Speeches before Servants and others, concerning the French Nation and Government, despising and cursing them.—I am sorry for these Things, but it is no Part of my Business to quarrell with any Body without Cause. It is no Part of my Duty to differ with one Party or another, or to give offence to any Body. But I must do my duty to the Public, let it give offence to whom it will.

The public Business has never been methodically conducted. There never was before I came, a minute Book, a Letter Book or an Account Book—and it is not possible to obtain a clear Idea of our Affairs.

Mr. D. lived expensively, and seems not to have had much order in his Business, public or private: but he was active, dilligent, subtle, and successfull, having accomplished the great Purpose of his Mission, to Advantage. . . . Mr. Gerard is his Friend, and I find that Dr. B. has the Confidence of Persons about the Ministry, particularly of the late Secretary to the Embassader to G.B.

MAY 8. FRYDAY.

This Morning Dr. Franklin, Mr. Lee, and Mr. Adams, went to Versailles, in Order that Mr. Adams might be presented to the King.—Waited on the Count De Vergennes, at his office, and at the Hour of Eleven the Count conducted Us, into the Kings Bed Chamber where he was dressing—one officer putting on his Sword, another his Coat &c.

The Count went up to the King, and his Majesty turned about, towards me, and smiled. Ce est il Monsieur Adams, said the King and then asked a Question, very quick, or rather made an Observation to me which I did not fully understand. The Purport of it was that I had not been long arrived.—The Count Vergennes then conducted me to the Door of another Room, and desired me to stand there which I did untill the King passed.—The Count told the King, that I did not yet take upon me to speak French. The King asked, whether I did not speak *at all* as yet—and passed by me, into the other Room.

This Monarch is in the 24th. Year of his Age, having been born the 23d of Aug. 1754. He has the Appearances of a strong Constitution, capable of enduring to a great Age. His Reign has already been distinguished, by an Event that will reflect a Glory upon it, in future Ages I mean, the Treaty with America.

We afterwards made a Visit to Count Maurepas, to Mr. Sartine, to the Chancellor, to Mr. Bertin &c.

The Chancellor, has the Countenance of a Man worn with severe Studies. When I was introduced to him he turned to Dr. F. and said Mr. Adams est un Person celebre en Amerique et en Europe.

We went afterwards to Dinner, with the Count de Vergennes. There was a full Table—no Ladies but the Countess. The Counts Brother, the Ambassador who lately signed the Treaty with Swisserland, Mr. Garnier the late Secretary to the Embassy in England, and many others, Dukes and Bishops and Counts &c.

Mr. Garnier and Mr.   asked me, with some Appearance of Concern, whether there was any foundation for the Reports which the Ministry had spread in England, of a Dispute between Congress and Gen. Washington. A Letter they say has been printed, from an officer in Phila. to that Purpose.

Mr. Garnier is the 1st. french Gentleman who has begun a serious political Conversation with me of any length. He is a sensible Man.

EUROPEAN AFFAIRS

To Samuel Adams

My dear Sir   Passi May 21. 1778

I have never yet paid my respects to you, since my Arrival in Europe, for which seeming Neglect of Duty, the total Novelty of the Scænes about me, and the incessant Avocations of Business and Ceremony and Pleasure, for this last I find in Europe, makes an essential part of both the other two, must plead my excuse.

The Situation of the general Affairs of Europe, is still critical and of dubious Tendency. It is still uncertain, whether there will be War, between the Turks and Russians; between the Emperor and the King of Prussia; and indeed between England and France, in the Opinion of many People; my own Conjecture however is, that a War will commence and that soon.

Before this reaches you, you will be informed, that a strong Squadron of thirteen Capital Ships and several Frigates, has sailed from Toulon, and that another Squadron is ordered to sail from Spithead. Whatever I may have heard of the destination of the first, I am not at Liberty to mention it. We have yet no intelligence that the latter has sailed.

Chatham the great is no more: but there is so much of his wild Spirit in his last Speech, yet left in the Nation, that I have no doubt but Administration will put all to the hazard.

We are happy to hear, by the Frigate Le Sensible, which has returned to Brest, that the Treaty arrived safe at Casco Bay. We hope to have the earliest Intelligence of the ratification of it. . . . The Commissioners from England, who sailed about the twenty second of April, will meet as We suppose with nothing but ridicule.

Prussia is yet upon the reserve concerning America, or rather, forgetting his Promise has determined not to acknowledge our Independance, at present. His Reason is obvious. He wants the Aid of those very German Princes who are most subservient to Great Britain, who have furnished her with Troops to carry on the War against Us, and therefore he does not choose to offend them by an Alliance with Us, at present.

Spain is on the reserve too: but there is not the least doubt entertained here, of her intentions to support America. In Holland there is more Friendship for Us, than I was aware before I came here. At least, they will take no part against Us.

Our Affairs in this Kingdom, I find in a State of confusion and darkness, that surprizes me. Prodigious Sums of money have been expended and large Sums are yet due. But there are no Books of Account, or any Documents, from whence I have been able to learn what the United States have received as an Equivalent.

There is one Subject, which lies heavily on my Mind, and that is the expence of the Commissioners. You have three Commissioners at this Court, each of whom lives at an Expence of at least Three thousand Pounds Sterling a Year, I fear at a greater Expence. Few Men in this World are capable of living at a less Expence, than I am. But I find the other Gentlemen have expended, from three to four Thousand a Year each, and one of them from five to six. And by all the Enquiries I have been able to make, I cannot find any Article of Expence, which can be retrenched.

The Truth is, in my humble Opinion, our System is wrong in many Particulars. 1. In having three Commissioners at this Court. One in the Character of Envoy is enough. At present each of the Three is considered in the Character of a Public Minister; a Minister Plenipotentiary, which lays him under an absolute Necessity of living up to this Character. Whereas one alone would be obliged to no greater Expence, and would be quite sufficient for all the Business of a Public Minister. 2. In Leaving the Salaries of these Ministers at an Uncertainty. You will never be able to obtain a satisfactory Account, of the public Monies, while this System continues. It is a Temptation to live at too great an Expence, and Gentlemen will feel an Aversion to demanding a rigorous Account. 3. In blending the Business of a public Minister with that of a Commercial Agent. The Businesses of various departments, are by this means so blended and the public and private Expences so confounded with each other, that I am sure no Satisfaction can ever be given to the Public, of the disposition of their Interests and I am very confident that Jealousies and Suspicions will hereafter arise against the Characters of Gentlemen, who may perhaps have Acted with perfect Integrity and the fairest Intentions for the public Good.

My Idea is this, seperate the Offices of Public Ministers from those of commercial Agents. . . . Recall, or send to some other Court, all the Public Ministers but one, at this Court. Determine with Precision, the Sum that shall be allowed to the remaining one, for his Expences and for his Salary, i.e. for his Time, Risque, Trouble &c., and when this is done see that he receives no more than his allowance.

The Inconveniences arising from the Multiplicity of Ministers and the Complications of Businesses are infinite.

Remember me, with the most tender Affection to my worthy Colleagues, and to all others to whom you know they are due. I am your Friend and Servant   John Adams
The Honourable Samuel Adams

CANADA AND PEACE

To James Warren

My dear Sir   Passi July 26. 1778

Yours of 7 June by Captain Barnes fortunately reached me, Yesterday. I was much Surprised, you may well imagine at its Contents. But I Suppose, the Cause of their not electing you to the Council, must have been your Engagements in the Navy Board.

I am unhappy to learn by the Newspapers, that our Constitution is likely to occasion much Altercation in the State, but notwithstanding all our Dissentions, there is a Mass of Prudence, and Integrity among our People, that will finally conduct them into the right Way.

I wish now that I had accepted of your polite offer of your son. It is however I presume for his Interest, because, he may pursue Business there to much better Profit. If Mr. Austin should leave me, I should have occasion for a Clerk, which would afford a young Gentleman, a decent subsistence and no more. The Frigates, the Merchandise, the Negociations and the vast Correspondence, we have, render a Clerk, indispensably necessary for each of the Commissioners, and for some of them more than one.

Mr. Hancock Mr. Adams, and my respectable successor Dr. Holten, are gone to Congress, but you dont mention Mr. Paine. Where is he? Earning Twenty thousand dollars a year at the Bar? If he is I wish him Joy, and hope in Time to arrive at some Post of the same Honour and Profit. Dana I suppose is earning Thirty thousands. Upon my Word I think these Gentry ought to through their rich Profits into Hotchpotch with a poor Brother at Passi.

Where is the Spirit and the Genius of America? To suffer the feeble Remnants of our Ennemis, in Philadelphia and Rhode Island, to come out with such Insolence, and burn Houses and Vessells, without Retaliation, is intollerable.

Will it ever do to think of Peace, while G. Britain has Canada, Nova Scotia and the Floridas, or any of them? Such a Peace will be but short. We shall have perpetual Wars with Britain while she has a foot of Ground in America. But if the belligerant Powers should be exhausted, so as to think of Peace, leaving Canada in the Hands of Britain, which I hope they will not, the Boundaries of Canada, must be ascertained, and of the Floridas too.

I believe I can tell you a Piece of News. The Cabinet at London, have determined to send to their Commissioners in America Instructions to offer you Independance, provided you will make Peace with them Seperate from France, and make a Commercial Treaty with them, by which they may retain something like their late Monopoly.

They certainly think that Americans are not Men of Honour. They believe them capable of violating their first Treaty, their first solemn sacred Faith, within a few Moments of its unanimous Ratification. Is it because they have seen, or heard any Thing like this Perfidy in Americans, or is it because they feel themselves capable of such Conduct and infer from thence that all other Men, are equally so?

Is there a Man in America, who would not run all hazards, who would not suffer the last Extremity rather than stain the first Page of our History with so foul a Breach of Faith? Is there who would confess and prove to the World that America has no Honour, no Conscience, no faith, no Pride, for the sake of avoiding the Evils of War?

But where and how did the King and Council obtain Authority to make Such an offer? They have no such Power. Parliament alone can do it.

But they mean no such Thing. They mean only to seduce soldiers to Desertion. They mean only to draw in Congress or some public Body to break their Faith with France and to do some Act which shall forfeit the Confidence of all Mankind, and then they think they can manage America. Their object in this Piece of Policy as in all their others towards America, appears to me to be to seduce, to deceive, and to divide. They must however be brought to mingle some sincerity with their Policy, before they will succeed. I am as ever, yours

THE FRANCO-AMERICAN ALLIANCE

To James Warren

My dear Sir   Passy August 4. 1778

Your kind Favor of July 1st. was brought here Yesterday from Bordeaux where Capt. Ayres has arrived, but was not deliver'd me till this day. This is only the second received from you. I have infinite Satisfaction in learning from all parts of America the prosperous Train of our Affairs and the Unanimity and Spirit of the people. Every Vessel brings us fresh Accessions of Ardour to the French and of Depression to the English in the War that is now begun in earnest.

The Resolutions of Congress upon the conciliatory Bills, the Address to the people, the Ratification of the Treaty, the Answer to the Commissioners, the Presidents Letter, the Message of G Livingston and the Letter of Mr. Drayton are read here with an Avidity that would surprise you. It is not one of the least Misfortunes, of G. Britain, that she has to contend with so much Eloquence, that there are such painters to exhibit her attrocious Actions to the World and transmit them to posterity, every publication of this kind seems to excite the Ardour of the French Nation and of their Fleets and Armies, as much as if they were Americans.

While American Orators are thus employed in perpetuating the Remembrance of the Injustice and Cruelty of G. Britain towards us, The French Fleet has been giving such a Check to her naval pride as she has not experienced before for many Ages. The Vessel which is to carry this will carry Information of a general Engagement between D'Orvielliers and Keppell which terminated in a disgracefull Flight of the British Fleet. We hope soon to hear of D'Estaing's Success which would demonstrate to the Universe that Britain is no longer Mistress of the Ocean. But the Events of War are always uncertain and a Misfortune may have happen'd to the French Fleet in America. But even if this should be the Case, which I dont believe, still Britain is not Mistress of the Sea, and every day will bring fresh proofs that she is not. The Springs of her Naval power are dried away.

I have hitherto had the Happiness to find that my Pulse beat in exact Unison with those of my Countrymen. I have venturd with some Freedom to give my Opinion what Congress would do with the Conciliatory Bills, with the Commissioners with the Treaty &c. &c. and every packet brings us proceedings of Congress, according in Substance, but executed in a Manner infinitely exceeding my Abilities.

Nothing has given me more Joy than the Universal Disdain that is express'd both in public and private Letters at the Idea of departing from the Treaty and violating the public Faith. This Faith is our American Glory, and it is our Bulwark, it is the only Foundation on which our Union can rest securely, it is the only Support of our Credit both in Finance and Commerce, it is our sole Security for the Assistance of Foreign powers. If the British Court with their Arts could strike it or the Confidence in it we should be undone forever. She would triumph over us after all our Toil and Danger. She would subjugate us more intirely than she ever intended. The Idea of Infidelity cannot be treated with too much Resentment or too much Horror. The Man who can think of it with Patience is a Traitor in his Heart, and ought to be execrated as one who adds the deepest Hypocrisy to the blackest Treason.

Is there a sensible Hypocrite in America who can start a Jealousy that Religion may be in danger? from whence can this danger arise? not from France, she claims no inch of Ground upon your Continent, she claims no legislative Authority over you, no negative upon your Laws, No Right of appointing you Bishops, nor of sending you Missionaries. Besides the Spirit for cruisading for Religion is not in France. The Rage of making Proselytes which has existed in former Centuries is no more. There is a Spirit more liberal here in this Respect than I expected to find. Where has been the danger to Religion of the protestant Cantons of Swisserland from an Alliance with France, which has subsisted with entire Harmony for 150 Years or thereabouts. But this Subject is fitter for Ridicule than serious Argument, as nothing can be clearer than that in this enlighten'd tollerant Age at this vast Distance, without a Claim or Colour of Authority, with an express Acknowledgement and Warranty of Sovereignty, this, I had almost said tollerant Nation can never endanger our Religion.

The longer I live in Europe and the more I consider our Affairs the more important our Alliance with France appears to me. It is a Rock upon which we may safely build, narrow and illiberal prejudices peculiar to John Bull with which I might perhaps have been in some degree infected when I was John Bull, have now no Influence with me. I never was however much of John Bull. I was John Yankee and such I shall live and die.

Is G. Britain to be annihilated? No such thing. A Revolution in her Government may possibly take place, but whether in Favor of Despotism or Republicanism is the Question. The Scarcity of Virtue and even the Semblance of it seems an invincible Obstacle to the latter. But the Annihilation of a Nation never takes place. It depends wholly on herself to determine whether she shall sink down into the Rank of the middling powers of Europe or whether she shall maintain the second place in the Scale, if she continues this War the first will be her Fate, if she stops short in her mad Career and makes peace she may still be in the second predicament. America will grow with astonishing Rapidity and England France and every other Nation in Europe will be the better for her prosperity. Peace which is her dear Delight will be her Wealth and her Glory, for I cannot see the Seed of a War with any part of the World in future but with Great Britain, and such States as may be weak enough, if any such there should be, to become her Allies.

That such a peace may be speedily concluded and that you and I may return to our Farms to enjoy the Fruits of them, spending our old Age in recounting to our Children the Toils and Dangers we have encounter'd for their Benefit is the Wish of Your Friend & very humble Servant,   John Adams

"THE FULL VALUE OF OUR LIBERTY"

To Abigail Adams

My dearest Friend   Passy Novr. 6 1778

We have received Information that so many of our Letters have been thrown overboard, that I fear you will not have heard so often from me, as both of us wish.

I have written often. But my Letters have not been worth so much as other Things which I have sent you. I sent you a small Present by Captain Niles. But he is taken by a Jersey Privateer. I sent you also, some other Things by Captain Barnes, and what affects me quite as much, I sent the Things that my dear Brother Cranch requested me to send, by the same Vessells. These Vessells were chosen because they were fast Sailers, and so small as to be able to see Danger before they could be seen, but all is taken and sent into Guernsy and Jersy.

By Captain Tucker I sent you the whole of the List you gave me of Articles for the Family. These I hope have arrived safe. But I have been so unlucky, that I feel averse to meddling in this Way. The whole Loss is a Trifle it is true: but to you, in the Convenience of the Family, and to Mr. Cranch in his Business they would have been of Value. If the Boston arrives, the little Chest she carries to you will be of service.

My Anxiety for you and for the public is not diminished by Time or Distance. The great Number of accidental Dissappointments in the Course of the last summer are afflicting. But We hope for better Luck another Year.

It seems to be the Intention of Heaven, that We should be

taught the full Value of our Liberty by the dearness of the Purchase, and the Importance of public Virtue by the Necessity of it. There seems to be also a further Design, that of eradicating forever from the Heart of every American, every tender Sentiment towards Great Britain, that We may sometime or other know how to make the full Advantage of our Independence by more extensive Connections with other Countries.

Whatever Syren songs of Peace may be sung in your Ears, you may depend upon it from me, (who unhappily have been seldom mistaken in my Guesses of the Intentions of the British Government for fourteen Years,) that every malevolent Passion, and every insidious Art, will predominate in the British Cabinet against Us.

Their Threats of Russians, and of great Reinforcements, are false and impracticable and they know them to be so: But their Threats of doing Mischief with the Forces they have, will be verified as far as their Power.

It is by no means pleasant to me, to be forever imputing malicious Policy to a Nation, that I have ever wished and still wish I could esteem: But Truth must be attended to: and almost all Europe, the Dutch especially, are at this day talking of G. Britain in the style of American sons of Liberty.

I hope the unfortunate Events at Rhode Island will produce no Heart Burnings, between our Countrymen and the Comte D'Estaing, who is allowed by all Europe to be a great and worthy Officer, and by all that know him to be a zealous friend of America.

I have enjoyed uncommon Health, since my Arrival in this Country and if it was Peace, and my family here, I could be happy. But never never shall I enjoy happy days, without either.

My little son gives me great Pleasure, both by his Assiduity to his Books and his discreet Behaviour. The Lessons of his Mamma are a constant Law to him, and the Reflexion that they are so to his sister and Brothers, are a never failing Consolation to me at Times when I feel more tenderness for them, than Words can express, or than I should choose to express if I had Power.

Remember me, in the most affectionate Manner to our

Parents, Brothers, Sisters, Unkles, Aunts, and what shall I say—Children.

My Respects where they are due, which is in so many Places that I cannot name them.

With Regard to my Connections with the Public Business here, which you will be naturally inquisitive to know something of, I can only say that We have many Disagreable Circumstances here, many Difficulties to accomplish the Wishes of our Constituents, and to give Satisfaction to certain half anglified Americains, and what is more serious and affecting to real and deserving Americans who are suffering in England and escaping from thence: But from this Court, this City, and Nation I have experienced nothing, but uninterupted Politeness.

It is not possible for me to express more Tenderness and Affection to you than will be suggested by the Name of

John Adams

INTERCEPTED LETTERS

To Abigail Adams

My dearest Friend   Passy Decr. 2 1778

Last Night an Express from M. De Sartine, whose Politeness upon this Occasion, was very obliging, brought me your Letters of September 29 and Octr. 10.

The Joy which the Receipt of these Packets afforded me, was damped, by the disagreable Articles of Intelligence, but still more so by the Symptoms of Grief and Complaint, which appeared in the Letters. For Heavens Sake, my dear dont indulge a Thought that it is possible for me to neglect, or forget all that is dear to me in this World.

It is impossible for me to write as I did in America. What should I write? It is not safe to write any Thing, that one is not willing should go into all the Newspapers of the World.—I know not by whom to write. I never know what Conveyance is safe.—Vessells may have arrived without Letters from me. I am 500 Miles from Bourdeaux and not much less distant from

Nantes. I know nothing of many Vessells that go from the Seaports, and if I knew of all there are some that I should not trust. Notwithstanding this, I have written to you, not much less I believe than fifty Letters. I am astonished that you have received no more. But almost every Vessell has been taken. Two Vessells by which I sent Goods to you for the Use of your Family and one by which I sent Mr. Cranches Things, We know have been taken, in every one of these I sent large Packetts of Letters and Papers for Congress, for you and for many Friends. God knows I dont spend my Time, in Idleness, nor in gazing at Curiosities. I never wrote more Letters, however empty they may have been. But by what I hear they have been all or nearly all taken or sunk.

My Friends complain that they have not received Letters from me. I may as well complain. I have received scarcely any Letters, from America. I have written three, where I have received one. From my Friend Mr. A. I have received only one short Card—from Mr. Gerry not a syllable—from Mr. Lovell only two or three very short.—What shall I say? I doubt not they have written oftener—but Letters miscarry. Drs. Cooper and Gordon write to Dr. F. not to me.

My Friend Warren has been good as usual, I have received several fine long Letters full of Sound sense, Usefull Intelligence and Reflexions as virtuous as wise, as usual, from him. I have answered them and written more, but whether they arrive I know not.

I approve very much of your draught upon me, in favour of your Cousin. The Moment it arrives it shall be paid. Draw for more as you may have Occasion. But make them give you Silver for your Bills.

Your Son is the Joy of my Heart, without abating in the least degree of my Affection for the young Rogue that did not seem as if he had a Father, or his Brother or sister. Tell Nabby, her Pappa likes her the better for what she tells her Brother, vizt. that she dont talk much, because I know she thinks and feels the more.—I hope the Boston has arrived—she carried many Things for you.

Last Night a Friend from England brought me the Kings Speech. Their Delirium continues, and they go on with the

War, but the Speech betrays a manifest Expectation that Spain will join against them, and the Debates betray a dread of Holland. They have Reason for both.

They have not, and cannot get an Ally. They cannot send any considerable Reinforcement to America.

Your Reflections upon the Rewards of the Virtuous Friends of the public are very just. But if Virtue was to be rewarded with Wealth it would not be Virtue. If Virtue was to be rewarded with Fame, it would not be Virtue of the sublimest Kind. Who would not rather be Fabricius than Cæsar? Who would not rather be Aristides, than even W the 3d? Who? Nobody would be of this Mind but Aristides and Fabricius.

These Characters are very rare, but the more prescious. Nature has made more Insects than Birds, more Butterflys than Eagles, more Foxes than Lyons, more Pebbles than Diamonds. The most excellent of her Productions, both in the physical, intellectual and moral World, are the most rare.—I would not be a Butterfly because Children run after them, nor because the dull Phylosophers boast of them in their Cabinets.

Have you ever read J. J. Rousseau. If not, read him—your Cousin Smith has him. What a Difference between him and Chesterfield, and even Voltaire? But he was too virtuous for the Age, and for Europe—I wish I could not say for another Country.

I am much dissappointed in not receiving Dispatches from Congress by this Opportunity. We expect Alterations in the Plan here. What will be done with me I cant conjecture. If I am recalled, I will endeavour to get a safe Opportunity, home. I will watch the proper Season and look out for a good Vessell. And if I can get safe to Penns Hill, shall never repent of my Voyage to Europe, because I have gained an Insight into several Things that I never should have understood without it.

I pray you to remember me with every Sentiment of Tenderness, Duty and Affection, to your Father and my Mother, Your and my Brothers and Sisters, Uncles, Aunts, Cousins and every Body else that you know deserves it. What shall I say too and of my dear young Friends by your Fireside, may God almighty bless them, and make them wise.

To James Warren

My dear Sir   Passy Decr 2 1778

Last Night, I received your Letter of Octr. 7th by a Special Messenger from M. De Sartine, who writes me that he knows not how where nor by whom it arrived. I mention this that it may serve as an Answer in some Measure to the Complaint in your Letter, that neither you nor my other Friends have heard from me. I have wrote very often, to you and them but there is Strange Management with Letters and most that We write are sunk in the Sea.

I Sincerely grieve for my Country in the News that you are not of either House. But it is Some Comfort to me to think that I shall be Soon a private Farmer, as well as you, and both pursueing our Experiments in Husbandry. The longer I live and the more I see of public Men, the more I wish to be a private one. Modesty is a Virtue, that can never thrive, in public. Modest Merit! is there Such a Thing remaining in public Life? It is now become a Maxim with some, who are even Men of Merit, that the World esteems a Man in Proportion as he esteems himself, and are generally disposed to allow him, to be what he pretends to be.

Accordingly, I am often astonished at the Boldness with which Persons make their Pretensions. A Man must be his own Trumpeter—he must write or dictate Paragraphs of Praise in the News Papers, he must dress, have a Retinue, and Equipage, he must ostentatiously publish to the World his own Writings with his Name, and must write even some Panegyricks upon them,—he must get his Picture drawn, his statue made, and must hire all the Artists in his Turn, to set about Works to Spread his Name, make the Mob stare and gape, and perpetuate his Fame. I would Undertake, if I could bring my Feelings to bear it, to become one of the most celebrated trumpeted, Admired, courted, worshipd Idols in the whole World in four or five Years. I have learned the whole Art I am a perfect Master of it. I learned a great deal of it from Hutchinson and the Tories, and have learned more of it since from Whigs and Tories both, in America and Europe. If you will learn the Art I will teach it you.

I have not yet begun to practice this. There is one Practice more which I forgot. He must get his Brothers, Cousins, sons and other Relations into Place about him and must teach them to practice all the same Arts both for them selves and him. He must never do any Thing for any Body who is not his Friend, or in other Words his Tool.

What I am going to say, will be thought by many to be practicing upon some of the above Rules. You and I have had an ugly Modesty about Us, which has despoyled Us of, almost all our Importance. We have taken even Pains to conceal our Names, We have delighted in the shade, We have made few Friends, no Tools, and what is worse when the Cause of Truth, Justice, and Liberty have demanded it We have even Sacrificed Those who called themselves our Friends and have made Ennemies.

No Man ever made a great Fortune in the World, by pursuing these Maxims, We therefore do not expect it, and for my own Part I declare, that the Moment, I can get into Life perfectly private, will be the happiest of my Life.

The little Art and the less Ambition with which I see the World full disgusts and shocks me more and more. And I will abandon it to its Course, the Moment I can do it with Honour and Conscience.

Remember me, Sir, in the most respectfull Manner to your good Lady, whose Manners, Virtues, Genius, and Spirit will render her immortal, notwithstanding the general Depravity. I am, her & your Friend   John Adams

"A THOUSAND THINGS TO DO"

To Abigail Adams

My dearest Friend   Passy Decr. 3 1778
    Your two Letters of the   of Sept. and of   Oct. gave me more Concern than I can express. I will not say a Fit of the Spleen. But last night I got a Letter from Mr. Vernon, in which

he acquaints me with the Arrival of the Boston, at Portsmouth. There were Letters from me on Board of the Boston, Providence or Ranger, and there was all the Things mentioned in the Memorandum, you gave me, this News has given me great Pleasure. I have sent other Things, on Board other Vessells since, with more Letters, which are all taken by the Ennemy, and among others all Mr. Cranchs Watch Materials.

You must not expect to hear from me so often as you used: it is impossible. It is impossible for me to write so often. I have so much to do here, and so much Ceremony to submit to, and so much Company to see, so many Visits to make and receive, that, altho I avoid as many of them as I possibly can with Decency and some People think, more, it is impossible for me to write to you so often as my Inclination would lead me.

I have been informed that Congress, on the 14 of September took up foreign Affairs and determined to have but one Minister, in France. By a Letter from Mr. Lovel we learn that Congress had foreign Affairs on the 12 of October, still under Consideration, but gives no Hint of what is done or intended. This keeps me in a State of Uncertainty that is very disagrable. I have applied every Moment of my Time when Awake, and not necessarily engaged otherwise in learning the Language, and the Laws, the Manners and Usages of this Nation, an occupation indisspensable in my situation. In order to avoid Expence, as much as possible, I have kept no Clerk altho every other Gentleman has constantly had two. In order to save Expences, and that I might be under the less Temptation to spend my Time unusefully, I have kept no Carriage, altho every other Gentleman has kept one Constantly and some Gentlemen two, and I am told I am the first public Minister that ever lived without a Carriage. By All these Causes together added to another Motive, viz. a Fear of Trusting our Books and Papers without a Keeper I have been almost constantly at home. Here are a Thousand Things to do, and no Body else to do them. The extensive Correspondence We have with Congress, with the Court, with our Frigates, our Agents, and with Prisoners, and a thousand others, employs a vast deal of my Time in Writing. You must therefore excuse me, if I dont write so often as I would. Yet I have written very often, but my Letters have miscarried.

By your Letter, and another, I suspect that Parties are forming among you. I expect also, by some Letters I have seen from the Weathersfield Family, that a certain fine Gentleman will join another fine Gentleman, and these some other fine Gentlemen, to obtain some Arrangement that shall dishonnour me. And by Hints that are given out here, I should not wonder if I should be recalled, or sent to Vienna which would be worse.

I am extreamly unhappy to see such Symptoms of Selfishness, Vanity and Ambition as manifest themselves in various Quarters, but I will neither indulge these Passions myself, nor be made the Instrument of them in others. Observing as I have a long Time the Characters of several Persons, I have long foreseen, that Parties must arise and this foresight has been the most forcible Motive with me to refuse a certain elevated Office. Because I knew, that my public Conduct, to which I was necessitated by the clearest Dictates of my Judgment, in the various intricate and hazardous Contingences of our Affairs, had exposed me to the Angry Passions of some Gentlemen of Consequence, who, altho obliged to cooperate with me, had often differed from me in Opinion. These I knew would render me, unhappy if not useless, in some situations, which determined me, to preserve my Independence, at the Expence of my Ambition, a Resolution in which I rejoice and ever shall rejoice.

The Conflicts of these Passions, I expect, will very soon relieve me from the Duties of this station, and enable me to return to my Family and my Garden, the Ultimate Object of all my Hopes, Wishes and Expectations, for myself. And happy indeed shall I be if by the favour of Heaven I can escape the danger of the Seas and of Ennemies, and return to the charming Office of Precepter to my Children.

FRENCH DIFFIDENCE

To Elbridge Gerry

Dr Sir   Passy Decr 5. 1778

It is necessary that you should be minutely informed, of the minutest and most secret Springs of Action here, if it is possible. Yet the Danger is so great of our Letters, being taken and getting into English News Papers, that it is very discouraging to a free Correspondence.

I will however take all the Precaution in my Power, to have the Letters sunk, but if all these fail and my Letters become public the World must take them as they find them, and I hope they will do more good upon the whole than Harm.

This Court and Nation appears to me, to be well convinced of the Utility to their Interests of the American Alliance. But notwithstanding this they appear to me to have too much Diffidence of Us. Too much Diffidence of the People of America, and too much Reserve towards the Commissioners here. I am not Satisfyed in the Cause of this.

Whether they think, that the obstacles of Language Religion, Laws, Customs and Manners are Obstacles in the Way of a perfect Friendship, which cannot be removed, and therefore that they shall loose our Connection as soon as Britain, comes to her senses, or whether they are Embarrassed by the Conduct of Spain, and are acting in this reserved manner, and with an Appearance of Irresolution in hopes of her coming in, or whether they have any Prejudices against the Personal Characters of the Commissioners, and are loth to be unreserved with them, for fear they should communicate either indiscreetly, or by design any Thing to the English, or to any Body here, who might convey it to England or whether all these Motives together have a share in it, I know not.

Thus much is certain, that ever since I have been here, I have never seen any Disposition in any Minister of state to talk with any of the Commissioners, either upon Intelligence from Spain, or England, upon the Designs or Negociations of Either, or any other Court in Europe, or upon the Conduct of the War by sea or Land, or upon their own Plans and Designs of Policy or War.

If this Reserve was ever thrown off, to any one, I should think, that putting it on to others, had some personal Motive. But it is exactly equal and alike to all three.

Each Commissioner here, before I came, had his own set of Friends, Admirers, and Dependants, both among the French and Americans. Two Households united in some degree against one, very unjustly I fear and impolitically. But this set the Friends of the two, to injuring the third, in Conversation, and they cant forbear to do it, to this day. This Dissention I suspect has made the Ministry cautious, lest in the Course of Altercations, improper Use should be made of free Communications.

For my own Part however Odd you may think it in me to say it I have no Friends, much less Dependants here, and am determined to have none, for I am convinced that Competitions among these have done the Evil: But I am determined, if I am continued here to have free Communication, with the Ministry upon these subjects and to search them to the Bottom. The Ministry are candid Men and sensible, and I am sure that some Ecclaircissements would do good.

However, I am reckoning without my Hoste, for by the Bruits which Mr. D's Letters have Scattered, I may expect that the first Vessell will bring my Recall, or Removal to some other Court. But wherever I am, my Heart will ever be axious for the good of our Country, and warm with Friendship for her Friends, among whom you will ever be reckoned, in the formost Rank, by your most obt

FRANKLIN, LEE, AND DEANE

To Samuel Adams

My dear Sir   Passy Decr 7 1778

On the 21 May, I wrote you a very long Letter, on the Subject of foreign Affairs in general, and particularly in this Country: on the 28 July, I wrote you another lengthy Letter, on the 7 August I wrote you again in answer to yours of 21 June, which is all I have ever received from you, on the 27 November I wrote you again. I hope Some of these have reached you, but So many Vessells have been taken that I fear Some have miscarried.

I wish I could unbosom myself to you without Reserve, concerning the State of Affairs here, but you know the danger. The two Passions of Ambition and Avarice, which have been the Bane of Society and the Curse of human Kind, in all ages and Countries, are not without their Influence upon our Affairs here, but I fancy the last of the two has done the most Mischief. Where the Carcass is there the Crows will assemble, and you and I have had too much Experience of the Greediness with which the Loaves and Fishes were aimed at under the old Government, and with which the Continental Treasury has been Sought for under the new, to expect that the Coffers of the American Banker here, would not make Some Mens Mouths Water. This appetite for the Bankers Treasure, I take to have been the Source of most of the Altercations and Dissentions here.

Your old Friend is a Man of Honour and Integrity, altho to be very frank and very impartial, he cannot, easily at all Times any more than your humble servant govern his Temper, and he has some Notions of Elegance Rank and Dignity that may be carried rather too far. He has been of opinion that the public Money has been too freely issued here, and has often opposed. The other you know personally, and that he loves his Ease, hates to offend, and seldom gives any Opinion untill obliged to do it. I know also and it is necessary you should be informed, that he is overwhelmed with a Correspondence from all Quarters, most of them upon trifling subjects, and in a more trifling Style; with unmeaning Visits from Multitudes of People, chiefly from the Vanity of Having it to say that they have Seen him. There is another Thing which I am obliged to mention, there are So many private Families, Ladies and Gentlemen that he visits So often, and they are So fond of him that he cannot well avoid it, and So much Intercourse with Academicians, that all these Things together keep his Mind in Such a constant State of Dissipation, that if he is left alone here, the public Business, will Suffer in a degree beyond Description, provided our Affairs are continued upon the present footing.

If indeed you take out of his Hands the public Treasury, and the Direction of the Frigates and continental Vessells that are sent here and all Commercial affairs, and intrust them to Persons to be appointed by Congress, at Nantes and Bourdeaux, I should think it would be best to have him here alone, with such a secretary as you can confide in, but if he is left here alone, even with such a secretary, and all maritime and Commercial and pecuniary as well as political affairs, are left in his Hands, I am perswaded, that France and America both will have Reason to repent it. He is not only so indolent that Business will be neglected: but you know that altho he has as determined a soul as any Man, yet it is his constant Policy, never to say Yes or no decidedly, but when he cannot avoid it: and it is certain, in order to preserve the Friendship between the two Countries your Minister here must upon some occasions speak freely and without Reserve, preserving Decency and Politeness at the same Time.

Both he and the other Colleague, were I am sorry to say it, in a constant opposition to your old Friend; and this Misunderstanding was no secret, at Court, in the City, or in the seaport Towns, either to French, English or Americans, and this was carried So far, that Insinuations, I have been told have been made at Court against your old Friend, not by Either of his Colleagues, that I have ever heard, but probably by somebody or other emboldened by and taking Advantage of the Misunderstanding among the three, that he was too friendly to the English, too much attached to Ld. Shelbourne, and even that he corresponded with his Lordship and communicated Intelligence to him. This whoever suggested it, I am perfectly confident was a cruel Calumny, and could not have made an Impression if the Colleagues had contradicted it, in the manner that you and I should have done. You and I had opportunity to know his invariable Attachment to our Cause long before Hostilities commenced, and I have not a Colour of Ground for Suspicion, that from that Time to this he has deviated an Iota from the Cause of his Country in Thought, Word, or Deed. When he left England or soon after, he wrote a Letter of mere Compliment to his Lordship, a mere Card to bid him farewell, and received such another in Return, which he assures me are all the Letters that ever passed between them, and I have not a doubt of the Truth of it.

The other Gentleman whom you know, I need not Say much of—You know his Ambition his Desire of making a Fortune and of promoting his Relations. You also know his Art and his Enterprise. Such Characters are often usefull, altho always to be carefully watched and controuled, especially in such a Government as ours.

There has been so much said in America, and among Americans here, about his making a Fortune by Speculating in English Funds, and by private Trade that it is saying nothing new to mention it. Our Countrymen will naturally desire to know if it is true, and it will be expected of me that I should say something of it. I assure you I know nothing about it. An intimate Friend of his, who recommended, the Major to you, certainly Speculated largely in the Funds, from whence the suspicion arose that, the other was concernd with him, but I know of no Proof that he was. Combinations, Associations, Copartnerships in Trade have been formed here, in which he and his Brothers are supposed to be connected, but I know nothing more than you do about them. But supposing it was proved that he speculated and traded, the Question is whether it was justifiable. Neither you nor I Should have done it, most certainly. Nor would it have been forgiven or excused in either of Us. Whoever makes Profits in public Life, neither of Us must be the Man. But does not prove it unlawful in him. If he did not employ the public Money, nor so much of his Time as to neglect the public Business, where is the Harm? That is the Question. And it ought to be remembered, that he was here a long Time, not as Ambassador, Envoy, Commissioner, Minister, or in any other Trust or Character from Congress, but merely as an Agent for the Committees of Commerce and Correspondence.

Some of the Gentlemen of Character, who are now in America from this Country, particularly the Minister and Consul, although their Characters are very good, it is to be feared, have had Prejudices insinuated into them, against your old Correspondent. I am extreamly Sorry for this, because I think it is against a worthy Character, and because it will be likely to have unhappy Effects both with you and abroad.

The other Gentleman, whose Consolation, when left out by his first Constituents was that he stood well with the Body to which he was sent, consoled himself also, when recalled by that Body, with the thought that he was esteemd by that Court, where he had resided. This no doubt will be displayed in all its variegated Colours. The Letter from the Minister, expressing high Esteem, the Present from an higher Personage, and above all the Fleet and the Magnificence that accompanied it, will be all repeated and rung in Changes in order to magnify Merit. Yet I am Sorry to see in the Newspapers such Expressions as these Mr. ____ "who was the principal Negociator"— such Expressions if true, ought not to be used, because they have only a Tendency to occasion Division and Animosity, and cannot do any Good. But there is Cause to doubt the Justice of them. In short I think upon an Examination of the Treaties and a Comparason of them with the Treaties and Instructions sent from Congress, I think it is probable that there was not much Discussion in the Case. I wish with all my Heart there had been more.

This Letter is not so free as I wish to write you, but still it is too free, to be used without Discretion. You will use it accordingly only for the public Good. Knowing the Animosity that has been in two against me here, which I believe to have been carried unwarrantable Lengths, knowing the Inveteracy of many subaltern and collateral Characters, which I think is injurious, to the Individual as much as the Public, and knowing that you will have these Things in Contemplation and much at Heart I have said thus much of my sentiments upon these subjects which I hope will do no Harm.

Believe me to be your Friend   John Adams

BRITISH DESPERATION

To Patrick Henry

My dear Friend   Passy Decr 8 1778
    Mr. Le Maire, writes me that he is about returning. I wrote you on the 9 July a long Letter in Answer to the one he brought, which is the only one I have received from you, altho

by a Letter from Lisbon, from a Master of a Vessell taken by the English and carried in there, I learn that he had Letters for me which he sunk.

I wish, I would give you hopes of Peace. And I would not excite a needless alarm. But by the Hints in both Houses of Parliament in the present session, and by possitive Information, from Persons in England who pretend to know, They the Cabinet, are not only determined to pursue the War, at all Hazzards, but to alter the Mode of it, and make it more bloody and fiery if that is possible. Clinton and Byron with their Army and Fleet are to ravage the sea coast and bombard the seaport Towns—the Army in Canada is to be reinforced, and Parties of Regulars, with as many Tories and Indians, and as they can perswade to join them, are to burn and massacre, upon the Frontiers of Mass Bay, N. York, N. Jersey, Pensylvania, Virginia the Carolinas &c.

This Kind of Sentiments it is pretty certain at present, occupy their Thoughts, please their Imaginations and warm their Hearts.

I know very well, that they have already done as much of this humane Work as they had Power to do, and dared to do. I know also that they must ask Leave of the French as well as Americans, and probably of other Powers, to do more Mischief than they have done. I know too that this Plan will be their certain and their Speedy destruction, because it will unite America more decisively, and it will excite that Earnestness Activity and Valour which alone is wanting to compleat their Destruction, and because, by relaxing their Discipline, and becoming less cautious and guarded than they have been, Desertions and Diseases will be more frequent among their Troops and they will more frequently expose themselves to the Snares and Attacks of ours.

The Spirits of the Nation are terribly sunk, the stocks are very low, lower than ever last War, and there is a Stronger Minority in both Houses than ever there was before. But they are now playing a desperate Game, and I think that the true Principle of their Conduct now, is not expecting ever to get America back, they mean to extinguish in the Hearts of the English Nation ever kind Sentiment towards America, that they may be and by wish to give them up and consider them forever in future with all the Envy, Jealousy and Hatred that they feel towards the French.

There is so great a Body of People in the Nation who are terrified at the Foresight of the Consequences of American Liberty—the Loss of the West India Islands of Canada Nova Scotia and the Floridas—a dangerous Rival in Commerce and naval Power, worming them out of their East India Trade, and other Branches—An Assylum, for all, Conspirators, and Minorities in Great Britain, that the Ministry expect such Disgrace and Danger to their Heads from giving it up, that they dare not do it, untill they have wrought the Nation into the rankest Hatred against America, and reduced her to the lowest possible degree of Weakness.

Many Persons, and I believe the Body of the Nation, foresee more Grandeur and Prosperity to America, and more Humiliation to themselves, in the Train of the Consequences of American Independence, than the Americans themselves do. It is certainly an Object worth contending for another Campaign, and many other Campaigns afterwards, if there was nothing in View but the future Grandeur, Glory and Prosperity of our Country. But We are contending for all the Ends of Government, for nothing less than the Difference between the best Form of Government, that ever existed, and the Worst that ever was formed even in Imagination, for Aristotle himself never thought of such a Government, as that of Ten or fifteen Men in a little Island, composing the Legislature of a vast Continent 3000 Miles off.

You cannot do me more Honour, or give me more Pleasure than by Writing often. Remember me, to all that I knew, particularly to Mr. Jefferson and Mr. Wyth two Characters, which no Circumstances of Time or Place will ever induce me to forget. I have the Honour to be, with great Respect, and Affection, your Friend and sert.

PAINFUL LETTERS

To Abigail Adams

Passy Decr. 18 1778

This Moment I had, what shall I say? the Pleasure or the pain of your Letter of 25 of Octr. As a Letter from my dearest Freind it gave me a pleasure that it would be in vain to attempt to describe: but the Complaints in it gave me more pain than I can express—this is the third Letter I have recd. in this complaining style. the former two I have not answer'd.—I had Endeavour'd to answer them.—I have wrote several answers, but upon a review, they appear'd to be such I could not send. One was angry, another was full of Greif, and the third with Melancholy, so that I burnt them all.—if you write me in this style I shall leave of writing intirely, it kills me. Can Professions of Esteem be Wanting from me to you? Can Protestation of affection be necessary? can tokens of Remembrance be desir'd? The very Idea of this sickens me. Am I not wretched Enough, in this Banishment, without this. What Course shall I take to convince you that my Heart is warm? you doubt, it seems.— shall I declare it? shall I swear to it?—Would you doubt it the less?—And is it possible you should doubt it? I know it is not? —If I could once believe it possible, I cannot answer for the Consequences.—But I beg you would never more write to me in such a strain for it really makes me unhappy.

Be assured that no time nor place, can change my heart: but that I think so often & so much, of the Blessings from which I am seperated as to be too unmindful of those who accompany me, & that I write to you so often as my Duty will permit.

I am extremely obliged to the Comte D'Estaing and his officers for their Politeness to you, and am very Glad you have had an opportunity, of seing so much of the french Nation. The accounts from all hands agree that there was an agreable intercourse, & happy harmony upon the whole between the inhabitants and the Fleet, the more this Nation is known, & the more their Language is understood, the more narrow Prejudices will wear away. British Fleet and Armys, are very different from theirs. in Point of Temperance and Politeness there is no Comparison.

This is not a correct Copy, but you will pardon it, because it is done by an Hand as dear to you as to your   John Adams

FRENCH WOMEN AND OLDER MEN

To Mercy Otis Warren

Madam   Passy Dec'r 18 1778

A few days ago I had the Pleasure of your obliging letter of the 15 of October. It came by the Post, and single, not a line from any other Person, so that I know not by what means it reach'd L'orient. It was not, however the less welcome to me, its intrinsic Excellence, would have recommended it, whoever had written it. The Merit of the writer would have made it dear to me if the Letter itself had been indifferent, a supposition not very easy to make in this case.

I am sorry very sorry for our Common Country that the unshaken Patriot you mention should think of retiring but I cannot blame him because my own thoughts are constantly running the same way and I am determined with submission to do the same thing.

I hope however Madam that there is not so total a change of Manners, as some appearances may indicate, paper Currency fluctuating in its Value will ever produce appearances in the Political, commercial, and even the Moral World, that are very shooking at first sight, but upon Examination they will not be found to proceed from a total Want of Principal but for the most part from Necessity.

Who will take the helm Madam, and indeed who will build the ship I know not but of one thing I am well convinced that a great part of the Evils you mention arise from the neglect to model the constitution and fix the Government. These things must be finished, and the dispute who shall be the head, is much less important than whether we shall have any. I am happy Madam to learn that so many of the most respectable strangers have had an opportunity to visit you. I am pleased with this because it has given you an opportunity of speculating upon those illustrious characters, and because it has given them an opportunity of observing that their new Ally can boast of Female Characters equal to any in Europe.

I have not the honor to know Mrs. Holker, she lives at Rouen at a distance however I have gratified Mr. H's father with a sight of his sons Portrait drawn by a Lady, which he could not read without the tears gushing from both his eyes.

As to Portraits Madam I dare not try my hand as yet. But my Design is to retire, like my Freind, and spend all my leisure hours in writing a history of this revolution. And with an Hand as severe as Tacitus, I wish to god it was as eloquent, draw the Portrait of every character that has figured in the business. But when it is done I will dig a Vault, and bury the Manuscript, with a positive injunction, that it shall not be opened till a hundred years after My Death.

What shall I say, Madam, to your Question whether I am as much in the good graces of the Ladies as my venerable Colleague. Ah No! Alas, Alas No.

The Ladies of this Country Madam have an unaccountable passion for old Age, whereas our Country women you know Madam have rather a Complaisance for youth if I remember right. This is rather unlucky for me for I have nothing to do but wish that I was seventy years old and when I get back I shall be obliged to wish myself back again to 25.

I will take the Liberty to mention an anecdote or two amongst a multitude to shew you how unfortunate I am in being so young. A Gentleman introduced me the other day to a Lady. Voila, Madame, says he, Monsieur Adams, notre Ami, Le Colleague de Monsieur Franklin! Je suis enchante de voir Monsieur Adams. Answer'd the Lady. Embrassez le, donc. Reply'd the Gentleman. Ah No, Monsieur, says the Lady, il est trop jeune.

So that you see. I must wait patiently, full 30 years longer before I can be so great a favorite.

Madam I can give you no news. The Lords and Commons have refused to censure the Manifests of the Comissionners. That unhappy Nation are going on in their Frenzy, but there is an awfull Gloom and Melancholy among them and with reason. I am Madam with every sentiment of Respect your affectionate Freind and humble servant   John Adams

Mrs. Warren will pardon my sending her a Letter, in another Hand Writing when she knows, that a little Friend of hers is the Clerk, who desires to send his profound Respects.

From the Diary: February 8–12, 1779

1779. FEB. 8.

In Conversation with Dr. Franklin, in the Morning I gave him my Opinion, of Mr. Deanes Address to the People of America, with great Freedom and perhaps with too much Warmth. I told him that it was one of the most wicked and abominable Productions that ever sprung from an human Heart. That there was no safety in Integrity against such a Man. That I should wait upon The Comte de Vergennes, and the other Ministers, and see in what light they considerd this Conduct of Mr. Deane. That if they, and their Representatives in America, were determined to countenance and support by their Influence such Men and Measures in America, it was no matter how soon the Alliance was broke. That no Evil could be greater, nor any Government worse, than the Toleration of such Conduct. No one was present, but the Doctor and his Grandson.

In the Evening, I told Dr. Bancroft, to the same Effect, that the Address appeared to me in a very attrocious Light, that however difficult Mr. Lees Temper might be, in my Opinion he was an honest Man, and had the utmost fidelity towards the united States. That such a Contempt of Congress committed in the City where they set, and the Publication of such Accusations in the Face of the Universe, so false and groundless as the most heinous of them appeared to me, these Accusations attempted to be coloured by such frivolous Tittle Tattle, such Accusations made too by a Man who had been in high Trust, against two others, who were still so, appeared to me, Evidence of such a Complication of vile Passions, of Vanity, Arrogance and Presumption, of Malice, Envy and Revenge, and at the same Time of such Weakness, Indiscretion and Folly, as ought to unite every honest and wise Man against him. That there appeared to me no Alternative left but the Ruin of Mr. Deane, or the Ruin of his Country. That he appeared to me in the Light of a wild boar, that ought to be hunted down for the Benefit of Mankind. That I would start fair with him, Dr. Bancroft, and give him Notice that I had hitherto been loath to give up Mr. Deane. But that this Measure of his appeared to Me to be so decisive against him that I had given him up to Satan to be buffeted.

In all this it is easy to see there is too much Declamation, but the substantial Meaning of it, is, as appears to me, exactly true, as such as I will abide by, unless, future Evidence which I dont expect should convince me, of any Error in it.

1779 FEB. 9.
    Abbe C.

> Terruit Hispanos, Ruiter, qui terruit Anglos
> Ter ruit in Gallos, territus ipse ruit.
>
> Cum fueris Romæ, Romano vivito more
> Si fueris alibi, vivito sicut ibi.

Any Thing to divert Melancholly, and to sooth an aking Heart. The Uncandor, the Prejudices, the Rage, among several Persons here, make me Sick as Death.

Virtue is not always amiable. Integrity is sometimes ruined by Prejudices and by Passions. There are two Men in the World who are Men of Honour and Integrity I believe, but whose Prejudices and violent Tempers would raise Quarrells in the Elisian Fields if not in Heaven. On the other Hand there is another, whose Love of Ease, and Dissipation, will prevent any thorough Reformation of any Thing—and his Silence and Reserve, render it very difficult to do any Thing with him. One of the others, whom I have allowed to be honest, has such a bitter, such a Sour in him, and so few of the nice feelings, that G knows what will be the Consequence to himself and to others. Besides he has as much Cunning, and as much Secrecy.

Called at Mr. Garniers—he not at home. At Mr. Grands. He and his Son began about the Address—bien fâché. &c. I said, cooly, that I was astonished at the Publication of it without sending it to congress. That I believed Mr. Lee a Man of Integrity, and that all Suggestions of improper Correspondences in England, were groundless. That my Br L was not of the sweetest disposition perhaps, but he was honest. That Virtue was not always amiable. . . . M. G. replyed, il est soupsonneux—il n'a du Confiance en Personne. Il croit que toute le Monde est —I cant remember the precise Word. . . . I believe this is a just Observation. He has Confidence in no body. He believes all Men selfish—And, no Man honest or sincere. This, I fear, is his Creed, from what I have heard him say. I have often in Conversation disputed with him, on this Point. However I never was so nearly in his Situation before. There is no Man here that I dare Trust, at present. They are all too much heated with Passions and Prejudices and party disputes. Some are too violent, others too jealous—others too cool, and too reserved at all Times, and at the same time, every day betraying Symptoms of a Rancour quite as deep.

The Wisdom of Solomon, the Meekness of Moses, and the Patience of Job, all united in one Character, would not be sufficient, to qualify a Man to act in the Situation in which I am at present—and I have scarcely a Spice of either of these Virtues.

On Dr. F. the Eyes of all Europe are fixed, as the most important Character, in American Affairs in Europe. Neither L. nor myself, are looked upon of much Consequence. The Attention of the Court seems most to F. and no Wonder. His long and great Rep to which L's and mine are in their infancy, are enough to Account for this. His Age, and real Character render it impossible for him to search every Thing to the Bottom, and L. with his privy Council, are evermore, contriving. The Results of their Contrivances, render many Measures more difficult.

1779. FEB. 11.

When I arrived in France, the French Nation had a great many Questions to settle.

The first was—Whether I was the famous Adams, Le fameux Adams?—Ah, le fameux Adams?—In order to speculate a little upon this Subject, the Pamphlet entituled Common sense, had been printed in the Affaires de L'Angleterre et De L'Amerique, and expressly ascribed to M. Adams the celebrated Member of Congress, le celebre Membre du Congress. It must be further known, that altho the Pamphlet Common sense, was received in France and in all Europe with Rapture: yet there were certain Parts of it, that they did not choose to publish in France. The Reasons of this, any Man may guess. Common sense undertakes to prove, that Monarchy is unlawful by the old Testament. They therefore gave the Substance of it, as they said, and paying many Compliments to Mr. Adams, his sense and rich Imagination, they were obliged to ascribe some Parts to Republican Zeal. When I arrived at Bourdeaux, All that I could say or do, would not convince any Body, but that I was the fameux Adams.—Cette un homme celebre. Votre nom est bien connu ici.—My Answer was—it is another Gentleman, whose Name of Adams you have heard. It is Mr. Samuel Adams, who was excepted from Pardon by Gen. Gage's Proclamation. —Oh No Monsieur, cette votre Modestie.

But when I arrived at Paris, I found a very different Style. I found great Pains taken, much more than the Question was worth to settle the Point that I was not the famous Adams. There was a dread of a sensation—Sensations at Paris are important Things. I soon found too, that it was effectually settled in the English News Papers that I was not the famous Addams. No body went so far in France or Ingland, as to say I was the infamous Adams. I make no scruple to say, that I believe, that both Parties for Parties there were, joined in declaring that I was not the famous Adams. I certainly joined both sides in this, in declaring that I was not the famous Adams, because this was the Truth.

It being settled that he was not the famous Adams, the Consequence was plain—he was some Man that nobody had ever heard of before—and therefore a Man of no Consequence—a Cypher. And I am inclined to think that all Parties both in

France and England—Whiggs and Tories in England—the Friends of Franklin, Deane and Lee, differing in many other Things agreed in this—that I was not the fameux Adams.

Seeing all this, and saying nothing, for what could a Man say?—seeing also, that there were two Parties formed, among the Americans, as fixed in their Aversion to each other, as both were to G.B. if I had affected the Character of a Fool in order to find out the Truth and to do good by and by, I should have had the Example of a Brutus for my Justification. But I did not affect this Character. I behaved with as much Prudence, and Civility, and Industry as I could. But still it was a settled Point at Paris and in the English News Papers that I was not the famous Adams, and therefore the Consequence was settled absolutely and unalterably that I was a Man of whom Nobody had ever heard before, a perfect Cypher, a Man who did not understand a Word of French—awkward in his Figure— awkward in his Dress—No Abilities—a perfect Bigot—and fanatic.

FEB. 12.

My Mind has been in such a State, since the Appearance of Mr. Deanes Address to the People, as it never was before. I confess it appeared to me like a Dissolution of the Constitution. It should be remembered that it first appeared from London in the English Papers—then in the Courier De L'Europe —and We had not received the Proceedings of Congress upon it. A few days after, Dr. Franklin received from Nantes, some Philadelphia Papers, in which were the Pieces signed Senex and Common Sense, and the Account of the Election of the New President Mr. Jay. When it was known that Congress had not censured Mr. Deane, for appealing to the People, it was looked upon as the most dangerous Proof that had ever appeared, of the Weakness of Government, and it was thought that the Confederation was wholly lost by some. I confess it appeared terrible to me indeed. It appeared to me that it would wholly loose us the Confidence of the French Court. I did not see how they could ever trust any of Us again—that it would have the worst Effects upon Spain, Holland and in England, besides endangering a civil War in America. In the

Agony of my Heart, I expressed myself to one Gentleman Dr. Bancroft, with perhaps too much warmth.

But this Day, Dr. Winship arrived here, from Brest, and soon afterwards, the Aid du Camp of Le Marquis de Fayette, with Dispatches, from Congress, by which it appears that Dr. Franklin is sole Plenipotentiary, and of Consequence that I am displaced.

The greatest Relief to my Mind, that I have ever found since the Appearance of the Address. Now Business may be done by Dr. Franklin alone. Before it seemed as if nothing could be done.

"ONCE MORE TO SEE OUR FIRESIDE"

To Abigail Adams

My dearest Friend   Passy Feb. 13 1779
Yours of 15 Decr. was sent me Yesterday by the Marquiss whose Praises are celebrated in all the Letters from America. You must be content to receive a short Letter, because I have not Time now to write a long one.—I have lost many of your Letters, which are invaluable to me, and you have lost a vast Number of mine. Barns, Niles, and many other Vessells are lost.

I have received Intelligence much more agreable, than that of a removal to Holland, I mean that of being reduced to a private Citizen which gives me more Pleasure, than you can imagine. I shall therefore soon present before you, your own good Man. Happy—happy indeed shall I be, once more to see our Fireside.

I have written before to Mrs. Warren and shall write again now.

Dr. J. is transcribing your scotch song, which is a charming one. Oh my leaping Heart.

I must not write a Word to you about Politicks, because you are a Woman.

What an offence have I committed?—a Woman!

I shall soon make it up. I think Women better than Men in

General, and I know that you can keep a Secret as well as any Man whatever. But the World dont know this. Therefore if I were to write any Secrets to you and the letter should be caught, and hitched into a Newspaper, the World would say, I was not to be trusted with a Secret.

I never had so much Trouble in my Life, as here, yet I grow fat. The Climate and soil agree with me—so do the Cookery and even the Manners of the People, of those of them at least that I converse with, Churlish Republican, as some of you, on your side the Water call me. The English have got at me in their News Papers. They make fine Work of me—fanatic—Bigot—perfect Cypher—not one Word of the Language—aukward Figure—uncouth dress—no Address—No Character—cunning hard headed Attorney. But the falsest of it all is, that I am disgusted with the Parisians—Whereas I declare I admire the Parisians prodigiously. They are the happiest People in the World, I believe, and have the best Disposition to make others so.

If I had your Ladyship and our little folks here, and no Politicks to plague me and an hundred Thousand Livres a Year Rent, I should be the happiest Being on Earth—nay I believe I could make it do with twenty Thousand.

One word of Politicks—The English reproach the French with Gasconade, but I dont believe their whole History could produce so much of it as the English have practised this War.

The Commissioners Proclamation, with its sanction from the Ministry and Ratification by both Houses, I suppose is hereafter to be interpreted like Burgoines—Speaking Daggers, but using none. They cannot send any considerable Reinforcement, nor get an Ally in Europe—this I think you may depend upon. Their Artifice in throwing out such extravagant Threats, was so gross, that I presume it has not imposed on any. Yet a Nation that regarded its Character never could have threatned in that manner.

Adieu.

FRENCH STRENGTH

To Samuel Adams

My dear Sir   Passy Feb. 14. 1779
The Marquiss de la Fayette did me, the Honour of a Visit, Yesterday, and delivered me, your Favour of the 25. of October. I am not sorry, as Things have been ordered, that mine of May 24 did not reach you till 24 Octr. because as the new Arrangement was previously made, it cannot be said that I had any Hand in accomplishing it. Yet I am glad the Letter has arrived because it will shew that the new system is quite agreable to me, i.e. the appointment of a single Minister here. Believe me Sir, it was become very necessary. How Congress will dispose of me, I dont know. If it is intended that I shall return, this will be very agreable to me: and I think this the most probable opinion, because Congress resolved soon after the 5 of december, to begin and go through, foreign affairs. The Alliance sailed the 14 Jan. and there is no Resolution arrived here respecting me. I think therefore it is my duty to return, and that is my present determination, but whether I shall go to Amsterdam and thence to St. Eustatia, or to Spain and thence, home, or in a French Man of War to Martinico or any other Way I know not. I have not decided.

Some Hint that I am to go to Holland—others to Spain—the last implies the Removal of Mr. Lee, which would give me much Paine. I think him an able and faithfull Man. Yet what the Determination, may be upon the Complaint, if it is decided before he answers I know not. This is a subject that I cannot write nor talk about. I would not have such another Sensation to be made a Prince. I confess I expected the most dismal Consequences, from it, because I thought it would render Business and Confidence between Us three, wholly impracticable. That it would destroy all Confidence between this Court and Us—that it would startle Spain—and allienate many in Holland. That it would encourage Ministry in England and disconcert opposition so much that they would even be able to make another vigorous Campaign, besides all the Evils it would produce among you.

But the arrival of Dr. F's Commission has relieved me from many of these Fears. This Court has Confidence in him alone: but I think they were cautious even of him when he had two Colleagues, to whom he was obliged to communicate every Thing, one of whom was upon as ill terms with him as with Mr. Deane. I have had a Kind of a Task here as my dear Brother Lovel expresses himself. Determined to be the Partisan of neither; yet the Friend of both as far as the service would Admit, I am fully perswaded that leaving the Dr. here alone, in a political Capacity only, is right and that Mr. Lee is an honest and faithfull Man.

You say that France should be our Pole Star in Case War should take Place. I was I confess, surprized at this Expression. Was not War sufficiently declared in the King of Englands Speech, and in the answers of both Houses, and in the Recall of Ambassadors, and in actual Hostilities in most Parts of the World?

I think there never will be any other Declaration of War— Yet there is in fact as compleat a War as ever existed, and it will continue, for you may depend upon it, the King of France is immoveably fixed in our support, and so are his Ministers. Every suspicion of a wavering Disposition in this Court, concerning the support of our Independance is groundless—is ridiculous—is impossible. You may remember that several Years ago, several Gentlemen were obliged to reason in order to shew that American Independance was the Interest of France. Since my Arrival here, I never yet found one Man, nor heard of more than one who doubted it. If the Voice of Popularity is any Thing, I assure you that this Voice was never so unanimous in America, in favour of our Independance as it is here. It is so much so that if the Court were to depart from its present system in this Respect, it is my clear opinion it would make this Nation very unhappy, and the Court too. But I repeat that the Court is as fixed as the Nation, and this Union in sentiment arises out of such Principles in Nature, as without a Miracle, cannot alter. Common sense in America supported Independance, Common sense in France supports the Alliance and will support it to the last—nay the Common sense of Europe supports the Common sense of France. By the Way my Love to Mr. P. and tell him, I cant agree with him perfectly in his Ideas about natural Ennemies. It is because England is the natural Ennemy of France, that America in her present situation is her natural Friend—at least this is one Cause altho there are many others, some of them more glorious for human Nature.

France Scarcely ever made a War before that was popular in Europe. Now there is not a state that I can hear of, but applauds her, and wishes her success. And in Point of Finance—and naval strength—in skill and Bravery of Officers, she seems to be superiour to England. You may be suprized at my saying naval strength. Yet if you consider, the wretched state of the British Navy, as to Masts, Yards, Rigging, and Men you will not wonder altho their Number of Ships may be superiour.

I therefore think that all is safe. We may have further Trouble and Tryals of our Patience. But Trouble is to you and me familiar, and I begin to think it necessary for my Health, for without it I should soon grow so fat as to go off in an Apoplexy.

There is one Thing, in one of my Letters to you exaggerated—the Expences of the Commissioners. I had been here but a short time and wrote according to the best guess I could make, from what I had heard. But I now think I put it too high. With much Affection yours

John Adams

Feb. 20. 1779

There is not the least appearance of the Embarkation of Troops, for America nor any Intelligence of Transports taken up. The national Discontent is very great, and Tumults, have arisen in Edinborough and in London. According to present Appearances, they will have Occasion for so many of their Troops to keep their Populace in fear, as to be able to spare few for America. Their Proclamations are all alike from Burgoines to those of the Commissioners. The Weaker they are the more they puff.

THE LEE-DEANE CONTROVERSY

To James Lovell

My dear Friend   Passy Feb. 20. 1779

I set down Simply to acknowledge over
again the Receipt of the Letters from you

1777 Decr 1   whose dates are in the Margin. These have
8   been answerd, and I have wrote you at other
21   Times. But there is a terrible Waste of Letters
1778 Jany. 20.   in the Sea.
Ap. 29.
May 15.   I cannot lay aside my Pen without Saying,
16   that the Accusations before Congress, against
Sept 25   the Messrs. Lees and I know not who besides
3 others which   distress me, beyond Measure. I fear it will
accompanied   perpetuate Altercation, without bringing any
some of the   great Truths to light for the Benefit of the
others without   Public. I have Sighed and mourn'd, and
dates   wept, for that Intemperance of Passions,
Oct. 24   which I very early discovered here, without
being able to Soften or to cool it in the least
degree. I wish I could draw the Portrait of
every Character here, as it appears in my
Eyes: But this would be imprudent, and if it should be known
would do public Mischief, full enough of which has been done
already by Indiscretion.

Our old incidental Agent, is an honest Man: faithfull and
zealous in our Cause: but there is an Acrimony in his Temper
—There is a Jealousy—there is an Obstinacy, and a Want of
Candor at times, and an Affectation of Secrecy the Fruit of
Jealousy, which renders him disagreable often to his Friends,
makes him Ennemies, and gives them infinite Advantages over
him.

That he has had great Provocations here I never doubted,
and Since the Appearance of the Address less than ever.

There is another Character here, exceedingly respectable in
Fortune, Education, Travel, Honour, Integrity, Love of his
Country and Zeal in its Cause: But Tacitus would say his Pas-

sions are always strong, often violent: and he has not Experience in public Life.

These two Gentlemen, have been very intimate, and have encouraged no doubt each other and often irritated. Another Thing I think that other Gentleman ought not to have been here. He should have been in Italy or in America, or being here, I really think he ought not to have interfered, so much. This is simply my opinion—I may be wrong. That Gentleman thought he was doing his Duty I am clear. But of this I am perswaded that if he had been in Italy Things would never have gone to the Lengths they have.

On the other Hand most of the old Connections of the Dr. and Mr. D. were filled with Prejudices against those two Gentlemen—one Party was striving to get the better of the other, to lessen its Reputation and diminish its Authority.

In this Chaos I found Things and have been tossed in it.

On the other Hand, there was a Monopoly of Reputation here, and an Indecency in displaying it, which did great Injustice to the real Merit of others, that I do not wonder was resented. There was an Indolence—there was a Dissipation— which gave just Occasion of Complaint—there was a Complaisance to interested Adventurers. There was an Intimacy, with stock jobbers, there was an Acquaintance with Persons from England, which gave just Occasion of Jealousy, however innocent the intentions were. I have learnd that total silence is enough to procure a Character for Prudence, whatever Indiscretions a Man may commit.

In this state of Things Congress have had the Wisdom and the Fortitude to do the only Thing, which could be done for putting Matters on a better Footing. But this will last a very little while, if Money matters are not seperated from political.

Some other Thing must be done. Some Resolution must be passed forbidding every Man, in the most positive Terms who has any Connection with your Minister here, from having any Connection with English Stocks, Insurances, &c and forbidding all Correspondence with them. There is in England a Practice of making Insurances on political Events, which has interested the whole Alley in American Politicks, and has thrown all into Distraction.

I have been wholly without Information of what was passing in Congress and indeed in America, especially in Philadelphia. My Friends I know have been engaged in doing the public Business, not in Strengthening the Hands of Individuals or Parties here. But Bushells of Letters, have come to Adventurers here, containing Information more exact in Some things, and not so true in others as they might.

THE NEED FOR TAXATION

To James Warren

Dear sir   Feb. 25. 1779

Yours of the 1. Jany. was delivered me, by the Marquis de la Fayette. I wish I was as happy as you, in not being obliged to copy my Letters. Sense or Nonsense frivolous or weighty, I must copy every line I write, for I know not what Accusations may be brought against me, grounded on my Letters if I do not. My Letters are lyable to more Misfortunes and foul Play too than yours, and I keep no Clerk, so that original and Copy, must be done with these weak Eyes almost blind with reading and writing: yet every Body complains of me for not writing enough, especially my Wife.

The Address you mention, produced astonishment, here and all over Europe. Yet it Seems to be not discountenanced: rather supported. You have Reason to be confident of Dr. L's Integrity and Fidelity—no Man more faithfull, and his Character must be vindicated or no Mans will be safe. I shall not however enter into this Business. He is able to justify himself and willing. You may tell your Lady however, she was not mistaken in the Character she gave me of him.

I shall not enter particularly into the Inconveniences, which must result from such an outrageous Measure as that Address. I wish to know, who will correspond with Us or any Body connected with Us, if they are to be thus exposed. What Prince, Minister or State will confide in Us, if Negociations are thus to be laid open? Where is our Secrecy, or a Possibility of it? Is the Confederation annihilated? Is the Union lost? Has Congress so little authority as to be obliged to endure this? God forbid. Yet I think the Probability is that he will succeed, get the two L's recalled, and himself appointed to some Trust abroad. If this should be the Case what is to become of Us? At least if this is done before they are asked if guilty or not guilty. Before they are allowed to defend themselves which I doubt not they can do.

This Publication gave the Ministry a Lift in England, and will hoist the Loan which before laboured. The Capture of St. Lucie, also which is just arrived, will give another Spur. Yet the Discontents in England, Scotland, Ireland, and Wales ought to be terrible to Administration. They can do not great Things against Us.

The only Ennemy, of any great Consequence which is left to Us is our Currency. TAXATION and ŒCONOMY, must be the Cry in America. A Depreciation and Appreciation Law must be made. The People will not Succumble to G.B. if the Bills depreciate, untill a Thousand Dollars, must be given for a silver shilling. They will not Succumbe to G.B. if our regular Army, was wholly disbanded.

For even then the English could not make an Excursion into the Country, from under the Guns of their Men of War, without Militia Men enough turning out to knock them in the Head. The Consumption of British soldiers and sailors in the West Indies is like to be such that you need not fear, any great force, with you. The Tories must now Act against every light of Conscience, for they know that we cannot now succumbe to G.B. without having France and Spain upon our Backs.

What C. will do with the Paper I dont know, but they had better, by a Vote annihilate it all, or call it in to be burned, infinitely, and go over the same ground again ten times than that G. B. should prevail. Burn it all with my good Will. My share shall go to the Flames with the Utmost cheerfulness. Call it all in, in a Loan if you will, but then dont let it stand at Sterling Standard to be redeemed. This would be greater Injustice than to burn it all.

This vile Paper discourages and disheartens the Whiggs, and emboldens the Tories, more than it ought. Blow it away, any way. Many have a Prejudice, that our Independance is connected with it. Convince both sides that our Independance dont depend upon that. That our Plate, our stocks and all shall go rather than our sovereignty depend upon it. It is worth them all and more, nay our Houses and Farms into the Bargain.

Our Remedy is so simple, that I am astonished, there should be the least Hesitation about it, in the Mind of the most ignorant and mean of the People.

Taxation alone, is amply Sufficient to carry on our share of the War in future. I am Sure that the 13 states can raise Money enough if they will to bear all their future Expences as they rise. If the People are so blind, blockish and stupid, as not to see it and be willing for it—it is a Pity.

But the Delirium that rages, is enough to discourage every Man of Virtue and Honour—The Foppery—the Avarice—the Ambition—the Vanity—the Rage—the Fury—is enough to induce every Man of sense and Virtue to abandon such an execrable Race, to their own Perdition. And if they could be ruined alone it would be just. There is Cause to fear that our Countrymen and Women, after having astonished the Universe by their Wisdom and Virtue, will become a Spectacle of Contempt and Derision to the foolish and wicked, and of Grief and shame to the wise among Mankind, and all this in the Space of a few Years.

I see so much Corruption, wherever I cast my Eyes. I see the virtuous few Struggling against it, with so little success, that a Retreat infinitely less Splendid than that of Pythagoras— at the Head of a little school, to teach a few Children the Elements of Knowledge would be a kind of Heaven to me.

I have the Honour to be reduced to a private Citizen and if I could remain there without an eternal Clamour, no Consideration in the World should induce me ever again to rise out of it. But you know the Noise—the Lyes—the slanders—the stupid Groans and Lamentations, that would be raised at such a Resolution.

However let them groan and hiss and curse as they will, I will never be again with my own Consent the sport of wise Men nor Fools.

GIVING NOTICE OF HIS RETURN

To John Jay

Sir   Passy Feb. 27. 1779

By the new Arrangement, which was brought by the Marquis de la Fayette I find myself restored to the Character of a private Citizen.

The Appointment of a single Minister, at the Court of Versailles was not unexpected to me, because I had not been two Months in Europe, before I was convinced of the Policy, and indeed of the Necessity of such a Measure. But I ever entertained hopes that when the News of Such an Alteration Should arrive the Path of my own Duty, would have been made plain to me by the Directions of Congress either to return home or go elsewhere. But as no Information we have received from Congress, has expressed their Intentions, concerning me, I am obliged to collect them by Implication, according to the best of my Understanding: And as the Election of the new Minister Plenipotentiary, was on the fourteenth of September, and the Alliance, Sailed from Boston the fourteenth of January, and in this Space of four Months no Notice appears to have been taken of me, I think the only Inference that can be made is, that Congress have no farther Service for me, on this Side the Water, and that all my Duties are on the other. I have accordingly given Notice to his Excellency M. De Sartine, and to his excellency the Minister Plenipotentiary here of my Intentions to return, which I Shall do by the first Frigate which Sails for any Part of the united States, unless I Should receive Counter orders in the mean time. In a Matter of so much Uncertainty, I hope I shall not incur the Disapprobation of Congress, even if I should not judge aright of their Intentions, which it is my Desire, as well as my Duty to observe, as far as I can know them.

By the Papers enclosed with this Congress will perceive, the discontented and tumultuous State of the three Kingdoms of England Scotland and Ireland, which is So great, and So rapidly increasing, that the united States, will have little to fear, from Reinforcements of their Ennemies, the ensuing Campaign. All their Forces will be necessary, to keep in order their own riotous Populace, and to replace those, which are daily consuming in the West Indies. There is however no Prospect of their evacuating either New York, or Rhode Island. The Possession of those Places, is So indispensible, for the Preservation of their West India and other Trade, as well as of their other Dominions in America that nothing but the last Necessity, will induce them to give them up.

The greatest Source of Danger and Unhappiness to the States then, probably will be, a depreciating Currency. The Prospect of a Loan in Europe, after every Measure, that has been, or could be taken, I think it my Duty to say frankly to congress, is very unpromising. The Causes of this are very obvious, and cannot be removed. The State of our Currency itself, and the Course of Exchange, would be Sufficient to discourage Such a Loan, if there was no other Obstruction: but there are many others. There are more Borrowers in Europe than Lenders, and the British Loan itself, will not be made this Year, at a less Interest than Seven and an Half Per Cent.

I See no Hope of Relief, but from Taxation and Œconomy: And these I flatter myself, will be found Sufficient, if the People are once convinced of the Necessity of them. When a People are contending not only for the greatest Object, that any People ever had in View, but for Security from the greatest Evil that any Nation ever had, to dread (for there is at this Hour no Medium between unlimited submission to Parliament, and entire Sovereignty) they must be destitute of sense as well as Virtue, if they are not willing to pay Sufficient Sums, annually to defray the necessary Expence of their Defence in future, Supported as they are by So powerfull an Ally, and by the Prospect of Others, against a Kingdom already exhausted, without any ally at all, or a Possibility of obtaining one.

As this is the first Time, I have had the Honour to address myself to Congress, Since We received the News, of your Excellencys Appointment to the Chair, you will please to accept of my Congratulations on that Event. I have the Honour to be with the highest Consideration, Sir, your most obedient, and most humble Servant   John Adams

"AN END OF OUR VIRTUOUS VISION"

To Arthur Lee

Dear Sir   Brest. March 24. 1779

I have this Moment the Honour of yours of 18.

I am perfectly of your Opinion that We have yet a hard Battle to fight. The Struggle will yet be long, and painfull, and the Difficulty of it will arise from nothing more than the weak Disposition in our Country men, as well as our Allies to think it will be short.

Long before, this War began I expected, a severe Tryal: but I never foresaw so much Embarrassement, from selfishness, Vanity, flattery and Corruption, as I find.

If these proceed much longer in their Career, it will not be worth the while of Men of Virtue, to make themselves miserable by continuing in the service.

If they leave it, the American system of Flattery and Corruption, will still prevail over the British. But there will be an End of our virtuous Vision of a Kingdom of the just.

I wrote Mr Issard from Nantes. My Regards to him and your Brother.

I am no Hand at a Cypher, but will endeavour, to unridel if you write in it. With much Esteem, your huml sert

John Adams

From the Diary: April 26–May 17, 1779

AP. 26. MONDAY.

Spent the Morning in translating with my Son the Carmen Seculare, and the Notes.

There is a Feebleness and a Languor in my Nature. My Mind and Body both partake of this Weakness. By my Physical Constitution, I am but an ordinary Man. The Times alone have destined me to Fame—and even these have not been able to give me, much. When I look in the Glass, my Eye, my Forehead, my Brow, my Cheeks, my Lips, all betray this Relaxation. Yet some great Events, some cutting Expressions, some mean Hypocrisies, have at Times, thrown this Assemblage of Sloth, Sleep, and littleness into Rage a little like a Lion. Yet it is not like the Lion—there is Extravagance and Distraction in it, that still betrays the same Weakness.

MONDAY MAY. 10.

This Morning the Wind at S.E. The Pilot came on board, the Alliance unmoored and set Sail, for L'orient. A gentle Breeze, fair Weather, and moderately warm.

The 1 Lt. I have made by this War £120 of Prize Money, for which I got six Months Imprisonment, and spent the little that I had. This is all I have got by the War.

The Sand Droguers and Chimney Sweepers in Boston have all turned Merchants and made Fortunes.

Ingraham. Otis says when the Pot boils the Scum rises to the Top.

Ego. The new Cyder, when it ferments sends all the Pummace, Worms, bruised seeds and all sorts of Nastiness to the Top.

People of Fortune have spent their Fortunes, and those who had none, have grown rich.

Ford. I came to France with the highest opinion of Dr. F.— as a Philosopher, a Statesman and as even the Pater Patriae. But I assure you Tempora mutantur.

He has very moderate Abilities, He knows nothing of Philosophy, but his few Experiments in Electricity: He is an Atheist, he dont believe any future State: Yet he is terribly afraid of dying.

This is Fords Opinion. This is his Character of the great Man.

I believe it is too much to say that he is an Atheist, and that he dont believe a future State: tho I am not certain his Hints, and Squibs sometimes go so far as to raise Suspicions:—and he never tells any Body, I fancy that he believes a G, a P or f s. It is too rank to say that he understands nothing of Philosophy, but his own electrical Experiments, altho I dont think him so deeply read in Philosophy, as his Name impute.

He has a Passion for Reputation and Fame, as strong as you

can imagine, and his Time and Thoughts are chiefly employed to obtain it, and to set Tongues and Pens male and female, to celebrating him. Painters, Statuaries, Sculptors, China Potters, and all are set to work for this End. He has the most affectionate and insinuating Way of charming the Woman or the Man that he fixes on. It is the most silly and ridiculous Way imaginable, in the Sight of an American, but it succeeds, to admiration, fullsome and sickish as it is, in Europe.

When I arrive, I must enquire—concerning Congress, Ennemys Army, R.I., N.Y., G, our Army, our Currency, Mass. Bay, Boston &c.

WEDNESDAY MAY 12TH.

L is jealous of every Thing. Jealous of every Body, of all his Officers, all his Passengers. He knows not how to treat his Officers, nor his Passengers nor any Body else.—Silence, Reserve, and a forbidding Air, will never gain the Hearts, neither by Affection nor by Veneration, of our Americans.

There is in this Man an Inactivity and an Indecision that will ruin him. He is bewildered—an Absent bewildered man—an embarrassed Mind.

This Morning he began "You are a great Man but you are deceived. The Officers deceive you! They never do their Duty but when you are on deck. They never obey me, but when you are on deck. The Officers were in a Plott vs. me at Boston, and the Navy Board promised to remove them all from the ship and yet afterwards let them all come on Board."

Conjectures, Jealousies, Suspicions.—I shall grow as jealous as any Body.

I am jealous that my Disappointment is owing to an Intrigue of Jones's. Jones, Chaumont, Franklin concerted the Scheme. Chaumont applied to Mr. De S. He wrote the Letter. If this Suspicion is well founded, I am to be made the Sport of Jones's Ambition to be made a Commodore. Is it possible that I should bear this? Another Suspicion is that this Device was hit upon by Franklin and Chaumont to prevent me from going home, least I should tell some dangerous Truths. Perhaps, Jones's Commodoreship, and my detention might both concur. Can I bear either? It is hard, very hard, but I must bear every Thing. I may as well make a Virtue of Necessity, for I cannot help my self.

Does the old Conjurer dread my Voice in Congress? He has some Reason for he has often heard it there, a Terror to evil doers.

I may be mistaken in these Conjectures, they may be injurious to J. and to F. and therefore I shall not talk about them, but I am determined to put down my Thoughts and see which turns out.

Mr. Chaumont and his son are here and have been 15 days. But no Chevalier de la Luzerne, nor any french Frigate.

It is decreed that I shall endure all Sorts of Mortifications. There is so much Insolence, and Contempt, in the Appearance of this. Do I see that these People despize me, or do I see that they dread me? Can I bear Contempt—to know that I am despized? It is my duty to bear every Thing—that I cannot help.

THURSDAY. MAY 13TH.

Went on Shore and dined with Captain Jones at the Epèe Royal. Mr. Amiel, Mr. Dick, Dr. Brooke, officers of the Poor Richard, Captain Cazneau, Captain Young, Mr. Ingraham, Mr. Blodget, Mr. Glover, Mr. Conant, Messrs. Moylans, Mr. Maese, Mr. Nesbit, Mr. Cummings, Mr. Tayler, made the Company, with Captain Landais, myself and my Son.

An elegant Dinner we had—and all very agreable.

No very instructive Conversation. But we practiced the old American Custom of drinking to each other, which I confess is always agreable to me.

Some hints about Language, and glances about Women, produced this Observation, that there were two Ways of learning french commonly recommended—take a Mistress and go to the Commedie. Dr. Brookes, in high good Humour—Pray Sir, which in your Opinion is the best? Answer in as good Humour—Perhaps both would teach it soonest, to be sure sooner than either. But, continued I, assuming my Gravity, the Language is no where better spoken than at the Comedie. The Pulpit, the Bar, the Accademie of Sciences, and the faculty of Medicine, none of them speak so accurately as the french Comedie.

After Dinner walked out, with Cs Jones and Landais to see Jones's Marines—dressed in the English Uniform, red and white. A Number of very active and clever Serjeants and Corporals are employed to teach them the Exercise, and Maneuvres and Marches &c.

After which Jones came on Board our ship.

This is the most ambitious and intriguing Officer in the American Navy. Jones has Art, and Secrecy, and aspires very high. You see the Character of the Man in his uniform, and that of his officers and Marines, variant from the Uniforms established by Congress. Golden Button holes, for himself—two Epauletts—Marines in red and white instead of Green.

Excentricities, and Irregularities are to be expected from him—they are in his Character, they are visible in his Eyes. His Voice is soft and still and small, his Eye has keenness, and Wildness and Softness in it.

MAY 17. MONDAY.

L. gave Us an Account of St. George at Paris, a Molatto Man, Son of a former Governor of Guadaloupe, by a Negro Woman. He has a sister married to a Farmer General. He is the most accomplished Man in Europe in Riding, Running, Shooting, Fencing, Dancing, Musick. He will hit the Button, any Button on the Coat or Waistcoat of the greatest Masters. He will hit a Crown Piece in the Air with a Pistoll Ball.

Mr. Gimaet came on Board, to go to Port Louis with C L. The Affectation, in the Eyes, features, laugh, Air, gate, Posture, and every Thing of this Gentleman is so striking, that I cannot but think I see C.J.Q. or C.B. whenever I see him.

Affectation proceeds from Vanity. EASE is the Opposite. Nature is easy, and simple. This Man thinks himself handsome, his Eyes, his Complexion, his Teeth, his Figure, his Step, and Air, have irresistable Charms, no doubt, in his Mind.

L. will never accomplish any great Thing. He has Honour—Delicacy—Integrity—and I doubt not Courage—and Skill, and Experience. But he has not Art.—And I firmly believe there never was, or will be a great Character, without a great deal of Art. I am more and more convinced every day of the Innocence, the Virtue and absolute Necessity of Art and

Design.—I have arrived almost at 44 without any. I have less than L. and therefore shall do less Things than even he.

This Evening L. said that Mathematicians were never good Company. That Mathematicks made a Man unhappy. That they never were good writers.

I said no nor the Lawyers—it had been often observed that Lawyers could not write.

L. said that Observation is not just, there are many other Instances of that besides you.—This looks like Art, but was too obvious.

I said, the Roman Lawyers were good Writers. Justinians Institutes were pure as Classicks. Several French Lawyers had been fine Writers as Cochin, &c.   and some English Lawyers as Bacon, Clarendon, Couper, Blackstone. But it was a common Observation in England, and I found it as common in Paris, that Lawyers were generally bad Writers.

"LITTLE TRICKS AND LOW DEVICES"

To Edmund Jenings

Dr. sir   L'orient May 22d. 1779

Yours of the 15 reached me, Yesterday. I am waiting here in anxious Expectation of the new Minister, with whom, it is said I am to embark. It would give me Pleasure to form an Acquaintance with this Gentleman, because his Character is good, and because, it would give me an opportunity of convincing him of the Importance of keeping himself disconnected with Parties. Not only the Benefits of the Alliance, but the Duration of the Confederacy of the states depends, upon the Neutrality of the French Court, in our internal Disputes.

The Object of the Armament that is fitting out, here, is a Secret of state. Who is to be at the Expence of it? Who directs it? Who is to have the Benefit of it?

I must Sing a little to the God of Love, let War and Politicks say what they will. Surely I may be allowed to hum a Tune to him, when I am not permitted to pay him any other Kind of Worship. This I may do without looking back, which I shall never do, whoever holds the Plough. As to your Idea of the *great Men*, there is not much in it. It is a great People, that does great Things. They will always find Instruments to employ that will answer their Ends. I am more and more convinced that every great Character in the World is a Bubble, and an Imposture, from Mahomet down to Governor Johnstone. It is made up of little Tricks and low Devices.

I thank you for the news from Holland and Sweeden. Every Article of News is important to me here, where nothing is to be learnd. I never felt the Want of it so much.

Mr. Ds. Permission to come over, to settle, his or the public Accounts is another Mistery. A new Device for Sliding into a public Character. Why permitted to do this? Is he to be a public Man? in public Pay? Why permitted to do what is his Duty? and was his Duty, to have done before? What Accounts are to settle? I am weary of these misterious Artifices. If he had been ordered to lay his Accounts, before Congress, without delay or as soon as he could get his Papers from France, and censured for leaving them there I should have understood this very well. I am convinced that a Construction will be put upon this that Congress never intended. And that he means to draw Consequences from it that they did not think of. Will Dr. F. pay Mr. Ds. Expences, who refused to pay Mr. Izards, and Mr. W. Lees?

With all my Professions of Neutrality and Impartiality I confess myself wholly against this Man. He will not have my Vote, to be in any very important office. His narrow Capacity and his immeasurable Vanity, to go no farther make such a Composition, as will not soon have my Confidence. With all this He has subtelty and Intrigue enough to do our affairs much Harm, if he comes to France. He has formd Connections in Trade, with some House or Houses or other in almost every State from G. to N.H. as I am informed. He has also formed very extensive Connections in the maritime Towns in France. These grasping Genius's are the Curse of human Kind. This Mans Conduct in particular has done our Cause in my humble opinion incredible Injuries. To his extravagant Projects, all the Disputes and Quarrells about our foreign affairs, are to be imputed. To him it is chiefly owing that Americans are tearing one anothers Characters in Pieces in this Country, mutually labouring to make each other appear to be Knaves. And a great Part of the

World, here, is now complaisant enough to take Us all at our Words.

For my own Part, instead of permitting Mr. D to come, I wish Congress had positively ordered Mr. L. to Spain, Mr. Izard to Tuscany and Dr. F. to attend wholly to his Negociations at Court.

If mercantile and maritime matters and the Disposition of all Money but his own salary, is not taken from the Minister, America will be ruined in Reputation as well as Credit very soon.

A Consul should be appointed at Nantes, with a Power of Deputation. This Consul, in Person or by Deputy should have the management of all our Commercial Concerns and the Direction of all the Vessells of War, and be made without Mercy to lay his Accounts before Congress once in two Months.

This is the substance of my system for American affairs in France. I beg your sentiments upon it, and your Reasons against any Part that you may disapprove, for I am open to Conviction.

The great Difficulty will be to find a proper Person for a Consul, I wish you would mention if you think of any.

This is writing freely to be sure, but you will make no improper Use of it, and the Times certainly demand a free Communication of Sentiments.

Adieu

Your Remembrancer is not yet arrived.

From the Diary: June 18–23, 1779

Mr. Marbois discovered an Inclination to day to slide into Conversation with me, to day. I fell down the Stream with him, as easily as possible. He Thought the Alliance beneficial, to both Countries, and hoped it would last forever. I agreed that the Alliance was usefull to both, and hoped it would last. I could not foresee any Thing that should interrupt the Friendship. Yes, recollecting myself, I could foresee several Things that might interrupt it.—Ay what were they?—I said it was possible, a King of France might arise, who being a wicked Man might make Attempts to corrupt the Americans. A King of France hereafter might have a Mistress, that might mislead him, or a bad Minister. I said I could foresee another Thing that might endanger our Confederation.—What was that?—The Court of France, I said, might, or their Ambassadors or Consuls might, attach themselves to Individuals or Parties, in America, so as to endanger our Union.—He caught at this, with great Avidity, and said it was a great Principle, not to join with any Party. It was the K's Determination and the Chevaliers, not to throw the Weight of the French Court into the Scale of any Individual or Party.

He said, he believed, or was afraid, it had been done: but it was disapproved by the King and would not be done again. . . . He said that the Chevalier and himself would have the favour of the greatest Part, the Generality of the honest People in France, altho there would be Individuals against them.

He said He hoped the United States would not think of becoming Conquerors. I said it was impossible they should for many Ages. It would be Madness in them to think of conquering foreign Countries, while they had an immense Territory, near them uncultivated. That if any one State should have a fancy for going abroad it would be the Interest of all the rest and their Duty to hinder her.—He seemed to be pleased with this.

He said We would explain ourselves wholly, on the Passage. I said, with all my Heart, for I had no Secrets.

All this Conversation was in french, but he understood me, very well, and I him.

He said Mr. Gerard was a Man of Wit, and had an Advantage of them in understanding the Language very well and speaking it easily. I said I believed not much. I had heard it affirmed, by some, that Mr. Gerard spoke English perfectly, but by others, very indifferently. That it was often affirmed that Mr. Franklin spoke French as fluently and elegantly, as a Courtier at Versailles, but every Man that knew and spoke sincerely, agreed that he spoke it very ill. Persons spoke of these Things, according to their Affections.

He said it was Flattery. That he would not flatter, it was very true that both Mr. F. and I spoke french, badly.

June 18, 1779

The Chevalier de la Luzerne, and M. Marbois are in raptures with my Son. They get him to teach them the Language. I found this Morning the Ambassador, Seating on the Cushing in our State Room, Mr. Marbois in his Cot at his left Hand and my Son streched out in his at his Right—The Ambassador reading out loud, in Blackstones Discourse, at his Entrance on his Professorship of the Common Law at the University, and my Son correcting the Pronunciation of every Word and Syllable and Letter. The Ambassador said he was astonished, at my Sons Knowledge. That he was a Master of his own Language like a Professor. Mr. Marbois said your Son teaches Us more than you. He has Point de Grace—Point d'Eloges. He shews us no Mercy, and makes Us no Compliments. We must have Mr. John.

This Evening had a little Conversation with the Chevalier, upon our American Affairs, and Characters, Mr. Samuel Adams, Mr. Dickinson, Mr. Jay—and upon American Eloquence in Congress and Assemblies as well as in Writing. He admired our Eloquence. I said that our Eloquence was not corrected. It was the Time of Ennius, with Us. That Mr. Dickinson and Mr. Jay had Eloquence, but it was not so chaste, nor pure, nor nervous as that of Mr. Samuel Adams. That this last had written some things, that would be admired more than any Thing that has been written in America in this Dispute.—He enquired after Mr. Dickinson, and the Reason why he disappeared. I explained, as well as I could in French, the Inconsistency of the Farmers Letters and his Perseverance in that Inconsistency in Congress. Mr. Dickensons Opposition to the Declaration of Independancy. I ventured as modestly as I could to let him know that I had the Honour to be the Principal Disputant in Congress against Mr. Dickinson upon that great Question. That Mr. Dickinson had the Eloquence, the Learning and the Ingenuity on his Side of the Question, but that I had the Hearts of the Americans on mine, and therefore my Side of the Question prevailed. That Mr. Dickinson had a good

Heart, and an amiable Character. But that his Opposition to Independency, had lost him the Confidence of the People, who suspected him of Timidity and Avarice, and that his Opposition sprung from those Passions: But that he had since turned out with the Militia, against the B Troops and I doubted not might in Time regain the Confidence of the People.

I said that Mr. Jay was a Man of Wit, well informed, a good Speaker and an elegant Writer. The Chevalier said perhaps he will not be President when We arrive. He accepted only for a short Time. I said I should not be sorry to hear of his Resignation, because I did not much esteem the Means by which he was advanced to the Chair, it appearing to me that he came in by the Efforts of a Faction at that Moment dominant by Means of an Influence which I was afraid to mention. That I did not care to say what I thought of it.

We fell into a great deal of other Conversation this Evening upon Litterature, and Eloquence ancient and modern, Demosthenes, Cicero, the Poets, Historians, Philosophers. The English, Bacon, Newton &c. Milton &c.

He said Milton was very ancient. I said no, in the Reign of Charles and the Protectorship of Cromwell and the Reign of Charles the Second.—He thought it was much more ancient.

I said there were three Epochas in the English History celebrated for great Men.—The Reign of Elizabeth, the Reign of C 1. and the Interregnum, and the Reign of Queen Anne.

The C. said Ld. Bolinbroke was a great Man. I said Yes and the greatest Orator that England ever produced.

Mr. Marbois upon this said, it would be easy in France to produce an Orator equal to Bolinbroke. I asked who? John Jac—No, Malesherbes. Malesherbes Orations might be placed on a Footing with Demosthenes and Cicero.

June 20, 1779

————————

The Chevalier de la Luzerne, the other day at Mr. De Thevenards Table, gave a terrible Stroke to M. Chaumont. Chaumont said, M. Franklin parle Francais bien.—Oh que non, said the Chevalier, fort mal. Mr. Adams parle mieux que lui.—Yesterday, in a long Conversation with the Chevalier, on the Quarter Deck, he said to me, Vous connoissez les Fondemens de notre Langue tres bien. Vous parlez lentement et avec difficulté, comme un homme qui cherche pour les mots: mais vous ne pechez pas contre la Prononciation. Vous prononcez bien. Vous prononcez, beaucoup mieux que Mr. Franklin. Il est impossible de l'entendre.

Mr. Marbois, with whom I fell into Conversation, this Afternoon very easily upon Deck, said a great many things that deserve Notice.

He said that Mr. Franklin had a great many Friends among the Gens des Lettres in France, who make a great Impression in France, that he had Beaucoup des Agremens, Beaucoup de Charlatagnerie, that he has Wit: But that he is not a Statesman. That he might be recalled at this Moment, and in that Case, that his Opinion was he would not return to America—But would stay in Paris.

That he heard many of the honest People in France lament that I left France, particularly the Count   and the Marquis de   . That I might possibly return to France or to some other Part of Europe. That the Court of France would have Confidence in any Gentleman, that Congress should have Confidence in. That there ought to be a Charge des Affairs or a Secretary, and a successor pointed out, in Case of the Death of Dr. F.

Mr. Marbois said some were of opinion, that as I was not recalled, I ought to have staid untill I was.

I told him that if Congress had directed me to return, I would have returned. If they had directed me to stay untill further orders I should have staid. But as they reduced me to a private Citizen I had no other Duties but those of a private Citizen to fulfill, which were to go home as soon as possible and take Care of my family. Mr. Franklin advised me to take a Journey to Geneva. My own Inclinations would have led me to Holland: But I thought my Honour concerned to return directly home.—He said I was right.

In the Evening I fell into Chat with the Chevalier. He asked me, about Governeur Morris. I said it was his Christian Name—that he was not Governor. The Chevalier said He had heard of him as an able Man. I said he was a young Man, chosen into Congress since I left it. That I had sat some Years with his Elder Brother in Congress. That Governeur was a Man of Wit, and made pretty Verses—but of a Character trés legere. That the Cause of America had not been sustained by such Characters as that of Governor Morris or his Colleague Mr. Jay, who also was a young Man about 30 and not quite so solid as his Predicessor Mr. Laurence, upon whose Resignation in the sudden Heat Mr. Jay was chosen. That Mr. Lawrence had a great landed Fortune free from Debt, that he had long Experience in public life and an amiable Character for Honour And Probity. That he is between 50 and 60 Years of Age.

June 22, 1779

JUNE 23. WEDNESDAY.

This Forenoon, fell strangely, yet very easily into Conversation with M.M.

I went up to him—M.M. said I, how many Persons have you in your Train and that of the Chevalier who speak the German Language?—Only my Servant, said he, besides myself and the Chev.—It will be a great Advantage to you said I in America, especially in Pensilvania, to be able to speak German. There is a great Body of Germans in P and M. There is a vast Proportion of the City of Philadelphia, of this Nation who have their Churches in it, two of which one Lutheran the other Calvinist, are the largest and most elegant Churches in the City, frequented by the most numerous Congregations, where the Worship is all in the German Language.

Is there not one Catholic, said M.M.?—Not a German Church said I. There is a Roman catholic Church in Philadelphia, a very decent Building, frequented by a respectable Congregation, consisting partly of Germans, partly of French and partly of Irish.—All Religions are tolerated in America, said M.M., and the Ambassadors have in all Courts a Right to a Chappell in their own Way. But Mr. Franklin never had any.— No said I, laughing, because Mr. F. had no—I was going to say, what I did not say, and will not say here. I stopped short and laughed.—No, said Mr. M., Mr. F. adores only great Nature, which has interested a great many People of both Sexes in his favour.—Yes, said I, laughing, all the Atheists, Deists and

Libertines, as well as the Philosophers and Ladies are in his Train—another Voltaire and Hume.—Yes said Mr. M., he is celebrated as the great Philosopher and the great Legislator of America.—He is said I a great Philosopher, but as a Legislator of America he has done very little. It is universally believed in France, England and all Europe, that his Electric Wand has accomplished all this Revolution but nothing is more groundless. He has done very little. It is believed that he made all the American Constitutions, and their Confederation. But he made neither. He did not even make the Constitution of Pensylvania, bad as it is. The Bill of Rights is taken almost verbatim from that of Virginia, which was made and published two or three Months before that of Philadelphia was begun. It was made by Mr. Mason, as that of Pensilvania was by Timothy Matlack, James Cannon and Thomas Young and Thomas Paine. Mr. Sherman of Connecticutt and Dr. F. made an Essay towards a Confederation about the same Time. Mr. Shermans was best liked, but very little was finally adopted from either, and the real Confederation was not made untill a Year after Mr. F. left America, and but a few Days before I left Congress.

Who, said the Chevalier, made the Declaration of Independance?—Mr. Jefferson of Virginia, said I, was the Draughtsman. The Committee consisted of Mr. Jefferson, Mr. Franklin, Mr. Harrison, Mr. R. and myself, and We appointed Mr. Jefferson a subcommittee to draw it up.

I said that Mr. Franklin had great Merit as a Philosopher. His Discoveries in Electricity were very grand, and he certainly was a Great Genius, and had great Merit in our American Affairs. But he had no Title to the Legislator of America.

Mr. M. said he had Wit and Irony, but these were not the Faculties of Statesmen. His Essay upon the true Means of bringing a great Empire to be a small one was very pretty.—I said he had wrote many Things, which had great Merit and infinite Wit and Ingenuity. His bonhomme Richard was a very ingenious Thing, which had been so much celebrated in France, gone through so many Editions, and been recommended by Curates and Bishops to so many Parishes and Dioceses.

Mr. M. asked, are natural Children admitted in America to all Priviledges like Children born in Wedlock.—I answered they are not Admitted to the Rights of Inheritance. But their fathers may give them Estates by Testament and they are not excluded from other Advantages.—In France, said M.M., they are not admitted into the Army nor any Office in Government.—I said they were not excluded from Commissions in the Army, Navy, or State, but they were always attended with a Mark of Disgrace.—M.M. said this, No doubt, in Allusion to Mr. Fs. natural Son and natural Son of a natural Son. I let myself thus freely into this Conversation being led on naturally by the Chevalier and Mr. Marbois, on Purpose because I am sure it cannot be my Duty nor the Interest of my Country that I should conceal any of my sentiments of this Man, at the same Time that I due Justice to his Merits. It would be worse than Folly to conceal my Opinion of his great Faults.

EUROPEAN POWERS AND AMERICAN INTERESTS

To John Jay

Sir   Braintree August 4th: 1779

At the Close of the Service, on which Congress have done me the Honour to Send me, it may not be amiss to Submit a few Reflections to their Consideration on the general State of Affairs in Europe, So far as they relate to the Interests of the united States. As the Time approaches, when our Relations, with the most considerable States in Europe, will multiply, and assume a greater Stability, they deserve the Attention of Americans in general, but especially of those composing their Supream Council.

France deserves the first Place, among those Powers with which our Connections will be the most intimate. And it is with Pleasure, that I am able to assure Congress, that from the Observations I have made during my Residence in that Kingdom, I have the Strongest Reasons to believe, that their august Ally, his Ministers and Nation, are possessed of the fullest Perswasion of the Justice of our Cause, of the great Importance of our Independance to their Interests, and the firmest Resolution, to preserve the Faith of Treaties inviolate, and to cultivate our Friendship with Sincerity and Zeal. This of the more

Consequence to Us, as this Power, enjoys in Europe at this Hour, an Influence, which it has not before experienced, for many Years.

Men, are So sensible of a constant Tendency, in others, to Excesses, that a Signal Superiority of Power, never appears, without exciting Jealousies, and Efforts to reduce it. Thus when Spain, under Charles the fifth and his successor, made herself dangerous, a great Part of Europe, united against her; assisted in Severing the united Provinces from her; and by degrees greatly diminished her Power. Thus when France, under Louis the fourteenth, indulged the Spirit of Conquest too far, a great Part of Mankind, united their Forces against her, with such success, as to involve her in a Train of Misfortunes, out of which she never immerged, before the present Reign. The English, in their Turn, by means of their Commerce, and extensive settlements abroad, arose to a Degree of Oppulence, and naval Power, which excited more extravagant Passions in her own Breast, and more tyrannical Exertions of her Influence than appeared in either of the other Cases. The Consequence has been Similar, but more remarkable. Europe Seems to be more universally and Sincerely united in the Desire of reducing her, than they ever were in any former Instance. This is the true Cause, why the French Court never made War, with so universal a Popularity among their own subjects, So general an Approbation of other Courts, and such unanimous Wishes among all Nations for her Success, as at this Time.

The Personal Character of the King, his declared Patronage of Morals and Œconomy, and the great strokes of Wisdom, which have marked the Commencement of his Reign; The active Spring that has been given to Commerce, by the Division of the British Empire and our new Connections with his subjects; all these Causes, together with the two Treaties of Peace, which have been lately signed under his Auspices and his Mediation, have given to this Power a Reputation, which the last Reign had lost her.

The first of these Treaties, has determined those Controversies, which had for a long Time divided Russia and the Port, and the Parties have been equally Satisfyed with the Conditions of their Reconciliation, a Circumstance the more honourable for the french Ministry, and the Chevalier de St. Priest their Ambassador at Constantinople, as it is uncommon. The ancient Confidence of the Porte in the Court of Versailles has revived and the Coolness, or rather Enmity, which had divided France and Russia for near Twenty Years, gives Place to a Friendship, which is at this Time in all its fervour, and will probably be durable, as these Powers, have no Interest to annoy each other, but, on the contrary, are able to assist each other in a manner, the most efficacious.

The Peace of Germany, Signed at Teschen, the thirteenth of last May, has not equally Satisfyed the Belligerent Powers, who were, on the one Part the Emperor, and on the other the King of Prussia, and the Elector of Saxony, his Ally. From the Multitude of Writings, which have appeared before and during this War, in which the Causes, the Motives, and the Right of it are discussed, it appears, that in 1778, at the Extinction of one of the Branches of the House of Bavaria, which has been Seperated from its Trunk for near five Centuries, the House of Austria, thought itself able, and Priests and Lawyers, among their own subjects, were complaisant enough to tell her she had a Right, to put herself, in Possession of the best Part of the Patrimony, of the extinguished Line. The King of Prussia, to whose Interests this Augmentation of Power, would have been dangerous, has crowned an illustrious Reign, by displaying all the Resources of military Genius, and profound Policy, in Opposition to it. While he contended in the Field, France negotiated, and the Work begun by his Arms, was compleated by the Cabinet of Versailles. The Palatine House of Bavaria, the Duke of Deux Ponts, and particularly the Elector of Saxony, have obtained all that they could reasonably demand, and the Empire has preserved its Ballance of Power, in Spight of the Ambition of its Head: the King of Prussia, has covered himself with Glory, to which he put the last finishing stroke, by not demanding any Compensation for the Expences of the War: All Parties have been Satisfied, except the Emperor, who has disordered his Finances; ruined his Kingdom of Bohemia; with immense Forces, has not obtained any Advantage over his Adversary and consequently has destroyed among his own Troops the opinion they had of their Superiority; and in fine, has sustained the Loss the most sensible for a young Prince, just beginning to Reign, the Reputation of Justice and Moderation.

It is the Influence, the Address, and Ability of the french Ministry, joined to the Firmness of Russia, which have compleated the Work: and Louis the Sixteenth has restored in Germany, to the Nation over which he reigns, that Reputation, which his Grand father had lost. The Merit of the Chevalier de la Luzerne, who was Ambassador, in Bavaria during the Transaction of this Business, and that of Mr. Marbois the Secretary to that Embassy, in accomplishing an Affair of Such Importance, which was rendered peculiarly delicate, by the late Family Connection, between the Courts of Vienna and Versailles was probably a Motive for sending them now to America, a Mission of no less importance, and no less Delicacy. It is not probable, however, that they could have succeeded so soon, if England could have afforded Subsidies to the Emperor.

The Revolution in America, in which, the French King has taken an earlier and a greater Part, than any other Sovereign in Europe, has operated so as to conciliate to him, a Consideration, that is universal. The new Minister, will give to Congress, Information the most precise in this Respect and touching the Part, which Spain is taking at this Time, for which Reason I shall refrain from entering into it, and content myself with observing That all these Considerations ought to induce Us to cherish the Alliance of France; and that every good Citizen of the United States ought to endeavour to destroy the Remains of those Prejudices, which our ancient Rulers have endeavoured to inspire into Us. That We have nothing to fear, and much to hope from France, while We conduct Ourselves with good sense, and Firmness, and that We cannot take too much Pains to multiply the Commercial Relations, and Strengthen the political Connections between the two Nations: Provided Always, that We preserve Prudence and Resolution enough, to receive implicitly, no Advice whatsoever, but to judge always for ourselves; and to guard Ourselves against those Principles in Government, and those Manners, which are So opposite to our own Constitution, and to our Characters, as a young People, called by Providence to the most honourable and important of all Duties, that of forming Establishments for a great Nation and a new World.

In the opinion of Some, the Power, with which We shall one Day, have a Relation the most immediate, next to that of

France, is Great Britain. But it ought to be considered that this Power, looses every Day her Consideration, and runs towards her Ruin. Her Riches in which her Power consisted, she has lost with Us, and never can regain. With Us, she has lost her Mediterranean Trade, her Affrican Trade, her German and Holland Trade, her Ally Portugal, her Ally Russia, and her natural Ally the House of Austria; at least by being unable to protect these as she once did, she can obtain no succour from them. In short, one Branch of Commerce has been lopped off, after another; and one political Interest Sacrificed after another, that she resembles the melancholly Spectacle of a great wide Spreading Tree that has been girdled at the Root. Her Endeavours to regain these Advantages, will continually keep alive in her Breast the most malevolent Passions towards Us. Her Envy, her Jealousy, and Resentment, will never leave Us, while We are, what We must unavoidably be, her Rivals, in the Fisheries, in various other Branches of Commerce, and even in naval Power. If Peace should unhappily be made, leaving Canada, Nova Scotia, the Floridas, or any of them, in her Hands, Jealousies, and Controversies will be perpetually arrising. The Degree therefore of Intercourse, with this Nation, which will ever again take Place, may justly be considered as problematical, or rather the Probability is that it will never be so great as some Persons imagine. Moreover, I think that every Citizen, in the present Circumstances, who respects his Country, and the Engagements she has taken ought to abstain from the Foresight of a Return of Friendship, between Us and the English, and Act as if, it never was to be.

But it is lawful to consider that which will probably be formed between the Hollanders and Us. The Similitude of Manners, of Religion and in Some Respects of Constitution; the Analogy, between the Means, by which the two Republicks arrived at Independancy; but above all the Attractions of commercial Interests, will infallibly draw them together. This Connection will not probably shew itself, in a public Manner before a Peace, or a near Prospect of Peace. Too many Motives of Fear or Interest place the Hollanders in a Dependance on England, to suffer her to connect herself openly, with Us, at present. Nevertheless, if the King of Prussia could be induced to take Us by the Hand, his great Influence, in the united

Provinces, might contribute greatly to conciliate their Friendship for Us. Loans of Money, and the operations of commercial Agents or Societies, will be the first Threads of our Connections with this Power.

From the Essays, and Inquirys, of your Commissioners at Paris, it appears that Some Money, may be borrowed there; and from the Success of Several Enterprizes by Way of St. Eustatia, it Seems, that the Trade, between the two Countries is likely to increase, and possibly Congress may think it expedient to send a Minister there. If they shall, it will be proper to give him a discretionary Power, to produce his Commission, or not, as he shall find it likely to suceed: to give him full Powers and clear Instructions concerning the Borrowing of Money: and the Man himself, above all, should have consummate Prudence; of a Caution and Discretion that will be Proof, against every Tryal.

If Congress could find any certain Means, of paying the Interest, annually in Europe, commercial and pecuniary Connections would Strengthen themselves, from day to day: and if the Fall of the Credit of England should terminate in Bankruptcy, the seven united Provinces having nothing further to dissemble, would be zealous for a Part of those rich Benefits which our Commerce offers to the maritime Powers; and by an early Treaty with Us, Secure those Advantages, from which they have already discovered strong symptoms of a Fear of being excluded, by Delays. It is Scarcely necessary to observe to Congress, that Holland has lost her Influence, in Europe to such a Degree, that there is little other Regard for her remaining, but that of a prodigal Heir, for a rich Usurer, who lends him Money, at an high Interest. The State, which is poor, and in Debt, has no political Stability: Their Army is very small, and their Navy less. The immense Riches of Individuals, may possibly be, in some future Time, the great Misfortune of the Nation, because her Means of Defence, are not proportioned to the Temptation which is held out, for some necessitious, avaricious and formidable Neighbour to invade her.

The active Commerce of Spain, is very inconsiderable: of her passive Commerce, We shall not fail to have a Part. The Vicinity of this Power, her Forces, her Resources, ought to make Us, attentive to her Conduct. But if We may judge of the future by the Past, I should hope, that We have nothing from it, to fear. The Genius and the Interest of the Nation, inclines it to repose. She cannot determine upon War, but in the last Extremity, and even then, she Sighs, for Peace. She is not possessed of the Spirit of Conquest, and We have Reason to congratulate ourselves that We have her, for the nearest, and the principal Neighbour. Her Conduct towards Us, at this Time, will perhaps appear equivocal and indecisive: her Determinations appear to be solely, the Fruit of the Negotiations of the Court of Versailles: But it ought to be considered, that she has not had Motives so pressing, as those of France to take in Hand our Defence. Whether she has an Eye upon the Florida's, or what other Terms she may expect from Congress, they are, no doubt, better informed than I am. To their Wisdom it must be submitted to give her satisfaction, if her Terms are moderate and her offers, in Proportion. This Conduct, may conciliate her Affection and shorten delays, a Point of great Importance, as the present Moment appears to be decisive.

Portugal, under the Administration of the Marquis de Pombal, broke Some of the shackles, by which she was held to England. But the Treaty, by which a permanent Friendship, is established, between the Crowns of Spain and Portugal, was made in 1777, an Event that the English deplore, as the greatest Evil, next to the irrecoverable Loss of the Colonies, arising from this War: because they will, now, no longer be able to play off Portugal against Spain, in order to draw away her Attention as well as her Forces, as in former Times. But as Portugal has not known how to deliver herself, entirely from the Influence of England, We shall have little to hope from her: on the other Hand, Such is her internal Weakness, that We have absolutely, nothing to fear. We shall necessarily have Commerce with her, but whether she will ever have the Courage to sacrifice the Friendship of England for the sake of it, is uncertain.

It would be endless to consider that infinite Number of little sovereignties, into which Germany is divided; and develope all their political Interests: This Task is as much beyond my Knowledge, as it would be useless to Congress, who will have few Relations, friendly, or hostile, with this Country, excepting in two Branches of Commerce, that of Merchandises and that of Soldiers. The latter infamous and detestible as it is, has been established between a Nation, once generous, humane and brave, and certain Princes as avaricious of Money, as they are prodigal of the Blood of their subjects: And such is the Scarcity of Cash, and the Avidity for it, in Germany, and so little are the Rights of Humanity understood or respected, that sellers will probably be found as long as Buyers. America will never be found in either Class.

The states of Germany, with which We may have Commerce of an honourable Kind, are, the House of Austria; one of the most powerfull in Europe. She possesses, very few Countries, however near the Sea. Ostend is the principal City, where she might have established a Trade of Some Consequence, if the Jealousy of the maritime Powers, had not constantly opposed it. France, Spain, Holland and England, have been all agreed in this opposition, and the Treaty of Utrecht, ratified more than once by subsequent Treaties, have so shackled this Port, that it will be impossible to open a direct Trade to it, without some new Treaty, which, possibly may not be very distant. England may possibly make a new Treaty with Austria and agree to Priviledges for this Port, in order to draw away Advantages of American Trade from France and Spain, and to such a Treaty Holland may possibly, acquiesce, if not acceed.

The Port of Triest, enjoys a Liberty, without Limits, and the Court of Vienna is anxious to make its Commerce flourish. Situated however as it is, at the Bottom of the Gulph of Triest, the remotest Part of the Gulph of Venice, tedious and difficult as the Navigation of those seas is, We could make little Use of it, at any Time, and none at all, while this War continues. This Court would seize with Eagerness, the Advantages that are presented to her by the Independance of America, but an Interest more powerfull restrains her, and altho She is certainly attentive to this Revolution, there is Reason to believe she will be one of the last Powers to acknowledge our Independance. She is so far from being rich that she is destitute of the Means of making War, without subsidies as is proved by the Peace which has lately been made. She has Occasion for the Succours of France or of England, to put in Motion her numerous Armies. She conceives easily, that the Loss of Resources and of Credit of the English, has dissabled them to pay the enormous subsidies, which in former Times they have poured out into the Austrian Coffers. She sees therefore, with a Secret Mortification, that she shall be hereafter more at the Mercy of France, who may choose her Ally, and prefer at her Pleasure, either Austria or Prussia, while neither Vienna nor Berlin, will be able, as in Times past, to choose between Paris and London, Since the latter has lost her past oppulence and pecuniary Ressources.

It is our Duty to remark these great Changes in the system of Mankind which have already happened in Consequence of the American War. The Allienation of Portugal from England, the Peace of Germany and that between Petersbourg and Constantinople, by all which Events England has lost and France gained Such a superiority of Influence and Power, are owing entirely to the blind Diversion of that Policy and Wealth which the English might have still enjoyed, from the Objects of their true Interest and Honour to the ruinous American War.

The Court of Berlin, flatters herself, that the Connections, which have heretofore so long united France and Prussia, will renew themselves sooner or later. This system is more natural, than that which subsists at this Day. The King of Prussia, may then wait without Anxiety, the Consequences of the present Revolution, because it tends to increase the Ressources of his natural Ally. The jealousy between the Emperor and the King of Prussia, and that between the Houses of Bourbon and Austria, are a natural Tye between France and Prussia. The Rivalry between France and Great Britain, is another Motive too natural and too permanent for the former to suffer the King of Prussia to be long the Ally of the latter. One of the favourite Projects of Prussia, that of rendering the Port of Embden a Place of flourishing Trade, interests him more powerfully in our Independance. Silesia, one of his best Provinces, has already felt the Influence of it, and, sensible of the Force that Empires derive from Commerce, he is earnestly desirous to see it introduced between America and his states, which gives ground to believe, that as Austria will be one of the last, so Prussia, will be one of the first to acknowledge our Independance, an Opinion, which is rendered more probable, by the Answer which was given by the Compte De Schulemberg, to Mr. A. Lee. And the Influence of the King of Prussia in the United Provinces, which is greater than that of any other Power, arising from his great military Force, the Vicinity of his Dominion and his near Relation to the stadholder, and the Prince of Brunswick, is an additional Motive with Us to cultivate his Friendship.

The Electorate of Saxony, with a fruitful soil, contains a numerous and industrious People, and most of the Commerce, between the East and West of Europe passes through it. The Fairs of Leipzic, have drawn considerable Advantages for these four Years from our Trade. This Power will see with Pleasure, the Moment which shall put the last Hand to our Independance.

The Rest of Germany, excepting Hamborough and Bremen, has no Means of opening a direct Commerce with Us. With the latter, We can have no Connection at present, in the former all the maritime Commerce of the lower Germany, is transacted. Here We shall have Occasion soon to establish an Agent or Consul.

Poland, depopulated by War, and a vicious Government, reduced by a shamefull Treaty to two thirds of her ancient Dominion; destitute of Industry and Manufactures, even of the first Necessity; has no Occasion for the Productions of America. Dantzic sees her ancient Prosperity diminish every day. There is therefore little Probability of Commerce, and less of any political Connection between that Nation and Us.

Russia, Sweeden and Denmark, comprehended under the Denomination of the Northern Powers, have been thought by some to be interested in our Return to the Domination of Great Britain. Whether they consider themselves in this Light or not, their late Declarations against the Right of England to interrupt their Navigation, and their Arming for the Protection of their Commerce, on the Ocean and even in the English Channel, are unequivocal Proofs of their Opinion concerning the Right, in our Contest, and of their Intentions not to interfere against Us. It is very true that the Objects of Commerce, which they produce, are in many Respects the Same, with those of America, yet if We consider that We shall have Occasion to purchase from them large Quantities of Hemp and Sail Cloth, and that our Productions of Timber, Pitch, Tar and Turpentine, are less profitable with Us, without Bounties, than some other Branches of Labour, it is not probable that We shall lower the Price of these Articles, in Europe so much as some Conjecture, and consequently our increased Demand upon those Countries for several Articles will be more than a Compensation to them, for the small Loss they may sustain, by a trifling Reduction in the Price of those Articles. It is not probable that the Courts of Petersbourg Stockholm and Copenhagen, have viewed with perfect Indifference the present Revolution. If they have been apprehensive of being hurt by it in some Respects, which however I think must have been a Mistaken Apprehension, Yet the Motive of humbling the Pride of the English, who have endeavoured to exercise their Domination even over the northern Seas, and to render the Sweedish and Danish Flagg, dependant on theirs, has prevailed over all others, and they are considered in Europe, as having given their Testimony against the English in this War.

Italy, a Country which declines every day, from its ancient Prosperity offers few Objects to our Speculations. The Priviledges of the Port of Leghorn, nevertheless, may render it usefull to our ships, when our Independance shall be acknowledged by Great Britain. If We once flattered ourselves, that the Court of Vienna might receive an American Minister, We were equally in Error respecting the Court of the Grand Duchy of Tuscany, where an Austrian Prince reigns, who receives all his Directions from Vienna in such a manner, that he will probably never receive any Person in a public Character, untill the Chief of his House, shall have set him the Example.

The King of the two Sicilies, is in the Same Dependance on the Court of Madrid, and We may depend upon it, he will conform himself to all that she shall suggest to him. This Prince has already ordered the Ports of his Dominions to be open to American Vessells public and private, and has ordered his Ambassador at Paris to apply to your Commissioners for a Description of the American Flagg, that our Vessells might be known and receive no Molestation, upon their Appearance, in his Harbours.

The Court of Rome, attached to ancient Customs, will be one of the last to acknowledge our Independance, if We were to solicit for it. But Congress will probably never send a Minister to his Holiness who can do them no service, upon Condition of receiving a Catholic Legate or Nuncio in Return, or in other Words an ecclesiastical Tyrant, which it is to be hoped the united States will be too wise ever to admit into their Territories.

The States of the King of Sardinia, are poor and their Commerce is very small. The little Port of Villa Franca, will probably See few American Vessells, nor will there be any close Relations either commercial or political between this Prince and Us.

The Republic of Genoa, is Scarcely known at this Day, in Europe but by those Powers, who borrow Money. It is possible that some Small Sums might be obtained here, if Congress could fall upon Means of insuring a punctual Payment of Interest in Europe.

Venice heretofore so powerfull, is reduced to a very inconsiderable Commerce, and is in an entire state of Decay.

Switzerland is another Lender of Money, but neither her Position nor her Commerce, can Occasion any near Relation with Us.

Whether there is any Thing in these Remarks, worth the Trouble of reading them, I shall submit to the Wisdom of Congress, and subscribe my self with the highest Consideration, Your most obedient and most humble servant.

John Adams

"LEFT SPRAWLING IN THE MIRE"

To James Lovell

My dear Sir   Braintree Septr. 10. 1779

By the last Post, I had the Pleasure of yours of August 20 and 24. It was not for Want of Affection, that I did not write particularly to you and to many other Gentlemen, but from Want of Time. And since my Arrival to this Time, I have been obliged to go to Boston, Cambridge &c., so often, my good old Town of Braintree having taken it into their Heads, upon my Arrival, to put me into the Convention, that I have not been able to write, excepting on the 13 of Aug. inclosing some Copies of Letters which I wish to hear you have received.

You tell me, that you send me three Gazettes, which you desire me to inclose to A. Lee: but I find but two Gazettes and in neither of them is there a Word relative to the subject You mention.

You say too, that you will send me, a Part of the Report of a Committee of 13 relative to me. But in the Journal you inclose, 19th to 24 July, there is nothing like it.

In a late Letter of yours to W. You quote a Letter to H. which says that I did not succeed extravagantly in France, because I attached myself to L. the Madman. Does Congress receive such Evidence as this? Anonimous Letters, from Frenchmen to Frenchmen? or even from Americans to Americans? do they encourage this? Do they expose the Characters of their servants so much? Do they encourage foreign Consuls or even Ministers to attack the Characters of their Ministers abroad with such Weapons? Do they permit, foreign Ministers, and even Consuls, or commercial agents to become Partisans for or against Persons or systems? Mr. H's Master will not encourage him in it, I am well perswaded? and Mr. Holker May depend upon it, his Master or rather his Masters' Master shall know it, if he does make himself busy in Party Matters. I wish to know whether this letter was from Monthieu or Chaumont, or from whom? If the Latter, I shall make you laugh: if the former, Swear. I hope it was from neither.

However, I hope my Countrymen, will believe the King, whose sentiments of me and my Conduct, are certified to me, by the Comte De Vergennes in the Letters I inclosed to you the 13 of August, rather sooner, than the anonimous Correspondent of Mr. H. The Chevalier de la Luzerne, and Mr. Marbois, will inform you, if you ask them, what my Character was in France, although I am perswaded, they will never be Party Men. I know they dare not, for they have positive Instructions against it from the King.

In your Letter of the 20th, you assure me in strong Terms that "I have not an Enemy, amongst you." I am very Sure, there is no Man there who has any just Cause, to be my personal Enemy: But I think there must be many, in political Opposition to me. By the Hint you give of Iz's over heat, I dont know what to guess. Is it possible that Iz. should have written, to my Disadvantage? It is very true, that I thought him, sometimes imprudent, and that I uniformly and firmly refused to have any Concern in the Dispute between him and F. either before or after my Arrival in France: But I always told him this and my Reasons for it, so frankly and I always preserved with him and he with me, So friendly a personal Acquaintance, that altho I am very sensible he thinks I ought to have inserted myself more in their Quarrells, yet I think it is impossible, he should have written against me. However I thought him too hot, and therefore it is very probable he thought me too cool. Reasonable Men will judge.

I never heard in my Life, of any Misunderstanding among any of the Commissioners, that I can recollect, untill my Arrival at Bourdeaux. I had not been on shore an Hour before I learn'd it. When I arrived at Paris I found that it had arrived to a great Hight. Each Party endeavoured, to get me to inquire into the subjects of their Quarrells, and to join them. But I refused to have any Thing to do with their personal Disputes, and determined to treat every one of them as the Representative of the united states, to endeavour to cool and soften their Animosities as far as I could, and in all public Questions, impartially to give my Judgment according to Justice and good Policy. These Maxims, I invariably pursued, and I could challenge any of them, of any side to say that I ever deviated from them.

If you recollect, what has been done—that I was struck, in an instant in the sight of all Europe and America out of political Existence, that the scaffold, was cutt away, and I left sprawling in the mire, that not a Word was said to me—that I was neither desired nor directed to Stay or go—that I was never impowerd to draw a farthing of Money, to subsist me in Europe or even to pay the Expences of my Journey to a seaport—nor for my Passage home. That Dr. F. was not even authorized to advance a shilling for me. That he is Strictly culpable for doing it, altho he genteelly ran the risque. That the World was left to conjecture, what had brought upon me this Vengeance of my sovereign: whether it was for Gambling in the stocks: whether it was for forming commercial Combinations for my private Interest in all the seaport Towns in France, and in all the states of America; or whether it was for Treason against my Country, or Selling her Interest for Bribes. And all this after, I had undertaken to obey the Commands of Congress, at many Hazards of my Life and Liberty, Commands unsolicited by me, and given when I was absent: I think you must reconsider your Opinion concerning my Friends and Enemies in Congress. However, I shall not whine to Congress much less storm in News Papers, concerning the personal Treatment of me—unless I should be driven to the Necessity of a candid Appeal to the World. This would oblige me to lay open So many Things and Characters that had better be concealed that such Necessity must be very evident before I shall venture upon it. I dont dread however, for myself, nor much for the publick, taking Mr. D in his own Way but I should go a little deeper than Mr. Paine did. But it is a melancholly Consideration, and of a very dangerous and destructive Tendency, that so many Characters, as meritorious as any that ever served this Continent, should be immolated not to Divinities but to a Gang of Pedlars. Write me, when you can & believe me your F.

I thank you, for your kind Attention to my dear Portia, in my Absence, but your Rogueries are so bewitching that I should, have some hesitation about trusting you nearer together, than Philadelphia and Braintree.

NEGOTIATIONS IN FRANCE

To Elbridge Gerry

Dear Sir   Braintree Septr. 11. 1779
Early last Fall, in Conversation with Several Gentlemen, who are acquainted with Ministers of State, I laboured to convince them of the Policy and Necessity of sending Strong Reinforcements to the Compte D'Estaing. Mr. Chaumont particularly, coming into my Chamber, one Morning in his Way to Versailles, I begged him to mention it to the Compte De Vergennes, and Mr. De Sartine and endeavoured to possess him with my Reasons. On his Return he told me he had done it, and that they had hearkened to him attentively. About the same Time I had a long Conversation with Mr. Garnier, late secretary to the French Embassy in England, who told me soon

afterwards that he had been to Versailles on Purpose to present my Reasoning to the Ministry and that they had heard him, with Pleasure. Soon afterwards I met Mr. Genet, who is the first Comis of the Office of foreign Affairs, at Mr. Izards. I began a Conversation with him, upon the same subject, and entered into the Reasons at large. Both these Gentlemen, I mean Genet and Izard appeared pleased with the Conversation. A few days afterwards I had a Letter from Genet, in which he informed me, that he had been impressed upon Reflection on what I had said to him, with such a sense of its Importance, that he had waited on Mr. De Sartine, and the Compte De Vergennes, the next Morning to propose it to them, that he had been very patiently heard by them, and desired to state his Reasons in Writing, in order to which he desired my Assistance. Upon considering the matter, I thought, that if I should enter into a Correspondence with a Comis, upon this subject alone, instead of proposing it, to my Colleagues, and joining with them, it would not have so much Weight, at Court; it would excite Jealousies in my Colleagues, and be against the Maxim by which I had invariably conducted My self, to do nothing with out consulting them.

Instead therefore of answering Genets Letter, I applied my self to get my Colleagues to join me, in a direct Application to Court. I proposed it to them. Mr. Lee entered into it with Zeal, Dr. F. with Moderation. I desired Mr. Lee to draw up, a Letter. He did, it was a very handsome one, but short. I told him I thought We had better be more particular, in our Reasons. He agreed, and desired me to attempt a Draught. I took a Time, and wrote a Treatise, which I shewed my Colleagues. They said that the Observations were very well, but too long for a Minister of State to read. I thought so too, and desired Dr. F. to take the Letter Book as he had an happy faculty of Writing shortly and clearly, and make a Draught. He took the Book, and after some short time, returned it with a few Corrections to my Treatise, saying that upon reading it again he thought it would do very well, and that it was not worth while to make a new Draught. However I thought the Length of it, would weaken it, and it was too hastily and incorrectly written. I therefore undertook to make a new Draught, Copy of which I send you. It was agreed to by my Colleagues, signed by all three of Us, sent to Court, and answered by the Compte De Vergennes, that it contained Matters of great Importance, and should be considered in due time.

Whether these Negotiations had any Influence at Court, I cant say, but it is certain that the Compte De Grass, was sent in December, with one Reinforcement to the Compte D'Estaing, and Mr. De la Motte Piquet, in the spring with another, besides some other scattering ships, and if the Compte D'Estaing is now upon this Coast, this fact may be another Commentary on the Letter.

On the first Arrival of the Marquis De la Fayette in Paris, I made him a Visit and finding him alone, had two Hours Conversation with him, in which I entered into all these Things, and had the Pleasure to find him well acquainted with our Affairs, and heartily disposed to serve Us. He told me, he would represent every one, of my Arguments as from himself to the Ministry, which was what I desired, because I knew that his Character was so high and he was so beloved at Court, that he would be always there, and constantly in Conversation on our affairs. The next Morning however, fearing he might forget, or not be perfectly possessed of my Meaning, I wrote him the Letter, Copy of which is inclosed, which he has since told me in Conversation he approved in every Part, and would represent at Court, and by his answer to my Letter, a little before I sailed, he told me, he had been constantly representing and had in some Measure succeeded.

I send these Things to you in Confidence—you will not expose me. I would not appear to arrogate to my self what belongs to others, nor would I wish to be thought by you and my other Friends to have been idle and Useless. As to being idle the public Letter Book, which is almost all in my Hand Writing, will sufficiently shew that I was not so.

You can have no adequate Idea of the Difficulty We had in doing Business, while We acted together. But although it was become necessary to appoint one Minister alone at that Court, it is still necessary to go farther, to appoint a secretary to the Commission, and to give the Management of all maritime and commercial Affairs to a Consul, to reside at Nantes. There is a Gentleman in Paris, whose Name I will venture to mention to you, Edmund Jennings Esqr., Councillor at Law of Maryland.

This Gentleman appears to me, to have Such Abilities, such extensive Knowledge, and so much Candor and Moderation, that I cannot but think he would be very usefull as secretary to the Commission. And I would fain hope he would accept it. He is not upon bad Terms with F. nor too much an Idolator of him, which is exactly the Character that a Secretary to the Commission ought to have, in Relation to the Minister. There are Gentlemen in Congress who know him. Mr. D's Wish is to have Dr. Bancroft made Secretary. If this should happen, America ought to retire and weep. F's Desire, no doubt would be to have his Grandson, but he is too young and too nearly connected. I rely upon your Discretion to make Use of this Letter only for the public Good, and am with great Affection your Frd   John Adams

"MY PRINCIPLES ARE NOT IN FASHION"

To Benjamin Rush

Dear Sir   Braintree Septr. 19. 1779
    I had the Pleasure of yours of August 19, by the last Post, and thank you for your kind Congratulations on my Return. You judge right, when you Suppose, that I cannot be idle, but my Industry will probably be directed, in a different manner, in future. My Principles are not in Fashion. I may be more usefull here, as you observe, than in the Cabinet of Louis the 16. But let me tell you, that that Cabinet, is of great Importance, and that there ought to be Somebody there, who knows Somewhat of the Affairs of America, as well as Europe, and who will take the Pains to think, and to advise that Cabinet, with all proper Delicacy, in certain Circumstances.
    I have little to Say about the Time and manner of my being Superceeded. Let those reflect upon them selves, who are disgraced by it, not I. Those who did it, are alone disgraced by it. The Man who can shew a long Series of disinterested Services to his Country, cannot be disgraced even by his Country. If she attempts it, she only brings a Stain upon her own Character and makes his Glory the more illustrious.

We have Cause to congratulate ourselves, on the favourable Appearance of Affairs in Europe and America. There is not one Symptom in Europe against Us. Yet I must own to you, that I think France and Spain are yet to be convinced, of the true Method of conducting this War. It is not by besieging Gibralter nor invading Ireland, in my humble Opinion, but by sending a clear Superiority of naval Power into the American Seas, by destroying or captivating the British Forces here by Sea and Land, by taking the West India Islands and destroying the British Trade, and by affording Convoys to Commerce between Europe and America, and between America and the french and Spanish Islands, that this War is to be brought to a Speedy Conclusion, happy for Us, and glorious as well as advantageous to our Allies.

These were the Objects of all my Negotiations, and I dare hazard all, upon the good Policy of them. I fear that these Ideas, will now be forgotten: I cannot but wish that Congress would give positive Instructions to their Minister, nay that they would make a direct Application themselves to their Ally, to this Purpose. Mr. Gerry can shew you, in Confidence, some Papers upon the subject.

I have a great Curiosity to know, the History of the political Proceedings, within and out of Doors, last Winter. I confess myself, unable to comprehend it. I am more puzzled at the Conduct of those who ought to have been my Friends than at any Thing else. However I have not Lights enough to form a Judgment.

You Speak French So perfectly, and love good Men so much, that I wish you to be acquainted with the Chevalier De la Luzerne, and Mr. Marbois. Those Gentlemen were making Enquiry after a certain Letter, that you was very partial to. I enclose it to you and request you to give it them from me, with my most affectionate and respectfull Compliments.

I am with much Affection, your Friend & sert

John Adams

FRANKLIN'S SHORTCOMINGS

To Thomas McKean

My dear sir   Braintree Septr. 20. 1779

It is a long Time, Since I had the Pleasure to see you, but my Esteem is not at all diminished. None of Us have any Thing to boast of in these Times, in Respect to the Happiness of Life. You have been in disagreable Scænes no doubt—mine have been much worse than I expected.

I never heard of any Jealousy, Envy or Malevolence, among our Commissioners, at Paris, untill my Arrival at Bourdeaux. Judge of my surprise, Grief and Mortification, then, when I heard at Bourdeaux, and found on my Arrival at Paris, the Heat and Fury to which it had arisen. Both Sides most earnestly besieged me, in order to get me to join their Party, but I Saw the only Part a Man who had either Conscience or Honour could take, in my Situation, was to join neither. Accordingly I invariably and firmly refused to have any Thing to do with their Disputes, before my Arrival, or after it, any farther than they might, unavoidably be intermixed, with the public Questions, in which my Office obliged me to give an Opinion, and then to give it impartially for the public Good. I accordingly lived, not only in Peace but in Friendship to all Appearance, with both Sides. If there was any Animosity, in either against me, personally, it was very artfully concealed from me, and certainly never had any just Cause. Since my Arrival here, I am informed that I have been honoured with a little of the Ill humour of both sides, and I beg your Assistance in Congress, that I may be informed of the Particulars as I have requested.

Congress have done the only Thing that could dissolve the Charm that is left one alone. An opposition in Parliament, in an Assembly, in a senate, in Congress is highly usefull and necessary to ballance Individuals, Bodies, and Interests one against another, to bring the Truth to Light and Justice to prevail. But an opposition in a foreign Embassy in the Circumstances of this Country and of Europe, is Ruin. There can be no secrecy, no Confidence, where such an opposition takes Place, much less where there now are Such infernal Quarrells, as were between my Colleagues. It would be better to employ a single Man of sense, even although he should be as selfish and interested as is possible consistent with Fealty to his Country, than three virtuous Men of greater Abilities, any two of whom should be at open Variance with each other. It would be better to employ a single Stockjobber, or Monopolizer. It is better still no doubt to employ one Man of Virtue and Ability.

I presume Congress intend to appoint a secretary to the Commission, and Consuls for the Management of Commercial and maritime matters. It is highly necessary. Franklin is a Wit and a Humourist, I know. He may be a Philosopher, for what I know, but he is not a sufficient Statesman, he knows too little of American Affairs or the Politicks of Europe, and takes too little Pains to inform himself of Either. He is too old, too infirm too indolent and dissipated, to be sufficient for the Discharge of all the important Duties of Ambassador, Secretary, Admiral, Commercial Agent, Board of War, Board of Treasury, Commissary of Prisoners, &c. &c. &c. as he is at present in that Department, besides an immense Correspondence, and Acquaintance, each of which would be enough for the whole Time of the most active Man in the Vigour of Youth.

Yet such is his Name on both Sides the Water, that it is best, perhaps that he should be left there. But a secretary and Consuls should be appointed to do the Business, or it will not be done, or if done it will not be done by him, but by busy People who insinuate themselves into his Confidence without either such Heads or Hearts as Congress should trust.

I took my Pen, chiefly to pay my Respects to you, but it ran insensibly into Politicks, in which the public is so much Interested, that I will neither blot, nor alter.

I am, with great Esteem and Respect sir, your most obedient servant   John Adams

PLANS FOR RETURNING TO EUROPE

To Elbridge Gerry

Secret as the Grave.

Mon cher Ami   Braintree Octr. 18 1779

Looking over your Letter again, I find several Things unanswered. I should be Sorry to think that Mr. D. was the only vote against me. I had rather believe it was Some other State, than that this Gentleman voted vs. from a personal Pique founded on so futile an Affair, So innocently intended and so unlukily divulged, as the only semblance of anything personal between me and him. In public Questions I never differed from that Gentleman in my Opinion, without carrying my Point, except in the 2d Petition, and Time has discovered that in this as well as all others, in which I differd from him I was right and he wrong. I had not then and never had since any personal Ill will or Dislike to that Gentleman, nor by the unluky Expression did I mean to express that he had not great Ingenuity, and a good Heart. But his Connections, or preconcieved Opinions at that time appeard to me to have drawn him from that great, masterly and daring System, that the Times appeared to me to make indispensible, and he had Influence enough at that time with one state S.C to carry the Point by a bare Majority, to the great Injury of the Cause, in my Anxiety and Mortification upon that Occasion to a bosom friend in Confidence, my Passions broke out into that ridiculous Expression, which I was then and have been ever since very sorry for—enough of this however.

I thank you for the History of my first Appointment, which gives me much Satisfaction, as a Gentleman Mr. B. Deane, wrote something by me to Dr. B, from Mr. Hancock which had given me some Uneasiness—that Mr. H. told him he was extreamly sorry Mr. D. was recalled—that Congress did not do it—that it was done after the Members were withdrawn and Congress very thin. But I find I was appointed by seven states, which is enough to remove this Imputation. I am glad I was absent, and more glad still that Mr. S. Adams was so—and more glad than all the rest that he was against my going. I have my Reasons. You know, if any Man knows, and I Swear that no human Being knows the Contrary, that I never solicited, this nor any other Employment abroad. If I had not refused to be nominated when F., D. and Lee were first appointed, it would have been because the four New England states, Virginia, Georgia, and I believe New Jersey, could not have made a Vote. But I refused as a whole Clubb knows, and insisted on Deane, and A. Lee. In F we all then agreed. If I had not declined when W. Lee and Is were appointed and when R. H. Lee nominated me, I believe there is no doubt I should have been chosen. But in Truth I was never very desirous of exposing myself, to the sea and the Ennemy, and had too much Diffidence of my own Qualifications to solicit this Honour. I have great Reason to believe, however, that I should have been nominated and appointed at different times, that I can recollect if it had not been for my Name sake. His motives are easier guessed than expressed. So much for this. But altho I have never before solicited, suffrages, I will now begin. I suspect that I shall go to France and live there, without much Negociation with England for some time, not in Idleness I promise you, for I am now as confident that I can render important services to my Country in Europe as I once was diffident of it. My Request is, that in Case there should be no Business to do as Negotiator with England, and in Case you should send to Holland or Prussia, that you would employ me to one of those Places, without any Additional salary, or Emoluments unless it should Occasion Additional Expences to be allowed by Congress. Or if there should be a Vacancy, in France or Spain, that I may fill it up—unless you think it is necessary that I should attend only to England and wait her Motions, in which Case I shall be content. I said before and repeat, that I dont mean to have double salaries or any Additional Emoluments. But I hate to live upon the public Bread without earning it, with the sweat of my Brow.

I must confess myself, very nearly of your Opinion in all the Articles of your Political Creed excepting as to the Recall of Dr. Franklin. I know as well as Dr. L. or Mr. Iz. every Thing that is to be said for this Measure, but his Name is so great in Europe and America and the People have rested upon him in their own Minds so long, however erroneously, it would take so much Time and Pains to let the People into the Grounds, Reasons and Motives of it, that I have ever hitherto hesitated at it.

The Recall of Dr. Lee and Mr. Izard, will give them Opportunity and Provocation, I suppose to go great Lengths in laying open foreign Affairs. And if they are restrained by that Delicacy Moderation and Discretion which ought to characterize, foreign Ministers from these Infant States, I shall be happy.

My dear Friend, there has been a kind of Fatality that has attended, the Representation of the Mass, from the Beginning. Her Delegates never stood by one another, like those of other States. There is a Jealousy if not an Envy, you know against her, which has appeared to me to endeavour to take Advantages against her, and her Advocates. I could mention innumerable Instances. In little Things this appears as well as in great. Let me mention some that are Personal to myself, in perfect Confidence to you insisting at the same time that you never shew this Letter to any living Being.

Silas Deane is but of Yesterday and of Nothing in this Cause in Comparison of me. I was known in Europe and celebrated as a Writer, in this Controversy vs. G.B more than fourteen Years ago. S. Ds Name was never heard in it, six years ago. I had been elected every Year with all most Unanimous Votes by a great state, D. was left out by an almost unanimous Vote by a middling state. In the first Commission S.D. was arranged before A. Lee. But when my Commission was made out, I was placed after A. Lee. Lee was a young student in Law, after being a Phicician and a Preceptor to Ld. Shelbournes Children, just beginning to open Cases at the Bar under the Auspices of Mr. Dunning. I had been a Barrister at Law from the year 1761, had been in the fullest Practice for fifteen Years at the Bar; had been Chief Justice of the Massachusetts Bay, by an unanimous Vote of Council to my Commission, had been in Congress from the Beginning, had been President of the Board of War from its Creation, had been long a Member and sometime President of your Committee of Appeals in maritime Causes, had been upon that Committee which laid the foundation of the Navy, and been on allmost all the Committees for establishing disciplining and healing the Army, had been on the Committee for declaring Independency, and that for preparing a Treaty with France, a Measure that you know I was forced, with your Aid to push aganst all the great Folks in Congress, even the deified Franklin. Yet I was placed in the Commission after Mr. Lee.

Is it possible, sir that the Massachusetts Bay, should ever be respected, or her Rights respected if the Men she most respects are thus to be slighted.

Is it possible that Congress should be respected, if she suffers those Men upon whom she has as her Records show most depended from the Beginning, those Men who have formed and disciplined her Navy and Army, who have supported her Independance, who have promoted and formed her Alliances, thus to be postponed.

In the present Instance, Mr. Jay is made Minister Plenipotentiary, I Commissioner. This no doubt is done to give Mr. Jay Rank of me, and a Title above me, in order to maintain the superiority of New York above the Massachusetts Bay. Mr. Jays Name was never heard till 1774, mine was well known in Politicks in 1764.

These Things are of more Importance in Europe than here to the Public, but these are of too much here. If the Mass. is to be made the Butt and Sport in this Manner you will soon see it abandoned by all Men of Spirit, or you will see it, break the Union, for myself I care Nothing at all, for my Children I care but little for these Things, but for the public I care much. It is really important that Congress should not dishonour their own Members, it is really important that the Delegates of Mass Bay should support each other's Honour and Characters, which never can be done if such little stigmas are suffered to be fixed upon them, so unjustly. It is really important that Congress should not dishonour, the Man in one Moment upon whom they confer in the same Moment the most important Commission for ought I know which they ever issued. I could return to my Practice at the Bar, and make Fortunes for my Children and be happier, and really more respected, than I can in the hazardous, tormenting Employments into which they have always put me. I can be easy, even under the Marks of Disgrace they put upon me, but they may depend upon it they either mistake their own Interest in putting me into these

Employments, or in putting these Brands upon me—one or the other.

I am not at all Surprized at your Impatience under the Reflections you mention. I had heard an hint of them, with great Regret. But I am sure, they must be unjust, and that they have made no Impressions here. You stand on sure ground that of eternal Justice and Truth in the Vote about me, and are very far from being chargeable with a Fault in the other Votes, altho I cannot say I should have voted with you in every one of them, I mean for recalling F. and L. Yet there are so many weighty Arguments for them that I cannot blame you.

It has been reported in Europe that Mr. Deane laid before Congress, a Testimony from the King of France in his own Hand Writing, highly in favour of Mr. Deane. This was so extraordinary, so out of all the Rules of the Court and Maxims of the Monarchy that it was disbelieved. I wish you would inform me of the Fact, and send me a Copy, if there is such an original.

ACCEPTING A NEW DIPLOMATIC COMMISSION

To Henry Laurens

My dear Sir   Braintree Octr. 25. 1779

Your Favour of the fourth of the Month, gave me great Pleasure. But I am afraid that you and Some others of my Friends felt more for me, in the Aukward Situation, you mention, than I did for myself, 'tho I cannot Say, I was wholly insensible. I could not help laughing a little at the figure I cutt, to be sure. I could compare it, to nothing, but Shakespeares Idea of Ariel, wedged by the Waist, in the Middle of a rifted Oak, for I was Sufficiently Sensible that it was owing to an unhappy Division in Congress, and Pains enough were taken to inform me, that one Side were for Sending me to Spain, and the other to Holland, So that I was flattered to find that neither Side had any decisive Objection against trusting me, and that the apparent Question was only, where? But I assure you, that all my Sprawling, Wriggling, and brandishing my Legs and Arms in the Air, like Ariel, never gave me half the

Pain, that the Picture of Congress in my Imagination at that time, excited. When I saw a certain Appeal to the People; that no Animadversion was made on it; that you resigned &c., Congress appeared to me to resemble a Picture in the Gallery of the C. De Vergennes and I trembled for the Union and safety of the states.

The Picture represents a Coach, with four Horses, running down a steep Mountain, and rushing on to the middle of a very high Bridge, over a large River. The Foundations of the whole Bridge, give Way, in a Moment, and the Carriage, the Horses, the Timbers, Stones and all, in a Chaos are falling through the Air down to the Water. The Horror of the Horses, the Coachman, the Footmen, the Gentlemen and Ladies in the Carriage, is Strongly painted in their Countenances and Gestures, as well as the Simpathy and Terror of others in Boats upon the River and many others on shore, on each side of the River.

That I was sent without any solicitation of mine, directly or indirectly, is certainly true; and I had such formidable Ideas of the Sea and of British Men of War, Such Diffidence of my own Qualifications to do service in that Way, and Such Uncertainty of the Reception I should meet, that I had little Inclination to Adventure. That I went against my pecuniary Interest is most certainly so, for I never yet served the public without loosing Money by it. I was not however, as you suppose kept unimployed. I had Business enough to do, as I could easily convince you. There is a great Field of Business there and I could easily shew you that I did my share of it. There is so much to do, and So much difficulty to do it well, that I rejoice with all my Heart to find a Gentleman, of such Abilities, Principles and Activity, as Coll. Laurens, without a Compliment, undoubtedly is, appointed to assist in it. I most Sincerely hope for his Friendship and an entire Harmony, with him, for which Reason, I should be very happy in his Company in the Passage, or in an Interview with him, as Soon as possible, in Europe. He will be, in a delicate situation, but not so much so, as I was, and plain sense, honest Intentions, and common Civility, will I think be sufficient to secure him and do much good.

Your kind Compliments on my Safe Return, and most honourable Re-Election, are very obliging.

I have received no Commission, nor Instructions, nor any particular Information of the Plan, but from the Advice and Information from you and Several others of my Friends at Philadelphia, and here, I shall make no Hesitation to say, that notwithstanding the Delicacy, and Danger of this Commission, I suppose, I shall accept it, without Hesitation, and trust Events to Heaven as I have been long used to do.

It is a Misfortune to me, to be deprived of the Pleasure of shaking Hands with you, at the Foot of Pens Hill, Eleven miles from Boston, where there lives a Lady, however, who desires me to present her best Respects, and ask the Favour of a Visit, when you come to Boston, that She may have an opportunity of Seeing a Gentleman, whose unshaken Constancy, does so much Honour and Such essential Service to his Country.

The Convulsions at Philadelphia, are very affecting and alarming but not entirely unexpected to me. The state of Parties and the Nature of their Government, have a long time given me disagreable Apprehensions. But I hope they will find some Remedy.

Methods will be found to feed the Army, but I know of none to cloath it, without Convoys to trade, which Congress, I think would do well to undertake, and perswade France and Spain, to undertake as soon as possible.

Your Packetts for your Friends in Europe, will give me Pleasure, and shall be forwarded with Care and dispatch. With great Truth and Regard, I am, sir, your Friend and servant

John Adams

The Report of a Constitution or Form of Government for the Commonwealth of Massachusetts

Agreed upon by the Committee—to be laid before the Convention of DELEGATES, assembled at CAMBRIDGE, on the First Day of *September*, A.D. 1779; and continued by Adjournment to the Twenty-eighth Day of *October* following.

To the Honorable the Convention of Delegates from the several Towns in the State of MASSACHUSETTS, appointed for the forming a new Constitution of Government for the said State.

GENTLEMEN,

YOUR Committee, in Pursuance of your Instructions, have prepared the Draught of a new Constitution of Government for this State; and now make Report of it: which is respectfully laid before you, in the following Pages, for your Consideration and Correction.

In the Name of the Committee,

JAMES BOWDOIN, Chairman.

A Constitution or Form of Government for
the Commonwealth of MASSACHUSETTS.

PREAMBLE.

THE end of the institution, maintenance and administration of government, is to secure the existence of the body-politic; to protect it; and to furnish the individuals who compose it, with the power of enjoying, in safety and tranquility, their natural rights, and the blessings of life: And whenever these great objects are not obtained, the people have a right to alter the government, and to take measures necessary for their safety, happiness and prosperity.

THE body politic is formed by a voluntary association of individuals: It is a social compact, by which the whole people covenants with each citizen, and each citizen with the whole people, that all shall be governed by certain laws for the common good. It is the duty of the people, therefore, in framing a

Constitution of Government, to provide for an equitable mode of making laws, as well as for an impartial interpretation; and a faithful execution of them, that every man may, at all times, find his security in them.

WE, therefore, the delegates of the people of Massachusetts, in general Convention assembled, for the express and sole purpose of framing a Constitution or Form of Government, to be laid before our Constituents, according to their instructions, acknowledging, with grateful hearts, the goodness of the Great Legislator of the Universe, in affording to this people, in the course of His providence, an opportunity of entering into an original, explicit, and solemn compact with each other, deliberately and peaceably, without fraud, violence, or surprize; and of forming a new Constitution of Civil Government, for themselves and their posterity; and devoutly imploring His direction in a design so interesting to them and their posterity, DO, by virtue of the authority vested in us, by our constituents, agree upon the following *Declaration of Rights, and Frame of Government*, as the CONSTITUTION of the COMMON-WEALTH of MASSACHUSETTS.

CHAPTER I
A DECLARATION of the RIGHTS of the Inhabitants of the Commonwealth of Massachusetts.

Art. I. ALL men are born equally free and independent, and have certain natural, essential, and unalienable rights: among which may be reckoned the right of enjoying and defending their lives and liberties; that of acquiring, possessing, and protecting their property; in fine, that of seeking and obtaining their safety and happiness.

II. IT is the duty of all men in society, publicly, and at stated seasons, to worship the SUPREME BEING, the great creator and preserver of the universe. And no subject shall be hurt, molested, or restrained, in his person, liberty, or estate, for worshiping GOD in the manner most agreeable to the dictates of his own conscience; or for his religious profession or sentiments; provided he doth not disturb the public peace, or obstruct others in their religious worship.

III. GOOD morals being necessary to the preservation of

civil society; and the knowledge and belief of the being of GOD, His providential government of the world, and of a future state of rewards and punishment, being the only true foundation of morality, the legislature hath therefore a right, and ought, to provide at the expence of the subject, if necessary, a suitable support for the public worship of GOD, and of the teachers of religion and morals; and to enjoin upon all the subjects an attendance upon their instructions, at stated times and seasons: Provided there be any such teacher, on whose ministry they can conscientiously and conveniently attend.

ALL monies, paid by the subject to the support of public worship, and of the instructors in religion and morals, shall, if he requires it, be uniformly applied to the support of the teacher or teachers of his own religious denomination, if there be such, whose ministry he attends upon: otherwise it may be paid to the teacher or teachers of the parish or precinct where he usually resides.

IV. THE people of this commonwealth have the sole and exclusive right of governing themselves, as a free, sovereign, and independent state; and do, and forever hereafter shall, exercise and enjoy every power, jurisdiction, and right, which are not, or may not hereafter, be by them expresly delegated to the United States of America, in Congress assembled.

V. ALL power residing originally in the people, and being derived from them, the several magistrates and officers of government, vested with authority, whether legislative, executive or judicial, are their substitutes and agents, and are at all times accountable to them.

VI. NO man, nor corporation or association of men, have any other title to obtain advantages, or particular and exclusive privileges, distinct from those of the community, than what arises from the consideration of services rendered to the public; and this title being in nature neither hereditary, nor transmissible to children, or descendents, or relations by blood, the idea of a man born a magistrate, law-giver, or judge, is absurd and unnatural.

VII. GOVERNMENT is instituted for the common good; for the protection, safety, prosperity and happiness of the people; and not for the profit, honor, or private interest of any one man, family, or class of men: Therefore the people alone have an incontestible, unalienable, and indefeasible right to institute government; and to reform, alter, or totally change the same, when their protection, safety, prosperity and happiness require it.

VIII. IN order to prevent those who are vested with authority from becoming oppressors, the people have a right, at such periods and in such manner as may be delineated in their frame of government, to cause their public officers to return to private life, and to fill up vacant places by certain and regular elections.

IX. ALL elections ought to be free; and all the male inhabitants of this commonwealth, having sufficient qualifications, have an equal right to elect officers, and to be elected for public employments.

X. EACH individual of the society has a right to be protected by it in the enjoyment of his life, liberty and property, according to standing laws. He is obliged, consequently, to contribute his share to the expence of this protection; to give his personal service, or an equivalent, when necessary: But no part of the property of any individual can, with justice, be taken from him, or applied to public uses, without his own consent, or that of the representative body of the people: In fine, the people of this commonwealth are not controulable by any other laws, than those to which their constitutional representative body have given their consent.

XI. EVERY subject of the commonwealth ought to find a certain remedy, by having recourse to the laws, for all injuries or wrongs which he may receive in his person, property or character: He ought to obtain right and justice freely, and without being obliged to purchase it; compleatly, and without any denial; promptly, and without delay; conformably to the laws.

XII. NO subject shall be held to answer for any crime or offence, untill the same is fully and plainly, substantially and formally, described to him: He cannot be compelled to accuse himself, or to furnish evidence against himself; and every subject shall have a right to be fully heard in his defence, by himself or his council, at his election; to meet the witnesses against him face to face, to produce all proofs that may be favourable to him; to require a speedy and public trial by an impartial jury of the country, without whose unanimous consent, or his own voluntary confession, he cannot finally be declared guilty, or sentenced to loss of life, liberty or property.

XIII. IN criminal prosecutions, the verification of facts in the vicinity where they happen, is one of the greatest securites of the life, liberty and property of the citizen.

XIV. NO subject of the commonwealth shall be arrested, imprisoned, despoiled, or deprived of his property, immunities or privileges, put out of the protection of the law, exiled, or deprived of his life, liberty or estate, but by the judgment of his peers or the law of the land.

XV. EVERY man has a right to be secure from all unreasonable searches and seizures of his person, his houses, his papers, and all his possessions. All warrants, therefore, are contrary to this right, if the cause or foundation of them be not previously supported by oath or affirmation; and if the order in the warrant to a civil officer, to make search in suspected places, or to arrest one or more suspected persons, or to seize their property, be not accompanied with a special designation of the persons or objects of search, arrest or seizure; and no warrant ought to be issued but in cases and with the formalities prescribed by the laws.

XVI. IN all controversies concerning property, and in all suits between two or more persons, the parties have a right to a trial by a jury; and this method of procedure shall be held sacred; unless, in causes arising on the high-seas, and such as relate to mariners wages, the legislature shall hereafter find it necessary to alter it.

XVII. THE people have a right to the freedom of speaking, writing and publishing their sentiments: The liberty of the press therefore ought not to be restrained.

XVIII. THE people have a right to keep and to bear arms for the common defence. And as in time of peace standing armies are dangerous to liberty, they ought not to be maintained without the consent of the legislature; and the military power shall always be held in an exact subordination to the civil authority, and be governed by it.

XIX. A FREQUENT recurrence to the fundamental principles of the constitution, and a constant adherence to those of piety, justice, moderation, temperance, industry and frugality, are absolutely necessary to preserve the advantages of liberty, and to maintain a free government: The people ought, consequently, to have a particular attention to all those principles, in the choice of their officers and representatives: And they have a right to require of their law-givers and magistrates, an exact and constant observance of them, in the formation and execution of the laws necessary for the good administration of the commonwealth.

XX. The people have a right, in an orderly and peaceable manner, to assemble to consult upon the common good; give instructions to their representatives; and to request of the legislative body by the way of addresses, petitions, or remonstrances, redress of the wrongs done them, and the grievances they suffer.

XXI. The power of suspending the laws, or the execution of the laws, ought never to be exercised but by the legislature, or by authority derived from it, to be exercised in such particular cases only as the legislature shall expresly provide for: and there shall be no suspension of any law for the private interest, advantage, or emolument, of any one man or class of men.

XXII. The freedom of deliberation, speech and debate in either house of the legislature, is so essential to the rights of the people, that it cannot be the foundation of any accusation or prosecution, action or complaint, in any other court or place whatsoever.

XXIII. The legislature ought frequently to assemble for the redress of grievances, for correcting, strengthening and confirming the laws, and for making new laws as the common good may require.

XXIV. No subsidy, charge, tax, impost or duties ought to be established, fixed, laid, or levied, under any pretext whatsoever, without the consent of the people or their representatives in the legislature.

XXV. Laws made to punish for actions done before the existence of such laws, and which have not been declared crimes by preceeding laws, are unjust, oppressive, and inconsistent with the fundamental principles of a free government.

XXVI. No man ought in any case or in any time, to be declared guilty of treason or felony by any act of the legislature.

XXVII. No magistrate or court of law shall demand excessive bail, or sureties, impose excessive fines, or inflict cruel or unusual punishments.

XXVIII. In time of peace, no soldier ought to be quartered in any house without the consent of the owner; and in time of war such quarters ought not to be made, but by the civil magistrate in a manner ordained by the legislature.

XXIX. No person can in any case be subjected to law martial, or to any penalties or pains, by virtue of that law, except those employed in the army or navy, and except the militia in actual service, but by authority of the legislature.

XXX. It is essential to the preservation of the rights of every individual, his life, liberty, property and character, that there be an impartial interpretation of the laws, and administration of justice. It is the right of every citizen to be tried by judges as free, impartial and independent as the lot of humanity will admit. It is therefore not only the best policy, but for the security of the rights of the people, and of every citizen, that the judges should hold their offices as long as they behave themselves well; and that they should have honorable salaries ascertained and established by standing laws.

XXXI. The judicial department of the State ought to be separate from, and independent of, the legislative and executive powers.

CHAPTER II.
The Frame of Government.

The people inhabiting the territory heretofore called the Province of Massachusetts-Bay, do hereby solemnly and mutually agree with each other, to form themselves into a free, sovereign, and independent body-politic or state, by the name of THE COMMONWEALTH OF MASSACHUSETTS.

In the government of the Commonwealth of Massachusetts, the legislative, executive, and judicial power, shall be placed in separate departments, to the end that it might be a government of laws and not of men.

SECTION I.

Art. I. The department of legislation shall be formed by two branches, *a Senate* and *House of Representatives*; each of which shall have a negative on the other.

They shall assemble once, on the last Wednesday in May, and at such other times as they shall judge necessary, every year; and shall be stiled, THE GENERAL COURT OF MASSACHUSETTS.

AND the first magistrate shall have a negative upon all the laws—that he may have power to preserve the independence of the executive and judicial departments.

II. THE General Court shall forever have full power and authority to erect and constitute judicatories and courts of record, or other courts, to be held in the name of the Commonwealth, for the hearing, trying, and determining of all manner of crimes, offences, pleas, processes, plaints, actions, matters, causes and things, whatsoever, arising or happening within the Commonwealth, or between or concerning persons inhabiting, or residing, or brought within the same; whether the same be criminal or civil, or whether the said crimes be capital or not capital, and whether the said pleas be real, personal, or mixt; and for the awarding and making out of execution thereupon: To which courts and judicatories, are hereby given and granted full power and authority from time to time to administer oaths or affirmations, for the better discovery of truth in any matter in controversy or depending before them.

III. AND further, full power and authority are hereby given and granted to the said General Court, from time to time, to make, ordain, and establish all manner of wholesome and reasonable orders, laws, statutes, and ordinances, directions and instructions, either with penalties or without; so as the same be not repugnant or contrary to this Constitution, as they shall judge to be for the good and welfare of this Commonwealth, and for the government and ordering thereof, and of the subjects of the same, and for the necessary support and defence of the government thereof; and to name and settle annually, or provide by fixed laws, for the naming and settling all civil officers within the said Commonwealth; such officers excepted, the election and constitution of whom are not hereafter in this Form of Government otherwise provided for; and to set forth the several duties, powers and limits of the several civil and military officers of this Commonwealth, and the forms of such oaths as shall be respectively administred unto them for the execution of their several offices and places, so as the same be not repugnant or contrary to this Constitution;

and also to impose fines, mulcts, imprisonments, and other punishments; and to impose and levy proportional and reasonable assessments, rates, and taxes, upon the persons of all the inhabitants of and residents within the said Commonwealth, and upon all estates within the same; to be issued and disposed of by warrant, under the hand of the Governor of this Commonwealth for the time being, with the advice and consent of the Council, for the public service, in the necessary defence and support of the government of the said Commonwealth, and the protection and preservation of the subjects thereof, according to such acts as are or shall be in force within the same; and to dispose of matters and things whereby they may be religiously, peaceably, and civilly governed, protected, and defended.

AND that public assessments may be made with equality, there shall be a valuation of estates within the Commonwealth taken anew once in every ten years at the least.

SECTION II.
SENATE.

I. THERE shall be annually elected by the freeholders and other inhabitants of this Commonwealth, qualified as in this Constitution is provided, forty persons to be Counsellors and Senators for the year ensuing their election, to be chosen in and by the inhabitants of the districts into which the Commonwealth may from time to time be divided by the General Court for that purpose: And the General Court, in assigning the numbers to be elected by the respective districts, shall govern themselves by the proportion of the public taxes paid by the said districts; and timely make known to the inhabitants of the Commonwealth, the limits of each district, and the number of Counsellors and Senators to be chosen therein; provided that the number of such districts shall be never more than sixteen nor less than ten.

AND the several counties in this Commonwealth shall, until the General Court shall determine it necessary to alter said districts, be districts for the choice of Counsellors and Senators (except that the counties of Dukes-County and Nantucket shall form one district for that purpose) and shall elect the following number for Counsellors and Senators, viz.

Suffolk	6	York	2
Essex	6	Dukes County and Nantucket	1
Middlesex	5		
Hampshire	4	Worcester	5
Plymouth	3	Cumberland	1
Barnstable	1	Lincoln	1
Bristol	3	Berkshire	2

II. THE Senate shall be the first branch of the legislature; and the Senators shall be chosen in the following manner, viz. There shall be a meeting on the first Monday in April annually, forever, of the inhabitants of all the towns in the several counties of this Commonwealth, to be called by the Selectmen, and warned in due course of law, at least seven days before the first Monday in April, for the purpose of electing persons to be Senators and Counsellors: And at such meetings every male person of twenty-one years of age and upwards, resident in such towns one year next preceeding the annual election of Senators, having a freehold estate within the Commonwealth, of the annual income of three pounds, or other real or personal estate of the value of sixty pounds, shall have a right to give in his vote for the Senators for the district.

THE Selectmen of the several towns shall preside at such meetings, and shall be under oath, as well as the Town-Clerk, to preside impartially, according to their best skill and judgment; and to make a just and true return.

THE Selectmen shall receive the votes of all the inhabitants of such towns qualified to vote for Senators, and shall sort and count them in open town-meeting, and in presence of the Town-Clerk, who shall make a fair record, in presence of the Selectmen, and in open town-meeting, of the name of every person voted for, and of the number of votes against his name; and a fair copy of this record shall be attested by the Selectmen and the Town-Clerk, and shall be sealed up, directed to the Secretary of the Commonwealth for the time being, with a superscription, expressing the purport of the contents thereof, and delivered by the Town-Clerk of such towns, to the Sheriff of the county in which such town lies, thirty days at least before the last Wednesday in May annually; or it shall be delivered into the Secretary's office seventeen days at least before the said last Wednesday in May; and the Sheriff of each county shall deliver all such certificates by him received into the Secretary's office seventeen days before the said last Wednesday in May.

AND the inhabitants of plantations unincorporated, qualified as this Constitution provides, who are or shall be empowered and required to assess taxes upon themselves toward the support of government, shall have the same privilege of voting for Counsellors and Senators in the plantations where they reside, as town inhabitants have in their respective towns; and the plantation-meetings for that purpose shall be held annually on the same first Monday in April, at such place in the plantations respectively, as the Assessors thereof shall direct; which Assessors shall have like authority for notifying the electors, collecting and returning the votes, as the Selectmen and Town-Clerks have in their several Towns by this Constitution. And all other persons living in places unincorporated (qualified as aforesaid) who shall be assessed to the support of government by the Assessors of an adjacent town, shall have the privilege of giving in their votes for Counsellors and Senators, in the town where they shall be assessed, and be notified of the place of meeting by the Selectmen of the town where they shall be assessed for that purpose accordingly.

III. AND that there may be a due convention of Senators on the last Wednesday in May annually, the Governor, with five of the Council, for the time being, shall, as soon as may be, examine the returned copies of such records; and fourteen days before the said day he shall issue his summons to such persons as shall appear to be chosen by a majority of voters, to attend on that day and take their seats accordingly: Provided nevertheless, that for the first year the said returned copies shall be examined by the President and five of the Council of the former Constitution of Government; and the said President shall, in like manner, issue his summons to the persons so elected, that they may take their seats as aforesaid.

IV. THE Senate, however, shall be the final judge of the elections, returns and qualifications of their own members; and shall, on the said last Wednesday in May annually, determine and declare who are elected by each district, to be Senators by a majority of votes: And in case there shall not appear to be the full number of Senators returned elected by a majority of votes for any district, the deficiency shall be supplied in the following manner, viz. The members of the House of Representatives, and such Senators as shall be declared elected, shall take the names of twice the number of Senators wanting, from those who shall be found to have the highest number of votes in such district, and not elected; and out of these shall elect, by ballot, a number of Senators, sufficient to fill up the vacancies in such district: And in this manner all such vacancies shall be filled up in every district of the Commonwealth; and in like manner all vacancies in the Senate, arising by death, removal out of the State, or otherwise, shall be supplied as soon as may be after such vacancies shall happen.

V. Provided nevertheless, that no person shall be capable of being elected as a Senator who is not of the christian religion, and seized in his own right of a freehold within this Commonwealth, of the value of three hundred pounds at least, and who has not been an inhabitant of this Commonwealth for the space of seven years, three of which immediately preceeding his election, and in the district for which he shall be chosen.

VII. The Senate shall have power to adjourn themselves, provided such adjournments do not exceed two days at a time.

VIII. The Senate shall choose its own President, appoint its own officers, and determine its own rules of proceedings.

IX. The Senate shall be a court with full authority to hear and determine all impeachments made by the House of Representatives, against any officer or officers of the Commonwealth, for misconduct and mal-administration in their offices. But previous to the trial of every impeachment, the members of the Senate shall respectively be sworn, truly and impartially to try and determine the charge in question, according to evidence. Their judgment, however, shall not extend further than to removal from office, and disqualification to hold or enjoy any place of honor, trust, or profit, under this Commonwealth: But the party so convicted, shall be, nevertheless, liable to indictment, trial, judgment, and punishment, according to the laws of the land.

SECTION III.
House of Representatives.

I. THERE shall be in the legislature of this Commonwealth, a representation of the people, annually elected, and founded in equality.

II. AND in order to provide for a representation of the citizens of this Commonwealth, founded upon the principle of equality, every corporate town, containing one hundred and fifty rateable polls, may elect one Representative: Every corporate town, containing three hundred and seventy-five rateable polls, may elect two Representatives: Every corporate town, containing six hundred rateable polls, may elect three Representatives; and proceeding in that manner, making two hundred and twenty-five rateable polls the mean increasing number for every additional Representative.

AND forever hereafter the least number of rateable polls necessary to entitle a corporate town to elect one Representative, when increased by the addition of a number equal to half the said least number shall be the mean increasing number of rateable polls for every additional Representative any corporate town may elect.

AND to prevent hereafter the House of Representatives from becoming unweildy, and incapable of debating, and deliberating by the great additions it would continually receive from the increasing settlement, and population of this Commonwealth, no corporate town shall, from and after the Year of our Lord one thousand seven hundred and ninety, be entitled to elect one Representative, unless it shall contain two hundred rateable polls; nor to elect two Representatives unless it shall contain five hundred rateable polls; nor to elect three Representatives unless it shall contain eight hundred rateable polls; and so proceeding in that manner, making by the aforesaid rule three hundred rateable polls the mean increasing number for every additional Representative. And every tenth year, from and after the said year of our Lord one thousand seven hundred and ninety, and until such time as the number of Representatives, which may be elected for this Commonwealth, shall not exceed the number of two hundred, the least number of rateable polls, which at that time any corporate town must contain to entitle it to elect one Representative: shall be increased by the addition of fifty; and the least number aforesaid, thus increased by the said addition, shall be the number of rateable polls any corporate town must contain to entitle it to elect one Representative: and the number of Representatives any corporate town may elect shall be regulated accordingly by the rules aforesaid.

THE freeholders and other inhabitants of this Commonwealth, qualified to vote for Representatives, living in corporate towns, which severally shall contain a less number of rateable polls than is necessary to entitle them respectively to elect one Representative, shall, nevertheless, have a right to associate with some town or towns adjoining, for the election of Representatives; and in such cases the voters thus united, shall have a right to elect the same number of Representatives as they would have done were they inhabitants of one corporate town; which Representatives may be elected out of either of the associated towns indifferently: And the legislature shall from time to time determine what towns shall thus associate, the manner of the association, and the method and manner of calling and conducting the meetings of the associated towns for the election of Representatives.

III. THE members of the House of Representatives shall be chosen by written votes; and no person shall be qualified, or eligible, to be a member of the said House, unless he be of the christian religion, and for one year at least next preceeding his election shall have been an inhabitant of, and have been seized in his own right of a freehold of the value of one hundred pounds within the town or towns he shall be chosen to represent; and he shall cease to represent the said town or towns, immediately on his ceasing to be a freeholder within the same.

IV. EVERY male person, being twenty-one years of age, and resident in any particular town in this Commonwealth for the space of one year next preceeding, having a freehold estate within the same town, of the annual income of three pounds, or other estate, real, or personal or mixt, of the value of sixty pounds, shall have a right to vote in the choice of a Representative or Representatives for the said town, or for the towns united as aforesaid.

V. THE members of the house of Representatives shall be chosen annually in the month of May, ten days at least before the last Wednesday of that month, from among the wisest, most prudent, and virtuous of the freeholders.

VI. THE house of Representatives shall be the Grand Inquest of this Commonwealth; and all impeachments made by them, shall be heard, and tried by the Senate.

VII. ALL money-bills shall originate in the house of Representatives; but the Senate may propose or concur with amendments, as on other bills.

VIII. THE house of Representatives shall have power to adjourn themselves; provided such adjournment shall not exceed two days at a time.

IX. NOT less than sixty members of the house of Representatives, shall constitute a quorum for doing business.

X. THE house of Representatives shall chuse their own Speaker, appoint their own officers, and settle the rules and orders of proceeding in their own house: They shall have authority to punish by imprisonment, every person who shall be guilty of disrespect to the house, in its presence, by any disorderly, or contemptuous behaviour; or by threatning or illtreating any of its members; or, in a word, by obstructing its deliberations; every person guilty of a breach of its privileges, in making arrests for debts, or by assaulting one of its members during his attendance at any session, or on the road, whether he be going to the house or returning home; in assaulting any one of its officers, or in disturbing him in the execution of any order, or procedure of the House; in assaulting or troubling any witness or other person, ordered to attend the House, in his way in going or returning, or in rescuing any person arrested by order of the House.

XI. THE Senate shall have the same powers in the like cases; and the Governor and Council shall have the same authority to punish in like cases. Provided that no imprisonment on the warrant or order of the Governor, Council, Senate, or House of Representatives, for either of the above-described offences, be for a term exceeding thirty days.

CHAPTER III.
Executive Power.

SECTION I.
Governor.

Art. I. THERE shall be a supreme executive Magistrate, who shall be stiled, THE GOVERNOR OF THE COMMONWEALTH OF MASSACHUSETTS; and whose Title shall be —HIS EXCELLENCY.

II. THE Governor shall be chosen annually; and no person shall be eligible to this office, unless at the time of his election, he shall have been an inhabitant of this Commonwealth for seven years next preceeding; and unless he shall at the same time be seized in his own right of a Freehold within the Commonwealth, of the value of One Thousand Pounds; and unless he shall be of the Christian Religion.

III. THOSE persons, who shall be qualified to vote for Senators and Representatives within the several towns of this Commonwealth, shall, at a meeting to be called for that purpose, on the first Monday of April annually, give in their votes for a Governor to the Selectmen, who shall preside at such meetings; and the Town-Clerk, in the presence and with the assistance of the Selectmen, shall, in open town-meeting, sort and count the votes, and form a list of the persons voted for, with the number of votes for each person against his name; and shall make a fair record of the same in the town books, and a public declaration thereof in the said meeting, and shall, in the presence of the inhabitants, seal up copies of the said list, attested by him and the Selectmen, and transmit the same to the Sheriff of the county thirty days at least before the last Wednesday in May; or shall cause returns of the same to be made to the office of the Secretary of the Commonwealth seventeen days at least before the said day, who shall lay the same before the Senate and the House of Representatives, on the last Wednesday in May, to be by them examined; and in case of an election by a majority of votes through the Commonwealth, the choice shall be by them declared and published: But if no person shall have a majority of votes, the House of Representatives shall, by ballot, elect two out of four persons who had the highest number of votes, if so many shall have been voted for, but if otherwise, out of the number voted for; and make return to the Senate of the two persons so elected; on which, the Senate shall proceed, by ballot, to elect one, who shall be declared Governor.

IV. THE person chosen Governor, and accepting the trust, shall, in the presence of the two Houses, and before he proceed to execute the duties of his office, make and subscribe the following declaration, and take the following oaths, to be administred by the President of the Senate: viz.—

I, A. B. being declared duly elected Governor of the Commonwealth of Massachusetts, do now declare, that I believe and profess the christian religion, from a firm persuasion of its truth; and that I am seized and possessed in my own right of the property required by law, as one qualification for that office.

I, A. B. do solemnly swear, that I bear faith and true allegiance to the Commonwealth of Massachusetts; that I will faithfully and impartially discharge and perform all the duties incumbent on me as a Governor of this Commonwealth, according to the best of my abilities and understanding, agreeably to the rules and regulations of the Constitution; and that I will not attempt or consent to a violation thereof. So help me GOD.

V. THE Governor shall have authority from time to time, at his discretion, to assemble and call together the Counsellors of this Commonwealth for the time being; and the Governor, with the said Counsellors, or five of them at least, shall and may, from time to time, hold and keep a Council, for the ordering and directing the affairs of the Commonwealth according to law.

VI. THE Governor, with advice of Council, shall have full power and authority, in the recess of the General Court, to prorogue the same from time to time, not exceeding ninety days in any one recess of the said Court; and during the Session of the said Court, to adjourn or prorogue it to any time the two Houses shall desire, and to dissolve the same at their request, or on the Wednesday next preceeding the last Wednesday in May; and to call it together sooner than the time to which it may be adjourned or prorogued, if the welfare of the Commonwealth shall require the same.

VII. IN cases of disagreement between the two Houses, with regard to the time of adjournment or prorogation, the Governor, with advice of the Council, shall have a right to adjourn or prorogue the General Court, as he shall determine the public good shall require.

VIII. THE Governor of this Commonwealth for the time being, shall be the commander in chief of the army, and navy, and of all the military forces of the State, by sea and land; and shall have full power by himself, or by any chief commander, or other officer or officers, to be appointed by him from time to time, to train, instruct, exercise, and govern, the militia and navy; and, for the special defence and safety of the Commonwealth, to assemble in martial array, and put in warlike posture, the inhabitants thereof, and to lead and conduct them, and with them to encounter, expulse, repel, resist, and pursue, by force of arms, as well by sea as by land, within or without the limits of this Commonwealth; and also to kill, slay, destroy, and conquer, by all fitting ways, enterprizes, and means whatsoever, all and every such person and persons as shall, at any time hereafter, in a hostile manner attempt, or enterprize the destruction, invasion, detriment, or annoyance of this Commonwealth; and to use and exercise, over the army and navy, and over the militia in actual service, the law-martial in time of war, invasion, or rebellion, as occasion shall necessarily require; and also from time to time to erect forts, and to fortify any place or places within the said Commonwealth, and the same to furnish with all necessary ammunition, provisions, and stores of war, for offence or defence; and to commit from time to time the custody and government of the same, to such person or persons as to him shall seem meet: and in times of emergency the said forts and fortifications to demolish at his discretion; and to take and surprize, by all ways and means whatsoever, all and every such person or persons, with their ships, arms, ammunition, and other goods, as shall, in a hostile manner, invade, or attempt the invading, conquering, or annoying this Commonwealth; and in fine, that the Governor be intrusted with all other powers incident to the offices of Captain-General and Commander in Chief, and Admiral, to be exercised agreeably to the rules and regulations of the Constitution, and the laws of the land.

PROVIDED, that the said Governor shall not, at any time hereafter, by virtue of any power by this Constitution granted, or hereafter to be granted to him by the legislature, transport any of the inhabitants of this Commonwealth, or oblige them to march out of the limits of the same, without their free and voluntary consent, or the consent of the General Court; nor grant commissions for exercising the law-martial upon any of the inhabitants of this Commonwealth, without the advice and Consent of the Council of the same.

IX. THE power of pardoning offences, except such as persons may be convicted of before the Senate by an impeachment of the House, shall be in the Governor, by and with the advice of Council: But no charter of pardon, granted by the Governor, with advice of the Council, before conviction, shall avail the party pleading the same notwithstanding any general or particular expressions contained therein, descriptive of the offence or offences intended to be pardoned.

X. ALL judicial officers, the Attorney-General, the Solicitor-General, all Sheriffs, Coroners, Registers of Probate, and Registers of Maritime Courts, shall be nominated and appointed by the Governor, by and with the advice and consent of the Council; and every such nomination shall be made by the Governor, and made at least seven days prior to such appointment.

XI. ALL officers of the militia shall be appointed by the Governor, with the advice and consent of the Council; he first nominating them seven days at least before the appointment.

XII. ALL monies shall be issued out of the treasury of this Commonwealth, and disposed of by warrant under the hand of the Governor for the time being, with the advice and consent of the Council, for the necessary defence and support of the Commonwealth; and for the protection and preservation of the inhabitants thereof, agreeably to the acts and resolves of the General Court.

XIII. ALL public Boards, the Commissary-General, all superintending Officers of public magazines and stores, belonging to this Commonwealth, and all commanding Officers of forts and garrisons within the same, shall once in every three Months officially, and without requisition, and at other times, when required by the Governor, deliver to him an account of all goods, stores, provisions, ammunition, cannon with their appendages, and small arms with their accoutrements, and of all other public property whatever under their care respectively; distinguishing the quantity, number, quality, and kind of each, as particularly as may be; together with the condition of such forts and garrisons: and the said commanding Officers shall exhibit to the Governor, when required by him, true and exact plans of such forts, and of the land and sea, or harbour or harbours, adjacent.

AND the said Boards, and all public Officers, shall communicate to the Governor, as soon as may be after receiving the same, all letters, dispatches, and intelligences, of a public nature, which shall be directed to them respectively.

XIV. AND to prevent an undue influence in this Commonwealth, which the first magistrate thereof may acquire, by the long possession of the important powers and trusts of that office; as also to stimulate others to qualify themselves for the service of the public in the highest stations, no man shall be eligible as Governor of this Commonwealth, more than five years in any seven years.

XV. As the public good requires, that the Governor should not be under the undue influence of any of the members of the General Court, by a dependence on them for his support—that he should, in all cases, act with freedom for the benefit of the public—that he should not have his attention necessarily diverted from that object to his private concerns—and that he should maintain the dignity of the Commonwealth in the character of its Chief Magistrate—it is necessary, that he should have an honorable stated salary, of a fixed and permanent value, amply sufficient for those purposes, and established by standing laws: and it shall be among the first acts of the General Court, after the commencement of this Constitution, to establish such salary by law accordingly.

PERMANENT and honorable salaries shall also be established by law for the Justices of the Superior Court.

AND if it shall be found, that any of the salaries aforesaid, so established, are insufficient, they shall, from time to time, be enlarged as the General Court shall judge proper.

SECTION II.

LIEUTENANT-GOVERNOR, and the ascertaining the Value of the Money mentioned in this Constitution, as Qualifications to Office, &c.

I. THERE shall be annually elected a Lieutenant-Governor of the Commonwealth of Massachusetts, whose title shall be— HIS HONOR—and who shall be qualified, in point of religion, property, and residence in the Commonwealth, in the same manner with the Governor. He shall be chosen on the same day, in the same manner, and by the same persons. The return of the votes for this officer, and the declaration of his election, shall be in the same manner: And if no one person shall be found to have a majority of votes, the vacancy shall be filled by the Senate and House of Representatives, in the same manner as the Governor is to be elected, in case no one person has a majority of the votes of the people to be Governor.

II. THE Lieutenant-Governor shall always be, ex officio, a member, and, in the absence of the Governor, President, of the Council.

III. WHENEVER the chair of the Governor shall be vacant, by reason of his death, or absence from the Commonwealth, or otherwise, the Lieutenant-Governor, for the time being, shall, during such vacancy, have and exercise all the powers and authorities, which by this Constitution the Governor is vested with, when personally present.

IV. THE respective values, assigned by the several articles of this Constitution, to the property necessary to qualify the subjects of this Commonwealth to be electors, and also to be elected into several offices, for the holding of which such qualifications are required, shall always be computed in silver at the rate of six shillings and eight pence per ounce.

V. AND it shall be in the power of the legislature from time to time, to increase such qualifications of the persons to be elected to offices, as the circumstances of the Commonwealth shall require.

SECTION III.

Council, and the Manner of setling Elections by the Legislature; Oaths to be taken, &c.

I. THERE shall be a Council for advising the Governor in the executive part of government, to consist of nine persons besides the Lieutenant-Governor, whom the Governor, for the time being, shall have full power and authority, from time to time, at his discretion, to assemble and call together. And the Governor, with the said Counsellors, or five of them at least, shall and may, from time to time, hold and keep a Council, for the ordering and directing the affairs of the Commonwealth, according to the laws of the land.

II. NINE Counsellors shall, out of the persons returned for Counsellors and Senators, be annually chosen, on the last Wednesday in May, by the joint ballot of the Senators and Representatives assembled in one room. The seats of the persons, thus elected into the Council, and accepting the trust shall be vacated in the Senate; and in this manner the number of Senators shall be reduced to thirty one.

III. THE Counsellors, in the civil arrangements of the Commonwealth, shall have rank next after the Lieutenant-Governor.

IV. NOT more than two Counsellors shall be chosen out of any one county of this Commonwealth.

V. THE resolutions and advice of the Council shall be recorded in a register, and signed by the members present; and this record may be called for at any time by either House of the legislature; and any member of the Council may insert his opinion contrary to the resolution of the majority.

VI. WHENEVER the office of the Governor and Lieutenant-Governor shall be vacant, by reason of death, absence, or otherwise, then the Council, or the major part of them, shall, during such vacancy, have full power and authority, to do, and execute, all and every such acts, matters and things, as the Governor or the Lieutenant-Governor might or could, by virtue of this Constitution, do or execute, if they, or either of them, were personally present.

VII. AND whereas the elections appointed to be made by this Constitution, on the last Wednesday in May annually, by the two Houses of the legislature, may not be compleated on that day, the said elections may be adjourned from day to day until the same shall be compleated. And the order of elections shall be as follows, the vacancies in the Senate, if any, shall first be filled up, the Governor and Lieutenant-Governor shall then be elected; provided there should be no choice of them by the people: and afterwards the two Houses shall proceed to the election of the Council.

VIII. THE Lieutenant-Governor, Counsellors, Senators, and Members of the House of Representatives, shall, before they enter on the execution of their respective offices, make and subscribe the same declaration, and take the same oath, (mutatis mutandis) which the Governor is directed by this Constitution to make, subscribe and take.

AND every person, appointed to any civil or military office of this Commonwealth, shall, previous to his entering on the execution of his office, make and subscribe the following declaration, (mutatis mutandis) viz.—

I, A. B. being appointed   do now declare, that I believe and profess the christian religion, from a firm persuasion of the truth thereof.

AND he shall likewise take an oath of the form following, (mutatis mutandis) viz.—

I, A. B. do solemnly swear, that I will bear faith, and true allegiance to the Commonwealth of Massachusetts; that I will faithfully and impartially discharge, and perform all the duties incumbent on me as   according to the best of my abilities and understanding, agreeably to the rules and regulations of the Constitution; and that I will not attempt, or consent to, a violation thereof. So help me GOD.

PROVIDED notwithstanding, that any person, so appointed, who has conscientious scruples relative to taking oaths, may be admitted to make solemn affirmation, under the pains and penalties of perjury, to the truth of the matters, contained in the form of the said oath, instead of taking the same.

SECTION IV.
Secretary, Treasurer, Commissary, &c.

I. THE Secretary, Treasurer and Receiver-General, and the Commissary-General, Notaries-Public, and Naval-Officers, shall be chosen annually, by joint ballot of the Senators and Representatives in one room. And that the citizens of this Commonwealth may be assured, from time to time, that the monies remaining in the public Treasury, upon the settlement, and liquidation of the public accounts, are their property, no man shall be eligible as Treasurer and Receiver-General more than five years successively.

II. THE records of the Commonwealth shall be kept in the office of the Secretary, who shall attend the Governor and Council, the Senate and House of Representatives, in person, or by his Deputies, as they shall respectively require.

CHAPTER IV
Judiciary Power.

Art. I.   THE tenure, that all commission officers by law hold in their offices, shall be expressed in their respective commissions. All judicial officers, duely appointed, commissioned and sworn, shall hold their offices during good behavior: Provided nevertheless, the Governor, with consent of the Council, may remove them upon the address of both Houses of the legislature: and all other officers, appointed by the Governor and Council, shall hold their offices during pleasure.

II. No Justice of the Superior Court of Judicature, Court of Assize, and General Goal Delivery, shall have a seat in the Senate, or House of Representatives.

III. THE Senate, nevertheless, as well as the Governor and Council, shall have authority to require the opinions of the Judges upon important questions of law, and upon solemn occasions.

IV. IN order that the people may not suffer from the long continuance in place of any Justice of the Peace, who shall fail of discharging the important duties of his office, with ability or fidelity, all commissions of Justices of the Peace shall expire, and become void, in the term of seven years, from their respective dates; and upon the expiration of any commission, the

Governor and Council may, if necessary, renew such commissions, or appoint another person, as shall most conduce to the well-being of the Commonwealth.

V. THE Judges of Probate of Wills, and for granting letters of administration, shall hold their courts at such place or places, on fixed days, as the convenience of the people shall require. And the legislature shall, from time to time, hereafter appoint such times and places: until which appointments, the said courts shall be holden at the times and places, which the respective Judges shall direct.

VI. ALL causes of marriage, divorce and alimony, shall be determined by the Senate; and all appeals from the Judges of Probate shall be heard, and determined, by the Governor and Council, until the legislature shall, by law, make other provision.

CHAPTER V.

Delegates to Congress, Commissions, Writs, Indictments, &c. Confirmation of Laws,—Habeas Corpus,—and enacting Style.

Art. I. THE delegates of this Commonwealth to the Congress of the United States of America, shall, on the second Wednesday of November, if the General Court be then sitting, or on the second Wednesday of the Session next after, be elected annually, by the joint ballot of the Senate, and House of Representatives, assembled together in one room. They shall have commissions under the hand of the Governor, and under the great seal of the Commonwealth; but may be recalled at any time within the year, and others chosen and commissioned, in the same manner, in their stead.

II. ALL commissions shall be in the name of the Commonwealth of Massachusetts, signed by the Governor, and attested by the Secretary, or his Deputy; and have the great seal of the Commonwealth affixed thereto.

III. ALL writs, issuing out of the clerk's office in any of the courts of law, shall be in the name of the Commonwealth of Massachusetts. They shall be under the seal of the court, from whence they issue. They shall bear test of the Chief Justice, or first, or senior Justice of the court, to which they shall be returnable, and be signed by the clerk of such court.

IV. ALL indictments, presentments, and informations, shall conclude, "against the peace of the Commonwealth and the dignity of the same."

V. ALL the statute-laws of the Province, Colony, or State, of Massachusetts-Bay, the common law, and all such parts of the English or British statutes, as have been adopted, used and approved in the said Province, Colony, or State, and usually practiced on in the courts of law, shall still remain and be in full force, until altered or repealed by the legislature; such parts only excepted as are repugnant to the rights, and liberties, contained in this Constitution.

VI. THE privilege and benefit of the writ of Habeas Corpus shall be enjoyed in this Commonwealth, in the most free, easy, cheap, expeditious, and ample manner; and shall not be suspended by the Legislature, except upon the most urgent and pressing occasions, and for a short and limited time.

VII. THE enacting Style, in making and passing all acts, statutes and laws, shall be—"Be it enacted by his Excellency the Governor, the Senate, and House of Representatives, in General Court assembled, and by the Authority of the same." —Or, "By his Honor the Lieutenant-Governor," &c. or, "The Honorable the Council," &c. as the case may be.

CHAPTER VI.
The University at Cambridge, and Encouragement of Literature, &c.

SECTION I.
The University.

Art. I. WHEREAS our wise and pious ancestors, so early as the year one thousand six hundred and thirty six, laid the foundation of Harvard-College, in which University many persons of great eminence have, by the blessing of GOD, been initiated in those arts and sciences, which qualified them for public employments, both in Church and State: And whereas the encouragement of Arts and Sciences, and all good literature, tends to the honor of GOD, the advantage of the christian religion, and the great benefit of this, and the other United States of America—It is declared, That the PRESIDENT and FELLOWS of HARVARD-COLLEGE, in their corporate capacity, and their successors in that capacity, their officers and servants, shall have, hold, use, exercise, and enjoy all the powers, authorities, rights, liberties, privileges, immunities and franchises, which they now have, or are entitled to have, hold, use, exercise and enjoy: and the same are hereby ratified and confirmed unto them, the said President and Fellows of Harvard College, and to their successors, and to their officers and servants, respectively, for ever.

II. AND whereas there have been at sundry times, by divers persons, gifts, grants, devises of houses, lands, tenements, goods, chattles, legacies and conveyances, heretofore made, either to Harvard-College in Cambridge, in New-England, or to the President and Fellows of Harvard-College, or to the said College, by some other description, under several Charters successively: IT IS DECLARED, That all the said gifts, grants, devises, legacies and conveyances, are hereby forever confirmed unto the President and Fellows of Harvard-College, and to their Successors, in the capacity aforesaid, according to the true intent, and meaning of the donor or donors, grantor or grantors, divisor or devisors.

III. AND whereas by an act of the General Court of the Colony of Massachusetts-Bay, passed in the year one thousand six hundred and forty two, the Governor and Deputy-Governor, for the time being, and all the magistrates of that jurisdiction, were with the President, and a number of the Clergy, in the said act described, constituted the Overseers of Harvard-College: And it being necessary, in this new Constitution of Government, to ascertain who shall be deemed Successors to the said Governor, Deputy-Governor, and Magistrates: IT IS DECLARED, That the Governor, Lieutenant-Governor, Council and Senate of this Commonwealth, are, and shall be deemed, their Successors; who, with the President of Harvard-College, for the time being, together with the Ministers of the congregational churches, in the towns of Cambridge, Watertown, Charlestown, Boston, Roxbury, and Dorchester, mentioned in the said act, shall be, and hereby are, vested with all the powers and authority belonging, or in any way appertaining to the Overseers of Harvard College; PROVIDED, that nothing herein shall be construed to prevent the Legislature of this Commonwealth from making such alterations in the government of the said university, as shall be conducive to its advantage, and the interest of the Republic of Letters, in as full a manner as might have been done by the Legislature of the Province of the Massachusetts-Bay.

SECTION II.
The Encouragement of Literature, &c.

WISDOM, and knowledge, as well as virtue, diffused generally among the body of the people, being necessary for the preservation of their rights and liberties; and as these depend on spreading the opportunities and advantages of education in the various parts of the country, and among the different orders of the people, it shall be the duty of legislators and magistrates, in all future periods of this Commonwealth, to cherish the interests of literature and the sciences, and all seminaries of them; especially the university at Cambridge, public schools, and grammar schools in the towns; to encourage private societies and public institutions, rewards and immunities, for the promotion of agriculture, arts, sciences, commerce, trades, manufactures, and a natural history of the country; to countenance and inculcate the principles of humanity and general benevolence, public and private charity, industry and frugality, honesty and punctuality in their dealings, sincerity, good humour, and all social affections, and generous sentiments among the people.

CHAPTER VII. and last.
Continuance of Officers, &c.

To the end there may be no failure of justice, or danger arise to the Commonwealth from a change of the form of government, all officers, civil and military, holding commissions under the government and people of Massachusetts-Bay, in New-England, and all other officers of the said government and people at the time this Constitution shall take effect, shall have, hold, use, exercise, and enjoy all the powers and authority to them granted or committed, until other persons shall be appointed in their stead: And all courts of law shall proceed in the execution of the business of their respective departments; and all the executive and legislative officers, bodies and powers, shall continue in full force, in the enjoyment and exercise of all their trusts, employments and authority, until the General Court, and the supreme and executive officers, under this Constitution, are designated, and invested with their respective trusts, powers and authority.

ERRATA.

Page 249. 8th Line of the Preamble, read, *Prosperity and Happiness.*

In Lieu of the first full Paragraph on Page 250, substitute the following.

"WE, therefore, the people of Massachusetts, acknowledging with grateful hearts, the goodness of the Great Legislator of the Universe, in affording us, in the course of His providence, an opportunity of entering into an original, explicit and solemn compact with each other, deliberately and peaceably, without fraud, violence, or surprize; and of forming a new Constitution of Civil Government for ourselves and posterity; and devoutly imploring His direction in so interesting a design, DO agree upon, ordain and establish, the following *Declaration of Rights,* and *Frame of Government,* as the CONSTITUTION OF THE COMMONWEALTH OF MASSACHUSETTS.

PAG. 250, Chap. I, Art. I. l. 1. Read "All men are born free and equal," omitting the words "equally and independent."

Art. 2. l. 1. Read, "It is the Right as well as the Duty." l. 5. Read, "in the manner and season most agreeable."

PAG. 255. Chap. II. Next under the 1st Section, insert the Contents of it, viz.—The Legislature, or General Court.

PAG. 260. For Art. VII. read VI. for VIII. r. VII. and for IX. r. VIII.

PAG. 270. l. 16 from bot. for "County," read "District."

November 1, 1779

A NECESSARY FORM OF GOVERNMENT

To Elbridge Gerry

My Friend   Braintree Novr. 4. 1779
    Yours of Octr. 12 has been, seven days, by me. Am happy to
learn that my Accounts and Vouchers arrived Safe, by Mr.
Lowell. I know not how the Board will explain, the three
Months after Notice of Recall, as applied to me. If they were
to allow three Months after my Arrival, it would be no more
than just.
    Mr. Dana, I presume will accept, and sail with me, in a few
days.
    I am clear for Three Branches, in the Legislature, and the
Committee have reported as much, tho aukwardly expressed. I
have considered this Question in every Light in which my
Understanding is capable of placing it, and my Opinion is decided in favour of Three Branches. And being, very unexpect-
edly called upon to give my Advice to my Countrymen,
concerning a Form of Government, I could not answer it to
myself, to them, or Posterity, if I concealed or disguised my real
Sentiments. They have been received with Candor, but perhaps
will not be adopted. In such a State as this, however, I am perswaded, We never shall have any Stability, Dignity, Decision, or
Liberty, without it. We have so many Men of Wealth, of ambitious Spirits, of Intrigue, of Luxury and Corruption, that incessant Factions will disturb our Peace, without it. And indeed
there is too much reason to fear with it. The Executive, which
ought to be the Reservoir of Wisdom, as the Legislature is of
Liberty, without this Weapon of Defence will be run down like
a Hare before the Hunters. But I have not Time to enlarge.
    I am more Solicitous about the Means of procuring, the
salary you mention, than the sum of it. I can make it do, if I
can get it. But I wish I had Power to borrow Money, and also
Power to draw upon, Dr. Franklin, or the American Banker, in
Case of Necessity. I should get it, in that Way.
    Mr. Jay, will have no Difficulty, for Spain will undoubtedly,
furnish him, as they did Mr. Lee, who I believe, but am not
certain, has some Spanish Money remaining in his Hands. I

know not how much, and may be mistaken in Supposing he has any.

You think my Appointment ought not to be divulged: but it was public in Boston and in every Bodys Mouth upon Change, before I heard a lisp of it. If it is generally approved I am happy. Happy and blessed indeed shall I be if I can accomplish my Errand, and give general Satisfaction in the End.

Let me beseech you by every Feeling of Friendship as well as Patriotism, to continue your Favours, and transmit me the Journals, News Papers, Pamphlets, as well as your Advice, from Time to Time. My Importance in that Country will depend much upon the Intelligence, that shall be sent me by my Friends, more than you can imagine. If you intend that I shall do you any good, keep me constantly informed, of every Thing. The Numbers, the Destinations of the Army, the state of Finance. The Temper of the People—military operations. The state and the Prospects of the Harvests, the Prices of Goods— the Price of Bills of Exchange—the Rate between silver and Paper. Nothing can come amiss. The Growth or decline of the Navy, the Spirit and success of Privateers, the Number of Prizes, —the Number, Position, Exertions and designs of the Enemy.

Your Election comes on, this Month, and it is sure. I wish I was as sure of getting safe to France. God bless you.

FRANKLIN'S THEORY OF COLDS

To Benjamin Rush

My dear Sir   Braintree Novr 4. 1779

Your favours of Octr. 12 and 19 are before me. I should not have left the first Seven days unanswered, if had not been for my new Trade of a Constitution monger. I inclose a Pamphlet as my Apology. It is only a Report of a Committee, and will be greatly altered no doubt. If the Committee had boldly made the Legislature consist of three Branches, I should have been better pleased. But I cannot enlarge upon this subject.

I am pained in my inmost soul, at the unhappy Affair, at Coll Wilsons. I think there ought to be an Article in the Declaration of Rights of every State, Securing Freedom of Speech, Impartiality, and Independance at the Bar. There is nothing on which the Rights of every Member of Society more depend. There is no Man so bad, but he ought to have a fair Tryal, and an equal Chance to obtain the ablest Council, or the Advocate of his Choice, to see that he has fair Play, and the Benefit of Truth and Law.

Dont be dismayed, you will yet find Liberty a charming Substance. I wish I had Leonidas, cant you send it, after me?

Thank you, for your Congratulations, on my new and most honourable Appointment. If it is possible, for Mortals to honour Mortals, I am honoured,—with an Honour, however, that makes me, tremble. Pray, help me, by corresponding constantly with me, and sending me, all the Pamphlets, Journals, News &c. to a little success, as well as honour.

Your Congratulations on the Count D'Estaings operations, are conceived in Terms flattering enough. I will please myself, with the Thought, untill the contrary appears, that I had Some Share in bringing him here. If he only liberates Georgia and Rhode Island, which Seems to be already done, it is a great success. Altho I go to make Peace, yet if the old Lady, Britania will not suffer me to do that, I will do all I can in Character, to Sustain the War, and direct it in a sure Course. I must be prudent, in this, however, which, I fear is not enough my Characteristick, but I flatter myself, I am rather growing in this Grace. In this Spirit, I think, that altho, We have had Provocations enough to excite the warmest Passions against Great Britain, yet it is our duty to silence all Resentments in our deliberations about Peace, and attend only to our Interests, and our Engagements with our allies.

Nothing ever gives me So much Pleasure, as to hear of Harmony in Congress. Upon this depends our Union, Strength, Prosperity and Glory. If the late Appointments give Satisfaction I am happy, and if the Liberties and Independance of our Country, are not safe in my Hands, you may Sware it is for Want of Brains, not of Heart. The Appointment of Mr. Dana, could not be mended. He will go, and I shall be happy. You have given me Pain by your Account of the Complaints against the Director. I am sorry, very sorry!

What will you say, if I should turn your Thoughts, from Pol-

iticks to Philosophy? What do you think of Dr. Franklins Theory of Colds. He is fixed in the opinion that We never take
Cold, from the cold Air. And wants the Experiments of Sanc-
torius tried over again. Suppose you should make a Statical
Chair, and try, whether Perspiration is most copious in a warm
bed, or stark naked, in the open Air. I assure you, these
Branches of Physicks, come within the Circle of the Sciences of
the statesman, for an unlucky Cold (which I have been much
subject to all my days) may stop him, in his Career, and dash
all his schemes; and it is a poor Excuse to say, he foresaw and
provided against every Event, but his own sickness.

My Partner, whose tender Health and numerous Family,
will not permit her, to make me, as happy, as Mr. Jay, joins
with me, in the kindest Compliments to you and Mrs. Rush.
Adieu   John Adams

PEACE NEGOTIATOR WITH
BRITAIN AND MINISTER TO
THE NETHERLANDS
1779–1783

To Abigail Adams 2nd

My dear Daughter   Ferrol Decr. 12. 1779

If I could send you some of the Lemons, Oranges, or Water Melons of this Place, it would give me more Pleasure than you. But there are very seldom merchant Vessells at this Place from America.

We are here in the Latitude of 43, which is better than half a degree farther north than Boston, yet there has not yet been the slightest frost. The Verdure on the Fields and in the Gardens is as fresh as ever. We see large Quantities of Indian Corn, hanging up in Bunches of Ears, about the higher Parts of the Houses, which shews Us that that Species of Grain grows and is cultivated here, altho the Ears and the Kernel is much smaller than with Us.

I have much Curiosity to see Madrid and a strong Inclination to go that Way: but it is a great Way farther and I have some doubts for several other Reasons whether I ought to go there. But I shall go through Bilboa from whence I shall again write to you if I can.

I have met with few Things more remarkable than the Chocolate which is the finest I ever saw. I will enquire whether it is the Superiour Quality of the Cocoa Nut, or any other Ingredient which they intermix with it, or a better Art of making it, which renders it so much superiour to any other.

I see very little, which would be entertaining to a young Lady of your Turn of thinking, in this Place, which seems to be wholly devoted to military Affairs. There is what they call, an Italien Opera: but neither the Theaters, nor the Actors, nor the Pieces, nor the Musick are very pleasing. I have been once there, but not understanding the Italien Language, and seeing very little Company, and scarcely any Ladies who are always to me the most pleasing ornaments of such Spectacles, I don't think it worth while for me to go again: but the Gentlemen, and your Brothers with them are about going this Evening. They may possibly learn a little of the Spanish Language, as the Piece tonight is to be in that Tongue.

In the Course of my Journeys, I shall embrace any Moments of Leisure, to inform you of any Thing that I observe which may contribute to your Improvement or Entertainment: But you must remember that my Voyages and Journeys are not for my private Information, Instruction, Improvement, Entertainment or Pleasure; but laborious and hazardous Enterprizes of Business. I shall never be much polished, by Travel, whatever your Brothers may be. I hope they will be improved. I hope they will increase in Knowledge as they go: but I am not anxious about their being very much polished.

Gold is very little more prescious for being burnished Silver and Steel are as usefull without polishing as with it.

I dont mean by this however to suggest, that Arts and Accomplishments which are merely ornamental, should be wholly avoided or neglected especially by your Sex: but that they ought to be slighted when in Comparison or Competition, with those which are useful and essential.

I hope your Attention will be fixed chiefly upon those Virtues and Accomplishments, which contribute the most to qualify Women to act their Parts well in the various Relations of Life, those of Daughter, Sister, Wife, Mother, Friend.— Yours Affectionately,   John Adams

TYRANNY AND "THE ELECTRICAL ROD"

To Elbridge Gerry

My dear Friend   Paris Feby. 23d. 1780
The Boston Committee of Correspondence, and the Military Associations which grew out of it, are likely to prove the greatest Engines for pulling down Tyranny, that were ever invented. The Electrical Rod, which deprives the Clouds of their Thunder, does it not so effectually, as these Committees wrest the Iron Rod out of the Hands of a Tyrant.

Ireland has already obtained, purely by the Use of this Machine, great Advantages, and as She has not yet laid it down, She will obtain more, or give England further Trouble. The

Counties in England are generally laying hold of it, as you will see by the public Papers.

I recieved your Letter relative to Mr. Dalton's Vessel that was sunk, since my Arrival in this City. Dr. F. applied in the Time of it, as he tells me, to the Minister, and obtained an Order for Compensation, which I hope Mr. Dalton has recieved. But if the Order miscarried, a Repetition of it may be obtained at any Time. Let me beg of You, to write Me by every Opportunity.

Your Friend & humble Servant   John Adams

RELATIONS WITH FRANCE AND SPAIN

To Samuel Adams

                         Paris Hotel de Valois, Rue de Richelieu
Dear Sir   March 4. 1780
This will be delivered to you by Mr. Izard, who goes out in the Alliance, with Mr. Lee, Mr. Wharton, Mr. Brown and others. He will wait on you of Course, and will be able to give you, good Information concerning the Intentions of the English and their military Preparations by sea and Land: and those of the French and Spaniards, at the same Time.

He will also give his Opinion very freely concerning American and other Characters here as well as Measures. In many Things his opinions may be just, but in some and those not a few I am sure they are wrong.

The great Principle, in which I have differed from him, is this, in the Mode of treating with this Court. He has been always of opinion that it was good Policy, and necessary to hold an high Language to this Court. To represent to them, the danger of our being subdued if they did not do this and the other Thing for Us, in order to obtain Money and other Aids from them. He is confident they would not have dared to refuse Us Any Thing.

Altho no Man in America or in the World, was earlier convinced than I was, that it was the Interest of France and Spain to support the Independence of America, and that they would Support it, and no Man is more sensible than I am of the Necessity they are under to support Us, yet I am not and never was of Opinion that we could with Truth or with good Policy, assume the Style of Menace, and threaten them with returning again to G. B. and joining against France and Spain—even tell them that We should be subdued, because I never believed this myself, and the Court here would not have believd it from Us.

The Court here have many Difficulties to manage as well as we, and it is a delicate and hazardous Thing, to push Things in this Country. Things are not to be negotiated here, as they are with the People in America, even the Tories in America, or as with the People of England.

There is a Frankness however that ought to be used with the Ministry, and a Candor, with which the Truth may be and has been communicated: but there is a harshness, that would not fail to ruin, in my opinion the fairest Negotiation in this Country.

We are anxious to hear from you having nothing since the Beg. of Decr. and very little since We left you.

Your Fred & Sert,

STUDYING LATIN AND GREEK

To John Quincy Adams

My dear Son   Paris March 17. 1780

I have received your Letter, giving an Account of your Studies for a day. You should have dated your Letter.

Making Latin, construing Cicero, Erasmus, the Appendix de Diis et Heroibus ethnicis, and Phædrus, are all Exercises proper for the Acquisition of the Latin Tongue; you are constantly employed in learning the Meaning of Latin Words, and the Grammar, the Rhetorick and Criticism of the Roman Authors: These Studies have therefore such a Relation to each other, that I think you would do well to pursue them all, under the Direction of your Master.

The Greek Grammar and the Racines I would not have you

omit, upon any Consideration, and I hope your Master will soon put you into the Greek Testament, because the most perfect Models of fine Writing in history, Oratory and Poetry are to be found in the Greek Language.

Writing and Drawing are but Amusements and may serve as Relaxations from your studies.

As to Geography, Geometry and Fractions I hope your Master will not insist upon your spending much Time upon them at present; because altho they are Useful sciences, and altho all Branches of the Mathematicks, will I hope, sometime or other engage your Attention, as the most profitable and the most satisfactory of all human Knowledge; Yet my Wish at present is that your principal Attention should be directed to the Latin and Greek Tongues, leaving the other studies to be hereafter attained, in your own Country.

I hope soon to hear that you are in Virgil and Tully's orations, or Ovid or Horace or all of them.

I am, my dear Child, your affectionate Father,

John Adams

P.S. The next Time you write to me, I hope you will take more care to write well. Cant you keep a steadier Hand?

"AMERICA IS THE CITY, SET UPON A HILL"

To Nathanael Greene

Dear Sir   Paris March 18th. 1780

Give me Leave, by the Opportunity of the Viscount de Noailles, to take this Method of reviving a Correspondence, which has been interupted almost three Years, but was one of the most pleasing I ever had.

It is unnecessary to say any thing of the Expedition with which this Letter is intended to go, because I hope it will reveal itself to You, in Accounts which will make themselves heard and understood by all the World.

As there is a probability that there will be more frequent Communication, with America this Summer, than there ever has been, let me beg the favor of your Sentiments both upon Subjects of Policy and War.

Every Operation of your Army has its Influence upon all the Powers of Europe in France, Spain, England, Ireland, Holland, Sweeden, Denmark, Russia, Prussia, Portugal, and even in the German Empire.

America is the City, set upon a Hill, I do not think myself guilty of Exaggeration, Vanity or Presumption, when I say, that the proceedings of Congress are more attended to, than those of any Court in Europe, and the Motions of our Armies than any of theirs. And there are more political Lies made and circulated about both, than all the rest: which renders genuine Intelligence, from good Authority, the more interesting and important.

There is a great Variety of Policy on foot, in England, Ireland, Holland, and among the Northern Powers, all tending to favor the Cause of America, which is promoted by nothing more than by prompt and accurate Intelligence.

I am, Sir, as much as ever, your Friend and Servant

ENCOURAGING NEWS FROM LONDON

To Samuel Huntington

Paris Hotel de Valois Ruë de Richelieu
Sir   March 23d. 1780

I have the Honor to inclose the English Papers of the eleventh thirteenth and fourteenth of March. The Courier de L'Europe and the Hague, Leiden and Amsterdam Gazettes.

We are in hourly Expectation of great News from Holland, Ireland, England, Spain, and above all from America and the West Indies. I have not a Letter from America, since I left it, except one from my Family of the tenth of December, and indeed, although several Vessels have arrived, I can hear of no Letters or News.

By the English Papers Congress will percieve the violent Fermentation in England, which has arisen to such an Height, as to produce a Congress in Fact, and it will soon be so in

Name. The Proceedings in the House of Commons on the fourteenth, which were terminated by a Resolution of the Committee of the whole House, to abolish the Board of Trade and Plantations, carried against the Ministry after a very long and warm Debate by a Majority of Eight Voices, is not only the most extraordinary Vote which has passed in the present Reign, but it leads to very extensive Consequences.

I believe it is very true, that this Board has been the true Cause of the Quarrel of Great Britain against the Colonies, and therefore may be considered as a natural Object of national Resentment; but a Resentment of this kind alone, would not probably have produced this Effect.

Whether it is the near Approach of an Election, that has intimidated the Members of the House of Commons; or whether the Committees, Petitions, Associations and Congress have alarmed them; or whether the Nation is convinced that America is indeed lost forever, and consequently that the Board will in future be useless, I dont know.

Be this as it may, the English Nation, and even the Irish and Scotch Nations—all parts of the World will draw this Inference from it, that even in the Opinion of the House of Commons America is lost. The free and virtuous Citizens of America, and even the slavish and vicious, if there are any still remaining of this Character, under the Denomination of Tories, must be convinced by this Vote, passed in the Heyday of their Joy for the Sucesses of Admiral Rodney's Fleet, that the House of Commons despair of ever regaining America. The Nations, subject to the House of Bourbon, cannot fail to put the same Interpretation upon this Transaction. Holland, and all the Northern Powers, with the Empress of Russia at their Head, who are all greatly irritated against England for their late Violences against the innocent Commerce of Neutral Powers, will draw the same Consequences. The Politicians of Great Britain are too enlightened in the History of Nations, and the Rise and Progress of Causes and Effects in the political World, not to see that all these Bodies of People will, in Consequence of this Vote, consider the Colonies as given up for lost by the House of Commons; and they are too well instructed not to know the important Consequences that follow, from having such points as these, thus settled among the Nations. I cannot therefore but consider this Vote, and the other respecting the Secretary of State for the American Department, which arose almost to a Ballance as a most important Declaration of the Sense of the Nation.

The first probable Consequence of it, will be one further Attempt, by offering some specious Terms, which they know we cannot in Justice, in Honor, in Conscience accept, to deceive seduce and divide America, throw all into Confusion there, and by this Means gain an Opportunity to govern.

There is nothing more astonishing than the Inconsistencies of the Patriots in England. Those, who are most violent against the Ministry, are not for making Peace with France and Spain, but they wish to allure America into a seperate Peace, and persuade her to join them against the House of Bourbon. One would think it impossible, that one Man of Sense in the World could seriously believe, that we could thus basely violate our Faith, thus unreasonably quarrel with our best Friends, thus madly attach ourselves to our bitterest Enemies. But thus it is.

Sir George Saville threw out in the House, that he wished to carry home to his Constituents the News of an Accommodation with America, and Mr David Hartley has given Notice of his Intention to make a Motion relative to Us. But I confess I have no Expectations. Mr Hartley's Motions and Speeches have never made any great Fortune in the House, nor been much attended to; from whence I conclude, if the present great Leaders of Opposition in the House, were seriously disposed to do any thing towards a Pacification, which we could attend to, they would not suffer Mr. Hartley to have the Honor of making the Motion.

The Heads of many People run upon a Truce with America, and Mr. Hartley's Motion may tend this Way: but a Truce with America cannot be made without a Peace with France and Spain; and would America accept of such a Truce? Give Great Britain time to encroach and fortify upon all our Frontiers? To send Emissaries into the States and sow the Seeds of Discord? To rise out of her present exhausted and ruined Condition? Suffer France and Spain to relax? Wait for Alterations by the Deaths of Princes, or the Changes in the Characters of Princes or Ministers in the System of Europe? I ask these Questions, that Congress may give me Instructions if they think necessary. At present I dont believe that my Powers are sufficient to agree to a Truce, if it was proposed; nor do I believe it would be for our Interest or Safety to agree to it, if I had. I dont mean however to give any decided Opinion upon such a great Question, in this hasty Letter. I am open to Conviction, and shall obey the Instructions of Congress with the most perfect Respect.

I have the Honor to be, with the Greatest Respect & Esteem, Sir, your most obedient, and most humble Servant,

John Adams

ANNOUNCING HIS MISSION

To Edmund Jenings

Dear Sir   Paris April 2. 1780

After Settling a Point or two here, I now think myself at Liberty to inform you, that I have indeed the Honour, to be a Minister plenipotentiary from the United States of America, "vested with full Powers and Instructions to confer, treat, agree and conclude with the Ambassadors or Plenipotentiaries of his most christian Majesty and of his Britannic Majesty, and those of any other Princes or states, whom it may concern, vested with equal Powers, relating to the Reestablishment of Peace and Friendship, and whatever shall be so agreed and concluded to Sign, and make a Treaty or Treaties and to transact every Thing that may be necessary for compleating, the great Work of Pacification." This you may affirm, without making Use of my Name as your Authority, at present unless to particular Friends.

My Mission was not the Effect of any sudden Joy or Sorrow, Hope or fear arising from any Event of War prosperous or Adverse: but a measure more than a year under Consideration of Congress, and it was thought very proper to have a Minister residing in Europe, Solely for the Purpose of attending to Propositions for Peace. Their Deliberations were long upon the Commission and Instructions, which were at last concluded, and the Choice to my utter astonishment fell upon me, by the Votes of Eleven states, twelve only being present.

This Unanimity, after all the Struggles and Divisions about our foreign Affairs, and the Certainty of still greater Divisions, which I was assured would be the Consequence of my Refusal, determined Me, to put myself once more to sea from a quiet and an happy Harbour. It is a situation that is and will be envyed. And I have Seen enough of what there is in human Bosoms to know that Envy is a formidable Ennemy. It is however more justly to be dreaded than envyed. I assure you it appalls me, when I reflect upon it. The Immensity of the Trust, is too great for every Thing but an honest Heart, and for that too, without a sounder Understanding, and profounder, sublimer and more extended Views, than I have any Pretentions too.

I should esteem it as a favour if you would take Measures, to have Some Paragraphs inserted in the English Newspapers, announcing the Purport of my Mission. The Nature of them I shall leave to your Discretion. I am with much affection yours,

John Adams

REPRINTING A "POLITICAL RHAPSODY"

To Edmund Jenings

Secret and confidential

My dear Sir   Paris April 20. 1778
There is a little Pamphlet, which was written by me in the Year 1765, and published at Boston, afterwards reprinted in England, under the Title of "a Dissertation on the Cannon and the feudal Law." It is a kind of philosophical and political Rhapsody, written when I was not very old, and when I had certainly Seen very little of this World, and knew but little of Men or Things. It was ascribed, in the time of it to Jeremiah Gridley Esq, the greatest Lawyer, that ever was in Boston, who was my Patron in my Youth. He died before the Pamphlet came over under his name or he would have publickly disclaimed it, because he was on the other side in Politicks. It was

printed, or bound up in a small Pamphlet under the Tittle of the true sentiments of America, with Letters from the House of Representatives of Mass Bay, to several great Men. I want to beg the favour of you to write to England to obtain it for me, and to get it printed in the Remembrancer. They may put my name to it, if they please. It may be thought vanity in me, perhaps to say it, but it had an Effect upon the People of New England beyond all Imagination. It appeared to them to point out the means by which human nature had been degraded in Europe, to shew them that their Ancestors had wisely and virtuously endeavored, to Screen them from those means, and perhaps no one thing that ever was written or done contributed more than that Publication, to unite the People of New England, as one Man in the Resolution of opposing force, to the stamp Act, and of having recourse to Arms rather than submit to it. I have Reasons of a public nature to wish to see this published at this time, which perhaps sometime or other you may know. I shall, take occasion to let you further, into some particulars of my History, which is altogether unknown I find in Europe. You will never find me any, very great Matter, but you will find, that I have been twenty Years, in the midst of Politicks and through the whole of it, invariably constant to the same Principles and the same system, through all Opprobriums, Obloquies, Dangers, Terrors, Losses, and Allurements.

I ask your Pardon sir, for giving you so much trouble, but I take Advantage of your friendly Professions, and I assure you confidence is a Plant of slow growth in my Bosom, Altho it was very far otherwise twenty years ago. I have not yet found in Europe another Person, to whom I can unbosom myself.

I shall put you to expence, perhaps for Postage or otherwise, which I shall be glad to repay.

Adieu.

April 20, 1780

CULTIVATING AMERICAN MANNERS

To Elkanah Watson Jr.

Paris Hotel de Valois Ruë de Richelieu
Sir   April 30. 1780

Your Letter of the 10th. of March, I recieved but Yesterday.
I recollect that General Warren mentioned to me, his having
given You Letters to me, but I cant recollect seeing those Letters. I am obliged to You for writing to me, and if it should be
in my power to be of any Service to You, it will give me pleasure to do it, altho' I have not the Satisfaction to know You
personally. I have been so long from home and so much longer
from Plymouth, that it is impossible for me to say any thing of
your Character, but this that I doubt not it is good, having no
Cause to suspect otherwise. Your Family I know very well to
be one of the most respectable in the County of Plymouth.
Your Father, I had the Honor to know very well, and I know
that he was, in those days universally respected to have an independent hereditary Fortune which I have no doubt he still
possesses undiminished, very probably, with large Additions to
it, by the profits of Business. I knew too, that in ancient Times
(for I must talk to you like an old Man), when the Friends to
the American cause were not so numerous, nor so determined
as they are now, we always found your Father firm and consistent, as a friend to his Country. This I know, for more than ten
Years before the Commencement of the War, and therefore
have no difficulty in believing, that he has been since that period uniformly strenuous in Support of Independence.

You tell me, Sir, You wish to cultivate your Manners, before
You begin your Travels; and since You have had so much Confidence in me, as to write to me upon this Occasion, permit
me, to take the Liberty of advising You to cultivate the Manners of your own Country, not those of Europe. I don't mean
by this that You should put on a long face, never dance with the
Ladies, go to a play, or take a Game of Cards. But you may depend upon this, that the more decisively You adhere to a
manly Simplicity in Your Dress, Equipage, and Behaviour, the
more You devote yourself to Business and Study, and the less

to Dissipation and Pleasure, the more You will recommend yourself to every Man and Woman in this Country whose Friendship or Acquaintance is worth your having or wishing. There is an Urbanity without Ostentation or Extravagance, which will succeed every where, and at all Times. You will excuse this freedom, on account of my friendship for your Father, and consequently for You, and because I know that some young Gentlemen have come to Europe with different Sentiments, and have consequently injured the Character of their Country as well as their own both here and at home. All Europe knows that it was American manners that have produced such great Effects from that young and tender Country. I should be glad to hear from You, as often as You please and shall be glad to recieve from You any Intelligence, from America or elsewhere, and to wait on You in Paris. You may show this Letter in whole or in Part, to Mr. Williams and Mr. Schweighauser, to both of whom You will please my Compliments, and to any others that You think proper.

I am with much Respect, Sir, your most obedient & humble Servant

John Adams

A NATURAL HISTORY COLLECTION

To Abigail Adams

My dear Portia

Yesterday We went to see the Garden of the King, Jardin du Roi, and his Cabinet of natural History, Cabinet d'Histoire naturell.

The Cabinet of natural History is a great Collection, of Metals, Minerals, shells, Insects, Birds, Beasts, Fishes, and presscious stones. They are arranged in good order, and preserved in good condition, with the name of every thing beautifully written on a piece of paper annexed to it. There is also a Collection of Woods and marbles.

The garden is large and airy, affording fine Walks between Rows of Trees. Here is a Collection from all Parts of the

World, of all the plants, Roots and Vegetables that are used in medicine, and indeed of all the Plants and trees in the World.

A fine Scæne for the studious youth in Physick or Philosophy. It was a public day. There was a great deal of Company, and I had opportunity only to take a cursory view. The whole is very curious. There is an handsome statue of Mr. Buffon, the great natural Historian whose Works you have, whose labours have given fame to this Cabinet and Garden. When shall We have in America, such Collections? The Collection of American Curiosities that I saw at Norwalk in Connecticutt made by Mr. Arnold, which he afterwards to my great mortification sold to Gov. Tryon, convinces me, that our Country affords as ample materials, for Collections of this nature as any part of the World.

Five midshipmen of the Alliance, came here last night, Marston, Hogan, Fitzgerald and two others, from Norway, where they were sent with Prizes, which the Court of Denmark were absurd and unjust enough, to restore to the English. They however treated the Officers and People well, and defrayed their Expences. They say the Norwegians were very angry, with the Court of Copenhagen, for delivering up these Vessells. It was the Blunder of Ignorance, I believe, rather than any ill Will.

Every day when I ride out, without any particular Business to do, or Visit to make, I order my servant to carry me to some place where I never was before, so that at last I believe I have seen all Paris, and all the fields and scenes about it, that are near it. It is very pleasant.

Charles is as well beloved here as at home. Wherever he goes, every body loves him. Mr. D is as fond of him, I think as I am. He learns very well.

There is a Volume in folio just published here, which I Yesterday, run over at a Booksellers shop. It is a description and a copper Plate of all the Engravings upon precious stones in the Collection of the Duke of Orleans. The stamps are extreamly beautiful, and are representations of the Gods and Heroes of Antiquity, with most of the fables of their Mithology. Such a Book would be very usefull to the Children in studiing the Classicks, but it is too dear—3 Guineas, unbound.

There is every Thing here that can inform the Understanding, or refine the Taste, and indeed one would think that could purify the Heart. Yet it must be remembered there is every thing here too, which can seduce, betray, deceive, deprave, corrupt and debauch it. Hercules marches here in full View of the Steeps of Virtue on one hand, and the flowery Paths of Pleasure on the other—and there are few who make the Choice of Hercules. That my Children may follow his Example, is my earnest Prayer: but I sometimes tremble, when I hear the syren songs of sloth, least they should be captivated with her bewitching Charms and her soft, insinuating Musick.

April–May 1780

"I MUST STUDY POLITICKS AND WAR"

To Abigail Adams

My dear Portia

The inclosed Dialogue in the Shades was written by Mr. Edmund Jennings now residing at Brussells, a Native of Maryland. I will send you the Rest when I can get it.

How I lament the Loss of my Packets by Austin! There were I suppose Letters from Congress of great Importance to me. I know not what I shall do without them. I suppose there was Authority to draw &c. Mr. T's Letter from his father, hints that Mr. L. is coming here. This will be excellent.

Since my Arrival this time I have driven about Paris, more than I did before. The rural Scenes around this Town are charming. The public Walks, Gardens, &c. are extreamly beautifull. The Gardens of the Palais Royal, the Gardens of the Tuilleries, are very fine. The Place de Louis 15, the Place Vendome or Place de Louis 14, the Place victoire, the Place royal, are fine Squares, ornamented with very magnificent statues. I wish I had time to describe these objects to you in a manner, that I should have done, 25 Years ago, but my Head is too full of Schemes and my Heart of Anxiety to use Expressions borrowed from you know whom.

To take a Walk in the Gardens of the Palace of the Tuilleries, and describe the Statues there, all in marble, in which the ancient Divinities and Heroes are represented with exquisite Art, would be a very pleasant Amusement, and instructive Entertainment, improving in History, Mythology, Poetry, as well as in Statuary. Another Walk in the Gardens of Versailles, would be usefull and agreable.—But to observe these Objects with Taste and describe them so as to be understood, would require more time and thought than I can possibly Spare. It is not indeed the fine Arts, which our Country requires. The Usefull, the mechanic Arts, are those which We have occasion for in a young Country, as yet simple and not far advanced in Luxury, altho perhaps much too far for her Age and Character.

I could fill Volumes with Descriptions of Temples and Palaces, Paintings, Sculptures, Tapestry, Porcelaine, &c. &c. &c.—if I could have time. But I could not do this without neglecting my duty.—The Science of Government it is my Duty to study, more than all other Sciences: the Art of Legislation and Administration and Negotiation, ought to take Place, indeed to exclude in a manner all other Arts.—I must study Politicks and War that my sons may have liberty to study Mathematicks and Philosophy. My sons ought to study Mathematicks and Philosophy, Geography, natural History, Naval Architecture, navigation, Commerce and Agriculture, in order to give their Children a right to study Painting, Poetry, Musick, Architecture, Statuary, Tapestry and Porcelaine.

Adieu.

after May 12, 1780

"AMERICA HAS TAKEN HER EQUAL STATION"

To Thomas Digges

May 13

I have to acknowledge, one of 14 Ap. and one 2d. May. The Parcells, have not yet seen nor heard of. You may Stop the London Evg. and the London Packet for the future, but send on the courant if you please. Have not yet received, the debate upon Cs motion. I have seen the paper and read the debate. It is the scene of the Goddess in the Dunciad reading Blackmore to her Children. The Commons are yawning, while the Ministry and Clinton, are cementing the Union of America, by the blood of every Province, and binding all to their Allies, By compelling them to shed theirs. All is well that ends well. These wise folk are giving F. and S. a Consideration in Europe too, that they had not, and are throwing away their own as nothing worth. Sweden and Denmark, are in the Same System with Russia and Holland. Indeed if the Ministry, had only common Information, they would have known that this Combination of the maritime powers, has been forming these 18 Months, and was nearly as well agreed a year ago as it is now. But when a Nation is once, fundamentally wrong, thus it is. Internal Policy, external defence, foreign negotiations, all go away to gether. The bad Consequences of a Principle essentially Wrong, are infinite. The Minority, mean only to try if they can make peace with America Separately, in order to revenge themselves, as they think they can upon F. and S., but this is as wrong and as absurd, and impracticable as the plans of the ministry. All Schemes for reconciliation with America short of Independance, and all plans for Peace with America, allowing her Independance, Seperate from her allies, are visionary, and delusive, disingenuous, corrupt and wicked. America has taken her equal Station, and she will behave with as much honour, as any of the nations of the Earth. To Say that the Americans are upon the Poise, are ballancing, and will return to their Allegiance to the King of England, is as wild as bedlam. If Witnesses cannot be believed, why dont they believe the nature of things. Ask the Newspapers, which are so free, that nothing is Spared, Congress, and every body is attacked. Yet never a Single paragraph, even hinting in the most distant manner, a wish to return. Ask the Town meetings. Those assemblies which dared readily enough, to think as they pleased and say what they would, dared attack the King, Lords Commons, Governors, Councils, Representatives, Judges and whole armies, under the old Government, and that attack, every body and every thing that displeases them of this day. Not one Vote, not one Instruction to a Representative, not one Motion, nor so much as one Single Speach, in favour of returning to the Leeks of Egypt. Ask the grand and petit Juries, who dared to tell the Judges to their faces, they were corrupted, and that they would not serve under them because they had betrayed and overturn'd the Constitution. Not a single Juror, has ever whispered a Wish to return after being washed to their wallowing in the mire. The Refugees you mention never did know the Character of the American people, but they knew it now less than ever. They have been long away. The Americans of this day, have higher notions of themselves than ever. They think, they have gone through the greatest Revolution that ever took Place among Men, that this revolution is as much for the benefit of the generality of Mankind in Europe, as for their own. They think they should act a base and perfidious part towards the World in general, if they were to go back, that they should manifestly counteract the designs of providence, as well as betray themselves, their posterity and mankind. The English manifestly think Mankind and the World made for their Use. Americans dont think so. But why proceed. Time alone can convince.

Adieu   F. R. S.

May 13, 1780

BRITISH ANIMOSITY TOWARD AMERICA

To Edmé Jacques Genet

Sir   Paris May 17th. 1780

Genl. Conway in his Speech in the House of Commons, on the 6th. of May, affirms that the Alliance between France and the United States is not natural. Whether it is or not, is no doubt a great question. In order to determine, whether it is or no, one should consider, what is meant by a natural Alliance. And I know of no better general Rule than this, when two Nations, have the same Interests in general they are natural Allies, when they have opposite Interests, they are natural Ennemies. The general Observes 1st. that Nature, has raised a Barrier between France and America, but Nature has raised no other Barrier, than the Occean, and the Distance, and this Barrier is equally great between England and America. The General will not pretend that nature in the constitution of American Minds or Bodies, has laid any foundation for friendship or Enmity, towards one nation more than another. The General observes further that Habit, has raised another Barrier between France and America. But he should have considered, that the Habit of Affection or of Enmity between nations, are easily changed, as Circumstances vary, and as essential Interests alter. Besides the fact is that the horrible Perfidy and Cruelty of the English, towards the Americans, which they have taken care to make universally felt, in that Country for a long Course of years past has allienated the american mind and Heart from the English, and it is now much to be doubted whether any nation of Europe is So universally and so heartily detested by them. On the contrary most of the other Nations of Europe have treated them with Civility, and France and Spain with Esteem, Confidence, and Affection, which has greatly changed the Habits of the Americans in this respect. The 3d. material of which the Generals Barrier is created is Language. This no doubt, occasions many difficulties in the Communication, between the Allies, but is lessening every day. Perhaps no Language was ever studied at once, by So many persons at a time, in Proportion as french is now studied in America. And, it is certain that English was never so much studied in France, as since the Revolution, so that the difficulties of understanding one another are lessening every day. Religion is the fourth part of the Barrier —but let it be considered first, that there is not enough of Religion of any kind among the Great in England, to make the Americans, very fond of them. 2d. that what Religion there is in England, is as far from being the Religion of America as that of France. The Hierarchy of England, is quite as disagreable to America, as that of any other Country. Besides the Americans knew very well, that the Spirit of propagating any Religion by Conquest, and of making Proselytes by force or by Intrigue is fled from all other Country of the World, in a great measure, and that there is more of this Spirit remaining in England, than any where else. And the Americans had, and have still more reason, to fear the Introduction of a Religion that is disagreable to them, at least as far as Bishops and an Hierarchy go, from a Connection with England than any other nation of Europe. The Alliance with France, has no Article respecting Religion, France neither claims nor desires any Authority, or Influence over America in this respect: whereas England claimed, and intended to exercise Authority, and force over the Americans, at least So far as to introduce Bishops, and the English society for propagating the Gospel in foreign parts, has in fact for a Century sent large sums of Money to America to support their religion there, which really operated as a Bribe upon many minds and was the principal source of Toryism. So that upon the whole the alliance with France is in fact more natural, as far as religion is concerned than the former Connection with Great Britain, or any other Connection that can be formed.

Indeed whoever considers, attentively this Subject will see, that these 3 Circumstances, of Habit Language and religion will for the future operate, as natural causes of Animosity between England and America, because they will facilitate migration. The Loss of Liberty the decay of religion, the horrible national debt, the decline of Commerce, and of political Importance in Europe and of maritime power, which cannot but take place in England will tempt numbers, of their best people to emigrate to America, and to this fashions, Language, and religion, will contribute. The British Government will therefore see themselves obliged, to restrain this, by many Ways, and among others by cultivating an Animosity and Hatred in the minds of their People against the Americans. Nature has already sufficiently discovered itself, and all the World sees, that the British Government have for many Years, not only indulged in themselves the most unsocial and bitter passions against Americans, but have systematically encouraged them in the People.

After all; the Circumstances of Modes, Language and Religion, have much less Influence in determining the friendship and Emnity of nations, than other more essential Interests. Commerce is more than all these and many more such Circumstances. Now it is easy to see that the Commercial Interests, of England and America will forever hereafter be incompatible. America will take away or at least diminish the Trade of the English in ship building, in Freight, in the Whale fisheries, in the Cod Fisheries in Furs and Skins, and in other particulars too many to enumerate. In this respect America will not interfere with France, but on the Contrary will facilitate and benefit the french Commerce and marine, to a very great degree.

Here then will be a perpetual rivalry and Competition between England and America, and a continual source of Animosity and War. America will have Occasion for the Alliance of France, to defend her against this ill Will of England, as France will stand in Need of that of America, to aid her against the natural and continual Jealousies and Hostility of England.

The Boundaries of Territory, will, also be another constant source of disputes. If a Peace should unhappily be made leaving England in Possession of Canada, Nova Scotia, the Floridas or any one spot of Ground in America, they will be perpetually encroaching upon the states of America: whereas France, having renounced all territorial Jurisdiction in America, will have no room for Controversy.

The People of America therefore, whose very Farmers appear to have considered, the Interests of nations more profoundly than General Conway, are therefore universally of opinion that from the time they declared themselves independent, England became their natural Ennemy, and as she has been for Centuries and will be, the natural Ennemy of France, and the natural Ally of other natural Ennemies of France, America became the natural Friend of France, and She the natural friend of the United States—Powers naturally united against a Common Enemy, whose Interests will continue long to be, reciprocally secured and promoted, by mutual friendship.

It is very Strange that the English should thus dogmatically judge of the Interests of all other nations. According to them the Americans are and have been many years acting directly against their own Interest; France and Spain, have been acting against their own Interests, Holland is acting against her own Interest—Russia and the northern Powers are all acting against their own Interests—Ireland is acting against hers &c. So that there is only that little Island of the whole World that understand their own Interest—and of the Inhabitants of that, the Committees and Associations and Assemblies, are all in the same Error with the rest of the World: So that there remains only the Ministry and his equivocal, undulating Majority among all the People upon the face of the Earth who act naturally, and according to their own Interests.

The rest of the World however, think they understand

themselves very well, and that it is the English, or scottish Majority that are mistaken.

Your Friend   John Adams

THE MASSACHUSETTS CONSTITUTION

To William Gordon

Paris Hotel de Valois Ruë de Richelieu
Dear sir   May 26. 1780

I am much obliged to you, for your Letter of the 8 and 11. of March, which is the more prescious for being in so little Company, having not a line from any other, except a kind Card from Mr. S. Adams.

I thank you for your account of the Proceedings of Convention, and am happy to learn, that they have gone through the Report of the Committee. Mr. Jackson, has obliged Us, by an enumeration of the Amendments made, which if they do not improve the Plan, I am persuaded will contribute much to its acceptance, and upon the whole, I think the Constitution will be very good. The Report of the Committee, has been published in the Courier de L'Europe, and exceedingly applauded. The Article respecting Religion, is more admired, here than I expected. They compliment the Mass. with having outdone all other outdoings, in this respect.

Your Friend J. A. by advising an Acquiesence in the first Essay, meant well. But his Countrymen, who mean equally well, Saw further, as they have often done. J. A. thinks the Massachusetts are exhibiting a Phenominon in the political World, that is new and Singular. It is the first People, who have taken So much Time to deliberate upon Government—that have allowed such Universal Liberty to all the People to reflect upon the subject, and propose their objections and Amendments— and that have reserved to themselves at large, the right of finally accepting or rejecting the form. It forms a Kind of Epocha, in the History of the Progress of Society. I doubt not their final determination will be wise. The explicit Reservation of a Right to call a Convention in 1795, I think is judicious—

for altho the right of the People to call a Convention at any time cannot be denied; yet they might be less likely to think of it, in Earnest if it had not been mentioned.

You demand, Something in the way of Barter for the News you sent me. I acknowledge the Justice of it. But you have now such Correspondences, with various Parts of the World, that you will probably have from other Quarters, all I can send you, before mine will arrive.

I have written to my Masters, every Thing, that has happend in Europe, that they are interested in, but whether they receive it I dont know. The substance of the whole detail is, that France and Spain appear convinced of the Policy and Necessity of pursuing the War in America, especially be Sea: that they are exerting themselves with Vigeur to this End—that 12 ships of the Line 5 frigates &c with 11,500 Troops have Sailed 28 April from Cadiz. 8 ships of the Line, besides frigates and 6,000 Troops have Sailed from Brest, 2 May. That a second division is to follow from Brest. That Ireland, is not composed to rest, notwithstanding the duplicity, or the Temperisation of their Parliament. That Committees, associations and a Congress are going on, with some timidity and Irresolution however, in England. That all the Maritime Powers, Holland, Sweeden Denmark, Portugal, with Russia at their Head, have formed a Confederation to support a Neutrality, and the right of neutral Powers with arms in their Hands. That however the English, still flatter themselves with the submission of America, or at least that She will make a Separate Peace, and join England to revenge her against France and Spain, or at least be a silent Spectater of their Vengence—but no honest Thoughts of Peace.

Now, Mr. Historiographer, please to tell, Prince Posterity, one Truth, for me, and that is, that I love my Wife, and that I have left her, to see Countries where I dont find any body I like so well, to serve my Country. Pray what Motive will you impute it to? Ambition I suppose and the Love of Glory, like Tacitus and the rest of the malignant Run of impartial Historians, who will never allow any higher motive to govern Men. But if you dont tell the Prince aforesaid, that I had not enough of this Taste for Glory, to make me leave my Wife and Children, and that nothing but a sense of duty, added to all the taste I could have produced this Effect, you will want penetration to discover the Motives of one Heart, and I will undertake to tell Posterity my self that you are not a perfect Historian. And this Prince, will believe me, as soon as you. I suspect, I shall be obliged to turn Historiographer too. So let us both take Care least We give the other any thing improper to say. Adieu in Haste.

THE ROLE OF PROVIDENCE

To Edmund Jenings

Dear Sir   Paris June 11th. 1780

I have recieved with great pleasure yours of the 5th. I have certainly seen those extremes of Confidence and of Diffidence that You saw. We ought to attend to proofs, but we ought to discountenance Suspicions without Grounds. In these points We are agreed.

I assure you, Sir, I am of your Mind, that Providence is working the general Happiness, and whether We co-operate in it, with a good Will, or without co-operate We must. We mortals feel very big sometimes, and think ourselves acting a grand Roll, when in Truth it is the irresistible Course of Events that hurries Us on, and We have in fact very little Influence in them. The utmost that is permitted to Us is to assist, and it is our Duty to be very cautious that what we do is directed to a right End. When We are sure of this, We are sure We are right, and need not fear that things will go wrong. When We read of blinded Eyes and hardened Hearts, in the Case of the Jews and Egyptians and many other Nations; when We read of Infatuation, to which many great Historians asscribe Examples of remarkable Folly, in the Government of Nations and signal Calamaties in Consequence of it, I do not think it necessary to bring in divine Interpositions, to account for such Occurrences in an extraordinary Manner.

When Nations are corrupted, and grown generally vicious when they are intoxicated with Wealth or Power, and by this means delivered over to the Government of the baser Passion of their Nature, it is very natural that they should act an irrational part. They are really as a Body in a State Drunkenness. They neither act nor think like men in sound Health, and in possession of their Senses. Ambition, Avarice and Pleasure, when they prevail among the Multitude of a Nation to a certain degree, produce the appearance of a general Delirium and Intoxication.

The Candor and Freedom, with which you have given me your Sentiments; upon the Observations made You upon Conways Speech, I assure you Sir, I consider as the most genuine Marks of Friendship. I wish I may be found in Experience to be mistaken in my apprehension that Britain will in future be unfriendly to Us. If She could have magnanimity enough to give up all America, I mean Canada, Nova Scotia and the Floridas as well as the United States, the natural Cause of Avidity and Hostility, which arises from Territory, would be removed. But can We obtain this? We shall I believe if She continues the War. But there is another Thing that comes upon me forever. English Sailors speak the American Language. They will find better Bread in our Service. They will find Beer and Grog and Beef and Pudding. What should hinder them from crouding to America? Will not the American Trade, once free, spread beyond even my most sanguine Expectations? England should have considered this long ago. Americans did, to my certain Knowledge, in great Numbers. Hostility will come from the Side of the English. America will have no Temptation to it, but the Provocations which England will give. The true American System will be Peace, eternal Peace: but this very System will provoke England. In future Times, America at Peace, and England at War, what will become of her? How many will fly, Sailors especially, to the standard of the Olive Branch. Will not this excite her Envy, her Jealousy; her Rage?

The Reasons however that You offer, are very forcible, for omitting this part, or softening of it. You know the People of England better than I. It is impossible however to conceal these things. The People of England now know them very well, but are silent about them least they should stimulate other Nations to be more active, and the Americans too. There are unthinking members in America no doubt, who please themselves with vain hopes of Friendship and Kindness again with England: but the considerate People of all Ranks despair of it.

I am sure action speaks louder than Words. There never was given by any Nation, more dreadful proofs of deadly Hate, than have been constantly given these five Years by the English to Americans. Lord Mansfield's Words have been adopted in all their Actions. Kill them, kill them, right or wrong, by fas and nefas, kill them or they will kill you. Delenda est Carthago —sink them all upon one plank—burn them up, that they may not be useful to their Allies, nor destructive to Us. These have been their Words and Actions. Do You know the deep political Motive for ringing the everlasting Knell of Rebel and Rebellion. Have you not considered that the Nation have habitually settled it in their minds and Hearts, that Rebels have no Rights, that every thing is lawful against them. They are Insects, they are Reptiles, they are Serpents, they are wild Boars and Tygers, they are Devils in the English Imagination. Have not Parliament, Gazettes, Pamphlets, Common Prayers, Sermons, and every thing for these six years, shot this Word down deep into the minds of the People of England and produced its Effect. The Government, the Church, the Nation itself means to establish an ineradicable Hatred and Animosity against us. I am sorry for it.

There is but one Way—that is make Peace—let Us live in Peace: in this Case We shall never designedly injure them. We shall trade with them, and in this Way help them to keep up some of their Importance. But they are in a right Way to drive away forever all our Trade, and make Us hostile too—for these horrible Passions engender the like in other Minds. I submit the whole to your Correction and am &c

Adieu.   John Adams

THE DEATH OF THOMAS HUTCHINSON

To Abigail Adams

My dear Portia   June 17. 1780
I yesterday received a Letter of 26 April from Brother Cranch, for which I thank him and will answer as soon as possible. He tells me you have drawn a little Bill upon me. I am

sorry for it, because I have sent and should continue to send you, small Presents by which you would be enabled to do better than by drawing Bills. I would not have you draw any more. I will send you Things in the family Way which will defray your Expences better. The Machine is horribly dear. Mr. C. desires to know if he may draw on me. I wish it was in my power to oblige him but it is not. I have no Remittances nor any Thing to depend on, not a Line from Congress nor any member since I left you. My Expences thro Spain, were beyond all Imagination, and my Expences here are so exorbitant, that I cant answer any Bill from any body not even from you, excepting the one you have drawn. I must beg you, to be as prudent as possible. Depend upon it, your Children will have Occasion for all your Œconomy. Mr. Johonnot must send me some Bills. Every farthing is expended and more. You can have no Idea of my unavoidable Expences. I know not what to do.

Your little affairs and those of all our Friends, Mr. Wibert &c. are on Board the Alliance and have been so these 4 months, or ready to be.—Pray write me by the Way of Spain and Holland as well as France. We are all well.—My Duty to your father, my Mother, and affections and Respects where due.

My affections I fear got the better of my Judgment in bringing my Boys. They behave very well however.

London is in the Horrors.—Governor Hutchinson fell down dead at the first appearance of Mobs. They have been terrible. A Spirit of Bigotry and Fanaticism mixing with the universal discontents of the nation, has broke out into Violences of the most dreadful Nature—burnt Lord Mansfields House, Books, Manuscripts—burnd the Kings Bench Prison, and all the other Prisons—let loose all the Debtors and Criminals. Tore to Pieces Sir G. Savilles House—insulted all the Lords of Parliament &c. &c. Many have been killed—martial Law proclaimed—many hanged—Lord George Gordon committed to the Tower for high Treason—and where it will end God only knows.—The Mobs all cryd Peace with America, and War with France—poor Wretches! as if this were possible.

In the English Papers they have inserted the Death of Mr. Hutchinson with severity, in these Words—Governor Hutchinson is no more. On Saturday last he dropped down dead. It is charity to hope that his sins will be buried with him in the

Tomb, but they must be recorded in his Epitaph. His Misrepresentations have contributed to the Continuance of the War with America. Examples are necessary. It is to be hoped that all will not escape into the Grave, without a previous Appearance, either on a Gibbet or a scaffold.

Govr. Bernard I am told died last fall. I wish, that with these primary Instruments of the Calamities that now distress almost all the World the Evils themselves may come to an End. For although they will undoubtedly End, in the Welfare of Mankind, and accomplish the Benevolent designs of Providence, towards the two Worlds; Yet for the present they are not joyous but grievous.

May Heaven permit you and me to enjoy the cool Evening of Life, in Tranquility, undisturbed by the Cares of Politicks or War—and above all with the sweetest of all Reflections, that neither Ambition, nor Vanity, nor Avarice, nor Malice, nor Envy, nor Revenge, nor Fear, nor any base Motive, or sordid Passion through the whole Course of this mighty Revolution, and the rapid impetuous Course of great and terrible Events that have attended it, have drawn Us aside from the Line of our Duty and the Dictates of our Consciences!—Let Us have Ambition enough to keep our Simplicity, or Frugality and our Integrity, and transmit these Virtues as the fairest of Inheritances to our Children.

Translation of Thomas Pownall's "Memorial to the Sovereigns of Europe"

A Translation of the "Memorial to the Sovereigns of Europe," into common Sense and intelligible English

A Pamphlet has been published in England, under the Title of "A Memorial to the Sovereigns of Europe, on the present State of Affairs, between the old and new World." It is said to have been written by Governor Pownal: and there are So many quaint Words, and dark Expressions, intermixed with So many good Thoughts and So much Knowledge of America that it seems worth translating.

The Memorialist begins, with observing very justly, that at the End of the last War, a new System was begun, both political and commercial, which is now compleatly formed: that the Spirit of Commerce has become a leading Power: that at that time, the Center of this System was Great Britain, whose Government might, if it had been wise, have preserved the Advantage of continuing the Center both of the Commerce and Politicks of the World: but being unwise, they disturbed the Course of Things, and have not only lost, forever, that dominion, which they had and might have held, but the extirnal Parts of the Empire are, one after another falling off, and it will be once more reduced to its insular Existence.

On the other hand, this new System of Power, moving round its own proper Center, which is, America, has dissolved all the Forces Sent against it by the English. and has formed natural Connections, with France and Spain, and other Countries. Founded in Nature, it is growing, by accellerated motions, into a great and powerfull Empire. It has taken its equal Station among the nations of the Earth. Video Solem orientem in Occidente. The Congress of The United States of North America is a new primary Planet, which taking its Course in its own orbit, must have an Effect upon the orbit of every other, and Shift the common Center of Gravity of the whole System of the European World. They are De Facto, an independant Power, and must be so de Jure.

The Politicians of Europe, may reason; and the Powers

of Europe may negotiate or fight: but such Reasonings, Negotiations, and Wars, will have no Consequence on the Right or the Fact. It would be just as wise to fight or negotiate for the dominion of the moon, which is common to them all; and all may profit of her reflected Light. The Independence of America, is as fixed as Fate. She is Mistress of her own Fortune; knows that She is So; and will manage that Power which She feels herself possessed of, to establish her own System, and change that of Europe.

If the Powers of Europe, will See the State of Things, and act accordingly, the Lives of Thousands may be Spared, the Happiness of millions Secured and the Peace of the World preserved: if not, they will be plunged into a Sea of Blood. The War, which is almost gorged, between Britain and America, will extend itself to all the maritime Powers, and most probably afterwards to all the Inland Powers, and like the thirty years War of the Sixteenth and Seventeenth Centuries, will not end, but by a general Resettlement of Interests, according to the Spirit of the new System, which has taken Place. Why may not all this be done, by a Congress, of all Nations, before, as well as after the War?

The final Settlement of Power, at a Peace, is never in Proportion to the Success of Arms. It depends upon the Interposition of Parties, who have not meddled in the War, but who come to the Treaty of Peace, brought forward by Intrigue, with the Aid of Jealousy, and counteract by Negotiation the Envied Effects of Arms.

The Britons have forced the present system into Establishment, before its natural Season. They might have Secured the Attachment of the Plantations for years to come: but it was a principal part of the Plan of the confidential Counsellors, in a general Reformation of the Kings Government, to reform the Constitutions of America. They were informed it would lead to War, but they thought it would be a good measure to force the Americans to Arms. Conquest of which they were sure, would give them the right of giving what Constitutions they thought fit, Such as that of Quebec, little foreseeing what a War it would prove, and Still less Suspecting, that France and Spain, and all the rest of the World, would interpose.

None of the Powers of Europe, and few of the most knowing Politicians have considered, what Effect this Revolution will have on the general System of Europe. (Note. Here it Should Seem, Governor Pownal is mistaken. Every Power in Europe, and every great Politician in Europe, except those in Great Britain, have digested this Subject.)

One Thing is certain, that on whatever Ground the War between G. Britain and Bourbon began, whatever course it may take, however long they may continue it, to their mutual destruction, the Americans will never belong to either Foedere inaquali. The Powers of Europe who will become Parties, before these affairs shall have been brought to the Issue will concur, in no other Settlement, than that these States are an independant Sovereign Power, holding a free Commerce equally with all.

In order to Shew how these matters will finally be Settled, he proposes to lay before, the Sovereigns, a View of Europe and America, and point out, what will be the natural Effects of the Seperation of them, and of the Independence of America, upon the commercial and political State of Europe; and finally to Shew how, the present Crisis, may be, by Wisdom and Benevolence, wrought into the greatest Blessing of Peace, Liberty and Happiness, which the World hath yet Seen.

He then proceeds to compare, the new and old World, in Point of Spirit, Magnitude and Power. In measuring the Magnitude of States too much is commonly ascribed, to Extent of Country and Fertility of Soil. That Extent of Dominion, which is most capable of a Systematical Connection and Communication, has the most natural Greatness. The three other Parts of the World, are naturally Seperated from each other, and altho, once under the dominion of the Romans, as this was an unnatural Exertion, beyond the Resources of human nature, it Soon dissolved, and they Seperated. Europe, Asia, and Africa, are not only Seperated by their local Positions but are inhabited by distinct Species of the human Being. North and South America, are, in like manner naturally divided. North America is possessed, by Englishmen, and this natural Circumstance forms this division of America into one great Society, the Basis of a great Dominion. There is nowhere in Europe So great and combined an Interest, communicating through So large a Territory, as that in North America. The northern and Southern

Parts of Europe, are possessed by different nations, actuated by different Sovereignties and Systems. Their Intercourse is interrupted: they are at perpetual Variance. Intercourse is difficult over Land, and by Sea. They are cutt off, by intervening nations. On the contrary, when North America is examined, you find every Thing united in it, which forms Greatness. The nature of the coast and the Winds renders communication by navigation perpetual. The Rivers open an Inland navigation, which carries on a Circulation through the whole. The Country thus united, and one part of it, communicating with another, by its Extent of Territory, and Variety of Climates, produces all that nature requires, that Luxury loves, or that Power can employ. All those Things, which the Nations of Europe, under every difficulty, that a defect of natural communication, under every Obstruction that a perverse artificial System throw in their Way, barter for; are in North America possessed, with an uninterrupted natural Communication, an unobstructed navigation and an universal Freedom of Commerce, by one Nation. The naval Stores, Timber, Hemp, Fisheries, and Salt Provisions of the North; the Tobacco, Rice, Cotton, Silk, Indigo, Fruits and perhaps Wines, Resin and Tar, of the South, form a Reciprocation of Wants and Supplies. The Corn, Flour, Manufactures &c. of the middle States, fill up the Communication and compleat its System. They unite those Parts, which were before connected, and organize the Several Parts, into one whole.

Civilization, next to Union of System and Communication of Parts constitute, what Lord Bacon calls, the Amplitude and Growth of State. The Civilization of America, may be compared to that of Europe. It is Superiour to that of Europe. Architecture, Painting, Statuary, Poetry, oratory, and the mechanick Arts are not So well understood and practiced nor are the Sciences, those of Government and Policy particularly, So learnedly mastered by any Individual in America, as they are by Some in Europe. But Arts, Sciences, Agriculture, Manufactures, Government, Policy, War, and Commerce, are better understood by the Collective Body of the People in America than they are by that of Europe, or any nation in it. And this is the only Way of Stating the Comparison of Civilization, and in this Respect America is infinitely further removed from Barbarity, than Europe.

Translation of the Memorial to the Sovereigns of Europe
upon the present State of Affairs between the
old and the new World, into common Sense,
and intelligible English, continued.

When the Spirit of Civilization began first in Europe, after the barbarous Ages of the northern Invaders; the Clergy were the blind Leaders to Light, and the feudal Lords, the Patrons of Liberty. What Knowledge! What Liberty! The Instruction of the first was more pernicious than Ignorance. The Patronage of the last was the Benevolence of the Grazier, who fattens his Cattle for the Profit of their Hides and Tallow. The People held their Knowledge, as they did their Lands, by a servile Tenure, which did not permit them to Use it as their own. Such was the Source of Civilization in Europe.

The first movement of Civilization, is the application of Labour to the Culture of the Earth, in order to raise that Supply of food, which is necessary for Men in Society. The application of Labour to Architecture, Cloathing, Tools and Instruments is concomitant with this. Marketts, in which a Reciprocation of Wants and surplusses, is accomplished, Succeed. Hence arise by a farther Improvement Artificers and Manufacturers: and in succession, a surplus is created beyond what is wanted by the Individuals or the Community which produces Commerce, by exchanging this surplus for Articles of Conveniency, or Enjoyment, which the Country does not produce. By the Violence of the military Spirit, under which Europe was a second Time peopled, the Inhabitants were divided into two Classes, Warriours and Slaves. Agriculture, was conducted by the latter; Wretches annexed to, not owners of the Soil; degraded Animals! Cattle! Property! Not Proprietors! *They* had no Interest in their own Reason, Labour or Time. *They* had neither Knowledge nor Motive to make an Effort of Improvement. Improvement in Agriculture, was therefore many hundred Years at a Stand. Altho in Some Countries of Europe it may Seem at present progressive, it is so slow, that for Ages, it can have no great Effect, except perhaps in England, yet even here the Farmer is absurdly and cruelly oppressed. Manufactures, or the Labour of Men, in Wool, Iron, Stone, or Leather, were held as the Servile offices of Society, and fit only for Slaves. These Artificers were mere Machines of the most arrogant and ignorant Masters. They would never make Experiments—so that Mechanicks and Arts went on for Ages without Improvements.

Upon the Dissolution of the Hanseatick League, the Sovereigns, who had Seen the Power, which arose from manufactures and Trade, began to encourage their Subjects and invite Strangers, to establish them. Civilization took a momentary Start. But the Policy of the Sovereigns, held the Manufacturers in a wretched Condition, by many obstructing Regulations. The same Policy affecting to encourage Manufactures, gave them a false help, by Setting assizes on the Produce of Land, which oppressed Agriculture. This Same System of Policy, confined Ingenuity, by making imposing Regulations, on every motion of Manufactures, on their coming from the Hand of the Workman; on the Carriage; on the Sale; on the Return, whether in goods or Money. This Policy was directed to draw into the Treasury of the State, all the Profit beyond the Labourers Subsistance. Commercial Legislation was directed wholly, to make the subject Sell, but not buy: export Articles, but import money of which the State must have the greatest share. Hence exclusive Property of certain materials of manufacture, which they called Staple Commodities—hence monopolies—exclusive Priviledges of Trade, to Persons, Articles and Places; exclusive Fisheries; hence the notions of the Ballance of Trade: and hence the whole Train of Retaliations, Restraints on Exportation; Prohibitions of Importation; alien Duties, Imposts. Having thus rendered Communication among themselves almost impracticable, they were forced to look out for foreign Settlements. Hence Colonies, which might be worked like out Farms for the exclusive Benefit of the Metropolis. Hence that wildest of all the wild Visions of Avarice and Ambition, the Attempt to render the Ocean an Object of Property; the Claim of Possession in it, and dominion over it. Thus Civilization was obstructed, the Spirit of Improvement checked, and the Light of Genius extinguished. Events *may* arise, which may induce, the Rulers of Europe, to revise and reform the hard Conditions of its Imprisonment, and give it Liberty.

In America, all the Inhabitants are free, and allow universal naturalization to all that wish to be so, and a perfect Liberty of using any mode of Life they choose, or any means of getting a Livelihood, that their Talents lead them to. Their Souls are their own. Their Reason is their own. Their Time is their own. They are their own Masters. Their Labour is employed on their own Property, and what they produce is their own. Where every man has the free and full Exertion of his Powers, and may acquire any Share of Profit or Power that his Spirit can work him up to, there is an unabated Application; and a perpetual Struggle of Spirits, sharpens the Wit, and trains the Mind. The Acquisition of Knowledge in Business, necessary to this mode of Life, gives the Mind a Turn of Investigation, which forms a Character peculiar to these People. This is called Inquisitiveness, which goes often to ridicule, but is in matters of Business and Commerce an usefull Talent. They are animated with the Spirit of the New Philosophy. Their Life is a Course of Experiments; and Standing on as high Ground of Improvement as the most enlightened Parts of Europe have advanced, like Eaglets commence the first Efforts of their Pinnions from a Towering Advantage.

In Europe the poor mans Wisdom is despized. The poor mans Wisdom is not Learning but Knowledge of his own Picking up, from Facts and nature, by Simple Experience. In America, the Wisdom and not the Man is attended to. America is the Poor Mans Country. The Planters there reason not from what they hear, but from what they See and feel. They follow what mode they like. They feel that they can venture to make Experiments, and the Advantages of their Discoveries are their own. They therefore try what the Soil claims, what the Climate permits, and what both will produce to the greatest Advantage. In this Way, they have brought into Cultivation, and Abundance of what no Nation of the old World ever did, or could. They raise not only plenty and Luxury for their internal Supply, but the Islands in the West Indies have been Supplied from their Superabundance, and Europe, in many Articles has profited of it. It has had its Fish from their Seas: its Wheat and Flour from one Part: its Rice from another part: its Tobacco and Indigo from another: its Timber and naval Stores from another. Olives, oranges and Wines are introducing by Experiments.

This Spirit of Civilization first attaches itself to mother

Earth, and the Inhabitants become Land Workers. You See them labouring at the Plough and the Spade, as if they had not an Idea above the Earth yet their minds are all the while enlarging all their Powers, and their Spirit rises as their Improvements advance. Many a real Phylosopher, Politician and Warriour, emerges out of this Wilderness, as the Seed rises out of the Ground.

They have also made many Improvements in Handicrafts, Tools and machines. Want of Tools and the Unfitness of Such as they had, have put these Settlers to their Shifts, and these shifts are Experiments. Particular Uses calling for Some Alteration, have opened many a new Invention. More new Tools and machines, and more new Forms of old ones, have been invented in America than were ever invented in Europe in the Same Space of Time. They have not turned their Labour into Arts and manufactures, because their Labour employed in its own natural Way can produce those Things which purchase Articles of Arts and manufactures, cheaper, than they could make them. But tho they dont manufacture for Sale, they find Fragments of Time which they cannot otherwise employ, in which they make most of the Articles of personal Ware and Household Use, for home Consumption. When the Field shall be filled with Husbandmen and the Classes of Handicraft fully Stocked, as there are no Laws, which impose Conditions, on which a Man is to become intituled to exercise this or that Trade, or by which he is excluded, from exercising the one or the other, in this or that Place: none that prescribe the manner in which or the Prices at which he is to work, or that confine him even to the Trade he was bred to; the moment that Civilization carried on in its natural Course, is ripe for it, the Branch of Manufactures, will take root, and grow with an astonishing Rapidity. Altho they do not attempt to force the Establishment of manufactures, yet, following the natural Progress of Improvement, they every Year produce a Surplus of Profit. With these Surplusses, and not with manufactures, they carry on their Commerce. Their Fish, Wheat, Flour, Rice, Tobacco, Indigo, Live Stock, Barrell Pork and Beef, Some of these being peculiar to the Country and Staple Commodities, form their Exports. This has given them a direct Trade to Europe and a circuitous one to Africa and the West Indies. The

Same Ingenuity, in mechanicks which accompanies their Agriculture, enters into their Commerce, and is exerted in Ship building. It is carried on, not only for their own Freight, and that of the West Indies, but for Sale, and to Supply a great Part of the Shipping of Britain; and if it continues to advance will Supply a great Part of the Trade of Europe with Ships, at cheaper Rates, than they can any where, or by any means Supply themselves. Thus their Commerce, altho under various Restrictions, while they were Subordinate Provinces, by its advancing Progress, in Shipbuilding, hath Struck deep Roots, and is now Shot forth into an active Trade, Amplitude of State and great Power.

It will be objected, that the Ballance of Trade has been at all Times against America So as to draw all the Gold and Silver from it, and for this Reason it cannot advance in commerce and opulence. It will be answered, that, America, Even while in depressd and restrained Provinces, has advanced its Cultivation to great Opulence, and constantly extending the Channells of its Trade, and increasing its Shipping. Tis a fallacious Maxim to judge of the general Ballance of Profit in Commerce, by the motions of one Article of Commerce, the prescious metals. These metals will always go to that Country that pays the most for them. That country which on any Sudden Emergency wants Money, and knows not how to circulate any other than Silver and gold, must pay the most for them. The Influx of them, therefore, into a Country, instead of being a Consequence of the Ballance of Trade being in its Favour, or the Efflux being a Mark of the Ballance being against it, may be a Proof of the Contrary. The Ballance of Trade, reckoned by the Import or Export of Gold and Silver, may in many Cases be Said to be against England and in Favour of the Countries to which its Money goes. If this Import or Export, was the Effect of a final Settled Account, instead of being only the Transfer of this Article to or from an Account currant (as it commonly is) yet it would not be a Mark of the Ballance of Trade. England, from the Nature of its Government, and Extent of its Commerce, has established a Credit, on which, in any Emergency, it can give Circulation to Paper Money, almost to any Amount. If it could not, it must at any Rate, purchase gold and Silver, and there would be a great Influx of the prescious Metals. Will any one Say, that this is a Symptom of the Ballance of Trade being in its favour! But, on the contrary having Credit, from a progressive Ballance of Profit, it can, even in Such an Emergency, Spare its Gold and Silver, and even make a Profit of it, as an Article of Commerce exported. Here We See, the Ballance of Profit creating a Credit, which circulates as money, even while its gold and Silver are exported. If any Event like the Recoignage of the Gold in England which called in the old Coin at a better Price, than that at which it was circulating abroad, Should raise the Price of this article, in England, it will for the Same reason, as it went out, be again imported into England, not as a Ballance of Accounts, but as an Article of Trade, of which, the best profit could at that moment be made. The Fact was, that at that period, Quantities of English Gold Coin, to a great Amount, were actually imported into England in bulk; and yet this was no mark of any Sudden Change of a Ballance of Trade in favour of that Country. The Ballance of Trade reckoned by this false Rule, has been always Said to be against North America: but the Fact is, that their Government, profiting of a Credit arising from the progressive Improvements, and advancing Commerce of the Country hath, by a refined Policy, established a Circulation of Paper money, to an Amount that is astonishing. That from the immense quantity it should depreciate, is nothing to this argument, for it has had its Effect. The Americans therefore can Spare their Gold and Silver as well as England, and Information Says, there is now locked up in America, more than three millions of English money, in Gold and Silver, which when their Paper is annihilated, will come forth. The Efflux, therefore of Gold and Silver, is no Proof of a Ballance against them: on the contrary, being able to go without Gold and Silver, but wanting other Articles without which they could not proceed in their Improvements, in Agriculture, Commerce, or War, the Gold and silver is, in Part hoarded, and part exported for these Articles. In Fact, this objection, which is always given as an Instance of Weakness in America, under which, she must Sink, turns out, in the true State of it, an Instance of the most extensive Amplitude and Growth of State. It would be well for England, if, while She tryumphs over this mote in her Sisters Eye, She would attend to the Beam in her own, and prepare for the Consequences of her own Paper Money.

From this Comparison of the State of Civilization, applied to Agriculture, Mechanicks and Commerce, extended through a large Territory, having a free Communication through the whole, it appears, that North America has advanced, and is every day advancing, to a Growth of State, with a constant and accellerating motion, of which there has never been any Example in Europe.

To be continued.

Translation of the Memorial
to the Souvereigns of Europe, continued.

The two Countries may be compared, in the Progress of Population. In North America Children are a Blessing. They are Riches and Strength to the Parents. In Europe, Children are a Burden. The Causes of which have been explained in the observations concerning the Increase of Mankind, the Peopling of Countries &c. Take a few Examples. The Massachusetts Bay, had, of Inhabitants in the Year 1722 Ninety four Thousands. In 1742 one hundred Sixty four Thousands. In 1751 when there was a great depopulation both by War and the Small Pox one hundred and Sixty four Thousand, four hundred and Eighty four. In 1761, 216,000. In 1765 255,500. In 1771 292,000. In 1773 300,000. In Connecticutt, in 1756 129,994. In 1774 257,356. These Numbers are not increased by Strangers, but decreased by Wars and Emigrations to the Westward, and to other States, yet they have nearly doubled in Eighteen years.

In N. York in 1756—96,776—in 1771—168,007. In 1774—182,251. In Virginia in 1756—173,316. In 1764—200,000. In 1774—300,000. In S. Carolina in 1750—64,000. In 1770—115,000. In R. Island in 1738—15,000. In 1748—28,439.

As there never was a militia in Pensilvania, with authentic Lists of the Population, it has been variously estimated on Speculation. There was a constant Importation for many years of Irish and foreign Emigrants, yet many of these Settled in other Provinces: but the Progress of Population, in the ordinary course advanced in a Ratio, between that of Virginia and that of Massachusetts Bay. The City of Philadelphia advanced more rapidly. It had in 1749—2076 Houses. In 1753—2300. In 1760—2969. In 1769—4474. From 1749 to 1753 from 16 to 18,000 Inhabitants; from 1760 to 1769 from 31,318 to 35,000. There were in 1754 various Calculations and Estimates made of the Numbers on the Continent. The Sanguine made the Numbers, one million and an half. Those who admitted less Speculation into the Calculation, but adhered closer to Facts and Lists, Stated them at one million, two hundred and fifty thousand. The Estimate Said to be taken in Congress in 1774 makes them 3,026,678. But there must have been great Scope of Speculation in that Estimate. Another after two or three years of War is Two Million Eight hundred and Ten Thousand. 2,141,307 would turn out nearest to the real amount in 1774. But what an Amazing Progress, which in 18 years has added a million to a million two hundred and fifty thousand, altho a War was maintained in that country for seven years of the Term. In this View one sees a Community unfolding itself beyond any Example in Europe.

But the Model of these Communities, which has always taken Place, from the Beginning, has enrolled, every Subject as a Soldier, and trained a greater Part or 535,326 of these People to Arms, which number the Community has, not Seperate from the civil, and formed into a distinct Body of regular Soldiers, but remaining united in the internal Power of the Society, a national Piquet Guard, always prepared for defence. This will be thought ridiculous by the regular Generals of Europe: But Experience hath evinced, that for the very Reason, that they are not a Seperate Body, but members of the Community, they are a real and effectual Defence. The true Greatness of a State consists in Population, where there is Valour, in Individuals, and a military Disposition in the Frame of the Community: where all, and not particular Conditions and degrees only, make Profession of Arms, and bear them in their Country's defence.

This Country is now an independent State, and has been avowedly and compleatly so, for more than four Years. It is indeed Six years, Since it was so in Effect. It hath taken its equal Station among the Nations. It is an Empire, the Spirit of whose Government, extends from the Center to the extream Parts. Universal Participation of Council, creates Reciprocation of universal Obedience. The Seat of Government, will be well informed of the State and Condition of the remote and extream Parts, which by Participation in the Legislature, will be informed and Satisfied in the Reasons and necessity of the Measures of Government. These will consider themselves as acting in every Grant that is made, and in every Tax imposed. This Consideration will give Efficacy to Government, that Consensus Obedientium, on which the permanent Power of Empire is founded. This is the Spirit of the new Empire in America. It is liable to many disorders, but young and Strong, like the Infant Hercules it will Strangle these Serpents in the Cradle. Its Strength will grow with Years. It will establish its Constitution and perfect Growth to Maturity. To this Greatness of Empire, it will certainly arise. That it is removed Three thousand miles from its Ennemy; that it lies on another Side of the Globe, where it has no Ennemy: that it is Earth born and like a Giant ready to run its Course, are not the only Grounds, on which a Speculatist may pronounce this. The fostering Care with which the Rival Powers of Europe will nurse it, ensures its Establishment, beyond all doubt or danger.

When a State is founded on such Amplitude of Territory; whose Intercourse is So easy; whose Civilization is So advanced; where all is Enterprize, and Experiment: where Agriculture has made So many discoveries of new and peculiar Articles of Cultivation: where the ordinary Produce of Bread Corn, has been carried to a degree, that has made it a Staple Export, for the Supply of the old World: whose Fisheries are mines, producing more Solid Riches than all the Silver of *Potosi*: where Experiment hath invented so many new and ingenious Improvements in mechanicks: where the Arts, Sciences, Legislation and Politicks, are Soaring with a Strong and Extended Pinion; where Population has multiplied like the Seeds of the Harvest: where the Power of these numbers, taking a military Form, shall lift itself up as a young Lion: where Trade of extensive orbit, circulating in its own Shipping, has wrought these Efforts of the Community to an active Commerce: where all these Powers have united and taken the Form of Empire; I may Suppose I cannot err, or give offence to the greatest Power in Europe, when upon a Comparison of the State of Mankind and of the Powers of Europe, with that of America, I venture to Suggest to their Contemplation, that America is growing too large for any Government in Europe to manage as subordinate. That the Government of Congress and the States is too firmly fixed in the Hands of their own Community to be either directed by other Hands, or taken out of those, in which it is. And that the Power in Men and Arms is too much to be forced, at the distance of Three Thousand miles. Were I to ask an Astronomer whether, if a Satellite Should grow, untill it could ballance with its Planet, whether it could be held any longer, by any of the Powers of nature in the orbit of a Satellite, and whether any external Force could keep it there, he will answer me directly, no. If I ask a Father, after his Son is grown up to full Strength of Body, Mind and Reason, whether he can be held in Pupillage, and will Suffer himself to be treated and corrected as a Child, he must answer, No. Yet, if I ask an European Politician, who learns by Hearsay and thinks by Habit, whether North America will remain dependent, he answers, Yes. He will have a Thousand reasons why it must be So, altho Fact rises in his Face to the very contrary. Politicians, instead of being employed to find out Reasons to explain Facts, are often employed with a Multitude about them, to invent and make Facts according to predetermined Reasonings. Truth, however, will prevail. This is not Said to prove, but to explain the Fact, So that the Consequences may be Seen. The present Combination of Events, whether, attended to or not, whether wrought by Wisdom into the System of Europe or not, will force its Way there, by the Vigour of natural causes. Europe, in the course of its commerce, and even in the internal order and Œconomy of its communities, will be affected by it. The Statesman cannot prevent its Existence, nor resist its operation. He may embroil his own Affairs, but it will become his best Wisdom, and his duty to his Sovereign and the People, that his measures coincide and cooperate with it.

The first Consequence of this Empire, is, the Effect it will have as a naval Power on the Commerce, and political System of Europe.

Whoever understands the Hanseatic League, and its Progress, in naval Power, by possessing the commanding Articles of the Commerce of the World; the command of the great Rivers;

its being the Carrier of Europe; that it could attract, resist and even command the landed Powers; that it was made up of Seperate and unconnected Towns, included within the dominions, of other States; that they had no natural communication, and only an artificial Union: whoever considers, not only the commercial but naval and political Power, which this League established throughout Europe, will See, on how much more Solid a Basis, the Power of North America Stands; how much faster it must grow, and to what an Ascendancy of Interest, carrying on the greatest Part of the Commerce, and commanding the greatest Part of the Shipping of the World, this great commercial and naval Power must Soon arrive. If the League, without the natural Foundation of a political Body, in Land, could grow by commerce and navigation to such Power: if, of Parts Seperated by nature and only joined by Art and Force, they could become a great political Body, acting externally with an Interest and Power, that took a lead and even an Asendancy, in Wars, and Treaties. What must North-America, removed at the Distance of half the Globe, from all the Obstructions of Rival Powers, founded in a landed Dominion peculiarly adapted for Communication of Commerce, and Union of Power, rise to in its Progress? As the Hanseatic League grew up to Power, Denmark, Sweeden, Poland, and France, Sought its Alliance, under the common Veil of Pride, by offers of becoming its Protectors. England also growing fast into a commercial Power, had commercial Arrangements, by Treaty with it. Just so now, will the Sovereigns of Europe; just so have, the Bourbon Compact, the greatest Power in Europe, courted the Friendship of America. Standing on Such a Basis, and growing up under Such Auspices, one may pronounce of America, as was said of Rome Civitas incredibile est memoratu, adepta Libertate, quantum brevi creverit.

In the Course of this American War, all the Maritime Powers of Europe, will one after another, as Some of the leading ones have already done, apply to the States of America, for a Share, in their Trade, and for a Settlement of the Forms, on which they may carry it, on, with them. America, will then become, the Arbitress of the Commercial, and perhaps as the Seven united Belgic Provinces were in the Year 1647 the Mediatrix of Peace, and of the political Business of the World.

If North America follows the Principles on which nature has established her; and if the European Alliances Which She has made do not involve her in and Seduce her to, a Series of Conduct, destructive of that System, which those Principles lead to, She must observe, that as nature hath Seperated her from Europe, and established her alone on a great Continent, far removed from the old World, and all its embroiled Interests, and wrangling Politicks, without an Ennemy or a Rival or the Entanglement of Alliances.—1. that it is contrary to her Interest, and the Nature of her Existence, that She Should have any Connections of Politicks with Europe, other than merely commercial; and even, on that Ground, to observe inviolably the caution of not being involved, in either the Quarrells, or the Wars of Europeans. 2. That the real State of America is, that of being the common Source of Supply to Europe in general, and that her true Interest is therefore, that of being a free Port to all Europe at large, and that all Europe, at large, Should be the common market for American Exports. The true Interest therefore of America, is, not to form any partial Connections with any Part, to the Exclusion of the rest. If England had attended to her true Interest, as connected with that of America, She would have known that it is the Commerce, and not the Conquest of America by which she could be benefited: and if She would even yet, with temper listen to her true Interest, She would Still find, that that Commerce, would in a great measure continue, with the Same benefit, were the two Countries as independent of each other as France and Spain, because in many Articles, neither of them can go to a better market. This is meant as under their present habits and Customs of Life. Alienation may change all this.

The first great leading Principle will be that North America, will become a free Port to all the nations of the World, indiscriminately; and will expect, insist on, and demand, in fair Reciprocity, a free market in all those nations with whom She trades. This will, if She forgets not, nor forsakes her real nature, be the Basis of all her commercial Treaties. If She adheres to this Principle, She must be in the course of Time, the chief Carrier of the commerce of the whole World, because unless the Several Powers of Europe, become to each other, likewise free Ports and free marketts, America alone will come to and act there, with an ascendant Interest, that must command every Advantage to be derived from them.

The Commerce of North America, being no longer, the Property of one Country only, her Articles of Supply will come freely, and be found now in all the Marketts of Europe: not only moderated by, but moderating the Prices of the like Articles of Europe. The Furs and Peltry will meet those of the North East Parts of Europe; and neither the one nor the other can any longer be estimated by the Advantages to be taken of an exclusive Vent. Advantages of this Kind, on Iron and naval Stores, have frequently been aimed at by Sweeden: and the Monopoly in them was more than once used as an Instrument of Hostility against England, which occasiond the Bounties on those articles, the Growth of America, which gave rise to the Export of them from America. When they come freely to the European Market co-operating with the Effect which those of Russia have, will break that monopoly. For Russia, by the Conquest of Livonia, and the Advancement of her Civilization has become a Source of Supply in these Articles, to a great Extent. All Europe by the Intervention of this American Commerce, will find the good Effects of a fair Competition, both in Abundance of Supply, and in moderation of Price. Even England who hath lost the Monopoly, will be no great Looser. She will find this natural Competition as advantageous to her, as the Monopoly, which in Bounties and other Costs of Protection, She paid so dear for.

Translation &c. continued.

Ship building and navigation having made Such Progress in America, that they are able to build and navigate cheaper, than any Country in Europe, even than Holland with all their Œconomy, there will arise a Competition in this Branch of Commerce. There will also be a Competition in the marketts of Europe, in the Branch of the Fisheries. The Rice and Corn, which the Americans have been able to export, to an amount that Supplied in the European Markett, the defect arising from Englands withholding her Exports will, when, that Export Shall again take Place, keep down depressed, the Agriculture of Portugal and Spain and in Some measure of France, if the

Policy of those countries does not change the Regulations, and order of their internal Œconomy. The particular Articles, to be had as yet from America only, which Europe So much Seeks after, will give the Americans the Command of the Markett in those Articles, and enable them, by annexing assortments of other Articles, to produce those also, with Advantage in these marketts. The Refuse Fish, Flour, Maize, Meat, Live Stock, Lumber &c. all carried in American Shipping to the West India Islands: the African Slaves, carried by a circuitous Trade, in American Shipping also to the West India Marketts: taking from thence the Molasses: aiding those Islands with American shipping in the Carriage of their produce, must ever command, and have the Ascendancy, in that Part of the World, if this ascendency even Stops here. The cheap manner, in which the Americans produce their Articles of Supply: the Low Rates, at which they carry them to Europe, Selling also their shipping there: the Small profits at which their Merchants are used to Trade, must lower the Price of the like Articles in Europe: oblige the European Merchants to be content with a less Profit: occasion Some reform in the Œconomy of Europe, in raising and Police in bringing to Markett, the active Articles of Supply. But further, the Americans by their principle of being a free Port in America and having a free Markett in Europe; by their Policy of holding themselves, as they are remote from all the wrangling Politicks, So neutral in all the Wars of Europe: by their Spirit of Enterprize, in all the quarters of the Globe, will oblige the nations of Europe to call forth within themselves Such a Spirit, as must entirely change its commercial System also.

But will a People whose Empire Stands Singly predominant, on a great Continent, who before they lived, under their own Government, had pushed their Spirit of Adventure in Search of a North West Passage to Asia, Suffer in their Borders the Establishment of Such a Monopoly as the European Hudsons Bay Company? Will that Spirit which has forced an extensive Commerce in the two Bays of Honduras and Campeachy, and on the Spanish main, and which has gone to Falkland's Islands in Search only of Whales, be Stopped at Cape horn, or not pass the Cape of Good Hope? It will not be long, after their Establishment as an Empire, before they will be found trading in the

South Sea and in China. The Dutch will hear of them in Spice Islands, to which the Dutch can have no Claim, and which those Enterprizing People will contest, on the very ground, and by the very Arguments, which the Dutch used to contest the Same Liberty against Portugal. By the Intercourse and correspondance, which there will be between Europe and America, it will be as well known, as Europe. By Attention, to the Winds, Currents, the Gulph Stream and its Lee Currents, the Passage will be better understood, and become shorter. America will Seem every day to approach nearer and nearer to Europe. When the Alarm which the Idea of going to a Strange and distant Country, gives to a Manufacturer or Peasant, or even a Country Gentleman, Shall thus be worn out; a thousand Attractive motives respecting a Settlement in America will raise a Spirit of Adventure, and become the irresistable Cause of a general Emigration to that World. Nothing but Some future, wise and benevolent Policy in Europe, or Some Spirit of the Evil one, which may mix itself in the Policy of America can prevent it. Many of the most usefull Enterprizing Spirits, and much of the active Property will go there. Exchange hath taught the Statesmen of the World long ago, that they cannot confine money: and the Governments of Europe, must fall back to the Feudal Tyranny, in which its own People are locked up, and from which all others are excluded, or Commerce will open a Door to Emigration.

These Relations of Things; these Leges et Foedera Rerum are forming the new System. The Sublime Politician, who ranges in Regions of predetermined Systems—the Man of the World, narrowed by a selfish Experience, worse than Ignorance, will not believe: and it is but Slowly, that nations relinquish any System, which hath derived Authority from Time and Habit. These Sovereigns of Europe, who have despized the awkward Youth of America, and neglected to form Connections, and interweave their Interests with these Rising States, will find the System of this new Empire, obstructing and Superseding the old System of Europe, and crossing all their maxims and measures. They will call upon their Ministers Come curse me this People, for they are too mighty for me. The Spirit of Truth will answer How shall I curse, whom God hath not cursed? How shall I defy, whom the Lord hath not defied? From the Top of the Rock, I See them, and from the Hills, I behold them. Lo! the People shall dwell alone, and shall not be reckoned among the nations. On the contrary those Sovereigns, who Shall See Things as they are, and form, if not the earliest, yet the most Sure and natural Connections with America, as an independent State; as the Market of and a free Port to Europe: as that being which must have a free Markett in Europe, will become the principal leading Powers in Europe, in regulating the Courses of the rest, and in Settling the common Center of all.

England is the State in those Circumstances, and in that Situation. Similar modes of living and thinking, Manners, and Fashions, Language and Habits, all conspire naturally to a Rejunction by Alliance. If England would treat America, as what She is, She might Still have the ascendency in Trade and navigation: might Still have a more Solid and less invidious Power than that Magni Nominis Umbra with which she braves the whole World. She might yet have an active leading Interest among the Powers of Europe. But She will not. As though the Hand of divine Vengeance was upon her, England will not See the Things which make for her Peace! France, who will be followed by other nations, acknowledging these States to be what they are, has formed Alliances, with Terms of perfect Equality and Reciprocity. And behold the Ascendant to which She directly arose, from that *politick Humiliation*. There never was a wiser or a firmer Step taken by any established Power, than that which the new States took for their first Footing in this Alliance. There never was more Address, Art, or Policy Shewn by any State, than France has given Proof of, in the Same, when both agreed and became allied on Terms, which exclude no other Power, from enjoying the Same Benefits by a like Treaty. Can it be Supposed that other States, conceiving that the exclusive Trade of England to America is laid open, will not desire, and have their Share? They certainly will. Here then are the Beginnings of Changes in the European System.

There are two Courses, in which this general Intercourse of Commerce, between Europe and North America, may come into operation: one, by particular Treaties of Commerce the other by all the maritime States of Europe, previous to their engaging in a War or upon the general settlement of a Peace, meeting in Some Congress, to regulate among themselves as well as with north America; the Free Port, on one Hand, and the free Markett on the other, as also general Regulations of Commerce and navigation, Such as must Suit this free Trader, now common to them all, indifferently, and without Preference. Such Regulations, must exclude all Monopoly of this source of Supply and course of Trade, and So far make an essential Change in the commercial system. Such Regulations, not having Reference only to America, but reciprocal References, between all the contracting Parties, trading now, under different Circumstances, and standing towards each other in different Predicaments, must necessarily change the whole of that System in Europe.

The American will come to Markett in his own ship, and will claim the Ocean as common: will claim a navigation restrained by no Laws, but the Laws of nations, reformed as the rising Crisis requires: will claim a free Markett, not only for his Goods but his ship, which will make a Part of his Commerce. America being a free Port to all Europe, the American will bring to Europe not only his own peculiar Staple Produce, but every Species of his produce which the Markett of Europe can take off: he will expect to be free to offer to Sale in the European Markett, every Species of wrought materials, which he can make to answer in that markett: and further as his Commerce Subsists, by a circuitous Interchange with other Countries, whence he brings Articles not Singly for his own Consumption, but as exchangeable Articles, with which he trades in foreign Marketts; he will claim as one of the Conditions of the free Markett, that these foreign Articles, as well as his own Produce, Shall be considered as free for him to import in his own shipping to such Market. Those States who refuse this at first, Seeing others acquiesce in it, and Seeing also how they profit by having Articles of Supply and Trade, brought so much cheaper to them, will be obliged, in their own defence, and to maintain their Balance in the commercial World, to accede to the Same Liberty. Hence again, even if the American should not, by these means, become the ascendant Interest in the carrying Trade and in shipping and Seamen, a most essential Change, must arise in the European System.

The American raises his produce and navigation cheaper,

than any other can: his Staples are Articles which he alone can
Supply. These will come to market assorted with others, which
he thus can most conveniently Supply; and unless the Same
freedom of Trade which he enjoys, be reciprocally given and
taken by the European Powers, among each other, he will
come to the European market, on Terms, which no other can:
but Europe will be affected, benefited, and improved by his
manner of trading. The peculiar Activity of the Americans, will
raise a Spirit and Activity among those, who come to the Same
market. That peculiar Turn of Character, that Inquisitiveness,
which in Business animates a Spirit of Investigation to every
Extent, and the minutest detail, enables them to conduct their
dealings in a manner more advantageous, than is usually practised by the European Merchant. They acquire a Knowledge
not only of the Marketts of Europe, that is of the Wants and
Supplies, how they correspond, and of their relative Values;
but they never rest, till they are possessed of a Knowledge of
every Article of Produce and Manufacture, which comes to
those Marketts; untill they know the Establishments, the operations and the Prices of Labour, and the Profits made on each,
as well, even better, than the Merchants of the Country themselves. A little before the War, Several of the American Merchants, especially those of Pensilvania, Sending some of their
own Houses to England, became their own Factors, went immediately to the Manufacturers in Birmingham, Wolverhamp-
ton, and Sheffield; to the woolen Manufacturers in Yorkshire,
and Lancashire: to those of Liverpool, and those in the West:
and opened an immediate Trafick with them at the first hand.
This Same Spirit of Investigation and Activity, will activate
their dealings in every other Country of Europe. The Effect
of this, instead of being disadvantageous to those Countries,
will become a general Blessing; by raising a more general
Competition, and diffusing a more proportional Share of
Profit, between all Ranks of the industrious. While Trade is
Solely in the Hands of the Merchant he bears hard on the Pur-
chaser, by his high Profit, and oppresses the Manufacturer by
the little share he allows him. The merchant grows rich and
magnificent, makes a great Bustle and Figure. It can never be
well where Merchants are Princes. The more the Merchant can

make by high Profit, the less quantity will he carry to markett. Whereas when Commerce Shall be free, and by the Mixture of this American Spirit, trade run with fair Competition in a broad Channell, the Merchant must make his Way by being content with small profit, and by doing a deal of Business, on those Small Profits. The Consumer and Manufacturer will come nearer together—the one will Save an unreasonable Advance, and the other obtain a more equal Share of Profit. More Work will be done: The Profits of Industry more equally distributed —The Circulation will Spread through the lesser Vessells, and Life, Health, and Growth be promoted.

If these operations take this Course, it will be needless to point out to the Shrewd Speculations of the Merchants, what their Conduct must necessarily be. But it will behove States-men, to be aware that they do not Suffer the Merchant to per-swade them, that the Commerce is languishing merely because there is not the Same Parade of Wealth, in such dazzling In-stances. Let them look to the Marketts of Supply, and See if there is not plenty. Next to the rude produce, which is the Basis of manufactures, and enquire, whether, while more and more Industry, is daily called forth, it is not employed, and more adequately paid, by a free and extended Vent? While the Num-bers and Ingenuity of Manufacturers increase they do not all live more comfortably, so as to have and maintain increasing Families? Whether Population does not increase? Let them in future guard against the exclusive Temper of Trade. The polit-ical Founders of the old System, were totally ignorant of this Principle of Commerce. It was Wisdom with them to render their neighbours and Customers poor. By a wretched System of Taxation they effectually prevented the Stock of Labour and Profit from accumulating. But if the Statesmen of the present enlightened Age, will follow, where Experience leads to Truth and Right, they will throw the Activity of mankind into its proper Course, of productive Labour. When Man has the Lib-erty of exerting his Industry and Ingenuity as he can make them the most productive; finds a free market, and his share of Profit; then is the Ground duely prepared for Population, Op-ulence and Strength. Then will the Sovereigns of Europe find their Interest and their Power, in their Peoples Happiness.

Translation &c

If the Sovereigns of Europe, Should find, that the System of Colonies in distant Regions, for the Purpose of monopolies, is at an End, and turn their Attention, to give Exertion to their own internal Powers, like the Police of China, cultivate their waste Lands, improve Agriculture, encourage manufactures, and abolish Corporations: as all the Remnants of Barbarism Shall be removed, the Powers of the Community will create those Surplusses which will become the Source, and open the Channels of Commerce. If they Should See the Dissappointments of attempts to establish a monopoly of navigation by the Force of Laws, instead of creating or maintaining it, by the Spirit of an active Commerce; that all the Prohibitions by which they labour to oppress their neighbours do but depress them Selves, they may come to think that giving Freedom and Activity to commerce, is the true System of every commercial Country. Suppose them checked in their Career of War, hesitating on the maxims of their old Systems, perceiving that the Œconomical Activity of Europe, is on the Turn to take a new Course, feeling the Force of an active Commerce, finding themselves under the Necessity of making Some Reform, Should begin to Speculate, how amidst a Number of Powers of Trade, Shifting their Scale, an even Ballance may be formed and Secured; how amidst a Number of Interests, floating on the Turn of this great Tide in the affairs of Men, an equal Level may be obtained, if, on a Review of their old System they should perceive how it is prepared for Change, they may find, that Commerce, which might have risen by Competition, Industry, Frugality, and Ingenuity, hath long been an exclusive Scrambling Rivalship. Instead of being an equal Communication, concentring the Enjoyments of all Regions and Climates, and a Consociation of all nations, in one Communion of the Blessings of Providence; when actuated as it has been by a Selfish Principle, it hath been to the nations an occasion of Jealousies, alternate depressions of each others Interests, and a never ceasing Source of Wars, perhaps they may also See that Treaties of Peace have been but Truces and Guarrantees so many entangling Preparations for future Wars. On the other Hand they Should See with Pleasure, that the manners of Mankind, Soft-

ening by degrees, have become more humanized; their Police
more civilized; and altho many of the old oppressive Institutions of Government, as they respect Husbandry, Manufactures, Merchants, Marketts and Commerce, have not yet been
formally abolished; yet that Practice, by various Accommodations, has abrogated their most mischievous operations; that
the Activity of Man finds every day, a freer Course; that there
are a Thousand Ways, which although Pride will not open Prudence will connive at; through which the Intercourse of Marketts finds every Year, a freer Vent; and that the active Spirit of
Commerce is like the Spirit of Life, diffusing itself through the
whole Mass of Europe. They will find there is an End of all
their monopolizing Systems: They will See that any one of the
Powers of Europe, who would aim to deal with the rest of mankind, with an unequal Ballance, will only find, that they have
raised among their Neighbours a Jealousy, that will conspire to
wrest that false Ballance out of their Hands, and to depress
them down again to a level with the rest of the World. The
Cities of Italy, the low Countries, Portugal, Holland, England,
have all, for their Period, as commercial Powers, arisen above
the common Level, but pressing, with a Weight which was felt
as unequal by those below them, they have each in its Turn
found, even in the moment of their highest Elevation, a general Rising all around them, and themselves Sinking to the
common Level. Statesmen must See, how much it is the Interest of all, to liberate each other, from the Restraints, Prohibitions, and Exclusions, by which they have aimed to depress
each other. They will See, that the most advantageous Way,
which a landed nation can take, to encourage and multiply Artificers, Manufacturers and Merchants of their own, is to grant
the most perfect Freedom, to the Artificers, Manufacturers,
and merchants of every other nation. That a contrary Practice
lowers the Value of their own internal Productions, by raising
the Prices of all Things, which must be bought with them; and
gives to the Artificers, Manufacturers and Merchants a monopoly against their own Farmers. Seeing this, they will encourage
Population, and an universal Naturalization, and Liberty of
Conscience. If Nature has so formed man and Policy, Society,
that each labouring in his Line, produces a Surplus of Supply,
it is both perfect Justice and Policy that Men and nations

Should be free, reciprocally to interchange it. This Communion of nations is a Right, which may be enjoyed in its genuine Spirit and utmost Extent, except in Time of War, and even then to a great degree, without interfering in the political and civil Power of the World. The Spirit of those exclusive Laws of navigation will appear as the Spirit of Piracy. The common Ocean, incapable of being defined, or of a Special Occupancy, or of receiving exclusively the Labour of any Individual, Person, or State, is incapable of becoming an Object of Property, never an Object of Dominion: and therefore the Ocean, Should in Policy, as it is in Fact, remain common and free. Pervium cunctis Iter. If it should be Seen, that the commercial System of Europe is changing, and in Wisdom and Policy ought to be changed: that the great Commerce of North America, emancipated from its provincial State, not only coincides with, but is a concurring Cause of this Change: that the present Combination of Events form a Crisis, which Providence, with a more than ordinary Interposition hath prepared: and that Heaven itself Seems to call upon Sovereigns to co-operate with its gracious Providence: if they should be convinced, that there is nothing so absurd, as warring against each other about an Object, which as it is Seperated from Europe, will have nothing to do with its Broils, and will not belong exclusively to any one of them: if listening to this Voice, which as that of an Angel, announcing Peace and good Will to Mankind, Summons them to leave off the endless, useless operations of War; to consider the present Crisis as an Object of Council and not of War, and therefore to meet in Communication and Intercourse of their reasoning Powers.

The maritime Powers must before Peace respecting America, and the mixed Interests of Europe and America, can be Settled, convene, by their ministers, in order to consider the Points on which they may Safely Suspend Hostilities, and those which must form the Basis of Treaty, and which will enter into the future System and on which Peace may not only be made, but established among the nations of the Atlantic Ocean.

Will not Reason and Benevolence, then, in which true Policy, and their Right and best Interest is included, Suggest to their Hearts, and actuate their Councils to convene a Congress, before they are engaged in further Hostilities; before the devastation of War, extends Ruin and Misery yet farther. Some Such measure, as led the great trading Bodies of Europe to convene in a Congress, which gave rise to the Hanseatic League, is not out of the Course of public Business but is what the nature of the present Crisis, in a more than ordinary Necessity requires. Whether Some general Council, on the Model of that concerted between the Great Henry of France and Elizabeth of England, two as noble Spirits and as wise Politicians as the World hath Since Seen, Should not now be proposed; not indeed a Council of Administration, for regulating and conducting a general political System of all Europe but a Council of Commerce for Europe and North America, exclusive of every Point of Politicks.

Such a Council might prevent future Occasions of War, from commercial Quarrells. The present vague State of the marine Law of Nations, Seems to be Such, as creates a necessity of Such a measure. At present, all Principle, Rule, and Law, Seem to be as much lost as if the nations were fallen back to the old State of Piracy under their old Barbarism. Europe cannot, even in War, go on under the present Abrogation of all Treaties, and all the Laws of Nations.

The Cardinal Points which will come under Deliberation, will be 1. how far, in Right and Policy, it may be best for all to establish the Mare liberum. And how far each nation, providing for the Property and Dominion, which they hold in Bays and Harbours, may accede to this Establishment, as a Law of Nations. 2. How far the universal Jus navigandi, may be established. 3. This will lead to Deliberation on the Libertas universalis Commerciorum; free Ports; and free Marketts. It will be best by degrees to abolish all Port Duties, and raise their Revenues by Excise, Tailles &c. and other internal Sources of Finance, immediately laid on the Consumer. This Measure would make that Country which adopted it a free Port, a Circumstance very desirable to every well wisher to his Country.

Voila tout ce qu'on peut, raisonablement, exiger. Il n'est au Pouvoir de l'humanité, que de preparer, et agir. Le Succés est l'ouvrage d'un main plus puissantt. Sully Liv. 30.

Finis

c. July 8–14, 1780

"Letters from a Distinguished American," No. I

SIR

I HAVE not till lately obtained a sight of a number of Pamphlets, ascribed indeed to Mr. Galloway but containing the mention of such circumstances, as convince me that they were written in concert between the American Refugees and the British Ministry. In some of them I perceive apparently unequivocal traces of the hand of the late Governor Hutchinson. I have read them with surprize, because it seems to me, that if their professed intention had been to convince America, that it is both her interest and duty to support her Sovereignty and her Alliances, and the interest and duty of all the maritime powers of Europe to support her in them, the writers could not have taken methods more effectual.

The Author of the "Cool Thoughts on the Consequences of American Independence" observes, that "an offensive and defensive alliance between France and America will naturally coincide with their several views and interests, as soon as American Independence shall be acknowledged by the powers in Europe. America will naturally wish, while she is rising from her infant state into opulence and power, to cover her dominions under the protection of France; and France will find new resources of strength in American commerce, armies, and naval force. The recovery of America, from the disasters and distresses of war, will be rapid and sudden; very unlike an old country, whose population is full, and whose cultivation, commerce, and strength have arrived at their height. The multiplication of her numbers, and the increase of her power, will surpass all expectation. If her sudden growth has already exceeded the most sanguine ideas, it is certain, that the increase of her strength, when supported and assisted by France, and pushed forward by the powerful motives, arising from her separate interest, her own preservation, and the prospect of her own rising glory and importance among nations, will far outrun any idea we have had of her late population."

It is pleasing to see the irresistible force of truth operating upon the minds even of the most inveterate and disingenuous of the enemies of America. It was impossible to deny, that the alliance between France and the United States is natural, and founded on their mutual interests. It was impossible to deny, that the resurrection of America from the distresses of this war will be sudden and surprizing. But *is this an argument for England to continue the war*? Will the resurrection of England out of the ruins of this war be *sudden*? If she continues it much longer, will she ever arise *again*? The present and future state of Great Britain, then, are decisive arguments (if reason could be heard) for making peace immediately: while the present and future state of America are arguments equally unanswerable for America to continue the war, until her Independence shall be acknowledged by all the world. It is equally an argument for France and Spain, and Holland, to exert themselves to support American Independence, because, by this means they will effectually secure her gratitude and good will: they will bind the connections between them closer, and the sudden rise of America out of her distresses into affluence and power, will enable her to repay those nations whatever debts may be contracted, and to become an able ally to defend them in case of need against their enemies; or, if the true American system of policy should be peace and neutrality, as no doubt it will, they will derive such commerce and naval supplies from America for ever, hereafter, as will secure them the freedom of the seas. This is also a powerful motive for all the maritime nations of Europe to favour and support American Independence. It is the true interest of all the maritime nations, that America should have a free trade with all of them, and that she should be neutral in all their wars. Every body now throughout the world sees, that a renewal of the English monopoly of the American trade, would establish an absolute tyranny upon the ocean, and that every other ship that sails would hold its liberty at the mercy of these Lordly Islanders. If the French or Spaniards were to obtain a monopoly of this trade, it would give them a superiority over all the other commercial nations, which would be dangerous to the freedom of navigators. It is obviously then the interest and duty of all the maritime powers to keep the American trade open and free to all, and to be sure to prevent its being monopolized by any one nation whatever.

Another inference that may fairly and must [   ] America will suddenly arise out of the distresses of the war to affluence and power, is this:—That all the monied men in Europe ought to transfer as fast as possible their stocks from British to American funds: For as it is certain, that England will not suddenly rise out of the disasters of the war, and it is at least dubious whether she will ever rise out of them; the interest neither of the capitalist, nor the speculator, is safe in the English funds; whereas, what ever money may be lent to America, is safe and sure, both for the principal and interest, and it will become easier every day for America to pay both.

Thus it appears, that Mr. Galloway is involuntarily forced to lay open truths, which supports her credit, and unites the interests of all the world in her favour against Great Britain.

This writer goes on: "Nor will it be the interest of America to check the ambition of France, while confined to Europe. Her distance, and the safety arising from it, will render her regardless of the fate of nations, on this side of the Atlantic, as soon as her own strength shall be established. The prosperity or ruin of kingdoms, from whose power she can have nothing to fear, and whose assistance she can never want, will be matters of equal indifference. She can wish for no other connection with Europe, than that of commerce; and this will be better secured in the hands of an ally, than in those with whom she holds other connections; so that it will be of little moment to her, whether Great Britain, Spain, Holland, Germany, or Russia, shall be ruled by one or more Monarchs."

Here again it is manifest, that this gentleman clearly sees her true interest and political system, in relation to Europe, and the true interest and political system of all Europe towards America. —*Both consist in two words, peace and commerce.*—It can never, after the conclusion of this war, and the final establishment of the independence of America, be her interest to go to war with any nation of Europe; and it can never be the interest of any one of the maritime powers to go to war with her, unless we should except Great Britain, and there is no sufficient reason, perhaps, for excepting her.—It is not improbable, however, that the selfish, unsocial, tyrannical spirit, which has hitherto dictated to her the maxim of making war with every nation, that has commerce and a considerable marine, may still prompt her to endeavour to destroy the navy of America. If it should, however, she will not succeed, and will only ruin herself by it.

But if it will not be the interest of America to go to war with any power of Europe, it will certainly be her interest to trade with every power of Europe, because the greater number and variety of markets are open to her, the greater will be the demand for her productions, the greater quantity of them she will sell, and she will obtain so much a better price, and the cheaper and easier will she obtain the commodities of the growth, production and manufacture of Europe that she wants. On the contrary, if it is not the interest of any nation of Europe to go to war with her, it will be the interest of every one of them to trade with her, because she has commodities that every one of them wants, and every one of them has commodities that she wants; so that a barter may be carried on advantageous on all sides; and, besides this, every maritime power in Europe must endeavour to have a share in American commerce, in order to maintain her share of the commerce of Europe, to maintain her marine upon a proportional footing, and maintain her rank among the other maritime powers.

This observation then, instead of being an argument for any one to continue the war, is a very forcible one to shew the danger to the other powers of Europe, arising from the former connection between America and England; and also to shew, that the other maritime powers ought to interfere in assisting America to maintain her independence, and also to maintain her true system of neutrality in future, that the blessings of her commerce may be open to all. As to the idea of the ambition of France, for universal monarchy, it is a chimera, fit to amuse the madness of Britains, which in this moment catches at any thing, however extravagant, to plague and harass herself with. But it is fit for the rest of the world to smile at.—Universal Monarchy at land is impracticable; but universal Monarchy at sea has been well nigh established, and would before this moment have been perfected, if Great Britain and America had continued united. France can never entertain an hope of it, unless the fury of Great Britain should be assisted by the folly, the indolence, and inactivity of the other maritime powers, so as to drive the American commerce wholly into the hands of France, which is not to be supposed; but, on the contrary, every trading nation will, no doubt, demand a share in American trade, and will consequently augment their riches and naval power in proportion.   ADIEU

July 1780

"Letters from a Distinguished American," No. II

SIR

EVERY American will agree with the writer on the consequence of American Independence, that the United States, when their Independence shall be no longer disputed, can wish for no other connection with Europe than that of commerce. No good American would wish to involve his country in the labyrinths of European negotiations, or in the iniquities of their wars. America will wish to be a common blessing to all the nations of Europe, without injuring any; and such will be her demand for the productions of each of them, that each one will derive material advantages in the increase of the means of subsistence, and consequent population, from supplying her wants. Each of them wants her commodities in exchange, and no one of them can reasonably wish to cramp the growth, and prevent the happiness of the human species in both worlds, by confining the advantages of this commerce to itself.

It is equally clear, that this commerce will be better secured by her own wisdom, than by the domination of any European power; and safer in the hands of an ally than a master. But it is amazing that this man's malice against his native country should have suffered such important truths in her favour to escape him. It shews that he knows not how to conduct the cause he has patronised, and that he is as wrong headed, as he is malicious and insidious.

"The new states are, and will continue the allies of France, our natural enemy, unless reduced." England ought to consider, whether all attempts to reduce the new States have not a tendency to rivet the alliance with France, and to drive the States to the necessity of forming closer connections with her than they have now; to make all America too the natural enemy of England for ever; to drive her to more rigorous renunciations of British trade; nay, to a final and total prohibition of it; to enter into engagements with France, Spain, Holland, and other maritime powers, to this effect. It ought to be considered, whether, the new States will not become soon the allies of Spain too, and continue so for ever, If this war is pursued much farther. As to reducing these States, the idea of it, at this day, is fit only for ridicule and contempt. It is derided in every town in America. This country will never again be in quiet and continual possession of one State of the thirteen, not even of Georgia. South Carolina, where we are melting into disease and death that army which ought to be defending the West India Islands, will never be ours a single month; no, not for an hour.

This writer goes on, "The far greater part of the people wish and hope for an union with this country." It is not possible to conceive any thing more barefacedly false than this. A Germain, or a Conway may be excused, on account of ignorance and misinformation; but this man knows better than he says. But having forfeited his life to the laws of his country, and by the black catalogue of his crimes, rendered himself unpardonable, he has vowed to revenge himself, not like Coriolanus, by his sword, but by misrepresentations.

But he adds, "the greater part of the people are ready to unite with the King's forces, in reducing the power of their tyrants," by which he means, no doubt, the Congress and the new government. Nothing can shew the complection of this assertion better than to recollect the orders which are constantly given by the Commanding Officers in New York, which are published in the newspapers. They dare not trust the Provincials and Volunteers, and Militia, &c. as they call them, of whom such an ostentatious parade is made in the dispatches of Commanding Officers and Court Gazettes. They exercise them in the day time with bits of wood in their musquets for flints; they take the arms from them every night, and pile them in the magazines; and they forbid them to be trusted with any quantity of powder. The truth is, the only consequence that the Commanders of the English troops have found, in giving arms and cloathing and ammunition to any of the inhabitants, whenever they have been, has been to cloath, arm, and supply their expences. General Burgoyne found it so in New England, and New York. General Howe found it so in New Jersey, Pennsylvania, Maryland, and Delaware; and Sir Henry Clinton and Earl Cornwallis found it so in Georgia and South Carolina. What encouragement could have been given that has not? Is exemption from plunder encouragement? Forbid plunder, and half your army will desert; nay, for the provisions, horses, cattle, you take, you enrich the country with English guineas, and enable the people to buy arms, ammunition, cloathing, and every thing they want from your own soldiers. By large bounties, and by commissions, a few banditti, who have no honour nor principle to bind them to any country, or any cause, may be collected, but these would betray their new masters the first opportunity, and will be very few in number. The great body of the people in every state revere the Congress, more sincerely, than British soldiers revere their. . . . They reverence it as the voice of their country, the guardians of its right, and the voice of God; and they esteem their Independence and alliance with France, as the two greatest blessings which Providence ever yet bestowed upon the new world. They think them equal blessings to Europe in general, as to America; and are universally of opinion, that a Council of Statesmen consulting for their good, and the good of mankind, could not have devised a plan, so much for their honour, interest, liberty and happiness, as that which has been derived, by the folly and imprudence of Great Britain. He goes on, "the treachery of this country, in not exerting its powers for their relief, will create permanent resentment." How many lives, and how many millions, has this country already sacrificed? Probably more lives, certainly more millions than the whole of the last war cost us. What was the fruit of the last war? Triumph and conquest by sea and land in every part of the world. What the effect of this? Defeat, disgrace, loss of America, West India Islands, African, Mediterranean, and German and Holland trade, the contempt of all nations, the Independence of Ireland, and a civil war in England; yet the war is to be continued!

"Gratitude to the nations which shall save them from our ravages, will stamp impressions never to be effaced." Stop the ravages then; and the further gratitude and impressions will be prevented. "Further Treaties of Alliance and Commerce will be made." No longer war, no further Treaties. This can only be the effect of British imprudence. The treaties already made are well known. What further treaties Ministry may drive them to, will depend upon themselves.

With the Independence of America, we must give up our fisheries "on the Banks of Newfoundland and in the American seas." Supposing this true, which it is not at present, but our infatuation in continuing the war may make it so, what follows? If Britain lose them, who will gain them? France and America. Have not France and America then as urgent a motive to contend for the gain, as we to prevent the loss? Are they not an object as important and desirable to France and America, as to us? Have they not as much reason to fight for them, as England? Will they easily give up the Independence of America, which is to bear such tempting fruit? One would think this writer was in the interest of France and America still, and labouring to persuade them, that they are fighting for a rich and a glorious prize. The question then is reduced to another, viz. which has the best prospect of contending for them successfully—America, France and Spain, favoured by all the world, or England, thwarted and opposed by all the world? And to whom did God and Nature give them? Ministry lay great stress upon the gift of God and Nature, when they consider the advantages of our insular situation, to justify their injustice and hostility against all the maritime powers. Why should Americans hold the blessings of Providence in a baser estimation, which they can enjoy, without injury to any nation whatever.

"With American Independence, says he, we must give up thirty-five thousand American seamen, and twenty-eight thousand more, bred and maintained in those excellent nurseries, the fisheries. Our valuable trade, carried on from thence with the Roman Catholic States, will be in the hands of America. These nurseries, and this trade, will ever remain the natural right of the people, who inhabit that country. A trade so profitable, and a nursery of seamen so excellent, and so necessary for the support of her naval force, will never be given up, or even divided by America with any power whatsoever."

If all this were true, what then? If Britain loses it all, by American Independence, who will gain it? These advantages are not to be lost out of the world. Who will find them, but America and France? These are the powers at war, for these very objects, if they are the necessary consequences of American Independence, will they not fight as bravely to obtain them, as the English? It is here admitted they are the natural right of America, will not she contend for it? Who then has the most power, one nation or three? Perhaps five or six before the end? Are 60,000 seamen a feebler bulwark for America or France, than for England? Are they feebler instruments of wealth, power and glory, in the service of America, than England? At the command of Congress, than the King? The question occurs then, who is the strongest? However, we need not lose so many seamen, nor the fishery, nor the trade with the Roman Catholick countries, by American Independence. America never thought of excluding England from the fishery; and even her seamen, her share of the fishery, and the profits of her trade to Roman Catholick countries would again, be useful to England, and center here, if peace were made now. But let it be remembered, America grows every day of this war more independent of England for manufactures, by the amazing increase of her own; and France, Spain, and even the states of Italy and Germany, and *Ireland too*, are every day putting themselves more and more in a condition to supply America; so that every day of the continuance of this ruinous war, increases the facility and the inclinations of America to supply herself elsewhere, and the capacity of other nations to supply her, and of consequence makes it more and more inevitable for England to lose the seamen, the fisheries, and the trade. The question recurs at every sentence, who is the ablest to hold out? America, that grows stronger every year, and that too in ways and degrees that England has no idea of, or England that grows weaker? But England's misfortune and ruin are, that *it never knew America*, nor her resources, nor the character of her people.

(*To be continued.*)

July 1780

"Letters from a Distinguished American," No. III

SIR

THE Writer on the Consequences of American Independence adds, "the British Islands in the West Indies must
fall of course. The same power that can compel Great Britain
to yield up America, will compel her to give up the West Indies. They are evidently the immediate objects of France."

It is very true, that if we continue the war, the West Indies
must fall into the hands of France.—England has held them by
no other tenure, than the courtesy of France and Spain, for
two years past. Britons, be not deceived! You can defend these
islands only by your Navy, and the friendship of North America. Your Navy is not what it was the last war. The loss of
America has put it out of your power, for ever, until you regain
the friendship of America, and a share of her trade, to have
such a Navy, as you once had. Your ships are weak and unable
to sustain the shocks of winds, and seas, and battles, as formerly. The masts and spars are not to be depended on as
heretofore. The rigging, notwithstanding the immense sums
granted for the sea service, is not as it was. Your ships are not
manned, as they were, either in the numbers or qualities of the
seamen. Your Officers then have not the same dependence
upon ships, spars, rigging, or men, which they had in former
wars, and consequently cannot perform what they once could.

The Navies of your enemies are as far from being what they
were. They are as much improved, as your's are declined. It is
also now plain, from a vast number of experiments, that the
science of naval tacticks is now quite as well understood, and
all the manœuvres as ably executed by the French Officers as
by the English. Add to this, the advantage that the French and
Spanish fleets and armies have over the English, in the supplies
of provisions, artificers, and materials, which they now draw
from the United States of North America, and every man must
see, that we hold these Islands at the mere mercy of our enemies, and if we continue this war, we shall infallibly lose them.
Our policy is plain then:—"Let us make peace, while these

Islands are our's, and America will never be obliged, nor inclined, in any future war, to assist France in obtaining them, as they are now bound to do by treaty, while this war continues. North America, it is plain, will never wish to govern these Islands. The reason is obvious: they will be as profitable to her as under the government of France, Spain or England, as they could be under her own, and she will be at no expence to protect, secure, or defend them."

If the British West India Islands should be taken by France and Spain, how are we to recover them at the peace? What have we taken, to exchange for them? What are we likely to take?

"Our only true policy is, to make peace, and save the Islands while we may."—Once taken, it will be more difficult to recover them. Are we able to keep peace at home, in Ireland, in the East Indies, and with the neutral maritime powers, who have unanimously declared against us, as clearly, as if they had declared war in favour of America; and continue the war long enough to annihilate the fleets of France and Spain, retake our lost Islands, and after that reduce the United States of America to submission? For these stubborn spirits will remain to be reduced, after France and Spain shall be beaten. Will our soldiers, seamen, and revenues, never fail till this is done? How many more years of war will this cost us?—And after all these miraculous feats shall be accomplished, will our resources enable us to maintain a sufficient force to keep down the power of France, Spain, and America? We have, hitherto, made it a maxim to go to war with France and Spain, whenever they had a fleet. The appearance of a formidable French fleet upon the ocean, has been offence enough to provoke a war. We must now add America; for America, if subdued, would be ever ready to revolt afresh.

"France, he subjoins, expects from the Independence of America, and the acquisition of the West India Islands, the sovereignty of the British seas, if not of Great Britain itself."

France expects only the freedom of the seas; and why should she not expect them? Have we any charter from above, for the government of the ocean? Sovereignity of the seas will never again be permitted to any nation. We have boasted of it, until we have revolted all mankind. America herself will never suffer

France to hold the sovereignty of the seas, any more than England. No nation that ever arose upon the globe, had such powerful motives to maintain a perfect freedom of navigation and of commerce among all nations as she has. No nation ever had such advantages and resources to assist the maritime powers to support it. She is as sensible of this as we are. If by our unbridled rage we drive her to the provocation, and the inactivity of the neutral powers should permit it, she may form such further connections with France and Spain, as may give them a superiority of naval power over us, that will be terrible to us. But America herself will never suffer any power of Europe again that decided superiority over all commercial nations, which we have vainly boasted of, and which the past tameness of mankind has permitted. And America, little as she is thought of, will, for ever have it in her power, by joining with a majority of maritime powers, to preserve their Freedom. The only possible means then of preventing France from obtaining and preserving for some time a superiority over us at sea, is to make peace, and regain not the domination, but the neutrality of America, and our share of her commerce. Thus, and thus only, we may save the West India islands, and an equal freedom on the seas. By making peace at present, we may have more of American trade in future than France, and derive more support to our navy than she will to her marine. But by pushing the war, we weaken ourselves, and strengthen France and Spain every day, to such a degree, that in the end they may acquire such a superiority as will endanger our liberty.

But if Great Britain is to lose the West-India islands, and the sovereignty of the seas, by the Independence of America, who is to gain them? If France is to gain them, are they not as valuable objects to her as to England? Are not their riches as glittering in the eyes of the French as the English? Are they not then as urgent a motive to them to continue the war as to us? We come again once more to the old question, who is likely to hold out longest? The immense resources of France, Spain and America, or the exhausted kingdom of Great Britain?

ADIEU

(*To be continued.*)

July 1780

"Letters from a Distinguished American," No. IV

THE writer, on the consequences of American Independence says that "France has long struggled to rival us in our manufactures in vain; this (i.e. American Independence) will enable her to do it with effect."

If England would awake out of her dream, and make peace, acknowledge American Independence, and acknowledge the American treaties with France, and make a similar treaty of commerce with the United States, upon the most generous principles of equality and reciprocity, neither France nor any other nation of Europe would be able to rival England in those manufactures which we most wanted in America, those of wool and iron: The English manufactures, in these articles are at present so much better, and the Americans are so much more accustomed to them, that this trade would return to its old channel, and the American demand for them, and for many other articles of our manufactures would increase in proportion, as the population increases in America, and as their commerce with each other and with other nations increases, and the consequent means of paying England for what they purchase. This nation would find themselves so far from being materially hurt, by American Independence, that they would see a prosperity introduced here in consequence of it, that would excite the utmost astonishment at our own obstinacy, in contending so long, at the expence of so much blood and treasure, against it, provided we are wise enough to lay aside our groundless jealousies, and that hostile disposition towards America which is once more indulged with so much rancour; and provided we take care at the peace to settle all questions about boundaries, so as to prevent our own people from encroaching upon them; and provided we do not meanly aim at excluding them from any branches of commerce, fisheries or naval powers which God and nature have destined to them. If we will indulge the base passions of envy, jealousy and hatred against them, we may depend upon a reciprocation of these passions from them, and we may depend upon a dreadful enemy in them: but if we had magnanimity enough to comply with what appears to be the settled digested system of all the other maritime powers of Europe relative to America, to treat them with candour and friendship, we shall find as much real advantage from them, and more too, than we ever did. All will depend upon ourselves. Nothing is wanting but common sense.

But if we pursue this war, destroying the lives and distressing the commerce of America, we shall feel from that country such shafts of deadly hate, as will finally ruin our credit, destroy our manufactures, reduce to nothing our influence in Europe, depress our naval power to such an inferiority to France and Spain, as we never shall recover; leave the East Indies and Ireland in a state of Independency too, and the West India Islands ready to petition any other power for protection, and indeed this island itself at the mercy of an invader. If we continue this war, France and Spain too will be able to rival us in manufactures. They are both attentive at this time to this object; they are not only endeavouring to introduce our manufactures, but to accommodate them more to the taste and use of the Americans. And the Americans are daily growing more familiar with French articles, and acquiring a taste for them. The advantages in trade, already granted to Ireland, and the consequent growth of manufactures there, will infinitely facilitate the introduction and improvement of manufactures; and the emigration of manufactures into France and Spain, by means of the intimate intercourse between Ireland and those kingdoms. In short, the continuance of the war will indeed be fatal: it will enable France to rival us in effect in our most essential interests; and there has hardly ever happened among mankind so obstinate and so blind a perseverance in error so obvious, for so long a time, as we have already pursued this ruinous war. Let us open our eyes. We are amused with insinuations that France is sick of the part she has acted. This is to suppose her sick of the wisest, most successful, most honourable, and noble part she ever acted.—Think as we will, all the rest of Europe and America are convinced of this:—and if we had sold ourselves to France, we could not serve her more essentially, in every interest, commercial, naval, political, or oeconomical, than by continuing this war.

Our cool thinker goes on. "We receive, say he, from the

West India Islands, certain commodities, absolutely necessary to carry on our manufactures to any advantage and extent, which we can procure from no other country. We must take the remains from France or America, after they have supplied themselves, and fullfilled their contracts with their allies at their own prices, and loaded with the expence of foreign transportation, if we are permitted to trade for them at all." If this was intended as an argument for continuing the war, I should have thought it the raving of the delirium of a fever, rather than a cool thought. Is it possible to urge an argument more clear for making peace now, while we may have our islands? How are we to supply our islands with lumber, and other necessaries, if we continue the war? A man who has really thought coolly upon the subject, would have advised us to make peace and save our West India islands. He would have told us, that by continuing the war, we should certainly lose them, and with them the articles so necessary to our manufactures. America does not wish the English Islands in the hands of the French. She is very ready to warrantee to the English all that are not taken, and very probably France would restore those which are, in exchange for other possessions which we have taken from them. America cannot wish to continue the war; because she gains nothing,* except in military skill; in the advancement of agriculture and manufactures, laying the strongest possible foundation for future commerce, prosperity and naval power. France and Spain indeed may be supposed to wish its continuance, because they are gaining every year conquest of territory, as well as augmentation of manufactures and commerce, naval power, and political consideration in Europe. THE ENGLISH MALADY IS UPON US.—THE DISPOSITION TO SUICIDE, WHICH DESTROYS SO MANY INDIVIDUALS AMONG US, HAS SEISED THE PUBLIC.—WHEN PEACE LEADS TO GLORY, AND WAR TO NOTHING BUT DIS-

---

*Nothing except these! Yes! and much more than what the letter writer has enumerated. She gains a glorious triumph over tyranny and ambition; a reparation, purchased gallantly with the best blood of her fellow citizens, for the violated rights of man; the power of establishing peace, freedom, virtue and independency, upon the spot, which was intended for the scene of their extinction; and of leaving an aweful and instructive lesson to the nations of the earth, for ever.

GRACE AND RUIN, WE FALL HEADLONG INTO THE
ABYSS OF THE ONE, AND LEAVE THE PLEASANT
AND SAFE PATH OF THE OTHER.   ADIEU
(*To be continued.*)

July 1780

"Letters from a Distinguished American," No. V

IF "we receive from the West India Islands certain commodities necessary to manufactures," as the cool reasoner on the
consequences of American Independence pretends, "which we
can procure from no other country;" is not this a motive for
France to continue the war, as forcible as for *us*? The rivalry,
and the enmity, between England and France, is so ancient,
and so deeply rooted in the hearts of the two nations, that
each considers the weakening of the other, as a strengthening
of itself, and a loss to the other as a gain to itself. The English
have, a long time, made it a maxim never to suffer France
either to have a navy, or a flourishing commerce. An active,
prosperous trade, or a formidable marine, have ever been considered as a legitimate cause of war. And whether we think of it
coolly or not, England would have been at war with France
before now, if we had never had any war with America, merely
to burn, sink, and destroy her Marine. Can we be so ignorant
of the human heart then, as not to know that depriving us of
these commodities, which we derive from the West India
Islands, and which are necessary to our manufactures, will be
an inducement to our enemies to continue the war? Depriving
us of a commodity, taking from us a manufacture, is motive
enough, if our enemies act upon the same maxims that we do;
but, adding the commodity or the manufacture to themselves,
is a double motive. In short, is it possible for this writer to ad-
duce one reason for us to continue the war, which is not also
a cool argument for France, Spain, and America to continue
it? The question still is, Which can hold out longest, France,
who has not yet laid on one new imposition, or we, who add

annually almost a million to our perpetual taxes? America, whose whole national debt does not amount to more than five millions, or we, whose debt is more than 200 millions, at least sixty of which have been already added by this war? *By making peace, we save the Islands, with their commodities; by continuing the war, we lose them infallibly.*

"But this is not all," says this cool declaimer: "We must add to our loss of seamen, sustained by the Independence of America, at least twenty thousand more, who have been bred and maintained in the trade from Great Britain to the West Indies, and in the West India trade among themselves, and with other parts, amounting in the whole to upwards of eighty thousand; a loss which cannot fail to affect the sensibility of every man who loves this country, and knows that its safety can only be secured by its Navy."

But has it been considered, that neither of the powers at war have any pretence of claim to these Islands now? That they will have pretences upon them if they take them, which we cannot hinder if we continue the war? That *once taken by France, America is bound by treaty to warrant them to her?* This treaty lasts no longer than this war. Another war, America will be under no such obligations, unless, by continuing the war, we should compel her into further treaties, which *may be*, though she would be averse to them. Is it prudency in us to hazard so much upon the events of war, which are always uncertain, where forces are equal? But we are now most impolitically entangling ourselves in a war where the forces and resources are two to one against us? But will France and Spain be the less zealous to conquer the English Islands, because, by this means, they shall certainly take away so many seamen, and share them with America? Annexing these Islands to France and Spain, will increase the trade of France, Spain, Denmark, the United Provinces of the Low Countries, and the United States of America, and the twenty thousand seamen will be divided in some proportion between all these powers. The Dutch and the Americans will have the carriage of a great part of this trade, in consequence of the dismemberment of these Islands from you, and annexation to France and Spain. Do we expect to save these things by continuing the war? If we do, I wish we could reflect *more coolly* upon things. Every success we have yet had, in the whole course of this war, has been owing to fortunate contingences, or the mistaken policy of our enemies. It is too much for us to presume, that a series of miracles will be wrought for our deliverance, or that our enemies will never discover where their strength lies. We may bless our stars, and not our wisdom, that we have now an army, a navy, or an island in the West Indies.

"Will not Great Britain lose much of her Independence, if obliged to other countries for her naval stores?" Has she lost her Independence? Has she not been obliged to other countries for naval stores these five years?

"In the time of Queen Anne, we paid 3£. a barrel for tar to the extortionate Swede; and such was the small demand of those countries for the manufactures of this, that the ballance of trade was greatly in their favour. The gold we obtained in other commerce, was continually pouring into their laps. But we have reduced that ballance, by our importation of large quantities of those supplies from America."

But what is to hinder Great Britain from importing these large quantities of pitch, tar, and turpentine, from America, after we shall be wise enough to acknowledge and guarantee her Independence, by an honourable and advantageous peace with her? Great Britain may be obliged to give a price somewhat higher, because other nations will import them too. But this augmentation of price will probably be very little. Will the prospect of this higher price induce America to give up her Independence, and her new Governments, which, whatever we may think, are more firmly and solidly established than ours is? Will not our manufacturers purchase pitch from independent America? Will the prospect which is opened to the other maritime powers, of drawing these supplies, as well as those of masts, yards, bowsprits, ship timber, and ready-wrought ships too, make them less zealous to support American Independence? Will the increase of the demand upon the Northern Powers for those Article, in consequence of the destruction of the British monopoly, in America, make these powers less inclined to American Independency?

The British monopoly and bounties, in fact, reduced the

price of these articles in the Northern markets. The ceasing of that monopoly, and those bounties, will rather raise the price in the Baltic: Because those States in America, where pitch and tar chiefly grow, have so many articles of more profitable cultivation, that, without bounties, it is not likely that trade will flourish to a degree, to reduce the prices in the North of Europe.

Every day shews us more and more, that we undertook this war too rashly; without considering ourselves; without knowing the character and resources of America, and without weighing the relations between America and Europe. [   ] they have all decided this question against us, and in favour of America, as fully as even France has done. They all think that the cause of America is just, and that every one of them is interested in supporting her Independence. They have not had motives so pressing as France, Spain, and Holland, to engage in open war; but the measures they are taking, are as clearly in favour of America. There is not a power upon earth so much interested as America in the capital point which they are establishing, That free ships make free goods.

"Should a war take place between us and the Northern Powers, where are we to procure our naval stores?" I answer, make peace with America, and procure them from her. But when you go to war with America and the Northern Powers at once, you will get them no where. This writer appears to have had no suspicion, when he wrote his book, of the real intentions of the Northern Powers. What he thinks now, after their confederation against Great Britain, I know not. It is remarkable that this confederation was known in Europe eighteen months, and in the American Congress twelve months (not indeed as an act executed, but as a sentiment and design in which they were all agreed, and for which they were all making preparations) before it was either known or attended to by that Administration, of which Lord North was the ostensible Premier. We may affect to be as much astonished as we will: We may cry: "How sharper than a serpent's tooth it is to have thirteen *thankless* children!" *We may growl amidst the tempest, like* Lear, and cry to the thunders: "Rumble your fill! Fight whirlwind! hail! and fire!" But we must submit to fate. Her ordinances cannot be repealed by our Parliament, which has not yet claimed jurisdiction over her in all cases whatsoever.

ADIEU

(*To be continued.*)

July 1780

"Letters from a Distinguished American," No. VI

THE Cool Thoughts go on. "Timber of every kind, iron, salt-petre, tar, pitch, turpentine, and hemp, are raised, and manufactured in America. Fields of an hundred thousand acres of hemp are to be seen spontaneously growing between the Ohio and Mississippi, and of a quality little inferior to the European."

And is not this enough to cool the English courage, in the pursuit of a chimera? Is it possible to keep one country that has an abundance of these articles, and skill to use them, dependent on another? It is a maxim among the sons of Neptune, that "with wood, iron, and hemp, mankind may do what they please." America not only has them in plenty, but artists and seamen to employ them, fifteen hundred miles of sea coast, and an hundred excellent harbours to use them in, at three thousand miles distance from her enemy, who is surrounded with nations that are courting her friendship. Are not these articles as precious to France, Spain, and Holland, as to England? Will not these powers be proportionably active to procure a share of them, or a liberty to trade in them, as England will be to defend her monopoly of them? And will not America be as alert to obtain the freedom of selling them to the best advantage in a variety of markets, as other nations will for that of purchasing them?

This writer is so cool, that he thinks of nothing. A little warmth of imagination would be of use to him; it would present to his view a variety of considerations that have never occurred to him. Three millions of people in America, and all the nations of Europe, have as great a right to the common blessings of Providence, as the inhabitants of this island, some of whom wish to lord it over all. The Americans have as good a claim to the use of the earth, air, and seas, as the Britons. What right has Britain to shut them up in the prison of a monopoly, and prevent them from giving and receiving happiness from the rest of mankind? Did the Creator make that quarter of the globe for the use of this Island exclusively? This may be a cool thought, but a very narrow one.—There is another very serious consideration, that our coolness, or our heat, makes us incapable of attending to. Great Britain, separated from America, has, in the course of this war, displayed a power and resources, vastly greater, especially at sea, than the other maritime powers ever before believed she possessed.—America, separated from Great Britain, has displayed a power and resources ten times greater than any power in Europe, (even Great Britain herself,) ever suspected her to have. These are two discoveries which the other maritime powers have made. They now see, to a demonstration, that if Great Britain and America should ever be again united under one domination, there would be an end of the liberty of all other nations upon the seas. All the commerce and navigation of the world would be swallowed up in one frightful despotism, in this island. The Princes of Europe, therefore, are now unanimously determined that America shall never again come under the English government. Even if the Americans themselves desired it, which it is most certain they do not, nor ever will, the powers of Europe would not suffer it. For what object then are the English shedding their blood, and spending their millions?

"Will the Coasting trade, that of the Baltic and Mediterranean, with the small intercourse the English have with other nations in our own bottoms, furnish seamen for a Navy, necessary for the protection of Great Britain and its trade?"

According to this supposition, Great Britain will have no other trade, than that of the Coast, the Mediterranean, and the Baltic to protect, and she may protect her trade in that case as well as Portugal and Holland, &c. protect theirs, and in the same manner. And to this situation she will certainly come, if she continues this war for any length of time. If the American

Congress should take the resolution of prohibiting the importation of British manufactures, directly or indirectly, from any part of the world, a part which they will be likely to take, in order to weaken Great Britain, and strengthen their allies; if she continues this war, she will perceive the sources of her trade drying away, and the waters gliding into other channels; her seamen lessening and consuming, those of her enemies increasing; her capacity to defend her Islands, and even her East India trade, every day lessening, and that of her enemies to invade them every day increasing. So that it must end in the very evil this writer suggests: Whereas, if Great Britain makes peace now, the evil is avoided.

"Will her mariners continue as they are, when her manufacturers are labouring under the disadvantage of receiving their materials at higher and exorbitant prices, and selling at foreign markets at a certain loss?"

I suppose the English will be able to purchase of the Americans their materials as cheap as other nations. But do they expect ever to recover her monopoly so as to prevent other nations from getting American materials? So as to prevent the Americans from getting manufactures, productions, and all sorts of merchandizes from other nations? Let us consider this coolly. How much trouble did it cost them to prevent this communication before the war, when the American mind was possessed with all that fear, which is essentially the characteristic of monopolized colonies? When the American merchants had never travelled but to England: When their masters of vessels and seamen were ignorant of the French coast, and were taught to dread it as unknown and dangerous: Were the English ever able, under all these advantages, to prevent the Americans from eluding our art of navigation? But what has happened since this war broke out? Young American merchants, from every one of the Thirteen States, have crouded to France, and other parts of Europe, in great numbers, have studied the wants of France, and the articles she has which America wants, and the prices of all are stated in journals and memorandum books, which we can never obliterate. When such numbers of American masters of vessels have now explored the whole coast of France, so as to conduct vessels, wherever they please, even without pilots: When young Physicians, and Divines, and Lawyers, have travelled to France, formed acquaintance with men of letters, and established correspondences, which never can be extinguished: When American merchants and mariners have explored the creeks, inlets, and harbours of North America itself, ten times more perfectly than they were ever known before, to elude our frigates and cruisers: After all this, can we coolly suppose that the English ever will regain our monopoly, and prevent smuggling? If the English were to conquer America; if she was to submit, (suppositions as wild as can well be made,) no Custom-house officer, of any candour, will give it as his opinion, that they ever should be able to execute the act of navigation again in America. Fifty thousand regular soldiers, posted on the sea coast, and fifty men of war constantly cruising, an expence that would be greater than the monopoly ever was worth, would not effect it. Be not deceived! Impossibilities cannot be performed by Great Britain, and if her monopoly be gone, what is she contending for? The seamen then, which were secured to her by the monopoly, are gone for ever; and her only policy is to be as generous and magnanimous as France: in this way she has it in her power to prevent America from getting any destructive advantage of her; but by continuing the war, she will infallibly compleat the triumph of America and her own humiliation,—for civil, political, military, literary, commercial, and naval connections between America in every part of it, and France, and Spain, and Holland, are multiplying every day, and never will be checked but by a peace.

But what is the tendency of this argument, about the loss of seamen? If it serves to convince Britain that she should continue the war, does it not convince the allies that they ought to continue it too? They are to get all that England is to lose; and America is to be the greatest gainer of all. Whereas, she is not only to lose these objects, but her liberty too, and the lives of her best men, in infamy, if she is subdued: France, Spain, and Holland, and all the other Maritime Powers, are to gain a share of the objects, if Britain loses them. Whereas they not only lose all share in them, but even the safety and existence of their flag upon the ocean may be lost, if America is reduced, and the British monopoly of American Trade, Fisheries, and Seamen revived.

But let us coolly consider a few of the consequences of the redoubtable English conquest of America! Multitudes of the most learned, ingenious, and at present reputable men in the Thirteen United States, must fly abroad. Some of them the English would arrest; some of them would not fly to save their lives, but would remain there, to exhibit to mankind spectacles that Sydney and Russell never exceeded; but multitudes would fly. What would be the policy of France and Spain? Would they not immediately form American Brigades, as they have done Irish Brigades? Would not these be asylums for American Officers and Soldiers? Would not these hold constant correspondence and commerce too with America, and keep America on tiptoe for fresh revolts? Would it not cost America the constant maintenance of a larger fleet and army, than have been employed in the conquest, to preserve it?

The English are pursuing the most absurd war, that ever was waged by rational beings. Their very successes are ruinous to them, and useful to America. If they take a city, they only establish disaffection, open a trade which supplies the Americans with every thing they want, and their soldiers teach the citizens, and even the children, every branch of the art of war, the discipline, manœuvres of troops, cavalry, artillery, &c. If their men of war and privateers take American ships, it only serves to form American naval officers and seamen, who are made prisoners, to as perfect a mastery of every branch of the sea service as their own. If American privateers take British seamen, they find beef and pudding, and grog and beer, among American sailors, and enlist with the utmost chearfulness into their service.

Let the English go on, and compleat the glorious work of destruction to themselves, and glory to America and the rest of mankind. Such infatuation is in the order of Providence. Our *Thinker* ought to excuse me, if I am as much too warm as he is too cool.

(TO BE CONTINUED.)

July 1780

"Letters from a Distinguished American," No. VII

T HE American Refugees, in England, are so great an obstacle in the way of peace, that it seems not improper for me to take notice of them. The first and greatest of them, the late Mr. Hutchinson, is no more. He was born to be the cause, the object, and the victim of popular rage; and he died the day after the commencement of the insurrections in London, and just soon enough to escape the sight of the vengeance against Lord Mansfield's house, which so exactly resembled that which was fifteen years ago inflicted on his own. Descended from an ancient and honourable American family; born and educated in that country; possessing all the zeal of the congregational religion; affecting to honour the character of the first planters; early initiated into public business; industrious and indefatigable in it; beloved and esteemed by the people; elected and entrusted by them, and their Representatives; his views opened and extended by repeated travels in Europe; minutely informed in the history of his country; author of an history of it, which was extensively read in Europe; engaged in much correspondence, in Europe, as well as America; favoured by the Crown of Great Britain, and possessed of its honours and emoluments; in these circumstances, and with these advantages, he was perhaps the only man, in the world, who could have brought on the controversy, between Great Britain and America, at the time, and in the manner, in which it was begun, and involved the two countries in an enmity, which must end in their everlasting separation. This was his character; and these his memorable actions. An inextinguishable ambition, which was ever discerned among his other qualities, which grew with his growth, and strengthened with his age and experience, at last predominated over ever other passion of his heart and principle of his mind: rendered him credulous of every thing which favoured his ruling passion, but blind and deaf to every thing that opposed it: to such a degree, that his representations, with those of his friend and instrument, Bernard, drew on the King, Ministry, Parliament and Nation to concert those measures, which must end in a reduction of the power of the English, if they do not change their conduct, but in the exaltation and glory of America.

There are visible traces of his councils in a number of pamphlets not long since published in England, and ascribed to Mr. Gallaway. It is most probable, they were concerted between Administration and the Americans in general here, and Mr. Galloway was given out as the ostensible, as he probably was the principal author.

The "Cool Thoughts, on the Consequences of American Independence," although calculated to inflame a warlike nation, are sober reasons for America to defend her Independence and her alliance.

The pamphlet says "It has often been asserted, that Great Britain has expended, in settling and defending America, more than she will ever be able to repay, and that it will be more to the profit of this kingdom to give her Independence, and to lose what we have expended, than to retain her a part of its dominions." To this he answers very justly, that the bounties on articles of commerce, and the expence of the last war, ought not to be charged to America; that the charge of colonial Governments, have been confined to New York, the Carolinas, Georgia, Nova Scotia, and East and West Florida. That New England, New Jersey, Pennsylvania, Delaware and Virginia, have not cost Great Britain a farthing; that the whole expence of the former, is no more than one million seven hundred thousand pounds; and that when we deduct the seven hundred thousand pounds, extravagantly expended in building a key at Hallifax, we can only call it one million."

But the true answer is, that America has already repaid to England an hundred fold for all that has been expended upon her. The profit of her commerce, for one year, has been more than all that this kingdom has expended upon her in one hundred and fifty years. Whence is all the pride of Great Britain? Whence her opulence? Whence her populous cities? Whence multitudes of her cloud-capt towers, her gorgeous palaces and solemn temples, but from the profits of American commerce? But all this would not content her; she must tax America, and rob her of her liberty, as well as monopolize her commerce. The latter she endured, but the former she would not bear, and who can blame her? None, none but those who are conscious of the guilt of forging shackles for her.

This commerce Great Britain might still enjoy, but will not. Why? Because she cannot enjoy it all. Where will be the injury to her from other nations enjoying with her a small share of the blessings of Heaven? If France alone were to possess a share, Great Britain might have some color for jealousy, that she would become dangerous to her; but when America herself in the treaty she sent to France, with a foresight, a refined and enlarged policy that does honour to human nature, so studiously and anxiously guard against excluding any other nation from an equal share in her commerce; when she had coolness and magnanimity enough, although under every provocation from Great Britain to resentment, to guard against excluding even her from an equal share of her commerce, what has Great Britain to fear. If she made peace with America, she would not be without friends in Europe; and if her enemies should profit by American commerce she and her friends would profit more. The balance will be preserved, and she will have nothing to fear. Commerce she may have with America, as advantageous as ever, if she does not lose the opportunity: But taxation, domination and monopoly, are gone for ever.

The writer proceeds, "Posterity will feel that America was not only worth all that was spent upon her but that a just, firm, and constitutional subordination of the Colonies, was absolutely necessary to the independence and existence of Great Britain."

He should have said, That the ancestors of the present English have already found that America was worth all that has been spent upon her; that they have received, and themselves enjoyed more from her, than all that has been spent: that besides this, they have amassed more solid wealth from her, and transmitted down, by inheritance to their children, an hundred fold more than all the cost: *And even now America remains ready to renew her commerce with England to as great an advantage as ever, if they will make a peace.* Are domination and taxation necessary to trade? By no means. Their trade to Portugal and Russia is as profitable, as if these were not independent States.

That a share in the commerce of America is necessary to

support long the independence and existence of Great Britain, I readily agree; but this share does not depend upon her having the government of that country, much less upon her drawing taxes from it. This depends upon the wants of America, and the capacity of Great Britain to supply them. Her wants will increase beyond all proportion to the ability of Great Britain to supply in time; and her *immediate* demand upon her would be greater than she could possibly supply at present, if she made peace.

The independence of America would have no more effect upon the independence of Great Britain, than it either has, or will have, upon that of France or Spain, if she would change our hostile character against America into friendship, as they have done. But writers, from private views and private passions, are drawing the English on in error and delusion against their clearest Interest, against the voice of Nature, of Reason, of all Europe, and of GOD!   ADIEU

(TO BE CONTINUED.)

July 1780

"Letters from a Distinguished American," No. VIII

LET us proceed with our cool meditations. The author says, "Another argument much relied on by the advocates for American Independence, is, that a similarity of laws, religion, and manners, has formed an attachment between the People of Great Britain and America, which will insure to Great Britain a preference in the trade of America."

A similarity of laws facilitates business. It may be done with more ease, expedition, and pleasure, and with less risque of loss, mistake, or imposition, and consequently with more profit, in a country whose laws are understood, than in another where they are not. A similarity of religion is a motive of preference to those persons who are conscientious, and some such there are among the men of business even of this philosophic age. A similarity of manners and language also prevents many perplexities, delays, and impositions in trade: besides that the pleasures of society and conversation are some motives to a man of business. Laws, religion, manners, and language, therefore, will be motives of preference, *cæteris paribus*. After all, however, the goodness and cheapness of commodities will be the only decisive temptations to Americans to come here to market. They can learn languages, enjoy their own religion, among a people of a different one; conform for a time to manners very different from their own, and acquire a knowledge of the laws of other countries sufficient to do business there, provided they find better and cheaper goods there to be bought, and a better price for those they have to sell. Can the English then give them a better price for their commodities than other nations, and sell them theirs cheaper than others? This is the main question; and there is no doubt that they can, in most articles, at present: it will not be long so. If they give other nations time to establish their manufactures by the continuance of the war, all this may be changed. Do the English expect ever to compel the Americans to take their commodities at an high price, when they can have them abroad at a lower? An American would laugh in your face if you were gravely to tell him so. Can the English trust their Custom House Officers, who are to be appointed in future, that they would not connive? Did they never hear of merchants privileged to smuggle? Did they never hear of Governors sharing profits? Do they expect that Juries in America will condemn? Do they expect their single Judges of Admiralty will be again admitted in America, to try seizures and questions of civil property at land, where the people have even insisted that Juries should be appointed to try all maritime causes? It is a chimera that the English pursue. If they could re-acquire the Government, they never could execute the laws which guarded the monopoly. They never could execute them before. Now both the knowledge, the temptation, and the facilities to evade and elude them are infinitely multiplied. If they could force a sufficient number of Americans to submit to regain the government, the great body of the people would think them usurpers and tyrants, and that they have a right to elude and evade their mandates by every art and every shift. It will be a forced government, maintained only by military power, detested and execrated by the people, even by the most of those who in a fright or a fit of delusion should now submit.

Their acts of trade never were executed in America, excepting only at Boston. At New York, at Philadelphia, at Charles Town, they were constantly evaded. The Custom House Officers never dared to put them in execution. Nay, they were never executed even in Rhode Island and New Hampshire. It was only at Boston, under a military power, and an innumerable host of Custom House Officers, where they were executed at all. And here, at the expence of constant lawsuits, riots, tumults, and thousands of other evils. Before this war, the Americans were almost as ignorant of each other, as they were of Europe. Now they have become acquainted with both. There was little communication or correspondence, and still less trade between one Colony and another since this war. Great numbers of gentlemen of the first characters in the States have met in Congress, where they have learned every thing respecting other States. Officers and armies have marched from one end of the Continent to the other; became intimately acquainted with each other, formed friendships and correspondences with each other that never will cease; became perfectly acquainted with the geography of every province, city river, creek, plain, and mountain. Waggons and waggoners have constantly passed from Maryland, Pennsylvania, New Jersey, New York, and all New England, to Boston. Do the English suppose they will ever prevent the trade between one Colony and another again? Will they prevent tilt hammers from being erected, wool from being waterborne, or tobacco from being sent from Virginia to Boston? An hundred thousand regular soldiers, and every man of war they have in the world, would not accomplish it. But the English are in a dream. They know not what they are contending for. *They think America is in the same situation she was ten years ago.* They either know not, or consider not, what has happened there within these six years. This cool writer himself has been too much warmed with some passion or other to recollect what has passed within his own observation. It is much to be wished he would give us his *cool Thoughts on the Consequences of American dependence, conquest, and submission.* If he were to reflect upon the subject, he might easily prove, that it would be a constant source of vexation and expence to England, without any profit or advantage. It would be but a momentary and that an armed, riotous, rebellious and distracted truce; a constant source of fresh American revolts, and fresh foreign wars. The English ought to dread the temporary submission of America, more than America herself. It would be the source of their certain, final ruin; whereas to them it might be only a temporary evil. Every rising country has infinite advantages over a declining one, in every view.   ADIEU

(*To be continued.*)

July 1780

"*Letters from a Distinguished American,*" No. IX

SIR

Aₙ uniformity of laws and religion, united with a subordination to the same supreme authority; forms the national attachment: but when the laws and supreme authority are abolished, the manners, habits, and customs derived from them, will soon be effaced. The Americans have already instituted governments opposite to the principles upon which the British government is established. New laws are made in support of their new political systems, and of course destructive of the national attachment. The new States, altogether popular, their laws resemble those of the democratical cantons of Switzerland, not those of Great Britain. Thus we find, in their first acts, the strongest of all proofs, of an aversion in their rulers to our national policy, and a sure foundation laid to obliterate all affection and attachment to this country among the people. The attachment, then arising from a similarity of laws, habits, and manners, will last no longer than between the United Provinces and Spain, or the Corsicans and Genoese, which was changed, from the moment of their separation, into an enmity that is not worn out to this day."

How it is possible for those rulers, in a government altogether popular, who are the creatures of the people, and constantly dependent upon them for their political existence, to have the strongest aversion to the national policy of Great Britain; and at the same time, for the far greater part of the people, to wish and hope for an Union with that country, and to be ready to unite in reducing the power of those rulers, as this writer asserts, I know not. I leave him to reconcile it. But his consistency, and his sincerity, are points of no consequence to the Public.

It is very true that there is no strong attachment in the minds of the Americans to the laws and government of Great Britain. The contrary is true; they have almost universally a strong aversion to those laws and that government. There is a deep and forcible antipathy to two essential branches of the British Constitution, the monarchichal and the aristocratical. —There is no country upon earth where the maxims, that all power ought to reside in the great body of the people, and all honours and authorities to be frequently derived from them, are so universally and sincerely believed as in America. All hereditary titles, powers, and dignities, are detested from one end of the Continent to the other; and nothing contributed more to unite all America in the late resistance, than the attempt, by an Act of Parliament, to render one branch of the legislature in the council of the Massachuset's, independent of the people and their representatives. The government of these Colonies have all been popular from their first establishment. It was wise, just, politic, and necessary, that they should be so. —Nothing but that importance that was given by these governments to the common people, even to artisans and labouring men, and that comfortable state of life which is the fruit of it, could ever have peopled America. The severe labours of the field, in a wild country, and the dangers of the wilderness, where Planters were forced to carry their arms and their instruments of husbandry together to raise their bread, would have totally discouraged these settlements, if life had not been sweetened by superior liberty for themselves, and the prospect of it for their children. The first Planters of New England, Winthcap, Winslow, Saltenstall, Cotton, Wilson, Norton, and many others, were great men: they modelled their governments professedly upon the plan of the ancient Republicks of Greece. Penn, who founded the colony which bears his name, was another, and his form of government was as popular, as any in New England. Sir Walter Rawleigh did nearly the same in Virginia; so that democratical sentiments and principles were not confined to one Colony, of one part of the Continent, but they run through it. Even in New York and Virginia and New Hampshire, &c. where the councils were appointed by the crown, these very counsellors were seized with a strong proportion of the spirit of the people, and were obliged always to give way to the popular torrent. It is no wonder then, that every State upon the Continent has instituted a democracy, and that the people are universally fond of their new government. And a philosopher, who considers their situtaion, planted in a new country, with immense regions to fill up, by increasing population and severe labour, will see and acknowledge, what these kinds of governments are the best adapted to their circumstances, but calculated to promote their happiness, their population, their agriculture, manufactures and commerce, as well as their defence. It is the interest of all Europe, that they should enjoy these forms of government. They are best adapted to preserve peace, for the people always sigh for peace, and detest war; and it is their interest as well as inclination. It is the interest, and ought to be the inclination of every nation in Europe to let them enjoy it. As to the affection and attachment to the country, there was always more noise made about it than sense in it. The affection of one nation for another, at 3000 miles distance, is never a strong passion. The Americans love and adore their country; but America is their country, not this Island. There are few connections by blood between that country and this, but what are worn out of memory by age. Why, then, should we amuse ourselves with unnatural expectations? We shall never have any hold on the love of America, but what we obtain, by making it their interest to be our friends, in a fair and equal commerce, and by favouring their benevolent views of planting freedom, toleration, humanity, and policy, in the new world, for the happiness of the human species in both worlds. They are a people whose feelings are too refined, whose views are too enlarged for us, sunk as we are in dissipation, avarice, and pleasure. They think the cause of their country a sacred trust deposited in their hands by Providence for the happiness of millions yet unborn. They now think their liberty can never be safe under government of any European nation, the idea of coming again under which strikes them with horror. The frozen souls of this country may scribble, speculate, and fight as they please, they never will have any future advantage from that, but in the way of a fair and equal commerce with them as independent states.

This author is certainly just in his sentiments, that the attachment to England, from a similarity of religion, is also very feeble. There is no predominant religion, and it is their policy that there never shall be. They are of all the religious societies in Europe; they are Churchmen, Lutherans, Calvinists, Methodists, Presbyterians, Moravians, Congregationalists, Quakers, Anabaptists, Menonists, Swinfielders, Dumplers, and Roman Catholicks.

If the attachments arising from laws and government, from religion, customs, habits, fashions, and language, are such feeble ties, as this writer very justly represents them, what authority can we ever have over them, but by their general interests in a fair and equal commerce, as independent states? Will this writer say, it is their interest to become again dependent upon us? He has many times admitted, in effect, in this very pamphlet, that it is not. An American, even a Tory in America, will readily admit, they ever have admitted that Independence would be the most prosperous and glorious event for America, if she could obtain it.—They never contended for any thing, but the American inability to preserve it against the power of Great Britain. What would the rest of Europe say, if we were gravely to tell them, that it is the interest of America to come again under our dominion and monopoly? The interest of America in her independence is too clear a point to be contested. How then are we to govern them? Are we to govern and monopolize them, against their interest and inclination, by force? With all their power and resources, and the aids of France and Spain, and Holland, favoured, encouraged and abetted by all the maritime powers of Europe? We have really a task beyond our forces. Surely, in such a situation, peace with

America, and a treaty of commerce upon terms of perfect equality and reciprocity, would be a safe, an honourable, and an advantageous peace.   ADIEU

(To be continued.)

July 1780

"Letters from a Distinguished American," No. X

SIR

THE writer on the consequences of American independency proceeds, "It has been asserted, that America will be led, from motives of interest, to give the preference in trade to this country, because we can supply her with manufactures cheaper than she can raise them, or purchase them from others."—He has not favoured us with his opinion, whether we can supply them cheaper than others. If we can, the consequence is certain, that though independent, they will trade with us, in preference to others. If we cannot, they will trade with others, in preference to us, though they should again become dependent.—They now know the world, and they will make use of it, and the world will make use of them. Dependent, or independent, it will make very little difference. It is not doubted, at present, that we can sell our commodities to them cheaper, and give them a better price for theirs than other nations. But how long will this last? Certainly not long, if the war continues.

That we, or any other nation in Europe, can supply her with manufactures cheaper than she can raise them, in time of peace, is most certain. Europe has a warrantee upon America for this for centuries to come, in the immense regions of uncultivated lands. It is demonstrably certain, that so long as wild land is to be had cheap, and it will be for centuries so long, America will continue to exchange the productions of her agriculture for the manufactures of Europe. So long the manufacturers, who may emigrate from Europe, will soon be metamorphosed into farmers, because they will find, as they always have found, that they can advance themselves and their children the faster by it.

It is very true, "that she possesses, and can produce a greater variety of raw materials, than any other country on the globe," but it by no means follows, that it will be her interest to manufacture them, because a day's labour, worth two shillings, in a manufacture, produces but two shillings, whereas a day's labour, on wild land, produces the two shillings in immediate production, and makes the land itself worth two shillings more. We may, therefore, absolutely depend, that at a peace, America will have her manufactures from Europe, and, if it is not our fault, from us.

But, continues the writer, "a commercial alliance is already ratified, greatly injurious to the trade of Great Britain." The commercial alliance with France engages a free trade between those two nations. We may make a commercial alliance with America, and engage a free trade with her too. There is no article in the treaty with France which gives her any exclusive privilege in trade, or that excludes Great Britain from any branch of American trade. It is at this moment as open and free to us, as any other nation, and it is our imprudence that we are throwing it away. Do we suppose that France will give up the benefit she has obtained by this treaty? Is not the commerce, the navy, the independence, and existence of France as a maritime power, at stake? Does it not depend upon American independence? If it does not, it will depend upon her rendering the Colonies, after a mock submission, useless to us, by fomenting continual broil, and wars between us and them; and upon getting that commerce clandestinely, that by the treaty she may have openly. Will she not contend as earnestly for her independence and existence as we do for a chimera? The commercial treaty with France is no otherwise injurious to the trade of Great Britain, than as it is a breach of our monopoly, which is broke in an hundred ways, and never to be repaired, if this treaty were annulled.

"Should France succeed in supporting American independence, no one can doubt that other treaties, still more injurious, will be added."—Does he mean that America will make treaties of commerce with other maritime nations? This she will do;

but upon the same footing of equality, freedom and reciprocity; without excluding us, unless we drive her to despair and revenge, and the same passions that we now indulge against her. Make peace now, and you are safe against all unequal treaties. Other nations must have an equal right to American trade with France and us. The maritime powers all see it, and we may depend upon it, they will take care to secure themselves both against us and France. "When America shall have a separate and distinct interest of her own to pursue, her views will be enlarged, her policy will become exerted to her own benefit."

Does this writer suppose the Americans so ignorant and stupid as not to know this, as well as he? Does he coolly think that they wish to have their views contracted, and their policy exerted against her own benefit, as it used to be, or to the benefit of others, exclusive of her own. It must be an icy soul indeed that can wish itself smaller, or that can desire to have its understanding employed against itself. Is this an argument to prove that the far greater part of the people wish to return to our Government? This would be narrowing their views indeed; but this writer may be assured that this evil, if it be one to us, is already done; their views are already enlarged, they know one another; they know us; and they know the rest of Europe better than ever they did. They know what they are capable of, and what Europe wants.

"Her interest, instead of being united with, will become not only different from, but opposite to that of Great Britain." While we continue her enemy, it is her interest to weaken us as much as she can. But nothing can be clearer, than that her interest will not be opposite to that of any power in Europe, that will trade with her. She will grow; and every power in Europe that trade with her, will grow too in consequence of that trade, and ours more than any other.

"She will perceive that manufactures are the great foundation of Commerce." The productions of agriculture are a foundation of commerce, as well as manufactures are.

"That commerce is the great means of acquiring wealth." But manufactures are not the foundations of her commerce, nor is commerce her great means of acquiring wealth. Agriculture, and the continued augmentation of the value of land by improvement, are the great source of her wealth: and agriculture and commerce are but secondary objects, which do not bear a proportion to the former of one to twenty. It is her interest to attend to manufactures for filling up interstices of time, and no farther: and to commerce, to send her superfluous productions abroad, and bring back what she wants, and to be carriers, for the sake of selling her ships and commodities; but all her commerce and manufactures center and terminate in the improvement of land, and will infallably continue to do so, as long as there shall remain wild land in America: so that it is politically impossible, that she should ever interfere with Europe, either in manufactures or commerce, for centuries to come. In the nature of things she can carry on no manufactures and no commerce which will not be useful to Europe, instead of interfering with it, and to us more than any other, if we would cease our absurd hostilities.

"Bounties will be granted to encourage manufactures, and duties laid to disencourage or prohibit foreign importations!" Will the farmers vote away their money to encourage manufactures, when they can import them cheaper? Will merchants give theirs to strip themselves of the profit of importing? And where is the manufacturing interest to vote at all? All this is against reason and universal experience; a clearer demonstration of this cannot be given than in the instances of salt petre and salt.

Bounties have been given this war upon these articles, manufactured in America, because we would not suffer them to import them. And such is the ingenuity and invention of these people, that hundreds of tons of salt petre were produced in a few months, and the women learned to make it in their families, as they make soap. Salt works were erected upon the sea coast of the whole Continent, and they are now able to supply themselves with these articles, when they can't get them from Europe; but it is at the expence of the interest of agriculture, and when their trade began to open again, these manufactures declined; and they now revive and decline, like ebb and tide, as there happens to be scarcity or plenty imported—and thus it must be.   ADIEU

(*To be continued.*)

July 1780

"Letters from a Distinguished American," No. XI

To illustrate his argument on the Consequences of American Independence, the Writer subjoins, a Comparison, between the united States and the West Indies. He Says the Exports from England were in 1771

	£ s d
To North America	4,586,882: 15: 5
To Dominica	170,623:19: 3
To St. Vincent	36,839:10: 7
To Grenada	123,919: 4: 5
	331,338:14: 3
Difference	4,255,500: 1: 2

"If We reflect on the Extent of Territory, improved and improvable, the Numbers of People, of Mariners, of Shipping, naval Force, raw materials, and Consumption of manufactures, he hopes We should confess the Continent of more Importance than the Islands." He compares them 1. in Point of Extent of Territory. 2. Salubrity of Clymates. 3. Numbers of Inhabitants capable of Warring for the Empire, whereas the Islands are a dead weight in case of War. 4. Variety of Clymates. If the West Indies furnish Rum, Sugar, Cocoa, Coffee, Pimento and Ginger. The Continent produces Wheat, Rye, Barley, Oats, Indian Corn, Rice, Flour, Biscuit, Salt Beef, Pork, Bacon, Venison, Cod, Mackarel, and other Fish and Tobacco. If the West Indies produce Some materials for Dyes, as Logwood, Fustick, Mahogany and Indigo; the Continent produces Indigo, Silk, Flax, Hemp; Furs and skins of the Bear, Beaver, otter, Muskrat, Deer, Tyger, Leopard, Wildcat, Fox, Raccoon; and Pot ash and Pearl ash, Copper, and Lead ore, Iron in Pigs and Bars, for our manufactures; besides all the Articles of naval Stores, Timber, Plank, Boards, Masts, Yards, ships for sale, Pitch, Tar, Turpentine, Hemp, and Salt Petre. Such of these Articles as are necessary for the manufactures and Commerce of England were sent there: the surplus only to other Marketts, and the proceeds of that surplus remitted in Bills of Exchange or Cash for British manufactures and foreign articles of Commerce."

As to the Consumption of Manufactures, America would demand and consume, if Peace were now made as many and more of our manufactures than she ever did, because her Numbers have greatly increased Since this Trade was interrupted. As to our supplying them again with foreign Articles of Commerce it is chimerical in Us, to expect it: neither America, nor foreign nations will submit to it. As to the long roll of Articles, which contribute to political, military and naval Power, it is extravagant to hope ever to regain them. All mankind are interested and have the most pressing Motives to Sunder them from Us. They would make Us an universal monarchy.

Power is intoxicating, encroaching and dangerous, in Nations, as well as Individuals. Surrounding nations are jealous, and envyous of a Power that they see growing too formidable for their Safety. Examples are innumerable. Spain under Charles the 5th.—France under Louis the 14th. were thought by the Powers of Europe to have become dangerous, and allmost all the World united to lessen their Power. How did Portugal break off from Spain? how did she maintain her Independency? how does she hold it now—but because that England, France Holland and other Powers, will not see her again annexed to the Spanish monarchy, Situated as Portugal is, if she were annexed to Spain it would make her dangerous to the other maritime Powers. How did Holland maintain her Independency? but by the determined Aid of England, and France? How did the Cantons of Switzerland maintain theirs?

We are arrived at the Period long since foreseen and foretold, by cooler and deeper Thinkers than this Pamphlateer. It is an Observation of a sage and amiable Writer of the French nation, who has as much respect for England and as little for America as any impartial man in Europe, De Mably, "That the Project of being sole Master of the Sea, and of commanding all the Commerce, is not less chimerical, nor less ruinous than that of Universall, Monarchy, on Land. And it is to be wished for the Happiness of Europe, that the English may be convinced of this Truth, before they shall have learned it by their own Experience. France has already repeated several Times, that it was necessary to establish an Equilibrium, or Ballance of

Power, at Sea: and she has not yet convinced any Body because she is the dominant Power, and because they suspect her to desire the Abasement of the English, only that she may domineer the more surely, on the Continent. But if England abuses her Power and would exercise a Kind of Tyranny over Commerce, presently all the States that have Vessells and sailors, astonished that they had not before believed France, will join themselves to her to assist her in avenging her Injuries. Principles of Negotiation" p. 90.

The Present Conjuncture of affairs, resembles so exactly the Case that is here Stated that it seems to be a litteral fulfillment of a Prophecy. A Domination upon the sea is so much the more dangerous to other commercial nations and maritime Powers, as it is more difficult to form Alliances and combine Forces at Sea, than at Land. For which Reason it is essential, that the sovereigns of every commercial state, should make his national Flagg be respected, in all the Seas and by all the nations of the World. The English have ever acted upon this Principle, in supporting the Honour of their own, but of late years, inflated with intoxicating dreams of Power, they have grown less and less attentive to it, as it respects the Honour of other Flaggs. Not content with making their Flagg respectable they have grown more and more ambitious of making it terrible. Unwilling to do as they would be done by, and to treat other commercial nations as they insisted Upon being treated by them, they have grown continually more and more haughty, turbulent, and insolent upon the seas, and are now never Satisfied untill they make all other nations see and feel, that they despise them upon that Element. We have not only invaded the universal Liberty of the Americans, by cutting up by the Roots their ancient forms of Government, and endeavouring to subject them to a foreign Legislature in all Cases: but We had endangered the Liberty of France upon the Seas. Her Commerce, her Navy, her West India Islands her Fisheries, her East India Possessions, had all been entirely at our mercy, if North America had continued to this day a Part of the British Empire: We equally endangered the Liberty of Spain, her Fleets, her Islands, and the Communication between her Country and her Colonies would have been in our Power. What would have become of Holland? With what unbounded Contempt have We treated her. Her Liberty upon the seas, is so little respected by Us, that We annull at Pleasure all Treaties ancient and modern, and seize ships without a Colour of Law. The other maritime Powers are all now more attentive to Commerce than ever. They see America is necessary to their Views of Commerce. Each one of them sees that she must have a share of American Commerce or she cannot maintain her maritime Independency, her Liberty upon the seas. She sees also that if any one commercial nation of Europe were to enjoy an exclusive monopoly in America, that no other maritime Power could preserve her Liberty. No Wonder then, that We see such Unanimity of Sentiment among the maritime Powers. No Wonder that all the sons of Neptune, are united to preserve the Independence, the Freedom and sovereignty of his Reign from our Invasions.

5. The Growing State of the Colonies, on the Continent which appears by the Exports.

The Value of the Exports from England to	£	s	d
North America was in 1763	1,867,285:	6:	2
in 1771	4,586,882:	17:	11
Increase in Eight Years	2,719,597:	11:	9

The Value of the Exports from England to the			
West Indies was in 1763	1,149,596:	12:	4
in 1771	1,155,658:	3:	11
Increase in 8 years	6,061:	11:	7

The Value of the Imports into England from			
the West Indies, was in 1763	3,268,485:	14:	6
in 1771	2,800,583:	14:	0
Decrease in 8 years	467,902:	0:	6

He could not obtain an Account of the general Exports from the West Indies, and therefore, cannot make a Comparison, with those from North America, which were.

		s	d
in 1766	3,924,606:	0:	0
in 1773	6,400,000:	0:	0
Increase in 7 Years	2,475,394:	0:	0

The Exports from Great Britain to foreign Countries have been generally computed at   7,000,000: 0: 0

	£ s d	
in 1771 from England to		
America	4,586,882:15: 5	
to the W. Indies	1,155,658: 3:11	5,742,530:19: 4
		12,742,530:19: 4

The Exports from Scotland to America are not included; when added they will increase the value of the Exports from Great Britain to Upwards of 6,000,000: 0: 0 which is nearly equal to the amount of all the foreign Exports of the Kingdom, and one half of the whole Commerce of the nation, exclusive only of that to Ireland and the East Indies.

It is reported that these Facts and Estimates were all laid before the American Congress in the Year 1774 when this Writer was a member. They were minutely examined and thoroughly weighed, and with the most unfeigned sincerity it was wished and prayed by all, and with the most Sanguine Confidence expected by many, that they would occur to our Parliament, and prevent them from disaffecting by a perseverance in Impolicy and Injustice, So precious a Part of the dominions. Others who had studied more attentively the Character of this nation, and the Relations of America with Europe, had Strong Fears that nothing would Succeed. They have been found to have judged right. The Americans lament the Misfortunes of the English, but they rejoice in the Prospect of Superiour Liberty, Prosperity and Glory to the new World, that now opens to View, in Consequence of our Errors. They rejoice also at the destruction of that selfish and contracted monopoly which confined the Blessings, of that Quarter of the World to a single nation and at the liberal Extension of them to all mankind.

I shall conclude all with one observation upon the ability and Resources of America to continue the War and finally support their Independency. By the Resolutions of Congress of the 18 of March last, they redeem their two hundred millions of Paper dollars, at the Ratio of 40 Paper for one silver, which it seems is a full allowance, which makes the whole Value of their Paper Bills abroad of the Value of five millions of silver dollars, or 1,102,500 £ sterling.

They have also resolved that the Loan office Certificates shall be paid in Proportion to the Value of money at the time they were issued, which is the only equitable Way, and these added to the 1,102,500 in Bills and to their debt contracted in Europe makes the whole amount of the national debt of the United states amount to about five millions sterling. Thus they have conducted this whole War, for five years for five millions, one Million a Year. According to the Estimate of this Writer the Exports from North America in 1773, were 6,400,000 Pounds. The whole Expence of five Years War, has not then amounted to the Value of one Years exports.

Compare this with our Expences. Lord Norths Loan only this Year is Twelve Millions. According to the Estimate of this Writer the whole Exports of Great Britain to foreign Countries North America and the West Indies, amounted in 1771 to 12,762,530:19: 4. Thus We borrow annually to maintain the War a sum equal nearly to our whole Exports.

Let a cool man judge, whether We or they can support the War longest. Let Us soberly reflect, what Burden this debt is to America. It has been said that all the Colonies together, contracted in the Course of the last French War a debt of Ten Millions, double their market. Which was all nearly discharged before this War began. Be this as it may, I am well informed that the Province of the Massachusetts Bay alone, raised by Taxes half a Million and by Loan half a Million more, in the Course of the last War, and that before this War broke out it was all paid off. The Province of Massachusetts now has double the Number of Inhabitants she had in the middle of last War. Let this War continue as long as it will our debt will accumulate twice as fast, four times as fast in Proportion to our Abilities, as the American will. And at the End this Affecting difference, that in a very few Years she will pay the Utmost Farthing of the Principal, and We shall be very happy, if We can pay the annual Interest.

We knew not the Resources of America. We knew not the Resources in their Minds and Hearts. There are deep and great Virtues and Profound abilities in that People that We have not yet put to Tryal nor called forth to Action. Her Agriculture Manufactures and Commerce, are Resources, that We have no Idea of. But she is now recurring to another Resource that We neither understand nor can bear to practice. Œconomy. They are striking off, every useless officer and office in their Army their navy, their civil departments and otherwise to save Expences, and in future they will conduct the War at half the Expence of the past. America is the best Friend We can have Upon Earth—and We shall find her, if We will not suffer her to be our Friend, our most fatal Ennemy.   Finis

July 1780

"Letters from a Distinguished American," No. XII

Before We dismiss these cool Thoughts it may not be amiss to Subjoin a few Reflections, upon the Certainty of American Independance.

We have repeated the Word Rebellion, untill the People have been wrought Up, to a Pitch of Passion and Enthusiasm, which has rendered them incapable of listening to the Still voice of Reason. Men are governed by Words, their Passions are inflamed by Words. Policy associates certain Passions with certain Words for its own Purposes. There are Words which command the Respect of nations, others irresistably allure their Esteem: others excite their Envy or their Jealousy: and there are others that Summon up all their Hatred, Contempt, Malice and Rancour. It is only necessary to let loose a Single Word, to Stir up Armies, Navies and nations to unlimited Rage.

The Word Rebellion has been too often repeated from the Throne, and ecchoed from both Houses of Parliament: too often repeated in the Prayers of the Church; in News Papers and Pamphlets, in private Conversation, and in the dispatches of our Generals and Admirals, not to have had its full Effect. It has wrought this nation, out of "its old good nature, and its old good Humour" to borrow Expressions of Lord Clarendon, into a Degree of Inhumanity, that cool Posterity will condemn to Shame, and our Armies and Navies to a series of Cruelties, which will form an indellible Blott in our History.

The Americans were fully aware, before this War broke out, of all the Consequences of the Cry of Rebellion. Our Governors and other Crown officers took Care to instruct them in the Nature and the Punishment of Treason, by elaborate Descriptions and Deffinitions in the Newspapers. There was not a circumstance in the Punishment of Treason but what was laid before the Eyes of the People at large. But all this did not Succeed. Their Love of Liberty was stronger than death. They did not Want to be informed in the last Speech from the Throne: that the Authors of all rebellious Resistance, to repeal or reform the Laws, must terminate in their Destruction or in the overthrow of the Constitution. This very cry with which we have annimated ourselves and our Forces to pursue the War will opperate as an eternal Barrier to any Reconciliation short of Independence. The People know, that however plausible and Specious, our Pretensions may be, if they ever submit to the Kings Government again, if it were but for an Hour, they shall be construed into Rebells and Traitors, Characters that they more universally and justly disdain, than the People of any one of the three Kingdoms.

In the civil Wars that have happened in these Kingdoms, in that for Example, which prevailed from 1641 to 1660, it originated in a Contraversy between different Branches of our Legislature, and each having been an undoubted Part of our Constitution, the nation was nearly equally divided. The Clergy were divided tho the greater Part took side with the Court. The Lawyers were equally divided. And this has ever been the position of this nation nearly ballanced between the Court and Country Party leaning Sometimes to one and Sometimes to the other, as the Constitution seemed to require.

But in America the Case was different. In all the Colonies the monarchical Part of their Constitutions, the Royal Governors, were generally little esteemed or confided in, by the Body of the People. The Aristocratical Part, their Councils, in those Colonies where they were elected by the Representatives, were esteemed only in Proportion as they conformed to the sentiments of the Representatives, in those where they were appointed by the Crown they were not esteemed at all, except by the few who flattered them in order to get offices and those in that Country where Men and Estates were so divided, were an inconsiderable Number: The predominant Spirit then of every Colony has been from the Beginning democratical, and the Party that ever could be obtained to decide in favour of Councils, Governors, the Royal Authority or that of Parliament has ever been inconsiderable. The People ever stood by their Representatives. And what is very remarkable, the Lawyers and Clergy have almost universally taken the same side.

This has been the popular Torrent, that like a River changing its bed, has irresistably born away every Thing before it. The Sentiments of this People therefore are not to be changed.

> Britain changefull as a Child at Play
> Now called in Princes and then drove away,

because the nation was so equally divided that a little good or bad success, a little Prosperity or Distress, was sufficient by changing the sentiments or the Professions of a small Number to alter the Ballance.

But if in that Case any foreign Power had intervened, if France, had taken the Side of the Patriotic Party against the Royal Family, or that of the Court against the Country and sent over to this Island Sixty thousand Men and Fifty sail of Men of War to its assistance, what would have been the Consequence? It is most certain that it would have decided the Contraversy at once.

In the Case of America, the popular Party, had a Majority in every Colony So divided, that all the offices and Authority under the King, when the Period of the Revolution came to a Crisis, were hurried away before it like Leaves and Straws before the Hurricane. We have sent over more than Sixty thousand Men, and a great naval Force to assist the Small Party of Royalists humbled in the Dust in order to make a Ballance. Were they able to succeed? Did They ever produce the least Simptom of Doubt or Hesitation in the Body of the People of the final success of their Cause. But now by the Interposition of France and Spain, our Forces by sea and Land, are so employed, our Resources so exhausted, We have called off So much of our Force for the defence of the West India Islands, that our whole Force is inconsiderable. The French themselves have a sea Force there perhaps equal to ours, and a Land Force, which amounts to a Great deal. What have We then to expect? It is obvious to all Europe that France and

Spain, or either of them have it in their Power to finish all our Hopes in North America, whenever they please, and compleat the Tryumph of the Patriotic Party there. And they have motives So urgent to do it, that We may depend upon it they will. Why then are We putting ourselves to an infinite Expence to keep New York and Charlestown? If We wait for the People to declare in our favour, We shall wait like the Jews, for a Messiah that will never come, or like the Countryman who waited for the last drops of the River. When We see that even the Inhabitants of New York are distrusted by our Generals; when they dare not confide to them Ammunition or Arms. When We see that all our Acts and all our Terrors, added to all the Joys of our Partisans, and all the sorrows of the Patriots, could obtain only 210 Names to an Address out of 120 thousand Inhabitants in Carolina, and when Clinton himself tells Us that Parties were lingering in the Province, and Magistrates under the late Government endeavouring to execute the Laws? Do You suppose the great states of N. Carolina, Virginia and Maryland will be idle? Will not the Congress exert themselves to relieve Carolina and Georgia at the very Time, when the Spaniards are marching with slow but sure steps through the Floridas, and New York will be blocked up with a French Fleet. The combined naval armaments of Spain and France may be an overmatch for Rodney, Gibralter is suffering in heroic Patience, and D'Estaing putting the channel Fleet and this Island in Danger.
Finis

July 1780

POLITICAL SPECULATIONS

To Benjamin Franklin

Sir   Amsterdam August 17. 1780
  I never was more amuzed with political Speculations, than Since my Arrival in this country. Every one has his Prophecy, and every Prophecy is a Paradox. One Says America will give France the Go By. Another that France and Spain, will abandon America. A Third that Spain will forsake France and

America. A Fourth that America, has the Interest of all Europe against her. A Fifth that She will become the greatest manufacturing Country, and thus ruin Europe. A Sixth that she will become a great and an ambitious military and naval Power, and consequently terrible to Europe.

In short it Seems as if they had Studied for every Impossibility, and agreed to foretell it, as a probable future Event.

I tell the first, that if the K. of France would release America from her Treaty and England would agree to our Independance, on condition we would make an Alliance offensive and defensive with her, America ought not to accept it and would not, because She will in future have no security for Peace even with England, but in her Treaty with France. I ask the Second, whether they think the Connection of America of So little Consequence to France and Spain, that they would lightly give it up? I ask the third, whether the Family compact added to the Connection with America is a trifling Consideration to Spain? To the fifth, that America will not make manufactures enough for her own Consumption, these 1000 years. To the sixth that We love Peace and hate War So much, that We can Scarcely keep up an army necessary to defend ourselves against the greatest of Evils, and to secure our Independance which is the greatest of Blessings; and therefore while We have Land enough to conquer from the Trees, Rocks and wild Beasts We shall never go abroad to trouble other nations.

To the fourth, I Say that their Paradox is like several others, viz. that Bachus and Ceres did mischief to mankind when they invented Wine and Bread, that Arts, Sciences and Civilization have been general Calamities &c.

That upon their Supposition all Europe ought to agree, to bring away the Inhabitants of America, and divide them among the nations of Europe to be maintained as Paupers, leaving America to grow up again, with Trees and Bushes, and to become again the Habitations of Bears and Indians, forbidding all navigation to that quarter of the globe in future. That Mankind in general, however are probably of a different opinion, believing that Columbus as well as Bachus and Ceres did a service to mankind, and that Europe and America will be rich Blessings to each other, the one Supplying a surplus of manufactures, and the other a surplus of raw materials, the Productions of Agriculture.

It is very plain, however, that Speculation and disputation, can do Us little service. No Facts are believed, but decisive military Conquests: no Arguments are seriously attended to in Europe but Force. It is to be hoped our Countrymen instead of amusing themselves any longer with delusive dreams of Peace, will bend the whole Force of their Minds to augment their Navy, to find out their own Strength and Resources and to depend upon themselves. I have the Honour to be, with great Respect, your most obedient servant

John Adams

AMERICA AND THE ENGLISH LANGUAGE

To Samuel Huntington

Duplicate

Sir   Amsterdam September 5th. 1780

As Eloquence is cultivated with more Care in free Republicks, than in other Governments, it has been found by constant Experience that such Republicks have produced the greatest purity, copiousness and perfection of Language. It is not to be disputed that the Form of Government has an Influence upon Language, and Language in its Turn influences not only the Form of Government but the Temper, the Sentiments and Manners of the People. The admirable Models, which have been transmitted through the World, and continued down to these days, so as to form an essential part of the Education of Mankind from Generation to Generation, by those two ancient Towns, Athens and Rome, would be Sufficient without any other Argument, to shew the United States the Importance to their Liberty, Prosperity and Glory of an early Attention to the subject of Eloquence and Language.

Most of the Nations of Europe, have thought it necessary to establish by public Authority, Institutions for fixing and improving their proper Languages. I need not mention the Academies in France, Spain, and Italy, their learned labours, nor their great Success. But it is very remarkable that although many learned and ingenious Men in England have, from Age to Age, projected Similar Institutions for correcting and improving the English Tongue, yet the Government have never found time to interpose in any manner so that to this day, there is no Grammar nor Dictionary, extant of the English Language, which has the least public Authority, and it is only very lately that a tolerable Dictionary has been published even by a private Person, and there is not yet a passable Grammar enterprised by any Individual.

The Honour of forming the first public Institution for refining, correcting, improving and ascertaining the English Language, I hope is reserved for Congress. They have every Motive that can possibly influence a public Assembly to undertake it.

It will have an happy effect upon the Union of the States, to have a public Standard for all persons in every part of the Continent to appeal to, both for the Signification and Pronunciation of the Language.

The Constitutions of all the States in the Union are so democratical that Eloquence will become the Instrument for recommending Men to their fellow Citizens, and the principal means of Advancement, through the various Ranks and Offices of Society.

In the last Century, Latin was the universal Language of Europe. Correspondence among the learned, and indeed among Merchants and Men of Business and the Conversation of Strangers and Travellers, was generally carried on in that dead Language. In the present Century, Latin has been generally laid aside, and French has been substituted in its place; but has not yet become universally established, and according to present Appearances, it is not probable that it will. English is destined to be in the next and succeeding Centuries, more generally the Language of the World, than Latin was in the last, or French is in the present Age. The Reason of this is obvious, because the increasing Population in America, and their universal Connection and Correspondence with all Nations will, aided by the Influence of England in the World, whether great or small, force their Language into general Use, in spight of all the Obstacles that may be thrown in their Way, if any such there should be.

It is not necessary to enlarge further to shew the Motives which the People of America have to turn their thoughts early to this Subject: they will naturally occur to Congress in a much greater detail, than I have time to hint at.

I would therefore submit to the Consideration of Congress, the Expediency and Policy of erecting by their Authority, a Society under the Name of "The American Academy, for refining, improving and ascertaining the English Language."

The Authority of Congress is necessary to give such a Society Reputation, Influence and Authority, through all the States and with other Nations.

The number of Members of which it shall consist: the manner of appointing those Members: whether each State shall have a certain Number of Members, and the Power of appointing them: or whether Congress shall appoint them: whether after the first Appointment the Society itself shall fill up vacancies—these and other Questions will easily be determined by Congress.

It will be necessary, that the Society should have a Library consisting of a compleat Collection of all Writing, concerning Languages of every sort ancient and modern. They must have some Officers, and some other Expences, which will make some small Funds indispensibly necessary. Upon a Recommendation from Congress, there is no doubt but the Legislature of every State in the Confederation, would readily pass a Law making such a Society a Body Politick, enable it to sue and be sued and to hold an Estate real or personal of a limited Value in that State.

I have the Honour to submit these Hints to the Consideration of Congress, and to be, with the greatest Respect, Sir, your moss obedient & most humble servt.

Replies to Hendrik Calkoen No. I

1st. Letter

Sir   Amsterdam Octr. 4. 1780

You desire an exact and authentic Information of the present Situation of American Affairs, with a previous concise Account of their Course before, during and after the Commencement of Hostilities.

To give a Stranger an adequate Idea of the Rise and Progress of the Dispute between Great Britain and America, would require much time and many Volumes. It comprizes the History of England, and the united states of America for twenty Years; that of France and Spain for five or Six; and that of all the maritime Powers of Europe for two or three. Suffice it to say, that immediately upon the Conquest of Canada from the French in the Year 1759, Great Britain Seemed to be Seized with a Jealousy against the Colonies and then concerted the Plan of changing their forms of Government, of restraining their Trade within narrower Bounds, and raising a Revenue within them by Authority of Parliament for the avowed or pretended Purpose of protecting, Securing, and defending them. Accordingly in the Year 1760 orders were sent from the Board of Trade, in England to the Custom house officers in America, to apply to the Supream Courts of Justice for Writs of Assistance, to enable them to carry into a more vigorous Execution certain Acts of Parliament called the Acts of Trade, among which the famous Act of navigation was one, the fruit of the ancient English Jealousy of Holland by breaking open Houses, ships or Cellars, Chests, stores and Magazines, to search for uncustomed Goods. In most of the Colonies these Writs were refused. In the Massachusetts Bay the Question, whether Such Writs were legal and constitutional, was Solemnly and repeated, Argued before the supream Court by the most learned Council in the Province.

The Judges of this Court held their Commissions during the Pleasure of the Governor and Council, and the Chief Justice dying at this Time, the famous Mr. Hutchinson was appointed, probably with a View of deciding this cause in favour of the Crown, which was accordingly done. But the Arguments advanced upon that occasion by the Bar and the Bench, opened to the People Such a View of the designs of the British Government against their Liberties and of the Danger they were in, as made a deep Impression upon the public which never wore out.

From this Moment, every Measure of the British Court and Parliament, and of the Kings Governors and other servants, confirmed the People in an opinion of a Settled design, to over turn, those Constitutions under which their Ancesters had emigrated from the old World, and with infinite Toil, Danger and Expence planted a new one. It would be endless to enumerate all the Acts of Parliament and Measures of Government, but in 1764 Mr. George Grenville moved a Number of Resolutions in Parliament which passed, for laying a vast Number of heavy duties upon stamped Paper, and in 1765 the Act of Parliament was made called the stamp Act. Upon this, there was an Universal rising of the People in every Colony compelling the stamp officers by Force to resign, and preventing the stamped Papers from being used, and indeed compelling the Courts of Justice to proceed in Business without them. My Lord Rockingham perceiving the Impossibility of executing this statute, moved by the Help of Mr. Pitt for the Repeal of it, and obtained it, which restored Peace, order and Harmony, to America, which would have continued to this Hour, if the evil Genius of Great Britain had not prompted her to revive the Resistance of the People by fresh Attempts upon their Liberties, and new Acts of Parliament imposing Taxes upon them.

In 1767, they passed another Act of Parliament, laying Duties upon Glass, Paper and Painters Colours, and Tea—this revived the Discontents in America But Government sent over a Board of Commissioners, to over see the Execution of this Act of Parliament, and all others imposing Duties with a Multitude of new officers for the same Purpose, and in 1768 for the first Time sent four thousand regular Troops to Boston to protect the Revenue Officers in the Collection of the Duties.

Loth to commence Hostilities the People had Recourse to Non Importation agreements, and a variety of other Measures, which in 1770 induced Parliament to repeal all the Duties upon Glass, Paper and Painters Couleurs, but left the Duty upon

Tea unrepealed. This produced an Association not to drink Tea. In 1770 the Animosity between the Inhabitants of Boston and the Kings Troops, grew so high, that a Party of the Troops fired upon a Crowd of People in the streets, killing 5 or 6 and wounding some others. This raised such a spirit among the Inhabitants that in a Body they demanded the instant Removal of the Troops, which was done the Governor ordering them down to Castle Island some miles from the Town.

In 1773 the British Government determined to carry into Execution the Duty upon Tea, impowrd the East India Company to export it to America. They sent some Cargoes to Boston, some to New York, some to Philadelphia and some to Charlestown. The Inhabitants of New York and Philadelphia, sent the ships back to London and they Sailed up the Thames to proclaim to all the Nation that N.Y. and Pen. would not be enslaved. The Inhabitants of Charlestown unloaded it and stored in Cellars where it could not be used and where it finally perished. The Inhabitants of Boston, after trying every Measure to send the ships back like N.Y. and Philadelphia, but not being permitted to pass the Castle, the Tea was all thrown into the sea.

This produced several Vindictive Acts of Parliament—one for starving the Town of Boston by shutting up the Port, another for abolishing the Constitution of the Province, by destroying their Charter, another for sending Persons to England to be tryed for Treason &c.

These Acts produced the Congress of 1774, who stated the Rights and Grievances of the Colonies and petitioned for Redress. Their Petitions and Remonstrances were all neglected and treated with Contempt.

General Gage had been sent over with an Army to in force the Boston Port Bill, and the Act for destroying the Charter. This Army on the 19 of April 1775 commenced Hostilities at Lexington, which have been continued to this day.

You see sir by this most imperfect and Hasty sketch that this War is already twenty years old. And I can truly say, that the People, through the whole Course of this long Period, have been growing constantly every Year more and more unanimous and determined to resist the designs of Great Britain.

I should be ashamed to lay before a Gentleman of Mr.

Kalkoens Abilities so rude a Sketch if I had not an equal Confidence in his Candor and discretion which will induce me as I may have leisure to continue to sketch a few Observations upon your Questions. I have the Honour to be   John Adams

Replies to Hendrik Calkoen No. II

2nd. Letter.

Sir   Amsterdam Octr. 5 1780

Your first Proposition is to prove by Striking Facts, "that an implacable Hatred and Aversion reigns throughout America."

In Answer to this, I beg leave to Say that the Americans are animated by higher Principles and better and Stronger Motives than Hatred and Aversion. They universally aspire after a free Trade with all the commercial World, instead of that mean Monopoly, in which they were shackled by great Britain, to the disgrace and Mortification of America, and to the Injury of all the rest of Europe, to whom it seems as if God and Nature intended, that So great a Magazine of Productions the raw Materials of Manufactures, So great a source of Commerce, and so rich a Nursery of Seamen as America is should be open. They despize, Sir, they disdain the Idea of being again Monopolized by any one Nation whatsoever: and this contempt is at least as powerfull a Motive of Action as any Hatred whatsoever.

Moreover Sir they consider themselves contending for the purest Principles of Liberty civil and religious: for those Forms of Government under the Faith of which their Country was planted: and for those great Improvements of them which have been made by their new Constitutions. They consider themselves not only as contending for these great Blessings but against the greatest Evils that any Country ever suffered, for they know if they were to be deceived by England, to break their Union among themselves and their Faith with their Allies, they would ever after be in the Power of England who would bring them into the most abject submission to the

Government of a Parliament, the most corrupted in the World in which they would have no Voice nor Influence, at 3000 miles distance from them.

But if Hatred must come into consideration, I know not how to prove their Hatred better than by shewing the Provocations they have had to Hatred.

If tearing up from the foundation, those Forms of Government under which they were born and educated and thrived and prospered, to the infinite Emolument of England—if imposing Taxes upon them, or endeavouring to do it for Twenty years without their consent, if commencing Hostilities upon them—burning their Towns—butchering their People—deliberately starving Prisoners, ravishing their Women—exciting Hosts of Indians to butcher and scalp them and purchasing Germans to destroy them, and hiring Negro servants to murder their Masters—if all these and many other things as bad are not Provocation enough to Hatred, I would request Mr. Calkoen to tell me what is or can be. All these Horrors, the English have practised in every Part of America from Boston to Savanna.

Replies to Hendrik Calkoen No. III

3d. Letter

Sir   Amsterdam October the 6. 1780

Your Third Proposition is to shew that America, notwithstanding the War, daily increases in Strength and Force."

It is an undoubted Fact that America, daily increases in Strength and Force: but it may not be so easy to prove this to the Satisfaction of an European, who has never been across the Atlantick. However some Things may be brought into Consideration, which may convince, if properly attended to.

1. It may be argued from the Experience of former Wars, during all which the Population of that country was so far from being diminished or even kept at a Stand, that it was always found at the End of a War that the Numbers of People, had increased during the Course of it, nearly in the Same

Ratio as in Time of Peace. Even in the last French War which lasted from 1755 to 1763, during which Time, the then American Colonies, made as great Exertions, had in the Field as great a Number of Men, and put themselves to as great an Expence, in Proportion to the Numbers of People, as the united States have done during this War; it was found that the Population had encreased nearly as fast as in times of Peace.

2. If you make Enquiry into the Circumstances of the different Parts of America at this day, you find the People in all the States pushing their Settlements out into the Wilderness, upon the Frontiers, cutting down the Woods and subduing new Lands, with as much Eagerness and Rapidity, as they used to do in former Times of War or Peace. This Spreading of the People into the Wilderness, is a decisive Proof of the increasing Population.

3. The only certain Way of determining the Ratio of the Increase of Population is by authentic Numerations of the People, and regular official Returns. This has I believe never been done generally in former Wars, and has been generally omitted in this. Yet some States have made these Returns. The Massachusetts Bay for Example, had a Valuation about the year 1773 or 1774, and again the last year 1779 they had another. In this Period of five years, that State was found to have encreased, both in Number of People and in Value of Property, more than it ever had grown before in the Same Period of Time. Now the Massachusetts Bay, has had a greater Number of Men employed in the War, both by Land and sea in Proportion to the Numbers of her Inhabitants than any other state of the thirteen. She has had more Men killed, taken Prisoners, and died of sickness, than any other state: Yet her growth, has been as rapid as ever—from whence it may be fairly argued that all the other States have grown in the same or a greater Proportion.

4. It has been found by Calculations, that America, has doubled her Numbers even by natural Generation alone, upon an Average, about once in Eighteen Years. This War has now lasted, near six Years. In the Course of it, We commonly compute in America that We have lost by sickness and the sword and Captivity, about five and thirty Thousand Men. But the Numbers of People have not increased less than Seven hundred

and Fifty thousand, souls, which give at least an hundred Thousand fighting Men. We have not less probably than seventy thousands of Fighting Men in America, more than We had, on the day that Hostilities were first commenced on the 19 of April 1775. There are near Twenty thousand Fighting Men Added to the Numbers in America every Year. Is this the Case with our Ennemy, Great Britain? Which then can maintain the War the longest?

5. If America increases in Numbers, she certainly increases in Strength. But her Strength increases in other respects. The Discipline of her Armies increase. The skill of her Officers, increase by Sea and Land—her skill in military Manufactures, such as those of Salt Peter, Powder, Fire Arms, Cannon, Musquets, increases. Her skill in Manufactures of Flax and Wool for the first necessity, increases—her Manufactures of salt also increases, and all these are Augmentations of Strength and Force to maintain her Independence. Further her Commerce increases every Year—the Number of Vessells She has had this Year in the Trade to the West Indies—the Number of Vessells arrived in Spain, France, Holland, and Sweeden, shew that Her Trade is greatly increased this Year.

But above all her Activity skill Bravery and success in Privateering, increases every Year. The Prizes she has made from the English this Year, will defray more than one half of the whole Expence of this Years War. I only submit to your consideration a few Hints which will enable you to Satisfy yourself by Reflection, how fast the Strength and Force of America increases.

I have the Honour to be

Replies to Hendrik Calkoen No. IV

4. Letter
Sir   Amsterdam October 7. 1780

Your fourth Question is, whether America, in and of itself, by means of purchasing or exchanging the Productions of the several Provinces, would be able to continue the War, for 6, 8 or 10 years, even if they were entirely deprived of the Trade with Europe, or their Allies exhausted by the War and forced to make a Seperate Peace were to leave them.

This is an extreme case. And where is the necessity of putting Such a Supposition! Is there the least appearance of France or Spain being exhausted by the War? Are not their Resources, much greater than those of England, Seperated as she is from America? Why should a Suspicion be entertained that France or Spain will make a seperate Peace? Are not these Powers Sufficiently interested in seperating America from England? All the World knows that their maritime Power, and the Possession of their Colonies depend upon Seperating them? Such Chimæras as these are artfully propagated by the English to terrify Stockjobbers, but thinking Men, and well informed Men know that France and Spain have the most pressing Motives to persevere in the War. Besides Infractions so infamous, of Solemn Treaties made and avowed to all Mankind are not committed by any nation. In short no Man who knows any Thing of the real Wealth and Power of England on one hand; and of the Power and Resources of France, Spain and America on the other, can believe it possible, in the ordinary Course of human Events and without the Interposition of Miracles, that France and Spain should be So exhausted by the War, as to be forced to make a Seperate Peace.

The other Supposition here made is equally extreme. It is in the nature of Things impossible that America should ever be deprived entirely of the Trade of Europe. In opposition to one extream I have a Right to advance another. And I Say that if all the maritime Powers of Europe, were to unite their Navies, to block up the American Ports and prevent the Trade of Europe they could not wholly prevent it. All the Men of War in Europe would not be sufficient to block up a seacoast of 2000 Miles in Extent, varied as that of America is by such an innumerable Multitude of Ports, Bays, Harbours, Rivers, Creeks, Inlets and Islands, with a Coast so tempestuous that there are many Occasions in the Course of the Year, when Merchant Vessells can push out and in altho Men of War cannot cruise. It should be remembered, that this War was maintained by America for Three Years, before France took Any Part in it.

During all that Time the English had fifty Men of War upon that Coast which is a greater Number than they ever will have again: yet all their Vigilance was not Sufficient to prevent American Trade with Europe. At the worst Time We ever saw, one Vessell in three went and came Safe. At present there is not one in four taken. It should also be remembered that the French Navy have never untill this Year, been many days together upon the American Coast. So that We have in a sense maintained the Trade of the Continent five Years against all that the English navy could do, and it has been growing every Year.

Why then should We put cases that We know can never happen. However I can inform you, that the Case was often put, before this War broke out. And I have heard the common Farmers in America reasoning upon these Cases seven years ago. I have heard them Say, if Great Britain could build a Wall of Brass, a thousand feet high all along the seacoast at low Water Mark, We can live and be happy. America is most undoubtedly capable of being the most independent Country upon Earth. It produces every Thing for the Necessity, Comfort and Conveniency of Life, and many of the Luxuries too. So that if there were an eternal Seperation between Europe and America—The Inhabitants of America would not only live but multiply, and for what I know be wiser, better, and happier, than they will be, as it is.

That it would be unpleasant, and burthensome to America to continue the War for 8 or 10 Years, is certain: but will it not be unpleasant and burdensome to Great Britain too? There are between 3 and four millions of People in America. The Kingdom of Sweeden, that of Denmark, and even the Republick of the united Provinces have not each of them many more than that Number. Yet these States can maintain large standing armies even in time of Peace, and maintain the Expences of Courts And Governments much more costly than the Government of America. What then should hinder America from maintaining an Army sufficient to defend her Altars, and her Firesides? The Americans are as active as industrious and as capable as other Men. America could undoubtedly maintain a regular Army of Twenty thousand Men forever. And a regular Army of Twenty thousand Men, would be Sufficient to keep

all the Land Forces that Great Britain can send there, confined
to the Seaport Towns under cover of the Guns of their Men of
War. Whenever the British Army shall attempt to penetrate far
into the Country the regular American Army will be joined by
such Reinforcements from the Militia, as will ruin the British
Force—By desertions, by Fatigue, by sickness and by the
sword in occasional skirmishes, their numbers will be wasted
and the miserable Remainders of them Burgoined.

I have the Honour to be &c.

Replies to Hendrik Calkoen No. V

5th. Letter

Sir   Amsterdam October 9. 1780

The fifth Enquiry is, whether a voluntary Revolt of any one
or more of the States, in the American Confederation is to be
apprehended: and, if one or more were to revolt, whether the
others would not be able to defend themselves?

This is a very judicious and material Question. I conceive
that the answer to it is easy, and decisive. There is not the least
danger of a voluntary Revolt, of any one State in the Union. It
is difficult to prove a negative however: and still more difficult
to prove a future Negative. Let us however consider the Subject a little.

Which State is the most likely to revolt, or Submit? Is it the
most ancient Colony as Virginia or the Massachusetts? Is it
the most numerous and powerful as Virginia, Massachusetts,
or Pensilvania? I believe no body will Say that any one of these
great States will take the Lead in a Revolt or a voluntary
Submission.

Will it be the Smallest, and weakest States, that will be most
likely to give up voluntarily? In order to Satisfy ourselves of this,
let Us consider what has happened, and by the Knowledge of
what is passed We may judge of what is to come. The Three
Smallest States are Rhode Island, Georgia, and Delaware. The

English, have plainly had it in view to bring one of these States to a submission and have accordingly directed very great Forces aginst them.

Let Us begin with Rhode Island. In the latter End of the Year 1776, General How sent a large Army of near seven thousand Men, by sea under a strong Convoy of Men of War, detached by Lord How, to take Possession of Newport, the Capital of Rhode Island. Newport stands upon an Island, and was neither fortified, nor garisoned sufficiently to defend itself against so powerfull a Fleet and Army and therefore the English made themselves Masters of the Place. But what Advantage did they derive from it? Did the Colony of Rhode Island, Small as it is, Submit? So far from it, that they were rendered the more eager to resist, and an Army was assembled at Providence, which confined the English to the Prison of Rhode Island, untill the fall of the year 1779 when they were obliged to evacuate it, and our Army entered it in Tryumph.

The next little state which the English attempted was Delaware. This state consists of three Counties only situated upon the River Delaware below Philadelphia, and is the most exposed to the English Men of War, of any of the states, because, they are open to Invasion not only upon the Ocean but all along the River Delaware. It contains not more than thirty Thousand Souls. When the English got Possession of Philadelphia, and had the command of the whole Navigation of the Delaware, These People were more in the Power of the English than any Part of America ever was, and the English Generals, Admirals, Commissioners and all the Tories used all their Arts to seduce this little state. But they could not succeed. They never could get the Appearance of a Government erected under the Kings Authority. The People continued their Delegation in Congress, and continued to elect their Governors, senate and assemblies, under their new Constitution, and to furnish their quota to the continental Army, and their Proportion to the Militia, untill the English were obliged to evacuate Philadelphia. There are besides, in this little state, from various Causes more Tories in Proportion than in any other. And as this state stood, immoveable, I think We have no reason to fear a voluntary submission of any other.

The next Small state that was attempted was Georgia. This

state is situated at the southern Extremity of all, and at such a distance from all the rest and such difficulties of Communication, being above an hundred Miles from Charlestown in South Carolina, that it was impossible for the neighbouring states to afford them any Assistance. The English invaded this little state and took the Capital Savanna, and have held it, to this day: but this Acquisition has not been followed by any submission of the Province. On the contrary they continue their delegation in Congress, and their new officers of Government. This Province moreover, was more immediately the Child of England than any other. The settlement of it cost England more than all the rest: from whence one might expect they would have more Friends here than any where.

New Jersey is one of the middling Sized States. New Jersey had a large British Army in Philadelphia, which is on one Side of them, and another in New York which is on the other Side, and the British Army has marched quite through it; and the English have used every Policy of Flattery, of Terror, and severity, but all in vain and worse than in vain. All has conspired to make the People of New Jersey some of the most determined against the English and some of the most brave and skillfull to resist them.

New York, before the Commencement of Hostilities, was supposed to be the most lukewarm, of the middling states in the Opposition to the designs of the English. The English Armys have invaded it, from Canada and from the Ocean, and have long been in Possession of three Islands, New York Island, long Island and staten Island, yet the rest of that Province has stood immoveable through all the Varieties of the Fortune of War for four Years, and increases in Zeal and Unanimity, every year.

I think therefore there is not even a Possibility that any one of the thirteen States should ever, voluntarily revolt or submit.

The Efforts and Exertions of General How, in New York, long Island, staten Island, New Jersey, Pensilvania, Delaware, and Mariland, to obtain Recruits, the vast Expence that he put his Master to, in appointing new Corps of officers, even General officers, the Pains they took, to inlist Men, among all the straglers in those Countries and among many Thousands of Prisoners which they then had in their Hands. All these measures, obtaining but 3600 Men and very few of these Americans, according to General Hows own Account, shews I think to a Demonstration, that no voluntary Revolt or submission is ever to be apprehended.

But even supposing that Rhode Island, should submit, what could this small Colony of 50,000 souls do, in the midst of Massachusetts, Connecticutt, and New Hampshire.

Supposing Delaware, 30,000 souls should submit, what Influence could it have upon the Great states of New Jersey, Pensilvania, Mary land And Virginia among which it lies.

If Georgia, at the Extremity of all should submit, what Influence could this little society of 20,000 souls have upon the two Carolinas and Virginia.

The Colonies are at such vast distances from one another, and the Country is so fortified every where by Rivers, Mountains, and Forests, that the Conquest or submission of one Part, has no Influence upon the rest.

Replies to Hendrik Calkoen No. VI

Letter 6
Sir   Amsterdam October 10. 1780

The sixth Task, is to shew that no Person, in America, is of so much Influence, Power, or Credit, that his Death, or Corruption by English Money could be of any nameable Consequence.

This question is very natural, for a Stranger to ask, but it would not occur to a native American who had passed all his Life, in his own Country: and upon hearing it proposed, he could only Smile.

It Should be considered, that there are in America, no Kings, Princes, or Nobles: no Popes, Cardinals, Patriarchs, Archbishops, Bishops, or other ecclesiastical Dignitaries. They are these and Such like lofty Subordinations, which place great Bodies of Men in a State of Dependance upon one, which enable one or a few Individuals in Europe to carry away after them, large Numbers, wherever they may think fit to go.

There are no hereditary Offices, or Titles, in Families nor even any great Estates that descend in a right Line, to the Eldest sons. All Estates of Intestates are distributed among all the Children. So that there are no Individuals, nor Families, who have either from office, Title or Fortune any Extensive Power, or Influence. We are all equal in America, in a political View, and as much alike as Lycurgus's Hay cocks. All publick offices and Employments are bestowed, by the free Choice of the People, and at present through the whole Continent are in the Hands of those Gentlemen who have distinguished themselves the most, by their Councils, Exertions, and sufferings, in the Contest with Great Britain. If there ever was a War, that could be called *the Peoples War* it is this of America, against Great Britain, it having been determined on by the People and pursued by the People in every step of its Progress.

But who is it in America, that has credit to carry over to the Side of Great Britain any Numbers of Men? General How tells Us, that he employed, Mr. Delancey, Mr. Cortland Skinner, Mr. Chalmers, and Mr. Galloway, the most influential Men they could find, and he tells you their ridiculous success.

Are they Members of Congress, who by being corrupted, would carry Votes in Congress in favour of the English? I can tell you of a Truth, there has not been one Motion made in Congress, Since the Declaration of Independancy, on the 4. of July 1776, for a Reconciliation with Great Britain, and there is not one Man in America, of sufficient Authority or Credit to make a Motion in Congress for a Peace with Great Britain upon any Terms short of Independance, without ruining his Character forever. If a Delegate from any one of the thirteen States were to make a Motion, for Peace upon any Conditions short of Independency, that delegate would be recalled with Indignation by his Constituents as soon as they shall know it. The English have artfully represented in Europe, that the Congress have been governed by particular Gentlemen: but you may depend upon it, it is false. At one Time the English would have made it believed that Mr. Randolph, the first President of Congress, was its Soul. Mr. Randolph died, and Congress proceeded, as well as ever. At another Time Mr. Hancock was all and all. Mr. Hancock left the Congress, And has Scarcely been there for three Years: yet Congress has proceeded with as much Wisdom, Honour and Fortitude as ever. At another Time, the English represented that Mr. Dickinson, was the Ruler of America. Mr. Dickinson opposed, openly and upon Principle, the Declaration of Independancy, but instead of carrying his Point, his Constituents differed with him so materially that they recalled him from Congress, and was absent for some years: yet Congress proceeded with no less Constancy, and Mr. Dickinson lately finding all America unalterably fixed in the system of Independancy has fallen in like a good Citizen and now supports it in congress with as much Zeal as others. At another Time, the English have been known to believe that Dr, Franklin, was the essential Member of Congress: but Dr. Franklin was sent to France in 1776, and has been there ever Since, yet Congress have been as active and as capable as before. At another Time Mr. Samuel Adams, was represented as the Man who did every Thing: Yet Mr. Samuel Adams has been, absent for the greatest Part of three Years, attending his Duty as Secretary of State in the Massachusetts Bay: yet it does not appear that Mr. Adams's Absence has weakened the Deliberations of Congress, in the least. Nay, they have sometimes been silly enough to represent your humble servant, Mr. John Adams, as an essential Member of Congress. It is now however, three Years Since Congress did him the Honour to send him to Europe as a Minister Plenipotentiary to the Court of Versailles, and he has never been in Congress since. Yet Congress have done better since he came away than they ever did before.

In short sir all these Pretences are the most ridiculous imaginable. The American Cause stands upon the essential, unalterable Character, of the whole Body of the People upon their Prejudices, Passions, Habits and Principles, which they derived from their Ancestors their Education, drew in with their Mothers Milk, and have been confirmed by the whole Course of their Lives, and the Characters whom they have made conspicuous by placing them in their publick Employments

> are but Bubbles on the Sea of matter born
> They rise: they break, and to that Sea return.

The Same Reasoning is applicable to all the Governors, Lt. Governors, secretaries of state, Judges, senators and Representatives of particular states. They are all eligible and elected every Year, by the Body of the People, and would loose their Characters and Influence, the Instant they should depart in their public Conduct from the political system that the People are determined to support.

But are there any officers of the Army, who could carry over, large Numbers of People? The Influence of these officers is confined to the Army. They have very little among the Citizens. But if We consider the Constitution of that Army, We shall see, that it is impossible that any officer could carry with him any Numbers even of soldiers. These officers are not appointed by a King, or a Prince, nor by General Washington. They can hardly be Said to be appointed by Congress. They have all Commissions from Congress it is true; but they are named and recommended and even generally appointed by the Executive Branch of Government in the particular state to which they belong, except the general officers who are appointed by Congress. The Continental Army, consists of the Quotas of officers and Troops, furnished by thirteen different states. If an officer of the Massachusetts Bay forces for Example should go over to the Ennemy, he might possibly carry with him half a dozen soldiers belonging to that state—yet I even doubt whether any officer whatever who should defect from that state could persuade so many as half a dozen soldiers to go with him.

Is it necessary to put the supposition, that General Washington should be corrupted? Is it possible that So fair a Fame as Washingtons should be exchanged for Gold or for Crowns? A Character so false so cruel, so blood thirsty, so detestible as that of Monk might betray a Trust. But a Character so just, so humane, so fair, so open honourable and amiable as Washingtons, never can be stained with so foul a Reproach.

Yet I am fully of opinion that if even Mr. Washington, should go over to the English which I know to be impossible, he would find none or very few officers or soldiers to go with him. He would become the Contempt and Execration of his own Army, as well as of all the rest of Mankind.

No sir! The American Cause is in no Danger from the Defection of any Individual. Nothing short of an entire Alteration in the sentiments of the whole Body of the People, can make any material Change in the Councils, or in the Conduct of the Army of the United States. And I am very sure that Great Britain has not Power or Art sufficient to change essentially the Temper the Feelings, and the opinions of between three and four Millions of People, at three thousand Miles distance, supported as they are by Powerfull Allies.

If such a Change could ever have been made, it would have been seven Years ago when offices, Employments and Power in America were in the Hands of the King. But every Ray of Royal Authority has been extinguished now between four and five years, and all civil and military Authority is in Hands determined to resist Great Britain to the last.

I have the Honour to be

Replies to Hendrik Calkoen No. VII

Letter 7
Sir   Amsterdam October 10th 1780

Your seventh Inquiry is, whether the common People in America, are not inclined, nor would be able to find sufficient means, to frustrate by Force, the good Intentions of the skilful Politicians?

In answer to this, it is sufficient to say, that the Commonalty have no need to have recourse to Force, to oppose the Intentions of the skillful: because the Law and the Constitution authorize the common People to choose Governors and Magistrates every year: so that they have it constantly in their power, to leave out any Politician however skillful, whose Principles, Opinions or Systems they don't approve.

The difference however in that Country is not so great as it is in some others between the Common People and the Gentlemen, for Noblemen they have none. There is no Country where the Common People, I mean the Tradesmen, the Husbandmen, and the labouring People have such Advantages of Education, as in that: and it may be truly said that their Education, their Understanding and their Knowledge is as nearly equal as their Birth, Fortune, Dignities and Titles.

It is therefore certain, that whenever the Common People shall determine upon Peace, or Submission, it will be done. But of this there is no danger. The Common People, are the most unanimously determined against Great Britain of any: it is the War of the Common People; it was undertaken by them, and has been and will be supported by them.

The People of that Country often rose in large Bodies, against the Measures of Government, while it was in the Hands of the King. But there has been no Example of this sort, under the new Constitutions, excepting one which is mentioned in General How's Narrative in the back part of North Carolina. This was owing to Causes so particular, that it rather serves to shew the Strength of the American Cause in that State, than the Contrary.

About the year 1772, under the Government of Tryon, who has since made himself so obnoxious to all America, there were some warm disputes in North Carolina concerning some of the internal Regulations of that Province, and a small number of People in the back parts rose in Arms under the name of regulators against the Government. Governor Tryon marched at the head of some Troops, drawn from the Militia, gave battle to the Regulators, defeated them, hanged some of their Ringleaders and publishing Proclamations against many others. Those People were all treated as having been in Rebellion, and they were left to solicit Pardons of the Crown. This established in the Minds of those Regulators such an hatred towards the rest of their Fellow-Citizens, that in 1775, when the War broke out, they would not join with them. The King has since promised them pardon for their former Treasons, upon Conditions that they commit fresh ones against their Country. In 1777, in conjunction with a Number of Scotch Highlanders, they rose, and Governor Caswell marched against them, gave them Battle and defeated them. This Year they have risen again and been again defeated. But these People are so few in Number: there is so much apparent Malice and Revenge, instead of any principle in their disaffection, that any one who knows any thing of the human Heart, will see, that instead of finally weakening the American Cause in North Carolina, it will only serve to give a keenness and an Obstinacy to those who support it.

Nothing indeed can shew the Unanimity of the People, throughout America, in a stronger light than this—that the British Army has been able to procure so few Recruits, to excite so few Insurrections and Disturbances. Nay, although the freedom of the Press and the freedom of Speech is carried to as great lengths in that Country as in any under the Sun, there has never been a Hint in a Newspaper, or even in a Hand Bill, nor a single Speech or Vote in any Assembly, that I have heard of, for submission or even for Reconciliation.

I have the Honor to be, Sir, your humble Servant.

Replies to Hendrik Calkoen No. VIII

Letter 8

Sir   Amsterdam October 16th. 1780

The eighth Enquiry is, what England properly ought to do, to force America to Submission, and preserve her in it? How much Time, Money, and how many Vessels would be wanted for that purpose?

I assure You, Sir, I am as much at a loss to inform You, in this particular, as Lord George Germaine would be. I can fix upon no Number of Men, nor any Sum of Money, nor any Number of Ships, that I think would be sufficient. But most certainly no Number of Ships or Men which Great Britain now has, or ever can have, nor any Sum of Money, that She will ever be able to command, will be sufficient.

If it were in the power of Great Britain to send an hundred thousand Men to America, and they had Men of War and Transports enough to convey them there in safety, amidst the dangers that await now from French, Spanish and American Men of War, they might possibly get possession of two or three Provinces, and place so many Garrisons in various parts as to prevent the People from exercising the functions of Government, under their new Constitutions, and they might set up a sham Appearance of a Civil Government under the King. But I dont believe that an hundred thousand Men, could gain and preserve them the Civil Government of any three States in the Confederation. The States are at such distances from one another; there are such difficulties in passing from one to another by land; and such a multitude of Posts are necessary to be garrisoned and provided, in order to command any one Colony, that an Army of an hundred thousand Men, would soon find itself consumed, in getting and keeping possession of one or two States. But it would require the Armies of Semiramis to command and preserve them all.

Such is the Nature of that Country and such the Character of the People, that if the English were to send ever so many Ships, and ever so many Troops, they never would subdue all the Americans. Numbers in every State would fly to the Mountains and beyond the Mountains, and there maintain a constant War against the English. In short the English, if they could conquer America, which they never can, nor any one State in it, it would cost them a standing Army of an hundred thousand Men to preserve their Conquest; for it is in vain for them ever to think of any other Governments taking place again under the King of England, but a military Government.

As to the Number of Ships it must be in proportion to the number of Troops: they must have transports enough to carry their Troops, and Men of War enough to convoy them, through their numerous French, Spanish and American Enemies upon the Seas.

As to the Sums of Money, You will easily see, that adding two hundred Millions more to the two hundred Millions they already owe, would not procure and maintain so many Ships and Troops.

It is very certain the English can never send any great Numbers more of Troops to America. The Men are not to be had: the Money is not to be had: the Seamen and even the Transports are not to be had.

I have the Honor to be

I give this to Mr. Calkoen as my private Opinion concerning the question he asks. As Mr. Calkoen observes, this is a Question that had better not be publickly answered. But time will shew the Answer here given is right. It would at present be thought Extravagance or Enthusiasm. Mr. Adams only requests Mr. Calkoen to look over this letter a few years hence, and then say what his Opinion of it is. Victories gained by the English, in taking Sea-port Towns, or in open field fighting will make no difference in my answer to this Question. Victories gained by the English will conquer themselves sooner than the Americans. Fighting will not fail in the End to turn to the Advantage of America, although the English may gain an Advantage in this or that particular Engagement.

Replies to Hendrik Calkoen No. IX

Letter 9
Sir   Amsterdam October 16. 1780

The ninth question is, how Strong the English Land Force, is in America? How Strong it was at the Beginning? and whether it increases, or diminishes?

According to the Estimates laid before Parliament the Army under General How, General Carleton, and General Burgoine, amounted to fifty five Thousand Men, besides, Volunteers, Refugees, Tories, in short all the Recruits raised in Canada, and all other Parts of America under whatever denomination. If We Suppose that all these in Canada and elsewhere amounted to 5000 Men, the whole According to this Computation amounted to sixty thousand Land Forces.

This Estimate however, must have been made from the Number of Regiments, and must have Supposed them all to be full.

General How himself however, in his Narrative Page 45 tells Us that his whole Force, at the Time when he landed on long Island in 1776, amounted to Twenty thousand, one hundred and Twenty one Rank and File, of which 1,677 were Sick.

By a Regular Return of General Burgoines Army, after its Captivity in 1777 it amounted in Canadians, Provincials, British and German Troops to upwards of Ten Thousand Men. We may suppose that four Thousand Men, were left in Canada for the Garrison of Quebec, Montreal and the great number of

other Posts in that Province. To these Numbers if We Add the
Officers, We may fairly allow the whole Land Force at that
Time to be forty Thousand Combattants.

This is all the Answer, that I am able to give from Memory,
to the Question how Strong the british Army was.

In order to give an Answer, to the other, how Strong it is,
let Us consider

1. There has been no large Reinforcement, ever Sent to
America, since that Time. They have Sent Some Troops every
year: but these never amounted to more than Recruits, and
probably rather fell short of filling up the Vacancies which
were made in the Course of the Year, by Desertion and Death,
by Sickness and by the sword. So that upon the whole I think
it may be Safely Said, that the Army never has been greater
than it was in 1776.

But We must deduct from this Ten Thousand Men taken
with Burgoine one Thousand Hessians Taken at Trenton and
Prince Town, and indeed many more taken by two or three
hundred at a Time upon other Occasions.

In the next Place We must deduct, I Suppose about Ten
Thousand more sent since the French War, to Jamaica, St.
Luce, Barbadoes and the other West India Islands.

So that upon the whole, I think We make an ample Allowance if We State the whole Number now in New York,
Carolina, and Georgia, including all Refugees &c. at Twenty
thousand Men, officers included.

This is in Part an Answer to the Question, whether their
Force increases or diminishes. But it should be further considered, that there is a constant and rapid Consumption of their
Men. Many die of sickness, Numbers desert, there have been
frequent skirmishes, in which they have ever had more Men
killed and wounded, than the Americans: and now, So many of
their Troops are in Carolina and Georgia, where the Climate is
so unhealthy that, there is great Reason to expect that the
greatest Part of that Army will die of Disease. And whoever
considers the Efforts the English have made, in Germany, Ireland, Scotland, and England, as well as America, for seven
Years successively to raise Men the Vast Bounties they have
offered: and the few they have obtained, Whoever considers
the Numbers they must loose this Year by the severity of Duty

and by Sickness in New York, Carolina, Georgia and the West India Islands, and the Numbers that have been taken going to Quebec, North America, the East and West Indies, will be convinced, that all the Efforts they can make will not enable them for the future to keep their Numbers good.

I have the Honour to be &c.   John Adams

Replies to Hendrik Calkoen No. X

Letter 10
Sir   Amsterdam Octr. 16. 1780

The Tenth Head of Inquiry is, how great is the Force of America? the Number of Men? their Discipline, &c. from the Commencement of the Troubles? Is there a good Supply of warlike Stores? are these to be found, partly or entirely in America? or must they be imported?

The Force of America, consists of a regular Army, and of a Militia. The regular Army, has been various at different Times. The first regular Army, which was formed in April 1775 was inlisted for Six months only. The next was inlisted for one year. The next for three Years. The last Period expired last February. At each of these Periods, between the Expiration of a Term of Enlistment, and the Formation of a new Army, the English have given themselves Airs of Tryumph, and have done Some brillant Exploits. In the Winter of 1775, 6 indeed, they were in Boston, and altho our Army, after the Expiration of the first Period of Inlistment for Six months, was reduced to a Small Number, yet the English were not in a condition to attempt any Thing. In the Winter of 1776, 7, after the Expiration of the Second Term of Inlistment, and before the new Army was brought together the English marched through the Jersies. After the Expiration of the last Term of Inlistment, which was for three Years and ended last January or February, the English went to their old Exultations again, and undertook the Expedition to Charlestown. In the Course of the last Spring and

Summer, however, it seems the Army has been renewed and they are now inlisted, in general during the War.

To State the Numbers of the regular Army, according to the Establishment, that is according to the Number of Regiments at their full Compliment, I suppose the continental Army has sometimes amounted, to Fourscore thousand Men. But the American Regiments have not often been full, any more than the English. There are in the War Office, at Philadelphia, regular Monthly returns, of the Army from 1775 to this day, but I am not able from Memory to give any accurate Account of them. It is sufficient to say, that the American regular Army has been generally Superiour to that of the English, and it would not be good Policy to keep a larger Army, unless We had a Prospect of putting an End to the British Power, in America by it. But, this, without a naval Superiority, is very difficult, if not impracticable. The English take Possession of a Seaport Town, fortify it in the Strongest manner, and cover it with the Guns of their Men of War, So that our Army cannot come at it. If France and Spain should cooperate with Us So far as to send Ships enough to maintain the Superiority at Sea, it would not require many Years, perhaps not many Months, to exterminate the English from the United States. But this Policy, those Courts have not adopted, which is a little Surprizing because it is obvious, that by captivating the British Fleet and Army in America, the most decisive Blow would be given to their Power, which can possibly be given in any quarter of the Globe.

What Number of regular Troops General Washington, has at this Time under his immediate Command, I am not able precisely to say. I presume, however that he has not less than Twenty Thousand Men, besides the french Troops under the Comte De Rochambeau. Nor am I able to say, how many General Gates has at the southward.

But besides the regular Army, We are to consider the Militia. Several of the Colonies were formed into a Militia, from the Beginning of their Settlement. After the Commencement of this War, all the others followed their Example, and made Laws, by which all the Inhabitants of America are now enrolled in a Militia, which may be computed at five hundred Thousand Men. But these are Scattered over a Territory of one hundred and fifty miles in Breadth, and at least fifteen hundred Miles in Length, lying all along upon the Sea Coast. This gives the English the Advantage, by means of their Superiority at Sea, to remove Suddenly and easily from one Part of the Continent to another, as from Boston to New York, from New York to Rhode Island, from New York to Cheasapeak or Delaware Bay, or to Savanna or Charles town, and the Americans the Disadvantage, of not being able to march either the regular Troops or the Militia, to such vast distances without immense Expence of Money and of Time. This puts it in the Power of the English to take so many of our Sea port Towns, but not to make any long and successfull Marches into the interiour Country, or make any permanent Establishments there.

As to Discipline, in the Beginning of the War, there was very little either among the Militia or the regular Troops. The American officers have however been industrious, they have had the Advantage of reading all the Books which have any Reputation concerning military Science, they have had the Example of their Ennemies the British Officers, before their Eyes a long Time, indeed from the Year 1768—and they have had the Honour of being joined by British, German, French, Prussian and Polish officers of Infantry and Cavalry, of Artillery and Engineering, So that the Art of War is now as well understood in the American Army, and military Discipline is now carried to as great Perfection, as in any Country whatever.

As to a Supply of Warlike Stores, At the Commencement of Hostilities, the Americans had neither Cannon, Arms, or Ammunition, but in Such contemptible Quantities as distressed them, beyond description. And they have all along been Streightened at Times, by a Scarcity of these Articles, and are so to this Day.

They have however at present an ample Field Artillery, they have Arms, and Powder, and they can never be again, absolutely destitute, because the Manufactures of all Sorts of Arms of Cannon of all sorts, of salt Peter and Powder, have been introduced and established. These Manufactures, altho very good, are very dear, and it is difficult to make enough for so constant and so great a Consumption. Quantities of these Articles are imported every Year. And it is certain they can be imported and paid for by American Produce, cheaper than they can be made.

But the Americans, to make their system perfect, want five hundred thousand stands of Arms, that is one at least for every Militia Man, with Powder, Ball and Accoutrements in Proportion. This however is rather to be wished for than expected. The French Fleet carried Arms to America, and if the Communication between America and France and Spain, should become more frequent by Frigates and Men of War, and especially if this Republick, should be compelled into a War with England, America will probably never again suffer much for Want of Arms or Ammunition.

The English began the War against the Northern Colonies. Here they found the Effects of ancient Militia Laws. They found a numerous and hardy Militia, who fought and defeated them upon many Occasions. They then thought it necessary to abandon these and fell upon the Middle Colonies, whose Militia had not been so long found. However after, several Years Experience, they found they were not able to do any Thing to the Purpose against them. They have lastly conceived the Design of attacking the Southern Colonies. Here the white People, and consequently the Militia are not so numerous, and have not yet been used to War. Here therefore they have had some apparent successes, but they will find in the End their own destruction in these very successes. The Climate will devour their Men, their first successes will embolden them to rash Enterprizes, the People there will become enured to War, and will finally, totally destroy them. For as to the Silly Gasconade, of bringing the southern Colonies to submission, there is not even a Possibility of it. The People of those states are as firm in Principle and as determined in their Tempers against the Designs of the English as the Middle, or the northern states.

I have the Honour to be &c.   John Adams

Replies to Hendrik Calkoen No. XI

Letter 11
Sir   Amsterdam October 17. 1780

Your eleventh Question, will give an Opportunity of making Some Observations upon a Subject, that is quite misunderstood, in every Part of Europe. I shall answer it with great Pleasure according to the best of my Information, and with the utmost Candour.

The Question is.

How great is the present Debt of America? What has she, occasion for yearly, to act defensively? Are those Wants Supplied, by the Inhabitants themselves, or by other Nations? If in the latter case, what does America loose of her Strength by it? Are they not in one manner or other, recompensed, again by some equivalent Advantage? If So, in what manner? What would be required, to act offensively? And by that means shorten the War?

All Europe has a mistaken Apprehension of the present Debt of America. This Debt is of two Sorts, that which is due from the thirteen United States, in Congress assembled: and that which is owing from each of the thirteen States in its Seperate Capacity. I am not able to Say, with Precision, what the Debt of each Seperate State is. But all these added together, fall far short, of the Debt of the United States.

The Debt of the United States consists of three Branches. 1. The Sums which have been lent them, by France and Spain, and by Mr. Beaumarchais and Company. These have been for purchasing some Supplies of Cannon, Arms, Ammunition, and Cloathing, for the Troops, for assisting Prisoners escaped from England, and for some other Purposes. But the whole Sum amounts to no great Thing.

2. The Loan Office Certificates, which are promissory Notes given to Individuals in America who have lent Paper Money to the Congress, and Are their Securities for the Payment of the Principal and Interest. These the Congress have equitably de-

termined Shall be paid, according to the Value of the Paper Bills in Proportion to Silver, at the Time of their dates.

3. The Paper Bills, which are now in Circulation, or which were in Circulation on the Eighteenth day of March last. These Bills, amounted to the nominal sum of Two hundred Millions of Dollars, but the real Value of them to the Possessors, is estimated at forty for one, amounting to five Millions of Spanish Dollars, or one Million and a quarter Sterling. This is the full Value of them, perhaps more. But this estimation of them has given Satisfaction in America to the Possessors of them, who certainly obtained them in general at a cheaper Rate.

These three Branches of Debt, which are the whole, According to a Calculation made last May, and sent me by a Member of Congress, who has been four Years a Member of their Treasury Board and is perfect Master of the subject, amount, in the whole to five Millions sterling, and no more. The national Debt of America, then is five Millions sterling.

In order to judge of the Burthen of this Debt, We may compare it with the Numbers of People. They are three Millions. The national Debt of Great Britain is two hundred Millions. The Number of People in England and Scotland is not more than Six millions. Why should not America, with three Millions of People be able to bear a Debt of one hundred Millions, as Well as Great Britain with six millions of People, a debt of two hundred Millions.

We may compare it, with the Exports of America. In 1774 The Exports of America, were Six millions sterling. In the same Year the Exports of Great Britain were twelve Millions. Why would not the Exports of America, of Six millions, bear a national Debt of one hundred Millions, as well as the twelve millions of British Exports bear a Debt of Two hundred Millions?

We may compare it, in this manner, with the national Debt of France, Spain, the United Provinces, Russia, Sweeden, Denmark, Portugal, and you will find, that it is but small in comparison.

We may compare it, in another Point of View. Great Britain, has already Spent in this War, Sixty Millions sterling—America five Millions. Great Britain has annually added, to her national

Debt, more than the whole Amount of her annual Exports. America has not added to hers, in the whole Course of five Years war, a sum equal to one Years Exports.

The Debt of Great Britain is, in a large Proportion of it, due to Foreigners, for which they must annually pay the Interest by sending Cash abroad. A very trifle of the American Debt is yet due to Foreigners.

Lord North borrowed last Year, Twelve Millions, and every future Year of the War, must borrow the Same or a larger Sum. America could carry on this Way, an hundred Years, by borrowing only one Million sterling a year.

The annual Expence of America has not hitherto exceeded one Million *a Year*—that of Great Britain, has exceeded Twenty Millions, some years. America may therefore carry on this War, an hundred Years, and at the End of it will be no more in Debt in Proportion to her present Numbers of People and her Exports in 1744 than Great Britain is now.

There is another Consideration of some Weight. The Landed Interest in America is vastly greater in Proportion to the mercantile Interest, than it is in Great Britain. The Exports of America are the Productions of the soil, *annually*, which increase every year. The Exports of Great Britain were Manufactures, which will decrease every Year, while this War with America lasts.

The only Objection to this Reasoning is this, that America, is not used to great Taxes, and the People there are not yet disciplined to such enormous Taxation as in England. This is true. And this makes all their Perplexity at present. But they are capable of bearing as great Taxes in Proportion as the English, and if the English force them to it, by continuing the War, they will reconcile themselves to it: and they are in fact, now taxing themselves more and more every Year, and to an Amount that a Man who knew America only twenty year ago would think incredible.

Her Wants have hitherto been supplied by the Inhabitants themselves, and they have been very little indebted to foreign Nations. But on Account of the Depreciation of her Paper, and in order to introduce a more stable Currency, she has now Occasion to borrow a sum of Money abroad, which would enable her to support her Credit at home, to exert herself more vigorously against the English both by sea and Land, and greatly assist her in extending her Commerce with foreign Nations especially the Dutch. America would not loose of her Strength by borrowing Money, but on the Contrary would gain vastly. It would enable her to exert herself more by Privateering, which is a Mine of Gold to her. She would make Remittances in Bill of Exchange to foreign Merchants for their Commodities, and it would enable Many Persons to follow their true Interest in Cultivating the Land instead of attending to Manufactures, which being indispensable, they are now obliged more or less to follow, tho less profitable. The true Profit of America, is the continual Augmentation of the Price and Value of Land. Improvement in Land, is her principal Employment, her best Policy, and the principal source of her growing Wealth.

The last Question is easily answered. It is. What would be required to act offensively, and by that means, shorten the War?

To this I answer, nothing is wanted, but a Loan of Money, and a Fleet of ships.

A Fleet of ships, only Sufficient to maintain a superiority over the English, would enable the Infant Hercules to Strangle all the Serpents that environ his Cradle. It is impossible to express in too Strong terms, the Importance of a few ships of the Line to the Americans. Two or three French or Dutch or Spanish ships of the Line, Stationed at Rhode Island, Boston, Delaware River, or Chesapeak Bay, would have prevented, the dreadful Sacrifice at Penobscot. Three or four ships of the Line would have prevented the whole Expedition to Charlestown. Three or four ships of the Line more, added to the Squadron of the Chevalier de Ternay, would have enabled the Americans to have taken New York.

A Loan of Money is now wanted, to give Stability to the Currency of America—to give Vigour to the Inlistments for the Army—to add Alacrity to the fitting out Privateers—and to give an Ample Extension to their Trade.

The Americans, will labour through, without a Fleet and without a Loan. But it is ungenerous and cruel, to put them to such Difficulties, and to keep Mankind embroiled in all the Horrors of War, for Want of such Trifles, which so many of the

Powers of Europe wish they had and could so easily furnish. But if Mankind must be embroiled and the Blood of Thousands must be shed, for want of a little Magnanimity in some, the Americans must not be blamed, it is not their Fault.

I have the Honour to be &c,   John Adams

Replies to Hendrik Calkoen No. XII

Letter 12th.
Sir   Amsterdam October 17. 1780

We are now come to your Twelfth Head of Inquiry, which is. What Countenance have the Finances? How much does the Expence exceed the Yearly Income? Does the annual Revenue, deriving from the Taxes, increase or diminish? in the whole, or in any Particulars? and what are the Reasons to be given for it?

Here I am apprehensive, I shall find a Difficulty to make my self under Stood, as the American Finances, and Mode of Taxation, differ so materially from any, that I know of in Europe.

In the Month of May, 1775, when the Congress came together, for the first Time, after the Battles of Lexington and Concord, they found it necessary, to raise an Army, or rather to adopt an Army already raised, at Cambridge, in order to oppose the British Troops and shut them up, in the Prison of Boston. But they found, that the Colonies, were but just got out of Debt, had just paid off the Debts contracted in the last French War. In the Several Treasuries of the Colonies, they found only a few Thousand Pounds. They had before them a Prospect of a Stagnation, or Interruption of their Trade, pretty universally, by the British Men of War. They had a thousand Perplexities before them, in the Prospect of passing through thirteen Revolutions of Government, from the Royal Authority to that under the People. They had Armies and Navies to form, they had new Constitutions of Government to attend to. They had, twenty Tribes of Indians to negotiate with. They had vast Numbers of Negroes to take care of. They had all sorts of Arms, Ammunition, Artillery to procure, as well as Blanketts and Cloathing, and subsistance for the Army, they had Negotiations to think of in Europe and Treaties to form of Alliance and Commerce, and they had even Salt to procure for the Subsistance of the Inhabitants and even of their Cattle as well as their Armies.

In this situation, with so many Wants and demands, and no Money, or Revenues to recur to, they had recourse to an Expedient, which had been often practiced in America, but no where else. They determined to emit, Paper Money.

The American Paper Money, is nothing but Bills of Credit, by which the Publick, the Community, promises to pay the Possessor, a certain Sum in a limited Time. In a Country where there is no Coin, or not enough in circulation, these Bills may be emitted to a certain Amount, and they will pass at Par, but as Soon as the Quantity exceeds, the Value of the ordinary Business of the People, it, will depreciate, and continue to fall in its Value in Proportion to the Augmentation of the Quantity.

The Congress on the 18 of March last, Stated this Depreciation at forty for one. This may be nearly the Average, but it often passes much lower. By this Resolution All the Bills in Circulation, on that day, and none have been emitted Since, amount to about one Million and a Quarter sterling. To this if you add the Money borrowed upon Loan Certificates, and the debt contracted abroad in France and Spain, the whole does not amount to but little more than five Millions.

Yearly Income, We have none, properly Speaking. We have no Imposts or Duties laid upon any Articles of Importation Exportation, or Consumption. The Revenue consists entirely in Grants annually made by the Legislatures, of Sums of Money for the current service of the Year and appropriated to certain Uses. These Grants are proportioned upon all the Polls and Estates, real and personal in the community, and they are levied and paid into the publick Treasury with great Punctuality, from whence they are issued in Payments of the demands upon the Public.

You see then that it is in the Power of the Legislatures, to raise what sums are wanted, at least as much as the People can bear, and they are usually proportioned to the publick Wants and the Peoples Abilities. They are now constantly laying on and paying very heavy Taxes, altho for the three or four first Years of the War, the Obstructions of Trade &c. made it difficult to raise any Taxes at all. The yearly Taxes, annually laid on have increased every Year, for these three Years past, and will continue to be increased in Proportion To the abilities of the People. This ability no doubt increases in Proportion as Population increases, as new Lands are cultivated, and as Property is in any Way added to the common stock. It will also increase as our Commerce increases, and as the Success in Privateering Increases.

But by the Method of Taxing you see that it is in the Power of the Legislature to increase the Taxes every Year, as the publick Exigences may require, and they have no other Restraint or Limit than the Peoples Ability.

I have the Honour to be, with great Esteem &c.

John Adams

Replies to Hendrik Calkoen No. XIII

13 Letter
Sir   Amsterdam October 26 1780

Your thirteenth Inquiry is, "Of what Resources might America hereafter Still make Use of?"

There are many Resources, yet untried, which would certainly be explored, if America Should be driven to the Necessity of them.

1. Luxury prevails in that young Country, not withstanding all the confident assertions of the English concerning their Distress, to a degree, that retrenching this alone would enable them to carry on the War. There are Expences in Wheel-carriages, Horses, Equipage, Furniture, Dress, and the Table, which might be Spared and would amount to enough to carry on the War.

2. The Americans might, and rather than the English should

prevail against them they would be brought to impose Duties upon Articles of Luxury, and Convenience and even of Necessity, as has been done by all the Nations of Europe. I am not able at present, and upon Memory to entertain you with accurate Calculations, but in general it may be said with Certainty that if as heavy Duties were laid, upon Articles of Consumption, and Importation as are laid in England, or even in Holland, it would produce a Revenue Sufficient to carry on this War, without borrowing at all. I hope however they will never come to this. I am clear they need not. Such Systematical and established Revenues are dangerous to Liberty, which is Safe, while the Revenue depends upon annual Grants of the People, because this secures publick Œconomy.

3. If there should be hereafter any Accession to the Population of America, by Migrations from Europe, this will be a fresh Resource, because in that Country of Agriculture, the Ability to raise a Revenue will bear a constant Proportion to the Numbers of People.

4. There are immense Tracts of uncultivated Lands. These Lands are all claimed by particular States. But if these States Should cede these Claims to the Congress, which they would do in case of Necessity, the Congress might Sell these Lands, and they would become, a great Resource. No Man can Say, how great or how lasting.

5. There is a great deal of Plate in America, and if she were driven to Extremities, the Ladies I assure you have Patriotism enough, to give up their Plate to the Publick, rather than loose their Liberties or run any great hazard of it.

6. There is another Resource Still. The War may be carried on, by means of a fluctuating Medium of Paper Money. The War has been carried on in this manner hitherto, and I firmly believe, if the People could not find a better Way—they would agree, to call in all the Paper, and let it lie as a demand upon the Public, to be hereafter equitably paid, according to its fluctuating Value in silver—and emit new Bills, to depreciate and carry on the War in the Same Way. This however would occasion many Perplexities, and much Unhappiness. It would do Injustice to many Individuals, and will and ought to be avoided, if possible.

7. A Loan in Europe, however, would be the best Resource,

as it would necessarily extend our Trade, and relieve the People from too great a present Burden. Very heavy Taxes, are hurtfull, because they lessen the Increase of Population by making the means of subsistence, more difficult.

8. There are Resources of Agriculture, Manufactures and Labour, that would produce much, if explored and attempted.

9. The Resources of Trade and Privateering, ought to be mentioned again. The real Cause of our doing So little hitherto is this. The Congress in 1774, agreed upon a Non Exportation to begin in September 1775. This induced the Merchants in every Part of America, to Send their ships and Sailors to England, from whence the most of them never returned.

The Consequence of which was that the Americans have been distressed for want of ships and Seamen ever since. But the Number of both has increased every Year, in Spite of all that English have taken and destroyed. The vast Number of ships and seamen taken this Year, will repair those Losses, and no man can say to what an Extent Trade and Privateering will be carried, the next and the succeeding Years.

I have the Honour to be &c.   John Adams

Replies to Hendrik Calkoen No. XIV

Letter 14
Sir   Amsterdam Octr. 26. 1780
The fourteenth Question is "What is the Quantity of Paper Money in Circulation? What Credit, the Inhabitants have for it, in their daily Business? What designs the Inhabitants have by maintaining its Credit? at by preventing its Increase? and in what manner do they realize it?"

The Quantity of Paper Bills, in Circulation on the 18 of March last, was Two hundred millions of Paper Dollars.

The Congress then Stated the Value of it, upon an average, at forty for one, amounting in the whole to five millions of silver Dollars, or one Million and a quarter sterling. This they did by resolving to receive one silver Dollar, in Lieu of forty Paper ones, in the Payment of Taxes. This was probably allowing more than the full Value for the Paper, because by all Accounts the Bills passed from hand to hand in private Transactions at Sixty or seventy for one.

The Designs of the Inhabitants, in preserving its Credit, as much as they can are very good and laudable. The Designs are that they may have a fixed and certain Medium both for external and internal Commerce. That every Man May have an equal Profit from his Industry, and for his Commodities. That private and publick Debts may be justly paid, and that every Man may pay an equal and proportional share of the Public Expences.

And this is their Design in preventing its Increase: because it is impossible, if the Quantity is increased to prevent the Depreciation of the whole in Circulation.

They realize it, in various Ways. Some have lent it to the Public, and received Loan Office Certificates for it, upon Interest, which are to be paid in Proportion to their Value in Silver at the Time of their Dates.

Some Purchase with it the Produce of the Country, which they export to the West Indies and to Europe, and by this means supply, the French and Spanish Fleets and Armies, both upon the Continent of America and in the West India Islands. Others Purchase Merchandizes imported with it. Others purchase Bills of Exchange upon France, Spain, &c. Others purchase silver and Gold with it—and others Purchase Houses and Lands. Others have paid their Debts with it, to such a degree, that the People of America, were never so little in debt, in their private Capacities as at present.

I have the Honour to be &c.   John Adams

Replies to Hendrik Calkoen No. XV

Letter 15th.
Sir   Amsterdam October 26. 1780

Your fifteenth Quære is "Does not the English Army, lay out its Pay, in America? at how much can the Yearly benefit be calculated? Are not the Prisoners, provided for in America? Who has the Care of their Maintenance? How was Burgoines Army supplied?"

When the English Army, was in Boston, they bought all that they could, and left considerable Sums there in silver and Gold. So they did at Rhode Island. Since they have been in New York, they have purchased every Thing they could of Provisions and Fuel, on Long Island, staten Island, New York Island, and in those Parts of the states of New York and New Jersey where they have been able to carry on any clandestine Trafick.

When they were in Philadelphia, they did the Same, and General How tells you, that he suspects that General Washington from Political Motives connived at the Peoples supplying Philadelphia, in order essentially to serve his Country by insinuating into it, large sums of silver and Gold. They are doing the Same now, more or less in South Carolina and Georgia, and they cant go into any Part of America, without doing the Same.

The British Prisoners, in the Hands of the Americans, receive their Cloathing chiefly from the English, and Flaggs of Truce are permitted to come out from their Lines, for this Purpose. They receive their Pay also from their Master, and Spend the most of it where they are. They also purchase Provisions in the Country and pay for it in hard Money.

I am not able to ascertain exactly the Yearly Benefit, but it must be considerable, and the Addition now of a French Fleet and Army, to supply will make a great Addition of Cash and Bills of Exchange, which will facilitate Commerce and Privateering.

And the more Troops and ships Great Britain and France send to America the greater will this Resource, necessarily be to the Americans.

I have the Honour to be &c.   John Adams

Replies to Hendrik Calkoen No. XVI

Letter 16th.
Sir   Amsterdam October 26. 1780

The Sixteenth, Inquiry is, "Who looses most by desertion? Do the English and German Deserters, Serve voluntarily and well in the American Army? How, can those who do not enter into the Army subsist?"

These Questions, I answer with great Pleasure. There has been, from the Beginning of the War to this day, Scarcely an Example of a native Americans deserting from the Army to the English. There have been in the American Army Some Scattering Scotch, Irish, and german soldiers, Some of these have deserted but never in great Numbers. And among the Prisoners they have taken it is astonishing how few they have ever been able to perswade, by all their Flatteries, Threatnings, Promisses and even Cruelties to enlist into their Service.

The Number of Deserters from them, has been all along Considerably more. Congress have generally prohibited their officers from inlisting Deserters. For some particular services Permission has been given, and they have served well.

Those who do not inlist, into the Army, have no Difficulty to subsist. Those of them who have any Trades, as Weavers, Tailors, Smiths, shoemakers, Tanners, Curriers, Carpenters, Bricklayers, in short any trade whatsoever, enter immediately into better Business than they ever had in Europe, where they gain a better subsistance and more Money, because Tradesmen of all denomination are now much wanted. Those who have no Trade, if they are capable of any Kind of Labour, are immediately employed, in Agriculture &c., labour being much wanted and very dear.

I am not able to tell the precise Numbers that have deserted, but if an hundred thousand were to desert they would find no difficulty in Point of subsistence or Employment, if they can and will work.

Sir yours   John Adams

Replies to Hendrik Calkoen No. XVII

Letter 17
Sir   Amsterdam October 26. 1780

The Seventeenth, Inquiry is "whether We have any Information that we can rely on, concerning the Population? has it increased or diminished, Since the War?"

In some former Letters, I have made Some Observations upon the Subject of the Increase of Mankind in America.

In the Year 1774, There was much private Conversation, among the Members of Congress, concerning the Numbers of Souls in every Colony. The Delegates of each, were consulted, and the Estimates made by them were taken down as follows.

In New Hampshire	150,000
Massachusetts	400,000
Rhode Island	59,678
Connecticut	192,000
New York	250,000
New Jersey	130,000
Pensilvania and Delaware	350,000
Maryland	320,000
Virginia	640,000
North Carolina	300,000
South Carolina	225,000
Total	3,026,678

This however, was but an Estimate, and Some Persons, have thought there was too much Speculation in it. It will be observed, that Georgia, was not represented in the first Congress, and therefore is not included in the Estimate.

In a Pamphlet published in England about a Year ago, intitled "A Memorial to the Souvereigns of Europe, on the present State of Affairs, between the old and new World," written by Mr. Pownal, a Member of Parliament and formerly Governor of Massachusetts and Lt. Governor of New Jersey We are told that "The Massachusetts, had in the year 1722, 94,000

Inhabitants, in 1742, 164,000—in 1751, when there was a great depopulation both by War and the Small Pox 164,484—in 1761—216,000—in 1765, 255,500—in 1771—292,000—in 1773—300,000.

In Connecticut, in 1756, 129,994—in 1774—257,356. These Numbers are not increased by Strangers, but decreased by Wars and Emigrations to the West ward, and to other States: yet they have nearly doubled in Eighteen Years.

In New York in 1756—96,776—in 1771—168,007 in 1774—182,251.

In Virginia in 1756—173,316—in 1764—200,000—in 1774—300,000.

In South Carolina in 1750—64,000, in 1770—115,000.

In Rhode Island in 1738—15,000, in 1748—28,439.

As there never was a Militia, in Pensilvania, before this War with authentic Lists of the Population, it has been variously estimated on Speculation. There was a continual Importation for many years, of Irish and german Emigrants, yet many of these Settled in other Provinces: but the Progress of Population, in the ordinary Course, advanced, in a Ratio, between that of Virginia and that of Massachusetts. The City of Philadelphia, advanced more rapidly. It had in 1749—2076 houses. In 1753, 2300—in 1760, 2969—in 1769—4474—From 1749 to 1753 from 16 to 18,000 Inhabitants, from 1760 to 1769 from 31,318 to 35,000.

There were in 1754 various Calculations, and Estimates made of the Numbers, on the Continent. The Sanguine, made the Numbers, one Million and an half. Those who admitted less Speculation into the Calculation, but adhered closer to Facts and Lists as they were made out, Stated them at one Million two hundred and Fifty thousand. Governor Pownal thinks that 2,141,307 would turn out nearest to the real Amount in 1774. But what an amazing Progress, which in Eighteen Years, has added a Million to a Million two hundred and fifty Thousand altho a War, was maintained in that Country, for Seven Years of the Term. In this View one Sees a Community unfolding itself, beyond any Example in Europe.

Thus you have the Estimates made by the Gentlemen in Congress in 1774, and that of Governor Pownal, for the Same

Epocha. That made in Congress is most likely to be right. If in their Estimate Some states were rated too high, it has been since made certain that others were too low.

But admiting Mr. Pownals Estimate to be just, the Numbers, have grown, since 1774 So much notwithstanding the War, and the Interruption of Migrations from Europe, that they must be well nigh three Millions—if the Calculation, made by the Members of Congress was right, the Numbers now, must be nearer four millions than three millions and an half.

I have observed to you in a former Letter that, the Massachusetts Bay, has been lately numbered and found to have increased in Numbers, as much as in former Periods, very nearly.

I now add that Delaware, which in 1774 was estimated at 30,000 but upon numbering the People Since, they appeared to be 40,000.

Pensilvania is undoubtedly set too low in both Estimates.

I have the honour to be, very respectfully &c.

John Adams

Replies to Hendrik Calkoen No. XVIII

Letter 18
Sir   Amsterdam October 26. 1780

Question 18. Does Sufficient Tranquility, Contentment and Prosperity reign, in those Places where the War does not rage? Can one Sufficiently Subsist there, without feeling the oppression of the Taxes? Does Plenty abound there? Is there more than is necessary for Consumption? Are the People well affected and encouraged to pursue the War, and endure its Calamities, or is there Poverty and Dejection?

There has been more of this Tranquility and Contentment, and fewer Riots, Insurrections and Seditions, throughout the whole War, and in the Periods of its greatest distress than there was for Seven Years before the War broke out, in those Parts that I am best acquainted with. As to subsistance, there never was or will be any difficulty. There never was any real Want of any Thing but warlike stores and Cloathing for the Army, and Salt and Rum both for the Army and the People: but they have Such Plentifull Importations of these Articles now, that there is no Want—excepting of Blanketts, Cloathing and Warlike stores for the Army.

The Taxes are rising very high, but there never will be more laid on than the People can bear, because the Representatives Who lay them tax themselves and their Neighbours in exact Proportion. The Taxes indeed fall heaviest upon the rich and the higher Classes of People.

The Earth produces Grain, and Meat in Abundance for the Consumption of the People, for the support of the Army, and for Exportation.

The People are more universally well affected and encouraged to pursue the War than are the People of England France or Spain, as far as I can judge.

As to Poverty there is hardly a beggar in the Country. As to Dejection, I never Saw, even at the Time of our greatest Danger and Perplexity, So much of it, as appears in England or France, upon every Intelligence of a disastrous Event.

The greatest Source of Grief and Affliction, is the fluctuation of the Paper Money, but this although it occasions Unhappinesses, has no violent or fatal Effects.

I have the Honour to be   John Adams

Replies to Hendrik Calkoen No. XIX

19 Letter
Sir   Amsterdam October 26. 1780

Question 19. Is not Peace very much longed for in America? might not this desire of Peace induce the People to hearken to Proposals appearing very fair, but which really are not So, which the People might be too quick in listening to, and the Government forced to accept?

The People, in all Ages and Countries wish for Peace, human Nature does not love War. Yet this does not hinder Nations from going to War, when it is necessary, and often indeed for frivolous Purposes of Avarice, Ambition, Vanity, Resentment and Revenge. I have never been informed of more desire of Peace in America than is common to all Nations, at War. They in general know that they cannot obtain it, without submitting to Conditions, infinitely more dreadful than all the horrors of this War.

If they are ever deceived it is by holding out to them false hopes of Independance and Great Britains Acknowledging it.

The People of America are too enlightened to be deceived, in any great Plan of Policy. They understand the Principles and Nature of Government too well to be imposed on, by any Proposals short of their own Object.

Great Britain has tryed So many Experiments to deceive them, without Effect that, I think it is Scarcely worth her while to try again. The History of these Ministerial and Parliamentary Tricks would fill a Volume. I have not records nor Papers to recur to: but if Mr. Calkoen desires it I could give him a Sketch from Memory, of these Artifices, and their success, which I think would convince him there is no danger from that Quarter.

I have the Honour to be &c.   John Adams

Replies to Hendrik Calkoen No. XX

20 Letter

Sir   Amsterdam October 26. 1780

Question 20. Has there not been different opinions in Congress, with Regard to this, (i.e. to Proposals appearing fair, which were not so) from whence Animosities have arisen?

There has never been any Difference of Sentiment in Congress, Since the Declaration of Independancy, concerning any

Proposals of Reconciliation. There has been no Proposals of Reconciliation made, Since the 4. of July 1776—excepting twice.

The first was made by Lord Howe, who together with his Brother the General, were appointed by the King, Commissioners for Some Purpose or other. The Public has never been informed, what Powers they had. Lord Howe sent a Message by General Sullivan, to Congress, desiring a Conference with Some of its Members. There were different Sentiments Concerning the Propriety of Sending any Members, untill We knew his Lordships Powers. A Majority decided to send. Dr. Franklin, Mr. John Adams and Mr. Rutledge were Sent. Upon their Report, there was a perfect Unanimity of sentiment in Congress.

The Second was the Mission of Lord Carlisle, Governor Johnson and Mr. Eden in 1778. Upon this Occasion again there was a perfect Unanimity in Congress.

Before the Declaration of Independency, Lord North moved Several conciliatory Propositions in Parliament, in which a good deal of Art was employed to Seduce, deceive and divide. But there was always an Unanimity in Congress upon all those Plans.

There were different opinions concerning the Petition to the King in the Year 1775 and before that concerning the Non Exportation Agreement—there have been different opinions concerning Articles of the Confederation—concerning the best Plans for the conduct of the War—concerning the best officers to conduct them—concerning territorial Controversies between particular states &c. But these Differences of opinion, which are essential to all Assemblies, have never caused greater Animosities, than those which arise in all Assemblies where there is Freedom of Debate.

I have the Honour to be &c.   John Adams

Replies to Hendrik Calkoen No. XXI

21. Letter

Sir　　　　　　　　　　　　　　　Amsterdam October 27. 1780

Question 21st. Are there no Malcontents in America? against the Government, who are otherwise much inclined for the american Cause, who may force the Nation, or Congress, against their Resolutions and Interests to conclude a Peace?

There is no Party formed in any of the thirteen States against the new Constitution, nor any opposition against the Government, that I have ever heard of, excepting in Pensylvania, and in North Carolina. These by no means deserve to be compared together.

In Pensilvania, there is a respectable Body of People, who are zealous against Great Britain, but yet wish for Some Alteration in their new Form of Government. Yet this does not appear to weaken their Exertions: it seems rather, to excite an Emulation in the two Parties, and to increase their Efforts.

I have before explained the History of the Rise and Progress, of the Party in North Carolina, consisting of Regulators and Scotch Highlanders, and General How has informed you of their Fate. This Party has ever appeared to make N. Carolina more stanch and decided, instead of weakening it.

The Party in Pensilvania will never have an Inclination, to force the Congress, against their Interests to make Peace, nor would they have the Power if they had the Will.

The Party in North Carolina, whose Inclination cannot be doubted is too inconsiderable to any Thing.

I have the Honour to be &c.　　　　　　　　　　John Adams

Replies to Hendrik Calkoen No. XXII

Letter 22.
Sir   Amsterdam October 27. 1780

Questions 22. and 23. General Monk repaired the Kings Government in England. Might not one American General or another, be able, by discontent or Corruption, to do the Same? Would the Army follow his orders on Such an Occasion? Could one or more Politicians, thro Intrigues undertake the Same, with any hopes of Success, Should even the Army assist him in Such a Case?

I have before observed that no Politicians, or General Officers in America, have any Such Influence. Neither the People, nor the soldiers would follow them. It was not attachment to Men but to a Cause, which first produced and has supported the Revolution. It was not attachment to officers but to Liberty which made the Soldiers inlist. Politicians in America can only intrigue with the People. Those are So numerous and so Scattered, that no statesman has any great Influence, but in his own Small Circle. In Courts Sometimes, gaining two or three Individuals may produce a Revolution: No Revolution in America can be accomplished without gaining the Majority of the People, and this, not all the Wealth of Great Britain is able to do, at the Expence of their Liberties.

Question 24. The Revolution must have made a great Change in affairs, So that many People, tho at present free of the Ennemies Incursions, have lost their daily subsistance. Are the occupations, which come instead of their old ones, been Sufficient to supply their Wants?

All the Difficulties which were ever apprehended, of this Sort, are long Since past. In 1774, Some were apprehensive, that the Fishermen, Sailors, and shipwrights would be idle. But Some went into the Army, Some into the Navy, and Some went to Agriculture. And if there had been twice as many, they would all have found Employment. The Building of Frigates and Privateers has employed all the Carpenters—Manufactures besides have been set up of Cannon, Arms, Powder, Salt Peter, Salt—Flax and Wool have been raised in greater Quantities and coarse Manufactures of Cloth and Linen been increased. In short the greatest Difficulty is that there are not hands enough. Agriculture alone in that Country would find Employment enough for Millions, and Privateering for thousands more than there are.

I have the Honour to be   John Adams

Replies to Hendrik Calkoen No. XXIII

Letter 23.
Sir   Amsterdam October 27. 1780

Question 25. Do they who have lost their Possessions and Fortunes by the War, endure it patiently as Compatriots, So that nothing can be feared from them?

Loosing Fortunes in America, has not such dreadful Consequences to Individuals or Families, as it has in Europe. The Reason is obvious because the means of Subsistance are easier to be obtained, So that nobody suffer for Want. As far as I am acquainted with the Sufferers, they have born their Losses both of Property and Relations with great Fortitude and so far from producing in their Minds a desire of submission they have only served to irritate them, to convince them more fully of the precarious and deplorable Situation they should be in under the Government of the English and to make them more eager to resist it.

Question 26. How has it gone, with the Cultivation of the Land, before the Troubles at their Commencement and at present? What Change has taken Place?

Agriculture ever was and will be the dominant Interest in America. Nevertheless before this War, perhaps, she run more into Commerce than was for her Interest. She depended too much perhaps upon Importations for her Cloathing, Utensiles &c. and indulged in too many Luxuries. When the Prospect opened in 1775 of an Interruption of her Commerce she applied her self more to Agriculture, and Many Places that depended upon the Lumber Trade the Fishery &c., for the Importation of even their Bread have turned their Labour and Attention to raising Corn Wool Flax and Cattle, and have lived better and advanced in Wealth and Independance faster than ever they did. For Example, the Towns in the Neighbourhood of the Sea in the Massachusetts Bay, used to depend upon the Fishery and Commerce, to import them their Wheat and Flour from Philadelphia, Maryland and Virginia and Rice from South Carolina and Georgia. The Communication being interrupted by Sea, Since the War, they have planted their own Corn.

The Eastern Parts of the Massachusetts Bay, before the War depended, on the Commerce of Lumber for the West India Market, and of Masts, Yards and Bowsprits for the Royal Navy of Great Britain, to procure them Cloaths, Meat and Strong Liquors. Since the War, they have cultivated their Lands raised their own Corn, Wool, Flax, and planted the Apple Tree instead drinking rum. In consequence of which they are more temperate, wealthy and independant than ever.

North Carolina depended upon the Commerce of Pitch, Tar and Turpentine and Tobacco, for the Importation of many Things. Since the War, they have turned their Labour, to raise more of the Things which they wanted.

Maryland, Virginia and N. Carolina, depended upon the Trade of Tobacco to import coarse Cloaths for their Negroes. Since the War they have raised less Tobacco and more Wheat, Wool and Cotton, and made the coarse Cloaths themselves.

So that upon the whole the Lessening of Commerce, and the Increase of Agriculture, has rendered America more independant than she ever was.

I have the Honour to be &c.   John Adams

Replies to Hendrik Calkoen No. XXIV

Letter 24
Sir   Amsterdam October 27. 1780

Question 27. How was the Situation of Manufactures, manual Art and Trade in general, at the Beginning of this War? What Change have they Suffered?

Manufactures in general, never flourished in America. They were never attended only by Women and Children who could not work in the Field, and by Men at certain Seasons of the Year, and at certain Intervals of Time when they could not be employed in the Cultivation of the Lands, because that Labour upon Land in that Country is more profitable, than in Manufactures. These they could import and purchase with the Produce of their Soil cheaper than they could make them. The Cause of this, is the Plenty of wild Land. A days Work worth two shillings upon wild Land, not only produced two shillings in the Crop, but made the Land worth too shillings more: whereas a days work of the Same Price applied to Manufactures, produced only the two shillings.

Since the War however, Freight and Insurance have been so high, that Manufactures have been more attended to. Manufactures of Salt Peter, Salt, Powder, Cannon, Arms, have been introduced. Cloathing in Wool and Flax has been made, and many other necessary Things, but these for the Reason before given will last no longer than the War, or than the Hazard of their Trade.

America is the Country of Raw Materials, and of Commerce enough to carry them to a good Market—But Europe is the Country for Manufactures and Commerce. Thus Europe and America will be Blessings to each other, if some malevolent Policy does not frustrate the Purposes of Nature.

I have the Honour to be &c.   John Adams

Replies to Hendrik Calkoen No. XXV

Letter 25
Sir
                                        Amsterdam October 27. 1780

Question 28. Has America gained or lost, by the mutual Capture of ships? How much is the Benefit or Prejudice of it by Calculation?

America has gained. She took early, from the English ordonnance and Ammunition ships, and supplied herself in that Way, with those Articles when she had them not, and could not otherwise obtain them. She has taken in this Way a great Number of British and German Soldiers. She has taken a vast number of Seamen, who have generally inlisted on board our Privateers. She has taken great quantities of Provisions, Cloathing, Arms, and warlike stores. She has taken every Year, more and more Since 1775, and will probably continue to take more and more every Year while the War lasts. I have certain Intelligence, that there have been this year carried into Boston and Philadelphia only, Ninety Nine Vessells in the Months of July and August. On board of these Vessells there were not less than Eight hundred Seamen, many of the ships were very rich. The Vessells the English have taken from the Americans were of Small Value—this year they have been few in Number.

I am not able to give you an exact Calculation. The Quebec ships were worth from thirty to forty thousand Pounds sterling each and there were two and twenty of them in Number.

Privateering is a great Nursery of Seamen, and if the Americans had not imprudently Sacrificed Such a Number of their Frigates and Privateers in the Attack and defence of Places, these alone, would by this Time, well nigh have ruined the British Commerce, Navy and Army.

I have the Honour to be &c.   John Adams

Replies to Hendrik Calkoen No. XXVI

26. Letter
Sir   Amsterdam October 27 1780

I believe you will be pleased when I tell you that We are now come to the 29th. and last Question, which is

What are the real Damages Sustained, or still to be suffered by the Loss of Charlestown? and what Influence it has had upon the Minds of the People?

An Interruption of the Commerce of Indigo and Rice. The Loss of many Negroes which the English will steal from the Plantations, and send to the West India Islands for Sale. A great deal of Plunder of every sort. Much Unhappiness among the People. And several Lives of very worthy Men will be lost. But the Climate will be Death to European Troops, and at an immense Expence of Men and Money they will ravage for a while and then disappear.

The Effect of the surrender of Charleston and the Defeat of Gates, has only been to awaken the People from their dreams of Peace.

The Artifices of the English, holding out Ideas of Peace, seems to have deceived both the Americans and their Allies, while they were only contriving means to succour Gibraltar, and invade Carolina. The People are now convinced of their Mistake, and generally roused. But these Disasters will have no more Effect, towards Subduing America, than if they had taken a Place in the East Indies.

I have the Honour to be &c.   John Adams

PERSONAL INDEPENDENCE

To Abigail Adams

My dearest Portia   Asterdam Decr. 18. 1780
I have this morning sent Mr. Thaxter, with my two Sons to

Leyden, there to take up their Residence for some time, and there to pursue their Studies of Latin and Greek under the excellent Masters, and there to attend Lectures of the celebrated Professors in that University. It is much cheaper there than here: the Air is infinitely purer; and the Company and Conversation is better.

It is perhaps as learned an University as any in Europe.

I should not wish to have Children, educated in the common Schools in this Country, where a littleness of Soul is notorious. The Masters are mean Spirited Writches, pinching, kicking, and boxing the Children, upon every Turn.

Their is besides a general Littleness arising from the incessant Contemplation of Stivers and Doits, which pervades the whole People.

Frugality and Industry are virtues every where, but Avarice, and Stingyness are not Frugality.

The Dutch say that without an habit of thinking of every doit, before you spend it, no Man can be a good Merchant, or conduct Trade with Success. This I believe is a just Maxim in general. But I would never wish to see a Son of Mine govern himself by it. It is the sure and certain Way for an industrious Man to be rich. It is the only possible Way for a Merchant to become the first Merchant, or the richest Man in the Place. But this is an Object that I hope none of my Children ever aim at.

It is indeed true, every where, that those who attend to small Expences are always rich.

I would have my Children attend to Doits and Farthings as devoutly as the meerest Dutchman upon Earth, if such Attention was necessary to support their Independence.

A Man who discovers a Disposition and a design to be independent seldom succeeds—a Jealousy arises against him. The Tyrants are alarmed on one side least he should oppose them. The slaves are allarmed on the other least he should expose their Servility. The Cry from all Quarters is, "He is the proudest Man in the World. He cant bear to be under Obligation."

I never in my Life observed any one endeavouring to lay me under particular Obligations to him, but I suspected he had a design to make me his dependant, and to have claims upon my Gratitude. This I should have no objection to—Because Gratitude is always in ones Power. But the Danger is that Men will expect and require more of Us, than Honour and Innocence and Rectitude will permit Us to perform.

In our Country however any Man with common Industry and Prudence may be independant.

But to put an End to this stuff Adieu, most affectionately Adieu.

THE CREDIT OF THE UNITED STATES

To Baron Van der Capellen

Sir   Amsterdam Jan. 21. 1781

I have not been able to find an opportunity to acknowledge the receit of the esteemed favour with which you honoured me on the 24 of December, untill now.

I think it is very probable that the Several Causes you have enumerated cooperate to lessen the Credit of the United States, but I think at the Same time that it is because the Facts are misrepresented and exagerated, by the Friends of England. Let Us consider them for a few Moments one by one.

The Invasion of Georgia and of South Carolina, is the first. But why should the Invasion of these two States affect the Credit of the 13 more than, the Invasion of any two others. Massachusetts and Rhode Island, have been invaded, by Armies much more formidable, New York, Connecticutt, N. Jersy, Pensyllvania, Delaware, Maryland and Virginia have been all invaded before: but what has been the Issue? Not conquest. Not submission. On the contrary, all those States, have learned the Art of War, and the Habits of Submission to military Discipline, and have got them selves well armed, nay cloathed and furnished with a great deal of hard Money by these very Invasions. And what is more than all the rest they have got over the Fears and Terrors, that are always occasioned by a first Invasion, and are a worse Ennemy than the English: and besides they have had Such Experience of the Tyranny and Cruelty of the English as have made them more resolute than ever against the English Government. Now why should not the Invasion of Georgia and Carolina have the Same Effect? It is very certain, in the opinion of the Americans them selves that it will. Besides the unexampled Cruelty of Cornwallis has been enough to revolt, even Negroes. It has been Such as will make the English objects of greater Horrour there than in any of the other States.

The Capture of Charlestown is the Second. But why should the Capture of Charlestown, have a greater Effect than that of Boston, or Philadelphia, the latter of which was of vastly more Importance to the common Cause than Charlestown.

The Loss of the Continental Frigates. This is a Grief to be Sure. But why were these 4 or 5 frigates of So much more Importance than, Several Times that Number that We had lost before. We lost Several Frigates with Philadelphia and shipping to a much greater value than at Charlestown. We lost Frigates with New York: but above all We lost at Penobscot, armed Vessells, to five times a greater amount than at Charlestown. Yet all these Losses, have been Suddenly repaired, in so much that our armed Vessells, in the Course of the last summer, have taken more Prizes than they ever did, by half. They did more dammage to the English than the whole maritime Power of France and Spain have done from the beginning of the War. We can afford to loose a great many Frigates, because they cost Us nothing. I am assured from an accurate Calculation from the publick Accounts, the Prizes taken by the Continental Navy have amounted to a large sum more than the whole Sum expended in Building equipping manning victualling and paying the ships from the Beginning of the War.

The Defeat of Gates. But why should this defeat, discourage America or weaken her Credit in Europe, more than the Defeat on Long Island—the Loss of Fort Washington,—the Defeat at Brandewine—at Germantown.—the Loss of Canada —Ticonderoga &c.—much greater Defeats and more deplorable Losses?

The Inaction of the combined Fleets of De Guichen and Solano. But if We consider, that the Spaniards got their Fleet and Army and Artillery Safe to America, to put their Dominions there in a State of Safety: that the French have convoyd home safe their Merchant Fleets—that De Guichen fought Rodney twice or three times, on equal Terms and the English gained no Advantage—and the French Fleet is now at Brest, under L'Estainge to keep the English in awe—perhaps it is better for the common Cause than if they had put more to hazard.

The decided Superiority of the English in the Islands. But if We consider the french and Spanish Ships that are still in the W. Indies and the disabled condition of the English Fleet, their Want of Men and especially the weakness of their Garrisons in their Islands and the Strength of the french and Spanish Garrisons We are sure the English are not in a Condition to attempt any Thing against them.

The Superiority of the English at N. York is but just sufficient to prevent their Ennemies from destroying them.

The Defection of Arnold, will be considered by every Man who considers all the Circumstances that attended it as a Proof of the Weakness of the English and the decisive Strength and Confidence of the Americans.

When We consider the Crimes he had committed and the Unpopularity into which he had justly fallen—When consider that an officer of his high Rank, long services and brillant Reputation, was not able to carry over with a single officer nor soldier, nor even his own Valet, nor his Wife nor his Child,—When We consider the Universal Execration in which his Treason was held by the whole Army and the whole Continent—When We consider the Firmness and Dignity with which Andre was punished, We must conclude that the American Army and People stand Strong, as strong against the Arts and Bribes as the Arms and Valour of their Ennemies.

The Discontent of the Army. There never was an Army without Anxiety and a constant Agitation of hopes and Fears. When the Officers think their Pay is not enough, what can they do but represent them to Government for Redress. This has constantly been done. But what are the Discontents in the English Army and Navy? much greater I assure you than in the American service.

The Jealousy between the Army and the Body Politick, is not to be dreaded. It only Shews that the Spirit of Liberty is still alive and active in the People. The Baron Van der Capellen I am Sure will applaud, the People, for keeping a Watchfull Eye over the Army, to see that it does not ravish from them that Liberty for which all have been contending.

Mr. Neckar Seems to stand upon firm Ground, and the Changes in the French Ministry, probably have been for the better. But it is scarcely possible to believe that any Change in the French Ministry should do any considerable Injury to the common Cause. The Changes already made were because enough was not done. France's Importance, nay her Existence as a maritime and commercial Power, are so much at stake in this Business, that it is impossible she should forsake the Cause.

The Depreciation of the Paper Money is the most difficult to be answerd, because it is the most difficult to explain to a Gentleman who has not been in the Country and seen its operation. The Depreciation of the Money has been a real Advantage, because it is a Tax upon the People, paid as it advances, and therefore prevents the publick from being found in debt. It is true it is an unequal Tax and therefore causes, what your Friend G. Livingston justly calls Perplexity, but by no means disables or weakens the People from carrying on the War. The Body of the People loose nothing by it. The Merchant, the Farmer, the Tradesmen the Labourer looses nothing by it. They are the Monied Men, the Capitalists, those who have Money at Interest, and live upon fixed Salaries, that is the officers of Government who loose by it, and who have born this Tax. This you see is an Ease and Relief to the People, at large. The Consequence of this depreciation has been, that while England has increased her national Debt Sixty Millions by this War, ours is not a tenth Part of it, not Six millions— who then can hold out longest?

This Depreciation has no Tendency to make the People Submit to G. Britain, because that submission would not relieve but increase the Perplexity—for submission would not procure Us Peace. We must raise Men and Money to fight France Spain Holland, Russia Sweden and Denmark. The Congress, instead of Attempting to Save the Paper Money, by hard Cash, has ordered it all in, at the depreciated Value, and this measure is adopted by the States, without any difficulty which is the only Method of Justice or Policy.

Nobody need fear that the English will seize the Moment when our Army shall be feeble for Want of Pay. There have been several Moments when our Army has been reduced to almost nothing, not for Want of Pay but from the Expiration of their Periods of Enlistment. These Moments the English Seized, and before they had sent half their Army to the West India Islands. But what was the Consequence? When our Army was reduced to a few Hundreds, and theirs more than double what it is now they marched through the Jerseys and what was the Consequence? Their Post at Trenton was attacked and taken, another Body of their Troops were attacked and defeated at Princetown, and G. Washington took Post at Morristown in their Rear, and they dared not move another Step the whole Winter.

The affairs of Trenton, Bennington and lately of the summit of Kings Mountain, prove beyond Reply, that if our Army is reduced ever so low, and theirs extend them selves ever so far their necessary advanced Posts are in our Power, in the Power even of an handfull of the Militia. No sir, their Power to hurt Us lies more in keeping hid in a fortified Seaport town protected by their Men of War, than by marching into the Country.

As to a total Failure of Specie, We are in no Danger of it. The English are furnishing Us with silver and Gold every day. What is become of all the Millions they have sent to America during this War? What of all the Cash that France Sends to pay and subsist their fleet and Army? The Truth is that silver and Gold now circulate freely in America, and there are greater Quantities of it than any body in Europe imagines.

As to the danger of the Peoples submitting, from Indigence, the danger of that if ever there was any is past. In 1776 and 7— The People suffered, very much and the Army too for Want of Salt, sugar, Rum, and Cloathing. But at this day their Trade is so far extended, they make such Numbers of Prizes, and have introduced and established so many necessary Manufactures, that they have a plentifull supply. We have been more distressed for Want of Salt and Powder than any Thing else. But there is now an Abundance of both, manufactured in the Country and imported too.

As to the Ability of America to pay—it depends upon a few Words. America has between 3 and 4 Millions of People. England and Scotland have between five and six. The Lands in America produce as much as any other Lands. The Exports of America in 1774 were Six millions. The Exports of Great

Britain in 1774 were 12 millions, including too a great Part of
the Commodities of the Growth of America. England is two
hundred millions in Debt. America is six Millions. England has
Spent Sixty Millions in this War—America Six. Which People
then are the Ablest to pay. Yet England has Credit America
not. Is this from Reasoning or Prejudice?

Numbers of People—their Industry—the Quantity and Fertility of their Lands and the Value of their Exports, are the only
Rules that I know of, to judge of the ability of a People to pay,
Taxes and Debts. In all these Respects American Credit will
bear the most rigorous Examination.

The Country that Lends them Money will get the most by
it—their Principal and Interest will be safe and what is more
they Money will be laid out among them in the Purchase of
Cloathing and supplies, so that the Trade will be promoted by it.

When England and every other Nation of Europe, is
obliged to borrow Money every year to carry on War, England
to the Amount of her whole annual Exports, it is not to be
wondered that America has occasion to borrow, a sum after 6
years War equal to a Twelfth or a twenty fourth Part of her annual Exports. With such a Loan We could carry on the War
more at our Ease—our poor soldiers would be more warm and
comfortable—but if We can not obtain it, We shall not have it
to pay. And I am positively certain We can carry on the War,
without a Loan, longer than G.B. can with.

You may depend upon it, sir I shall be cautious, and maintain the most Sacred Regard to Truth in my Representations
to Congress. But I dare not deceive them with false hopes. No
Man living has more at heart than I have a friendly and a lasting Connection between the two Republicks. The Religion
the Government and the Commerce of the two Countries,
point out such a Connection—old Prejudices and Habits of
Veneration for Holland in the Minds of all Americans, who
have ever considered the Dutch as their Friends and Allies, (for
it should be rememberd that We have been as long in Alliance
and Friendship with this Country as England, and have as
good a Right for what I know to the Benefit of the Treaties as
the English) make the Americans wish for such a Connection.
And therefore if the Truth will not warrant me in representing
to Congress, so much Zeal and Warmth in this Nation for a

Connection with America as I could wish, it will not be my
fault but my Misfortune and my Grief.

EUROPEAN FEAR OF AMERICAN LIBERTY

To Edmund Jenings

Dear Sir

On my Return from a little Excursion, I received yours of 18.

I dont know whether Calkoens, Pamphlet is unanswerable
or not. There are two very sharp Pamphlets written against it,
as they say. These People dont understand their own Constitution alike.

There is a Part of the Pamphlet, which disgusted me, as well
as you. It is a Dutch affectation of Shrewdness. Nothing can
be a greater Folly. However—The French Marine have it, to
my certain Knowledge as well as Calkoen and the Spanyards.
There is in Deed and in Truth an European Jealousy, and Envy
of America. Weak wretched Man! Sagacious only to find out
and make Causes of thine own Misery.

It has been, these two or three years, a philosophical Speculation as well as a political, to discover the true Cause of this
European Suspicion. Is it natural? Men dont usually disquiet
themselves about Evils, so distant in Futurity.

Who ever made himself uneasy about a Thing which was to
happen 3 hundred years hence? However the Evil here Apprehended, never will nor can happen, unless a Silly Jealousy,
should induce the Europeans to take unfriendly Measures, So
as to excite ill Will.

I Suspect, that this Jealousy is artificial. That it is artfully
managed by the Courts of Europe. These dread the Forms of
Government in America. They dread that high Sense and Spirit
of Liberty, and those popular Principles, with which America is
full. They are afraid of their Spreading in Europe and propagating like a Contagion, So as to produce Revolutions.

But the People of Europe, and the Men of Letters ought for
the opposite Reasons, to cherish America as their only remain-

ing Barrier against Despotism. For if the Spirit of Liberty is Subdued in America there is now an end of it in the World.

I am weary however of Speculation. I See that our poor Country must bid farewell to all Ideas of Peace. Warlike she must be or not exist. For she will be involved in eternal War, that is plain. Britains and French and Spanyards, and others will keep poor America the constant Sport of their infernal Politicks. Let Us warn our Countrymen therefore to be Soldiers and Seamen, and teach them to love War Since Europe will oblige them to it.

It will depend entirely upon Europe, whether America shall ever hurt it or not. If she treats America with Suspicion and Jealousy, Envy and Malice, she will necessarily, produce the Same Passions in America towards her. And she will bring it, to this question whether America shall be, desolated and totally depopulated, or not? It is easy to see that this is not in the Power of all Europe. European Jealousy however will have one Effect. It will keep America longer United. Without Unkind and ungenerous Treatment from Europe, God knows America will too soon divide and quarell with itself.

But it is not the Part of Policy or Philosophy, to torment itself with Prospects into such distant Futurities, I dont expect that America will turn the Earth into an Heaven or an Hell. This World will continue to be Earth and its Inhabitants Men, and Wars and Follies will abound as much as ever. We have full enough to do with those of the present Age. Dont let Us distress ourselves about those which are to happen a thousand Years hence.

Can you help me to borrow Some Money. This is the best Way to treat America, lend them some Money, which will all come back again, twice over with Interest. In the first Place it will all be Spent here—in the next it must all be paid here again. Will your Friend insert my Plan in his Leaf and give Us some Remarks upon American Credit? The Population, Industry, and the Extent and Variety of her Productions and Commerce, are the sources of her Wealth and Ability to pay. And Where there is Ability there is seldom wanting Inclination.

My Plan of a Loan, is a political Machine, which will set many Wheels in Motion. We shall See what Effect it will have.

I hope, to see the Speculations of all the Journalists upon it. If it Succeeds it will promote Commerce, Politicks, and War, in our favour. If not it will compell Congress against their Inclination, to tax all Europe by laying Duties on their Exports. We might in this Way oblige Europe to pay the Expences of the War, for our Productions they must and will have at any Rate. If the Loan dont Succeed, America may be forced to make an American Act of Navigation. We have it in our Power to manage Europe if she will be ill natured, but I hope she will be wise.

As to the present State of America, her Governments are now compleetly established and have as much Force as any in Europe at least. Her Army, is as numerous as usual, but the Cowardice of the English in keeping hid in New York and skulking about in their ships leaves our Army nothing to do, but grow discontented with an inactive Life, I suppose. The Navy of the Continent, seems neglected but the Privateers fare the better, for that, and make an incredible Number of Prizes. The Paper Money seems to be little talked of, as the silver and gold, Spent there by the English and french, are now circulating in sufficient quantities to serve for a Medium.

February 27, 1781

EUROPE'S UNFAIR TREATMENT OF AMERICA

To Benjamin Franklin

Sir   Leyden April 16th. 1781

I yesterday had the honour of your's of the seventh. The letter inclosed is a bitter satire on the nation which produced it. Is it possible that Arnold should shew his Face among Men after such a Letter? If it is not a bribe it is robbery committed in the American Service: for it is well known, that Arnold had no such Sum when the War began. He is now employed in stealing Tobacco and Negroes—so is Cornwallis: a fair employment for Peers—for Arnold is the Peer of them all. I think the Southern States will have the Honour after all, of putting the Continent in a right Way to finish the Business of the War.

All the Papers English, French and Dutch assure the World that I have succeeded in a Loan. I wish they would prove their Words. I am told it will do by and by: so I am that the nation will act vigorously by and by. I wish both may prove true: but I have not one Grain of your Faith nor Hope.

There are Capitalists who believe Us able and honest to pay, and that We shall prevail, and they have Inclinations enough they say, to the Loan: but the true motive of their Conduct is fear of being pointed out to Mobs and Soldiers, as Persons who have contributed to the Commencement or Continuance of the War with England.

I wrote You some days ago that I had not succeeded at all and requesting your Orders how the Bills accepted should be paid. Some of them become payable the beginning of May, and on the fifteenth of that Month, the sixty six Bills amounting to ten thousand pounds sterling, which were drawn in favor of Mr. Tracy, become due. I congratulate You on your Success at Versailles. If Spain would make a Treaty with Mr. Jay it would assist Us here. Every body asks, why does Spain delay? You and I know very well but cannot tell. But so it is— one always negotiates ill when one is not in a Condition to make oneself feared. If America could dissemble enough to threaten other Nations with a return to Great Britain they would be ready to hang themselves to prevent it: but America is too honest and sincere to play this Game. England would have all the Mountains of Mexico and Peru in a few Years if America should join her. Yet We are slighted. God forgive them, and enable America to forget their Ungenerosity.

America has fought Great Britain and Ireland for Years and not only Great Britain, but many States of Germany, many Tribes of Indians, and many Negroes their Allies. Great Britain has been moving Earth and Hell to obtain Allies against Us, yet it is improper in Us to propose an Alliance. Great Britain has borrowed all the superfluous Wealth of Europe in Italy, Germany, Holland, Switzerland, and some in France to murder Us, yet it is dishonourable in Us to propose to borrow Money. By Heaven I would make a Bargain with all Europe, if it lay with me. Let all Europe stand still, neither lend Men nor Money nor Ships to England nor America, and let them fight it out alone. I would give my Share of Millions for such a Bargain. America is treated unfairly and ungenerously by Europe. But thus it is. Mankind will be servile to Tyrannical Masters and basely devoted to vile Idols.

With Great Respect, Sir, Your obedient Servant.

John Adams

Memorial to the States General of the Netherlands

Copy

Leyden April 19. 1781

A Memorial To their High Mightinesses, the States General of the United Provinces of the Low Countries.

High and Mighty Lords

The Subscriber has the Honour to propose to your High Mightinesses, that the United States of America, in Congress Assembled, have lately thought fit to send him a Commission (with full Powers and Instructions) to confer with your High Mightinesses, concerning a Treaty of Amity and Commerce, an authentic Copy of which he has the Honour to annex to this Memorial.

At the Times, when the Treaties between this Republick and the Crown of Great Britain, were made, the People, who now compose the United States of America, were a Part of the English Nation; as such, Allies of the Republick, and Parties to those Treaties; entitled to all their Benefits, and chearfully submitting to all their Obligations.

It is true, that when the British Administration, renouncing the ancient Character of Englishmen for Generosity, Justice and Humanity, concieved the design of subverting the political Systems of the Colonies; depriving them of the Rights and Liberties of Englishmen, and reducing them to the worst of all Forms of Government; starving the People, by blockading the Ports and cutting off their Fisheries and Commerce; sending Fleets and Armies to destroy every Principle and Sentiment of Liberty, and to consume their Habitations and their Lives; making Contracts for foreign Troops and Alliances with savage Nations to assist them in their Enterprise; casting, formally, by Act of Parliament, three Millions of People at once out of the Protection of the Crown: then, and not 'till then, did the United States of America, in Congress Assembled, pass that memorable Act, by which they assumed an equal Station among the Nations.

This immortal Declaration, of the fourth of July one thousand

seven hundred and seventy six, when America was invaded by
an hundred Vessels of War, and, according to Estimates laid
before Parliament, by fifty five thousand of veteran Troops,
was not the Effect of any sudden Passion, or Enthusiasm; but
a Measure, which had been long in deliberation among the
People, maturely discussed in some hundreds of popular Assemblies, and by public Writings in all the States: it was a Measure, which Congress did not adopt, until they had recieved
the positive Instructions of their Constituents: it was then
unanimously adopted by Congress, subscribed by all its Members, transmitted to the Assemblies of the several States, and
by them respectively accepted, ratified and recorded among
their Archives: so that no Decree, Edict, Statute, Placart or
fundamental Law of any Nation was ever made with more
Solemnity, or with more Unanimity or Cordiality adopted, as
the Act and Consent of the whole People, than this: and it has
been held sacred to this day by every State with such unshaken
Firmness, that not even the smallest has ever been induced to
depart from it; although the English have wasted many Millions, and vast Fleets and Armies in the vain Attempt to in-
validate it. On the contrary, each of the thirteen States has
instituted a Form of Government for itself, under the Authority of the People; has erected its Legislature in the several
Branches; its Executive Authority with all its Offices; its Judiciary Departments and Judges; its Army, Militia, Revenue, and
some of them their Navy: and all these Departments of Government have been regularly and constitutionally organized
under the associated Superintendency of Congress, now these
five Years, and have acquired a Consistency, Solidity and Activity, equal to the oldest and most established Governments. It
is true, that in some Speeches and Writings of the English it is
still contended, that the People of America are still in Principle
and Affection with them: but these Assertions are made
against such evident Truth and Demonstration, that it is surprising they should find at this day one Believer in the World.
One may appeal to the Writings and recorded Speeches of the
English for the last seventeen Years to shew, that similar Misrepresentations have been incessantly repeated through that
whole Period, and that the Conclusion of every Year has in fact
confuted the confident Assertions and Predictions of the

beginning of it. The Subscriber begs Leave to say from his own Knowledge of the People of America, (and he has a better right to obtain Credit, because he has better Opportunities to know than any Briton whatsoever) that they are unalterably determined to maintain their Independence. He confesses, that notwithstanding his Confidence through his whole Life in the virtuous Sentiments and Uniformity of Character among his Countrymen, their Unanimity has surprised him: that all the Power, Arts, Intrigues and Bribes, which have been employed in the several States, should have seduced from the Standard of Virtue so contemptible a few, is more fortunate than could have been expected. This Independence stands upon so firm and broad a Bottom of the Peoples Interests, Honour, Consciences and Affections, that it will not be affected by any Successes that the English may obtain either in America, or against the European Powers at War, nor by any Alliances they can possibly form, if indeed in so unjust and desperate a Cause they can obtain any.

Nevertheless, although compelled by Necessity, and warranted by the fundamental Laws of the Colonies, and of the British Constitution; by Principles avowed in the English Laws, and confirmed by many Examples in the English History; by Principles interwoven into the History and public Right of Europe in the great Examples of the Helvetic and Batavian Confederacies and many others, and frequently acknowledged and ratified by the Diplomatic Body; Principles founded in eternal Justice and the Laws of God and Nature: to cut asunder forever all the Ties which had connected them with Great Britain; yet the People of America did not consider themselves as seperating from their Allies, especially the Republick of the United Provinces, or departing from their Connections with any of the People under their Government: but, on the contrary, they preserved the same Affection, Esteem and Respect for the Dutch Nation in every Part of the World, which they and their Ancestors had ever entertained.

When sound Policy dictated to Congress the Precaution of sending Persons to negotiate natural Alliances in Europe, it was not from any failure in Respect, that they did not send a Minister to your High Mightinesses with the first whom they sent abroad: but, instructed in the Nature of the Connections between Great Britain and the Republick, and in the System of Peace and Neutrality, which She had so long pursued, they thought proper to respect both so far, as not to seek to embroil her with her Allies, to excite Divisions in the Nation or lay Embarrassments before it. But, since the British Administration, uniform and persevering in Injustice, despising their Allies, as much as their Colonists and fellow Subjects; disregarding the Faith of Treaties, as much as that of Royal Charters; violating the Law of Nations, as they had before done the fundamental Laws of the Colonies, and the inherent Rights of British Subjects; have arbitrarily set aside all the Treaties between the Crown and the Republick, declared War, and commenced Hostilities, the settled Intentions of which they had manifested long before, all those Motives, which before restrained the Congress, cease, and an Opportunity presents of proposing such Connections, as the United States of America have a Right to form, consistent with those already formed with France and Spain, which they are under every Obligation of Duty, Interest and Inclination to observe sacred and inviolate; and consistent with such other Treaties as it is their Intention to propose to other Sovereigns.

A natural Alliance may be formed between the two Republicks, if ever one existed among Nations.

The first Planters of the four Northern States found in this Country an Asylum from Persecution, and resided here from the Year one thousand six hundred and eight to the Year one thousand six hundred and twenty, twelve Years preceeding their Migration. They ever entertained, and have transmitted to Posterity a grateful Remembrance of that Protection and Hospitality, and especially of that religious Liberty they found here, though they had sought them in vain in England.

The first Inhabitants of two other States, New York and New Jersey, were immediate Emigrants from this Nation, and have transmitted their Religion, Language, Customs, Manners and Character. And America in general, until her Relations were formed with the House of Bourbon, has ever considered this Nation as her first Friend in Europe, whose History and the great Characters it exhibits, in the various Arts of Peace, as well as Atchievements in War by Sea and Land, have been particularly studied, admired and imitated in every State.

A Similitude of Religion, although it is not deemed so essential in this as it has been in former Ages to the Alliance of Nations, is still, as it ever will be thought a desirable Circumstance. Now it may be said with Truth, that there are no two Nations whose Worship, Doctrine and Discipline are more alike, than those of the two Republicks. In this particular therefore, as far as it is of Weight, an Alliance would be perfectly natural.

A Similarity in the Forms of Government is usually considered as another Circumstance, which renders Alliances natural: and although the Constitutions of the two Republicks are not perfectly alike, there is yet Analogy enough between them to make a Connection easy in this respect.

In general Usages, and in the Liberality of Sentiments in those momentous Points, the Freedom of Inquiry, the Right of private Judgment and the Liberty of Conscience, of so much Importance to be supported in the World, and imparted to all Mankind, and which at this Hour are in more danger from Great Britain, and that intolerant Spirit which is secretly fermenting there, than from any other Quarter, the two Nations resemble each other more than any others.

The Originals of the two Republicks are so much alike, that the History of one seems but a Transcript from that of the other: so that every Dutchman, instructed in the Subject, must pronounce the American Revolution just and necessary, or pass a Censure upon the greatest Actions of his immortal Ancestors; Actions which have been approved and applauded by Mankind, and justified by the Decision of Heaven.

But the Circumstance, which, perhaps in this Age, has stronger Influence than any other in the formation of Friendships between Nations, is the great and growing Interest of Commerce; of the whole System of which through the Globe, your High Mightinesses are too perfect Masters for me to say any thing that is not familiarly known. It may not however be amiss to hint, that the central Situation of this Country; her extensive Navigation; her Possessions in the East and West Indies; the Intelligence of her Merchants; the Number of her Capitalists and the Riches of her Funds, render a Connection with her desirable to America. And on the other Hand, the Abundance and Variety of the Productions of America; the

Materials of Manufactures, Navigation and Commerce; the vast Demand and Consumption of the Manufactures of Europe, of Merchandizes from the Baltic, and from the East Indies, and the Situation of the Dutch Possessions in the West Indies, cannot admit of a doubt, that a Connection with the United States would be useful to this Republick. The English are so sensible of this, that, notwithstanding all their Professions of Friendship, they have considered this Nation as their Rival in the American Trade: a Sentiment which dictated and maintained their severe Act of Navigation, as injurious to the Commerce and Naval Power of this Country as it was both to the Trade and the Rights of the Colonists. There is now an Opportunity offered to both to shake off this Shackle forever. If any Consideration whatever could have prevailed with the English to have avoided a War with your High Mightinesses, it would have been an Apprehension of an Alliance between the two Republicks: and it is easy to foresee, that nothing will contribute more to oblige them to a Peace than such a Connection once completely formed. It is needless to point out particularly, what Advantages might be derived to the Possessions of the Republick in the West Indies, from a Trade opened, protected and encouraged between them and the Continent of America: or what Profits might be made by the East India Company by carrying their Effects directly to the American Market: how much even the Trade of the Baltic might be secured and extended by a free Intercourse with America, which has ever had so large a Demand, and will have more for Hemp, Cordage, Sail Cloth and other Articles of that Commerce: how much the national Navigation would be benefited by building and purchasing Ships there: how much the Number of Seamen might be increased, or how much Advantage to both Countries to have their Ports mutually opened to their Men of War and Privateers and their Prizes.

If therefore an Analogy of Religion, Government, Original, Manners and the most extensive and lasting Commercial Interests can form a Ground and an Invitation to political Connection, the Subscriber flatters himself, that in all these Particulars, the Union is so obviously natural, that there has seldom been a more distinct Designation of Providence to any two distant Nations to unite themselves together.

It is further submitted to the Wisdom and Humanity of your High Mightinesses, whether it is not visibly for the Good of Mankind, that the Powers of Europe, who are convinced of the Justice of the American Cause (and where is one to be found that is not?) should make haste to acknowledge the Independence of the United States, and form equitable Treaties with them, as the surest Means of convincing Great Britain of the Impracticability of her Pursuits: whether the late Marine Treaty, concerning the Rights of neutral Vessels, noble and useful as it is, can be established against Great Britain, who never will adopt it nor submit to it but from Necessity, without the Independence of America: whether the Return of America, with her Nurseries of Seamen and Magazines of Materials for Navigation and Commerce, to the Domination and Monopoly of Great Britain, if that were practicable, would not put the Possessions of other Nations beyond Seas wholly in the Power of that enormous Empire, which has long been governed wholly by the feeling of its own Power; at least without a proportional Attention to Justice, Humanity or Decency. When it is obvious and certain that the Americans are not inclined to submit again to the British Government on one hand, and that the Powers of Europe ought not and could not with Safety consent to it, if they were, on the other: why should a Source of Contention be left open for future Contingencies to involve the Nations of Europe in still more Bloodshed; when, by one decisive Step of the Maritime Powers, in making Treaties with a Nation long in Possession of Sovereignty, by Right and in Fact, it might be closed.

The Example of your High Mightinesses would, it is hoped, be followed by all the Maritime Powers, especially those, which are Parties to the late Marine Treaty: nor can an Apprehension, that the Independence of America would be injurious to the Trade of the Baltic be any Objection. This Jealousy is so groundless, that the reverse would happen. The Freight and Insurance in Voyages across the Atlantic are so high, and the Price of Labour so dear in America, that Tar, Pitch, Turpentine and Ship Timber can never be transported to Europe at so cheap a Rate, as it has been and will be afforded by Countries round the Baltic. This Commerce was supported by the English before the Revolution with difficulty and not without large Parliamentary Bounties. Of Hemp, Cordage and Sail Cloth, there will not probably be a Sufficiency raised in America for her own Consumption in many Centuries, for the plainest of all Reasons, because those Articles can be imported from Amsterdam, or even from Petersbourg or Archangel cheaper than they can be raised at Home. America will therefore be for Ages a Market for these Articles of the Baltic Trade.

Nor is there more Solidity in another Supposition, propagated by the English to prevent other Nations from pursuing their true Interests, that other Colonies will follow the Example of the United States. Those Powers, which have as large Possessions as any beyond Seas, have already declared against England, apprehending no such Consequences. Indeed there is no Probability of any other Power of Europe following the Example of England, in attempting to change the whole System of the Government of Colonies, and reducing them by Oppression to the Necessity of governing themselves. And without such manifest Injustice and Cruelty on the Part of the Metropolis, there is no danger of Colonies attempting Innovations. Established Governments are founded deeply in the Hearts, the Passions, the Imaginations and Understandings of the People, and without some violent Change from without to alter the Temper and Character of the whole People, it is not in human Nature to exchange Safety for Danger, and certain Happiness for very precarious Benefits.

It is submitted to the Consideration of your High Mightinesses, whether the System of the United States, which was minutely considered and discussed and unanimously agreed on in Congress in the Year one thousand seven hundred and seventy six, in planning the Treaty they proposed to France, to form equitable Commercial Treaties with all the Maritime Powers of Europe, without being governed or monopolized by any: a System which was afterwards approved by the King, and made the Foundation of the Treaties with his Majesty: a System to which the United States have hitherto constantly adhered, and from which they never will depart, unless compelled by some Powers declaring against them, which is not expected; is not the only means of preventing this growing Country from being an Object of everlasting Jealousies, Rivalries and Wars among the Nations. If this Idea is just, it follows, that it is the Interest of every State in Europe, to acknowledge American Independency immediately. If such benevolent Policy should be adopted, the new World will be a proportional Blessing to every Part of the old.

The Subscriber has the further Honour of informing your High Mightinesses, that the United States of North America in Congress Assembled, impressed with an high Sense of the Wisdom and Magnanimity of your High Mightinesses, and of your inviolable Attachment to the Rights and Liberties of Mankind, and being desirous of cultivating the Friendship of a Nation, eminent for its Wisdom, Justice and Moderation, have appointed the Subscriber to be their Minister Plenipotentiary to reside near You, that he may give You more particular Assurances of the great Respect they entertain for your High Mightinesses, beseeching your High Mightinesses to give entire Credit to every thing, which their said Minister shall deliver on their Part, especially when he shall assure You of the Sincerity of their Friendship and Regard. The original Letter of Credence, under the Seal of Congress, the Subscriber is ready to deliver to your High Mightinesses, or to such Persons as You shall direct to recieve it. He has also a similar Letter of Credence to his most Serene Highness the Prince Stadtholder.

All which is respectfully submitted to the Consideration of your High Mightinesses, together with the Propriety of appointing some Person or Persons, to treat on the Subject of his Mission, by

John Adams

CONGRESS AND FOREIGN AFFAIRS

To the Comte de Vergennes

Paris July 21. 1781

Since my Letter of the nineteenth, Sir, another Point has occurred to me, upon which it seems necessary, that I Should Say Something to your Excellency, before my Departure for Holland, which will be on Monday Morning.

An Idea has, I perceive been suggested, of the several States of America, choosing Agents seperately, to attend the Congress, at Vienna, in order to make Peace, with Great Britain, so that there would be thirteen instead of one.

The Constitution or Confederation of the United States, which has been Solemnly adopted and ratified by each of them Seperately and by all of them jointly has been officially and authentically notified to their Majesties the Kings of France and Spain, and to their High Mightinesses, the States General of the United Provinces of the Low Countries, and communicated to all the other Courts and Nations of the World, as far as the Gazettes of Europe are able to Spread it: So that it is now as well and universally known as any Constitution of Government in Europe.

By this Constitution, all Power and Authority, of negotiating with foreign Powers is expressly delegated to the United States, in Congress assembled. It would therefore be a publick Disrespect and Contempt offered, to the Constitution of the Nation if any Power Should make any Application, whatever, to the Governors, or Legislatures of the Separate States. In this respect the American Constitution is very different from the Batavian.

If the two Imperial Courts Should address their Articles to the States Seperately No Governor or President of any one of those Commonwealths, could even communicate it to the Legislature. No President of a Senate could lay it, before the Body, over which he presides. No Speaker of an House of Representatives could read it to the House.

It would be an Error, and a Misdemeanour, in any of these officers, to receive and communicate any Such Letter. All that he could do would be, after breaking the Seal and reading it, to Send it back. He could not, even, legally transmit it to Congress. If Such an Application, therefore, Should be made and Sent back, it would consume, much time to no Purpose, and perhaps have other worse Effects.

There is no method for the Courts of Europe, to convey any Thing to the People of America but through the Congress of the United States, nor any Way of negotiating with them, but by means of that Body. I must therefore intreat your Excellency, that the Idea of Summoning Ministers from the thirteen States may not be countenanced at all.

I know very well, that if each State, had in the Confederation, reserved to itself a right of negotiating with foreign Powers, and Such an Application Should have been made to them, Seperately upon this occasion, they would all of them Seperately refer it to Congress, because the People universally know, and are well agreed, that all Connections with foreign Countries, must, in their Circumstances, be under one Direction. But all these Things, were very maturely considered in framing the Confederation, by which, the People of each State, have taken away from themselves, even the right of deliberating and debating upon these Affairs, unless they should be referred to them by Congress for their Advice, or unless they should think proper to instruct their Delegates in Congress, of their own Accord.

This matter may not appear to your Excellency, in so important a Light as it does to me: and the Thought of such an Application to the United states may not have been seriously entertained: but, as it has been mentioned, though only in a Way of transient Speculation, I thought I could not excuse myself from Saying Something upon it, because I knew it would be considered in so unfavourable a Light, in America, that I am persuaded Congress would think them selves bound to remonstrate against it, in the most Solemn manner.

I have the Honour to be, with the greatest Respect, sir your most obedient and most humble Servant   John Adams

JUSTIFYING HIS DIPLOMATIC CONDUCT

To Robert R. Livingston

Duplicate
Secret and confidential

Sir   Amsterdam Feby. 21st 1782
I know very well the Name of the Family where I spent the Evening with my worthy Friend Mr. — before We set off, and have made my Alphabet accordingly: but I am on this occasion as on all others hitherto utterly unable to comprehend the

sense of the Passages in Cypher. The Cypher is certainly not taken regularly under the two first Letters of that Name. I have been able sometimes to decypher Words enough to show that I have the Letters right: but upon the whole I can make nothing of it, which I regret very much upon this occasion, as I suppose the Cyphers are a very material part of the Letter.

The friendly and patriotic Anxiety, with which You enquire after my Motives and Reasons for making the Proposition of the 4th. of May and for printing the Memorial, has put me upon recollecting the Circumstances. If the Series of my Letters had arrived, I think the Reasons would have appeared; but not with that Force, in which they existed at the Time. I have never expressed in writing those Reasons so strongly as I felt them. The Hopes have never been strong in anybody, of inducing the Republick to a sudden Alliance with France and America. The utmost Expectation, that many of the well-intentioned have entertained, has been to prevent the Government from joining England. I am sorry to be obliged to say it, and if it should ever be made public it might be ill taken. But there is no manner of doubt, that the most earnest Wish of the Cabinet has been to induce the Nation to furnish the Ships and Troops to the English according to their Interpretation of the Treaty. Amsterdam distinguished itself, and its ancient and venerable Burgomaster Temmink, and its eldest Pensionary Mr. Van Berkel, have distinguished themselves in Amsterdam. When Mr. Laurens's Papers were discovered, they were sent forthwith to the Hague. The Prince in Person laid them before the States. Sir Joseph York thundered with his Memorials against Amsterdam, her Burgomasters and Pensionary. The Nation was seized with an Amazement, and flew to the Armed Neutrality for Shelter against the fierce Wrath of the King. Instantly Sir Joseph York is recalled and a Declaration of War appears, levelled against the City, against the Burgomaster and Mr. Van Berkel, and Sir G. Rodney in his dispatches pursues the same Partiality and Personality against Amsterdam. What was the drift of all this? Manifestly to excite Seditions against Temmink and Van Berkel. Here then is a base and scandalous System of Policy, in which the King of Great Britain and his Ministry and Admiral all condescend to engage, manifestly concerted by Sir Joseph York at the Hague and I am sorry to add too much favoured by the Cabinet, and even openly by the Prince by his presenting Laurens's Papers to the States, to sacrifice Temmink and Van Berkel to the Fury of an enraged Populace. This Plan was so daringly supported by Writers of the first Fame on the side of the Court, that Multitudes of Writings appeared attempting to shew that what Temmink and Van Berkel had done was high Treason. All this had such an Effect, that all the best Men seemed to shudder with Fear. I should scarcely find Credit in America, if I were to relate Anecdotes. It would be ungenerous to mention Names as well as unnecessary: I need only say that I was avoided like a Pestilence by every Man in Government. Those Gentlemen of the Rank of Burgomasters, Schepens, Pensionaries, and even Lawyers, who had treated me with great Kindness and Sociability and even Familiarity before, dared not see me; dared not be at home when I visited at their Houses; dared not return my Visit; dared not answer in writing even a Card that I wrote them. I had several Messages in a round about way and in Confidence, that they were extremely sorry they could not answer my Cards and Letters in writing, because on fait tout son possible pour me sacrifier aux Anglomanes. Not long after arrived the News of the Capture of St. Eustatia &ca. This filled up the Measure. You can have no Idea, Sir. No Man who was not upon the Spot, can have any Idea of the Gloom and Terror that was spread by this Event. The Creatures of the Court openly rejoiced in this, and threatened in some of them in the most impudent Terms. I had certain Information that some of them talked high of their Expectations of popular Insurrections against the Burgomasters of Amsterdam and Mr. Van Berkel, and did Mr. Adams the honor to mention him as one, that was to be hanged by the Mob in such Company.

In the midst of the Confusion and Terror, my Credentials arrived from Paris thro' an hundred Accidents and Chances of being finally lost. As soon as I read my despatches, and heard the History of their Escape by Post, Diligence and Trech Schoots, it seemed to me as if the hand of Providence had sent them on purpose to dissipate all these Vapours.

With my Dispatches arrived from Paris Intimations of their Contents, for there are no Secrets kept at Paris. The People, who are generally eager for a Connection with America, began to talk, and Paragraphs appeared in all the Gazettes in Dutch and French and German, containing a thousand ridiculous Conjectures about the American Ambassador and his Errand. One of my Children could scarcely go to School, without some pompous Account of it in the Dutch Papers. I had been long enough in this Country to see tolerably well where the Ballance lay, and to know that America was so much respected by all Parties, that no one would dare to offer any Insult to her Minister as soon as he should be known. I wrote my Memorial and presented it, and printed it in English, Dutch and French. There was immediately the most universal and unanimous Approbation of it expressed in all Companies and Pamphlets and Newspapers, and no Criticism ever appeared against it. Six or seven months afterwards a Pamphlet appeared in Dutch, which was afterwards translated into French, called Considerations on the Memorial: but it has been read by very few, and is indeed not worth reading.

The Proposition to the President being taken ad referendum, it became a Subject of the Deliberation of the Sovereignty The Prince therefore and the whole Court are legally bound to treat it with respect, and me with decency, at least it would be criminal in them to treat me or the Subject with Indecency.

If it had not been presented and printed, I am very sure I could not long have resided in the Republick, and what would have been the Consequence to the Friends of Liberty here I know not. They were so disheartened and intimidated, and the Anglomanes were so insolent, that no Man can say, that a sudden Phrenzy might not have been excited among the Soldiery and the People to demand a Junction with England, as there was in the Year 1748. Such a Revolution would have injured America and her Allies, have prolonged the War and have been the total Loss and Ruin of the Republick.

Immediately upon the Presentation of my Memorial, Mr. Van Berkel ventured to present his Requete and Demand for a Trial. This contributed still further to raise the Spirits of the good People, and soon afterwards the Burgomasters of Amsterdam appeared with their Proposition for giving the Prince a Committee for a Council, and in Course their Attack upon the Duke, all which together excited such an Enthusiasm in the

Nation and among the Officers of the Navy, as produced the Battle of Doggersbank, which never would have happened in all Probability, but would have been eluded by secret Orders and various Artifices, if the Spirit raised in the Nation by this Chain of Proceedings, of which the American Memorial was the first and an essential Link, had not rendered a display of the national Bravery indispensible for the honor of the Navy, and perhaps for the Safety of the Court.

The Memorial, as a Composition, has very little Merit, yet almost every Gazette in Europe has inserted it, and most of them with a Compliment, none with any Criticism. When I was in Paris and Versailles afterwards, no Man ever expressed to me the smallest disapprobation of it, or the least apprehension that it could do any harm. On the contrary, several Gentlemen of Letters expressed higher Compliments upon it than it deserved. The King of Sweden has done it a most illustrious honor, by quoting one of the most material Sentiments in it, in a public Answer to the King of Great Britain; and the Emperor of Germany has since done the Author of it the honor to desire in the Character of Count Falkenstein to see him, and what is more remarkable has adopted the sentiment of it concerning religious Liberty into a Code of Laws for his Dominions, the greatest Effort in favor of Humanity, next to the American Revolution, which has been produced in the eighteenth Century.

As my Mission to this Republick was wisely communicated to the Court of Versailles, who can say that this Transaction of Congress had not some Influence in producing de Grasse in Cheasapeak Bay. Another thing I ought to mention. I have a Letter from Mr. Jay, informing me that in the Month of June last Mr. del Campo was appointed by the Court of Madrid to treat with him—the exact time when my Memorial appeared at Madrid. You may possibly say, that my Imagination and Self-Love carry me extraordinary lengths, but when one is called upon to justify an Action, one should look all round. All I contend for is, that the Memorial has certainly done no harm. That it is probable it has done some Good, and that it is possible it has done much more than can be proved. A Man always makes an aukward figure when he is justifying himself and his own Actions, and I hope I shall be pardoned. It is easy to say, il abonde trop dans son sens—il est vain et glorieux—il est plein de lui même—il ne voit que lui, and other modest things of that sort, with which even your Malsherbes's, your Turgots and Neckars are sometimes sacrificed to very small Intrigues.

Your Veterans in Diplomaticks and in Affairs of State consider Us as a kind of Militia, and hold Us perhaps, as is natural, in some degree of Contempt, but wise Men know that Militia sometimes gain Victories over regular Troops, even by departing from the Rules.

Soon after I had presented the Memorial, I wrote to the Duke de la Vauguyon upon the subject of inviting or admitting in Concert the Republick to accede to the Alliance between France and America. The Duke transmitted that Letter to the Count de Vergennes, which produced the offer to Congress from the King to assist Us in forming a Connection with the Republick, and the Instructions upon the Subject, which I shall execute as soon as the French Ambassador thinks proper. With him it now lies, and with him thank God I have hitherto preserved a perfectly good Understanding, altho' I differed from him in opinion concerning the point of time to make the former Proposition.

The Evacuation of the Barrier Towns has produced an important Commentary upon the Conversation I had with the Duke, and his Opinion upon that occasion. How few Weeks was it, after the publication of my Memorial, that the Roman Emperor made that memorable Visit to Brussells, Ostend, Bruges, Antwerp and all the considerable maritime Towns in his Provinces of Brabant and Flanders? How soon afterwards his memorable Journies to Holland and to Paris? Was not the American Memorial full of Matter for the Emperor's Contemplation, when he was at Ostend, Antwerp and Bruges? Was it not full of Matter, calculated to stimulate him to hasten his Negotiations with France concerning the Abolition of the Barrier Towns? Was not the same Matter equally calculated to stimulate France to finish such an Agreement with him, as We have seen the Evidence of in the actual Evacuation of those Towns? If this Evacuation is an Advantage to France and to America, as it undoubtedly is, by putting this Republick more in the Power of France, and more out of a Possibility of pursuing the System of Orange by joining England, and my Memorial is supposed to have contributed any thing towards it, surely it was worth the while.

The Period, since the 4th. of May 1781, has been thick sown with great Events, all springing out of the American Revolution, and connected with the Matter contained in my Memorial. The Memorial of Mr. Van Berkel, the Proposition of the Burgomasters of Amsterdam; their Attack upon the Duke of Brunswick and the Battle of Doggersbank; the Appointment of Senior del Campo to treat with Mr. Jay; the Success of Colo. Laurens in obtaining Orders for the French Fleet to go upon the Coast of America; their Victory over Graves and the Capture of Cornwallis; the Emperor's Journey to his maritime Towns, to Holland and to Paris; his new Regulations for encouraging the Trade of his maritime Towns; his Demolition of the Barrier Fortifications; and his most liberal and sublime Ecclesiastical Reformation; and the King of Sweeden's Reproach to the King of England for continuing the War, in the very Words of my Memorial: these Traits are all subsequent to that Memorial, and they are too sublime and decisive proofs of the Prosperity and Glory of the American Cause, to admit of the Belief that that Memorial has done it any material hurt.

By comparing Facts and Events and Dates, it is impossible not to believe, that the Memorial had some Influence in producing some of them. When Courts and Princes and Nations have been long contemplating a great system of affairs, and their Judgments begin to ripen, and they begin to see how things ought to go and are agoing, a small Publication, holding up these objects in a clear point of View, sometimes sets a vast Machine in motion at once like the springing of a mine. What a Dust We raise, said the Fly upon the Chariot Wheel? It is impossible to prove that this whole Letter is not a similar delusion to that of the Fly. The Councils of Princes are enveloped in impenetrable Secrecy. The true Motives and Causes, which govern their Actions little or great, are carefully concealed. But I desire only that these Events may be all combined together, and then that an impartial Judge may say, if he can, that he believes, that that homely harmless Memorial had no share in producing any part of this great Complication of Good.

But be all these Speculations and Conjectures as they will,

the foresight of which could not have been sufficiently clear to have justified the Measure, it is sufficient for me to say, that the Measure was absolutely necessary and unavoidable. I should have been contemptible and ridiculous without it. By it I have secured to myself and my Mission universal Decency and Respect, tho' no open Acknowledgment or Avowal.

I write this to You in Confidence. You may entirely suppress it, or communicate it in Confidence, as You judge for the public Good.

I might have added, that many Gentlemen of Letters of various Nations have expressed their Approbation of this Measure. I will mention only two. Mr. D'Alembert and Mr. Raynal, I am well informed, have expressed their Sense of it in Terms too flattering for me to repeat. I might add the Opinion of many Men of Letters in this Republick.

The Charge of Vanity is the last Resource of little Wits and mercenary Quacks, the vainest Men alive, against Men and Measures that they can find no other Objection to: I doubt not but Letters have gone to America, containing their weighty Charge against me: but this Charge, if supported only by the Opinion of those who make it, may be brought against any Man or Thing.

It may be said, that this Memorial did not reach the Court of Versailles until after Colo. Laurens had procured the Promise of Men and Ships: but let it be considered Colo. Laurens brought with him my Credentials to their high Mightinesses, and Instructions to Dr. Franklin to acquaint the Court of Versailles with it and request their Countenance and Aid to me. Colo. Laurens arrived in March. On the 16th. of April I acquainted the Duke de la Vauguyon at the Hague, that I had recieved such Credentials, and the next day waited on him in Person, and had that day and the next two Hours Conversation with him each day upon the subject, in which I informed him of my Intention to go to their high Mightinesses. All this he transmitted to the Comte de Vergennes; and tho' it might procure me the Reputation of Vanity and Obstinacy, I shall forever believe that it contributed to second and accelerate Colo. Laurens's Negotiations, who succeeded to a Marvel, tho' Dr. Franklin says he gave great offence. I have long since learned that a Man may give offence and yet succeed. The very Measures necessary for Success may be pretended to give offence.

The earnest Opposition made by the Duke de la Vauguyon, only served to give me a more full and ample persuasion and assurance of the Utility and Necessity of the Measure. His Zeal convinced me, that he had a stronger Apprehension that I should make a great Impression somewhere, than I had myself. "Sir, says he, the King and the United States are upon very intimate Terms of Friendship. Had not You better wait until We can make the Proposition in Concert?" God grant they may ever continue in perfect friendship says I: but this friendship does not prevent your Excellency from conducting your Negotiations without consulting me. Why then am I obliged, in proposing a simple Treaty of Commerce, which the United States have reserved the entire Right of proposing, to consult your Excellency? If I were about to propose an Alliance, or to invite or admit the Dutch to accede to the Alliance between the King and the States, I should think myself obliged to consult your Excellency.

"But, says he, there is a Loan talked of to be opened by the United States here under the Warranty of the King. How will it look for You to go to the States without my Concurrence?" Of this I know nothing, says I, but one thing I know, that if such a Loan should be proposed, the Proposition I propose to make to the States, instead of obstructing will facilitate it, and your Proposal of a Loan will rather countenance me.

"Is there not danger, says he, that the Empress of Russia and the other Northern Powers will take offence at your going to the States General before them?" Impossible says I. They all know that the Dutch have been our old Friends and Allies: that We shall have more immediate Connections of Commerce with Holland than with them. But what is decisive in this matter is America and Holland have now a common Enemy in England at open War, which is not the Case of the Northern Powers.

"Had you not better wait, until I can write to the Comte de Vergennes and have his Opinion?" I know already beforehand says I, what his Opinion will be. "Ay what?" Why directly against it. "For what Reason?" Because the Comte de Vergennes will not commit the Dignity of the King, or his own Reputation, by advising me to apply until he is sure of Success; and in this he may be right: but the United States stand in a different Predicament. They have nothing to lose by such a Measure, and may gain a great deal.

"But, says he, if Holland should join England in the War, it will be unfortunate." If there was danger of this, says I, a Proposition from the United States would be one of the surest means of preventing it: but the Situation of Holland is such, that I am persuaded they dare not join England. It is against their Consciencies, and they are in bodily Fear of an hundred thousand Men from France. "God, says he, You have used an Argument now that You ought to speak boldly and repeat peremptorily in all Companies, for this People are governed very much by Fear." I have however spoken upon this Subject with delicacy upon all occasions, and shall continue to do so, says I, but shall make no Secret that I am sensible of it.

After turning the Subject in all the Lights it could bear, I told him, that I believed he had urged every objection against the Measure that could be thought of, but that I was still clear in my former Opinion. "Are You decided to go to the States?" Yes Sir. I must say I think it my Duty. "Very well. In that Case, says he, You may depend upon it, I will do all in my Power as a Man to countenance and promote your Application."

DUTCH RECOGNITION

To Benjamin Rush

My dear Sir   The Hague April 22. 1782

Mr Peter Paulus, is seized with an enthusiasm to go to Philadelphia, with his Journeymen.

I Should be much obliged to you, for any Advice or Civility you may Show him.

The Batavian Spirit is at last arroused, and has uttered its Voice, with Majesty, for the Souvereignty of the United States of America. The 19 of April, was the memorable day, when their High Mightinesses took, the Resolution. You will see in the Gazettes, the Petitions and Maneuvres, which ushered in this Event with Such Solemnity, as to make it the most Signal Epocha, in the History of a Century. We shall have in this Nation, if I am not infinitely mistaken a faithfull and affectionate and most usefull Ally.

In order to be Steady and persevering in my known Character for Vanity which however I have acquired Since I came to Europe, by the Help of Friends I must tell you that Don Liano, the Spanish Minister has this Moment gone out of my appartment, after having Said to me, "You have made Sir, the grandest Step that has ever yet been taken. It is you, who have filled this Nation with Enthusiasm for your Cause and turned their Heads. It is a most important, and a most decisive Measure, and it is due, to you."

Voila! a flour of diplomatick Rhetorick, enough to turn my Head, whether I have turned those of the Dutchmen or not.

Yours Affectionately   J. Adams

"PRESERVE YOUR INNOCENCE"

To John Quincy Adams

My Child

Yours of March 20/31 I have received.

I am well pleased with your learning German for many Reasons, and principally because I am told that Science and Literature flourish more at present in Germany than any where. A Variety of Languages will do no harm unless you should get an habit of attending more to Words than Things.

But, my dear Boy, above all Things, preserve your Innocence, and a pure Conscience. Your morals are of more importance, both to yourself and the World than all Languages and all Sciences. The least Stain upon your Character will do more harm to your Happiness than all Accomplishments will do it good.—I give you Joy of the safe Arrival of your Brother, and the Acknowledgment of the Independance of your Country in Holland. Adieu.

April 28, 1782

"I AM NO KING KILLER"

To the Marquis de Lafayette

Hotel des Etats Unis de L'Amerique, a la Haye

My dear General   May 21. 1782

Yours of the Seventh of this month, was yesterday brought me, by Mr Ridley, and I thank you for your kind Congratulations, on the Progress of our Cause in the Low Countries. Have a Care, however, how you profess Friendship for me: there may be more danger in it, than you are aware of.

I have the Honour, and the Consolation to be a Republican on Principle. That is to Say, I esteem that Form of Government, the best, of which human Nature is capable. Almost every Thing that is estimable in civil Life, has originated under Such Governments. Two Republican Towns, Athens and Rome, have done more honour to our Species, than all the rest of it. A new Country, can be planted only by Such a Government. America would at this moment have been an howling Wilderness in habited only by Bears and Savages, without Such forms of Government. And it would again become a Wilderness under any other. I am not however an enthusiast, who wishes to overturn Empires and Monarchies, for the Sake of introducing Republican Forms of Government. And therefore I am no King Killer, King Hater or King Despizer. There are Three Monarcks in Europe for whom I have as much Veneration as it is lawfull for one Man to have for another. The King of France, the Emperor of Germany and the King of Prussia, are constant objects of my Admiration, for Reasons of Humanity Wisdom and Beneficence which need not be enlarged on. You may well think then, that the Information you give me, that "the King of France was pleased the other day to Speak to you, of me in terms of the highest Regard," gave me great Pleasure.

I Shall do all in my Power to obtain here a Loan of Money but with very faint hopes of Success. In Short, there is no Money here but what is already promised to France, Spain, England Russia Sweeden Denmark, the Government here, and what will be fatal to me is the East India Comany have just opened a Loan for Nine Millions of florins under the Warrantee of the States of Holland and with an augmented Interest.

My Hopes of a Speedy Peace, are not Sanguine. I have Suspicions of the Sincerity of Lord Shelburne, Dunning and others of his Connections which I wish may prove groundless: but untill they are removed, I shall not expect a Peace. Shelbourne affects to be thought, the Chatham of the Day, without any of his great Qualities. I much fear that all their Maneuvres about Peace will turn out, but Artifices, to raise the stocks. The British Cabinet is so divided, that my Expectations are not very high. Let us be upon our Guard and prepared for a Continuance of the War. The Spaniards will demand Cessions and the Dutch Restitutions, which the English will not yet agree to, if they should get over all the Claims of France and America.

I Should be very happy to have a personal Conversation with you, but this will hardly take Place, untill full Powers arrive in Paris from London and I know very well that whether in America or Versailles or Paris, you will be constantly usefull, to America, and Congress will easily approve of your Stay where you are, untill you shall think it more for the publick Good to go elsewhere.

With great Affection and Esteem I have the Honour to be &c

"THE DIVINE SCIENCE OF POLITICKS"

To James Warren

dear Sir   The Hague June 17. 1782
Broken to Pieces and worn out, with the Diseases engendered by the tainted Atmosphere of Amsterdam operating upon the Effects of fatiguing Journeys dangerous Voyages, a Variety of Climates and eternal Anxiety of Mind, I have not been able to write you so often as I wished: But now I hope the fine Season and the pure Air of the Hague, will restore me. Perhaps You will say that the Air of a Court is as putrid as that of Amsterdam. In a moral and political sense perhaps, but I am determined that the bad Morals and false Politicks of other People shall no longer affect my Repose of Mind, nor disturb my

Physical Constitution. What is it to me, after having done all I can to set them right whether other People go to Heaven or to the Devil? I may howl and weep but this will have no Effect. I may then just as well Sing and laugh.

Pray how do you like your new Allies the Dutch? Does your Imagination rove into futurity and Speculate and combine, as it used to do? It is a pretty Amusement to play a Game with Nations, as if they were Fox and Geese—or Corns upon a Checkerboard—or the Personages at Chess, is it not? It is however, the real Employment of a statesman to play such a Game sometimes, a sublime one truly, enough to make a Man serious, however Addicted to sport. Politicks are the divine Science after all. How is it possible that any Man should ever think of making it Subservient to his own little Passions, and mean private Interests? Ye base born sons of fallen Adam! Is the End of Politicks a Fortune a Family, a gilded Coach, a Train of Horses a troup of Livery servants—Balls at Court—Splendid Dinners and suppers? Yet the divine Science of Politicks is at length in Europe reduced to a mechanical system composed of these Materials—what says the Muse Mrs Warren?

What is to become of an independent Statesman? One, who will bow the Knee to no Idol? who will worship nothing as a Divinity, but Truth, Virtue and his Country? I will tell you, he will be regarded more, by posterity than those who worship Hounds and Horses, and although he will not make his own Fortune he will make the Fortune of his Country. The Liberties of Corsica, sweeden and Geneva may be over turned, but neither his Character can be hurt nor his Exertions rendered ineffectual. Oh Peace, when wilt thou permit me to Visit Penshill Milton Hill and all the Blue Hills? I love every Tree and every Rock upon all those Mountains. Roving among these and the Quails Partridges squirrells &c that inhabit them shall be the amusement of my declining Years God willing. I wont go to Vermont. I must be within the Scent of the sea.

I hope to send along a Treaty in two or three Months. I love the Dutchmen with all their Faults. There is a strong Spirit of Liberty among them, and many excellent Qualities. Next year, their Navy will be so strong as to be able to do a great deal. They may do some thing this.

I am going to Court to sup with Princes, Princesses and

Ambassadors. I had rather sup with you at one of our Hills, though I have no Objection to Supping at Court. Adieu.

"ENGLAND DESERVES TO BE DAMNED"

To Philip Mazzei

Sir   The Hague July 3. 1782
    I have received the Letter, which you did me the Honour to write me the 21. May, and thank you for your Congratulations, on the Tryumph the American Cause has gained, in this Country. I call it a Tryumph because, it prevailed over great obstacles, long Habits of Friendship, vast Interests of Capitalists in the Stocks, intimate ancient and modern Connections of ruling Families, and multifarious little Intrigues, from Several other Courts; I cannot call them refined as you do: to me, they appear gross.
    I am not able to give you any Advice in the World. I dont believe you will succeed in any Attempt to borrow Money, but you may know better than my belief.
    England is not cured of her Delirium, as yet. But the Devil is in the other Powers of Europe, if they Suffer the war to continue much longer. We shall have Ireland, in Alliance with America, France, Spain and Holland, very soon for what I know: and a lucky or unlucky Game and Cards may throw all Europe together by the Ears.
    It is so easy and Simple to pacify the Universe that it is amazing it is not done. The System of Mankind is arranged exactly for the Purpose. There is nothing wanting, but for the confederated Neutral Powers, to admit the United States of America, to acceed to the Principles of the armed Neutrality, and the Business is done. England herself would rejoice in it, and, in her Heart thank those Powers, and the belligerent Powers, after this, would chicane but a very little time about Peace.
    By keeping open this Dispute, the Neutral Powers may begin to think England too much weakened, and France and Spain too much Strengthened and by and by all may be embroiled. I dont know that America, need distress herself much about

this, for the more miserable the Powers of Europe make their Subjects at home, the more will emigrate.

England is So equally divided into Parties, that neither has an Influence decided enough to acknowledge American Independence: but if the Example were set by the neutral Powers, the honest Party in England, would gain by it, Sufficient Authority to venture on the step.

If you are in a Situation to learn the refined Intrigues, as you call them, here, I wish you would explain them to me, for one can learn more in such a round about way, of such Things, than is to be got directly, nearer home.

We may make ourselves very easy, for neither "refined Intrigues" nor crude Intrigues, nor gross Intrigues, nor wicked Intrigues, can much injure Us. The Rescources of our Country appear greater and greater, every Year and the Population, Wealth, and Power of the United States, augment every day, in the midst of the War. I have recd a Letter within four days from Boston which informs me, that the Numbers of People, have increased by many Thousands, Since a Valuation in 1778, according to a new one lately taken, that the Property was proportionally increased, and that even the horned Cattle had increased by many Thousands, notwithstanding the immense Consumption of Beef, by the American Army, the French, Spanish and even English Fleets and Armies, in the West Indies, and in the United States, for all those derive a great Part of their supplies of Provisions, directly or indirectly from New England.

Old England deserves to be damned, and will be, without Repentance for having ever indulged the desire or conceived the Thought of enslaving such a Country: and a great Part of Europe deserve little less, for having viewed the accursed Project, with so much Indifference and Lukewarmness. I never could find an Image to represent the wickedness of this attempt in Britain. Herods murder of the Innocents was a trifle in comparison. Lady Macbeth uttered a Sentiment a little like it.

> "I have given Suck; and know how tender tis to love
> the Babe that milks me: yet would I: even when 'twas
> smiling in my face; have plucked my Nipple from its
> boneless Gums and dash'd the Branis out."

Stop Mother! You may pluck away the Nipple, if you please But the Boy is too big for the rest—have a Care, Mamma!

Such a total Deprivation of all the Moral Sentiments and natural Feelings, must and ever will be punished. Let Us lament that human Nature is capable of such Baseness, but let Us rejoice too, that it is capable of Elevation enough to resist it.

But I am wandering while I should asure you of the Esteem &c.

"I MUST BE AN INDEPENDENT MAN"

To Abigail Adams

My dearest Friend   The Hague July 1. 1782

Your charming Letters of April 10 and 22d were brought me, Yesterday. That of 22d is upon Business. Mr. Hill is paid I hope. I will honour your Bill if you draw. But be cautious—dont trust Money to any Body. You will never have any to lose or to spare. Your Children will want more than you and I shall have for them.

The Letter of the 10 I read over and over without End—and ardently long to be at the blue Hills, there to pass the Remainder of my feeble days. You would be surprised to see your Friend—he is much altered. He is half a Century older and feebler than ever you knew him. The Horse that he mounts every day is of service to his Health and the Air of the Hague is much better than that of Amsterdam, and besides he begins to be a Courtier, and Sups and Visits at Court among Princesses and Princes, Lords and Ladies of various Nations. I assure you it is much wholesomer to be a complaisant, good humoured, contented Courtier, than a Grumbletonian Patriot, always whining and snarling.

However I believe my Courtierism will never go any great Lengths. I must be an independent Man, and how to reconcile this to the Character of Courtier is the Question.

A Line from Unkle Smith of 6. of May makes me tremble for my Friend and brother Cranch! I must hope he is recoverd.

I can tell you no News about Peace. There will be no

Seperate Peaces made, not even by Holland—and I cannot think that the present English Ministry are firm enough in their Seats to make a general Peace, as yet.

When shall I go home? If a Peace should be made, you would soon see me.—I have had strong Conflicts within, about resigning all my Employments, as soon as I can send home a Treaty. But I know not what is duty as our Saints say. It is not that my Pride or my Vanity is piqued by the Revocation of my envied Commission. But in such Cases, a Man knows not what Construction to put. Whether it is not intended to make him resign. Heaven knows I never solicited to come to Europe. Heaven knows too what Motive I can have, to banish my self from a Country, which has given me, unequivocal Marks of its Affection, Confidence and Esteem, to encounter every Hardship and every danger by Sea and by Land, to ruin my Health, and to suffer every Humiliation and Mortification that human Nature can endure.

What affects me most is the Tryumph given to Wrong against Right, to Vice against Virtue, to Folly vs. Wisdom, to Servility against Independance, to base and vile Intrigue against inflexible Honour and Integrity. This is saying a great deal, but it is saying little more than Congress have said upon their Records, in approving that very Conduct for which I was sacrificed.—I am sometimes afraid that it is betraying the Cause of Independence and Integrity or at least the Dignity, which they ought to maintain, to continue in the service. But on the other Hand I have thought, whether it was not more dangerously betraying this Dignity, to give its Ennemies, perhaps the compleat Tryumph which they wished for and sought but could not obtain.

You will see, the American Cause has had a signal Tryumph in this Country. If this had been the only Action of my Life, it would have been a Life well spent. I see with Smiles and Scorn, little despicable Efforts to deprive me of the Honour of any Merit, in this Negotiation, but I thank God, I have enough to shew. No Negotiation to this or any other Country was every recorded in greater detail, as the World will one day see. The Letters I have written in this Country, are carefully preserved. The Conversations I have had are remembered. The Pamphlets, the Gazettes, in Dutch and French, will shew to Posterity, when it comes to be known what share I have had in them as it will be, it will be seen that the Spanish Ambassador expressed but the litteral Truth, when He said

"Monsieur a frappé la plus grand Coup de tout L'Europe.— Cette Reconnaisance fait un honneur infinie a Monsieur.— C'est lui qui a effrayée et terrassee les Anglomanes. C'est lui qui a rempli cet nation d'Enthusiasm."—&c.

Pardon a Vanity, which however is conscious of the Truth, and which has a right to boast, since the most Sordid Arts and the grossest Lies, are invented and propagated, by Means that would disgrace the Devil, to disguise the Truth from the sight of the World. I laugh at this, because I know it to be impossible. Silence!

Draft of the Memorial to the Sovereigns of Europe

Sir   The Hague July 1782
    This War has already continued so many Years, been extended to so many Nations, and been attended with so many unnatural and disagreable Circumstances that Every Man, who is not deficient in the Sentiments of Philanthropy, must wish to see Peace, restored upon just Principles, to Mankind: I shall therefore make no other Apology, for the Liberty I take in Writing this Letter, not in a public ministerial Character, but in a private and confidential Manner So that it is not expected or desired that you should make any further Use of it, then for your private amusement, unless you should judge it proper, to take any publick steps in Consequence of it, in which Case you are at Liberty to make what Use of it you think proper.
    All the World professes to wish for Peace: England professes Such a Desire, France, Spain, Holland and America, profess it. The neutral Powers, profess it, and Some of them are giving themselves much Trouble, by Negotiations and offers of Mediation to accomplish, it, either generally or at least partially. All the Nations at War with England seem to be be very well

agreed in the Sentiment, that any partial or Seperate Peace, would only retard a general Peace, and therefore do more harm than good, and this Sentiment, is past all doubt perfectly just.

What Measures than can be taken, with any plausible appearance of Probability to bring about a General Peace?

Great Britain, is in a Situation as critical as any Nation was ever known to Stand in. Ireland and all her foreign Dominions discontented, and almost ripe to follow the Example of the United states of America in throwing off, all their Connections with her. The Nation at home, nearly equally divided between the old Ministry and the New, and between the old System and the new, So that no Party, has an Influence sufficiently clear to take any decided Step. A Sentiment of Compassion for England, may take Place in Some of the neutral Powers, and after sometime induce them, especially if any new Motive should turn up, to become Parties to the War, and thus involve all Nations in a flame.

America has perhaps the least to dread, perhaps the most to gain by Such an Event of any of the Nations of the World. She would wish however to avoid it. But the Question is, in what manner?

If England could be unanimous, in the only Plan of Wisdom she might easily resolve this Question, by instantly declaring the United states of America, A souvereign and independent state—and by inviting them as Such to a Congress, for a general Pacification, under the Mediation of the two Imperial Courts as was proposed last Year. But the present british Ministers are not Sufficiently Seated in the Confidence of the King or the Nation to venture upon so Striking a Measure. The King would be displeased, the Nation allarmed, and the old Ministry and their Partisans, would raise a popular Cry against them, that they had Sacraficed the Honour and Dignity of the Crown and the essential Interests of the Nation.

Something is therefore wanting, to enable the Government in England to do what is absolutely necessary for the Safety of the Nation. In order to discover what that is, it is necessary to recollect, a Resolution of Congress of the

5th. of October 1780, in these Words

"Her Imperial Majesty of all the Russias, attentive to the Freedom of Commerce, and the Rights of Nations, in her

Declaration to the belligerent and neutral Powers, having proposed Regulations founded on Principles of Justice, Equity and Moderation, of which their most Christian and Catholic Majestys, and most of the neutral maritime Powers of Europe, have declared their Approbation, Congress willing to testify their Regard to the Rights of Commerce, and their Respect for the Sovereign, who hath proposed, and the Powers who have approved the said Regulations.

Resolve, that the Board of Admiralty prepare and Report Instructions for the Commanders of armed Vessells, commissioned by the United States, conformable to the Principles contained in the Declaration of the Empress of all the Russias, on the Rights of neutral Vessells.

That the Ministers Plenipotentiary, from the United States, if invited thereto, be, and hereby are, respectively impowerd to accede to Such Regulations, conformable to the Spirit of the Said Declaration, as may be agreed upon, by the Congress expected to assemble in pursuance of the Invitation of her imperial Majesty."

This Resolution, I had the Honour on the 8th of March 1781 of communicating to their High Mightinesses, and to the Ministers of Russia, Sweeden and Denmark residing at the Hague, and to inform them, that I was ready and desirous of pledging the Faith of the United states, to the Observances of the Principles of the armed Neutrality, according to that Resolution of Congress.

Now I Submit it to your Consideration sir, whether the Simplest and most natural Method of bringing this War to a General Conclusion is not, for the neutral Powers to admit a Minister from Congress to acceed to the Principles of the marine Treaty of Neutrality in the Same manner as France and Spain have done.

But it will be Said this is Acknowledging the Souvereignty of the United States of America. Very true—and for this very Reason it is desirable, because it settles the main question of the Controversy, it immediately reconciles, all the illdisposed Part of the English Nation to the Measure, it prepares the Way to the two Imperial Courts to invite the Ministers of the United states of America to a Congress, for making Peace under their Mediation, and enables the British Ministry to reconcile the

King and the present opposition to an Act of Parliament declaring America independent, and most probably is the only Method of Saving Great Britain herself from all the Horrors of an internal civil war.

This great Point once decided, the Moderation of the belligerent Powers and the impartial Equity of the two imperial mediating Courts, would leave no room to doubt of a Speedy general Peace.

Without Some such Interposition of the Neutral Powers, the War will probably be prolonged untill a civil War breaks out in England, for which the Parties there appear to be nearly ripe. The Vanity of that Nation will always enable artfull Men to flatter it, with illusive hopes of Divisions among their Ennemies, of Reconciliation with America, and of Seperate Peace with some that they make take vengeance on others. But these are all Delusions—America will never be unfaithfull to their Allies nor to herself.

I wish therefore, Sir, for your Advice, whether it would not be prudent for the States General to take Some Steps. To propose this matter to the Considerations of the Empress of Russia, the Emperor of Germany and all the other Neutral Courts —or at least to instruct their Ambassadors at all those Courts, to promote, the Admission of the United states of America to become Parties to the late Marine Treaty.

"NO FRIENDSHIP FOR FRANKLIN"

To Edmund Jenings

Sir   The Hague 20. July 1782

The more I reflect upon the late Revolution in the British Ministry the more I am Struck, with the Conduct of Mr Fox. I am become, upon certain Conditions his Admirer. The Conditions are two

1. That his Conduct has been the Result of Deliberation and Judgment, not of mere Jealousy Ambition, or Resentment.

2. That he has Patience and Fortitude enough to persevere, to the End.

His Conduct, appears to me Such, as that of a Man whose large Mind embraced, the whole Scheme of the Affairs and Relations of his Country, and capable of Seizing the only Clue which remained for extricating her out of that Entanglement in which the old Ministry had left her, ought to have been. If he stands fast upon the Ground he has taken, he will Shew himself worthy to be the Man of the People, and must finally prevail, if his Idea had been adopted and America declared a Sovereign State by Act of Parliament, the Way would have been clear, for the King to consent, that the two Imperial Courts Should immediately acknowledge American Independence by Admitting Mr Dana to Sign the Treaty of armed Neutrality, or otherwise as they pleased and invite Dr Franklin and Mr Jay to a Congress, for a general Peace, under their Mediation. These Combinations of Objects, are easy and natural although one of the Objects is unweildy, I mean the Armed Neutrality. As it is in the Power of this body So easily to pacify the World, it is their Duty to do it, by acknowledging the United states. Peace would soon follow.

Pray has not Parliament Seperated without agreeing to the Taxes for Paying the Interest of the last Loan? Is not this unprecedented? and what will be the Consequence? Will it not wound public Credit?

Lord Shelburne, had it in his Power to have pacified the World, and has failed. Mr Fox saw how to do it, but shelburnes opposition took away from him the Power. But shelburne would not have opposed, if Franklin had not piddled. If Vergennes and Franklin had decidedly refused to see any Agent about Peace, who had not a Commission and full Powers to treat with the United states of America the British stocks and Spirits would have fallen so low that shelburne and all the rest would have been compelled to have adopted Mr Fox's present Idea. But F. must make himself a Man of Consequence by piddling with Men who had no Title. But thus it is, that Men of great Reputations may do as many Weak Things as they please, and to remark their Mistakes is to envy them. I neither envy him however, nor his confidential Agent Mr Alexander. His base Jealousy of me and his Sordid Envy of my Commission for making Peace, and especially of my Commission for making a Treaty of Commerce with Great Britain have Stimulated him to attempt to commit an assassination upon my Character at Philidelphia, of which the World has not Yet heard, and of which it cannot hear untill the Time shall come when many voluminous state Papers may be laid before the Publick, which ought not to be, untill We are all dead. But this I Swear, I will affirm when and where I please that he has been actuated and is still by a low Jealousy and a meaner Envy of me, let the C. Vergennes or F. himself complain of it again to congress if they please, it would be my Joy to answer there in Person or by Letter. The anonimous scribbler charged me with clandestinely hurting Franklin. I have done nothing clandestinely. I have complained of Franklins Behaviour, in Company with Americans so I have in Company with the French and Spanish Ambassadors, without any Injunctions or desires of Seccresy. This is an odd Sort of Clandestinity. That I have no Friendship for Franklin I avow. That I am incapable of having any with a Man of his moral Sentiments, I avow. As Far as cruel Fate shall compell me to act with him in publick affairs, I shall treat him with decency and perfect Impartiallity, further than that I can feel for him no other sentiments than Contempt or Abhorrence. In my Soul I believe of him all that Burke says of shelburne. Yet to undertake to lay before the public all the Reasons I have for believing so would do more hurt at present than his Neck and mine too are both worth, and therefore I have Said and shall say as little about it, as is consistent with my Honour. Will you give my affectionate Regards to Mr Laurens and tell him, that all that is said by the anonimous scribbler is a Lye. That if he will accept of this Mission I will resign it in a Moment. That I love and esteem him, and ever did, and have ever openly publickly and privately avowed it.

Adieu, my dear sir Adieu   J. Adams

DIPLOMATIC SUCCESS

To James Warren

Dear Sir   The Hague Septr. 6th. 1782
   I thank You for the Papers and your Card of 22d July. The

Letters inclosed I shall send along. My Friends have all become as tender of me as You are; and to save me trouble send me no Letters: so I know nothing about You. I hope You have not been all sick as I have. I hope You have not all quite so much Business as I have to do; at least I hope it is to better effect, and to more profit, both public and private.

To negotiate a Loan of Money, to sign the obligations for it, to make a thousand Visits, some idle, some not idle, all necessary —to write Treaties in English, and be obliged to have them translated into French and Dutch, and to reason and discuss every Article to— to— to— to— to— &ca &ca. &ca. is too much for my Patience and Strength.

My Correspondence with Congress and their Ministers in Europe is a great deal of work. In short I am weary, and nobody pities me. Nobody seems to know any thing about me. Nobody knows that I do any thing or have any thing to do.

One thing, thank God, is certain. I have planted the American Standard at the Hague. There let it wave and fly! in Triumph over Sir Joseph York and British Pride. I shall look down upon the Flagg Staff with pleasure from the other World.

Not the Declaration of American Independence—not the Massachusetts Constitution—not the Alliance with France, ever gave me more Satisfaction or more pleasing Prospects for our Country than this Event. It is a Pledge against Friends and Enemies. It is an eternal Barrier against all Dangers from the House of Bourbon, as well as a present Security against England. Perhaps every Imagination dont rove into futurity, as much as mine, nor care so much about it.

My best Respects to Mrs. Warren and the Family, and believe me your Friend   John Adams

HAPPINESS AND SIMPLICITY

To Abigail Adams 2nd

My dear Daughter   The Hague, September 26, 1782
    I have received your charming letter, which you forgot to date, by Mrs. Rogers. Your proposal of coming to Europe to

keep your papa's house and take care of his health, is in a high strain of filial duty and affection, and the idea pleases me much in speculation, but not at all in practice. I have too much tenderness for you, my dear child, to permit you to cross the Atlantic. You know not what it is. If God shall spare me and your brother to return home, which I hope will be next Spring, I never desire to know of any of my family crossing the seas again.

I am glad you have received a small present. You ask for another; and although it would be painful for me to decline the gratification of your inclination, I must confess, I should have been happier if you had asked me for Bell's British Poets. There is more elegance and beauty, more sparkling lustre to my eyes, in one of those volumes, than in all the diamonds which I ever saw about the Princess of Orange, or the Queen of France, in all their birth-day splendour.

I have a similar request under consideration, from your brother at P. I don't refuse either, but I must take it *ad referendum*, and deliberate upon it as long as their H M do upon my propositions. I have learned caution from them, and you and your brother must learn patience from me.

If you have not yet so exalted sentiments of the public good as have others more advanced in life, you must endeavour to obtain them. They are the primary and most essential branch of general benevolence, and therefore the highest honour and happiness both of men and Christians, and the indispensable duty of both. Malevolence, my dear child, is its own punishment, even in this world. Indifference to the happiness of others must arise from insensibility of heart, or from a selfishness still more contemptible, or rather detestable. But for the same reason that our own individual happiness should not be our only object, that of our relatives, however near or remote, should not; but we should extend our views to as large a circle as our circumstances of birth, fortune, education, rank, and influence extend, in order to do as much good to our fellow men as we can.

You will easily see, my dear child, that jewels and lace can go but a very little way in this career. Knowledge in the head and virtue in the heart, time devoted to study or business, instead of show and pleasure, are the way to be useful and consequently happy.

Your happiness is very near to me. But depend upon it, it is simplicity, not refinement nor elegance that can obtain it. By conquering your taste, (for taste is to be conquered, like unruly appetites and passions, or the mind is undone,) you will save yourself many perplexities and mortifications. There are more thorns sown in the path of human life by vanity, than by any other thing.

I know your disposition to be thoughtful and serene, and therefore I am not apprehensive of your erring much in this way. Yet no body can be guarded too much against it, or too early.

Overwhelmed as I have been ever since you was born, with cares such as seldom fall to the lot of any man, I have not been able to attend to the fortunes of my family. They have no resource but in absolute frugality and incessant industry, which are not only my advice, but my injunctions upon every one of them.

With inexpressible tenderness of heart, I am Your affectionate father,   John Adams

From the Diary:
October 27–December 10, 1782

1782 OCT. 27. SUNDAY.

Went into the Bath, upon the Seine, not far from the Pont Royal, opposite the Tuilleries. You are shewn into a little Room, which has a large Window looking over the River into the Tuilleries. There is a Table, a Glass and two Chairs, and you are furnished with hot linnen, Towels &c. There is a Bell which you ring when you want any Thing.

Went in search of Ridley and found him. He says F has broke up the Practice of inviting every Body to dine with him on Sundays at Passy. That he is getting better. The Gout left him weak. But he begins to sit, at Table.

That J insists on having an exchange of full Powers, before he enters on Conference or Treaty. Refuses to treat with D'Aranda, untill he has a Copy of his Full Powers. Refused to treat with Oswald, until he had a Commission to treat with the Commissioners of the United States of America.—F. was afraid to insist upon it. Was afraid We should be obliged to treat without. Differed with J. Refused to sign a Letter &c. Vergennes wanted him to treat with D'Aranda, without.

The Ministry quarrel. De Fleury has attacked De Castries, upon the Expences of the Marine. Vergennes is supposed to be with De Fleury.—Talk of a Change of Ministry.—Talk of De Choiseul, &c.

F. wrote to Madrid, at the Time when he wrote his pretended Request to resign, and supposed that J. would succeed him at this Court and obtained a Promise that W. should be Sec. Jay did not know but he was well qualified for the Place.

Went to the Hotel D'orleans, Rue des petites Augustins, to see my Colleage in the Commission for Peace, Mr. Jay, but he and his Lady were gone out.

Mr. R. dined with me, and after dinner We went to view the Appartements in the Hotel du Roi, and then to Mr. J. and Mrs. Iz, but none at home. R. returned, drank Tea and spent the Evening with me. Mr. Jeremiah Allen, our Fellow Passenger in the leaky Sensible, and our Fellow Traveller through Spain, came in and spent the Evening. He has been home since and returned.

R. is still full of Js. Firmness and Independance. Has taken upon himself, to act without asking Advice or even communicating with the C de V—and this even in opposition to an Instruction. This Instruction, which is alluded to in a Letter I received at the Hague a few days before I left it, has never yet been communicated to me. It seems to have been concealed, designedly from me. The Commission to W. was urged to be filled up, as soon as the Commission came to O to treat with the Mins of the united States, and it is filled up and signed. W. has lately been very frequently with J. at his house, and has been very desirous of perswading F. to live in the same house with J.—Between two as subtle Spirits, as any in this World, the one malicious, the other I think honest, I shall have a delicate, a nice, a critical Part to Act. F.s cunning will be to divide Us. To this End he will provoke, he will insinuate, he will intrigue, he will maneuvre. My Curiosity will at least be employed, in observing his Invention and his Artifice. J. declares roundly, that he will never set his hand to a bad Peace. Congress may appoint another, but he will make a good Peace or none.

The present Conduct of England and America resembles that of the Eagle and Cat. An Eagle scaling over a Farmers Yard espied a Creature, that he thought an Hair. He pounced upon him and took him up. In the Air the Cat seized him by the Neck with her Teeth and round the Body with her fore and hind Claws. The Eagle finding Herself scratched and pressed, bids the Cat let go and fall down.—No says the Cat: I wont let go and fall, you shall stoop and set me down.

November 3, 1782

NOVEMBER 10. SUNDAY.

Accordingly at 8 this Morning I went and waited on the Comte. He asked me, how We went on with the English? I told him We divided upon two Points the Tories and Penobscot, two ostensible Points, for it was impossible to believe that My Lord Shelburne or the Nation cared much about such Points. I took out of my Pocket and shewed him the Record of Governour Pownals solemn Act of burying a Leaden Plate with his Inscription, May 23. 1759. Province of Massachusetts Bay. Penobscot. Dominions of Great Britain. Possession confirmed by Thomas Pownal Governor.

This was planted on the East Side of the River of Penobscot, 3 miles above Marine Navigation. I shew him also all the other Records—the Laying out of Mount Desert, Machias and all the other Towns to the East of the River Penobscot, and told him that the Grant of Nova Scotia by James the first to Sir William Alexander, bounded it on the River St. Croix. And that I was possessed of the Authorities of four of the greatest Governors the King of England ever had, Shirley, Pownal, Bernard and Hutchinson, in favour of our Claim and of Learned Writings of Shirley and Hutchinson in support of it. —The Comte said that Mr. Fitzherbert told him they wanted it for the Masts: but the C. said that Canada had an immense quantity. I told him I thought there were few Masts there, but that I fancied it was not Masts but Tories that again made the Difficulty. Some of them claimed Lands in that Territory and others hoped for Grants there.

The Comte said it was not astonishing that the British Ministry should insist upon Compensation to them, For that all the Precedents were in favour of it. That there had been no Example of an Affair like this terminated by a Treaty, without reestablishing those who had adhered to the old Government in all their Possessions. I begged his Pardon in this, and said that in Ireland at least their had been a Multitude of Confiscations without Restitution.—Here We ran into some Conversation concerning Ireland, &c. Mr. Rayneval, who was present talked about the national honour and the obligation they were under to support their Adherents.—Here I thought I might indulge a little more Latitude of Expression, than I had done with Oswald and Stratchey, and I answered, if the Nation thought itself bound in honour to compensate those People it might easily do it, for it cost the Nation more Money to carry on this War, one Month, than it would cost it to compensate them all. But I could not comprehend this Doctrine of national honour. Those People by their Misrepresentations, had deceived the Nation, who had followed the Impulsion of their devouring Ambition, until it had brought an indelible Stain on the British Name, and almost irretrievable Ruin on the Nation, and now that very Nation was thought to be bound in honour to compensate its Dishonourers and Destroyers. Rayneval said it was very true.

The Comte invited me to dine. I accepted. When I came I found the M. de la Fayette in Conference with him. When they came out the M. took me aside and told me he had been talking with the C. upon the Affair of Money. He had represented to him, Mr. Morris's Arguments and the Things I had said to him, as from himself &c. That he feared the Arts of the English, that our Army would disbande, and our Governments relax &c. That the C. feared many difficulties. That France had expended two hundred and fifty Millions in this War &c. That he talked of allowing six millions and my going to Holland with the Scheme I had projected, and having the Kings Warranty &c. to get the rest. That he had already spoken to some of Mr. De Fleury's Friends and intended to speak to him &c.

We went up to Dinner. I went up with the C. alone. He shewed me into the Room where were the Ladies and the Company. I singled out the Comtesse and went up to her, to make her my Compliment. The Comtess and the Ladies rose up, I made my Respects to them all and turned round and bowed to the reste of the Company. The Comte who came in after me, made his Bows to the Ladies and to the Comtesse last. When he came to her, he turned round and called out Monsieur Adams venez ici. Voila la Comtesse de Vergennes. A Nobleman in Company said Mr. Adams has already made his Court to Madame la Comtess. I went up again however and spoke again to the Comtess and she to me.—When Dinner was served, the Comte led Madame de Montmorin, and left me to conduct the Comtesse who gave me her hand with extraordinary Condescention, and I conducted her to Table. She made me sit next her on her right hand and was remarkably attentive to me the whole Time. The Comte who sat opposite was constantly calling out to me, to know what I would eat and to offer me petits Gateaux, Claret and Madeira &c. &c.— In short I was never treated with half the Respect at Versailles in my Life.

In the Antichamber before Dinner some French Gentlemen came to me, and said they had seen me two Years ago. Said that I had shewn in Holland that the Americans understand Negotiation, as well as War.

The Compliments that have been made me since my Arrival in France upon my Success in Holland, would be considered as a Curiosity, if committed to Writing. Je vous felicite sur votre Success, is common to all. One adds, Monsieur, Ma Foi, vous avez reussi, bien merveilleusement. Vous avez fait reconnoitre votre Independance. Vous avez fait un Traité, et vous avez procuré de l'Argent. Voila un Succés parfait.—Another says, vous avez fait des Merveilles en Hollande. Vous avez culbuté le Stathouder, et la Partie angloise. Vous avez donné bien de Mouvement. Vous avez remué tout le Monde.—Another said Monsieur vous etes le Washington de la Negotiation.—This is the finishing Stroke. It is impossible to exceed this.

Compliments are the Study of this People and there is no other so ingenious at them.

1782 NOVEMBER II. MONDAY.

Mr. Whitefoord the Secretary of Mr. Oswald came a second Time, not having found me at home Yesterday, when he left a Card, with a Copy of Mr. Oswalds Commission attested by himself (Mr. Oswald). He delivered the Copy and said Mr. Oswald was ready to compare it to the original with me. I said Mr. Oswalds Attestation was sufficient as he had already shewn me his original. He sat down and We fell into Conversation, about the Weather and the Vapours and Exhalations from Tartary which had been brought here last Spring by the Winds and given Us all the Influenza. Thence to french Fashions and the Punctuality with which they insist upon Peoples wearing thin Cloaths in Spring and fall, tho the Weather is ever so cold, &c. I said it was often carried to ridiculous Lengths, but that it was at Bottom an admirable Policy, as it rendered all Europe tributary to the City of Paris, for its Manufactures.

We fell soon into Politicks. I told him, that there was something in the Minds of the English and French, which impelled, them irresistably to War every Ten or fifteen Years. He said the ensuing Peace would he believed be a long one. I said it would provided it was well made, and nothing left in it to give future Discontents. But if any Thing was done which the Americans should think hard and unjust, both the English and French would be continually blowing it up and inflaming the American Minds with it, in order to make them join one Side or the other in a future War. He might well think, that the French would be very glad to have the Americans join them in future War. Suppose for Example they should think the Tories Men of monarchical Principles, or Men of more Ambition than Principle, or Men corrupted and of no Principle, and should therefore think them more easily seduced to their Purposes than virtuous Republicans, is it not easy to see the Policy of a French Minister in wishing them Amnesty and Compensation? Suppose, a french Minister foresees that the Presence of the Tories in America will keep up perpetually two Parties, a French Party and an English Party, and that this will compell the patriotic and independant Party to join the French Party is it not natural for him to wish them restored? 3. Is it not easy to see, that a French Minister cannot wish to have the English and Americans perfectly agreed upon all Points before they themselves, the Spaniards and Dutch, are agreed too. Can they be sorry then to see us split upon such a Point as the Tories? What can be their Motives to become the Advocates of the Tories? The french Minister at Philadelphia has made some Representations to Congress in favour of a Compensation to the Royalists, and the C. de Vergennes no longer than Yesterday, said much to Me in their favour. The Comte probably knows, that We are instructed against it, that Congress are instructed against it, or rather have not constitutional Authority to do it. That We can only write about it to Congress, and they to the States, who may and probably will deliberate upon it 18 Months, before they all decide and then every one of them will determine against it.—In this Way, there is an insuperable Obstacle to any Agreement between the English and Americans, even upon Terms to be inserted in the general Peace, before all are ready.—It was the constant Practice of The French to have some of their Subjects in London during the Conferences for Peace, in order to propagate such Sentiments there as they wished to prevail. I doubted not such were there now. Mr. Rayneval had been there. Mr. Gerard I had heard is there now and probably others. They can easily perswade the Tories to set up their Demands, and tell them and the Ministers that the Kings Dignity and Nations honour are compromised in it.

For my own Part I thought America had been long enough involved in the Wars of Europe. She had been a Football between contending Nations from the Beginning, and it was easy to foresee that France and England both would endeavour to involve Us in their future Wars. I thought it our Interest and Duty to avoid as much as possible and to be compleatly independent and have nothing to do but in Commerce with either of them. That my Thoughts had been from the Beginning constantly employed to arrange all our European Connections to this End, and that they would be continued to be so employed and I thought it so important to Us, that if my poor labours, my little Estate or (smiling) sizy blood could effect it, it should be done. But I had many fears.

I said the King of France might think it consistent with his Station to favour People who had contended for a Crown, tho it was the Crown of his Ennemy. Whitefoord said, they seem to be, through the whole of this, fighting for Reputation. I said they had acquired it and more. They had raised themselves high from a low Estate by it, and they were our good Friends and Allies, and had conducted generously and nobly and We should be just and gratefull, but they might have political Wishes, which We were not bound by Treaty nor in Justice or Gratitude to favour, and these We ought to be cautious off. He agreed that they had raised themselves very suddenly and surprisingly by it.

We had more Conversation on the State of Manners in France, England, Scotland and in other Parts of Europe, but I have not Time to record this.

1782 NOVEMBER 12. TUESDAY.

Dined with the Abby Chalut and Arnoux. The Farmer General, and his Daughter, Dr. Franklin and his Grand Son, Mr. Grand and his Lady and Neice, Mr. Ridley and I with one young French Gentleman made the Company. The Farmers Daughter is about 12 Years old and is I suppose an Enfant trouvee. He made her sing at Table, and she bids fair to be an accomplished Opera Girl, though she has not a delicate Ear. . . .

The Compliment of "Monsieur vous etes le Washington de la Negotiation" was repeated to me, by more than one Person. I answered Monsieur vous me faites le plus grand honour et la Compliment le plus sublime possible.—Eh Monsieur, en Verite vous l'avez bien merité.—A few of these Compliments would kill Franklin if they should come to his Ears.

This Evening I went to the Hotel des treize Etats Unis to see the Baron de Linden, to the Hotel de York to see the Messrs. Vaughans, and to the Hotel D'orleans to see Mr. Jay, but found neither. Returned through the Rue St. Honorée to see the decorated Shops, which are pretty enough. This is the gayest Street in Paris, in point of ornamented Shops, but Paris does not excell in this respect.

The old Farmer General was very lively at dinner. Told Stories and seemed ready to join the little Girl in Songs like a Boy.—Pleasures dont wear Men out in Paris as in other Places.

The Abby Arnoux asked me at Table, Monsieur ou est votre Fils Cadet qui chant, come Orphée.—Il est du retour en Amerique.—To Mademoiselle Labbard, he said Connoissez vous que Monsieur Adams a une Demoiselle tres aimable en Amerique?

NOVEMBER 17. SUNDAY.

Have spent several Days in copying Mr. Jays dispatches.

On Fryday the 15, Mr. Oswald came to Visit me, and entered with some Freedom into Conversation. I said many Things to him to convince him that it was the Policy of my Lord Shelburne and the Interest of the Nation to agree with Us upon the advantageous Terms which Mr. Stratchey carried away on the 5th. Shewed him the Advantages of the Boundary, the vast Extent of Land, and the equitable Provision for the Payment of Debts and even the great Benefits stipulated for the Tories.

He said he had been reading Mr. Paines Answer to the Abby Raynal, and had found there an excellent Argument in favour of the Tories. Mr. Paine says that before the Battle of Lexington We were so blindly prejudiced in favour of the English and so closely attached to them, that We went to war at any time and for any Object, when they bid Us. Now this being habitual to the Americans, it was excuseable in the Tories to behave upon this Occasion as all of Us had ever done upon all the others. He said if he were a Member of Congress he would shew a Magnanimity upon this Occasion, and would say to the Refugees, take your Property. We scorn to make any Use of it, in building up our System.

I replied, that We had no Power and Congress had no Power, and therefore We must consider how it would be reasoned upon in the several Legislatures of the separate States, if, after being sent by Us to Congress and by them to the several States in the Course of twelve or fifteen Months, it should be there, debated. You must carry on the War, Six or Nine months certainly, for this Compensation, and consequently spend in the Prosecution of it, Six or Nine times the Sum necessary to make the Compensation for I presume, this War costs every

Month to Great Britain, a larger Sum than would be necessary
to pay for the forfeited Estates.

How says I will an independant Man in one of our Assemblies consider this. We will take a Man, who is no Partisan of
England or France, one who wishes to do Justice to both and
to all Nations, but is the Partisan only of his own.

Have you seen says he, a certain Letter written to the C. de
V. wherein Mr. S.A. is treated pretty freely.—Yes says I and several other Papers in which Mr. J. Adams has been treated so
too. I dont know, what you may of heard in England of Mr.
S.A. You may have been taught to believe, for what I know,
that he eats little Children. But I assure you he is a Man of Humanity and Candour as well as Integrity, and further that he is
devoted to the Interest of his Country and I believe wishes
never to be, after a Peace, the Partisan to France or England,
but to do Justice and all the good he can to both. I thank you
for mentioning him for I will make him my orator. What will
he say, when the Question of Amnesty and Compensation to
the Tories, comes before the Senate of Massachusetts. And
when he is informed that England makes a Point of it and that
France favours her. He will say here are two old, sagacious
Courts, both endeavouring to sow the Seeds of Discord
among Us, each endeavouring to keep Us in hot Water, to
keep up continual Broils between an English Party and a
french Party, in hopes of obliging the Independent and patriotic Party, to lean to its Side. England wishes them here and
compensated, not merely to get rid of them and to save them
selves the Money, but to plant among Us Instruments of their
own, to make divisions among Us and between Us and
France, to be continually crying down the Religion, the Government, the Manners of France, and crying up the Language,
the Fashions, the Blood &c. of England. England also means
by insisting on our compensating these worst of Ennemies to
obtain from Us, a tacit Acknowledgment of the Right of the
War—an implicit Acknowledgment, that the Tories have been
justifiable or at least excuseable, and that We, only by a fortunate Coincidence of Events, have carried a wicked Rebellion
into a compleat Revolution.

At the very Time when Britain professes to desire Peace, Reconciliation, perpetual Oblivion of all past Unkindnesses, can

She wish to send in among Us, a Number of Persons, whose very Countenances will bring fresh to our Remembrance the whole History of the Rise, and Progress of the War, and of all its Atrocitys? Can she think it conciliatory, to oblige Us, to lay Taxes upon those whose Habitations have been consumed, to reward those who have burn'd them? upon those whose Property has been stolen, to reward the Thieves? upon those whose Relations have been cruelly destroyed, to compensate the Murtherers?

What can be the design of France on the other hand, by espousing the Cause of these Men? Indeed her Motives may be guessed at. She may wish to keep up in our Minds a Terror of England, and a fresh Remembrance of all We have suffered. Or She may wish to prevent our Ministers in Europe from agreeing with the British Ministers, untill She shall say that She and Spain are satisfyed in Points.

I entered largely with Mr. Oswald, into the Consideration of the Influence this Question would have upon the Councils of the British Cabinet and the Debates in Parliament. The King and the old Ministry might think their personal Reputations concerned, in supporting Men who had gone such Lengths, and suffered so much in their Attachment to them.—The K. may say I have other dominions abroad, Canada, Nova Scotia, Florida, the West India Islands, the East Indies, Ireland. It will be a bad Example to abandon these Men. Others will loose their Encouragement to adhere to my Government. But the shortest Answer to this is the best, let the King by a Message recommend it to Parliament to compensate them.

But how will My Lord Shelburne sustain the shock of Opposition? When Mr. Fox and Mr. Burke shall demand a Reason why the Essential Interests of the Nation, are sacrificed to the unreasonable demands of those very Men, who have done this great Mischief to the Empire. Should these Orators indulge themselves in Philippicks against the Refugees, shew their false Representations, their outragious Cruelties, their innumerable demerits against the Nation, and then attack the first Lord of the Treasury for continuing to spend the Bood and Treasure of the Nation for their Sakes.

Mr. Vaughan came to me Yesterday, and said that Mr. Oswald had that morning called upon Mr. Jay, and told him, if he
had known as much the day before as he had since learned, he
would have written to go home. Mr. V. said Mr. Fitzherbert
had received a Letter from Ld. Townsend, that the Compensation would be insisted on. Mr. Oswald wanted Mr. Jay to go to
England. Thought he could convince the Ministry. Mr. Jay said
he must go, with or without the Knowledge and Advice of this
Court, and in either Case it would give rise to jealousies. He
could not go. Mr. Vaughan said he had determined to go, on
Account of the critical State of his Family, his Wife being probably abed. He should be glad to converse freely with me, and
obtain from me, all the Lights and arguments against the Tories,
even the History of their worst Actions, that in Case it should
be necessary to run them down it might be done or at least expose them, for their true History was little known in England.
—I told him that I must be excused. It was a Subject that I had
never been desirous of obtaining Information upon. That I
pitied those People too much to be willing to aggravate their
Sorrows and Sufferings, even of those who had deserved the
Worst. It might not be amiss to reprint the Letters of G Bernard, Hutchinson and Oliver, to shew the rise. It might not be
amiss to read the History of Wyoming in the Annual Register
for 1778 or 9, to recollect the Prison Ships, and the Churches at
New York, where the Garrisons of Fort Washington were
starved in order to make them inlist into Refugee Corps. It
might not be amiss to recollect the Burning of Cities, and The
Thefts of Plate, Negroes and Tobacco.

I entered into the same Arguments with him that I had used
with Mr. Oswald, to shew that We could do nothing, Congress
nothing. The Time it would take to consult the States, and the
Reasons to believe that all of them would at last decide against
it. I shewed him that it would be a Religious Question with
some, a moral one with others, and a political one with more,
an Economical one with very few. I shewed him the ill Effect
which would be produced upon the American Mind, by this
Measure, how much it would contribute to perpetuate Alienation against England, and how french Emmissaries might by
means of these Men blow up the flames of Animosity and War.
I shewed him how the Whig Interest and the Opposition

might avail themselves of this Subject in Parliament, and how they might embarrass the Minister.

He went out to Passy, for a Passport, and in the Evening called upon me again. Said he found Dr. Franklins Sentiments to be the same with Mr. Jays and mine, and hoped he should be able to convince Lord Shelburne. He was pretty confident that it would work right.—The Ministry and Nation were not informed upon the Subject. Ld. Shelburne had told him that no Part of his office gave him so much Paine as the Levy he held for these People, and hearing their Stories of their Families and Estates, their Losses, Sufferings and Distresses. Mr. V. said he had picked up here, a good deal of Information, about those People, from Mr. Allen and other Americans.

Ridley, Allen and Mason, dined with me, and in the Evening Capt. Barney came in, and told me that Mr. Vaughan went off to day at noon. I delivered to Barney, Mr. Jays long Dispatches, and the other Letters.

In the Evening the Marquis de la Fayette came in and told me, he had been to see Mr. de Fleuri, on the Subject of a Loan. He told him that he must afford America this Year a Subsidy of 20 millions. Mr. de Fleuri said France had already spent 250 millions in the American War, and that they could not allow any more Money to her. That there was a great deal of Money in America. That the Kings Troops had been subsisted and paid there. That the British Army had been subsisted and paid there, &c. The Marquis said that little of the Subsistance or pay of the British had gone into any hands but those of the Tories within their Lines. I said that more Money went in for their Goods than came out for Provisions or any Thing. The Marquis added to Mr. Fleury that Mr. Adams had a Plan for going to the States General, for a Loan or a Subsidy. Mr. Fleury said he did not want the Assistance of Mr. Adams to get Money in Holland, he could have what he would. The M. said Mr. A. would be glad of it. He did not want to go, but was willing to take the Trouble, if necessary.

The Marquis said he should dine with the Queen tomorrow and would give her a hint, to favour Us. That he should take Leave in a few days and should go in the fleet that was to sail from Brest. That he wanted the Advice of Mr. F., Mr. J. and me before he went, &c. Said there was a Report that Mr. Gerard had been in England, and that Mr. de Rayneval was gone. I told him I saw Mr. Gerard at Mr. Jays a few Evenings ago.

He said he did not believe Mr. Gerard had been. That he had mentioned it to C. de V. and he did not appear confused at all, but said Mr. Gerard was here about the Limits of Alsace.

The Marquis said that he believed, the Reason why C. de Vergennes said so little about the Progress of Mr. Fitsherbert with him, was because the difficulty about Peace was made by the Spaniards and he was afraid of making the Americans still more angry with Spain. . . . He knew the Americans were very angry with the Spaniards.

NOVEMBER 18. MONDAY.

Returned Mr. Oswalds Visit. He says Mr. Stratchey who sat out the 5 did not reach London until the 10. . . . Couriers are 3, 4, or 5 days in going according as the Winds are.

We went over the old ground, concerning the Tories. He began to use Arguments with me to relax. I told him he must not think of that, but must bend all his Thoughts to convince and perswade his Court to give it up. That if the Terms now before his Court, were not accepted, the whole negotiation would be broken off, and this Court would probably be so angry with Mr. Jay and me, that they would set their Engines to work upon Congress, get us recalled and some others sent, who would do exactly as this Court would have them. He said, he thought that very probable. . . .

In another Part of his Conversation He said We should all have Gold Snuff Boxes set with Diamonds. You will certainly have the Picture. I told him no. I had dealt too freely with this Court. I had not concealed from them any usefull and neces-sary Truth, although it was disagreable. Indeed I neither ex-pected nor desired any favours from them nor would I accept any. I should not refuse any customary Compliment of that Sort, but it never had been nor would be offered me. . . . My fixed Principle never to be the Tool, of any Man, nor the Partisan of any Nation, would forever exclude me from the Smiles and favours of Courts.

In another Part of the Conversation, I said that when I was

young and addicted to reading I had heard about dancing on the Points of metaphisical Needles. But by mixing in the World, I had found the Points of political Needles finer and sharper than the metaphisical ones.

I told him the Story of Josiah Quincys Conversations with Lord Shelburne in 1774, in which he pointed out to him, the Plan of carrying on the War, which has been pursued this Year, by remaining inactive at Land and cruising upon the Coast to distress our Trade.

He said he had been contriving an artificial Truce since he found we were bound by Treaty not to agree to a separate Truce. He had proposed to the Ministry, to give Orders to their Men of War and Privateers, not to take any unarmed American Vessells.

I said to him, supposing the armed Neutrality should acknowledge American Independence, by admitting Mr. Dana who is now at Petersbourg with a Commission for that Purpose in his Pocket, to subscribe the Principles of their marine Treaty? The K. of G.B. could find no fault with it. He could never hereafter say, it was an Affront or Hostility. He had done it himself. Would not all Newtral Vessells have a right to go to America?—and could not all American Trade be carried on in Neutral Bottoms.

I said to him that England would always be a Country which would deserve much of the Attention of America, independently of all Considerations of Blood, Origin, Language, Morals &c. Merely as a commercial Country, She would forever claim the Respect of America, because a great Part of our Commerce would be with her provided She came to her Senses and made Peace with Us without any Points in the Treaty that should ferment in the Minds of the People. If the People should think themselves unjustly treated, they would never be easy, and they were so situated as to be able to hurt any Power. The Fisheries, the Mississippi, the Tories were points that would rankle. And that Nation that should offend our People in any of them, would sooner or later feel the Consequences.

Mr. Jay, Mr. Le Couteulx and Mr. Grand came in. Mr. Grand says there is a great Fermentation in England, and that they talk of uniting Lord North and Mr. Fox in Administration. D of Portland to come in and Keppel go out.—But this is wild.

You are afraid says M. Oswald to day of being made the Tools of the Powers of Europe.—Indeed I am says I.—What Powers says he.—All of them says I. It is obvious that all the Powers of Europe will be continually maneuvring with Us, to work us into their real or imaginary Ballances of Power. They will all wish to make of Us a Make Weight Candle, when they are weighing out their Pounds. Indeed it is not surprizing for We shall very often if not always be able to turn the Scale. But I think it ought to be our Rule not to meddle, and that of all the Powers of Europe not to desire Us, or perhaps even to permit Us to interfere, if they can help it.

I beg of you, says he, to get out of your head the Idea that We shall disturb you.—What says I do you yourself believe that your Ministers, Governors and even Nation will not wish to get Us of your Side in any future War?—Damn the Governors says he. No. We will take off their Heads if they do an improper thing towards you.

Thank you for your good Will says I, which I feel to be sincere. But Nations dont feel as you and I do, and your nation when it gets a little refreshed from the fatigues of the War, when Men and Money are become plenty and Allies at hand, will not feel as it does now.—We never can be such damned Sots says he as to think of differing again with you.—Why says I, in truth I have never been able to comprehend the Reason why you ever thought of differing with Us.

NOV. 20 WEDNESDAY.

Dr. Franklin came in, and We fell into Conversation. From one Thing to another, We came to Politicks. I told him, that it seemed uncertain whether Shelburne could hold his Ground without leaning Upon Ld. North on one hand or Fox on the other. That if he joined North, or North & Co. should come in, they would go upon a contracted System, and would join People at this Court to deprive Us of the Missisippi and the Fisheries &c. If Fox came in or joined Shelburne they would go upon a liberal and manly System, and this was the only Choice they had. No Nation had ever brought itself into such a Labyrinth perplexed with the demands of Holland, Spain, France and America. Their Funds were failing and the Money undertaken to be furnished was not found. Franklin said, that the Bank came in Aid, and he learned that large Sums of Scrip were lodged there.—In this Situation says I they have no Chance but to set up America very high—and if I were King of G.B. I would take that Tone. I would send the first Duke of the Kingdom Ambassador to Congress, and would negotiate in their favour at all the Neutral Courts &c. I would give the strongest Assurances to Congress of Support in the Fisheries, the Missisippi &c. and would compensate the Tories myself.

I asked what could be the Policy of this Court in wishing to deprive Us of the Fisheries? and Missisippi? I could see no possible Motive for it, but to plant Seeds of Contention for a future War. If they pursued this Policy they would be as fatally blinded to their true Interests as ever the English were.

Franklin said, they would be every bit as blind. That the Fisheries and Missisippi could not be given up. That nothing was clearer to him than that the Fisheries were essential to the northern States, and the Missisippi to the Southern and indeed both to all. I told him that Mr. Gerard had certainly appeared to America, to negotiate to these Ends, vizt. to perswade Congress to give up both. This was the Reason of his being so unpopular in America, and this was the Cause of their dislike to Sam Adams, who had spoken very freely both to Gerard and Congress on these heads. That Marbois appeared now to be pursuing the same Objects. Franklin said he had seen his Letter. I said I was the more surprized at this, as Mr. Marbois, on our Passage to America, had often said to me, that he thought the Fisheries our natural Right and our essential Interest, and that We ought to maintain it and be supported in it. Yet that he appeared now to be maneuvring against it.

I told him that I always considered their extraordinary Attack upon me, not as arising from any Offence or any Thing personal, but as an Attack upon the Fishery. There had been great debates in Congress upon issuing the first Commission for Peace, and in Setting my Instructions—that I was instructed not to make any Treaty of Commerce with Britain, without an express Clause acknowledging our Right to the Fishery. This Court knew that this would be, when communicated to the English, a strong Motive with them to acknowledge our Right, and to take away this they had directed their Intrigues against me, to get my Commission annulled, and had succeeded. They hoped also to gain some Advantage in these Points by associating others with me in the Commission for Peace. But they had failed in this for the Missisippi and Fishery were now much securer than if I had been alone. That Debates had run very high in Congress. That Mr. Drayton and Governieur Morris had openly espoused their Plan and argued against the Fishery. That Mr. Laurens and others of the Southern Gentlemen, had been staunch for them, and contended that as Nurseries of Seamen and Sources of Trade the Southern States were as much interested as the Northern. That Debates had run so high that the Eastern States had been obliged to give in their Ultimatum in Writing and to say they would withdraw, if any more was done, and that this Point was so tender and important that if not secured it would be the Cause of a Breach of the Union of the States—and their Politicks might for what I knew be so profound as to mean to lay a foundation for a rupture between the States, when in a few Years they should think them grown too big. I could see no possible Motive they had, to wish to negotiate the Missisippi into the hands of Spain, but this. Knowing the fine Country in the Neighbourhood, and the rapidity with which it would fill with Inhabitants, they might force their Way down the Missisipi and occasion another War. They had certainly Sense enough to know too that We could not and would not be restrained from the Fishery. That our People would be constantly pushing for it, and thus plunge themselves into another War, in which We should stand in need of France.

If the old Ministry in England should come in again, they would probably join this Court in attempting to deprive Us. But all would not succeed. We must be firm and steady, and should do very well.—Yes he said he believed We should do very well, and carry the Points.

I told him I could not think that the K. and Council here had formed any digested Plan against Us upon these Points. I hoped it was only the Speculation of Individuals.

I told him, that if Fox should know that Shelburne refused to agree with Us merely because We would not compensate the Tories, that he would attack the Minister upon this Ground and pelt him so with Tories as to make him uncomfortable. I thought it would be very well to give Fox an hint.—He said he would write him a Letter upon it. He had sometimes corresponded with him, and Fox had been in Conversation with him here, before I arrived.

I walked before Dinner to Mr. Jays, and told him, I thought there was danger, that the old Ministry would come in, or Shelburne unite with North. That the King did not love Us, and the old Ministry did not love Us: but they loved the Refugees, and thought probably their personal Characters concerned to support them. Rayneval was gone to England, and I wanted to have him watched to see, if he was ever in Company with North, Germain, Stormont, Hillsborough, Sandwich, Bute or Mansfield. If the wing clipping System and the Support of the Tories should be suggested by this Court to any of them it would fall in with their Passions and Opinions, for several of the old Ministry, had often dropped Expressions in the Debates in Parliament, that it was the Interest of England to prevent our Growth to Wealth and Power.

It was very possible, that a Part of the old Ministry might come in, and Richmond, Keppel, Townsend and Cambden go out, and in this Case, tho they could not revoke the Acknowledgment of our Independence, they would certainly go upon the contracted plan of clypping our Wings. In this Case it is true, England would be finally the Dupe, and it would be the most malicious Policy possible against her. It is agreed that if the Whigs go out, and Richmond, Keppell, Townsend, Cambden &c. join Fox and Burke in Opposition, there will be great Probability of a national Commotion and Confusion.

Mr. Jay agreed with me, in all I had said, and Added that six days would produce the Kings Speech. If that Speech should inform Parliament that he had issued a Commission to treat with the United States, and the two Houses should thank him for it, it would look as if a good Plan was to prevail: but if not, We should then take Measures to communicate it far, and wide.

I told him I thought, in that Case We should aid Opposition

as much as We could, by suggesting Arguments, to those who would transmit them in favour of America, and in favour of those who had the most liberal Sentiments towards America, to convince them that the Wing clipping Plan was ruinous to England, and the most generous and noble Part they could Act towards America, the only one that could be beneficial to the Nation, and to enable them to attack a contracted Ministry with every Advantage, that could be.

I thought it was now a Crisis, in which good Will or Ill will towards America would be carried very far in England, a time perhaps when the American Ministers may have more Weight in turning the Tide of Sentiment, or influencing the Changes of Administration than they ever had before and perhaps than they would have again. That I thought it our Duty, Upon this Occasion to say every Thing We could, to the Englishmen here, in order that just Sentiments might prevail in England at this Moment, to countenance every Man well disposed, and to disabuse and undeceive every body.

To drive out of Countenance and into Infamy, every narrow Thought of cramping, stinting, impoverishing or enfeebling Us. To shew that it is their only Interest to shew themselves our Friends, to wear away, if possible, the Memory of past Unkindnesses. To strike with Us now upon our own Terms, because tho We had neither Power nor Inclination to make Peace, without our Allies, yet the very report that We had got over all our difficulties would naturally make all Europe expect Peace, would tend to make Spain less exorbitant in her demands, and would make Holland more ardent for Peace, and dispose France to be more serious in her Importunities with Spain and Holland, and even render France herself easier, tho I did not imagine she would be extravagant in her Pretentions. To shew them the ruinous Tendency of the War if continued another Year or two.—Where would England be if the War continued 2 Years longer? What the State of her Finances? What her Condition in the E. and W. Indies, in N. America, Ireland, Scotland and even in England? What hopes have they of saving themselves from a civil War? If our Terms are not now accepted, they will never again have such offers from America. They will never have so advantageous a Line—never their Debts—never so much for the Tories, and perhaps a rigorous demand of Compensation for the Devastations they have committed.

Mr. Jay agreed with me in Sentiment, and indeed they are the Principles he has uniformly pursued thro the whole Negotiation before my Arrival. I think they cannot be misunderstood or disapproved in Congress.

There never was a Blunder in Politicks more egregious than will be committed by the present Ministry, if they attempt to save the Honour of the old Ministry and of the Tories. Shelburne may be too weak to combat them: but the true Policy would be to throw all the Odium of the War, and all the Blame of the Dismemberment of the Empire upon the old Ministers and the Tories. To run them down, tarnish them with Votes, envey against them in Speeches and Pamphlets, even strip them of the Pensions and make them both ridiculous, insignificant and contemptible, in short make them as wretched as their Crimes deserve. Never think of sending them to America. —But Shelburne is not strong enough. The old Party with the King at their Head, is too powerful, and popular yet.

I really pitty these People, as little as they deserve it. For surely no Men ever deserved worse of Society.

If Fox was in, and had Weight enough, and should take this decided Part which is consistent enough with the Tenor of his Speeches, which have been constant Phillippicks against the old Ministry and frequent Sallies against the Refugees, and should adopt a noble Line of Conduct towards America, grant her all She asks, do her honnour and promote her Prosperity, he would disarm the hostile Mind, and soften the resentful heart, recover much of the Affection of America, much of her Commerce, and perhaps equal Consideration and Profit and Power from her as ever. She would have no Governors nor Armies there and no Taxes, but She would have Profit, Reputation and Power.

Today I received a Letter from my Excellent Friend Mr. Laurens 12 Nov. London in answer to mine of the 6. agreeing as speedily as possible to join his Colleagues. "Thank God, I had a Son, who dared to die for his Country!"

Breakfasted at Mr. Jays, with Dr. Franklin, in Consultation upon the Propositions made to Us Yesterday by Mr. Oswald. We agreed unanimously, to answer him, that We could not consent to the Article, respecting the Refugees as it now stands. Dr. F. read a Letter upon the Subject which he had prepared to Mr. Oswald, upon the Subject of the Tories, which We had agreed with him that he should read as containing his private Sentiments.—We had a vast deal of Conversation upon the Subject. My Colleagues opened themselves, and made many Observations concerning the Conduct, Crimes and Demerits of those People.

Before Dinner Mr. Fitsherbert came in, whom I had never seen before. A Gentleman of about 33, seems pretty discreet and judicious, and did not discover those Airs of Vanity which are imputed to him.

He came in Consequence of the desire, which I expressed Yesterday of knowing the State of the Negotiation between him and the C. de Vergennes, respecting the Fishery. He told Us that the C. was for fixing the Boundaries, where each Nation should fish. He must confess he thought the Idea plausible, for that there had been great dissentious between the Fishermen of the two nations. That the french Marine Office had an whole Appartment full of Complaints and Representations of disputes. That the French pretended that Cape Ray was the Point Riche.

I asked him if the French demanded of him an exclusive Right to fish and dry between Cape Bona Vista and the Point riche. He said they had not expressly, and he intended to follow the Words of the Treaty of Utrecht and Paris without stirring the Point.

I shewed him an Extract of a Letter from the Earl of Egremont to the Duke of Bedford, March 1. 1763, in which it is said that by the 13 Art of the Treaty of Utrecht, a Liberty was left to the French to fish, and to dry their fish on Shore; and for that Purpose to erect the Necessary Stages and Buildings, but with an express Stipulation de ne pas sejourner dans la dite Isle, au dela du tems necessaire pour pêcher et sêcher le Poisson.— That it is a received Law among the Fishermen, that whoever arrives first, shall have the Choice of the Stations. That the Duke de Nivernois insisted, that by the Treaty of Utrecht the French had an exclusive Right to the Fishery from Cape Bona Vista to Point Riche. That the King gave to his Grace the D. of Bedford express Instructions to come to an Ecclaircissement upon the Point with the French Ministry, and to refuse the Exclusive Construction of the Treaty of Utrech &c.

I also shew him a Letter, from Sir Stanier Porteen, Lord Weymouths Secretary, to Ld. Weymouth, inclosing an Extract of Ld. Egremonts Letter to the Duke of Bedford, by which it appears that the Duke of Nivernois insisted

"That the French had an exclusive right to the Fishery from Cape Bona Vista to Point Riche, and that they had, on ceding the Island of Newfoundland to G. Britain by the 13 Article of the Treaty of Utrecht, expressly reserved to themselves such an exclusive Right, which they had constantly been in Possession of, till they were entirely driven from North America in the last War."

For these Papers I am obliged to Mr. Izard. Mr. Fitsherbert said it was the same Thing now Word for Word: but he should endeavour to have the Treaty conformable to those of Utrecht and Paris. But he said We had given it up, by admitting the Word "exclusive" into our Treaty.—I said perhaps not, for the whole was to be conformable to the true Construction of the Treaties of Utrecht and Paris, and that if the English did not now admit the exclusive Construction they could not contend for it vs. Us. We had only contracted not to disturb them, &c.

I said it was the Opinion of all the Fishermen in America that England could not prevent our Catching a fish without preventing themselves from getting a Dollar. That the 1st. Fare was our only Advantage. That neither the English nor French could have it. It must be lost if We had it not.

He said, he did not think much of the Fishery as a Source of Profit, but as a Nursery of Seamen. I told him the English could not catch a fish the more, or make a Sailor the more, for restraining Us. Even the French would rival them in the Markets of Spain and Portugal. It was our Fish which they ought to call their own, because We should spend the Profit with them.

That the southern States had Staple Commodities, but N. England had no other Remittance but the Fishery. No other Way to pay for their Cloathing. That it entered into our Distilleries and West India Trade as well as our European Trade, in such a manner that it could not be taken out or diminished, without tearing and rending. That if it should be left to its natural Course We could hire or purchase Spots of Ground on which to erect Stages, and Buildings, but if We were straightened by Treaty, that Treaty would be given in Instructions to Governors and Commodores whose duty it would be to execute it. That it would be very difficult to restrain our Fishermen, they would be frequently transgressing, and making disputes and Troubles.

He said his principal Object was to avoid sowing Seeds of future Wars.—I said it was equally my Object, and that I was perswaded, that if the Germ of a War was left any where, there was the greatest danger of its being left in the Article respecting the Fishery.

The rest of the Day, was spent in endless Discussions about the Tories. Dr. F. is very staunch against the Tories, more decided a great deal on this Point than Mr. Jay or my self.

NOV. 28. THURSDAY.

This Morning I have drawn up, the following Project

Art. 3.

That the Subjects of his Britannic Majesty, and the People of the said United States, shall continue to enjoy, unmolested, the Right to take Fish of every kind, on the Grand Bank and on all the other Banks of Newfoundland: also in the Gulph of St. Laurence, and in all other Places, where the Inhabitants of both Countries, used at any time heretofore to fish; and the Citizens of the said United States shall have Liberty to cure and dry their Fish, on the Shores of Cape Sables, and of any of the unsettled Bays, Harbours or Creeks of Nova Scotia, or any of the Shores of the Magdalene Islands, and of the Labradore Coast: And they shall be permitted in Time of Peace to hire Pieces of Land, for Terms of Years, of the legal Proprietors in any of the Dominions of his said Majesty, whereon to erect the necessary Stages and Buildings and to cure and dry their Fish.

1782 NOVEMBER 29. FRYDAY.

Met Mr. Fitsherbert, Mr. Oswald, Mr. Franklin, Mr. Jay, Mr. Laurens and Mr. Stratchey at Mr. Jays, Hotel D'Orleans, and spent the whole Day in Discussions about the Fishery and the Tories. I proposed a new Article concerning the Fishery. It was discussed and turned in every Light, and multitudes of Amendments proposed on each Side, and at last the Article drawn as it was finally agreed to. The other English Gentlemen being withdrawn upon some Occasion, I asked Mr. Oswald if he could consent to leave out the Limitation of 3 Leagues from all their Shores and the 15 from those of Louisbourg. He said in his own Opinion he was for it, but his Instructions were such, that he could not do it. I perceived by this, and by several Incidents and little Circumstances before, which I had remarked to my Colleagues, who were much of the same opinion, that Mr. Oswald had an Instruction, not to settle the Articles of the Fishery and Refugees, without the Concurrence of Mr. Fitsherbert and Mr. Stratchey.

Upon the Return of the other Gentlemen, Mr. Stratchey proposed to leave out the Word Right of Fishing and make it Liberty. Mr. Fitsherbert said the Word Right was an obnoxious Expression.

Upon this I rose up and said, Gentlemen, is there or can there be a clearer Right? In former Treaties, that of Utrecht and that of Paris, France and England have claimed the Right and used the Word. When God Almighty made the Banks of Newfoundland at 300 Leagues Distance from the People of America and at 600 Leagues distance from those of France and England, did he not give as good a Right to the former as to the latter. If Heaven in the Creation gave a Right, it is ours at least as much as yours. If Occupation, Use, and Possession give a Right, We have it as clearly as you. If War and Blood and Treasure give a Right, ours is as good as yours. We have been constantly fighting in Canada, Cape Breton and Nova Scotia for the Defense of this Fishery, and have expended beyond all

Proportion more than you. If then the Right cannot be denied, Why should it not be acknowledged? and put out of Dispute? Why should We leave Room for illiterate Fishermen to wrangle and chicane?

Mr. Fitsherbert said, the Argument is in your Favour. I must confess your Reasons appear to be good, but Mr. Oswalds Instructions were such that he did not see how he could agree with Us. And for my Part, I have not the Honour and Felicity, to be a Man of that Weight and Authority, in my Country, that you Gentlemen are in yours (this was very genteelly said), I have the Accidental Advantage of a little favour with the present Minister, but I cannot depend upon the Influence of my own Opinion to reconcile a Measure to my Countrymen. We can consider our selves as little more than Pens in the hands of Government at home, and Mr. Oswalds Instructions are so particular.

I replied to this, The Time is not so pressing upon Us, but that We can wait, till a Courier goes to London, with your Representations upon this Subject and others that remain between Us, and I think the Ministers must be convinced.

Mr. Fitsherbert said, to send again to London and have all laid loose before Parliament was so uncertain a Measure—it was going to Sea again.

Upon this Dr. Franklin said, that if another Messenger was to be sent to London, he ought to carry Something more respecting a Compensation to the Sufferers in America. He produced a Paper from his Pocket, in which he had drawn up a Claim, and He said the first Principle of the Treaty was Equality and Reciprocity. Now they demanded of Us Payment of Debts and Restitution or Compensation to the Refugees. If a Draper had sold a Piece of Cloth to a Man upon Credit and then sent a servant to take it from him by Force, and after bring his Action for the Debt, would any Court of Law or Equity give him his Demand, without obliging him to restore the Cloth? Then he stated the carrying off of Goods from Boston, Philadelphia, and the Carolinas, Georgia, Virginia &c. and the burning of the Towns, &c. and desired that this might be sent with the rest.

Upon this I recounted the History of G Gages Agreement with the Inhabitants of Boston, that they should remove with their Effects upon Condition, that they would surrender their Arms. But as soon as the Arms were secured, the Goods were forbid to be carried out and were finally carried off in large Quantities to Hallifax.

Dr. Franklin mentioned the Case of Philadelphia, and the carrying off of Effects there, even his own Library.

Mr. Jay mentioned several other Things and Mr. Laurens added the Plunders in Carolina of Negroes, Plate &c.

After hearing all this, Mr. Fitsherbert, Mr. Oswald and Mr. Stratchey, retired for some time, and returning Mr. Fitsherbert said that upon consulting together and weighing every Thing as maturely as possible, Mr. Stratchey and himself had determined to advise Mr. Oswald, to strike with Us, according to the Terms We had proposed as our Ultimatum respecting the Fishery and the Loyalists.—Accordingly We all sat down and read over the whole Treaty and corrected it and agreed to meet tomorrow at Mr. Oswalds House, to sign and seal the Treaties which the Secretaries were to copy fair in the mean time.

I forgot to mention, that when We were upon the Fishery, and Mr. Stratchey and Mr. Fitsherbert were urging Us to leave out the Word Right and substitute Liberty, I told them at last In Answer to their Proposal, to agree upon all other Articles, and leave that of the Fishery to be adjusted, at the definitive Treaty. I said, I never could put my hand to any Articles, without Satisfaction about the Fishery. That Congress had, 3 or 4 Years ago, when they did me the Honour to give me a Commission, to make a Treaty of Commerce with G. Britain, given me a positive Instruction, not to make any such Treaty, without an Article in the Treaty of Peace, acknowledging our Right to the Fishery, that I was happy that Mr. Laurens was now present who I believed was in Congress at the Time, and must remember it.

Mr. Laurens upon this said, with great Firmness, that he was in the same Case, and could never give his Voice for any Articles without this.

Mr. Jay spoke up and said, it could not be a Peace, it would only be an insidious Truce without it.

NOVEMBER 30. SATURDAY. ST. ANDREWS DAY.

We met first at Mr. Jays, then at Mr. Oswalds, examined and compared the Treaties. Mr. Stratchey had left out the limitation of Time, the 12 Months, that the Refugees were allowed to reside in America, in order to recover their Estates if they could. Dr. Franklin said this was a Surprize upon Us. Mr. Jay said so too. We never had consented to leave it out, and they insisted upon putting it in, which was done.

Mr. Laurens said there ought to be a Stipulation that the British Troops should carry off no Negroes or other American Property. We all agreed. Mr. Oswald consented.

Then The Treaties were signed, sealed and delivered, and We all went out to Passy to dine with Dr. Franklin. Thus far has proceeded this great Affair. The Unravelling of the Plott, has been to me, the most affecting and astonishing Part of the whole Piece.—

As soon as I arrived in Paris I waited on Mr. Jay and learned from him, the rise and Progress of the Negotiation. Nothing that has happened since the Beginning of the Controversy in 1761 has ever struck me more forcibly or affected me more intimately, than that entire Coincidence of Principles and Opinions, between him and me. In about 3 days I went out to Passy, and spent the Evening with Dr. Franklin, and entered largely into Conversation with him upon the Course and present State of our foreign affairs. I told him without Reserve my Opinion of the Policy of this Court, and of the Principles, Wisdom and Firmness with which Mr. Jay had conducted the Negotiation in his Sickness and my Absence, and that I was determined to support Mr. Jay to the Utmost of my Power in the pursuit of the same System. The Dr. heard me patiently but said nothing.

The first Conference We had afterwards with Mr. Oswald, in considering one Point and another, Dr. Franklin turned to Mr. Jay and said, I am of your Opinion and will go on with these Gentlemen in the Business without consulting this Court. He has accordingly met Us in most of our Conferences and has gone on with Us, in entire Harmony and Unanimity, throughout, and has been able and usefull, both by his Sagacity and his Reputation in the whole Negotiation.

I was very happy, that Mr. Laurence came in, although it

was the last day of the Conferences, and wish he could have been sooner. His Apprehension, notwithstanding his deplorable Affliction under the recent Loss of so excellent a Son, is as quick, his Judgment as sound, and his heart as firm as ever. He had an opportunity of examining the whole, and judging, and approving, and the Article which he caused to be inserted at the very last that no Property should be carried off, which would most probably in the Multiplicity and hurry of Affairs have escaped Us, was worth a longer Journey, if that had been all. But his Name and Weight is added which is of much greater Consequence.

These miserable Minutes may help me to recollect, but I have not found time amidst the hurry of Business and Crowd of Visits, to make a detail.

I should have before noted, that at our first Conference about the Fishery, I related the Facts as well as I understood them, but knowing nothing Myself but as an Hearsay Witness, I found it had not the Weight of occular Testimony, to supply which defect, I asked Dr. Franklin if Mr. Williams of Nantes could not give Us Light. He said Mr. Williams was on the Road to Paris and as soon as he arrived he would ask him. In a few days Mr. Williams called on me, and said Dr. Franklin had as I desired him enquired of him about the Fishery, but he was not able to speak particularly upon that Subject, but there was at Nantes a Gentleman of Marblehead, Mr. Sam White, Son in Law to Mr. Hooper, who was Master of the Subject and to him, he would write.

Mr. Jeremiah Allen a Merchant of Boston, called on me, about the same time. I enquired of him. He was able only to give such an hearsay Account as I could give myself, but I desired him to write to Mr. White at Nantes, which he undertook to do and did. Mr. White answered Mr. Allens Letter by referring him to his Answer to Mr. Williams, which Mr. Williams received and delivered to Dr. Franklin, who communicated it to Us, and it contained a good Account.

I desired Mr. Thaxter to write to Messrs. Ingraham and Bromfield, and Mr. Storer to write to Captn. Coffin at Amsterdam. They delivered me the Answers. Both contained Information, but Coffins was the most particular, and of the most importance, as he spoke as a Witness. We made the best Use of these Letters, with the English Gentlemen and they appeared to have a good deal of Weight with them.

From first to last, I ever insisted upon it, with the English Gentlemen, that the Fisheries and the Missisippi, if America was not satisfied in those Points, would be the sure and certain Sources of a future War. Shewed them the indispensible Necessity of both to our Affairs, and that no Treaty We could make, which should be unsatisfactory to our People upon these Points, could be observed.

That the Population near the Missisippi would be so rapid and the Necessities of the People for its navigation so rapid, that nothing could restrain them from going down, and if the Force of Arms should be necessary it would not be wanting. That the Fishery entered into our Distilleries, our coasting Trade, our Trade with the Southern States, with the West India Islands, with the Coast of Affrica and with every Part of Europe in such a manner, and especially with England, that it could not be taken from Us, or granted Us stingily, without tearing and rending. That the other States had Staples. We had none but fish. No other Means of remittances to London or paying those very Debts they had insisted upon so seriously. That if We were forced off, at 3 Leagues Distance, We should smuggle eternally. That their Men of War might have the Glory of sinking now and then a fishing Schooner but this would not prevent a repetition of the Crime, it would only inflame and irritate and inkindle a new War. That in 7 Years We should break through all restraints, and conquer from them the Island of Newfoundland itself and Nova Scotia too.

Mr. Fitsherbert always smiled and said, it was very extraordinary that the British Ministry and We should see it, in so different a Light. That they meant the Restriction, in order to prevent disputes and kill the Seeds of War, and We should think it so certain a Source of disputes, and so strong a Seed of War. But that our Reasons were such that he thought the Probability of our Side.

I have not time to minute the Conversations about the Sea Cow Fishery, the Whale Fishery, the Magdalene Islands and the Labradore Coasts and the Coasts of Nova Scotia. It is sufficient to say they were explained to the Utmost of our Knowledge and finally conceeded.

I should have noted before the various deliberations, between the English Gentlemen and Us, relative to the Words "indefinite and exclusive" Right, which the C. de Vergennes and Mr. Gerard had the Precaution to insert in our Treaty with France. I observed often to the English Gentlemen that aiming at excluding Us, from Fishing upon the North Side of Newfoundland, it was natural for them to wish that the English would exclude Us fro the South Side. This would be making both alike, and take away an odious Distinction. French Statesmen must see the Tendency of our Fishermen being treated kindly, and hospitably like Friends by the English on their Side of the Island, and unkindly, inhospitably and like Ennemies on the French Side. I added, farther, that it was my Opinion, neither our Treaty with the French, nor any Treaty or Clause to the same Purpose which the English could make, would be punctually observed. Fishermen both from England and America would smuggle, especially the Americans in the early Part of the Spring before the Europeans could arrive. This therefore must be connived at by the French, or odious Measures must be recurred to, by them or Us, to suppress it, and in either Case it was easy to see what would be the Effect upon the American Mind. They no doubt therefore wished the English to put themselves upon as odious a footing, at least as they had done.

Dr. Franklin said there was a great deal of Weight in this Observation, and the Englishmen shewed plainly enough that they felt it.

I have not attempted in these Notes to do Justice to the Arguments of my Colleagues all of whom were, throughout the whole Business when they attended, very attentive, and very able, especially Mr. Jays, to whom the French, if they knew as much of his negotiations as they do of mine, would very justly give the Title with which they have inconsiderately decorated me, that of Le Washington de la Negotiation, a very flattering Compliment indeed, to which I have not a Right, but sincerely think it belongs to Mr. Jay.

I hope it will be permitted to me or to some other who can do it better, some Ten or fifteen Years hence, to collect together in one View, my little Negotiations in Europe. Fifty Years hence it may be published, perhaps 20. I will venture to say, however feebly I may have acted my Part or whatever Mistakes I may have committed, yet the Situations I have been in between angry Nations and more angry Factions, have been some of the most singular and interesting that ever happened to any Man. The Fury of Ennemies as well as of Elements, the Subtilty and Arrogance of Allies, and what has been worse than all, the Jealousy, Envy, and little Pranks of Friends and CoPatriots, would form one of the most instructive Lessons in Morals and Politicks, that ever was committed to Paper.

December 4, 1782

———————

1782. DECEMBER 9. MONDAY.

Visited C. Sarsfield who lent me his Notes upon America. Visited Mr. Jay, Mr. Oswald came in. We slided, from one Thing to another into a very lively Conversation upon Politicks.—He asked me what the Conduct of his Court and Nation ought to be, in Relation to America. I answered the Alpha and Omega of British Policy, towards America, was summed up in this one Maxim—See that American Independence is independent, independant of all the World, independent of yourselves as well as of France, and independent of both as well as of the rest of Europe. Depend upon it, you have no Chance for Salvation but by setting up America very high. Take care to remove from the American Mind all Cause of Fear of you. No other Motive but Fear of you, will ever produce in the Americans any unreasonable Attachment to the house of Bourbon.—Is it possible, says he that the People of America should be afraid of Us, or hate Us?—One would think Mr. Oswald says I, that you had been out of the World for these 20 Years past. Yes there are 3 millions of People in America who hate and dread you more than any Thing in the World.—What says he now We are come to our Senses?—Your Change of System, is not yet known in America, says I.—Well says he what shall We do to remove these Fears, and Jealousies?

In one Word says I, favour and promote the Interest, Reputation and Dignity of the United States in every Thing that is consistent with your own. If you pursue the Plan of cramping, clipping and weakening America, on the Supposition that She will be a Rival to you, you will make her really so, you will make her the natural and perpetual Ally of your natural and perpetual Ennemies.—But in what Instance says he have We discovered such a disposition?—In the 3 Leagues from your Shores and the 15 Leagues from Cape Breton, says I to which your Ministry insisted so earnestly to exclude our Fishermen. Here was a Point that would have done Us great harm and you no good, on the contrary harm. So that you would have hurt yourselves to hurt Us. This disposition must be guarded against.—I am fully of your Mind about that, says he. But what else can We do?—Send a Minister to Congress, says I, at the Peace, a clever Fellow, who Understands himself, and will neither set Us bad Examples, nor intermeddle in our Parties. This will shew that you are consistent with yourselves, that you are sincere in your Acknowledgment of American Independence, and that you dont entertain hopes and designs of overturning it. Such a Minister will dissipate many fears, and will be of more Service to the least obnoxious Refugees than any other Measure could be. Let the King send a Minister to Congress and receive one from that it Body. This will be acting consistently and with Dignity, in the Face of the Universe.

Well what else shall We do says he?—I have more than once already says I, advised you to put your Ministers upon negotiating the Acknowledgment of our Independence by the Neutral Powers.—True says he and I have written about it, and in my Answers, says he, laughing, I find myself charged with Speculation. But I dont care, I will write them my Sentiments. I wont take any of their Money. I have spent already twelve or thirteen hundred Pounds, and all the Reward I will have for it shall be the Pleasure of writing as I think. My opinion is that our Court should sign the armed Neutrality, and announce to them what they have done with you, and negotiate to have you admitted to sign too. But I want to write more fully upon the Subject, and I want you to give me your Thoughts upon it, for I dont understand it so fully as I wish. What Motives can be thrown out to the Empress of Russia? or what Motives may she be supposed to have to acknowledge your Independence? and what Motives can our Court have to interfere, or interceed with the Newtral Powers to receive you into their Confederation?

I will answer all these Questions says I, to the best of my Knowledge and with the Utmost Candour. In the first Place, there has been with very little Interruption a Jealousy, between the Courts of Petersbourg and Versailles for many Years. France is the old Friend and Ally of the Sublime Port the natural Ennemy of Russia. France not long since negotiated a Peace between Russia and the Turk, but upon the Empresses late Offers of Mediation, and especially her Endeavours to negotiate Holland out of the War, France appears to have been piqued, and as the last Revolution in the Crimea happened soon after, there is Reason to suspect that French Emissaries excited the Revolt against the new independent Government which the Empress had taken so much Pains to establish. Poland has been long a Scæne of Competition between Russian and French Politicks, both Parties having spent great Sums in Pensions to Partisans untill they have laid all Virtue and public Spirit prostrate in that Country.

Sweeden is another Region of Rivalry between France and Russia, where both Parties spent such Sums in Pensions, as to destroy the Principles of Liberty and prepare the Way for that Revolution which France favoured from a Principle of Œconomy rather than any other. These hints were sufficient to shew the opposition of Views and Interests between France and Russia, and We see the Consequence of it, that England has more Influence at Petersbourg than France. The Empress therefore would have two Motives, one to oblige England, if they should interceed for an Acknowledgment of American Independence, and another to render America less dependent upon France. The Empress moreover loves Reputation, and it would be no small Addition to her Glory, to undertake a Negotiation with all the neutral Courts to induce them to admit America into their Confederacy. The Empress might be further tempted. She was bent upon extending her Commerce and the Commerce of America, if it were only in Hemp and Duck, would be no small Object to her.

As to the Motives to your Court. Princes often think themselves warranted if not bound to fight for their Glory. Surely they may lawfully negotiate for Reputation. If the Neutral

Powers should acknowledge our Independence now, France will have the Reputation, very unjustly, of having negotiated it. But if your Court now takes a decided Part in favour of it, your Court will have the Glory of it, in Europe and America, and this will have a good Effect upon American Gratitude.

But says he, this would be negotiating for the Honour and Interest of France, for no doubt France wishes all the World to acknowledge your Independence.

Give me leave to tell you, Sir, says I, you are mistaken. If I have not been mistaken in the Policy of France from my first Observation of it to this hour, they have been as averse to other Powers acknowledging our Independence as you have been.— Mr. Jay joined me in the same Declaration.—God! says he I understand it now. There is a Gentleman going to London this day. I will go home and write upon the Subject by him.

DECEMBER 10. TUESDAY.

Visited Mr. Oswald, to enquire what News from England. He had the Courier de L'Europe in which is Mr. Secretary Townsends Letter to the Lord Mayor of London dated the 3d. of this Month in which he announces the Signature of Preliminaries on the thirtieth of November, between the Commissioner of his Majesty and the Commissioners of the U. States of America.

He had also received the Kings Speech, announcing the same Thing.

Mr. Oswald said that France would not seperate her Affairs from Spain. That he had hoped that America would have assisted them, somewhat, in compromising Affairs with France &c. Dr. Franklin, who was present, said he did not know any Thing of the other Negotiations. He said that neither Mr. Fitsherbert, nor the C. de Vergennes, nor the C. D'Aranda communicated any Thing to him. That he understood, the Dutch were the farthest from an Agreement.

Upon this I said, Mr. Oswald, Mr. Fitsherbert cant, I think, have any diffiuculty, to agree with Mr. Brantzen. There are 3 Points. 1. The Liberty of Navigation. 2. Restitution of Possessions. 3. Compensation for Damages. The Liberty of Navigation I suppose, is the Point that sticks. But why should it stick?

When all Nations are agreed in the Principle, why should England stand out? England must agree to it! She has already in Effect agreed to it, as it affects all Nations but Holland and America, and if She were disposed, She could not prevent them from having the Benefit.

Upon this Dr. Franklin said the Dutch would be able in any future War, to carry on their Commerce even of naval Stores, in the Bottoms of other neutral Powers.

Yes says Mr. Oswald, and I am of Opinion that England ought to subscribe the armed Neutrality.

Very well, says I, then let Mr. Fitsherbert agree this Point with Mr. Brantzen, and let Mr. Harris at Petersbourg, take Mr. Dana in his hand, and go to the Prince Potempkin or the C. D'osterman, and say the K my Master has authorized me to subscribe the Principles of the armed Neutrality, and instructed me to introduce to you Mr. Dana, Minister from the United States of America, to do the same; let him subscribe his Name under mine.—At this they all laughed very heartily. Mr. Oswald however recollecting himself, and the Conversation between him and me Yesterday on the same Subject, very gravely turned it off, by saying he did not see a necessity to be in a hurry about that. America was well enough.

I said, as to Restitution of the Dutch Territories, I suppose your Court wont make much difficulty about that if this Court does not, as it is not probable she Will. And as to Compensation for damages, the Dutch will probably be as easy as they can about that.

Dr. Franklin said he was for beginning early to think about the Articles of the difinitive Treaty. We had been so happy as to be the first in the Preliminaries, and he wished to be so in the definitive Articles.—Thus We parted.

It may be proper for me to minute here some Points to propose in the difinitive Treaty.

1. The Liberty of Navigation. 2. That no Forts shall be built or Garrisons maintained upon any of the Frontiers in America, nor upon any of the Land Boundaries. 3. That the Island of Bermudas be ceeded to Us—or independent, or not fortified, or that no Privateers be fitted or sent out from thence or permitted to enter there, or prizes carried in. 4. That the Isle of

Sables remain the Property of its present owner, and under the Jurisdiction of the United States or Massachusetts. 5. That the Account of Prisoners be ballanced, and the Sums due for their subsistence &c. be paid, and the Ballance of Prisoners paid for according to the Usages of Nations.

A PRELIMINARY PEACE TREATY

To James Warren

Dear Sir   Paris Dec.ʳ 15. 1782

This goes with the Preliminary Treaty between the Crown of G. Britain and the United States of America—it is not to be in force untill France and Great Britain Shall agree and sign. When this will be is not yet known, it is Supposed that the principal Points remaining are Spanish or Dutch.

The great Interests of our Country in the West and in the East are Secured as well as her Independence. St Croix is the Boundary against Nova Scotia. The Fisheries are very Safe. the Missisippi and Western Lands to the middle of the great Lakes, are as well secured to Us as they could be by England.—All these Advantages would not have been obtained if We had litterally pursued our Instructions, the Necessity of departing from which in some degree will I hope be our Excuse. The King of Sweeden is the first Power in Europe who has invited Us to an alliance—the Commissioners are Arrived here, and the Treaty will be soon made. The other neutral Powers may possibly acknowledge our Independence all together.—it is possible, that England herself may advise it, but this is no more than Conjecture. The K. of Sweeden has inserted in his Commission an handsome Compliment to Us. Says that he had a great desire to form a Connection with a People who had So well established their Independence, and by their Wisdom and Bravery So well deserved it.

England has been wise to be the third Power in Europe to acknowledge Us. Is it my Vanity which makes me believe that the Dutch Negotiation has wrought this mighty Reverse, and

carried Us tryumphantly to the End of all our Wishes? without
this, the War would have continued for years, and the House
of Bourbon so pressed for Peace and We so dependent on
them that We should have lost the Western Country and the
Fisheries. and very probably been left in a Truce, in a state of
Poverty and Weakness, which would have made Us long the
miserable satellites of some great European Planet.

It is the Providence of God, not the good Will of England
of France, nor yet the Wisdom and Firmness of Congress that
has done this.—To that Providence let us with humble Gratitude and Adoration ascribe it.—Without making an ostentation
of Piety upon the occasion however, let Us turn our Thoughts
to what is future. The Union of the states, an Affectionate Respect and Attachment among all their Members, the Education of the rising Generation, the Formation of a national
system of Œconomy Policy, and Manners are the great Concerns which still lye before us.—We must guard as much as
Prudence will permit against the Contagion of European
Manners, and that excessive Influx of Commerce Luxury and
Inhabitants from abroad, which will soon embarrass Us.

with great Esteem, your Fnd.

From the Diary: January 11–12, 1783

JANUARY II. SATURDAY.

Mr. W. T. Franklin came in to talk with me, about a Subject
which he said he did not often talk about, and that was himself. He produced a Commission, drawn up, for Messrs.
Franklin and Jay to sign, when they only were here, before I
arrived, and in fact signed by them. I took the Commission
and read it. He asked me to sign it. I told him, that I considered myself as directly affronted in this Affair. That considering
that I came out to Europe without any Solicitation of mine,
single in the Commission for Peace, and considering that Congress had done me the Honour to place me at the head of the
new Commission, I had a right to be consulted in the Appoint-

ment of a Secretary to the Commission. But that without saying or writing a Word to me, Dr. Franklin had wrote to Mr. Jay
at Madrid and obtained a Promise from him. That considering
the Relation to me in which Mr. Thaxter came out, and his
Services and Sufferings in the Cause and the small Allowance
he had received, I thought he had a better right to it. That I
thought my self ill treated in this as in many other Things.
That it was not from any disrespect to him, Mr. W.T.F., that I
declined it. That I should not, if my Opinion had been asked,
have named Mr. Thaxter but another Gentleman.

He told me, how his Grandfather was weary, that he had renewed his Solicitation to Congress, to be relieved. That he
wanted to be with his Family at Philadelphia &c. &c. &c.

I told him I was weary too, and had written an uncondi-
tional Resignation of all my Employments in Europe. That an
Attack had been made upon me by the C. de Vergennes, and
Congress had been induced to disgrace me. That I would not
bear this disgrace if I could help it. That I would wear no Livery with a Spot upon it. The Stain should be taken out or I
would not wear the Coat. That Congress had placed me now in
a Situation, that I could do nothing without being suspected
of a sinister Motive, that of aiming at being restored to the
Mission to Great Britain. The Conduct of the American Cause
in Europe had been a constant Scramble for Offices and was
now likely to be a new and more passionate Scæne of Factions
for Places. That I would have nothing to do with it, had not
been used to it.

He said that Congress would have now a Number of Places
and would provide for Mr. Thaxter. That they would undoubtedly give me full Satisfaction &c.

I told him that the first Wish of my Heart was to return to
my Wife and Children &c.

He shewed me, Extract of a Letter of Dr. F. to Congress
concerning him, containing a studied and long Eulogium—
Sagacity beyond his Years, Diligence, Activity, Fidelity, genteel
Address, Facility in speaking French. Recommends him to be
Secretary of some Mission, thinks he would make an excellent
Minister, but does not propose him for it as yet.

This Letter and other Circumstances convince me, that the

Plan is laid between the C. de Vergennes and the Dr., to get Billy made Minister to this Court and not improbably the Dr. to London. Time will shew.

JANUARY 12. SUNDAY.

Mr. B. Vaughan came in. I told him, I had some Facts to communicate to him in Confidence. They affected my personal Interest, Character, and Feelings so intimately, that it was impossible for me to speak of them without being suspected of personal Resentments and sinister Motives. But that these Facts were at the same time so connected, with public Affairs, with the Interests of the House of Bourbon, and with the essential Interests of Great Britain and America and the true System of Policy, which the two last ought in future to pursue towards each other, that it was my indispensable Duty to communicate them to some English Gentleman who might put their Government upon their Guard.

The two Facts I should now mention were two Instances of the Policy of the C. de Vergennes to defeat the good Intentions of Congress, towards G. Britain. I then shewed him my two original Commissions—one as Minister Plenipotentiary for making Peace, the other as Minister Plenipotentiary to make a Treaty of Commerce with the Ambassador or Plenipotentiary of his Britannic Majesty, vested with equal Powers, and whatever shall be so agreed and concluded for Us and in our Name to sign and thereupon make a Treaty of Commerce, and to transact every Thing that may be necessary for compleating, securing and strengthening the same, in as ample Form and with the same Effect, as if We were personally present and acted therein, 29. Sept. 1779.

Mr. Vaughan said he was astonished at my Secrecy and Patience, in never communicating this before. That they never had any Idea of this in London. I told him the C. de Vergennes had required me in the name of the King not to communicate it.

I then shew him the Resolution of Congress of 12 July 1781, by which the Commission and Instructions for negotiating a Treaty of Commerce between the U. States and G. Britain given me on the 29. day of Sept. 1779, were revoked.

I then read to him the following Part of my Instructions of the 16. Oct. 1779, vizt. That the common Right of Fishing shall in no Case be given up. That it is essential to the Welfare of all these United States, that the Inhabitants there of, at the Expiration of the War should continue to enjoy the free and undisturbed Exercise of their common Right to fish on the banks of Newfoundland and the other fishing Banks and Seas of North America. That our Faith be pledged to the Several States, that without their unanimous Consent no Treaty of Commerce shall be entered into nor any Trade or Commerce whatever carried on with G. Britain without the Explicit Stipulation herein after mentioned. You are therefore not to consent to any Treaty of Commerce with G. Britain, without an explicit Stipulation on her Part not to molest or disturb the Inhabitants of the United States of America in taking fish on the Banks of Newfoundland and other Fisheries in the American Seas &c.—Here I stopped.

You see here says I Mr. Vaughan, a proof of a great Confidence in me. And what was the Cause of it? No other than this, My Sentiments were known in Congress, to be unalterable for Independence, our Alliance, Fisheries and Boundaries. But it was known also to be a fixed Principle with me, to hurt G. Britain no farther than should be necessary to secure our Independence, Alliance and other Rights.

The C. de Vergennes knew my Character, both from his Intelligences in America and from my Conversation and Correspondence with him. He knew me to be a Man who would not yield to some of the designs he had in View. He accordingly sets his Confidential Friend Mr. Marbois, to negotiating very artfully with Congress. They could not get me removed or recalled, and the next Scheme was to get the Power of the Commission for Peace into the hands of Dr. Franklin.

To this End the Choice was made to fall upon him, and four other Gentlemen who could not attend. They have been however mistaken, and no Wrestler was ever so compleatly thrown upon his Back as the C. de Vergennes.

But their Policy did not stop here. I had still a Parchment, to make a Treaty of Commerce with G. Britain, and an Instruction annexed to it, which would be a powerfull Motive with G.B. to acknowledge our Right to the Fisheries. This

Commission and these Instructions were to be and were revoked.

Mr. Vaughan said this was very important Information and entirely new. That he was much enlightened and had Sentiments upon the Occasion. That he would write it to the E. of Shelburne, and his Lordship would make great Use of it, without naming me, &c.

WRITING THE HISTORY OF THE REVOLUTION

To the Abbé de Mably

Sir   Paris January 15. 1783

It was with Pleasure, that I learn'd your Design of Writing upon the American Revolution, because your other Writings which are much admired by the Americans, contain Principles of Legislation, Polity and Negotiation perfectly conformable to theirs: so that it is impossible for you to write upon the Subject without producing a Work which will be entertaining an instructive to the Public, and especially to America. But I hope you will not think me guilty of Presumption nor Affectation of Singularity, if I venture to give you my Opinion that it is too Soon to attempt a compleat History, of this great Event and that there is no Man in Europe or America, who is as yet qualified for it, and furnished with the necessary Materials.

To accomplish Such a Work a Writer Should divide the History of North America into Several Periods 1. From the first Settlement of the Colonies in 1600, to the Commencement of the Controversy between them and Great Britain in 1761.— 2. From this Commencement, which was by an order of the Board of Trade and Plantations in Great Britain to the Custom house officers in America, to carry into a more rigorous Execution the Acts of Trade, and to apply to the Courts of Justice for Writs of Assistance for that Purpose, to the Commencement of Hostilities on the 19 of April 1775. during this Period of 14 Years, it was a Controversy upon Paper. 3. From the Battle of Lexington, to the Signature of the Treaty with France on the 6 of February 1778, during which Period, of 3 Years the

War was carried on Singly between Great Britain and the United States. 4. From the Treaty with France to the Hostilities between Great Britain and France, first & then Spain, then to the Completion of the neutral Confederation and the War against Holland, all of which Movements at last Unravelled themselves in the present Negotiations for Peace.

Without a distinct Knowledge of the History of the Colonies, in the first Period a Writer will find himself constantly puzzled, through his whole Work to account for Events and Characters which will occur to him in every step of his Progress through the Second, third and fourth.

To acquire a competent Knowledge of the first Period, one must read all the Charters to Colonies, and the Commissions and Instructions to Governors, all the Law Books of the Several Colonies, and thirteen folio Volumes of dry Statutes are not perused with Pleasure, nor in a short time; all the Records of the Legislatures of the Several Colonies, which are only to be found in Manuscript, and by travelling in Person from New Hampshire to Georgia; the Records of the Board of Trade and Plantations in Great Britain, from its Institution to its dissolution, as well as the Papers in the offices of some of the Secretaries of State.

There is another Branch of Reading too, which cannot be dispensed with, if the former might, I mean of those Writings which have appeared in America, from time to time, Some of which may be hinted at though I pretend not in this Place, absent from all Books and Papers to recollect them all. The Writings of the ancient Governors Winthrop and Winslow, Dr Mather, Mr Prince, Neals History of New England Douglas's Summary of the first planting progressive Improvement & present State of the British Colonies, Hutchinsons History of the Massachusetts Bay, Smiths History of New York, Smiths History of New Jersey William Penns Works, Dummers Defence of the New England Charters The History of Virginia, and many others. all these are previous to the present dispute which began in 1761.

During the Second Period, the Writings are more numerous and more difficult to obtain.—There are extant in print, Writings of great Importance in this Controversy, of the following Persons, who were all of them living Actors in the Scæne at the times when they wrote, and Persons of great Consideration. These were the Royal Governors Pounal, Bernard and Hutchinson, Lieutenant Governor Oliver, Mr Sewal Judge of Admiralty for Halifax, Jonathan Mayhew D. D. James Otis, Oxenbridge Thatcher Samuel Adams, Josiah Quincy, Joseph Warren Esq^rs. and perhaps of equal Importance to any are the Writings of Mr Dickinson Mr Wilson and Dr Rush of Philadelphia, Mr Livingston and McDougal of New York, C^oll Bland and Arthur Lee of Virginia and many others. The Records of the Town of Boston, and especially of its Committee of Correspondence, of the Board of Commissioners of the Customs, of the House of Representatives, and Council Board of the Massachusetts Bay Besides all these the Gazettes of the Town of Boston, at least if not of New York and Philadelphia, ought to be collected and examined from the Year 1760. All this is necessary, in order to write, with Precision and in detail the History of the Controversy, before Hostilities commenced, comprehending the Period from 1761 to the 19 of April 1775.

During the 3^d and 4th Periods, the Records, Pamphlets and Gazettes of the thirteen States ought to be collected together with the Journals of Congress, part of which however are yet Secret and the Collection of the new Constitutions of the Several States.—The Remembrancer, and annual Registers, periodical Papers published in England Les Affaires de L'Angleterre et de L'Amerique, and the Mercure de France, published in Paris and Le Politique Hollandais printed at Amsterdam.— The whole Series of General Washingtons Correspondence with Congress, from the Month of July 1775 to this Day, which has not yet been published and cannot be, untill Congress Shall order or permit it. And I beg Leave to Say, that untill this vast Source of Information Shall be opened, it will be to little Purpose for any body to attempt an History of the American War. There are other Papers of Importance in the offices of the Secret Committee, the commercial Committee the Committee of foreign Affairs, the Committee on the Treasury the Marine Committee and the Board of War, while they Subsisted, and of the Offices of War, Marine, Finances and foreign Affairs Since their Institution. There are also Letters from American Ministers in France, Spain, Holland and other Parts of Europe.

The most material Documents being yet Secret, it is too

early to attempt any Thing like a general History of the American Revolution, but nobody can begin too Soon or be too industrious in collecting Materials.—There have however been already two or three general Histories of the American War and Revolution published in London and two or three others in Paris. Those in English are masses of Party Billingsgate and those in English and those in French both mere Monuments of the total Ignorance of their Authors of their Subject.

It would require the whole of the longest Life, to begin at Twenty Years of Age, to assemble from all the Nations and Parts of the Globe in which they are deposited, the Documents to form a compleat History of the American War, because it is nearly the History of Mankind for the whole Epocha of it. The History of France Spain Holland, England and the Neutral Powers, as well as America are at least comprized in it. Materials must be collected from all these Nations, and the most important Documents of all, Such as Shew the Characters of Actors and the Secret Springs of Action, are yet locked up in Cabinets and in Cyphers.

Whether you Sir, however, Shall undertake to give a general History, or only Remarks and observations like those upon the Greeks and Romans, you will produce a Work highly interesting and instructive both in Morals, Politicks and Legislation, and I should esteem it an Honour as well as a Pleasure to furnish you with any little Helps in my Power in your Researches. —I am not able to Say however, whether the Government of this Country would wish to See any Thing very profoundly written, and by any Author of Great Name, in the French Tongue.—Principles and Systems of Religion and Government, must be laid open, So different from any Thing which is to be found in Europe, especially in France, that perhaps it would be Seen with a Jealous Eye.—of this however, I am no competent Judge.

Let me close this Letter, Sir, by giving you a Clue to the whole Mistery. There is a general Analogy, in the Governments and Characters of all the thirteen States: But as the Controversy and the War, began in the Massachusetts Bay, the principal Province of New England, their Institutions had the first operation. Four of those Institutions, Should be Studied and fully examined by any one, who would write with any Intelligence upon the Subject because they produced the decisive Effect, not only by the first decisions of the Controversy in publick Councils, and the first determinations to resist in Arms, but by Influencing the Minds of the other Colonies to follow their Example and to adopt, in a greater or less degree the Same Institutions and Similar Measures.

The four Institutions intended are, 1. the Towns. 2. The Churches. 3. The Schools. and 4. the Militia.

1. The Towns are certain Pieces of Land or Districts of Territory, into which the Massachusetts Bay, Connecticut, New Hampshire and Rhode Island are divided.—Each Town contains upon an Average Six miles or two Leagues Square. The Inhabitants who live within its Limits are erected by Law into a Corporation or Body Politick and are vested with certain Powers and Priviledges, Such as repairing the Roads, maintaining the Poor, choosing the Select Men Constables Collectors of Taxes, and other Officers, and above all their Representatives in the Legislature; and that of Assembling, whenever warned to it by their select Men, in Town Meeting to deliberate upon the publick affairs of the Town, or to instruct their Representatives. The Consequence of this Institution has been, that all the Inhabitants have acquired from their Infancy, an Habit of debating, deliberating and judging of public Affairs. it was in these Town Meetings that the Sentiments of the People were first formed, and their Resolutions taken from the Beginning to the End of this Controvesy and War.

2. The Churches are the religious Societies, which comprehend the whole People. each Town composes one Parish and one Church at least. most of them have more than one, and many of them Several. Each Parish has a Meeting house and a Minister, Supported at its own Expence. The Constitutions of the Churches are extreamly popular and the Clergy have little Authority or Influence, except such as their own Piety, Virtues and Learning naturally give them. They are chosen by the People of the Parish and ordained by the neighbouring Clergy. They all marry and have families, and live with their Parishes in mutual Friendship and good Offices. They visit the sick are charitable to the Poor, attend all Marriages & Funerals and preach, twice on every sunday. The least Reproach to their moral Character, ruins their Influence and forfeits their Liv-

ings, so that they are a wise virtuous and pious set of Men. Their sentiments are generally popular and they are zealous Friends of Liberty.

3. The Schools are in every Town. By an early Law of the Colony, every Town consisting of Sixty Families, is obliged, under a Penalty to maintain constantly a School House and a school Master, who teaches Reading, Writing Arithmetick and the Rudiments of Latin and Greek. To this public school the Children of all the Inhabitants poor as well as rich, have a Right to go. In these Schools are formed schollars for the Colleges at Cambridge New Haven, Warwick and Dartmouth, and in those Colledges are educated, Masters for the schools, Ministers for the Churches, Practitioners in Law and Physick, and Magistrates and officers for the Government of the Country.

4. The Militia comprehends the whole People.—By the Law of the Land every Male Inhabitant between Sixteen and Sixty Years of Age is enrolled in a Company and a Regiment of Militia, compleatly organized with all its officers, is obliged to keep at his own Expence constantly in his House, a Firelock in good order, a Powder Horn with a Pound of Powder, twelve Flynts four and Twenty Bullets, a Cartouch Box and an Havresack.— so that the whole Country is ready to march for their Defence at a short Warning. The Companies and Regiments are obliged to assemble certain Times of the Year, at the Command of their Officers, for the View of their Arms and Ammunition and to go through the military Exercises.

Thus, Sir you have a Brief Sketch of the four Principal Sources of that Wisdom in Council, and that skill and Bravery in War, which have produced the American Revolution and which I hope will be Sacredly preserved as the foundations of a free, happy and prosperous People.

If there is any other Particular in which I can give you any Information, you will do me a favour to mention it.

With very great Esteem I have the Honour to be, sir your most obedient and most humble servant

From the Diary: January 20, 1783

JANUARY 20. MONDAY.

Mr. Franklin and I met the Comte de Vergennes at his office at Ten. He told us, he was going to sign Preliminaries and an Armistice. At Eleven the C. D'Aranda came in, and Mr. Fitsherbert. After examining the Papers, D'Aranda and Fitsherbert signed the Preliminary Treaty, between the Crowns of G. Britain and Spain. De Vergennes and Fitsherbert that between Britain and France. Then Fitsherbert on one Part and Adams and Franklin on the other, signed, sealed and exchanged Declarations of Armistice between the Crown of Great Britain and the United States of America.

Previous to the Signature all the original Commissions were shewn. The C. D'Aranda shewed his. The C. de Vergennes his. Mr. Fitsherbert his—and Adams and Franklin theirs. Fitsherbert agreed to exchange Copies with Us.—Thus was this mighty System terminated with as little Ceremony, and in as short a Time as a Marriage Settlement.

Before the British and Spanish Ministers came in I asked the C. de Vergennes what was to become of Holland. He smiled and said, that We had nothing to do with that. I answered, with a Smile too, it was very true We had nothing to do with it, but that I interested myself very much, in the Welfare and Safety of that People. He then assumed an affected Air of Seriousness and said he interested himself in it too a good deal, and then told me, that the English had first wished to retain Demerary and Essquibo, but the king would not hear to that. Then they wanted Trincamale in the East Indies. But the King would not agree to that. Then they wanted Negapatnam. This the King left them to settle with the Dutch, but insisted on a Declaration from the King of G. Britain that he would restore all the other Possessions.

Fitsherbert told me afterwards it was the Severity of the Spaniards, that obliged his Court to be so hard with the Dutch. The Spaniards would do nothing without Minorca and the Floridas.

Returned to Paris and dined with the Duchess D'Anville and the Duke de la Rochefaucault.

DISMISSING A SUITOR

To Abigail Adams

My dearest Friend   Paris Jan. 22. 1783

The Preliminaries of Peace and an Armistice, were Signed at Versailles on the 20 and on the 21. We went again to pay our Respects to the King and Royal Family upon the Occasion. Mr. Jay was gone upon a little Excursion to Normandie and Mr. Laurens was gone to Bath, both for their health, so that the signature was made by Mr. Franklin and me. I want an Excursion too.

Thus drops the Curtain upon this mighty Trajedy. It has unravelled itself happily for Us. And Heaven be praised. Some of our dearest Interests have been saved, thro many dangers. I have no News from my son, Since the 8th. december, when he was at Stockholm, but hope every hour to hear of his Arrival at the Hague.

I hope to receive the Acceptance of my Resignation So as to come home in the Spring Ships.

I had written thus far when yours of 23 decr. was brought in. Its Contents have awakened all my sensibility, and shew in a stronger Light than ever the Necessity of my coming home. I confess I dont like the Subject at all. My Child is too young for such Thoughts, and I dont like your Word "Dissipation" at all. I dont know what it means, it may mean every Thing. There is not Modesty and Diffidence enough in the Traits you Send me. My Child is a Model, as you represent her and as I know her, and is not to be the Prize, I hope of any, even reformed Rake. A Lawyer would be my Choice, but it must be a Lawyer who spends his Midnights as well as Evenings at his Age over his Books not at any Ladys Fire side. I Should have thought you had seen enough to be more upon your Guard than to write Billets upon such a subject to such a youth. A Youth who has been giddy enough to Spend his Fortune or half his Fortune in Gaieties, is not the Youth for me, Let his Person, Family, Connections and Taste for Poetry be what they will. I am not looking out for a Poet, nor a Professor of belle Letters.

In the Name of all that is tender dont criticise Your Daughter for those qualities which are her greatest Glory her Reserve, and her Prudence which I am amazed to hear you call Want of Sensibility. The more Silent She is in Company, the better for me in exact Proportion and I would have this observed as a Rule by the Mother as well as the Daughter.

You know moreover or ought to know my utter Inability to do any Thing for my Children, and you know the long dependence of young Gentlemen of the most promising Talents and obstinate Industry, at the Bar. My Children will have nothing but their Liberty and the Right to catch Fish, on the Banks of Newfoundland. This is all the Fortune that I have been able to make for myself or them.

I know not however, enough of this subject to decide any Thing. Is he a Speaker at the Bar? If not he will never be any Thing. But above all I positively forbid, any Connection between my Daughter and any Youth upon Earth, who does not totally eradicate every Taste for Gaiety and Expence. I never knew one who had it and indulged it, but what was made a Rascall by it, sooner or later.

This Youth has had a brother in Europe, and a detestible Specimen he exhibited. Their Father had not all those nice sentiments which I wish, although an Honourable Man.

I think he and you have both advanced too fast, and I should advise both to retreat. Your Family as well as mine have had too much Cause to rue, the Qualities which by your own Account have been in him. And if they were ever in him they are not yet out.

This is too Serious a Subject, to equivocate about. I dont like this method of Courting Mothers. There is something too fantastical and affected in all this Business for me. It is not nature, modest, virtuous, noble nature. The Simplicity of Nature is the best Rule with me to Judge of every Thing, in Love as well as State and War.

This is all between you and me.

I would give the World to be with you Tomorrow. But there is a vast Ocean. No Ennemies. But I have not yet Leave from my Masters. I dont love to go home in a Miff, Pet or Passion nor with an ill Grace, but I hope Soon to have leave. I can never Stay in Holland—the Air of that Country chills every drop of

Blood in My Veins. If I were to stay in Europe another Year I would insist upon your coming with your daughter but this is not to be and I will come home to you.

Adieu ah ah Adieu.

CHOOSING A MINISTER TO GREAT BRITAIN

To Elias Boudinot

Sir, Paris Feby. 5th. 1783.

The Resolution of Congress of the 12th. July 1781,—"That the Commission and Instructions, for negociating a Treaty of Commerce between these United States and Great Britain, given to the Honorable John Adams on the 29th day of September 1779, be and they are hereby revoked," was duly recieved by me in Holland; but no Explanation of the Motives to it, or the Reasons on which it was founded, was ever transmitted to me by Congress, or the Committee of foreign Affairs, or any individual Member—Nor has any-body in Europe or America ever once attempted, that I know of, to guess at the reason.—Whether it was intended as a Punishment to me, or with a charitable design not to lead me into Temptation— Whether it was intended as a Punishment to the English for their Insolence and Barbarity—Whether it was intended to prevent or remove Suspicions of Allies, or the Envy and green eyed Jealousy of Co-Patriots, I know not.—Of one thing, however, I am fully satisfied, that Congress had Reasons and meant well—But whether those Reasons were founded on true or mistaken Information, I know not.

When I recollect the Instructions, which were given and revoked with that Commission, I can guess, and only guess, at some Considerations, which might, or might not, operate with Congress.—In these Instructions, Congress determined. 1st. That the common right of Fishing should in no Case be given up.—2dly. That it is essential to the Welfare of all these United States, that the Inhabitants thereof, at the Expiration of the War, should continue to enjoy the free and undisturbed Exercise of their common right to fish on the Banks of

Newfoundland, and the other fishing Banks of Newfoundland, and the other fishing Banks and Seas of North America, preserving inviolate the Treaties between France and the said States &$^{ca.}$ &$^{ca.}$—And 3$^{dly.}$ "That our Faith be pledged to the several States, that without their unanimous Consent no Treaty of Commerce shall be entered into, nor any Trade or Commerce whatever carried on with Great Britain, without the explicit Stipulation herein after mentioned.—You are therefore not to consent to any Treaty of Commerce with Great Britain, without an explicit Stipulation on her Part, not to molest or disturb the Inhabitants of the United States of America in taking Fish on the Banks of Newfoundland, and other Fisheries in the American Seas, any where excepting within the distance of three Leagues of the Shores of the Territories remaining to Great Britain at the close of the War, if a nearer distance cannot be obtained by Negociation:—And in the Negociation You are to exert your most strenuous Endeavours to obtain a nearer distance in the Gulph of S$^{t.}$ Laurence, and particularly along the Shores of Nova Scotia; as to which latter, We are desirous that even the Shores may be occasionally used for the purpose of carrying on the Fisheries by the Inhabitants of these States."

These Instructions are very decisive in favor of our indubitable right to the Fisheries: and it is possible, that Congress might be of Opinion, that Commerce would be the strongest Inducement to the English to make Peace, and at the same time, that there was something so Naval in the Fisheries, that the dread of acknowledging our right to them would be the strongest Obstacle in the way of Peace.—They might think too, that Peace was of more Importance to the United States, than a British Acknowledgment of our right to the Fisheries, which to be sure would have been enjoyed by our People in a good degree without it.—Reasonings like these might influence Congress to revoke the Commission and Instructions in question—But whatever Probability there might appear in them at that time, Experience has since shewn, that they were not well founded. On the contrary, Arguments have been found to convince the British Ministers themselves, that it was the Interest of their King and Country, not only to acknowledge the American Right to the Fisheries, but to encourage the unre-strained Exercise of it—These Considerations therefore can be no longer of any weight against a Treaty of Commerce with Great Britain, or against accrediting a Minister to the Court of S^t. James's—Nor can I concieve of any Motive now existing, against these Measures—On the contrary, so many Advantages present themselves to view, that I think it my Duty to recommend them to Congress, as proper to be adopted without loss of time.

If there are in Congress any of those Gentlemen, with whom I had the honor to serve in the Years 1775 and 1776, they may possibly remember, that in arguing in favor of sending Ministers to Versailles to propose a Connection with that Court, I laid it down as a first principle, that We should calculate all our Measures and foreign Negociations, in such a manner, as to avoid a too great dependence upon any one Power of Europe —to avoid all Obligations and Temptations to take any part in future European Wars—That the business of America with Europe was Commerce, not Politicks nor War—And that above all it never could be our Interest to ruin Great Britain, or injure or weaken her any farther, than should be necessary to support our Independence and our Alliances—And that as soon as Great Britain should be brought to a Temper to acknowledge our Sovereignty and our Alliances, and consent that We should maintain the one and fulfil the others, it would be our Interest and Duty to be her Friends; as well as the Friends of all the others Powers of Europe, & Enemies to none.—We are now happily arrived, through many tremendous Tempests, at that period—Great Britain repects Us as Sovereign States, and respects all our political Engagements with foreign Nations; and as long as She continues in this Temper of Wisdom, it is our Duty to respect her.—We have accordingly made a Treaty with her and mutually sworn to be Friends.—Through the whole period of our Warfare and Negociations, I confess I have never lost Sight of the Principles and the System, with which I sat out, which appeared to me too to be the Sentiments of Congress with great Unanimity, and I have no Reason to suppose that any Change of Opinion has taken place; and if there has not, every one will agree with me, that no Measure We can pursue will have such a Tendency to preserve the Government and People of England in the right System for their own and our Interest, and the Interest of our Allies too, well understood, as sending a Minister to reside at the Court of London.

In the next place, the Court of London is the best Station to collect Intelligence from every part; and, by means of the Freedom of the Press, to communicate Information for the benefit of our Country to every part of the World.—In time of Peace, there is so frequent travelling between Paris, London and the Hague, that the Correspondence of our Ministers at those Courts may be carried on by private Hands, without hazarding any thing from the Infidelity of the Posts, and Congress may reasonably expect Advantages from this Circumstance.

In the third place, a Treaty of Commerce with Great Britain is an Affair of great Importance to both Countries.—Upon this Occasion I hope I shall be excused, if I venture to advise, that Congress should instruct their Minister not to conclude such a Treaty; without sending the Project to them for their Observations and fresh Instructions—And I should think it would not be improper upon this Occasion to imitate the Dutch Method, take the Project ad referendum and transmit it to the Legislatures of all the States for their Remarks, before Congress finally resolve.—Their Minister may be authorized and instructed in the mean time, to enter into a temporary Convention for regulating the present Trade for a limited period of Months or Years, or until the Treaty of Commerce shall be compleated.—

In the fourth place, it is our part to be the first to send a Minister to Great Britain, which is the older, and as yet the superior State.—It becomes Us to send a Minister first, and I doubt not the King of Great Britain will very soon return the Compliment—Whereas if We do not begin, I believe there will be many Delicacies at S$^{t.}$ James's about being the first to send. —I confess, I wish a British Minister at Philadelphia, and think We should derive many benefits from his Residence.—While We have any foreign Ministers among Us, I wish to have them from all the great Powers, with whom We are much connected. —The Corps Diplomatick at every Court is, or ought to be, a System representing at least that part of the System of Europe, with which that Court is most conversant. In the same manner, or at least for similar Reasons, as long as We have any one

Minister abroad at any European Court, I think We ought to have one at every one, to which We are most essentially related, whether in Commerce or Policy, and therefore while We have any Minister at Versailles, the Hague, or London, I think it clear We ought to have one at each—Tho' I confess I have sometimes thought, that, after a very few Years, it will be the best thing We can do to recall every Minister from Europe, and send Embassies only on special Occasions.

If, however, any Members of Congress should have any Delicacies, lest an American Minister should not be recieved with a Dignity becoming his Rank and Character, at London, they may send a Commission, to make a Treaty of Commerce with Great Britain, to their Minister at Madrid, or Versailles, or the Hague, or S$^{t.}$ Petersbourg, and instruct him to carry on the Negociation from the Court where he may be, until he shall be invited to London,—Or a Letter of Credence may be sent to one of these with Instructions to go to London, as soon as the King shall appoint a Minister to go to Philadelphia.—After all however, my own Opinion is, that none of these Manœuvres are necessary, but that the best way will be, to send a Minister directly to S$^{t.}$ James's, with a Letter of Credence to the King as a Minister Plenipotentiary, and a Commission to treat of a Treaty of Commerce; but with Instructions not to come to any irrevocable Conclusion, until Congress and all the States have an Opportunity to consider of the Project, and suggest their Amendments.

There is one more Argument in favor of sending a Minister forthwith—It is this—While this Mission lies open, it will be a Source of Jealousy among present Ministers, and such as are or may be Candidates to be foreign Ministers—a Source of Intrigue and Faction among their Partizans and Adherents, and a Source of Animosity and Division among the People of the States.—For this Reason, it is a Pity that the first Choice had not been such as Congress could have continued to approve, and the first Measure such as Congress could have constantly persevered in.—If this had been the Case, the Door of Faction would have been kept shut.

As this however was once my Department by the Voice of Eleven States in twelve present, and as I will be answerable at any hazard, it will never be again the Department of any one by a greater Majority, there seems to be a Propriety in my giving my Advice concerning it, on taking Leave of it, if such is the Will of Congress, as I have before done in this Letter, according to the best of my Judgment.

And if it should not be thought too presumptuous, I would beg Leave to add, what is my Idea of the Qualifications necessary for an American foreign Minister in general, and particularly and above all to the Court of S^t. James's.—In the first place—He should have had an Education in classical Learning and in the Knowledge of general History, ancient and modern, particularly the History of France, England, Holland and America.—He should be well versed in the Principles of Ethicks; of the Law of Nature and Nations; of Legislation and Government; of the civil Roman Law; of the Laws of England and the United States; of the public Law of Europe, and in the Letters, Memoirs and Histories of those great Men, who have heretofore shone in the Diplomatick Order, and conducted the Affairs of Nations and the World. He should be of an Age to possess a Maturity of Judgment arising from Experience in Business—He should be active, attentive and industrious; and above all he should possess an upright Heart and an independent Spirit, and should be one, who decidedly makes the Interest of his Country, not the Policy of any other Nation nor his own private Ambition or Interest, or those of his Family, Friends and Connections, the Rule of his Conduct.

We hear so much said about a genteel address, and a Facility in speaking the French Language, that one would think a Dancing Master and French Master, the only Tutors necessary to educate a Statesman.—Be it remembered, the present Revolution, neither in America or Europe, has been accomplished by elegant Bows, nor by Fluency in French—Nor will any great thing ever be effected by such Accomplishments alone.—A Man must have something in his Head to say, before he can speak to effect, how ready soever he may be at Utterance— And if the Knowledge is in the Head and the Virtues, are in his Heart, he will never fail to find a way of communicating his Sentiments to good Purpose.—He will always have excellent Translators ready, if he wants them, to turn his Thoughts into any Language he desires.—As to what is called a fine Address, it is seldom attended to after the first or second Conversation, and even in these, it is regarded no more by Men of Sense of any Country, than another thing, which I once heard disputed with great Vivacity among the Officers of the French Frigate Le Sensible.—The Question was, what were the several Departments of an Ambassador and a Secretary of Legation? After a long and shrewd Discussion, it was decided by a Majority of Votes, "that the Secretary's Part was to do the Business, and that of the Ambassador to keep a Mistress."—This Decision produced a Laugh among the Company, and no Ideas of the kind will ever produce any thing else among Men of Understanding.

It is very true, that it is possible a Case may happen, that a Man may serve his Country by a Bribe well placed, or an Intrigue of Pleasure with a Woman—But it is equally true, that a Man's Country will be sold and betrayed a thousand Times by this infamous Commerce, where it will be one served.—It is very certain, that We shall never be a Match for European Statesmen in such Accomplishments for Negotiation, any more than, I must & will add, they will equal Us in any solid Abilities, Virtues & Application to Business; if We choose wisely among the excellent Characters, with which our Country abounds.—

Among the Ministers, which have already crossed the Atlantic to Europe, there have been none exceed^g M^r. Jay and M^r. Dana in all the Qualifications I have presumed to enumerate and I must say; that if I had the Honor to give my Vote in Congress, for a Minister at the Court of Great Britain, provided that Injustice must finally be done to him, who was the first Object of his Country's Choice, such have been the Activity, Intelligence, Address and Fortitude of M^r. Jay, as well as his Sufferings in his Voyage, Journies and passed Services, that I should think of no other Object of my Choice, than that Gentleman.

If Congress should neglect all their old Ministers, and send a fresh one from America, they cannot be at a loss—for there are in that Country great Numbers of Men well qualified for the Service—These are most certainly better known by Name to Congress, than to me, and therefore I shall venture no further, but conclude by wishing this arduous Business well settled, and by Assurances to Congress, and to You, Sir, of my warmest

Attachment and Respect.—your most obedient and most
humble Servant   John Adams

From the Diary:
February 18–March 9, 1783

1783 TUESDAY. FEB. 18.

Received a Letter from my Son John, dated at Gottenburgh
the 1. of Feb. This Letter gave me great Joy, it is the first I have
received from him since he left Petersbourg, and the first News
I have had of him since the Beginning of December, when he
was at Stockholm.—I have suffered extream Anxiety on his
Account.

I have omitted my Journal, and several Things of some Consequence, but I am weary, disgusted, affronted and disappointed. This State of Mind I must alter—and work while the
day lasts.

I have been injured, and my Country has joined in the Injury. It has basely prostituted its own honour by sacrificing
mine. But the Sacrifice of me for my Virtues, was not so servile,
and intollerable as putting Us all under Guardianship. Congress surrendered their own Sovereignty into the Hands of a
French Minister. Blush blush! Ye guilty Records! blush and
perish! It is Glory, to have broken such infamous orders. Infamous I say, for so they will be to all Posterity. How can such a
Stain be washed out? Can We cast a veil over it, and forget it?

In this Country, the Demon of Monarchy haunts all the
Scænes of Life. It appears in every Conversation, at every
Table and upon every Theatre. This People can attend to no
more than one Person at a Time. They can esteem but one,
and to that one their Homage is Adulation and Idolatry.

I once heard the Baron Van der Capellen de Poll say that the

Dæmon of Aristocracy appeared every where in that Republick. That he had collected together a Number of Merchants to sign a Requête. They agreed upon the Measure but insisted upon appointing a Committee to sign it. Many of them declared they would not sign it, with a Crowd, avec une foule.

Thus it is that the human Mind contracts habits of thinking from the Example of the Gouvernment. Accustomed to look up to a few as all in an Aristocracy, they imitate the same practice in private Life, and in common Things. Accustomed in monarchies to look up to one Man in great Affairs, they contract a similar disposition in little ones.

In the same manner in Democracies We contract an habit of deciding every Thing by a Majority of Votes. We put it to vote whether the Company will sing a Song or tell a Story. In an Aristocracy they ask 2 or 3 of the better Sort. In a Monarchy they ask the Lady or the Gentleman, in whose honour the feast was made.

March 9, 1783

AMERICA AND THE BALANCE OF POWER

To James Warren

confidential

Sir,   Paris March 20th, 1783.—

I was in hopes that the Peace would have put Us at ease; but it has not as yet much diminished our Anxiety.—The long interval, in which we have not been able to obtain any Intelligence from America, either by the way of Spain, France, Holland or England—The unsettled State of Parties and Councils in London, where there has been no responsible Minister this fortnight at least—The delay of the definitive Treaty, which it is now given out will not be signed for sometime, as there is to be a Congress and a Mediation here—And many other Causes, leave us in a painful state of Suspence and Solicitude.

The Revocation of the Commission to make a Treaty of Commerce with Great Britain, without issuing another, appears in Experience to be one of the most unfortunate measures, which Congress ever adopted.—My Lord Shelburne and his Colleagues had been convinced by various Arguments, that it was the Interest and best Policy of the British Nation to culti-vate the Friendship of America, and to allow her the amplest advantages in Trade; and the Voice of the Nation was falling in with this Principle: so that if there had been a Commission in being we should have had a provisional Treaty of Commerce with Great Britain, signed at the same time with the provi-sional Articles of Peace—But now there is great danger, that a new Ministry will come in, tainted with Passions, Prejudices and Principles as unfriendly to Us, as they are contracted in their Nature.—If any portion of foreign Influence contributed to the Revocation in question, the same will undoubtedly be employed in England; for it insinuates itself everywhere to em-broil Affairs there, and to prevent if possible a friendly Dis-position towards Us from prevailing. Can We blame this Influence? We ought only to blame ourselves for giving way to it.—It is not founded in our Interests, nor in any Interests that We are under any Obligation to favor. We are under no Ties of Honor, Conscience or good Faith, nor of Policy, Gratitude or Politeness, to sacrifice any profits which We can obtain in Trade with Great Britain, merely to promote the Trade of France. It is of the last Importance to Us in a political Light, that our Commerce should be impartial in future, and be drawn to no Country by any other Attraction than the best Bargains. The Price and Quality of Goods should be our only Criterion.—Let the Rivalry of our Trade be free and unre-strained—Let Nations contend which shall furnish Us the best Goods at the cheapest Rate, and Detur digniori.—

This is the only principle, which can warrant Us from too close an Attachment to one Scale in the Ballance of Europe, which will excite Jealousies in the other.—Gentlemen can never be too often requested to recollect the Debates in Con-gress in the Years 1775 & 1776, when the Treaty with France was first in Contemplation.—The Nature of those Connections, which ought to be formed between America and Europe, will never be better understood than they were at that time. It was then said, there is a Ballance of Power in Europe—Nature has formed it—Practice and Habit have confirmed it, and it must forever exist.—It may be disturbed for a time, by the accidental Removal of a Weight from one Scale to the other; but there will be a continual Effort to restore the Equilibrium.—The Powers of Europe now think Great Britain too powerful— They will see her Power diminished with pleasure—But they cannot see Us throw ourselves headlong into the Scale of Bourbon without Jealousy and Terror.—We must therefore give no exclusive priviledges in Trade to the House of Bourbon.—If We give exclusive priviledges in Trade, or form perpetual Alliances offensive and defensive with the Powers in one Scale, We infallibly make Enemies of those in the other, and some of these at least will declare War in favor of Great Britain.— Congress adopted these Principles and this System in its purity, and by their Wisdom have succeeded most perfectly in preventing every Power in the World from taking Part against them.—I hope I shall not give offence, if I humbly request Congress to take a review of the original Report of the Committee, which I think I remember very well as it is in my hand writing, and of the Alterations made in it, after debating it paragraph by paragraph in Congress.—Compare the Plan of a Treaty, which was sent over by Dr Franklin, with the Treaty as it was signed, and remark in how many particulars the distresses of our affairs have compelled Us to depart from the purity of our first Principle.—It is most certain We have now no Motive to depart farther from it.—One principal Duty of our Ministers abroad should have been to keep the several Courts informed that this was our System, which would have greatly facilitated & accelerated the progress of our Cause in Europe—But the Instructions, with which those Ministers have been bound, and the artful Obstructions thrown in their way, have rendered them much less useful than they might have been.—

I am very sorry to say, but my Duty obliges me to say, that in my poor Opinion our foreign Affairs have been very ill conducted.

Had I been permitted, on my Arrival in Paris in 1780, to open a Negociation with the British Ministry, if it had only been so far as to communicate to them, and if they had neglected to take Notice, to the Nation, Copies of my Commission to make Peace and a Treaty of Commerce with Great

Britain—Had M^r. Dana been permitted to communicate his Commission to the Ministers of the several Courts to which he is destined—Had M^r. Jay, M^r. Dana and myself been encouraged and countenanced as We ought to have been, instead of being opposed, obstructed, neglected and slighted, as We have been in our several Departments, many thousands of Lives would have been saved, many Millions of Money, and the War would have come to a Conclusion much sooner, upon Terms quite as advantageous to America, more equitable to Holland, and more glorious for France.—I must and do most solemnly deliver it as my Opinion, that French Policy has obstructed the progress of our Cause in Europe, more than British.—It is high time that We should be upon our Guard, and not mistake Evil for Good.

M^r. Marbois has not been alone in his Idea, *"that the independent Party will always stand in great Want of our Support,"* nor in his Endeavors to keep the independent Party always in want of such Support.

Every Step, which our Negociations advanced in Europe, diminished this "Want of Support."—It was a Crime in me to wish to do something in Holland to render Us less dependent on France, as it was in M^r. Samuel Adams to toast, "May the United States ever maintain their Right to the Fisheries."—

But I venture to say, the Authors of this shackling and clipping System, this enfeebling and impoverishing Plan, have been very bad French Politicians.—They have been ignorant of America, the Character of her People and her Resources.—They must reform their Policy, or their Master and his Country will have Cause to repent it.—They must change their System; and the sooner they are plainly and honestly told so, the better—The United States of America are not a Power to be trifled with.—There has been too much trifling in many Respects.

There are Intimations of a Desire of Commercial Treaties and Connections at present in various Parts of Europe.—The United States have been admitted to dance amongst the proudest Powers of Europe at a Masquerade Ball at the Court of Turin, and Portugal has acknowledged their Independence by the Act inclosed.—

With great Respect and Esteem, I have the Honour to be Sir, your most obedient and most humble servant

John Adams

HOPING TO RETURN HOME

To Abigail Adams

My dearest Friend   Paris March 28. 1783

On the 30 Nov. our Peace was Signed. On the 28. March We dont know that you have Yet heard of it. A Packet Should have been Sent off. I have not yet received the Ratification of my Dutch Treaty. I know not when I Shall be able to embark for home. If I receive the Acceptance of my Resignation, I Shall embark in the first ship, the first good ship I mean, for I love you too well, to venture my self in a bad one, and I love my own Ease to well to go in a very Small one.

I am Sometimes half afraid, that those Persons who procured the Revocation of my Commission to King George, may be afraid I shall do them more harm in America, than in England, and therefore of two Evils to choose the least and manoeuvre to get me sent to London. By several Coaxing hints of that Kind, which have been written to me and given me in Conversation, from Persons who I know are employed to do it, I fancy that Something of that is in Contemplation. There is another Motive too—they begin to dread the Appointment of some others whom they like less than me. I tremble when I think of such a Thing as going to London. If I were to receive orders of that sort, it would be a dull day to me. No Swiss ever longed for home more than I do. I Shall forever be a dull Man in Europe. I cannot bear the Thought of transporting my Family to Europe. It would be the Ruin of my Children forever. And I cannot bear the Thought of living longer Seperate from them. Our foreign Affairs, are like to be in future as they have been in times past an eternal Scæne of Faction. The fluctuation of Councils at Philadelphia have encouraged it, and even good Men Seem to be Seized with the Spirit of it.

The definitive Treaty is yet delayed, and will be for any Thing I can see till Mid Summer. It may however be signed in a few Weeks. If it should be signed I could go home with the Dutch Ambassador, in a Frigate which will sail from the Texel in June. But So many Points are uncertain, that I cannot determine on any thing. Dont think of coming to Europe however, unless you should receive a further desire from me, which is not at all probable. My present Expectations are to pay my Respects to you, at Braintree, before Midsummer.

My dear Daughters happiness employs my Thoughts night and Day. Dont let her form any Connections with any one, who is not devoted entirely to study and to Business. To honour and Virtue. If there is a Trait of Frivolity and Dissipation left, I pray that She may renounce it, forever. I ask not Fortune nor Favour for mine, but Prudence, Talents and Labour. She may go with my Consent whenever she can find enough of these.

My Son, has been another Source of Distress to me. The terrible Weather has made his Journey from Petersbourg very long. But I have a Letter from him at Hamborough the 14th. and hope he is at the Hague by this day. I am much relieved on his Account. My Charles and Thomas how are they? Fine Boys I dare Say? Let them take Care how they behave if they desire their Fathers Approbation. My Mother and your Father enjoy I hope a good Share of Health and Spirits. Mr. Cranch's Health is perfectly restored I hope, and Uncle Quincy and Dr. Tufts as good and as happy as ever. Why should not my Lot in Life be as easy as theirs? So it would have been if I had been as wise as they and staid at home as they do. But where would have been our Cod and Haddock, our Bever skins Deer skins and Pine Trees? Alass all lost, perhaps. Indeed I firmly believe so, in a good Conscience. I cannot therefore repent of all my fatigues, Cares, Losses, Escapes, anxious Days and Sleepless nights.

Nothing in Life ever cost me so much Sleep, or made me so many grey Hairs, as the Anxiety, I have Suffered for these Three Years on the Score of these Objects. No body knows of it: Nobody cares for it. But I shall be rewarded for it, in Heaven I hope. Where Mayhew, and Thatcher and Warren are rewarded I hope, none of whom however were permitted to suffer so much. They were taken away from the Evil to come.

I have one favour for you to ask of Mr. Adams the President

of the senate. It is that he would make a compleat Collection
of his Writings and publish them in Volumes. I know of no
greater service that could be rendered to the Rights of Mankind. At least that he would give you a List of them. They
comprize a Period of forty Years. And although they would
not find so many Rakes for Purchasers, as the Writings of
Voltaire, they would do infinitely more good to mankind especially in our rising Empire. There Posterity will find a Mass of
Principles, and Reasonings, Suitable for them and for all good
Men. The Copy, I fancy would Sell to Advantage in Europe.

Yours most affectiatly and eternally.

FRANKLIN'S DECEITFULNESS

To James Warren

Confidential.

Dear Sir,   Paris April 13[th.] 1783.
    I have in some late Letters opened to You in Confidence the
Dangers, which our most important Interests have been in, as
well as the Opposition and Jealousy and Slanders, which your
Ministers have met with, from the vain, ambitious and despotic
Character of one Minister, I mean the C. de Vergennes—But
You will form but an imperfect Idea after all of the Difficulties
We have had to encounter, without taking into Consideration
another Character equally selfish and interested—equally vain
and ambitious—more jealous and envious, and more false &
deceitful, I mean D[r.] Franklin.

    It is a Saying of Algernoon Sidney concerning Sir Walter
Rawleigh, that "his Morals were not sufficiently exact for a
great Man"—And the Observation can never be applied with
more propriety than to D[r.] Franklin.—His whole Life has been
one continued Insult to good Manners and to Decency. His
Son, and Grandson, as he calls him with characteristic Modesty; the Effrontery with which he has forced these his off-
spring up in the World, not less than his Speech of Polly Baker,
are Outrages to Morality & Decorum, which would never

have been forgiven in any other American—These things however are not the worst of his Faults—They shew however the
Character of the Man; in what Contempt he holds the Opinions of the World, and with what Haughtiness he is capable of
persevering through Life in a gross & odious System of Falsehood and Imposture.

A sacred regard to Truth is among the first and most essential Virtues of a public Man—How many Kings have involved
themselves and their Kingdoms in Misfortunes, by a Laxness
in this particular? How much Mischief has been done in all
Ages by Ministers of State, who have indulged themselves in a
Duplicity and Finesse, or in other Words, in an Hipocrisy and
Falsehood, which some are even abandoned enough to recommend and prescribe to Politicians, but which never yet did any
thing but Harm and Mischief.—I am sorry to say, but strict
and impartial Justice obliges me to say, that from five complete
Years of Experience of Dr Franklin, which I have now had in
Europe, I can have no Dependence on his Word. I never know
when he speaks the Truth, and when not. If he talked as much
as other Men, and deviated from the Truth as often in proportion as he does now, he would have been the Scorn of the Universe long ago—But his perpetual Taciturnity has saved him.

It would be Folly to deny, that he has had a great Genius,
and that he has written several things in Philosophy and in
Politicks, profoundly—But his Philosophy and his Politicks
have been infinitely exaggerated, by the studied Arts of Em-
piricism, until his Reputation has become one of the grossest
Impostures, that has ever been practised upon Mankind since
the Days of Mahomet.

A Reputation so imposing in a Man of Artifice and Duplicity, of Ambition and Vanity, of Jealousy and Envy, is as real a
Tyranny as that of the Grand Seignior. It is in vain to talk of
Laws of Justice, of Right, of Truth, of Liberty, against the Authority of such a Reputation. It produces all the Servility of
Adulation—all the Fear, all the Expectation & Dependence in
common Minds, that is produced by the imposing Pomp of a
Court and of Imperial Splendour. He has been very sensible of
this, & has taken Advantage of it.

As if he had been conscious of the Laziness, Inactivity and
real Insignificance of his advanced Age, he has considered

every American Minister, who has come to Europe, as his natural Enemy. He has been afraid that some one would serve his Country, acquire a Reputation, and begin to be thought of by Congress to replace him.—

Sensible that his Character has not been so much respected in America as in Europe, he has sought an Alliance to support him with Mr de Sartine and the C. de Vergennes and their "Autours" Satellites. It is impossible to prove, but from what I know of him, I have no doubt, that he is the Man, who, by means of the Emissaries or Satellites just alluded to, made to those Ministers all the malicious Insinuations against M^r. Lee & M^r. Izard, which, altho' absolutely false and groundless, have made as much Noise in the World, & had almost the same Effects, as if they had been true—From the same detestable Source came the Insinuations and Prejudices against me, and the shameless abandoned Attack upon me, the History of which You know better than I.—Hence too the Prejudices against M^r. Dana, M^r. Jay & every other. These are my Opinions, tho' I cannot prove them, otherwise than by what I have seen and heard myself, what results from a long Series of Letters & Transactions, and what I know of the Characters of the Men. The C. has had his Head filled with so many Prejudices against others, and in favor of him, and has found him so convenient a Minister,—ready always to comply with every Desire, —never asking any thing but when ordered and obliged to ask for Money—never proposing any thing—never advising any thing, that he has adopted all his Passions, Prejudices & Jealousies, and has supported him, as if his own Office depended upon him—He and his Office of Interpreters have filled all the Gazettes of Europe with the most senseless Flattery of him, and by means of the Police set every Spectacle, Society, and even private Club and Circle to clapping him with such Applause, as they give to Opera Girls.—This being the unfortunate Situation of foreign Affairs, what is to be done?

Franklin has, as he gives out, asked Leave to resign—He does not mean to obtain it, but to save the Shame of being recalled. I wish with all my Soul he was out of public Service, and in Retirement, repenting of his past Life, and preparing, as he ought to be, for another World. But as the Peace is made, and he is old, and it will make a horrid Wonder in the World to remove him, and it would be impossible to publish the whole Truth in Justification of it to the People of America as well as of Europe, perhaps it may be as well to let him alone.—But at least Congress should firmly and steadily support their other Ministers against his insidious Manœuvres—They should add no more Feathers to his Cap. This will however be difficult. He will watch Opportunities, and French Influence will forever aid him, and both will be eternally attacking openly and secretly every other Minister—so that I am persuaded he will remain as long as he lives, the Demon of Discord among our Ministers, and the Curse and Scourge of our foreign Affairs.

France has suffered as much as America, by the unskilful & dishonest Conduct of our foreign Affairs. They have had no Confidence in any but him—And he either knew nothing or cared nothing about Affairs—They have not only not confided in any other, but they have persecuted every other—By which Means France has not derived half the Advantage from the Alliance in the War, nor will She hold half the Benefit after the Peace, which She might have done, if She had vouchsafed to hearken to the Advice of those, who would have given it honestly and wisely.

To enter into the contemptible detail of all the unworthy Artifices, the Follies and Impositions, that have been the Fruit of these Characters; the "petit Commerce" of—&c—&c—the Arts in Holland, Spain, Russia, Sweeden, Denmark and all the rest of Europe, to prevent the progress of our Cause, and defeat our Negociations; to straiten in the Article of Money, and distress Us in the War; to keep Us humble, tame and dependent; to strip Us of the Fishery and Western Lands; the Millions of Affronts, Neglects, Contempts, or, in one French Word, "Desagremens," which have been put upon the Servants of Congress, would fill Volumes.

The Moral and the Politick of all is—"See with your own Eyes—judge with your own Understanding—repeal every shackling Instruction to your Ministers—support them inflexibly against all foreign Influence, and all little spiteful Intrigues."

For my own part, I have been made a Sacrifice to such Intrigues in so gross a manner, that unless I am restored and supported, I am unalterably determined to retire—So resolves your invariable Friend   J. Adams

THE ENEMIES OF SIMPLE INTEGRITY

To Abigail Adams

My dearest Friend   Paris April 16. 1783

If Congress when they revoked my Commission had appointed another to make a Treaty of Commerce with Great Britain, We should have had the Business all done on the 30 of Nov. Shelburnes Ministry would not have been condemned in the H. of Commons, and the definitive Treaty would have been signed before now and I Should be ready to embark for the Blue Hills, where I must go to recover my health, repose my Spirits, take a little Care of my Sons and Daughter, and be made much of, by their Mother.

My last Voyage and Residence in Europe has broken me very much. Millions of Contrivances are used, by some invisible Spirit, with Arrows shot in darkness to render an honest Mans Life uncomfortable to him, in every Part of Europe. In England the only Place where I could go with honour, I should live the Life of a Man in a Barrell Spiked with Nails. The Vanity, Pride, Revenge, of that People, irritated by French and Franklinian Politicks, would make it Purgatory to me. I sometimes feel Seriously afraid that Congress will send me, a Credence to that Court. I should be terrified at the sight of such a Thing.

My Health, to Speak to you Seriously, demands a Voyage home, my native Air and Repose from Business. You know very well that those Remedies alone have heretofore saved my Life. The Consequences of that Amsterdam Fever, are still upon me in Swelled Ankles, Weakness in my Limbs, a Sharp humour in my Blood, lowness of Spirits, Anxieties &c. I exercise every day on horse back or on foot, and take every Precaution in my Power, but all does not avail.

I begin to suspect that french and franklinian Politicks will now endeavour to get me sent to England, for two Reasons, one that I may not go to America where I should do them more Mischief as they think than I could in London. 2. That the Mortifications which they and their Tools might give me there might disembarrass them of me sooner than any where.

Is it not Strange and Sad that Simple Integrity should have so many Ennemies? that a Man should have to undergo so many Evils merely because he will not betray his Trust? If I would have given up the Fisheries and Illinois and Louisiana and Ohio, I might have had Gold snuff Boxes, Clappings at the Opera, I dont mean from the Girls, millions of Paragraphs in the Newspapers in praise of me, Visits from the Great, Dinners Wealth, Power Splendor, Pictures Busts statues, and every Thing which a vain heart, and mine is much too vain, could desire. Mais Je ne Scais pas, me donner aux tells Convenances et Bienseances.

I have found by Experience, that in this Age of the World that Man has an awfull Lot, who "dares to love his Country and be poor."

Liberty and Virtue! When! oh When will your Ennemies cease to exist or to persecute!

Our Country will be envied, our Liberty will be envied, our Virtues will be envied. Deep and subtle systems of Corruption hard to prove, impossible to detect, will be practised to sap and undermine Us and the few who penetrate them will be called suspicious, envious, restless turbulent ambitious—will be hated unpopular and unhappy.

But a Succession of these Men must be preserved, for these are the salt of the Earth. Without these the World would be worse than it is. Is not this after all the noblest Ambition. Such Ambition is Virtue. Cato will never be Consull but Catos Ambition was sublimer than Cæsars, and his Glory and even his Catastrophy more desirable.

I have Sometimes painted to myself my own Course for these 20 Years, by a Man running a race upon a right line barefooted treading among burning Ploughshares, with the horrid Figures of Jealousy Envy Hatred Revenge, Vanity Ambition, Avarice Treachery Tyranny Insolence, arranged on each side of his Path and lashing him with scorpions all the Way, and attempting at every Step to trip up his Heels.

I have got through, however to the Goal, but maimed scarrified and out of Breath.

From the Diary: April 30–May 2, 1783

1783. APRIL 30. WEDNESDAY.

Mr. Hartley did me the Honour of a Visit to assure me, as he said of the Satisfaction he had in reflecting, upon what passed Yesterday, and upon what We had agreed upon. He thought it was exactly as it should be. I was glad to hear of his Satisfaction and expressed my own. I told him that I was so convinced, that Great Britain and America would soon feel the Necessity and Convenience of a right Plan of Commerce that I was not anxious about it. That it was simply from a pure regard to Great Britain, and to give them an opportunity of alluring to themselves as much of our Commerce, as in the present State of Things would be possible, that I should give myself any Trouble about it. That I had never had but one Principle and one System, concerning this Subject, before, during or since the War, and that had generally been the System of Congress viz. That it was not our Interest to hurt Great Britain any further than was necessary to support our Independence and our Alliances. That the French Court had sometimes endeavoured to warp us from this System, in some degrees and particulars, that they had sometimes succeeded with some American Ministers and Agents, Mr. Deane particularly, and I must add that Dr. Franklin had not adhered to it at all times with so much Firmness as I could have wished, and indeed Congress itself from the Fluctuation of its Members, or some other Cause had sometimes appeared to loose Sight of it. That I had constantly endeavoured to adhere to it, but this Inflexibility had been called Stubbornness, Obstinacy, Vanity &c. and had exposed me to many Attacks, and disagreable Circumstances. That it had been to damp the Ardour of returning Friendship as I supposed, which had induced the French Minister, to use his Influence to get the Commission to make a Treaty of Commerce with Great Britain, revoked without appointing another. That I did not care a Farthing for a Commission to Great Britain, and wished that the one to me had never existed, but that I was very sorry it was revoked without appointing another. That the Policy of this Court he might well think would be, to lay every stumbling Block between

G. Britain and America. They Wished to deprive Us of the Fisheries and Western Lands for this Reason. They espoused the Cause of the Tories for this Reason.

I told him the Comte de Vergennes and I were pursuing different Objects. He was endeavouring to make my Countrymen meek and humble and I was labouring to make them proud. I avowed it was my Object, to make them hold up their Heads, and look down upon any Nation that refused to do them Justice. That in my Opinion Americans had nothing to fear, but from the Meekness of their own Hearts. As Christians I wished them Meek, as Statesmen I wished them proud, and I thought the Pride and the Meekness very consistent. Providence had put into our hands such Advantages, that We had a just Right and it was our Duty to insist upon Justice from all Courts, Ministers and Nations.

That I wished him to get his Commission as soon as possible and that We might discuss every Point and be perfectly ready to sign the definitive Treaty.

He said his Commission would come as soon as the Courier could go and return, and that he would prepare his Propositions for the definitive Treaty, immediately. He said he had not imagined that We had been so *stout* as he found Us.—But he was very silent and attentive. He has had hints I suppose, from Laurens and Jay, and Franklin too. He never before discovered a Capacity to hearken. He ever before took all the Talk to himself. I am not fond of talking, but I wanted to convey into his Mind a few Things, for him to think upon. None of the English Gentlemen have come here apprized of the Place where their danger lay.

FRYDAY. MAY 2.

Mr. Hartley came in to introduce to me his Secretary Mr. Hammond, whom he introduced also to mine, Mr. Thaxter and Storer.

He told me that the C. de Vergennes had been treating with Mr. Fitsherbert about the Post of Panmure at the Natches, which is within the Limits which England has acknowledged to be the Bounds of the United States. The Spaniards want to keep it, and the C. de Vergennes wants to make a Merit of procuring it for them with a few Leagues round it.—I told Mr. Hartley that this Subject was within the exclusive Jurisdiction of Mr. Jay. That the Minister for Peace had nothing to say in it.

I told Mr. Hartley the Story of my Negotiations with the C. de Vergennes about communicating my Mission to Ld. G. Germaine 3 Years ago and the subsequent Intrigues and Disputes &c. It is necessary to let the English Ministers know where their danger lies, and the Arts used to damp the Ardour of returning friendship.

Mr. Jay came, with several Pieces of Intelligence. 1. The Story of Panmure. 2. The Marquis de la Fayette told him that no Instructions were ever sent by the C. de Vergennes to the C. Montmorrin to favour Mr. Jays Negotiations at Madrid and that Montmorrin told la Fayette so.

Mr. Jay added that the Marquis told him, that the C. de Vergennes desired to ask Mr. Jay why he did not come and see him? Mr. Jay says he answered how can he expect it? when he knows he has endeavoured to play Us out of the Fisheries and vacant Lands? Mr. Jay added that he thought it would be best to let out by degrees, and to communicate to some French Gentlemen, the Truth and shew them Marbois's Letter. Particularly he mentioned C. Sarsefield.

Mr. Jay added, every Day produces some fresh Proof and Example of their vile Schemes. He had applied to Montmorin, to assist him, countenance him, support him, in his Negotiation at Madrid, and shewed him a Resolution of Congress by which the King of France was requested to Aid him. Montmorin said he could not do it, without Instructions from his Court, that he would write for Instructions, but Mr. Jay says he never heard any farther about it. But Yesterday La Fayette told him that Montmorin told him, no such Instruction had ever been sent him.

In Truth Congress and their Ministers have been plaid upon like Children, trifled with, imposed upon, deceived. Franklin's Servility and insidious faithless Selfishness is the true and only Cause why this Game has succeeded. He has aided Vergennes with all his Weight, and his great Reputation, in both Worlds, has supported this ignominious System and blasted every Man and every Effort to shake it off. I only have had a little Success against him.

To John Quincy Adams

My dear Child   Paris May 14. 1783

Mr. Hardouin has just now called upon me, and delivered me your Letter of the 6 Instant.

I find that, although, your hand Writing is distinct and legible, yet it has not engaged So much of your Attention as to be remarkably neat. I Should advise you to be very carefull of it: never to write in a hurry, and never to let a Slovenly Word or Letter go from you. If one begins at your Age, it is easier to learn to write well than ill, both in Characters and Style. There are not two prettier accomplishments than a handsome hand and Style, and these are only to be acquired in youth. I have Suffered much, through my whole Life, from a Negligence of these Things in my young days, and I wish you to know it. Your hand and Style, are clear enough to Shew that you may easily make them manly and beautifull, and when a habit is got, all is easy.

I See your Travells have been expensive, as I expected they would be: but I hope your Improvements have been worth the Money. Have you kept a regular Journal? If you have not, you will be likely to forget most of the Observations you have made. If you have omitted this Usefull Exercise, let me advise you to recommence it, immediately. Let it be your Amusement, to minute every day, whatever you may have seen or heard worth Notice. One contracts a Fondness of Writing by Use. We learn to write readily, and what is of more importance We think, and improve our Judgments, by committing our Thoughts to Paper.

Your Exercises in Latin and Greek must not be omitted a Single day, and you should turn your Mind, a little to Mathematicks. There is among my Books a Fennings Algebra. Begin it immediately and go through it, by a Small Portion every day. You will find it as entertaining as an Arabean Tale. The Vulgar Fractions with which it begins, is the best extant, and you should make yourself quite familiar with it.

A regular Distribution of your Time, is of great Importance.

You must measure out your Hours, for Study, Meals, Amusements, Exercise and Sleep, and suffer nothing to divert you, at least from those devoted to study.

But above all Things, my son, take Care of your Behaviour and preserve the Character you have acquired, for Prudence and Solidity. Remember your tender Years and treat all the World with Modesty, Decency and Respect.

The Advantage you have in Mr. Dumas's Attention to you is a very precious one. He is himself a Walking Library, and so great a Master of Languages ancient and modern is very rarely Seen. The Art of asking Questions is the most essential to one who wants to learn. Never be too wise to ask a Question.

Be as frugal as possible, in your Expences.

Write to your Mamma Sister and brothers, as often as you have opportunity. It will be a Grief to me to loose a Spring Passage home, but although I have my fears I dont yet despair.

Every Body gives me a very flattering Character of your Sister, and I am well pleased with what I hear of you: The principal Satisfaction I can expect in Life, in future will be in your good Behaviour and that of my other Children. My Hopes from all of you are very agreable. God grant, I may not be dissappointed.

Your affectionate Father   John Adams

From the Diary: June 1, 1783

1783 JUNE 1. SUNDAY.

The Loadstone is in Possession of the most remarkable, wonderfull and misterious Property in Nature. This Substance is in the Secret of the whole Globe. It must have a Sympathy with the whole Globe. It is governed by a Law and influenced by some active Principle that pervades and operates from Pole to pole, and from the Surface to the Center and the Antipodes. It is found in all Parts of the Earth. Break the Stone to Pieces, and each Morcel retains two Poles, a north and a south Pole, and does not loose its Virtue. The Magnetic Effluvia are too subtle, to be seen by a Microscope, yet they have great

Activity and Strength. Iron has a Sympathy with Magnatism and Electricity, which should be examined by every Experiment, which Ingenuity can devise.

Has it been tryed whether the Magnet looses any of its Force in Vacuo? in a Bottle charged with Electrical Fire? &c. This Metal called Iron may one day reveal the Secrets of Nature. The primary Springs of Nature may be too subtle for all our Senses and Faculties. I should think however that no Subject deserved more the Attention of Philosophers or was more proper for Experiments than the Sympathy between Iron and the magnetical and Electrical Fluid.

It would be worth while to grind the Magnet to Powder and see if the Dust still retained the Virtue. Steep the Stone or the Dust in Wine, Spirits, Oyl and other fluids to see if the Virtue is affected, increased or diminished.

Is there no Chimical Proscess, that can be formed upon the Stone or the Dust to discover, what it is that the magnetic Virtue resides in.

Whether boiling or burning the Stone destroys or diminishes the Virtue.

See whether Earth, Air, Water or Fire any wise applied affects it, and how.

Mr. Laurens came in, in the Morning and We had a long Conversation upon his proposed Journey to England to borrow some Money. I explained to him the Manner and Conditions of my Loan in Holland.

Dined at the Spanish Ambassadors with the Corps Diplomatick. Mr. Markoff was there, and was very civil.

D'Aranda lives now in the End of the New Buildings which compose the Façade de la Place de Louis 15. From the Windows at the End you look into the grand Chemin, the Champs eliseés, and the Road to Versailles. From the Windows and Gallery in the Front you see the Place de Louis 15, the Gardens of the Tuilerries, the River and the fine Rowe of Houses beyond it, particularly the Palais du Bourbon and the Dome of the Invalids. It is the finest Situation in Paris.

Mr. Fitzherbert told me, I might depend upon it the present Ministry would continue, at least untill the next Meeting of Parliament. He says there is little to be got in the Company of the Corps Diplomatick. They play deep, but there is no Conversation.

He says he is acquainted with half a Dozen of the Women of the Town, who live in houses which with their Furniture could not have cost less than twenty five Thousand Pounds. They live in a style he says which cannot be supported for less than two Thousand a Year. These are kept by grave People, Men of the Robe, &c. He says there is nothing like this in London. That the Corruption of manners, is much greater here, than there.

Mr. De Stutterheim the Minister from Saxony came to me and said, he had received orders from his Court to propose a Treaty of Commerce with the United States. He said he had spoken to Mr. Franklin about it. I asked him if Mr. Franklin had written to Congress upon it. He said he did not know. I told him that I thought Mr. Dana at Petersbourg had Power to treat tho not to conclude. He said he would call upon me, some Morning at My House, to consult about it.

Herreria dined there and the Duke of Berwick.

MISTRUST OF THE FRENCH

To Robert R. Livingston

Sir,   Paris July 10th. 1783.

In the present violent heat of the Weather, and feverish state of my own health, I cannot pretend to sit long at my Pen, and must pray you to accept of a few short hints only.

To talk, in a general stile, of Confidence in the French Court &ca. is to use a general language, which may mean almost any thing, or almost nothing.—To a certain degree, and as far as the Treaties and Engagements extend, I have as much Confidence in the French Court, as Congress has, or even as you, Sir, appear to have.

But if by Confidence in the French Court is meant, an Opinion that the French Office of foreign Affairs would be Advocates with the English for our rights to the Fishery, or the Mississippi River, or our Western Territory, or Advocates to persuade the British Ministers to give up the Cause of the Refugees, and make a parliamentary provision for them, I own I have no such Confidence, and never had.—Seeing and hearing what I have seen and heard, I must have been an Idiot to have entertained such Confidence—And having no such Confidence, I should be more of a Machevilian, or a Jesuit, than I ever was, or will be, to counterfeit it to you or to Congress.

Mr Marbois Letter is to me full proof of the principles of the C. de Vergennes. Why? Because I know, (for it was personally communicated to me upon my passage home by Mr Marbois himself) the Intimacy and the Confidence there is between these two—And I know farther, that that Letter contains Sentiments concerning the Fisheries diametrically opposite to those, which Mr Marbois repeatedly expressed to me upon the Passage, vizt "That the Newfoundland Fishery was our right, and we ought to maintain it." From whence I conclude, that Mr Marbois Sentiments have been changed by the Instructions of the Minister. To what purpose is it, where this Letter came from? Is it less genuine, whether it came from Philadelphia, Versailles, or London? What if it came thro' English Hands? Is there less weight, less evidence in it, for that? Are the Sentiments more just, or more friendly to Us, for that?

Mr Rayneval's Correspondence too with Mr Jay. Mr Rayneval is a Chef du Bureau. But we must be very ignorant of all Courts not to know, that an Under Secretary of State dares not carry on such a Correspondence without the Knowledge, Consent and Orders of the Principal.

There is another point now in agitation, in which the French will never give Us one good word. On the contrary, they will say every thing they can think of to persuade the English to deprive Us of the Trade of their West India Islands. They have already, with their Emissaries, been the chief Cause of the Change of Sentiments in London on this head against Us.

In general, they see with pain every appearance of returning real & cordial Friendship, such as may be permanent between Us and Great Britain. On the contrary they see with pleasure every Seed of Contention between Us. The Tories are an excellent Engine of Mischief between Us, and therefore very precious.—Exclusion from the West India Islands, will be another.

I hold it to be the indispensible duty of my Station, not to conceal from Congress these Truths. Dont let Us be Dupes, under the Idea of being grateful. Innumerable Anecdotes happen daily to shew that these Sentiments are general.

In Conversation a few Weeks ago with the Duke de la Vauguyon, upon the subject of the West India Trade, I endeavoured to convince him, that France & England both ought to admit Us freely to their Islands. He entered into a long Argument, to prove that both ought to exclude Us. At last I said, "the English were a parcel of Sots to exclude Us—for the consequence of it would be, that in 15 or 20 Years we should have another War with them." "Tant mieux! Tant mieux! Tant mieux! Je vous en felicite—" cried the Duke, with great pleasure. "Tant mieux pour nous," says I, because we shall conquer from the English in that Case all their Islands, the Inhabitants of which would now declare for Us, if they dared—But it will be not the better for the English. They will be the Sots and Dupes, if they lay a foundation for it.—"Oui Monsieur, says the Duke, je crois que vous aurez une autre guerre contre les Anglais."—And in this wish he expressed the feelings and the Vows of every Frenchman upon the face of the Earth.

If therefore We have it in Contemplation to avoid a future War with the English, dont let Us have too much Confidence in the French, that they will favor Us in this View.

I have the honor to be, with great Respect and Esteem, Sir, your most obedient & most humble Servant.   John Adams.

AMERICAN OBLIGATIONS TO FRANCE

To Robert R. Livingston

Sir   Paris July 11ᵗʰ· 1783.

As there are certain particulars, in which it has appeared to me that the friendship of a French Minister has been problematical at least, or rather not to exist at all, I have freely mentioned them to Congress; because I hold it to be the first duty of a public Minister in my Situation, to conceal no important Truth of this kind from his Masters.

But Ingratitude is an odious Vice, & ought to be held in detestation by every American Citizen. We ought to distinguish therefore between those points, for which We are not obliged to our Allies, from those in which We are.

I think then We are under no particular Obligations of Gratitude to them for the Fisheries, the Boundaries, Exemption from the Tories, or for the progress of our Negotiations in Europe.

We are under Obligations of Gratitude for making the Treaty with Us when they did; for those Sums of Money which they have generously given Us, and for those even which they have lent Us, which I hope We shall punctually pay, and be thankful still for the Loan; for the Fleet & Army they sent to America, & for all the important Services they did. By other mutual Exertions a dangerous Rival to them, and I may almost be warranted in saying, an imperious Master both to them and Us, has been brought to Reason, and put out of the Power to do Harm to either. In this respect, however, our Allies are more secure than we. The House of Bourbon has acquiered a great Accession of Strength, while their hereditary Enemy has been weakened one half, and incurably crippled.

The French are besides a good natured and humane Nation, very respectable in Arts, Letters, Arms and Commerce, and therefore Motives of Interest, Honour & Convenience join themselves to those of friendship and gratitude to induce Us to wish for the Continuance of their friendship & Alliance. The Provinces of Canada & Nova Scotia, in the hands of the English, are a constant warning to Us to have a Care of ourselves, & therefore a Continuance of the friendship and Alliance of France is of Importance to our Tranquility & even to our Safety. There is nothing will have a greater effect to overawe the English, and induce them to respect Us and our Rights, than the Reputation of a good Understanding with the French. My Voice and Advice will therefore always be for discharging, with the utmost Fidelity, Gratitude & Exactness, every Obligation We are under to France, & for cultivating her friendship and Alliance by all sorts of good Offices—But I am sure that to do this effectually, We must reason with them at times, enter into particulars and be sure that We understand one another. We must act a manly, honest independent, as well as a sensible part.

With great Respect, I have the honor to be, Sir, your most obedient & most humble Servant.   John Adams.

To Robert Morris

Sir   Paris July 11. 1783

In my Letter to you of Yesterday, I hinted in Confidence at an Application to the House of Hope. This is a very delicate Measure. I was induced to think of it merely by a Conversation which Mr Van Berkel who will be Soon with you as he Sailed the 26 June from the Texel, had with Mr Dumas.—it would be better to be Steady to the three houses already employed, if that is possible. You will now be able to converse freely with that Minister upon the Subject. I Should not advise you to take any decisive Resolution at Philadelphia but leave it to your Minister to Act as shall appear to him best upon the Spot. The Houses now employed are well esteemed and I hope will do very well. But no House in the Republick has that force in the Reins of that of Hope.

All depends, however, upon the Measures to be taken by Congress and the States for ascertaining their Debts and a regular discharge of the Interest.—The Ability of the People to make such an Establishment cannot be doubted: and the Inclination of no Man who has a proper Sense of publick Honour can be called in Question. The Thirteen States in Relation to the discharge of the Debts of Congress, must consider them Selves as one Body, animated by one Soul.—The Stability of our Confederation at home, our Reputation abroad, our Power of Defence, the Confidence and affection of the People of one state towards those of another all depend upon it. Without a Sacred Regard to publick Justice no Society can Subsist. it is the only Tie which can unite Mens Minds and Hearts in pursuit of the common Interest.

The Commerce of the World is now open to Us, and our Exports and Imports are of So large amount, and our Connections will be so large and extentensive that the least Stain upon our Character in this respect will loose Us in a very short time Advantages of greater pecuniary Value than all our Debt amounts to.—The Moral Character of our People is of infinitely greater worth than all the sums in question. Every hesitation every Uncertainty about paying or receiving a just Debt, diminishes that Sense of the Moral Obligation of publick Justice which ought to be kept pure and carefully cultivated in every American Mind. Creditors at home and abroad, the Army the Navy, every Man who has a well founded Claim upon the Publick, has an unalienable Right to be Satisfied, and this by the fundamentable Principles of Society. Can there ever be Content and Satisfaction? can there ever be Peace and order? Can there ever be Industry, or Decency without it.? To talk of a Spung to wipe out this Debt, or of reducing or diminishing it, below its real Value in a Country so abundantly able to pay the last farthing, would betray a total Ignorance of the first Principles of national Duty and Interest.—Let Us leave these odious Speculations to Countries that can plead a Necessity for them, and where Corruption has arrived at its last Stages. Where Infamy is Scarcely felt, and Wrong may as well assume one Shape as another Since it must prevail in Some.

I have &c

"THIS STATE OF UNCERTAINTY"

To Abigail Adams

My dearest Friend   Paris July 17. 1783
No Letter from you, yet. I believe I shall Set off Tomorrow or next day, for the Hague, and Shall bring John with me back to Paris in about 3 Weeks. There will be an Interval, before the Signature of the definitive Treaty and Several publick Concerns oblige me to go to the Hague for a Short time. When I get my Son with me, I shall be ready to go to any Place, where I may embark for home, as soon as I get Leave.

I am weary beyond all Expression of waiting in this State of
Uncertainty about every Thing. It is at this Moment as uncertain as it was six months ago when the definitive Treaty will be
signed. Mr. Laurens and Mr. Dana have leave to go home. Mr.
Danas is upon a Condition, however, which is not yet fullfilled
so that he will not go home for some time. Dr. Franklin Says
he is determined to go home, and Mr. Jay talks of going next
Spring.

In Short it is a terrible Life We lead. It wearies out the Patience of Job, and affects the health of Us all.

Mr. Smith writes me that Charles and Thomas are gone or
were going to Haverhill, under the Care of Mr. Shaw. I approve of this very much. They will learn no Evil there. With
them at Haveril, yourself and Miss Nabby and Mr. John with
me, I could bear to live in Europe another Year or two. But I
cannot live much longer without my Wife and Daughter and I
will not. I want two Nurses at least: and I wont have any, at
least female ones but my Wife and Daughter.

I tremble too, least a Voyage and change of Climate should
alter your health. I dare not wish you in Holland for there my
Charles, Mr. Thaxter, My servants and myself were forever
Sick. I am half a Mind to come home with the definitive
Treaty, and then if Congress dismiss me, well—. If they send
me back again I can take you and your Daughter with me.
However I can determine upon nothing. I am now afraid We
shall not meet till next Spring. I hear, by Word of Mouth that
Congress will not determine upon my Resignation till they
have received the definitive Treaty. Heaven know when this
will be. It will be a Mercy to Us all, if they let me come home:
for if you and your Daughter come to Europe you will get into
your female Imaginations, fantastical Ideas that will never wear
out, and will Spoil you both.

The Question is whether it is possible for a Lady, to be once
accustomed to the Dress, Shew &c. of Europe, without having
her head turned by it? This is an awfull Problem. If you cannot
be Mistress enough of yourself, and be answerable for your
Daughter, that you can put on and put off these Fooleries like
real Philosophers, I advise you never to come to Europe, but
order Your husband home, for this you may depend on, your
Residence in Europe will be as uncertain as the Wind. It cannot

be depended on for one Year no nor for Six Months. You have Seen two or three very Striking Instances of the Precariousness, of Congress Commissions, in my first, second and third. The Bread that is earned on a Farm is simple but sure. That which depends upon Politicks is as uncertain as they.

You know your Man. He will never be a Slave. He will never cringe. He will never accommodate his Principles, sentiments or Systems, to keep a Place, or to get a Place, no nor to please his Daughter, or his Wife. He will never depart from his Honour, his Duty, no nor his honest Pride for Coaches, Tables, Gold, Power or Glory. Take the Consequences then. Take a Voyage to Europe if the Case should so happen that I shall write to you to come live three Months. Let your Man See something in a different Light from his Masters, and give them offence, be recalled. You and he return back to the Blue Hills, to live upon a Farm. Very good. Let Lyars and slanderers without any of this, write Reports and nourish Factions behind his back, and the same effect is produced. I repeat it. It will be a Blessing to Us all, if I am permitted to return.

Be cautious my Friend, how you Speak upon these subjects. I know that Congress are bound, from regard to their own honour as well as mine, to send me to England, but it is the most difficult Mission in the Universe, and the most desperate, there is no Reputation to be got by it, but a great deal to be lost. It is the most expensive and extravagant Place in Europe, and all that would be allowed would not enable one to live, as a set of insolent Spendthrifts would demand. I am quite content to come home and go to Farming, be a select Man, and owe no Man any Thing but good Will. There I can get a little health and teach my Boys to be Lawyers.

I hope New York and Penobscot will be evacuated before this reaches you. That will be some Comfort. You must pray Mr. Storer or your Unkle Smith to send Your Letters to me, by Way of New York Philadelphia, London Bilbao, Holland France or any way. If they inclose them to any of their Friends in London they will get to me.

Farewell, my dearest Friend Farewell.

THE NEED FOR CONGRESSIONAL AUTHORITY

To Robert R. Livingston

Sir,   Paris. 18th. July. 1783.

There is cause to be solicitous about the State of things in England. The present Ministry swerve more & more from the true System for the prosperity of their Country & ours. M^{r:} Hartley, whose Sentiments are at bottom just, is probably kept here, (if he was not sent at first) merely to amuse us, & to keep him out of the way of embarrassing the Coalition, in Parliament.

We need not fear that France & England will make a common Cause against us, even in relation to the Carrying-Trade to & from the West-Indies; altho' they may mutually inspire into each other false notions of their Interests at times, yet there can never be a Concert of operation between them. Mutual emnity is bred in the blood & bones of both—and Rivals & Enemies at heart they eternally will be—In order to induce both to allow us our natural right to the carrying Trade, we must negotiate with the Dutch, Danes, Portuguese, & even with the Empires; for the more friends & resources we have, the more we shall be respected by the French & English—and the more freedom of trade we enjoy with the Dutch possessions in America, the more will France & England find themselves necessitated to allow us—

The present Ministers in England have very bad advisers; the Refugees & Emissaries of various other Sorts—and we have nobody to watch, to counteract, to correct, or prevent any thing—

The U: States will soon see the necessity of uniting in measures to conteract their Enemies, & even their friends. What powers Congress sh^{d.} have for governing the Trade of the whole —for making or recommending prohibitions or Imposts, deserves the serious Consideration of every man in America. If a constitutional, legislative Authority cannot be given them, a sense of common danger & necessity should give to their recommendations all the energy upon the minds of the people, which they had 6. years ago—

If the union of the States is not preserved, & even their

unity in many great points, instead of being the happiest people under the Sun, I don't know but we may be the most miserable. We shall find our foreign Affairs the most difficult to manage of any of our Interests—We shall see—feel them disturbed by invisible agents & Causes, by secret Intrigues, by dark & misterious insinuations, by concealed Corruptions of a thousand sorts, Hypocrisy & Simulation will assume a million shapes,—we shall feel the evil, without being able to prove the Cause—Those, whose penetrations reach the true Source of the evil will be called suspicious, envious, disappointed, ambitious: In short, if there is not an authority sufficiently decisive to draw together the minds, affections, & forces of the States in their common foreign Concerns, it appears to me we shall be the sport of trans-atlantic Politicians, of all denominations, who hate liberty in every shape, & every man who loves it, & every Country that enjoys it. If there is no common Authority, nor any common Sense to secure a revenue for the discharge of our engagements abroad for money, what is to become of our honor, our justice, our faith, our Credit, our universal, moral, political & commercial Character? If there is no common power to fulfill engagements with our Citizens, to pay our Soldiers & other Creditors, can we have any moral Character at home? Our Country will become the Region of everlasting discontents, reproaches & animosities, and, instead of finding our Independence a blessing, we shall soon become Cappadocians enough to wish it done away—

I may be tho't gloomy; but this ought not to discourage me from laying before Congress my apprehensions.—The dependence, of those who have designs upon us, upon our want of affection to each other, & of authority over one another, is so great, that, in my opinion, if the U: S: do not soon shew to the world a proof that they can command a common revenue, to satisfy their Creditors at home & abroad—that they can act as one people, as one nation, as one man in their transactions with foreign nations, we shall be soon so far despised, that it will be but a few years, perhaps but a few m^{ths:} before we are involved in another war—What can I say in Holland, if a doubt is started, whether we can repay the money we wish to borrow. I must assure them in a tone, that shall exclude all doubt that the money will be repaid. Am I to be hereafter reproached with deceiving the Moneylenders? I cannot believe there is a man in America who w$^{d.}$ not disdain the supposition, & therefore I shall not scruple to give the strongest assurances in my power: But, if there is a doubt in Congress, they ought to recall their Borrowers of money.—

I shall set off tomorrow for Holland, in hopes of improving my health, at the same time that I shall endeavor to assist the loan & to turn the Speculations of the Dutch Merch$^{ts:}$, Capitalists & Statesmen towards America. It is of vast importance that the Dutch sh$^{d.}$ form just ideas of their Interests, respect$^{g:}$ their Communication between us & their Islands & other Colonies in America. I beg that no time may be lost in commencing Conferences, with M$^{r:}$ Van Berkel upon this Subject as well as that of money—but this sh$^{d.}$ not be communicated to the French or English; because, we may depend upon it, both will endeavor to persuade the Dutch to adopt the same plan with themselves. There are jealousies, on both sides the Pas of Calais, of our Connections & Negotiations with the Dutch: But while we avoid, as much as we can, to enflame this jealousy, we must have Sense, firmness & Independance enough not to be intimidated by it from availing ourselves of advantages that Providence has placed in our power. There ever have been & ever will be, suspicions of every honest, active & intelligent American, & there will be, as there has been, insidious attempts to destroy, or lessen your Confidence in every such Character. But if our Country does not support her own Interests & her own Servants they will assuredly fall. Persons, who study to preserve or obtain the Confidence of America by the favor of European Statesmen or Courts, must betray their Country to preserve their places.—

For my own part, I wish M$^{r:}$ Jay & myself almost any where else but here. There is scarce any other place, where we might not do some good. Here we are in a state of annihilation—

I have the honor to be, Sir, Your hum$^{le:}$ serv$^{t.}$ John Adams.

To Abigail Adams

My dearest Friend   Paris August 14. 1783
     I have received your two favours of 7 May and 20 June. I
had received no Letter from you for so long an Interval that
these were really inestimable. I always learn more of Politicks
from your Letters, than any others. I have lost all my Correspondents in Congress. I wrote to Mr. Jackson and Gen. Warren Supposing they were Members. Mr. Gerry is there now, to
my Great Joy. Beg of him to write to me, if I stay in Europe.
     I learn with great Satisfaction the Wisdom of my Daughter,
whom I long to see. What is to be my Fate I know not. We
have not received any joint Commission to make a Treaty of
Commerce with Great Britain. I hate to force my self home
without Leave, and Congress have not given me Leave as Mr.
Lee gave you Reason to expect. My Son is with me, at present,
and you will be as proud of him as I shall be of my Daughter,
when I see her. He is grown up a Man, and his Steadiness and
Sobriety, with all his Spirits are much to his honour. I will
make of him my Secretary while I Stay.
     I like the Situation of Charles and Tom.
     Your Purchase of Land tho of only the Value of 200 Dollars
gives me more Pleasure than you are aware. I wish you had described it. I Suppose it to be that fine Grove which I have
loved and admired from my Cradle. If it is, I would not part
with it, for Gold. If you know of any Woodland or salt Marsh
to be sold, purchase them and draw upon me for the Money.
Your Bills shall be paid upon Sight. Direct the Bills to be presented if I should be returned home, to Messrs. Wilhem and
Jan Willink Merchants Amsterdam, who will accept and pay
them for the Honour of the Drawer. Pray dont let a Single
Tree be cutt upon that Spot. I expect, very soon, to be a private Man, and to have no other Resource for my Family but
my Farm, and therefore it is my Intention when I come home
to sell my House in Boston and to collect together all the
Debts due to me and all other little Things that I can convert
into Money and lay it out in Lands in the Neighbourhood of

our Chaumiere. The whole will make but a Small Farm, Yet it will be large enough for my Desires if my Children are content. You Speak of a high Office. In Gods Name, banish every Idea of such a Thing. It is the Place of the Greatest slavery and Drudgery in the World. It would only introduce me to endless Squabbles and Disputes, and expose me to eternal obloquy and Envy. I wish that all Parties would unite in the present one who has the Hearts of that People and will keep them. The Opposition will only weaken and distress his Administration, and if another were chosen in his Place, the Administration of that other would be weakened and distressed by a Similar Opposition. I have not health to go through the Business, nor have I Patience to endure the Smart. I beg that neither You nor yours would ever encourage in yourselves or others such a Thought. If after my Return home, the state should think proper to send me to Congress and you will go with me, I will go, for a short time, but not a long one. After that if I should be chosen into the senate or House, I should be willing to contribute my Mite, to the publick service in that Way. At home, upon my Farm and among my Books assisting in the Education of my Children, and endeavouring to introduce them into Business to get their Bread and do some service in the World, I wish to pass the feeble Remnant of my Days. But I am too much hurt, by those Exertions to which the Times have called me, to wish or to be capable of any great active Employment whatsoever. You know not how much your Friend is altered. The Fever burnt up half his Memory and more than half his Spirits, and has left him, with scorbutic Disorders about him that are very troublesome. Without Repose, if with it, he can never hope to get the better of them. This is said to you my friend in Confidence and is to be communicated to no one else. After having seen so many of my friends, thro Life fall Victims to the great Contest, I think my self very happy to have got through it, in no worse a Condition. Adieu.

To Abigail Adams 2nd

My Dear Daughter   Paris, August 13th, 1783
  I have received your affectionate letter of the 10th of May, with great pleasure, and another from your mother of the 28th and 29th of April, which by mistake I omitted to mention in my letter to her to-day. Your education and your welfare, my dear child, are very near my heart; and nothing in this life would contribute so much to my happiness, next to the company of your mother, as yours. I have reason to say this by the experience I have had of the society of your brother, whom I brought with me from the Hague. He is grown to be a man, and the world says they should take him for my younger brother, if they did not know him to be my son. I have great satisfaction in his behaviour, as well as in the improvements he has made in his travels, and the reputation he has left behind him wherever he has been. He is very studious and delights in nothing but books, which alarms me for his health; because, like me, he is naturally inclined to be fat. His knowledge and his judgment are so far beyond his years, as to be admired by all who have conversed with him. I lament, however, that he could not have his education at Harvard College, where his brothers shall have theirs, if Providence shall afford me the means of supporting the expense of it. If my superiors shall permit me to come home, I hope it will be soon; if they mean I should stay abroad, I am not able to say what I shall do, until I know in what capacity. One thing is certain, that I will not live long without my family, and another is equally so, that I can never consent to see my wife and children croaking with me like frogs in the Fens of Holland, and burning and shivering alternately with fevers, as Mr. Thaxter, Charles, Stephens, and myself have done: your brother John alone had the happiness to escape, but I was afraid to trust him long amidst those pestilential steams.
  You have reason to wish for a taste for history, which is as entertaining and instructive to the female as to the male sex. My advice to you would be to read the history of your own

country, which although it may not afford so splendid objects as some others, before the commencement of the late war, yet since that period, it is the most interesting chapter in the history of the world, and before that period is intensely affecting to every native American. You will find among your own ancestors, by your mother's side at least, characters which deserve your attention. It is by the female world, that the greatest and best characters among men are formed. I have long been of this opinion to such a degree, that when I hear of an extraordinary man, good or bad, I naturally, or habitually inquire who was his mother? There can be nothing in life more honourable for a woman, than to contribute by her virtues, her advice, her example, or her address, to the formation of an husband, a brother, or a son, to be useful to the world.

Heaven has blessed you, my daughter, with an understanding and a consideration, that is not found every day among young women, and with a mother who is an ornament to her sex. You will take care that you preserve your own character, and that you persevere in a course of conduct, worthy of the example that is every day before you. With the most fervent wishes for your happiness, I am your affectionate father,

John Adams

August 14, 1783

SIGNING THE FINAL PEACE TREATY

To Elbridge Gerry

My dear Mʳ Gerry   Paris. September 3. 1783.

The third of September, will be more remarkable for the Signature of the definitive Treaties than for the Battle of Naseby or Worcester or the Death of Oliver Cromwell.—We could obtain no Alteration from the Provisional Articles. We could Obtain no explanation of the Articles respecting the Tories nor any Limitation respecting Interest or Execution for Debts. I am however less anxious about these Things than others.

Our first object is to secure the Liberties of our Citizens in the Seperate States. Our second to maintain and Strengthen the Confederation. Our Third to purge the Minds of our People of their Fears, their diffidence of themselves and Admiration of strangers, and our fourth to defend ourselves against the Wiles of Europe. My Apprehensions of the Importance of our foreign Affairs, have been much increased by a Residence of five or Six Years in Europe—I see so much Enmity to the Principle of our Governments, to the Purity of our Morals, the Simplicity of our Manners, the honest Integrity, and Sincerity of our hearts, to our Contentment with Poverty, our Love of Labour, our Affection for Liberty and our Country. I see so many Proofs of their Hatred of all this, and of their Dread of it, both as a dangerous Example among their own corrupted debauched Subjects, and as a sure and certain source of Power and Grandeur; I see so many Artifices practised to debauch every Body you send, or who comes to Europe; so many practised by them in America itself hidden, covered up, disguised under all shapes, and I see they will ever have it in their Power to Practice so many of these arts, and to succeed to such a Degree, that I am convinced no Pains or Expences should be spared to defend ourselves.

But how shall we defend ourselves? We cannot refuse to receive foreign Ministers from Sovereign Powers: Shall we recall, all our own Ministers from Europe? this is a serious Question —I confess I am for the affirmative, and would give my Voice for recalling every one, if I could not secure two Points. The first is to send Men of independent Minds, who will not be Tools, Men of Virtue and Conscience: the second is to perswade Congress to support them firmly. it is infintely better to have none in Europe, than to have Artfull unprincipled Impostors, or Men debauched with Women You may depend upon this, the Moment an American Minister gives a loose to his Passion for Women that Moment, he is undone, he is instantly at the Mercy of the Spies of the Court, and the Tool of the most profligate of the human Race. This will be called Pedantry but it is Sacred Truth, and our Country will feel it to her Sorrow if she is not aware of it in Season. if you make it a Principle that your Ministers should be agreeable, at the Court, and have the good Word of the Courtiers you are undone. No Man will ever be pleasing at a Court in General, who is not debauched in his Morals, or warped from your Interests. if therefore, you can carry Elections for Men of pure Intregrity, and unshaken firmness, it will be for your Interest to have a Number of them at the Principal Courts of Europe for some time, two or three years at least. if you cannot, you had better send none. Men of any other Character, will be called amiable, and be said to be beloved, & esteemed and to have your Confidence but they will be made the Instruments of the most insidious and destructive designs upon your Liberties, I mean upon your Morals and Republican Virtues, which are the only Qualities which can Save our Country. for myself I dont care a Farthing. the most agreeable Thing to me would be to come home. But I pray one Thing only for myself, it is that you would determine immediately, whether I may come home or not.

It is the true Interest of our Country, to cultivate the Friendship of the Dutch: We have nothing to fear from them, as we have from the French and English. it is their Policy as well as ours to cultivate Peace and Neutrality, & we may aid each other in it.

With Sincere Affection your Friend   John Adams

MAINTAINING AMERICA'S REPUTATION

To Elias Boudinot

Sir,   Paris Septr 5th: 1783.
On Wednesday the third day of this Month, the American Ministers met the British Minister at his Lodgings at the Hôtel de York, and signed, sealed and delivered the Definitive Treaty of Peace between the United States of America and the King of Great Britain. Altho' it is but a Confirmation or Repetition of the Provisional Articles, I have the honor to congratulate Congress upon it, as it is a Completion of the work of Peace, and the best we could obtain. Nothing remains now to be done but a Treaty of Commerce—But this in my opinion cannot be negociated without a new Commission from Congress to some one or more Persons. Time, it is easy to foresee, will not be

likely to render the British Nation more disposed to a Regulation of Commerce favorable to Us, & therefore my Advice is to issue a Commission as soon as may be.

There is another Subject, on which I beg leave to present to Congress my Sentiments, because they seem to me of Importance, and because they differ from many sanguine Opinions, which will be communicated to the Members of that Assembly from Partisans both of England and France. In the late deliberations concerning an Acceptance of the Mediation of the two Imperial Courts, the British Minister refused it; and in the Conferences We had with the Comte de Vergennes upon this Subject, it was manifest enough to me, that he was not fond of our accepting it—For altho' he maintained a perfect Impartiality of Language, neither advising Us for nor against the Measure, yet at last, when it was observed that M^r. Hartley was averse to it, he turned to D^r. Franklin and said that we must agree with M^r. Hartley, about it, with such a Countenance, Air and Tone of Voice, (for from these you must often collect the Sentiments of Ministers) as convinced me, he did not wish the Mediation should take place. It was not a Subject, which would bear insisting on either way. I therefore made no difficulty— But I am upon recollection fully of Opinion, that We should have done wisely to have sent our Letter to the Imperial Ministers, accepting the Mediation on our Part. The Signature of those Ministers would have given Us Reputation in Europe, and among our own Citizens. I mention these because I humbly concieve, that Congress ought in all their Proceedings to consider, the Opinion that the United States or the People of America will entertain of themselves. We may call this national Vanity or national Pride, but it is the main Principle of the national Sense of its own Dignity, and a Passion in human Nature, without which Nations cannot preserve the Character of Men. Let the People lose this Sentiment, as in Poland, and a Partition of their Country will soon take place. Our Country has but lately been a dependent one, and our People, altho' enlightened and virtuous, have had their Minds and Hearts habitually filled with all the Passions of a dependent, subordinate People, that is to say, with Fear, with Diffidence and Distrust of themselves, with Admiration of Foreigners &^ca.— Now I say, that it is one of the most necessary & one of the most difficult Branches of the Policy of Congress, to eradicate from the American Mind every remaining Fibre of this Fear and Self-Diffidence on the one hand, and of this excessive Admiration of Foreigners on the other. It cannot be doubted one moment, that a solemn Acknowledgment of Us, by the Signature of the two Imperial Courts, would have had such a Tendency in the Minds of our Countrymen—But we should also consider, upon every Occasion, how our Reputation will be affected in Europe. We shall not find it easy to keep up the Respect for Us, that has been excited by the continual Publication of the Exploits of the War. In the Calm of Peace little will be said about Us in Europe, unless We prepare for it, but by those who have designs upon Us. We may depend upon it every thing will be said in Europe, and in the Gazettes, which any Body in Europe wants to have repeated in America, to make such Impressions upon the Minds of our Citizens as he desires. It will become Us therefore to do every thing in our Power, to make reasonable & just Impressions upon the public Opinion in Europe. The Signature of the two Imperial Courts would have made a deep & important Impression in our favor, upon full one half of Europe, as Friends to those Courts, and upon all the other half, as Enemies. I need not explain myself farther: I may however add, that Americans can scarcely concieve the decisive Influence of the Governments of Europe upon their People. Every Nation is a Piece of Clock-Work—Every Wheel is under the absolute direction of the Sovereign as its Weight or Spring. In Consequence of this, all that Moiety of Mankind, that are subject to the two Imperial Courts and their Allies, would, in Consequence of their Mediation, have been openly and decidedly our Friends at this Hour, and the other half of Europe would certainly have respected Us the more for this.— But at present, the two Imperial Courts, not having signed the Treaty, all their Friends are left in a state of Doubt and Timidity concerning Us. From all the Conversations I have had with the Comte de Mercy and M$^{r.}$ Markoff, it is certain, that the two Courts wished, as these Ministers certainly were ambitious, to sign our Treaty. They and their Sovereigns wished that their Names might be read in America, and there respected as our Friends. But this is now past. England and France will be most perfectly united in all Artifices and Endeavors to keep down our Reputation at Home and abroad—to mortify our self-Conceit, and to lessen Us in the Opinion of the World. If We will not see, We must be the Dupes—We need not for We have in our own Power, with the common blessing, the Means of every thing We want. There is but one Course now left to retrieve the Error, and that is to send a Minister to Vienna, with Power to make a Treaty with both the Imperial Courts. Congress must send a Minister first, or it never will be done. The Emperor never sends first, nor will England ever send a Minister to America, until Congress shall send one to London.

To form immediate commercial Connections with that half of Europe, which ever has been, and, with little Variations, ever will be opposite to the House of Bourbon, is a fundamental Maxim of that System of American Politicks, which I have pursued invariably from the beginning of this War. It is the only means of preserving the Respect of the House of Bourbon itself—It is the only means, in conjunction with our Connections with the House of Bourbon already formed, to secure Us the Respect of England for any long time, and to keep Us out of another War with that Kingdom. It is in short the only possible means of securing to our Country that Peace, Neutrality, Impartiality and Indifference in European Wars, which in my opinion We shall be unwise in the last degree if We do not maintain. It is besides the only way, in which We can improve and extend our commercial Connections to the best Advantage.

With great Respect, I have the honor to be, Sir, your most obedient & most humble Servant.   John Adams.

FRANKLIN'S EXCESSIVE INFLUENCE

To Elbridge Gerry

My dear Friend   Paris Sept.ʳ 5. 1783
You remember the Contract with Du Coudrai, and his hundred officers, and with many other officers. Coudrai was to take Rank of allmost all our Generals, to have the Command of all our Artillery and military Manufactures, and be Subject

to no orders, but those of Congress or the Commander in Chief, and the Marshall M. was wanted to be that Commander in Chief—Let me beg of you that those Papers of Mr Deans may be looked up copied and preserved.—hæc olim meminisse juvabit.—You knew the History of our foreign affairs from that Time to this. All has proceeded from the Same Source, and all has been calculated to hold Us at Mercy. The System has appeared in the Same Light to every Minister you have had in Europe, except one.—Izard, Lee, Jay, Dana, Laurens and my self, and even Deane has at last let out the Cat.—No wonder then that the one, is flattered and the rest coldly received. No wonder that every Thing is desired to be thrown into the hand of that one. To this End the Ministers and Courts of Sweeden, Denmark and Portugal, have been told that this one has Power to treat with them and he alone. This is false, but Still they have been told so.—I doubt not congress have been told that those Courts & Kings, have desired, to treat personally with the Great Philosopher. This I dont believe. because it would be an Impropriety, altogether beneath the Dignity of those Kings to dictate to Congress, to designate Persons, or attempt to influence the Elections of Congress. But if it is true, it ought to allarm and be refused for that very Reason. "Rome, n'a pas accoutumé des Rois a une telle Audace." Kings ought not to be indulged in Such Impertinence.—Republicks Should be jealous of the Influence of Kings, and cannot be too delicate in the perfect freedom of their own Elections. They Should oblige Kings to more delicacy than to suggest their Predilections.— But it is not credible that in these Cases they have done it. What is it to them, whether the Minister they treat with, is a mere Statesman, or whether he affects a skill in Metalurgy, Mineralogy, or Electricity.

The Truth is, they have been told that one Gentleman alone is impowered by you to treat with them, which is not true. The ancient Resolution that the Commissioners at Versailles, should have Power to treat with the Courts of Europe is in force for Mr Lee Mr Deane & me as much as for Dr F.—but it is fallen and superceeded by the new Commissions with regard to Us all.—I rely upon it, therefore that you will insert us all, who are obliged to reside here at least upon other affairs, in the Commission you send to treat with other Powers.

You have told all Europe, that Jay was C. J. of N. York, President of Congress, Minister to Madrid—that I was C. J. of Massachusetts, Delegate in Congress, Commissioner at Versailles, Minister in holland, and at the Peace.—when it was known that Franklin was treating with Sweeden So slyly, the Inquiry was why were not Jay and Adams, Men of such Trust under their Country, present in Paris joined in this Business as well as that of Peace.—Comis and Understrappers gave what Answers they pleased. a few Shruggs of the shoulders were Answer enough to answer their Purposes. This must be prevented. —if you chain Us together treat Us impartially. Support Us, or call Us home.—Such distinctions are but an artfull, Method of Libelling Us, by letting loose Tongues and Pens, which if not paid for abusing Us, will make a Merit of doing it.—Firmness, Steadiness and Impartiallity on your Part is all that is wanting, to support Us effectually. For there is nobody that dares to attack Us openly. they all know We stand upon too strong Ground. But Secret Insinuations, indirect Implications from the Proceedings of Congress which they labour a thousand Ways to influence to their Purposes are the only Means they venture on.—it is not King, Court, nor Nation. it is wholly owing to one french and one American Minister and their Tools. I am very happy to find you in Congress, I hope you will Stay there. You will soon see Mr Dana. He will unfold to you Scenes which will convince, if any Thing can.

My dear Friend Adieu   J. Adams

THE NEED FOR COMMERCIAL TREATIES

To Elbridge Gerry

Dear Sir   Paris Septr. 6 1783

I Shall never know when I have done writing to you. Our Affairs are so unsettled, and I am So uninformed, and uncertain about every Thing in America, that you will excuse me if I give you, more Trouble than usual.

I take it for granted, that you will not recall all your present Ministers, and neglect to Send new ones, altogether. This would be to Suppose that you dont mean to make any Treaty of Commerce with England, Denmark, Portugal, Spain, or either of the Empires.—for you may depend upon it that neither the Emperor of Germany, the Empress of Russia, the King of England or of Spain will ever Send a Minister to you first. This is a Point of Delicacy and Etiquette which they will never give up. England would not give it up to France nor Vice Versâ.—it was lately agreed, that the Duke of Manchester and the Comte D'Adhemar Should cross the Pass of Calais at the Same time or at least in the Same Boat one as it went and the other as it returned. I judge from Hints from Dr Franklin that he will insinuate in his Letters to Members of Congress, that they ought not to Send to London a Minister, untill the K. of G. Britain Sends one to Congress. if this is insinuated it is insidiously done, to recommend himself to Vergennes by defeating the Measure. now in my opinion it is of more Importance you should have a Minister in London, than in all the rest of Europe and will be so for Some time. if you do not Send a Minister there I presume you will Send a Commission, for making a Treaty of Commerce with G. B. to some one or to all of your Ministers for Peace.—it should be most natural and honourable to insert in it all your Ministers in Europe.— perhaps there may be Some objection about the order in which they now Stand. This may be obviated by resolving upon the Commission, and the Number of Ministers to be inserted in it, and then proceeding to elect them in the Usual Way and let him Stand first who is chosen first or has the most Votes according to your usual Rule. in this Case neither would refuse or be offended, whichever Stood first. if you intend to make a Treaty of Commerce with Denmark or Portugal, and that such Treaty shall be made with, the Comte de Souza Baron Waltensdorf or other Minister at the Court of Versailles, it is infinitely best that the Names of all your Ministers in Europe, Shall be inserted, and the Power given to them jointly & severally as it was in the Commission for Peace, so that all may attend if they can, or at least notified and have oppertunity to send their Hints and Advice in Writing, if you mean to have a Treaty with the two Empires or either of them, you may Send a Commission, in the Same manner, if you do not chose to Send a Minister to either of those Courts.—in this Way the

Expence will be no greater than it has been, and all necessary Treaties may be made in the Course of about one Year, or a Year & an half, and then if you please you may recall every Minister you have in Europe. But I think you ought not to recall all your Ministers till this is done. our Commercial and political Systems depend too much upon having these Treaties made to have them neglected. You may Send fresh hands it is true. But fresh Hands I know by woefull Experience have so many Timidities, so many difficulties arising from a clumsiness in the Language, and are so little respected at first and untill they have learned the Language, and made themselves taken Notice of. Every Man who comes new from America has a Reputation to make, I assure you, and Connections to form before he can do much, upon the whole therefore I think it will be best that at least Some of the old Hands should be employed.

For my own Part, my first Wish is very Sincerely to go home, and the greatest Pleasure you can do me is to send me, the Acceptance of my Resignation. But if it is thought proper to refuse or neglect to send me this Acceptance, that is Letters of Recall to their High Mightinesses and the Prince of orange, I think, the Honour of Congress as well as my own honour requires that you should revive my old Commission to make a Treaty of Commerce with Great Britain. But if you insert me with the rest in a general Commission to make Treaties at Paris with England Portugal Denmark the Empires or any of these, and continue me in my Post in Holland, I will not refuse. in this Case I can ride, from Paris to the Hague and from the Hague to Paris often enough to do the necessary Duty in both, and can take good Care of your Loan in Amsterdam. or if you think proper to send me to Vienna, I will not refuse.—But I am determined not to be shut up croaking with the Froggs in Holland, doing nothing, or very little while others are employed to do all your Business of Importance, in the rest of Europe. *My* Health besides would sink in that Country, in which I can not bear a constant Residence. Besides if Franklin is suffered to go on with his clandestine Schemes of Smuggling Treaties and thus Sacrificing the Interest and Honour of his Country and the Reputations of all her faith full servants to his own Vanity as he has done, I am determined at all Events

Leave or no Leave to come home. But above all Things I pray you to determine, if you send me my Letters of Recall all is well I come home. if you send me to England, Vienna, or continue me in holland inserting me at the Same time in a Commission at Paris to make Treaties with England, the Empires Denmark Portugal or any of them, Send me my Family, for I am decidedly God willing, never to live another Year without my Wife.—But if I get no Answer or if I am left to grope and moap in holland, I will go home in the first Spring Ships, Leave or no Leave.—Thus my dear Friend I have laid open my Thoughts to you with Freedom, you will communicate them to whom and in what manner you think proper.—Jay is so good and wise a Man So thoroughly able and willing, that I wish him any Thing you can make him. You can find no better Materials for your choicest Work.

If you make a general Commission, and appoint a secretary to it, no Man living is fitter for it, or deserves it more than Thaxter.

My dear Friend Farewell   John Adams.

A NEW DIPLOMATIC COMMISSION

To Abigail Adams

My dearest Friend   Paris September 7. 1783
    This Morning for the first Time, was delivered me the Resolution of Congress of the first of May, that a Commission and Instructions Should be made Out, to Me, Dr. Franklin and Mr. Jay to make a Treaty of Commerce with Great Britain. If this Intelligence had been Sent Us by Barney, who Sailed from Philadelphia a Month after, the 1st of May, and has now been Sailed from hence on his return home above a Month it would have Saved me and others much Anxiety. I am now even at a Loss. It is of great Importance that Such a Treaty Should be well made. The Loan in Holland must be attended to, and when the present one is full, another must be opened, which cannot be done but by me or my Successor. There are other Things too to be done in Europe of great Importance. Mr.

Laurens has Leave to go home, and Mr. Dana is gone so that there remain in service only Mr. Franklin Mr. Jay and my self. In these Circumstances I must stay another Winter. I cannot justify going home. But what Shall I do for Want of my Family. By what I hear, I think Congress will give Us all Leave to come home in the Spring. Will you come to me this fall and go home with me in the Spring? If you will, come with my dear Nabby, leaving the two Boys at Mr. Shaws, and the House and Place under the Care of your Father Uncle Quincy or Dr. Tufts, or Mr. Cranch. This Letter may reach you by the middle of October, and in November you may embark, and a Passage in November, or all December will be a good Season. You may embark for London, Amsterdam, or any Port of France. On your Arrival, you will find Friends enough. The Moment I hear of it, I will fly with Post Horses to receive you at least, and if the Ballon, Should be carried to such Perfection in the mean time as to give Mankind the safe navigation of the Air, I will fly in one of them at the Rate of thirty Knots an hour. This is my Sincere Wish, although the Expence will be considerable, the Trouble to you great and you will probably have to return with me in the Spring. I am So unhappy without you that I wish you would come at all Events. You must bring with you at least one Maid and one Man servant.

I must however leave it with your judgment, you know better than I the real Intentions at Philadelphia, and can determine better than I whether it will be more prudent to wait untill the Spring. I am determind to be with you in America or have you with me in Europe, as soon as it can be accomplished consistent with private Prudence and the publick Good. I am told that Congress intend to recall Us all, as soon as a few Affairs are finished. If this should be the Case, all will be well. I shall go home with infinite Pleasure. But it may be longer than you think of, before all their necessary Affairs will be dispatched. The Treaty of Commerce with G. B. must take Time. A Treaty will be wanted with Portugal and Denmark if not with the Emperor and Empress. If you come to Europe this Fall, in my Opinion you will be glad to go home in the Spring. If you come in the spring you will wish to return the next fall. I am sure I shall, but Six months of your Company is worth to me, all the Expences and Trouble of the Voyage.

This Resolution of Congress deserves my Gratitude; it is highly honourable to me, and restores me, my Feelings, which a former Proceeding had taken away. I am now perfectly content to be recalled whenever they think fit, or to Stay in Europe, untill this Business is finished, provided you will come and live with me. We may Spend our Time together in Paris London or the Hague, for 6 or 12 Months as the Public Business may call me and then return to our Cottage, with contented Minds. It would be more agreable to my Inclinations to get home and endeavour to get my self and Children into a Settled Way, but I think it is more necessary for the Publick that I should stay in Europe, untill this Piece of Business is finished. You dont probably know the Circumstances which attended this Proceeding of Congress. They are so honourable to me, that I cannot in Gratitude or Decency refuse.

I must Submit your Voyage to your Discretion and the Advice of your Friends, my most earnest Wishes are to see you but if the Uncertainties are such as to discourage you, I know it will be upon reasonable Considerations and must submit. But if you postpone the Voyage for this Fall, I shall insist on your coming in the Spring, unless there is a certainty of my going home to you. Congress are at such grievous Expences, that I Shall have no other Secretary than my son. He however is a very good one. He writes a good hand very fast, and is very Steady, to his Pen and his Books. Write me by every Ship to Spain France Holland or England, that I may know. You give me more public Intelligence than any body. The only hint in Europe of this Commission was from you to yours forever

John Adams

EUROPEAN DIPLOMATS

To Elbridge Gerry

My dear M^r. Gerry,   Paris Sept. 8th. 1783.

Yesterday morning, D^r. Franklin produced a Resolution of Congress, that A. F. & J. should be joined in a Commission to treat of Commerce with Great Britain. This is well, & I hope you will pursue the plan & send another Commission to the same Persons to treat with Joseph, Catharine, Denmark & Portugal. Jay & I do admirably well with the old Man. We go on very smoothly, & make him know what is right & do it, for absolutely he does not know of himself.

If you appoint a Secretary will you let it be Thaxter? He has richly merited it. You need not give him a thousand a year, as you did Carmichael, Dana & W. T. Franklin—five hundred a year would do—But with less it would be impossible to live. Three hundred a year is really as little as a private Clerk can live upon with Decency, even when he has his Rent; his Board, Washing, Lodging, Coach when he wants it, &ᶜᵃ, in the Family of a Minister. I hint at Mʳ· Thaxter, because I think him from Experience the fittest for it—But this is the Affair of Congress, & they must do as they judge best. I hope none will complain of Expence, when it is necessary & reasonable. Compute how much my Residence in Holland has cost you—not more than five thousand pounds—Indeed it has not cost you any thing, for you must have been at the same Expence for me as Minister of Peace, if I had lain idle at Paris. Compute next, how many Millions of Dollars the Capture of Burgoyne or Cornwallis cost you—nay how many Millions sterling? Now I say, and I can demonstrate, that the Negotiation in Holland advanced the American Cause more than the Capture of either of those Armies did. If Congress had indulged more Confidence in their Negotiations & Negotiators, they would have made more Advantage of them. I am as parsimonious of public Money, in principle & by habit, as any Man ought to be— But there is an œconomy at the Spigot & a Profusion at the Bung sometimes. Parsimony should not prevent your finishing your European System, by which you may save twenty Millions sterling in a future War. I am clear in this opinion, that, by the Expence of a few thousand pounds in Europe for two or three years to come, you will save many many Millions both in Commerce, Negotiation and War in future years. One thing more I beg may be attended to—The French dont wish you should have Ministers in Europe—They wish you may employ their little Agents to solicit for you every thing—They will therefore probably fall in with the Shoestring Ideas, in order to take you in, and secretly foment the Cry against Expence.

Timeo Danaos, et dona ferentes. I dont think it worth while to send Ambassadors, but would continue Ministers Plenipotentiary. But I really think the Error would be less expensive in the end, to send Ambassadors to every great Court in Europe, with Salaries of six thousand sterling a year, than to recal all your Ministers, & appoint Residents only with one thousand a year, at present, & for two or three years to come. I beg you would not think of sending Residents only to the great Courts —It would sink the Reputation of our Country infinitely more than recalling all your Ministers, & sending no Residents at all. In Europe, Appearance is so decidedly necessary, that nothing can be done without it.—Your Resident could keep no Company with Ambassadors or Ministers—They would be the Scorn & Ridicule of every Commis in Office—These Commis have sixty thousand Livres a year, besides all their innumerable & unknown Perquisites.

When I was first in Holland, I used to make Visits with one Footman behind my Coach. The plainest Republicans, the severest of them all, came to me to remonstrate. M^r. Adams, Said they, you must never make a Visit with less than two Servants in Livery behind your Coach. You can neither keep up your own Reputation with our People, nor that of your Country, nor our Reputation who associate with you & call you the American Minister, without it. "C'est trop en Bourgeois" This is the Fact.—It is seen and felt by every one.

The foreign Ministers at European Courts may be divided into three Classes. *First.*— Noblemen of high Rank and great Fortune in their Countries, who have six, eight or ten thousand Pounds from their Courts—some of whom are supposed to spend as much more out of their private Fortunes. These are commonly more fit for Parade than any thing else, or have particular Reasons for wishing to live out of their own Countries, or whose Courts have such Reasons for wishing them away. *Secondly*— Others who have smaller Salaries, but still handsome ones, & who spend twice as much, which they acquire by Speculations in Stocks, by making use of their Prerogatives in saving Duties upon Goods, even by secret Connections with Smugglers, by gaming & many other ways equally unfit to mention or suspect. All these Practices have been used, & perhaps are still—But Congress ought to execrate & condemn, in the most decided manner, every such thing in their Ministers. *Thirdly*—There are others, who have honorable Salaries, spend them honorably & are industrious & attentive to the Rights and Honor of their Country and their Masters.—Such and such only ought to be the American Ministers. The present Allowance to your Ministers, with an addition of 300. a year for a Clerk, is in my opinion as little as will possibly bear.—For besides all the expensive Articles of House, Coach, Livery Servants, Domestick Servants, Presents to the Servants at Courts, and the Pilferings of Servants, Tradesmen, Shopkeepers &$^{ca.}$, a great & inevitable deduction, your Ministers must keep an handsome Table, suitable to entertain genteel Company at all times, & great Company very often.

Let me beg of you, my Friend, to write to my Wife, and advise her, whether it is prudent for her to come to me or not this Fall, or next Spring—Of this you will make no Words with any one, as it is not necessary to trouble others with the Cares of my Family.

With great Esteem & sincere Affection, your Friend.

John Adams.

"COME TO EUROPE"

To Abigail Adams

My dearest Friend   London Nov. 8. 1783

I have this Day, by Special Permission from their Majesties obtained by Mr. West the Painter who with Mr. Copely do so much honour to our Country, Seen the Appartements in the Queens House, as it is called, or Buckingham House. It is a great Curiosity indeed. There is an inestimable Collection of Paintings by the greatest Masters, Raphael, Rubens, Vandyke, and many others.

There is one Room which the King calls Mr. Wests, as it is ornamented with a Collection of his Works—the Return of Regulus—The Death of Epaminondas—The Death of Bayard —The Death of General Wolf—and &c.

The Cartons of Raphael, are a wonderfull Production of Art.

The Library is the most elegant Thing I ever saw. But the Kings Military and Naval Room, pleased me best as it is a Collection of Plans, and Models of every Dockyard, Fortress and Man of War in his Empire.

Come to Europe with Nabby as soon as possible, and Satisfy your Curiosity, and improve your Taste, by viewing these magnificent Sceenes. Go to the Play—see the Paintings and Buildings—visit the Manufactures for a few Months—and then, if Congress pleases return to America with me to reflect upon them.

I am in earnest. I cannot be happy, nor tolerable without you. Besides I really think one Trip across the Sea would be of Service to you and my Daughter to whom my Love. I Shall expect you constantly untill you arrive.

I mourn the Loss of my Father, but it was time to expect it, from his Age. You must be melancholly and afflicted, and I hope that the Voyage, will divert your Thoughts.

Mr. Thaxter is in America before this no doubt. My dear Son, is the only Secretary, I have or propose to have at present. I believe I Shall go to the Hague, and reside chiefly there but write to me untill you embark by Portugal Spain France England or Holland. The nearer you Arrive to the Hague, the nearer I believe you will be to me, yet I may be in Paris. I shall stay but a Short time in London.

You will read in the Newspapers, innumerable Lyes about Jay and me. Regard them as little as I do. I have met with an agreable Reception here, as agreable as I wish. In short I have been received here, exactly as I wished to be.

Yours with Tenderness unutterable   J. Adams

THE POLITICAL SITUATION IN BRITAIN

To the President of Congress

Sir   London November 13. 1783.
    If any one should ask me what is the System of the present administration? I should answer, "to keep their places"—Every Thing they say or do appears evidently calculated to that End,

and no Ideas of public Good no national Object is suffered to interfere with it.

In order to drive out Shelburne, they condemned his Peace which all the Whig Part of them, would have been very glad to have made, and have gloried in the Advantages of it. in order to avail themselves of the old Habits and Prejudices of the Nation, they now pretend to cherish the Principles of the Navigation act, and the King has been advised to recommend this in his Speech, & the Lords have echoed it, in very strong terms.

The Coalition appears to stand on very strong Ground, the Lords, and great Commoners, who compose it, count a great Majority, of Members of the House of Commons, who are returned by themselves, every one of whom is a dead Vote. They are endeavouring to engage the Bedford Interest with them, in order to strengthen themselves still more, by perswading Thurloe to be again Chancellor, and M[r.] Pitt, whose personal Popularity and Family Weight with the Nation, is very desirable for them, is tempted with the Place of Chancellor of the Exchequer which Lord John Cavendish from mere Aversion to Business, wishes to resign.

While they are using such means to augment their Strength, they are manifestly intimidated at the sight of those great national Objects, which they know not how to manage; Ireland is still in a State of Fermentation, throwing off the Admiralty Post office, and every other relick of British Parliamentary Authority; and contending for a free Importation of their Woollen Manufactures into Portugal, for the Trade to the East Indies, to the United States of America and all the rest of the World. in as ample manner as the English enjoy these Blessings the Irish Volunteers are also contending for a Parliamentary Reform, and a more equal Representation in their House of Commons, and are assembling by their Delegates in a Congress at Dublin to accomplish it. This Rivalry of Ireland is terrible to the Ministry. They are supposed to be at Work to sow Jealousies and Divisions between the Protestants and Catholics in Ireland.

The East Indies exhibit another Scene, which will be formidable to the Ministers Here center the Hopes of England; and it is certain that no System can be pursued which will give universal Satisfaction—Some require the Government to take that whole Country into their own Hands others demand aids in Cash, and Troops to the Company: Opposition will be first formed probably upon Indian affairs.

Public Credit, is the greatest Object of all—The necessary annual Expence, comprehending the Interest of the whole national Debt funded and unfunded, and the Peace establishment, will amount to near Seventeen Millions: the annual Receipts of Taxes have never yet amounted to Thirteen Millions: Here will be a deficiency then of near four Millions a year: which will render an annual Loan necesary, untill the debt will be so increased and the Stocks so sunk, that no Man will lend his Money—The Judicious, call upon Ministers for a Remedy and will embarass them with their Reproaches: but the Stock Jobbers are more numerous than the Judicious and more noisy. These live upon loans, and as long as Ministers borrow twelve Millions a Year, and employ the Stockjobbers to raise it, however certainly the Measure tends to Ruin, their Clamours will be for Ministers, an enormous Loan is the most popular Thing a Statesman can undertake so certain is the Bankruptcy of this Country. opposition will declame upon this Topick, but will make no Impression.

The United States of America, are another Object of Debate. if an Opposition should be formed, and concerted, I presume, that one fundamental of it, will be a Liberal Conduct towards us. they will be very profuse in Professions of Respect and affection for Us Will pretend to wish for Measures which may throw a veil over the past and restore, as much as possible the ancient good will. They will be advocates for some freedom of Communication with the West Indies, and for our having an equitable share of that carrying Trade &c.

Administration on the other hand I am confident will with great difficulty be perswaded to abandon the mean contemptible Policy which their Proclamations exhibit.

In my humble Opinion the only suitable Place for us to negotiate the Treaty in is London—Here with the most perfect politeness to the Ministry, we may keep them in awe, a Visit to a distinguished Member of Opposition, even if nothing should be said at it, would have more Weight with Ministers than all our Arguments—M$^{r:}$ Jay is I believe, of the same opinion: But we shall not conduct the Negotiation here, unless

Dr Franklin should come over: indeed if Congress should join us in a Commission to treat with other Powers, in my opinion, we might conduct the Business better here than at Paris—I shall however chearfully conform to the sentiments of my Colleagues.

The Delay of the Commission is to me a great embarassment, I know not whether to stay here return to Paris or the Hague. I hope every moment to receive advices from Congress which will resolve me.

I receiv'd yesterday a Letter from Mr Hartley, with the Compliments of Mr Fox and that he should be glad to see me, proposing the hour of Eleven to day which I agreed to. Mr Jay saw him, one day this Week. Mr Jay made him, and the Duke of Portland a Visit on his first Arrival.—they were not at home But he never heard from them untill my arrival, ten days or a fortnight after. informed of this, I concluded not to visit them and did not. But after a very long time, and indeed after Mr Hartley's return from Bath, Messages have been sent to Mr Jay & me that Mr Fox would be glad to see us.—it is merely for Form, and to prevent a Cry against him in Parliament for not having seen us, for not one Word was said to Mr Jay of publick affairs, nor will a word be said to me.

The real Friendship of America seems to me the only Thing which can redeem this Country from total Destruction: there are a few who think so, here, and but a few and the present Ministers are not among them: or at least, if they are of this Opinion, they conceal it, and behave as if they thought America of small Importance. The Consequence will be, that little Jealousies and Rivalries, & Resentments will be indulged, which will do essential injury to this Country as they happen, and they will end in another War, in which will be torn from this Island all her Possessions in Canada, Nova Scotia, and the East and west Indies.

With great Respect I have the honour to be, Sir your most obedient, and most humble Servant   John Adams.

SELECTIONS FROM THE
AUTOBIOGRAPHY

Congress assembled and proceeded to Business, and the Members appeared to me to be of one Mind, and that mind after my own heart. I dreaded the danger of disunion and divisions among Us, and much more among the People. It appeared to me, that all Petitions, Remonstrances and Negotiations, for the future would be fruitless and only occasion a Loss of time and give Opportunity to the Ennemy to sow divisions among the States and the People. My heart bled for the poor People of Boston, imprisoned within the Walls of their City by a British Army, and We knew not to what Plunder or Massacres or Cruelties they might be exposed. I thought the first Step ought to be, to recommend to the People of every State in the Union, to Seize on all the Crown Officers, and hold them with civility, Humanity and Generosity, as Hostages for the Security of the People of Boston and to be exchanged for them as soon as the British Army would release them. That We ought to recommend to the People of all the States to institute Governments for themselves, under their own Authority, and that, without Loss of Time. That We ought to declare the Colonies, free, Sovereign and independent States, and then to inform Great Britain We were willing to enter into Negotiations with them for the redress of all Grievances, and a restoration of Harmony between the two Countries, upon permanent Principles. All this I thought might be done before We entered into any Connections, Alliances or Negotiations with forreign Powers. I was also for informing Great Britain very frankly that hitherto we were free but if the War should be continued, We were determined to seek Alliances with France, Spain and any other Power of Europe, that would contract with Us. That We ought immediately to adopt the Army in Cambridge as a Continental Army, to Appoint a General and all other Officers, take upon ourselves the Pay, Subsistence, Cloathing, Armour and Munitions of the Troops. This is a concise Sketch of the Plan, which I thought the only reasonable one, and from Conversation with the Members of Congress, I was then convinced, and have been ever since convinced, that it was the General Sense, at least of a considerable Majority of that Body. This System of Measures I publicly and privately avowed, without Reserve.

When congress had assembled I rose in my place and in as short a Speech as the Subject would admit, represented the State of the Colonies, the Uncertainty in the Minds of the People, their great Expectations and Anxiety, the distresses of the Army, the danger of its dissolution, the difficulty of collecting another, and the probability that the British Army would take Advantage of our delays, march out of Boston and spread desolation as far as they could go. I concluded with a Motion in form that Congress would Adopt the Army at Cambridge and appoint a General, that though this was not the proper time to nominate a General, yet as I had reason to believe this was a point of the greatest difficulty, I had no hesitation to declare that I had but one Gentleman in my Mind for that important command, and that was a Gentleman from Virginia who was among Us and very well known to all of Us, a Gentleman whose Skill and Experience as an Officer, whose independent fortune, great Talents and excellent universal Character, would command the Approbation of all America, and unite the cordial Exertions of all the Colonies better than any other Person in the Union. Mr. Washington, who happened to sit near the Door, as soon as he heard me allude to him, from his Usual Modesty darted into the Library Room. Mr. Hancock, who was our President, which gave me an Opportunity to observe his Countenance, while I was speaking on the State of the Colonies, the Army at Cambridge and the Ennemy, heard me with visible pleasure, but when I came to describe Washington for the Commander, I never remarked a more sudden and sinking Change of Countenance. Mortification and resentment were expressed as forcibly as his Face could exhibit them. Mr. Samuel Adams Seconded the Motion, and that did not soften the Presidents Phisiognomy at all.

General Ward was elected the second and Lee the third. Gates and Mifflin, I believe had some Appointments, and General Washington took with him Mr. Reed of Philadelphia, a Lawyer of some Eminence for his private Secretary. And the Gentlemen all sett off for the Camp. They had not proceeded twenty miles from Philadelphia before they met a Courier with the News of the Battle of Bunkers Hill, the Death of General

Warren, the Slaughter among the British Officers and Men as well as among ours and the burning of Charlestown. Mr. Hancock however never loved me so well after this Event as he had done before, and he made me feel at times the Effects of his resentment and of his Jealousy in many Ways and at diverse times, as long as he lived, though at other times according to his variable feelings, he even overacted his part in professing his regard and respect to me. Hitherto no Jealousy had ever appeared between Mr. Samuel Adams and me. But many Years had not passed away before some Symptoms of it appeared in him, particularly when I was first chosen to go to Europe, a distinction that neither he nor Mr. Hancock could bear. Mr. Adams however disguised it under a pretence that I could not be spared from Congress and the State. More of this Spirit appeared afterwards, when I had drawn up at his and Mr. Bowdoins desire a Constitution for Massachusetts, and it was about to be reported in my hand Writing. But after the Coalition between Mr. Hancock and him in 1788, both these Gentlemen indulged their Jealousy so far as to cooperate in dissiminating Prejudices against me, as a Monarchy Man and a Friend to England, for which I hope they have been forgiven, in Heaven as I have constantly forgiven them on Earth, though they both knew the insinuations were groundless.

An Event of the most trifling nature in Appearance, and fit only to excite Laughter, in other Times, struck me into a profound Reverie, if not a fit of Melancholly. I met a Man who had sometimes been my Client, and sometimes I had been against him. He, though a common Horse Jockey, was sometimes in the right, and I had commonly been successfull in his favour in our Courts of Law. He was always in the Law, and had been sued in many Actions, at almost every Court. As soon as he saw me, he came up to me, and his first Salutation to me was "Oh! Mr. Adams what great Things have you and your Colleagues done for Us! We can never be gratefull enough to you. There are no Courts of Justice now in this Province, and I hope there never will be another!" . . . Is this the Object for which I have been contending? said I to myself, for I rode along without any Answer to this Wretch.

Are these the Sentiments of such People? And how many of them are there in the Country? Half the Nation for what I know: for half the Nation are Debtors if not more, and these have been in all Countries, the Sentiments of Debtors. If the Power of the Country should get into such hands, and there is great danger that it will, to what purpose have We sacrificed our Time, health and every Thing else? Surely We must guard against this Spirit and these Principles or We shall repent of all our Conduct. However The good Sense and Integrity of the Majority of the great Body of the People, came in to my thoughts for my relief, and the last resource was after all in a good Providence.—How much reason there was for these melancholly reflections, the subsequent times have too fully shewn. Opportunities enough had been presented to me to convince me that a very great Portion of the People of America were debtors: but that enormous Gulf of debt to Great Britain from Virginia and some other States, which have since swallowed up the Harmony of all our Councils, and produced the Tryumph of Principles too nearly resembling those of my Client, was not known to me at that time in a tenth part of its extent. When the Consequences will terminate No Man can say.

At the appointed time, We returned to Philadelphia and Congress were reassembled. Mr. Richard Penn had sailed for England, and carried the Petition, from which Mr. Dickenson and his party expected Relief. I expected none, and was wholly occupied in measures to support the Army and the Expedition into Canada. Every important Step was opposed, and carried by bare Majorities, which obliged me to be almost constantly engaged in debate: but I was not content with all that was done, and almost every day, I had something to say about Advizing the States to institute Governments, to express my total despair of any good from the Petition or any of those Things which were called conciliatory measures. I constantly insisted that all such measures, instead of having any tendency to produce a Reconciliation, would only be considered as proofs of our Timidity and want of Confidence in the Ground We stood on, and would only encourage our Ennemies to greater Exertions against Us. That We should be driven to the Necessity of Declaring ourselves independent States, and that We ought now to be employed in preparing a Plan of Confederation for the Colonies, and Treaties to be proposed to foreign Powers particularly to France and Spain, that all these Measures ought to be maturely considered, and carefully prepared, together with a declaration of Independence. That these three Measures, Independence, Confederation and Negotiations with foreign Powers, particularly France, ought to go hand in hand, and be adopted all together. That foreign Powers could not be expected to acknowledge Us, till We had acknowledged ourselves and taken our Station, among them as a sovereign Power, and Independent Nation. That now We were distressed for Want of Artillery, Arms, Ammunition, Cloathing and even for Flynts. That the People had no Marketts for their Produce, wanted Cloathing and many other things, which foreign Commerce alone could fully supply, and We could not expect Commerce till We were independent. That the People were wonderfully well united and extreamly Ardent: their was no danger of our wanting Support from them, if We did not discourage them by checking and quenching their Zeal. That there was no doubt, of our Ability to defend the Country, to support the War, and maintain our Independence. We had Men enough, our People were brave and every day improving in all the Exercises and Discipline of War. That we ought immediately to give Permission to our Merchants to fit out Privateers and make reprisals on the Ennemy. That Congress ought to Arm Ships and Commission Officers and lay the foundations of a Navy. That immense Advantages might be derived from this resource. That not only West India Articles, in great Abundance, and British Manufactures of all kinds might be obtained but Artillery, Ammunitions and all kinds of Supplies for the Army. That a System of Measures taken with unanimity and pursued with resolution, would insure Us the Friendship and Assistance of France. Some Gentlemen doubted of the Sentiments of France, thought She would frown upon Us as Rebells and be afraid to countenance the Example. I replied to these Gentlemen, that I apprehended they had not attended to the relative Situation of France and England. That it was the unquestionable Interest of France that the British continental Colonies should be independent. That Britain by the Conquest of Canada and their naval Tryumphs during the last War, and by her vast Possessions in America and the East Indies, was exalted to a height of Power and Preeminence that France must envy and could not endure. But there was much more than pride and Jealousy in the Case. Her Rank, her Consideration in Europe, and even her Safety and Independence was at stake. The Navy of Great Britain was now Mistress of the Seas all over the Globe. The Navy of France almost annihilated. Its Inferiority was so great and obvious, that all the Dominions of France in the West Indies and in the East Indies lay at the Mercy of Great Britain, and must remain so as long as North America belonged to Great Britain, and afforded them so many harbours abounding with Naval Stores and Resources of all kinds and so many Men and Seamen ready to assist them and Man their Ships. That Interest could not lie, that the Interest of France was so obvious, and her Motives so cogent, that nothing but a judicial Infatuation of her Councils could restrain her from embracing Us. That our Negotiations with France ought however, to be conducted with great caution and with all the foresight We could possibly obtain. That We ought not to enter into any Alliance with her, which should entangle Us in any future Wars in Europe, that We ought to lay it down as a first principle and a Maxim never to be forgotten, to maintain an entire Neutrality in all future European Wars. That it never could be our Interest to unite with France, in the destruction of England, or in any measures to break her Spirit or reduce her to a situation in which she could not support her Independence. On the other hand it could never be our Duty to unite with Britain in too great a humiliation of France. That our real if not our nominal Independence would consist in our Neutrality. If We united with either Nation, in any future War, We must become too subordinate and dependent on that nation, and should be involved in all European Wars as We had been hitherto. That foreign Powers would find means to corrupt our People to influence our Councils, and in fine We should be little better than Puppetts danced on the Wires of the Cabinetts of Europe. We should be the Sport of European Intrigues and Politicks. That therefore in preparing Treaties to be proposed to foreign Powers and in the Instructions to be given to our Ministers, We ought to confine ourselves strictly to a Treaty of Commerce. That such a Treaty would be an ample Compensation to France, for all the Aid We should want from her. The Opening of American Trade, to her would be a vast resource for her Commerce and Naval Power, and a great Assistance to her in protecting her East and West India Possessions as well as her Fisheries: but that the bare dismemberment of the British Empire, would be to her an incalculable Security and Benefit, worth more than all the Exertions We should require of her even if it should draw her into another Eight or ten Years War.—When I first made these Observations in Congress I never saw a greater Impression made upon that Assembly or any other. Attention and Approbation was marked on every Countenance. Several Gentlemen came to me afterwards to thank me for that Speech, particularly Mr. Cæsar Rodney of Delaware and Mr. Duane of New York. I remember those two Gentlemen in particular because both of them said, that I had considered the Subject of foreign Connections more maturely than any Man they had ever heard in America, that I had perfectly digested the Subject, and had removed, Mr. Rodney said all, and Mr. Duane said, the greatest part of his objections to foreign Negotiations. Even Mr. Dickinson said to Gentlemen out of Doors, that I had thrown great light on the subject.

In the Course of this Winter appeared a Phenomenon in Philadelphia *a Star of Disaster* (Disastrous Meteor), I mean Thomas Paine. He came from England, and got into such company as would converse with him, and ran about picking up what Information he could, concerning our Affairs, and finding the great Question was concerning Independence, he gleaned from those he saw the common place Arguments concerning Independence: such as the Necessity of Independence, at some time or other, the peculiar fitness at this time: the Justice of it: the Provocation to it: the necessity of it: our Ability to maintain it &c. &c. Dr. Rush put him upon Writing on the Subject, furnished him with the Arguments which had been urged in Congress an hundred times, and gave him his title of common Sense. In the latter part of Winter, or early in the Spring he came out, with his Pamphlet. The Arguments in favour of Independence I liked very well: but one third of the

Book was filled with Arguments from the old Testiment, to prove the Unlawfulness of Monarchy, and another Third, in planning a form of Government, for the seperate States in One Assembly, and for the United States, in a Congress. His Arguments from the old Testiment, were ridiculous, but whether they proceeded from honest Ignorance, or foolish Superstition on one hand, or from willfull Sophistry and knavish Hypocricy on the other I know not. The other third part relative to a form of Government I considered as flowing from simple Ignorance, and a mere desire to please the democratic Party in Philadelphia, at whose head were Mr. Matlock, Mr. Cannon and Dr. Young. I regretted however, to see so foolish a plan recommended to the People of the United States, who were all waiting only for the Countenance of Congress, to institute their State Governments. I dreaded the Effect so popular a pamphlet might have, among the People, and determined to do all in my Power, to counter Act the Effect of it. My continued Occupations in Congress, allowed me no time to write any thing of any Length: but I found moments to write a small pamphlet which Mr. Richard Henry Lee, to whom I shewed it, liked so well that he insisted on my permitting him to publish it: He accordingly got Mr. Dunlap to print it, under the Tittle of Thoughts on Government in a Letter from a Gentleman to his Friend. Common Sense was published without a Name: and I thought it best to suppress my name too: but as common Sense when it first appeared was generally by the public ascribed to me or Mr. Samuel Adams, I soon regretted that my name did not appear. Afterward I had a new Edition of it printed with my name and the name of Mr. Wythe of Virginia to whom the Letter was at first intended to have been addressed. The Gentlemen of New York availed themselves of the Ideas in this Morsell in the formation of the Constitution of that State. And Mr. Lee sent it to the Convention of Virginia when they met to form their Government and it went to North Carolina, New Jersey and other States. Matlock, Cannon, Young and Paine had influence enough however, to get their plan adopted in substance in Georgia and Vermont as well as Pennsilvania. These three States have since found them, such Systems of Anarchy, if that Expression is not a contradiction in terms, that they have altered them and made them more conformable to my plan.—Paine soon after the Appearance of my Pamphlet hurried away to my Lodgings and spent an Evening with me. His Business was to reprehend me for publishing my Pamphlet. Said he was afraid it would do hurt, and that it was repugnant to the plan he had proposed in his Common Sense. I told him it was true it was repugnant and for that reason, I had written it and consented to the publication of it: for I was as much afraid of his Work as he was of mine. His plan was so democratical, without any restraint or even an Attempt at any Equilibrium or Counterpoise, that it must produce confusion and every Evil Work. I told him further, that his Reasoning from the Old Testament was ridiculous, and I could hardly think him sincere. At this he laughed, and said he had taken his Ideas in that part from Milton: and then expressed a Contempt of the Old Testament and indeed of the Bible at large, which surprized me. He saw that I did not relish this, and soon check'd himself, with these Words "However I have some thoughts of publishing my Thoughts on Religion, but I believe it will be best to postpone it, to the latter part of Life." This Conversation passed in good humour, without any harshness on either Side: but I perceived in him a conceit of himself, and a daring Impudence, which have been developed more and more to this day. . . . The third part of Common Sense which relates wholly to the Question of Independence, was clearly written and contained a tollerable Summary of the Arguments which I had been repeating again and again in Congress for nine months. But I am bold to say there is not a Fact nor a Reason stated in it, which had not been frequently urged in Congress. The Temper and Wishes of the People, supplied every thing at that time: and the Phrases, suitable for an Emigrant from New Gate, or one who had chiefly associated with such Company, such as "The Royal Brute of England," "The Blood upon his Soul," and a few others of equal delicacy, had as much Weight with the People as his Arguments. It has been a general Opinion, that this Pamphlet was of great Importance in the Revolution. I doubted it at the time and have doubted it to this day.

I was incessantly employed, through the whole Fall, Winter and Spring of 1775 and 1776 in Congress during their Sittings and on Committees on mornings and Evenings, and unquestionably did more business than any other Member of that house. In the Beginning of May I procured the Appointment of a Committee, to prepare a resolution recommending to the People of the States to institute Governments. The Committee of whom I was one requested me to draught a resolve which I did and by their Direction reported it. Opposition was made to it, and Mr. Duane called it a Machine to fabricate independence but on the 15th of May 1776 it passed. It was indeed on all hands considered by Men of Understanding as equivalent to a declaration of Independence: tho a formal declaration of it was still opposed by Mr. Dickinson and his Party.

Not long after this the three greatest Measures of all, were carried. Three Committees were appointed, One for preparing a Declaration of Independence, another for reporting a Plan of a Treaty to be proposed to France, and a third to digest a System of Articles of Confederation to be proposed to the States.—I was appointed on the Committee of Independence, and on that for preparing the form of a Treaty with France: on the Committee of Confederation Mr. Samuel Adams was appointed. The Committee of Independence, were Thomas Jefferson, John Adams, Benjamin Franklin, Roger Sherman and Robert R. Livingston. Mr. Jefferson had been now about a Year a Member of Congress, but had attended his Duty in the House but a very small part of the time and when there had never spoken in public: and during the whole Time I satt with him in Congress, I never heard him utter three Sentences together. The most of a Speech he ever made in my hearing was a gross insult on Religion, in one or two Sentences, for which I gave him immediately the Reprehension, which he richly merited. It will naturally be enquired, how it happened that he was appointed on a Committee of such importance. There were more reasons than one. Mr. Jefferson had the Reputation of a masterly Pen. He had been chosen a Delegate in Virginia, in consequence of a very handsome public Paper which he had written for the House of Burgesses, which had given him the Character of a fine Writer. Another reason was that Mr. Richard Henry Lee was not beloved by the most of his Colleagues from Virginia and Mr. Jefferson was sett up to rival and supplant him. This could be done only by the Pen, for Mr. Jefferson could stand no competition with him or any one else in Elocution and public debate. Here I will interrupt the narration for a moment to observe that from all I have read of the History of Greece and Rome, England and France, and all I have observed at home, and abroad, that Eloquence in public Assemblies is not the surest road, to Fame and Preferment, at least unless it be used with great caution, very rarely, and with great Reserve. The Examples of Washington, Franklin and Jefferson are enough to shew that Silence and reserve in public are more Efficacious than Argumentation or Oratory. A public Speaker who inserts himself, or is urged by others into the Conduct of Affairs, by daily Exertions to justify his measures, and answer the Objections of Opponents, makes himself too familiar with the public, and unavoidably makes himself Ennemies. Few Persons can bare to be outdone in Reasoning or declamation or Wit, or Sarcasm or Repartee, or Satyr, and all these things are very apt to grow out of public debate. In this Way in a Course of Years, a Nation becomes full of a Mans Ennemies, or at least of such as have been galled in some Controversy, and take a secret pleasure in assisting to humble and mortify him. So much for this digression. We will now return to our Memoirs. The Committee had several meetings, in which were proposed the Articles of which the Declaration was to consist, and minutes made of them. The Committee then appointed Mr. Jefferson and me, to draw them up in form, and cloath them in a proper Dress. The Sub Committee met, and considered the Minutes, making such Observations on them as then occurred: when Mr. Jefferson desired me to take them to my Lodgings and make the Draught. This I declined and gave several reasons for declining. 1 That he was a Virginian and I a Massachusettensian. 2. that he was a southern Man and I a northern one. 3. That I had been so obnoxious for my early and constant Zeal in promoting the Measure, that any draught of mine, would undergo a more severe Scrutiny and Criticism in Congress, than one of his composition. 4thly and lastly and that would be reason enough if there were no other, I had a great Opinion of the Elegance of his pen and none at all of my own. I therefore insisted that no hesitation should be made on his part. He accordingly took the Minutes and in a day or two produced to me his Draught. Whether I made or suggested any corrections I remember not. The Report was made to the Committee of five, by them examined, but whether altered or corrected in any thing I cannot recollect. But in substance at least it was reported to Congress where, after a severe Criticism, and striking out several of the most oratorical Paragraphs it was adopted on the fourth of July 1776, and published to the World.

The Committee for preparing the Model of a Treaty to be proposed to France consisted of   When We met to deliberate on the Subject, I contended for the same Principles, which I had before avowed and defended in Congress, viz. That We should avoid all Alliance, which might embarrass Us in after times and involve Us in future European Wars. That a Treaty of commerce, which would opperate as a Repeal of the British Acts of Navigation as far as respected Us and Admit France into an equal participation of the benefits of our commerce; would encourage her Manufactures, increase her Exports of the Produce of her Soil and Agriculture, extend her navigation and Trade, augment her resources of naval Power, raise her from her present deep humiliation, distress and decay, and place her on a more equal footing with England, for the protection of her foreign Possessions, and maintaining her Independence at Sea, would be an ample Compensation to France for Acknowledging our Independence, and for furnishing Us for our money or upon Credit for a Time, with such Supplies of Necessaries as We should want, even if this Conduct should involve her in a War. If a War should ensue, which did not necessarily follow, for a bare Acknowledgement of our Independence after We had asserted it, was not by the Law of Nations an Act of Hostility, which would be a legitimate cause of War. Franklin although he was commonly as silent on committees as in Congress, upon this Occasion, ventured so far as to intimate his concurrence with me in these Sentiments, though as will be seen hereafter he shifted them as easily as the Wind ever shifted: and assumed a dogmatical Tone, in favour of an Opposite System. The Committee after as much deliberation upon the Subject as they chose to employ, appointed me, to draw up a Plan and Report.

Franklin had made some marks with a Pencil against some Articles in a printed Volume of Treaties, which he put into my hand. Some of these were judiciously selected, and I took them with others which I found necessary into the Draught and made my report to the Committee at large, who after a reasonable Examination of it, agreed to report it. When it came before Congress, it occupied the Attention of that Body for several days. Many Motions were made, to insert in it Articles of entangling Alliance, of exclusive Priviledges, and of Warrantees of Possessions: and it was argued that the present Plan reported by the Committee held out no sufficient temptation to France, who would despize it and refuse to receive our Ambassador. It was chiefly left to me to defend my report, though I had some able Assistance, and We did defend it with so much Success, that the Treaty passed without one Particle of Alliance, exclusive Priviledge, or Warranty.

Fryday May 10. 1776. Congress resumed the Consideration of the Resolution reported from the Committee of the whole, and the same was agreed to as follows:

Resolved, That it be recommended to the respective Assemblies and Conventions of the United Colonies, where no Government sufficient to the Exigencies of their Affairs, hath been hitherto established, to adopt such Government as shall in the Opinion of the Representatives of the People best conduce to the Happiness and Safety of their Constituents in particular, and America in general.

Resolved that a Committee of three be appointed to prepare a Preamble to the foregoing Resolution. The Members chosen Mr. J. Adams, Mr. Rutledge and Mr. Richard Henry Lee.

Marshall in his Life of Washington says this Resolution was moved by R. H. Lee and seconded by J. Adams. It was brought before the Committee of the whole House, in concert between Mr. R. H. Lee and me, and I suppose General Washington was informed of it by Mr. Harrison the Chairman or some other of his Correspondents: but nothing of this Appears upon the Journal. It is carefully concealed like many other Things relative to the greatest Affairs of the Nation which were before Congress in that Year.

This Resolution I considered as an Epocha, a decisive Event. It was a measure which I had invariably pursued for a whole Year, and contended for, through a Scæne and a Series of Anxiety, labour, Study, Argument, and Obloquy, which was then little known and is now forgotten, by all but Dr. Rush and a very few who like him survive. Millions of Curses were poured out upon me, for these Exertions and for these Tryumphs over them, by the Essex Juntoes, for there were such at that time and have continued to this day in every State in the Union; who whatever their pretences may have been have never forgotten nor cordially forgiven me. By this Term which is now become vulgarly and politically technical, I mean, not the Tories, for from them I received always more candour, but a class of People who thought proper and convenient to themselves to go along with the Public Opinion in Appearance, though in their hearts they detested it. Although they might think the public opinion was right in General, in its difference with G. Britain, yet they secretly regretted the Seperation, and above all Things the Connection with France. Such a Party has always existed and was the final Ruin of the Federal Administration as will hereafter very plainly appear.

A Committee of the whole again. Mr. Harrison reported no Resolution. I mention these Committees to shew how all these great questions laboured. Day after day consumed in debates without any Conclusion.

Saturday May 11. 1776. A Petition from John Jacobs in behalf of himself and others was presented to Congress and read. Ordered that it be referred to a Committee of three. The Members chosen Mr. John Adams, Mr. Lee and Mr. Rutledge.

A Committee of the whole. Mr. Harrison reported no Resolution. This days Journal of this Committee shews, with what Art other matters were referred to these Committees of the whole, in order to retard and embarrass the great questions.

Monday May 13. 1776. Sundry Petitions were presented to Congress and read, viz. one from Dr. Benjamin Church, and one from Benjamin, Samuel and Edward Church, with a Certificate from three Physicians respecting the health of Dr. B. Church. Here I am compelled, much against my Inclination to record a Fact, which if it were not necessary to explain some things I should rather have concealed. When this Petition was before Congress, Mr. Samuel Adams said something, which I thought I confess too favourable to Dr. Church. I cannot recollect that I said any Thing against him. As it lies upon my Mind I was silent. Mr. Hancock was President, and Mr. Harrison Chairman of the Committee of the whole and a constant confidential Correspondent of General Washington. Neither of them friendly to me. I cannot suspect Mr. Samuel Adams of writing or insinuating any Thing against me to the Friends of Dr. Church, at that time. But Mr. Samuel Adams told me that Dr. Church and Dr. Warren, had composed Mr. Hancocks oration on the fifth of March, which was so celebrated, more than two thirds of it at least. Mr. Hancock was most certainly not friendly to me at that time, and he might think himself in the Power of Dr. Church. When Mr. Edward Church printed his poetical Libel against me at New York in 1789 or 1790, I was told by an Acquaintance of his that he was full of Prejudices against me on Account of Dr. Church his Brother. I leave others to conjecture how he came by them. I know of no other Way to account for his Virulence, and his Cousin Dr. Jarvis's Virulence against me, having never injured or offended any of them. Misrepresentation at that day was a Pestilence that walked in darkness. In more modern times it has stalked abroad with more impudence at Noon day.

Tuesday May 14. 1776. A Letter of the 11th. from General Washington inclosing sundry Papers; a Letter of the 3d from General Schuyler; and a Letter of the 9th. from Daniel Robertson were laid before Congress and read. Resolved that they be referred to a Committee of three. The Members chosen Mr. W. Livingston, Mr. Jefferson and Mr. John Adams.

William Ellery Esqr. appeared a Delegate from Rhode Island, in the place of Governor Ward, and being an excellent Member, fully supplied his place.

The Committee appointed to prepare a Preamble, thought it not necessary to be very elaborate, and Mr. Lee and Mr. Rutledge desired me as Chairman to draw something very short which I did and with their Approbation.

On Wednesday May 15. 1776 reported the following which was agreed to

Whereas his Britannic Majesty, in conjunction with the Lords and Commons of Great Britain, has, by a late Act of

Parliament, excluded the Inhabitants of these united Colonies from the Protection of his Crown; and whereas no Answer whatever to the humble Petitions of the Colonies for redress of Grievances and reconciliation with Great Britain has been or is likely to be given, but the whole force of that Kingdom aided by foreign Mercenaries is to be exerted for the destruction of the good People of these Colonies; and whereas it appears absolutely irreconcileable to reason, and good Conscience, for the People of these Colonies now to take the Oaths and Affirmations necessary for the support of any Government under the Crown of Great Britain, and it is necessary that the Exercise of every kind of Authority under the said Crown should be totally suppressed, and all the Powers of Government exerted under the Authority of the People of the Colonies, for the preservation of internal peace, Virtue and good order, as well as for the defence of their Lives, Liberties and Properties against the hostile Invasions and cruel depredations of their Ennemies; therefore

Resolved That it be recommended to the respective Assemblies and Conventions of the United Colonies, where no Government sufficient to the Exigencies of their affairs hath been hitherto established, to adopt such Government as shall in the Opinion of the Representatives of the People best conduce to the happiness and Safety of their Constituents in particular and America in General.

Ordered that the said Preamble, with the Resolution passed the 10th. instant, be published.—Mr. Duane called it, to me, a Machine for the fabrication of Independence. I said, smiling, I thought it was independence itself: but We must have it with more formality yet.

———————

I am not able to recollect, whether it was on this, or some preceeding day, that the greatest and most solemn debate was had on the question of Independence. The Subject had been in Contemplation for more than a Year and frequent discussions had been had concerning it. At one time and another, all the Arguments for it and against it had been exhausted and were become familiar. I expected no more would be said in public but that the question would be put and decided. Mr.

Dickinson however was determined to bear his Testimony against it with more formality. He had prepared himself apparently with great Labour and ardent Zeal, and in a Speech of great Length, and all his Eloquence, he combined together all that had before been written in Pamphlets and News papers and all that had from time to time been said in Congress by himself and others. He conducted the debate, not only with great Ingenuity and Eloquence, but with equal Politeness and Candour: and was answered in the same Spirit.

No Member rose to answer him: and after waiting some time, in hopes that some one less obnoxious than myself, who had been all along for a Year before, and still was represented and believed to be the Author of all the Mischief, I determined to speak.

It has been said by some of our Historians, that I began by an Invocation to the God of Eloquence. This is a Misrepresentation. Nothing so puerile as this fell from me. I began by saying that this was the first time of my Life that I had ever wished for the Talents and Eloquence of the ancient Orators of Greece and Rome, for I was very sure that none of them ever had before him a question of more Importance to his Country and to the World. They would probably upon less Occasions than this have begun by solemn Invocations to their Divinities for Assistance but the Question before me appeared so simple, that I had confidence enough in the plain Understanding and common Sense that had been given me, to believe that I could answer to the Satisfaction of the House all the Arguments which had been produced, notwithstanding the Abilities which had been displayed and the Eloquence with which they had been enforced. Mr. Dickinson, some years afterwards published his Speech. I had made no Preparation beforehand and never committed any minutes of mine to writing. But if I had a Copy of Mr. Dickinsons before me I would now after Nine and twenty Years have elapsed, endeavour to recollect mine.

Before the final Question was put, the new Delegates from New Jersey came in, and Mr. Stockton, Dr. Witherspoon and Mr. Hopkinson, very respectable Characters, expressed a great desire to hear the Arguments. All was Silence: No one would speak: all Eyes were turned upon me. Mr. Edward Rutledge came to me and said laughing, Nobody will speak but you, upon this Subject. You have all the Topicks so ready, that you must satisfy the Gentlemen from New Jersey. I answered him laughing, that it had so much the Air of exhibiting like an Actor or Gladiator for the Entertainment of the Audience, that I was ashamed to repeat what I had said twenty times before, and I thought nothing new could be advanced by me. The New Jersey Gentlemen however still insisting on hearing at least a Recapitulation of the Arguments and no other Gentleman being willing to speak, I summed up the Reasons, Objections and Answers, in as concise a manner as I could, till at length the Jersey Gentlemen said they were fully satisfied and ready for the Question, which was then put and determined in the Affirmative.

A Committee of the whole on the Articles of Confederation. Mr. Morton reported that the Committee had gone through the same, and agreed to sundry Articles which he was ordered to submit to Congress.

Ordered that Eighty Copies of the Articles of Confederation, as reported from the Committee of the whole, be printed under the same Injunctions as the former Articles, and delivered to the Members under the like Injunctions as formerly.

Thus We see the whole Record of this momentous Transaction. No Motions recorded. No Yeas and Nays taken down. No Alterations proposed. No debates preserved. No Names mentioned. All in profound Secrecy. Nothing suffered to transpire: No Opportunity to consult Constituents. No room for Advice or Criticisms in Pamphlets, Papers or private Conversation. I was very uneasy under all this but could not avoid it. In the Course of this Confederation, a few others were as anxious as myself. Mr. Wilson of Pennsylvania, upon one Occasion moved that the debates should be public, the Doors opened, galleries erected, or an Adjournment made to some public Building where the People might be accommodated. Mr. John Adams seconded the Motion and supported it, with Zeal. But No: Neither Party were willing: some were afraid of divisions among the People: but more were afraid to let the People see the insignificant figures they made in that Assembly. Nothing indeed was less understood, abroad among the People, than the real Constitution of Congress and the Characters of those who conducted the Business of it. The Truth is, the Motions, Plans, debates, Amendments, which were every day brought forward in those Committees of the whole House, if committed to Writing, would be very voluminous: but they are lost forever. The Preservation of them indeed, might for any thing I recollect be of more Curiosity than Use.

On this day, Mr. Franklin, Mr. Edward Rutledge and Mr. John Adams proceeded on their Journey to Lord Howe on Staten Island, the two former in Chairs and the last on Horseback; the first night We lodged at an Inn, in New Brunswick. On the Road and at all the public Houses, We saw such Numbers of Officers and Soldiers, straggling and loytering, as gave me at least, but a poor Opinion of the Discipline of our forces and excited as much indignation as anxiety. Such thoughtless dissipation at a time so critical, was not calculated to inspire very sanguine hopes or give great Courage to Ambassadors: I was nevertheless determined that it should not dishearten me. I saw that We must and had no doubt but We should be chastised into order in time.

The Taverns were so full We could with difficulty obtain Entertainment. At Brunswick, but one bed could be procured for Dr. Franklin and me, in a Chamber little larger than the bed, without a Chimney and with only one small Window. The Window was open, and I, who was an invalid and afraid of the Air in the night shut it close. Oh! says Franklin dont shut the Window. We shall be suffocated. I answered I was afraid of the Evening Air. Dr. Franklin replied, the Air within this Chamber will soon be, and indeed is now worse than that without Doors: come! open the Window and come to bed, and I will convince you: I believe you are not acquainted with my Theory of Colds. Opening the Window and leaping into Bed, I said I had read his Letters to Dr. Cooper in which he had advanced, that Nobody ever got cold by going into a cold Church, or any other cold Air: but the Theory was so little consistent with my experience, that I thought it a Paradox: However I had so much curiosity to hear his reasons, that I

would run the risque of a cold. The Doctor then began an harrangue, upon Air and cold and Respiration and Perspiration,
with which I was so much amused that I soon fell asleep, and
left him and his Philosophy together: but I believe they were
equally sound and insensible, within a few minutes after me,
for the last Words I heard were pronounced as if he was more
than half asleep. . . . I remember little of the Lecture, except, that the human Body, by Respiration and Perspiration,
destroys a gallon of Air in a minute: that two such Persons, as
were now in that Chamber, would consume all the Air in it, in
an hour or two: that by breathing over again the matter
thrown off, by the Lungs and the Skin, We should imbibe the
real Cause of Colds, not from abroad but from within. I am
not inclined to introduce here a dissertation on this Subject.
There is much Truth I believe, in some things he advanced:
but they warrant not the assertion that a Cold is never taken
from cold air. I have often conversed with him since on the
same subject: and I believe with him that Colds are often taken
in foul Air, in close Rooms: but they are often taken from cold
Air, abroad too. I have often asked him, whether a Person
heated with Exercise, going suddenly into cold Air, or standing still in a current of it, might not have his Pores suddenly
contracted, his Perspiration stopped, and that matter thrown
into the Circulations or cast upon the Lungs which he acknowledged was the Cause of Colds. To this he never could
give me a satisfactory Answer. And I have heard that in the
Opinion of his own able Physician Dr. Jones he fell a Sacrifice
at last, not to the Stone but to his own Theory; having caught
the violent Cold, which finally choaked him, by sitting for
some hours at a Window, with the cool Air blowing upon him.

The next Morning We proceeded on our Journey, and the
Remainder of this Negotiation, will be related from the Journals of Congress, and from a few familiar Letters, which I
wrote to my most intimate Friends before and after my Journey. The abrupt uncouth freedom of these, and all others of
my Letters, in those days require an Apology. Nothing was farther from my Thoughts, than that they would ever appear
before the Public. Oppressed with a Load of Business, without
an Amanuensis, or any Assistance, I was obliged to do every
Thing myself. For seven Years before this I had never been

without three Clerks in my Office as a Barrister: but now I had no Secretary nor servant whom I could trust to write: and every thing must be copied by myself, or be hazarded without any. The few that I wrote upon this Occasion I copied; merely to assist my memory as Occasion might demand.

There were a few Circumstances which appear neither in the Journals of Congress nor in my Letters, which may be thought by some worth preserving. Lord How had sent over an Officer as an Hostage for our Security. I said to Dr. Franklin, it would be childish in Us to depend upon such a Pledge and insisted on taking him over with Us, and keeping our Surety on the same side of the Water with Us. My Colleagues exulted in the Proposition and agreed to it instantly. We told the Officer, if he held himself under our direction he must go back with Us. He bowed Assent, and We all embarked in his Lordships Barge. As We approached the Shore his Lordship, observing Us, came down to the Waters Edge to receive Us, and looking at the Officer, he said, Gentlemen, you make me a very high Compliment, and you may depend upon it, I will consider it as the most sacred of Things. We walked up to the House between Lines of Guards of Grenadiers, looking as fierce as ten furies, and making all the Grimaces and Gestures and motions of their Musquets with Bayonets fixed, which I suppose military Ettiquette requires but which We neither understood nor regarded.

The House had been the Habitation of military Guards, and was as dirty as a stable: but his Lordship had prepared a large handsome Room, by spreading a Carpet of Moss and green Spriggs from Bushes and Shrubbs in the Neighbourhood, till he had made it not only wholesome but romantically elegant, and he entertained Us with good Claret, good Bread, cold Ham, Tongues and Mutton.

I will now proceed to relate the Sequel of this Conference, 1st from the Journal of Congress. 2d from the Letters written to some of my friends at the time: and 3dly a Circumstance or two which are not preserved in the Journals or Letters.

Fryday September 13. 1776. The Committee appointed to confer with Lord Howe, having returned made a verbal Report.

Ordered that they make a report in Writing as soon as conveniently they can.

Tuesday. September 17th. 1776. The Committee appointed to confer with Lord Howe, agreable to the order of Congress, brought in a report in Writing, which was read as follows:

In Obedience to the orders of Congress, We have had a meeting with Lord Howe. It was on Wednesday last upon Staten Island, opposite to Amboy, where his Lordship received and entertained Us, with the Utmost politeness.

His Lordship opened the Conversation by Acquainting Us, that, tho' he could not treat with Us as a Committee of Congress, yet, as his Powers enabled him to confer and consult with any private Gentlemen of Influence in the Colonies, on the means of restoring Peace, between the two Countries, he was glad of this Opportunity of conferring with Us, on that Subject, if We thought ourselves at Liberty to enter into a Conference with him in that Character. We observed to his Lordship, that, as our Business was to hear, he might consider Us, in what Light he pleased, and communicate to Us, any propositions he might be authorised to make, for the purpose mentioned; but that We could consider Ourselves in no other Character than that, in which We were placed, by order of Congress. His Lordship then entered into a discourse of considerable Length, which contained no explicit proposition of Peace, except one, namely, That the Colonies should return to their Allegiance and Obedience to the Government of Great Britain. The rest consisted principally of Assurances, that there was an exceeding good disposition in the King and his Ministers, to make that Government easy to Us, with intimations, that, in case of our Submission, they would cause the Offensive Acts of Parliament to be revised, and the Instructions to Ministers to be reconsidered; that so, if any just causes of complaint were found in the Acts, or any Errors in Government were perceived to have crept into the Instructions, they might be amended or withdrawn.

We gave it, as our Opinion to his Lordship, that a return to the domination of Great Britain, was not now to be expected. We mentioned the repeated humble petitions of the Colonies to the King and Parliament, which had been treated with Contempt, and answered only by additional Injuries; the Unexampled Patience We had shewn, under their tyrannical Government, and that it was not till the late Act of Parliament, which denounced War against Us, and put Us out of the Kings Protection, that We declared our Independence; that this declaration had been called for, by the People of the Colonies in general; that every colony had approved of it, when made, and all now considered themselves as independent States, and were settling or had settled their Governments accordingly; so that it was not in the Power of Congress to agree for them, that they should return to their former dependent State; that there was no doubt of their Inclination for peace, and their Willingness to enter into a treaty with Britain, that might be advantageous to both Countries; that, though his Lordship had at present, no power to treat with them as independent States, he might, if there was the same good disposition in Britain, much sooner obtain fresh Powers from thence, for that purpose, than powers could be obtained by Congress, from the several Colonies to consent to a Submission.

His Lordship then saying, that he was sorry to find, that no Accommodation was like to take place, put an End to the Conference.

Upon the whole, it did not appear to your Committee, that his Lordships commission contained any other Authority, than that expressed in the Act of Parliament, namely, that of granting Pardons, with such exceptions as the Commissioners shall think proper to make, and of declaring America or any part of it, to be in the Kings Peace, upon Submission: for as to the Power of enquiring into the State of America, which his Lordship mentioned to Us, and of conferring and consulting with any Persons the Commissioners might think proper, and representing the result of such conversation to the Ministry, who, provided the Colonies would subject themselves, might, after all, or might not at their pleasure, make any Alterations in the former Instructions to Governors, or propose in Parliament any Amendment of the Acts complained of, We apprehended any expectations from the Effects of such a Power would have been too uncertain and precarious to be relied on by America, had she still continued in her State of dependence.

Ordered that the foregoing Report, and also the Message from Lord Howe as delivered by General Sullivan, and the Resolution of Congress, in consequence thereof, be published by the Committee, who brought in the foregoing report.

Ordered that the said Committee publish Lord Drummonds Letters to General Washington and the Generals Answers.

Two or three Circumstances, which are omitted in this report, and indeed not thought worth notice in any of my private Letters, I afterwards found circulated in Europe, and oftener repeated than any other Part of this whole Transaction. Lord How was profuse in his Expressions of Gratitude to the State of Massachusetts, for erecting a marble Monument in Westminster Abbey to his Elder Brother Lord How who was killed in America in the last French War, saying "he esteemed that Honour to his Family, *above all Things in this World*. That such was his gratitude and affection to this Country, on that Account, that he felt for America, as for a Brother, and if America should fall, he should feel and lament it, like the Loss of a Brother." Dr. Franklin, with an easy Air and a collected Countenance, a Bow, a Smile and all that Naivetee which sometimes appeared in his Conversation and is often observed in his Writings, replied "My Lord, We will do our Utmost Endeavours, to save your Lordship that mortification." His Lordship appeared to feel this, with more Sensibility, than I could expect: but he only returned "I suppose you will endeavour to give Us employment in Europe." To this Observation, not a Word nor a look from which he could draw any Inference, escaped any of the Committee.

Another Circumstance, of no more importance than the former, was so much celebrated in Europe, that it has often reminded me of the Question of Phocion to his Fellow Citizen, when something he had said in Public was received by the People of Athens with a clamorous Applause, "Have I said any foolish Thing?"—When his Lordship observed to Us, that he could not confer with Us as Members of Congress, or public Characters, but only as private Persons and British Subjects, Mr. John Adams answered somewhat quickly, "Your Lordship may consider me, in what light you please; and indeed I should be willing to consider myself, for a few moments, in any Character which would be agreable to your Lordship, *except that of a British Subject*." His Lordship at these Words turn'd to Dr. Franklin and Mr. Rutledge and said "Mr. Adams is a decided Character:" with so much gravity and solemnity: that I now believe it meant more, than either of my Colleagues or myself understood at the time. In our report to Congress We supposed that the Commissioners, Lord and General Howe, had by their Commission Power to except from Pardon all that they should think proper. But I was informed in England, afterwards, that a Number were expressly excepted by Name from Pardon, by the privy Council, and that John Adams was one of them, and that this List of Exceptions was given as an Instruction to the two Howes, with their Commission. When I was afterwards a Minister Plenipotentiary, at the Court of St. James's The King and the Ministry, were often insulted, ridiculed and reproached in the Newspapers, for having conducted with so much folly as to be reduced to the humiliating Necessity of receiving as an Ambassador a Man who stood recorded by the privy Council as a Rebell expressly excepted from Pardon. If this is true it will account for his Lordships gloomy denunciation of me, as "a decided Character."—Some years afterwards, when I resided in England as a public Minister, his Lordship recollected and alluded to this Conversation with great politeness and much good humour. Att the Ball, on the Queens Birthnight, I was at a Loss for the Seats assigned to the foreign Ambassadors and their Ladies. Fortunately meeting Lord How at the Door I asked his Lordship, where were the Ambassadors Seats. His Lordship with his usual politeness, and an unusual Smile of good humour, pointed to the Seats, and manifestly alluding to the Conversation on Staten Island said, "Aye! Now, We must turn you away among the foreigners."

TRAVELS, AND NEGOTIATIONS.

Quincy December 1. 1806.

1777

When I asked Leave of Congress to make a Visit to my Constituents and my Family in November 1777, it was my intention to decline the next Election, and return to my practice at the Bar. I had been four Years in Congress, left my Accounts in a very loose condition, my Debtors were failing, the paper Money was depreciating, I was daily loosing the fruits of seventeen Years industry, my family was living on my past Acquisitions which were very moderate, for no Man ever did so much Business for so little profit. My Children were growing up without my care in their Education: and all my imoluments as a Member of Congress for four Years, had not been sufficient to pay a labouring Man upon my farm. Some of my Friends, who had more compassion for me and my family than others, suggested to me what I knew very well before, that I was loosing a fortune every Year by my Absence. Young Gentlemen who had been Clerks in my Office and others whom I had left in that Character in other Offices were growing rich, for the Prize Causes, and other Controversies had made the profession of a Barrister more lucrative than it ever had been before. I thought therefore that four Years drudgery, and Sacrifice of every thing, were sufficient for my Share of Absence from home and that another might take my place. Upon my Arrival at my home in Braintree I soon found that my old Clients had not forgotten me and that new ones had heard enough of me to be ambitious of engaging me in Suits which were depending. I had applications from all quarters in the most important disputes. Among others Coll. Elisha Doane applied to me to go to Portsmouth in New Hampshire, upon the Case of a large Ship and Cargo which had been seized and was to be tried in the Court of Admiralty before Judge Brackett. At the Tryal of the Cause at Portsmouth and while I was speaking in it, Mr. Langdon came in from Phyladelphia and leaning over the Bar whispered to me, that Mr. Deane was recalled, and I was appointed to go to France. As I could scarcely believe the News to be true, and suspected Langdon to be sporting with me, it did not disconcert me. As I had never solicited such an Appointment, nor intimated to any one, the smallest inclination for it, the News was altogether unexpected. The only hint I ever had of such a design in Congress was this. After I had mounted my horse for my Journey home Mr. Gerry at Yorktown, came out of the House of Mr. Roberdeau where We lodged together, and said to me, between him and me, that I must go to France. That Mr. Deanes Conduct had been so intollerably bad, as to disgrace himself and his Country and that Congress had no other Way of retrieving the dishonour but by recalling him. I answered that as to recalling Mr. Deane Congress would do as they thought fit, but I entreated him that neither Mr. Gerry nor any one else would think of me for a Successor for I was altogether unqualified for it. Supposing it only a sudden thought of Mr. Gerry and that when he should consider it a moment he would relinquish it, I knew not that I recollected it, again, till Mr. Langdone brought it to remembrance. At Portsmouth Captain Landais was introduced to me, as then lately arrived from France, who gave me an Account of his Voyage with Bougainville round the World and other particulars of his Life. Upon my return to Braintree I found to my infinite Anxiety that Mr. Langdons intelligence was too well founded. Large Packetts from Congress, containing a new Commission to Franklin, Lee and me as Plenipotentiaries to the King of France, with our instructions and other papers, had been left at my House, and waited my Arrival. A Letter from the President of Congress informed me of my Appointment, and that the Navy Board in Boston was ordered to fit the Frigate Boston, as soon as possible to carry me to France. It should have been observed before that, in announcing to me the Intelligence of my Appointment, Langdon neither expressed Congratulation nor regret: but I soon afterwards had evidence enough that he lamented Mr. Deanes recall, for he had already formed lucrative connections in France by Mr. Deanes recommendation, particularly with Mr. Le Ray de Chaumont who had shipped Merchandizes to him to sell upon Commission, an Account of which rendered to Chaumont by Langdon, was shewn to me by the former at Passy in 1779, in which allmost the whole Capital was sunk, really or pretendedly, by the depreciation of paper money.

When the Dispatches from Congress were read, the first question was whether I should accept the Commission or return it to Congress. The dangers of the Seas and the Sufferings of a Winter passage, although I had no experience of either, had little Weight with me. The British Men of War, were a more serious Consideration. The News of my Appointment, I had no doubt were known in Rhode Island, where a part of the British Navy and Army then lay, as soon as they were to me, and transmitted to England as soon as possible. I had every reason to expect, that Ships would be ordered to intercept the

Boston from Rhode Island and from Hallifax, and that Intelligence would be secretly sent them, as accurately as possible of the time when she was to sail. For there always have been and still are Spies in America as well as in France, England and other Countries. The Consequence of a Capture would be a Lodging in New Gate. For the Spirit of Contempt as well as indignation and vindictive rage, with which the British Government had to that time conducted both the Controversy and the War forbade me to hope for the honor of an Appartment in the Tower as a State Prisoner. As their Act of Parliament would authorise them to try me in England for Treason, and proceed to execution too, I had no doubt they would go to the extent of their power, and practice upon me all the Cruelties of their punishment of Treason. My Family consisting of a dearly beloved Wife and four young Children, excited Sentiments of tenderness, which a Father and a Lover only can conceive, and which no language can express. And my Want of qualifications for the Office was by no means forgotten.

On the other hand my Country was in deep distress and in great danger. Her dearest Interest would be involved in the relations she might form with foreign nations. My own plan of these relations had been deliberately formed and fully communicated to Congress, nearly two Years before. The Confidence of my Country was committed to me, without my Solicitation. My Wife who had always encouraged and animated me, in all antecedent dangers and perplexities, did not fail me on this Occasion: But she discovered an inclination to bear me Company with all our Children. This proposal however, she was soon convinced, was too hazardous and imprudent.

It was an Opinion generally prevailing in Boston that the Fisheries were lost forever. Mr. Isaac Smith, who had been more largely concerned in the Cod Fishery than any Man excepting Mr. Hooper and Mr. Lee of Marblehead, had spoken to me on the Subject, and said that whatever should be the termination of the War he knew We should never be allowed to fish again upon the Banks. My Practice as a Barrister in the Counties of Essex, Plymouth and Barnstable had introduced me to more Knowledge both of the Cod and whale fisheries and of their importance both to the commerce and Naval Power of this Country than any other Man possessed, who would be sent abroad if I refused, and this consideration had no small Weight in producing my determination. After much Agitation of mind and a thousand reveries unnecessary to be detailed, I resolved to devote my family and my Life to the Cause, accepted the Appointment and made preparation for the Voyage. A longer time than I expected was required to fit and man the Frigate. The News of my Appointment was whispered about, and General Knox came up to dine with me, at Braintree. The design of his Visit was As I soon perceived to sound me in relation to General Washington. He asked me what my Opinion of him was. I answered with the Utmost Frankness, that I thought him a perfectly honest Man, with an amiable and excellent heart, and the most important Character at that time among Us, for he was the Center of our Union. He asked the question, he said, because, as I was going to Europe it was of importance that the Generals Character should be supported in other Countries. I replied that he might be perfectly at his ease on the Subject for he might depend upon it, that both from principle and Affection, public and private I should do my Utmost to support his Character at all times and in all places, unless something should happen very greatly to alter my Opinion of him, and this I have done from that time to this. I mention this incident, because that insolent Blasphemer of things sacred and transcendent Libeller of all that is good Tom Paine has more than once asserted in Print, the scandalous Lye, that I was one of a Faction in the fall of the Year 1777, against General Washington. It is indeed a disgrace to the moral Character and the Understanding of this Age, that this worthless fellow should be believed in any thing. But Impudence and Malice will always find Admirers.

This day six Weeks We had sailed from Nantaskett Road. How many dangers, distresses, and hairbreadth escapes had We seen. There was one however which has been omitted. One Evening when We were approaching the French Coast, I was sitting in the Cabin, when Captain McIntosh our Prisoner came down to me and addressed me, with great solemnity "Mr. Adams this ship will be captured by my Countrymen, in less than half an hour. Two large British Men of War are bearing directly down upon Us, and are just by, you will hear from them I warrant you in six minutes. Let me take the Liberty to say to you that I feel for you more than any one else. I have always liked you since I came on board, and have always ascribed to you chiefly the good treatment I have received as well as my People; and you may depend upon it, all the good Service I can render you with my Countrymen shall be done with pleasure." I saw by his Countenance, Gestures, Air, Language and every Thing that he believed what he said, that he most heartily rejoiced in his own prospect of deliverance and that he heartily pitied me. . . . I smiled however at his Offers of kind Offices to me, knowing full Well that his Prayers and tears would be as unavailing as my own if he should be generous and I weak enough to employ them, with British Officers, Ministers, Judges or King, in the then Circumstances of Things and Temper of the Britons. I made him a bow expressive of my Sense of his politeness, but said nothing. Determined to see my danger before I would be intimidated at it, I took my hat and marched up to the Quarter Deck. I had before heard an uncommon trampling upon Deck and perceived Signs of some Alarm and confusion, but when upon Deck I saw the two ships indeed. They both appeared larger than our Frigate and were already within Musquet Shot of Us. The Air was clear and the Moon very bright. We could see every thing even the Men on board. We all expected every moment to be hailed, and possibly saluted with a broadside. But the two ships passed by Us without speaking a Word, and I stood upon Deck till they had got so far off as to remove all Apprehensions of danger from them. Whether they were English or French, or Spanish or Dutch, or whether they were two American Frigates which had been about that time in France We never knew. We had no inclination to inquire about their business or destination, and were very happy that they discovered so little curiosity about ours.

April 2 Thursday. Walked round the Town to see the Parliament which was sitting, where We heard but understood not the Counsel, then to see the Council and chamber of Commerce. Then We went round to the Ship Yards, made many

Visits, dined at the Hotel D'Angleterre, visited the Custom house, the Post Office, the Chatteau Trompette a famous Fortification of Vaubans and its Commandant. Then visited the Premier President of the Parliament of Bourdeaux. Here I met a reception that was not only polite and respectfull but really tender and seemingly affectionate. He asked Permission to embrace me A la francaise. He said he had long felt for me an Affection resembling that of a Brother. He had pitied me and trembled for me, and was cordially rejoiced to see me. He could not avoid sympathizing with every sincere friend of Liberty in the World. He knew that I had gone through many dangers and Sufferings in the cause of Liberty, and had felt for me in them All. He had reason he said to feel for the Sufferers in the Cause of Liberty, because he had suffered many Years in that cause himself. He had been banished for cooperating with Mr. Malsherbs, and the other Courts and Parliaments of the Kingdom in the time of Louis the fifteenth, for their Remonstrances against the arbitrary Conduct and pernicious Edicts of the Court &c. He envied the Count de Viralade his Son the pleasure, that he intended himself by accompanying me that Evening to the Commedy. But the Parliament was sitting and the press of Business rendered it impossible. Otherwise he should certainly attend me himself. Mr. Bondfield had to interpret all this Effusion of Compliments and I thought it never would come to an End. But it did and I concluded upon the whole there was a fund of Sincerity in it decorated and almost suffocated with French Compliments. Then We went to the Coffee House, then to the Comedie where We saw the two Misers (Les deux Avares). After which We supped with Messieurs Reuilles De Basmarein and Raimbeaux. Here I expected nothing but a common Supper and a small Company; but found myself much disappointed. Among many others in a large Company of both Sexes, were the Count de Viralade, the eldest Son of the first President whom I had just visited. Le Moine, the first Commissary of the Navy, Le Moine his Son a Commissary of the Navy. Cornie a Captain in the Navy and a Knight of Saint Louis. John Baptiste Nairac, a Deputy of commerce from La Rochelle. Paul Nairac a Merchant. Elisee Nairac a Merchant. La Tour Feger a Merchant; Menoire a Merchant, Conturier a Merchant, and many others with their Ladies; and

Mr. Bondfield and Major Fraser. The Company their dresses, Equipages, and the furniture were splendid and the Supper very sumptuous. The Conversation at and after Supper was very gay, animated, chearfull and good humoured as it appeared to my Eyes and Ears and feelings but my Understanding had no Share in it. The Language was altogether incomprehensible. The Company were more attentive to me, then I desired; for they often addressed Observations and questions to me, which I could only understand by the Interpretation of Mr. Bond, and the returns of civility on my part could only be communicated to me through the same Channel, a kind of conviviality so tædious and irksome, that I had much rather have remained in silent Observation and Reflection. One Anecdote I will relate, because among many others I heard in Bourdeaux it was Characteristic of the manners at that time. One of the most elegant Ladies at Table, young and handsome, tho married to a Gentleman in the Company, was pleased to Address her discourse to me. Mr. Bondfield must interpret the Speech which he did in these Words "Mr. Adams, by your Name I conclude you are descended from the first Man and Woman, and probably in your family may be preserved the tradition which may resolve a difficulty which I could never explain. I never could understand how the first Couple found out the Art of lying together?" Whether her phrase was L'Art de se coucher ensemble, or any other more energetic, I know not, but Mr. Bondfield rendered it by that I have mentioned. To me, whose Acquaintance with Women had been confined to America, where the manners of the Ladies were universally characterised at that time by Modesty, Delicacy and Dignity, this question was surprizing and shocking: but although I believe at first I blushed, I was determined not to be disconcerted. I thought it would be as well for once to set a brazen face against a brazen face and answer a fool according to her folly, and accordingly composing my countenance into an Ironical Gravity I answered her "Madame My Family resembles the first Couple both in the name and in their frailties so much that I have no doubt We are descended from that in Paradise. But the Subject was perfectly understood by Us, whether by tradition I could not tell: I rather thought it was by Instinct, for there was a Physical quality in Us resembling the Power of Electricity or of the Magnet, by which when a Pair approached within a striking distance they flew together like the Needle to the Pole or like two Objects in electric Experiments." When this Answer was explained to her, she replied "Well I know not how it was, but this I know it is a very happy Shock." I should have added "in a lawfull Way" after "a striking distance," but if I had her Ladyship and all the Company would only have thought it Pedantry and Bigottry. This is a decent Story in comparison with many which I heard in Bourdeaux, in the short time I remained there, concerning married Ladies of Fashion and reputation. The decided Advances made by married Women, which I heard related, gave rise to many reflections in my mind which may perhaps be detailed hereafter on some similar Occasions. The first was if such are the manners of Women of Rank, Fashion and Reputation in France, they can never support a Republican Government nor be reconciled with it. We must therefore take great care not to import them into America.

April 3. Fryday. 1778. We Visited the Intendant, dined at Mr. Bondfields and supped at Mr. Le Texiers, a Duch Merchant from Amsterdam, long settled in Trade at Bourdeaux. He was an inquisitive sensible Man with some considerable Information. He professed a regard for America, but seemed to be perplexed with many doubts and difficulties. He could not see how it was possible We could contend successfully against the Power of Great Britain, so irresistable by Sea and Land, with Armies and Navies so brave, experienced and disciplined and assisted with such Alliances. I answered that The Americans had no doubt of their Abilities. Very few entertained any doubt, and I had none at all, that We could defend ourselves as long as England could maintain the Contest even without Assistance; but I had hopes We should obtain Friends and perhaps Allies as powerful as Great Britain. We had more Men than she could ever send to America with the Assistance of all her Hessian and Anspach Allies who sold her their Subjects like Cattle to be slaughtered in America for the humane purpose of butchering Us.

Mr. Le Texier I found had a regard for England too. He said that they in Holland had regarded England as the Bulwark of

the Protestant Religion and the most important Weight in the
Ballance of Power in Europe against France. I answered that I
had been educated from my Cradle in the same Opinion and
had read enough of the History of Europe to be still of the
same Opinion. There would therefore be no difference of Opinion between Us on these Points. We in America however, were
not sufficiently acquainted with this subject, to see that the
failure or the Weakening of the Protestant Cause, or a revolution in the ballance of Power in Europe would be the necessary consequence of our Liberty or even of our Independence.
This would depend altogether upon the Conduct of England
And her friends in Europe. If they should drive Us against our
inclinations into permanent and indissoluble connections with
one Scale of the ballance of Power, that would be the fault of
Britain and her Friends that would be a misfortune to Us, but
not our fault. Our Plan was to have no Interest, Connection or
Embarassment in the Politicks or Wars of Europe, if We could
avoid it. But it ought not to be expected that We should
tamely suffer Great Britain to tear up from the foundations all
the Governments in America, and violate thirteen solemn and
sacred Compacts under which a Wilderness had been subdued
and cultivated, and submit to the unlimited domination of
Parliament who knew little more of Us than they did of
Kamshatska and who cared not half so much for Us, as they
did for their flocks and herds. The Inhumanity too, with which
they conducted the War, betrayed such a Contempt of Us as
human Nature could not endure. Not only hiring European
Mercenaries, but instigating Indians and corrupting Domesticks as if We were fit for nothing but to be cutt to Pieces by
Savages and Negroes. Americans would not submit to these
Things, merely from Prophecies and precarious Speculations
about the Protestant Interest and the ballance of Power in Europe. This Conversation was extended into a much wider field
of discussion and was maintained on both Sides with entire civility and good humour, till I took leave of Mr. Le Texier and
retired to my Lodgings. Twenty months afterwards passing
through Bourdeaux in my Journey from Ferrol to Paris, Mr.
Le Texier called upon me again And I found was still embarrassed with the same Prejudices and Scruples. But as I had not
time to enlarge I only said I was surprized to find him still

think it possible that We should ever come under the Government of England again when the Affections of the People were entirely alienated from it and We had pledged our Faith to France to maintain our Independence, an Engagement that would be sacredly fullfilled.

April 10. Fryday. 1778. The first moment Dr. Franklin and I happened to be alone, he began to complain to me of the Coolness as he very coolly called it, between the American Ministers. He said there had been disputes between Mr. Deane and Mr. Lee. That Mr. Lee was a Man of an anxious uneasy temper which made it disagreable to do business with him: that he seemed to be one of those Men of whom he had known many in his day, who went on through Life quarrelling with one Person or another till they commonly ended in the loss of their reason. He said Mr. Izard was there too, and joined in close friendship with Mr. Lee. That Mr. Izard was a Man of violent and ungoverned Passions. That each of these had a Number of Americans about him, who were always exciting disputes and propagating Stories that made the Service very disagreable. That Mr. Izard, who as I knew had been appointed a Minister to the Grand Duke of Tuscany, instead of going to Italy remained there with his Lady and Children at Paris, and instead of minding his own Business, and having nothing else to do he spent his time in consultations with Mr. Lee and in interfering with the Business of the Commission to this Court. That they had made strong Objections to the Treaty, and opposed several Articles of it. That neither Mr. Lee nor Mr. Izard were liked by the French. That Mr. William Lee his Brother, who had been appointed to the Court of Vienna, had been lingering in Germany and lost his Papers, that he called upon the Ministers at Paris for considerable Sums of Money, and by his Connection with Lee and Izard and their party, increased the Uneasiness &c. &c. &c.

I heard all this with inward Grief and external patience and Composure. I only answered, that I was personally much a Stranger to Mr. Izard and both the Lees. That I was extreamly sorry to hear of any misunderstanding among the Americans and especially among the public Ministers, that it would not become me to take any part in them. That I ought to think of nothing in such a Case, but Truth and Justice, and the means of harmonizing and composing all Parties: But that I foresaw I should have a difficult, dangerous and disagreable part to Act, but I must do my duty as well as I could.

It so happened or had been so contrived, that We Were invited to dine at Monsieur Brillons, a Family in which Mr. Franklin was very intimate, and in which he spent much of his Time. Here We met a large Company of both Sexes and among them were Monsieur Le Vaillant and his Lady. Madam Brillion was one of the most beautifull Women in France, a great Mistress of Musick, as were her two little Daughters. The Dinner was Luxury, as usual in that Country. A large Cake was brought in with three flaggs flying. On one of them "Pride subdued": on another "Hæc dies, in qua fit Congressus, exultemus et potemus in eâ." Mr. Brillon was a rough kind of Country Squire. His Lady all softness, sweetness and politeness. I saw a Woman in Company, as a Companion of Madam Brillon who dined with her at Table, and was considered as one of the Family. She was very plain and clumzy. When I afterwards learned both from Dr. Franklin and his Grandson, and from many other Persons, that this Woman was the Amie of Mr. Brillion and that Madam Brillion consoled herself by the Amitie of Mr. Le Vailliant, I was astonished that these People could live together in such apparent Friendship and indeed without cutting each others throats. But I did not know the World. I soon saw and heard so much of these Things in other Families and among allmost all the great People of the Kingdom that I found it was a thing of course. It was universally understood and Nobody lost any reputation by it. Yet I must say that I never knew an Instance of it, without perceiving that all their Complaisancy was external and ostensible only: a mere conformity to the fashion: and that internally there was so far from being any real friendship or conjugal Affection that their minds and hearts were full of Jealousy, Envy, revenge and rancour. In short that it was deadly poison to all the calm felicity of Life. There were none of the delightful Enjoyments of conscious Innocence and mutual Confidence. It was mere brutal pleasure.

April 15. Wednesday. 1778. Dined with Madam Helvetius. One Gentleman and one Lady, besides Dr. Franklin, his Grandson and myself, made the Company. An elegant Dinner. This was a Lady of established Reputation also: The Widow of the famous Helvetius, who, as Count Sarsefield once said to me, if he had made a few millions of Livres the more as one of the Farmers General, and written a few Books the less as a Philosopher it might have been better for France and the World. She has erected a Monument to her Husband, a Model of which She has in her House. It is a Statue of herself, weeping over his Tomb with this Inscription.

> Toi dont l'ame sublime et tendre
> A fait ma gloire, et mon bonheur
> Je t'ai perdu: pres de ta cendre,
> Je viens jouer de ma douleur.

That She might not be, however, entirely without the Society of Gentlemen, there were three or four, handsome Abby's who daily visited the House and one at least resided there. These Ecclesiasticks, one or more of whom reside in allmost every Family of Distinction, I suppose have as much power to Pardon a Sin as they have to commit one, or to assist in committing one. Oh Mores! said I to myself. What Absurdities, Inconsistencies, Distractions and Horrors would these Manners introduce into our Republican Governments in America: No kind of Republican Government can ever exist with such national manners as these. Cavete Americani.

This day We dined at Mr. La Fretés. A splendid House, Gardens and Furniture. The Family were fond of Paintings and exhibited a Variety of exquisite Pieces, but none of them struck me more than one Picture of a Storm and another of a Calm at Sea. I had not forgotten the Gulph Stream, the English Channel nor the Bay of Biscay.

At this dinner the Conversation turned upon the Infrequency of Marriage in France. Go into any company they said and you would find very few who were married, and upon Examination of the numerous Company at Table I was found the only married Person in Company except the Heads of the Family. Here We were shewn a manuscript History of the Revolution in Russia in the Year 1762. The Author was asked why he did not publish it. He answered that he had no mind to be assassinated as he certainly should be if he printed it and was known to be the Writer. Mr. Franklin retired to another room and read it. When he returned it to the Author he made many Eulogies of the Style, Arrangement, Perspicuity &c. and added "You have followed the manner of Sallust, and you have surpassed him."—I thought this as good a french Compliment as the best of the Company could have made.

At Table there was much conversation about the Education of daughters at the Convents, and I found the discreetest people, especially among the Ladies, had a very bad Opinion of such Education. They were very bad Schools for Morals. It was then News to me that they were thought such in France.

The greatest part of the Conversation was concerning Voltaire. He was extolled to the Skies as a Prodigy. His Eminence in History, Epick Poetry, Dramatick Poetry, Phylosophy, even the Neutonian Phylosophy: His Prose and Verse were equally admirable. No Writer had ever excelled in so many Branches of Science and Learning, besides that astonishing multitude of his fugitive Pieces. He was the grand Monarch of Science and Litterature. If he should die the Republick of Letters would be restored. But it was now a Monarchy &c. &c. &c.

April 17. Fryday. We dined home with Company. Mr. Platt and his Lady, Mr. Amiel and his Lady, Mr. Austin, Mr. Alexander &c. There were two Alexanders, one a Batcheller, the other with a Family of several Daughters, one of whom Mr. Jonathan Williams afterwards married. They lived in a House not far from Us, were from Scotland, and had some connection with Mr. Franklin, which I never understood and took no pains to investigate.

After dinner We went to see the Fete de long Champ, or the feast of the long Field. This was good Fryday. On this Week, all the Theatres of Paris are shutt up and the Performers forbidden to play. By this decree, whether of the Church or State, or both, All the fashionable People of Paris and its Environs are deprived of their daily Amusements and loose their ordinary topicks of conversation. The consequence of which is that they are si ennuiée, so weary of themselves that they cannot live. To avoid this direfull calamity they have invented this new Spectacle and have made it fashionable for every Person who owns a Carriage of any kind that rolls upon Wheels, and all those who can hire one to go out of Town and march their Horses slowly along one side of the great Road to the End of it, then they come about and return on the other Side, and in this manner the Carriages are rolling all day. It was asserted on that day that there was not a pair of Wheels left in the City. For some Years, the Ladies who were not acknowledged to have established reputations, were observed to appear in unusual splendor in these Processions, and the indecency increased from Year to Year till one of the most beautifull but one of the most infamous Prostitutes in Paris had sold her Charms to such profit that she appeared in the most costly and splendid Equipage in the whole Row: six of the finest horses in the Kingdom, the most costly Coach that could be built, more numerous Servants and richer Liveries than any of the Nobility or Princes. Her own Dress in Proportion. It was generally agreed to be the finest Shew that had ever been exhibited. This was so audacious an Insult to all modest Women and indeed to the national morality and Religion, that the Queen to her honor sent her a Message the next morning, that if she ever appeared again, any where, in that Equipage she should find herself in Bicêtre the next morning. Yet even this was a modest fancy in comparison with the palace of Bellvue. This was another Symptom of the pure virtuous manners which I was simple enough to think would not accord with our American Republican Institutions. To be sure it had never yet entered my thoughts, that any rational Being would ever think of demolishing the Monarchy and creating a Republick in France.

This Day Mr. David Hartley, a Member of the British House of Commons, with Mr. George Hammond the Father of Mr. George Hammond who was afterwards Hartleys Secretary at the Negotiation of the definitive Treaty of Peace, and after that Minister Plenipotentiary to the United States, came to Visit Us, under pretence of visiting Dr. Franklin. This mysterious Visit, I did not at all admire. I soon saw that Hartley was a Person of as consummate Vanity as Hammond was a plain honest Man: but I considered both as Spies, and endeavoured to be as reserved and as much on my guard as my nature would admit. Although I endeavoured to behave to both with entire civility, I suppose as I did not flatter Mr. Hartley with professions of confidence, which I did not feel, and of so much Admiration of his Great Genius and Talents as he felt himself, he conceived a disgust at me, and told Sir John Temple and others after his return to London "Your Mr. Adams that you represent as a Man of such good Sense, If he has that, he is the most ungracious Man I ever saw." I had not expressed so much astonishment at his Invention of Fire Plates, and Archimides's Mirrors, as he thought they deserved. I knew him to be intimate with Lord North by his own confession as well as by the Information of Dr. Franklin and others: and although he was numbered among the Opposition in Parliament and professed to be an Advocate for the American cause, yet I knew very well that Opposition to the Ministry was the only solid Ground, on which all the Friendship for America, that was professed in England, rested. I did not therefore think it safe, to commit myself to a Man, who came to Us without any pretence of Authority from his Sovereign or his Ministers. I say without any pretence of Authority because he made none. But I then supposed and still believe, that he came with the secret privity if not at the express request of Lord North to sound the American Ministers, and see if there were no hopes of seducing Us from our connection with France, and making a seperate Accommodation with Us, the very idea of which as the Treaty was already made appeared to me to be an Insult to our honor and good faith. What were the Subjects or the Objects of his freequent private Conferences with Franklin I know not. If either or both of them ever made any minutes of them I hope they will one day appear in publick. I neither then nor ever since suspected any unfair practice in Franklin except some secret Whispers against Lee and possibly against myself, for he had by this time found that I was not to be sufficiently complyant with his Views. He had indeed seen enough of me in Congress, to know that I was not a Man to swear, in the Words of another at all times.

This Evening Mr. Chaumont took me in his Carriage to The Concert Spirituel, in the Royal Pallace of the Tuilleries. A vast Number of Instruments were performing to an immense Crowd of Company. There were Men Singers and Women Singers. One Gentleman sung alone and then a young Lady. The Musick however did not entirely satisfy me. I had read that the French Ear was not the most delicate, and I thought the Observation verified. There was too much sound for me. The Gardens of the Tuilleries were full of Company of both Sexes walking.

April 20. Monday 1778. My Son had been with me since Saturday. This was delicious repast for me: but I was somewhat mortified to find that this Child among the Pupills at the Pension and my American Servant among the Domesticks of the Hotel, learned more french in a day than I could learn in a Week with all my Books.

April 21. Tuesday. 1778. Dined at Mr. Chaumonts, with the largest collection of great Company, that I had yet seen. The Marquis D'Argenson, The Count de Noailles, the Marshall de Mailbois, the Brother of Count de Vergennes, Mr. and Mrs. Foucault, the Son in Law and Daughter of Mr. Chaumont, who were said to have a fortune of four or five thousand Pounds Sterling a Year in St. Domingo, Mr. [   ] the first Officer, that is, a premier Comis under Mr. De Sartine, Mr. Chaumonts own Son and his other daughter with so many others that I found it impracticable to get their names and qualities.

But these incessant Dinners, and dissipations were not the Objects of my Mission to France. My Countrymen were suffering in America, and their Affairs were in great confusion in Europe. With much Grief and concern, I received daily and almost hourly information, of the disputes between the Americans in France. The bitter Animosities between Mr. Deane and Mr. Lee: between Dr. Franklin and Mr. Lee: between Dr. Franklin and Mr. Izzard: between Dr. Bancroft and Mr. Lee and Mr. Izzard: and between Mr. Charmichael and all of them.

Sir James Jay was there too, a Brother of Mr. John Jay, and an able Physician as well as a Man of Letters and information. He had lately come over from England, and although he seemed to have no Animosity against any of the Gentlemen, he confirmed many of the Reports that I had heard from several Persons before, such as that Mr. Deane had been at least as attentive to his own Interest, in dabbling in the English funds, and in trade, and in fitting out Privateers as to the Public, and said that he would give Mr. Deane fifty thousand Pounds Sterling for the fortune he had made here. That Dr. Bancroft too had made a fortune here, by speculating in the English Stocks and by gambling Policies in London. Mr. McCrery too, had adopted the Cry of Mr. Lees Ennemies, and said that the Lees were selfish, and that this was a Family misfortune. Dr. Franklin, Mr. Deane and Dr. Bancroft were universally considered as indissoluble Friends. The Lees and Mr. Izzard were equally attached in friendship to each other. The Friends and followers of each party both among the french and Americans were equally bitter against each other. Mr. Deane appeared to me, to have made himself agreable here, to Mr. De Chaumont, Mr. Beaumarchais, Mr. Monthieu, and Mr. Holker, Persons of importance and influence at that time, and with that Ministry, particularly the Count de Vergennes and Mr. De Sartine. Mr. Deane was gone home in great Splendor, with Compliments, Certificates and Recommendations in his favour from the King and Minister, and many other Persons French and American, among whom was Dr. Franklin who shewed me his Letter of recommendation in very strong terms. Mr. Deane had been active, industrious, subtle and in some degree successfull, having accomplished some of the great purposes of his Mission. Mr. Gerard and Mr. Holker were also his Friends: and although he had little order in his Business public or private, had lived very expensively and spent great Sums of Money that no body could Account for, and allthough unauthorised Contracts had well nigh ruined our Army, embarrassed Congress more than any thing that had ever happened and put his Country to a great and useless expence, I was still apprehensive there would be great Altercations excited by him in America, both in and out of Congress.

On the other hand it was said of Mr. Lee, that he had not

the confidence of the Ministry, nor of the Persons of influence here, meaning as before Mr. Chaumont, Mr. Beaumarchais, Mr. Monthieu and Mr. Holker: that he was suspected of too much Affection for England, and of too much intimacy with Lord Shelbourne: that he had given Offence, by an unhappy disposition, and by indiscreet Speeches before Servants and others, concerning the French Nation and Government, despizing and cursing them.

I was extreamly sorry for these Altercations and Calumnies, knowing that Parties and divisions among Americans here, must have disagreable and pernicious Effects both at home and abroad. I was wholly untainted with these prejudices and unalterably determined to preserve myself from them. It was no part of my Business to quarrel with any one without cause, to differ with one Party or the other, or give offence to any body. But I must and would do my duty to the Public, let it give offence to whom it might.

In this place it is necessary to introduce a few portraits of Characters that the subsequent narration may be better understood.

Dr. Franklin one of my Colleagues is so generally known that I shall not attempt a Sketch of his Character at present. That He was a great Genius, a great Wit, a great Humourist and a great Satyrist, and a great Politician is certain. That he was a great Phylosopher, a great Moralist and a great Statesman is more questionable.

Mr. Arthur Lee, my other Colleague, was a Native of Virginia. His Father had been long a Councillor under the Crown and sometime commander in Chief of the Colony and ancient Dominion of Virginia. He left several Sons, Thomas, Richard Henry, William, Francis Lightfoot and Arthur, with all of whom except Thomas I have been intimately acquainted. Their Father had given them all excellent Classical Educations and they were all virtuous Men. Arthur had studied and practiced Physick but not finding it agreable to his Genius he took Chambers in the Temple in England, and there was admitted to practice as a Barrister, and being protected by several Gentlemen of Rank among the Opposition was coming fast into importance. Animated with great Zeal in the Cause of his native Country, he took a decided part in her favour and became a Writer of some Celebrity by his Junius Americanus and other publications. Becoming known in America as a zealous Advocate for our Cause, the two Houses of the Legislature of Massachusetts Bay appointed him provisionally their Agent to the Court of Great Britain, in case of the death, Absence or dissability of Dr. Franklin, in which capacity he corresponded with some of the Members of that Assembly, particularly with Mr. Samuel Adams, and with the Assembly itself, transmitting from time to time information of Utility and Importance. After a Congress was called in 1774, 5 and 6 He continued to transmit to Us some of the best and most authentic Intelligence, which We received from England. In 1776 when the Election of Ministers to the Court of France was brought forward and after I had declined the nomination, and Mr. Jefferson had refused the Election and Appointment sent him by Congress, Mr. Arthur Lee was elected in his place. He came immediately over to Paris and joined his Colleagues in Commission. His manners were polite, his reading extensive, his Attention to Business was punctual, and his Integrity without reproach.

Mr. Ralph Izzard was a native of South Carolina. His Grandfather or Great Grandfather was One of Mr. Lockes Landgraves, and had transmitted to his Posterity an ample landed Estate. Mr. Izzard had his Education, I believe at Westminster or Eaton School, certainly at the University of Cambridge in England. When he came to the Possession of his fortune he married Miss De Lancy a Daughter of Chief Justice De Lancy, who was so long at the head of the Party in New York in Opposition to the Livingstones, a Lady of great beauty and fine Accomplishments as well as perfect purity of conduct and Character through Life. This accomplished Pair had a curiosity to Travel. They went to Europe, and passed through Italy, Germany, Holland and I know not how many other Countries. Mrs. Izzard, an excellent Domestic Consort, was very prolific, and it was often jocularly said that she had given Mr. Izzard a Son or a Daughter in every great City in Europe. When the American War commenced they were in England, and Mr. Izzard embracing the Cause of his Country with all the Warmth of his Character, passed with his Family over to France in his Way to America. Congress had been advised, by

Persons who knew no better, to send a Minister to the Emperor and to the Grand Duke of Tuscany because they were brothers to the Queen of France. In this measure there was less Attention to the Political Interests and Views of Princes than to the Ties of Blood and Family Connections. Congress however adopted the Measure, and Mr. Izzard was nominated by Mr. Arthur Middleton in the Name of South Carolina and highly recommended for his Integrity, good Sense and Information. The Members from New York and other States supported the nomination and concurred in all the particulars of his Character. Mr. Izzard was accordingly appointed and when he arrived in Paris he found his Commission to the Grand Duke. With an high Sense of honor, and great Benevolence of heart as well as integrity of Principle, Mr. Izzard had a Warmth of Temper and sometimes a violence of Passions, that were very inconvenient to him and his Friends, and not a little dangerous to his Enemies.

Dr. Edward Bancroft was a Native of Massachusetts Bay in the Town of Suffield. He had been a School Boy under Mr. Silas Deane, when he was a Schoolmaster, whether in any Town of the Massachusetts or Connecticutt I do not recollect. After some Education at School he had been bound an Apprentice to a Trade: but being discontented he had ran away and gone to Sea, carrying away with him, some property of his master. After some years of Adventures, the history of which I have not heard, he had acquired Property enough to return to his native Town, made his Apologies to his master, paid him honourably all his demands, and went to Sea again. The next information I have of him, was that he was in England and had published his Essay towards a natural History of Guiana, which I have in a handsome Volume presented me with his own hand, and it is a Work, considering the Advantages of the Author, of great merit. He wrote also in England The History of Sir Charles Wentworth, a Novel which no doubt was recommended to many readers, and procured a considerably better Sale, by the plentifull Abuse and vilification of Christianity which he had taken care to insert in it. He had also been in the Intimacy and Confidence of Dr. Franklin, who had recommended him to the Editors and Proprietors of the Monthly Review, in which his standing Share was to review all

Publications relative to America. This Information I had from Dr. Franklin himself. I understood this very well, as I thought —to wit that Bancroft was the ostensible Reviewer, but that Franklin was always consulted before the publication. Bancroft was a meddler in the Stocks as well as Reviews, and frequently went into the Alley, and into the deepest and darkest retirements and recesses of the Brokers and Jobbers, Jews as well as Christians, and found Amusement as well perhaps as profit by listening to all the News and Anecdotes true or false that were there whispered or more boldly pronounced. This information I had from his own mouth. When Mr. Deane arrived in France, whether he wrote to Bancroft or Bancroft to him, I know not, but they somehow or other sympathised with each other so well that Bancroft went over to Paris and became a confidential associate with his old Friends Franklin and Deane. Bancroft had a clear head and a good Pen. He wrote some things relative to the Connection between France and America, with the Assistance of Franklin and Deane as I presume, which were translated into French by Mr. Turgot or the Duke de la Rochefaucault I forget which and printed in a Publication called Affaires de L'Angleterre et Amerique and which were very well done. After the Peace he obtained a Patent in France for the exclusive Importation of the Bark of the Yellow Oak for the Dyers and then he went to England and procured a similar Patent there, by both which together he is said to have realised an Income of Eight hundred a Year. He has resided in England to this time and has renewed his ancient connections with the Monthly Reviewers, as I conclude from several Circumstances, among others from the Review of my first Volume of The Defence &c. and from that of my Sons Travels in Silesia, in both which the Spirit of Franklin, Deane and Bancroft, is to me very discernible.

This Man had with him in France, a Woman, with whom he lived, and who by the french was called la Femme de Monsieur Bancroft. She never made her Appearance. She had several Children very handsome and promising whom I saw in France and two of whom I have since seen in America, with complexions as blooming as they had in their Childhood. One of them behaved very well—the other has been much censured, I know not how truly. Bancrofts intimacy with Franklin brought him daily to our house, and he often came to my Appartment where I received him always with Civility for he was sensible, social and in several Things well informed. He often dined with Us especially when We had company. Here I was not so well pleased with his Conversation, for at Table he would season his food with such enormous quantities of Chayan Pepper, which assisted by a little generous Burgundy, though he drank not a great deal, would sett his tongue a running at a most licentious rate both at Table and after dinner, as gave me great paine. The Bible and the Christian Religion were his most frequent Subjects of Invective and ridicule, but he sometimes fell upon Politicks and political Characters, and not seldom expressed Sentiments of the Royal Family and the Court of France, particularly of the Queen, which I thought very improper for him to utter or for Us to hear. Much as Mr. Lee was censured for freedoms of Speech, I never heard a tenth part so much from him as from Bancroft. The Queens Intrigues with Madame the Duchess of Polinac, her constant dissipation, her habits of expence and profusion, her giddy thoughtless conduct were for a long time almost constant Topicks of his Tittle Tattle.

Another Personage who must be introduced upon the Scene, was a Dr. Smith. He told me he was a Native of New York, and of honourable descent for his Father had been a Member of his Majestys Council in that Province, and his Brother was William Smith who also had been a Royal Councillor. This Brother was afterwards Chief Justice in Canada. The Dr. had received a good Education in Letters, I know not where, and was a tollerable Writer. He had been a Wanderer and an Adventurer in the West Indies and in England, but had not well succeeded in the practice of Physick. He had married a Lady, a most perfect Antithesis to beauty in the face and to Elegance in Person. She was however infinitely too good for him, for she had some property in the West Indies, enough I suppose to afford them a bare Subsistance, and she was what is much more, a discreet, decent, virtuous and worthy Woman. This Man was supposed to come over from England, either to solicit some Employment, or to embarrass and perplex the American Ministers, or to be a Spy both upon the Americans and the French. Which of the three was his Errand, or whether either of them I know not. When he first arrived in Paris he visited Franklin and brought him some English Newspapers containing a Number of Pieces upon Liberty which he said he had written. Franklin told me that he read them and found them to contain some good common place principles of Liberty and that they were moderately well written, but of very little value or consequence. Whether Franklin neglected to return his Visit or to answer his Letter or whether he had not expressed so much Admiration of Smiths Talents as he thought they deserved, or whatever was the offence, he soon became very Angry with Franklin and wrote him many petulant and offensive Letters, which he complained of to me, till at length he received one which [   ] him very highly. When he came in to Breakfast he said to Us at Table "This Envy is the worst of all distempers. I hope I shall never catch it. I had rather have the Pox and Dr. Smith for my Physician," and then gave Us an Account of an insolent Letter he had just received and read from Smith, which had thus put him out of Temper. For some time he continued to persecute Mr. Lee much in the same manner, and once when he asked an Audience of the three Commissioners together, he told Mr. Lee that if ever he found him out of commission he would call him out into the Field of honour. Lee only smiled at this, but Smith continued in such a Strain of provoking Insolence both to Franklin and Lee, although he had carefully avoided saying an offensive Word to me, that I thought it time for me to speak and I said Dr. Smith your Conduct and Language to Dr. Franklin and Mr. Lee are excessively abusive and insufferable, and if my Colleagues are of my Mind you shall commit no more such offences here without being turned out of the house. Perceiving the determined Tone and Air with which I spoke and easily believing that Mr. Franklin and Mr. Lee would not leave me in a minority in this resolution, he changed his tone and said he did not mean to give Offence.—We had frequent Accounts of his violent invectives in Paris against my Colleagues and of his violent quarrells with the french at his Lodgings, cursing and swearing and raving as if he was beside himself: but concerning me he was always respectful in his Language and frequently said neither Deane, Franklin or Lee were fit to represent America at the Court of France: that Adams was the only Man that Congress had yet sent to Europe, who was qualified for his Station. Such Compliments from Dr. Smith, knowing so much of him as I did, although they were frequently repeated to me, were not very flattering to me. He continued as long as he staid in France to behave inoffensively to me. But he not long afterwards addressed Letters and remonstrances to Us all jointly as commissioners containing Remonstrances and misrepresentations, which only shewed his Ignorance of our Affairs, his Envy of our Situation and the iracible intemperance of his nature.

Another Character ought to be introduced here: although he was gone to America before my Arrival at Passi and I never had an Opportunity of seeing him. A letter or two may have passed between him and me when he was Charge des Affairs at Madrid, but no misunderstanding ever occurred between Us, and I never received to my knowledge any Injury or Offence from him. He was a native of Maryland of Scotch Extraction; wherever he had his Education, he was in England or Scotland, when the Revolution commenced, and in this Year 1778 came over to Paris, and as I was informed commenced an Opposition to all the Commissioners Franklin, Deane and Lee, and indeed to all who had any Authority in American Affairs, and was very clamorous. Mr. Deane and Dr. Franklin and Dr. Bancroft, however a little before or after his departure found means to appease him in some degree, and after his Arrival in America he was chosen one of the Delegates in Congress for Maryland, where in a Year or two he got an Appointment as Secretary of Legation and Charge Des Affaires to Mr. Jay when in 1779 he was appointed Minister to the Court of Spain, where he remained many Years and finally died. He had Talents and Education, but was considered by the soundest Men who knew him as too much of an Adventurer. What was his Moral Character and what was his Conduct in Spain I shall leave to Mr. Jay. But he was represented to me as having contributed much to the Animosities and Exasperations among the Americans at Paris and Passi. There were great divisions in Spain among the Americans and Mr. Jay had as much Trouble with his own Family Mr. Carmichael, Mr. Brokholst Livingston and Mr. Littlepage as I had at Paris. I shall leave this Scene to be opened by the memorials of the Actors in it, if any such should ever see the light.

I have now given a faint Sketch of the French and American Personages who had been concerned in our Affairs at and before the Time of my Arrival.

I may have said before, that Public Business had never been methodically conducted. There never was before I came, a minute Book, a Letter Book or an Account Book, or if there had been Mr. Deane and Dr. Franklin had concealed them from Mr. Lee, and they were now no where to be found. It was utterly impossible to acquire any clear Idea of our Affairs. I was now determined to procure some blank books, and to apply myself with Diligence to Business, in which Mr. Lee cordially joined me. To this End it was necessary to alter the Course of my Life. Invitations were sent to Dr. Franklin and me, every day in the Week to dine in some great or small Company. I determined on my part to decline as many as I could of these Invitations, and attend to my Studies of french and the Examination and execution of that public Business which suffered for want of our Attention Every day.

April 29. Wednesday. 1778. Dined with the Marshall De Maillebois, with a great deal of Company. Here also We were shewn the Marshalls Amie seated at the Table, with all his great Company. Mr. Lee and I had a good deal of conversation with her. Mr. Lee spoke french with tolerable ease. I could say little: but I understood her as well as any one I had heard in french. It appeared to me that the Marshall had chosen her rather for her Wit and Sense than personal charms. . . . I was soon informed that this Marshall Maillebois and Marshall Brolie had the reputation of the two most intriguing Men in France; and I was the more disposed to believe it, of the former, because I knew of his Intrigue with Mr. Deane, to be placed over the head of General Washington in the Command in Chief of our American Army. It is proper in this place to insert an Anecdote. Mr. Lee and I waited on the Count de Vergens, one day to ask a favour for our Country, I forget what it was. The Count said it was in the Department of War. It was on one of the Feasts of the Cordon blue, when the Count had been kneeling on marble Pavements in Church for some hours and his Knees aked to such a degree that he said he would take a Walk with Us to the Minister of War and ask the favour for Us. As We walked across the Court of the Castle of Versailles We met the Marshall Maillebois. Mutual Bows were exchanged as We passed, and Mr. Lee said to the Count de Vergennes That is a great General Sir. Ah! said the Count de Vergennes, I wish he had the Command with You! Mr. Lee's Observation was in French "C'est un grand General, Monsieur!" The Count de Vergennes's Answer was Ah! Je souhaite qu'il avait le Commandment chez vous. This escape was in my Mind a confirmation strong of the design at Court of getting the whole Command of America into their own hands, and a luminous Commentary on Mr. Deans Letters which I had seen and heard read in Congress, and on his mad Contract with Monsieur Du Coudray and his hundred Officers. My feelings on this Occasion were kept to myself: but my reflection was, I will be buried in the Ocean or in any other manner sacrificed, before I will voluntarily put on the Chains of France when I am struggling to throw off those of Great Britain. If my Life should be spared to continue these memorials, more of this Marshall De Maillebois will be recorded. Puffers he had found who represented him as one of the greatest Generals of Europe, but in Holland where I saw him in Command he proved himself as mean and mercenary as he was imbecille and unskillfull.

After dinner We went to the Accademy of Sciences, and heard Mr. D'Alembert as Secretary perpetual, pronounce Eulogies on several of their Members lately deceased. Voltaire and Franklin were both present, and there presently arose a general Cry that Monsieur Voltaire and Monsieur Franklin should be introduced to each other. This was done and they bowed and spoke to each other. This was no Satisfaction. There must be something more. Neither of our Philosophers seemed to divine what was wished or expected. They however took each other by the hand. . . . But this was not enough. The Clamour continued, untill the explanation came out "Il faut s'embrasser, a la francoise." The two Aged Actors upon this great Theatre of Philosophy and frivolity then embraced each other by hugging one another in their Arms and kissing each others cheeks, and then the tumult subsided. And the Cry immediately spread through the whole Kingdom and I suppose over all Europe Qu'il etoit charmant. Oh! il etoit enchantant, de voir Solon et Sophocle embrassans. How charming it was! Oh! it was enchanting to see Solon and Sophocles embracing!

After the Secretary's Eulogies were finished, one of which if I remember well was upon Mr. Jurieu and another on Mr. Duhamel, a number of Memoirs were publickly read by their Authors, upon various Subjects. One was upon the Art of making good Wine. As soon as he had read the Title The Audience compelled him to stop, which he did I presume with pleasure, for it was to hear a loud Applause, for the Choice of his Subject before they knew how he had treated it. It seemed to be a chymical Analysis of all the ingredients which enter into the composition of Wine, and a proscess by which it might be made in its greatest perfection. It was much applauded as were the Eulogies and most of the other Memoires. I remarked in all these compositions a kind of affectation that surprized me. The Authors seemed to search for Opportunities to introduce hints and sarcastical Allusions to the frivolities, Vanity, Affectation, follies and prejudices of their own Nation. This I should have expected would have been hissed at least, if no more. But on the contrary nothing was more loudly applauded, and nothing seemed to produce more gaiety and good humour. Is this an honourable trait, or is it not? More Liberties of this kind were taken in France, I believe than in any other country. In America at that time they would not have been endured. In England some freedoms may be used with John Bull, but you must be very careful to respect his essential Characteristicks of Integrity, good Sense, sound Judgment, great Courage and humanity. If you touch these you touch an Englishman to the quick. I have somewhere read that it is a proof of the last degree of depravity: when a Nation will laugh at their own Vices and then go away and repeat them. But I have some doubt of this.

May 1. Fryday. 1778. Dined with the Duke D'Ayen, the Brother of the Duke de Mouchy and the Father of the Marchioness de la Fayette. The House, the Gardens, the Walks, the Pictures and Furniture all in the highest Style of magnificence. The Portraits of the Family of Noailles, were ancient and numerous. Among them was a Picture of Noailles the Ambassador, in England at the time of the Regency when the Duke of Sommersett was at the head of it. The Negotiations of this Ambassador are in print and in my Possession. We were shewn into the Library, which was very large, and into all the Rooms and first Suite of Chambers in the house. The Rooms were very elegant and the furniture very rich. The Library was begun by the Ambassador and augmented by Cardinal Noailles in the Time of Lewis the fourteenth and Madame De Maintenon, who was his great friend. He is represented by Mr. Malesherbes in two Volumes which he wrote upon Toleration in the latter part of his Life to have contributed much to the revocation of the Edict of Nantes. The Cardinals Picture We also saw.

The Duchess D'Ayen had five or six Children contrary to the Custom of the Country, I saw no Amie there and this family appeared to be the most regular and exemplary of any that I had seen.

When I began to attempt a little conversation in french I was very inquisitive concerning this great Family of Noailles and I was told by some of the most intelligent Men in France, ecclesiasticks as well as others, that there were no less than six Marshalls of France of this Family, that they held so many Offices under the King that they received Eighteen millions of Livres annually from the Crown. That the Family had been remarkable for Ages, for their harmony with one another and for doing nothing of any consequence without a previous Council and concert. That, when the American Revolution commenced, a family Council had been called to deliberate upon that great Event and determine what part they should take in it, or what Conduct they should hold towards it. After they had sufficiently considered, they all agreed in Opinion that it was a Crisis of the highest importance, in the Affairs of Europe and the World. That it must affect France in so essential a manner, that the King could not and ought not to avoid taking a capital Interest and part of it. That it would therefore be the best policy of the Family, to give their Countenance to it as early as possible. And that it was expedient to send one of their Sons over to America to serve in her Army under General Washington. The Prince de Poix as the Heir apparent, of the Duke de Mouchy, they thought of too much importance to their Views and expectations to be risked in so hazardous a Voyage and so extraordinary a Service, and therefore it was concluded, to offer the Enterprize to the Viscount de Noailles, and if he should decline it, to the Marquis de la Fayette. The Viscount after due consideration, thought it most prudent to remain at home for the present. The Marquis, who was represented as a youth of the finest Accomplishments and most amiable disposition, panting for Glory, ardent to distinguish himself in military Service, and impatient to wipe out a slight imputation which had been thrown, whether by Truth or Calumny upon the Memory of his father who though he had been slain in Battle was suspected to have lost his Life by too much caution to preserve it, most joyfully consented to embark in the Enterprize. All France pronounced it to be the first page in the History of a great Man.

It is now high time to introduce some Facts, which occurred within the first Week or ten days of my residence at Passi. I have omitted them till this time because I was unable to ascertain the precise days, when they happened. I have before observed that Dr. Franklin, from my first Arrival had taken all opportunities to prejudice me against the Lees, Mr. Izzard &c., that Mr. Lee had been very silent and reserved upon the Subject of Parties &c. But within a few days after I had got settled in my Lodgings Mr. Izzard came out to Passi, and requested some private conversation with me. I accordingly attended him alone. Mr. Izzard began upon the Subject of the disagreable Situation of our Affairs in France and the miserable Conduct of them by Mr. Deane and Dr. Franklin, and their subordinate Agents, Adherents and Friends, upon the pillage that was committed upon Us, to gratify petty french Agents and Emissaries and Instruments, of whom nobody knew. Enlarged upon the Characters of Holker, Monthieu, Baumarchais and Chaumont. Represented the enormous Waste of Money by Mr. Deane, whom Dr. Franklin supported in all Things. Talked about the Money that was offered by Beaumarchais to Mr. Lee in London as a free Gift from the King, and for the Use of the United States in presence of Mr. Wilks and others: complained of foul play by intercepting dispatches, and of frauds in the qualities and Prices of Articles which had been purchased and shipped to America &c. &c. &c. He then introduced Dr. Bancroft, said he had known him in England and had there entertained an high Opinion of his Talents and had thought him an honest Man. But here, he found him a mere Tool and Dupe of Mr. Deane, Dr. Franklin and their French Satellites, and as unprincipled as any of them. Then he represented the whole Group of them as in a Conspiracy to persecute him and the two Lees and all their friends, and related to me an amazing number of Calumnies they had propagated concerning them at Court, in Paris, Passi and the Country. That they had not confined their Lies and Slanders to Americans in France, but had extended them to Mr. Richard Henry Lee in America and to Dr. Berkenhout in London &c.

As he enlarged upon the defamations and Persecutions against himself and his Friends he grew Warm. Mr. Izzard, with great honor and integrity, had irritable Nerves and very strong Passions. He either had or at least was reputed to have great pride. There was however more of the Appearance of this Vice in his external behaviour, than in his heart. A hesitancy in his Speech and an appearance of impatience that was often occasioned by it, contributed very much to the Suspicion and imputation of hautiness. In enumerating the detractions against himself and his friends, his passions transported him beyond all bounds. He declared and with asseverations which I will not repeat but which all who knew Mr. Izard may easily imagine, that Dr. Franklin was one of the most unprincipled Men upon Earth: that he was a Man of no Veracity, no honor, no Integrity, as great a Villain as ever breathed: as much worse than Mr. Deane as he had more experience, Art, cunning and Hypocricy. Mr. Izzard dilated on many of these particulars and his harrangue was extended to a great length.

I was thunderstruck and shuddered at the Situation I was in. By Dr. Franklins continual insinuations to me, I was convinced that the rancour in his heart was not less, though his Language had not been so explicit. I said nothing of this however to Mr. Izzard. I only observed to him, that Dr. Franklin, the two Mr. Lees and Mr. Izzard himself, all held Commissions from Congress and it was my duty to respect them all. That the conduct of Mr. Deane, I knew by his dispatches and contracts which had been read in congress before I left it, had been wild, irregular and pernicious, but that I had been desirous of imputing it to want of Judgment rather than any Thing worse. That my knowledge of Dr. Franklin personally had been only in Congress. That although I knew there had been great disputes in Pennsilvania formerly concerning his moral and political Character, as there had been in England, yet I knew at the same time that he had been in publick Life when Parties run high and that he had generally maintained an honourable Character in the World. That it was impossible for me to enter into any examination of what had passed before my Arrival, because I could find no books, Letters or documents of any kind to inform or guide me. That he must be sensible my Situation was delicate, difficult and dangerous in the extream, between two fires. I was a Stranger to the Country, the Language and the manners of the French: and not much less a Stranger to the Characters of the Americans in France. In this predicament I found myself necessarily an Umpire between two bitter and inveterate Parties, for in all questions that should come before the commissioners, if Dr. Franklin and Mr. Lee should differ in Opinion my Voice must decide. That it was easy to foresee that I should make both parties my Enemies: but no choice was left me, but to examine diligently every favour or affection to any man or party: and this course I was determined to pursue at all hazards. I entreated him to collect himself and by no means to allow himself to talk in the Style he had used to me to any other Person. That Dr. Franklin possessed the Confidence of the French Court and of his own Country, and held her Commission and Authority: and therefore it was the duty of all of Us, to treat him with respect.

May 6. Wednesday. 1778. Franklin told Us one of his Characteristic Stories. A Spanish Writer of certain Vissions of Hell, relates that a certain evil Spirit he met with who was civil and well bred, shewed him all the Apartments in the place. Among others that of deceased Kings. The Spaniard was much amused at so illustrious a Sight, and after viewing them for sometime, said he should be glad to see the rest of them. The rest? said the Dæmon. Here are all the Kings who ever reigned upon earth from the creation of it to this day, what the Devil would the Man have?

This Anecdote was in the Spirit of those times for the Philosophers of the last Age had raised a king killing Spirit in the World. I wrote the Story down in the Evening with a Note upon it not less Characteristick of myself. It was this. This Fable is not so charitable as Dr. Watts, who in his view of Heaven says "here and there I see a King," which seems to imply that Kings are as good as other men, since it is but here and there that We see a King upon Earth.

The Truth is that neither then nor at any former time, since I had attained any maturity in Age, Reading and reflection had I imbibed any general Prejudice against Kings, or in favour of them. It appeared to me then as it has done ever since, that there is a State of Society in which a Republican Government is the best, and in America the only one which ought to be adopted or thought of, because the morals of the People and Circumstances of the Country not only can bear it, but require it. But in several of the great nations of Europe, Kings appeared to me to be as necessary as any Government at all. Nor had I ever seen any reason to believe that Kings were in general worse than other Men.

———————

May 26. Tuesday. 1778. Dined at the Seat in the Country of Monsieur Bertin, a Secretary of State. Madam Bertin, the Lady of the Ministers Nephew, invited Dr. Franklin, Mr. William Temple Franklin and me to ride with her in her Coach with four Horses, which We did. This was one of the pleasantest rides, I had seen. We rode near the Backside of Mount Calvare, which is the finest Hill near Paris, though Mont Martre is a very fine Elevation. The Gardens, Walks and Waterworks of Mr. Bertin were in a Style of magnificence, like all other Seats of the Gentlemen in this Country. He was a Batchelor. His House and Gardens were situated upon the River Seine. He shewed his Luxury, as he called it, which was a collection of misshapen Rocks, at the End of his Garden, drawn together, from great distances, at an Expence of several Thousands of Guineas. I told him I would sell him a thousand times as many for half a Guinea. His Water Works were curious, four Pumps going by means of two horses. The Mechanism was simple and ingenious. The Horses went round as in a Mill. The four Pumps empty themselves into a square Pond, which contains an Acre. From this Pond the Water flows, through Pipes, down to every Part of the Garden.

I enquired of a certain Ecclesiastick, who sat next to me at dinner, who were the purest Writers of French. He took a Pencil and gave me in Writing, The Universal History of Bossuet, La Fontaine, Moliere, Racine, Rousseau, Le petit Cærene of Massillon, and the Sermons of Bourdaloue.

May 27th. Wednesday. I must now, in order to explain and justify my own Conduct give an Account of that of my Colleague Dr. Franklin. It is and always has been with great reluctance, that I have felt myself under the Necessity of stating any facts which may diminish the Reputation of this extraordinary Man, but the Truth is more sacred than any Character, and there is no reason that the Character of Mr. Lee and Mr. Izzard not to mention my own, should be sacrificed in unjust tenderness to that of their Ennemy. My quondam Friend Mrs. Warren is pleased to say that "Mr. Adams was not beloved by his Colleague Dr. Franklin." To this Accusation I shall make no other Answer at present than this, that "Mr. Deane was beloved by his Colleague Dr. Franklin."

I found that the Business of our Commission would never be done, unless I did it. My two Colleagues would agree in nothing. The Life of Dr. Franklin was a Scene of continual discipation. I could never obtain the favour of his Company in a Morning before Breakfast which would have been the most convenient time to read over the Letters and papers, deliberate on their contents, and decide upon the Substance of the Answers. It was late when he breakfasted, and as soon as Breakfast was over, a crowd of Carriges came to his Levee or if you like the term better to his Lodgings, with all Sorts of People; some Phylosophers, Accademicians and Economists; some of his small tribe of humble friends in the litterary Way whom he employed to translate some of his ancient Compositions, such as his Bonhomme Richard and for what I know his Polly Baker &c.; but by far the greater part were Women and Children, come to have the honour to see the great Franklin, and to have the pleasure of telling Stories about his Simplicity, his bald head and scattering strait hairs, among their Acquaintances. These Visitors occupied all the time, commonly, till it was time to dress to go to Dinner. He was invited to dine abroad every day and never declined unless when We had invited Company to dine with Us. I was always invited with him, till I found it necessary to send Apologies, that I might have some time to study the french Language and do the Business of the mission. Mr. Franklin kept a horn book always in his Pockett in which he minuted all his invitations to dinner, and Mr. Lee said it was the only thing in which he was punctual. It was the Custom in France to dine between one and two O Clock: so that when the time came to dress, it was time for the Voiture to be ready to carry him to dinner. Mr. Lee came daily to my Appartment to attend to Business, but we could rarely obtain the Company of Dr. Franklin for a few minutes, and often when I had drawn the Papers and had them fairly copied for Signature, and Mr. Lee and I had signed them, I was frequently obliged to wait several days, before I could procure the Signature of Dr. Franklin to them. He went according to his Invitation to his Dinner and after that went sometimes to the Play, sometimes to the Philosophers but most commonly to visit those Ladies who were complaisant enough to depart from the custom of France so far as to procure Setts of Tea Geer as it is called and make Tea for him. Some of these Ladies I knew as Madam Hellvetius, Madam Brillon, Madam Chaumont, Madam Le Roy &c. and others whom I never knew and never enquired for. After Tea the Evening was spent, in hearing the Ladies sing and play upon their Piano Fortes and other instruments of Musick, and in various Games as Cards, Chess, Backgammon, &c. &c. Mr. Franklin I believe however never play'd at any Thing but Chess or Checquers. In these Agreable and important Occupations and Amusements, The Afternoon and Evening was spent, and he came home at all hours from Nine to twelve O Clock at night. This Course of Life contributed to his Pleasure and I believe to his health and Longevity. He was now between Seventy and Eighty and I had so much respect and compassion for his Age, that I should have been happy to have done all the Business or rather all the Drudgery, if I could have been favoured with a few moments in a day to receive his Advice concerning the manner in which it ought to be done.

But this condescention was not attainable. All that could be had was his Signature, after it was done, and this it is true he very rarely refused though he sometimes delayed.

———————

The Disposition of the People of this Country for Amusements, and the Apparatus for them, was remarkable in this House, as indeed it was in every genteel House that I had seen in France. Every fashionable House had compleat Setts of Accommodations for Play, a Billiard Table, a Bacgammon Table, a Chesboard, a Chequer Board, Cards, and twenty other Sorts of Games, that I have forgotten. I often asked myself how this rage for Amusements of every kind, and this disinclination to serious Business, would answer in our republican Governments in America. It seemed to me that every Thing must run to ruin.

May 30. Saturday 1778. Dr. Franklin, who had no Business to do, or who at least would do none, and who had Mr. William Temple Franklin for his private Secretary, without consulting his Colleagues and indeed without saying a Word to me, who lived in the same house with him and had no private Secretary, though I had all the Business to do, thought fit to take into the Family a French private Secretary, a young Man of civil deportment however and good Understanding. He had some Knowledge of the Italian, German and English Languages. For what reason or for what Purpose he was introduced I never knew. Whether it was to be a Spy upon me, or whether Franklin was persuaded by some of his French Friends to give him Employment, or whether it was to save Mr. William Temple the trouble of Copying the Letters when I had written them, I gave myself no trouble to enquire. I thought his Salary and his Keeping an unnecessary expence. The young Man however continued with Us, as long as I remained at Passi, and conducted himself with propriety. This day I dined at home, with this young Gentleman only. Having some Inclination to look a little into the Italian Language, I asked him which was the best Dictionary and Grammar of it. He said those of Veneroni: and the best Dictionary and Grammar of the German, were those of Gottshed. I asked many questions about French books, and particularly enquired about their

Prosody, as I wished to understand something of their Versification. He said the best Treatise of French Prosody was The Poetique Francoise of Mr. Marmontell.

June 2. Tuesday. 1778. Went to Versailles, and found it deserted, the Court being gone to Marli. . . . We went to Marli, met the Count de Vergennes and did some Business with him, then went to Mr. De Sartine and after doing some business dined with him. His Lady was at home and dined with the Company. The Prince de Monbarry, then Secretary of War, dined there. After dinner went to the Spanish Ambassadors, the Count D'Aranda's Caffee, as they call it, where he gives Coffee, Ice Creams and Cakes to all the World. Marli was the most curious and beautiful place I had yet seen. In point of Magnificence it was not equal to Versailles but in Elegance and Taste, superiour. The Machinery, which conveys such a great body of Water from the Seine to Versailles, and through the Gardens of Marli is very complicated, and magnificent. The Royal Palace is handsome and the Gardens before it are grand. There are six Pavillions, on each side of the Garden, that is six Houses for the Residence of the Kings Ministers, while the Royal Family is at Marli, which is only for three Weeks. There is nothing prettier than the play of the fountains in the Garden. I saw a Rainbow in all its glory in one of them. The Shades, the Walks, the Trees were the most charming I had yet seen.

We had not time to visit Lucienne, the elegant retreat for devotion, Penitence and Mortification of Madam Dubarry: and indeed I had been in such a Reverie in the morning in passing Bellvue, that I was not averse to postpone the Sight of another Object of the same kind to a future Opportunity.

On the Road from Paris and from Passi to Versailles, beyond the River Seine and not far from St. Cleod but on the opposite side of the Way, stood a pallace of uncommon beauty in its Architecture, situated on one of the finest Elevations in the neighbourhood of the River, commanding a Prospect as rich and variegated as it was vast and sublime. For a few of the first times that I went to Versailles I had other Things to occupy my Attention: but after I had passed through my Ceremonies and began to feel myself more at Ease, I asked some Questions about this place and was informed that it was called Bellevue and was the Residence of the Kings Aunts Adelaide and two of the surviving Daughters of Louis the fifteenth. That this palace had been built and this Establishment made by that Monarch for Madame Pompadour, whom he visited here, almost every night for twenty Years, leaving a worthy Woman his virtuous Queen alone at Versailles, with whom he had sworn never to sleep again. I cannot describe the feelings, nor relate half the reflexions which this object and history excited. Here were made Judges and Councillors, Magistrates of all Sorts, Nobles and Knights of every order, Generals and Admirals, Ambassadors and other foreign Ministers, Bishops, Archbishops, Cardinals and Popes, in the Arms of a Strumpet. Here were directed all Eyes that wished and sought for Employment, Promotion and every Species of Court favour. Here Voltaire and Richelieu and a thousand others of their Stamp, obtained Royal favour and Commissions. Travellers of all Ranks and Characters from all Parts of Europe, were continually passing from Paris to Versailles and spreading the Fame of this House, its Inhabitants and Visitors and their Commerce, infamous in every point of view, civil, political, moral and religious, all over the World. The Eyes of all France had been turned to Bellevue, more than to Paris or Versailles. Here Letters de Cachet, the highest Trust and most dangerous Instrument of arbitrary Power in France were publickly sold, to any Persons who would pay for them, for any the vilest Purposes of private Malice, Envy, Jealousy or Revenge or Cruelty. Here Licences were sold to private Smugglers to contravene the Kings own Laws, and defraud the public Revennue. Here were sold Dukedoms and Peerages, and even the Cordon blue of the Knights of the Holy Ghost. Here still lived the Daughters of the last King and the Aunts of the present. Instead of wondering that the Licentiousness of Women was so common and so public in France, I was astonished that there should be any Modesty or Purity remaining in the Kingdom, as there certainly was, though it was rare. Could there be any Morality left among such a People where such Examples were set up to the View of the whole Nation? Yes there was a Sort of Morality, there was a great deal of humanity, and what appeared to me real benevolence. Even their politeness was benevolence. There was a great deal of Charity and tenderness for the poor.

There were many other qualities that I could not distinguish from Virtues. . . . This very Monarck had in him the Milk of human Kindness, and with all his open undisguised Vices was very superstitious. Whenever he met the Host, he would descend from his Coach and [   ] down upon his Knees in the Dust or even in the Mud and compell all his Courtiers to follow his Example. Such are the Inconsistencies in the human Character.

From all that I had read of History and Government, of human Life and manners, I had drawn this Conclusion, that the manners of Women were the most infallible Barometer, to ascertain the degree of Morality and Virtue in a Nation. All that I have since read and all the observations I have made in different Nations, have confirmed me in this opinion. The Manners of Women, are the surest Criterion by which to determine whether a Republican Government is practicable, in a Nation or not. The Jews, the Greeks, the Romans, the Swiss, the Dutch, all lost their public Spirit, their Republican Principles and habits, and their Republican Forms of Government, when they lost the Modesty and Domestic Virtues of their Women.

What havock said I to myself, would these manners make in America? Our Governors, our Judges, our Senators, or Representatives and even our Ministers would be appointed by Harlots for Money, and their Judgments, Decrees and decisions be sold to repay themselves, or perhaps to procure the smiles of profligate Females.

The foundations of national Morality must be laid in private Families. In vain are Schools, Accademies and universities instituted, if loose Principles and licentious habits are impressed upon Children in their earliest years. The Mothers are the earliest and most important Instructors of youth. . . . The Vices and Examples of the Parents cannot be concealed from the Children. How is it possible that Children can have any just Sense of the sacred Obligations of Morality or Religion if, from their earliest Infancy, they learn that their Mothers live in habitual Infidelity to their fathers, and their fathers in as constant Infidelity to their Mothers. Besides the Catholic Doctrine is, that the Contract of marriage is not only a civil and moral Engagement, but a Sacrament, one of the most solemn

Vows and Oaths of Religious devotion. Can they then believe Religion and Morality too any thing more than a Veil, a Cloak, an hypocritical Pretext, for political purposes of decency and Conveniency?

June 7. 1778. Went to Versailles in Company with Mr. Lee, Mr. Izard and his Lady, Mr. Lloyd and his Lady and Mr. Francis, a Gentleman who spoke the English Language very well, having resided many Years in England in some diplomatique Character, and who undertook upon this Occasion to conduct Us. Our Objects were to see the Ceremonies and the Procession of the Knights of the Holy Ghost, or the Chevaliers of the Cordon blue, and in the Evening the public Supper of the Royal Family at the grand Couvert. The Kneelings, the Bows, and the Curtesies of the Knights of the Saint Esprit, the Dresses and Decorations, The King seated on his Throne, his investiture of a new created Knight with the Badges and Ornaments of the Order, and his Majesty's profound and reverential Bow before the Altar as he retired, were Novelties and Curiosities to me, but surprized me much less, than the Patience and Perseverance with which they all kneeled for two hours together upon the hard Marble, of which the Floor of the Chapel was made. The distinction of the blue ribbon, was very dearly purchased at the price of enduring this painful Operation, four times in a Year. The Count De Vergennes confessed to me, that he was almost dead, with the pain of it. And the only insinuation I ever heard, that the King was in any degree touched by the Philosophy of the Age was, that he never discovered so much impatience under any of the Occurrences of his Life, as in going through those tedious Ceremonies of Religion to which so many hours of his Life were condemned by the Catholic Church.

The Queen was attended by her Ladies to the Gallery opposite to the Altar, placed in the Center of the Seat, and there left alone by the other Ladies, who all retired. She was an Object too sublime and beautiful for my dull pen to describe. I leave this Enterprize to Mr. Burke. But in his description there is more of the orator than of the Philosopher. Her Dress was every Thing that Art and Wealth could make it. One of the

Maids of honor told me, she had Diamonds upon her Person to the Value of Eighteen millions of Livres, and I always thought her Majesty much beholden to her Dress. Mr. Burke saw her probably but once. I have seen her fifty times perhaps and in all the Varieties of her Dresses. She had a fine Complexion indicating perfect health, and was an handsome Woman in her face and figure. But I have seen Beauties much superiour both in Countenance and form, in France, England and America. After the Ceremonies of this Institution are over there is a collection for the Poor and that this closing Scene may be as elegant as any of the former, a young Lady of some of the first Families in France is appointed to present the Box to the Knights. Her dress must be as rich and elegant in Proportion as the Queens, and her Air, motions and Curtesies must have as much Dignity and Grace as those of the Knights. It was a curious Entertainment to observe the Easy Air, the graceful Bow and the conscious Dignity of the Knight in presenting his contribution, and the correspondent Ease, Grace and Dignity of the Lady in receiving it were not less charming. Every Muscle, Nerve and Fibre of both seemed perfectly disciplined to perform its functions. The Elevation of the Arm, the bend of the Elbow and every finger in the hand of the Knight, in putting his Louis Door into the Box, appeared to be perfectly studied because it was perfectly natural. How much devotion there was in all this I know not, but it was a consummate School to teach the rising Generation the Perfection of the French Air and external Politeness and good Breeding. I have seen nothing to be compared to it, in any other Country. The House of Lords in England I thought the most likely to rival this: But seven Years afterwards when I had seen that Assembly on two extraordinary Occasions, the first the Introduction of the Prince of Wales to his Seat in Parliament and the second the Tryal of Mr. Hastings, I concluded the Peers of Great Britain were too intent on the great Interests of the Nation, to be very solicitous about the Charms of the exteriour Exhibition of a Spectacle. The Procession of the Peers and the Reverences they made to the Throne in conformity to the Usage of their Ancestors, as they passed to their Seats in Westminster Hall, were decent and graceful enough.

At nine O Clock in the Evening We went to the grand

Couvert, and saw the King, Queen and Royal Family at Supper. Whether Mr. Francis had contrived a plott to gratify the Curiosity of the Spectators, or whether the Royal Family had a fancy to see the raw American at their leisure, or whether they were willing to gratify him with a convenient Seat, in which he might see all the Royal Family and all the Splendors of the Place, I know not. But the Scheme could not have been carried into Execution certainly without the orders of the King. I was selected and summoned indeed from all my Company, and ordered to a Seat close beside the Royal Family. The Seats on both Sides of the Hall, arranged like the Seats in a Theater, were all full of Ladies of the first Rank and Fashion in the Kingdom and there was no room or place for me but in the midst of them. It was not easy to make room for one more Person. However Room was made and I was situated between two Ladies, with Rows and Ranks of Ladies above and below me, and on the right hand and on the left hand Ladies only. My Dress was a decent French Dress, becoming the Station I held, but not to be compared with the Gold and Diamonds and Embroidery about me. I could neither speak nor understand the Language in a manner to support a Conversation: but I had soon the Satisfaction to find it was a silent Meeting, and that nobody spoke a Word but the Royal Family to each other, and they said very little. The Eyes of all the Assembly were turned upon me, and I felt sufficiently humble and mortified, for I was not a proper Object for the criticisms of such a Company. I found myself gazed at, as We in America used to gaze at the Sachems who came to make Speeches to Us in Congress, but I thought it very hard if I could not command as much Power of face, as one of the Chiefs of the Six Nations, and therefore determined that I would assume a chearful Countenance, enjoy the Scene around me and observe it as coolly as an Astronomer contemplates the Starrs. Inscriptions of Fructus Belli were seen on the Ceiling and all about the Walls of the Room among Paintings of the Trophies of War, probably done by the order of Louis the fourteenth, who confessed in his dying Hour as his Successor and Exemplar Napoleone will probably do, that he had been too fond of War. The King was the Royal Carver for himself and all his Family. His Majesty eat like a King and made a Royal Supper of solid Beef and other Things in Proportion. The Queen took a large spoonful of Soupe, and displayed her fine Person and graceful manners, in alternately looking at the Company in various parts of the Hall, and ordering several kinds of Seasoning to be brought to her, by which she fitted her Supper to her Taste. When this was accomplished, her Majesty exhibited to the admiring Spectators, the magnificent Spectacle of a great Queen swallowing her Royal Supper in a single Spoonful, all at once. This was all performed like perfect Clockwork, not a feature of her face, nor a Motion of any part of her Person, especially her Arm and her hand could be criticised as out of order. A little and but a little Conversation seemed to pass among the Royal Personages of both Sexes, but in so low a voice that nothing could be understood by any of the Audience.

The Officers about the Kings Person brought him many Letters and Papers from time to time, while he was at Table. He looked at these, some of them he read or seemed to read, and returned them to the same Officers who brought them or some others.

These Ceremonies and Shows may be condemned by Philosophy and ridiculed by Commedy, with great reason. Yet the common Sense of Mankind has never adopted the rigid decrees of the former, nor ever sincerely laughed with the latter. Nor has the Religion of Nations in any Age, approved of the Dogmas or the Satyrs. On the Contrary it has always overborne them all and carried its Inventions of such Exhibitions to a degree of Sublimity and Pathos which has freequently transported the greatest Infidels out of themselves. Something of the kind every Government and every Religion has and must have: and the Business and Duty of Lawgivers and Philosophers is to endeavour to prevent them from being carried too far.

July 5. 1778. I have neglected to introduce, in the proper time, because I cannot precisely ascertain the Day, an Anecdote which excited my Grief, my Pitty and somewhat I confess of my resentment. Mr. Deane had left orders with Dr. Bancroft to receive and open all Letters which might arrive, addressed to him, after his departure. Among others he brought one to

me addressed to Mr. Deane from Mr. Hancock, highly compli-
mentary to Mr. Deane, professing great Friendship and Esteem for Mr. Deane, lamenting his Recall, complaining of the
cruel Treatment he had received, and assuring him that it was
not Congress that had done it. I pitied the weakness, grieved
at the meanness and resented the Malice of this Letter. He had
left Congress long before I did. He must have been ignorant
of the most urgent motives of Congress to the Measure. He
must have been blind not to have seen the egregious faults and
Misconduct of Mr. Deane before this. If Congress had not
done it, who had done it? Congress was unanimous in his Recall. In short the whole Letter was the Effect of a miserable
Jealousy and Envy of me. I felt no little Indignation, at the ill
Will, which had instigated this Persecution against me across
the Atlantic, from a Man who had been under great Obligations to me for defending him and his Fortune, and whom I
had never injured nor justly offended. The Letter was a fawn-
ing flattery of Deane, a Calumny against Congress, and had a
tendency to represent me in an unfavourable light in foreign
Countries and to embarrass and obstruct me in the discharge
of the Duties of my Mission.

Mr. Gerry a Member of Congress.

My Dear Friend   Passi July 9. 1778

I was disappointed in my Expectations of receiving Letters
from You by the two Vessells, The Saratoga and the Spy, which
have arrived. Although I know your time is every moment of
it, wisely and usefully employed, yet I cannot but wish for a
little of it, now and then. Europe is eager, at all times, for news
from America, and this Kingdom in particular enjoys every
Syllable of good News from that Country.

Great Britain is really a Melancholly Spectacle. . . . Destitute of Wisdom and Virtue to make Peace; burning with malice and revenge; yet affrighted and confounded at the Prospect
of War. . . . She has reason; for if she should be as successfull
in it, as she was in the last, it would weaken and exhaust her,
and she would not, even in that Case recover America, and
consequently her Superiority at Sea. . . . But humanly speaking it is impossible, she should be successful.

It is with real Astonishment that I observe her Conduct. . . . After all Experience, and altho' her true Interest, and her only safe plan of Policy is as obvious as the Sun, yet she cannot see it. . . . All Attention to the Welfare of the Nation seems to be lost, both by the Members of Administration and Opposition, and among the People at large. . . . Tearing one another to Pieces for the Loaves and Fishes, and a universal Rage for gambling in the Stocks, seem to take up all their Thoughts.

An Idea of a fair and honourable Treaty with Congress, never enters their Minds. In short Chicanery seems to have taken Possession of their hearts so entirely, that they are incapable of thinking of any Thing fair.

We had an Example, here last Week. . . . A long Letter, containing a Project for an Agreement with America, was thrown into one of our Grates. . . . There are Reasons to believe, that it came with the Privity of the King. . . . You may possibly see it, sometime. . . . Full of Flattery, and proposing that America should be governed by a Congress, of American Peers, to be created and appointed by the King. . . . And of Bribery, proposing that a Number not exceeding two hundred American Peers should be made, and that such as had stood foremost, and suffered most, and made most Enemies in this Contest, as Adams, Handcock, Washington and Franklin by Name, should be of the Number. . . . Ask our Friend, if he should like to be a Peer?

Dr. Franklin, to whom the Letter was sent, as the Writer is supposed to be a Friend of his, sent an Answer, in which they have received a Dose that will make them sick. John Adams
  Mr. Gerry

This Letter requires a Commentary. . . . The Reasons for believing that it came with the Privity of the King, were derived wholly from Dr. Franklin, who affirmed to me that there were in the Letter infallible Marks, by which he knew that it came from the King, and that it could not have come from any other without the Kings Knowledge. What these Marks were he never explained to me. I was not impertinently inquisitive, and he affected to have reasons for avoiding any more particular devellopement of the Mystery. Many other hints have been dropped by Franklin to me, of some Mysterious Intercourse or

correspondence between the King and him, personally. . . .
He often and indeed always appeared to me to have a personal
Animosity and very severe Resentment against the King. In all
his conversations and in all his Writings, when he could naturally and sometimes when he could not, he mentioned the
King with great Asperity. He wrote certain Annotations on
Judge Fosters discourse on the Legality of the Impressment of
Seamen, in the Margin of the Book, and there introduced his
habitual Accrimony against his Majesty. A thousand other Occasions discovered the same disposition. Among the ancient
disputes between Franklin and the Proprietary Governors of
Pensilvania, I have read, that Franklin, upon hearing of a report in Circulation against his Election as Agent for the
Province at the Court of St. James's that he had no Influence
with the Ministry, and no Acquaintance with Lord Bute, broke
out into a Passion and swore, contrary to his usual reserve,
"that he had an Influence with the Ministry and was intimate
with Lord Bute." It is not generally known that the Earl of
Bute was a Philosopher, a Chymist and a natural Historian.
That he printed seven or Eight Volumes of natural History of
his own Composition, only however for the Use of his particular confidential Friends. This kind of Ambition in the Earl
might induce him to cultivate the Acquaintance with Franklin,
as it did afterwards Rochefoucault, Turgot and Condorcet in
France. And at the Earl of Butes some mysterious Conferences
between the King and Franklin might have been concerted:
and in these Interviews Franklin might have conceived himself
deceived or insulted. I mention this merely as conjecture, Suggestion or Surmise. Franklins Memorials, if they ever appear
may confirm or confute the Surmise, which however after all,
will be of very little Consequence. Without the Supposition of
some kind of Backstairs Intrigues it is difficult to account for
that mortification of the pride, affront to the dignity and Insult to the Morals of America, the Elevation to the Government of New Jersey of a base born Brat.

July 25. 1778. I was much amused, among some People here
who understand a little English, to hear them puzzling each
other with Samples of English Sentences, very difficult to be

pronounced by a Frenchman. Among many others I remarked the following and very curious indeed were the Attempts to pronounce them. "What think the chosen Judges?" "I thrust this Thistle through this Thumb." "With an Apple in each hand and a third in my Mouth." But of all the Words I ever heard essayed by a French Man, the Words "General Washington" produced the greatest Variety of difficulties. I know not that I ever heard two Persons pronounce them alike, except the Marquis de La Fayette and his Lady. They had studied and practised them so long that they had mastered the great Subject. In my second Voyage to France, I carried with me a Friend as a private Secretary, Mr. John Thaxter. His name was a new Problem of Pronunciation. I could have filled a Sheet of Paper with the Varieties of Sounds, which these two Names suggested to my French Friends. "VAUGSTAINGSTOUNG" was one of the Sounds for Washington: and "TAUGISTEY," was another for Thaxter. But enough of this in this place.

On the Thirteenth day of November 1779, I had again the melancholly Tryal of taking Leave of my Family, with the Dangers of the Seas and the Terrors of British Men of War before my Eyes, with this additional Aggravation that I now knew by Experience, how serious they were, much better than I had when I embarked in Nantasket Road in 1778. We went to Boston and embarked on Board the Frigate whose Yards were manned, in Honour of the Passengers. We found the Ship crouded, full 350 Sailors, a great number of whom had been recruited in America: and a great many Passengers, among whom were Mr. Jeremiah Allen and Samuel Cooper Johonnot, Grandson of Dr. Cooper.

I shall not consume much time in the Narration of this second Voyage to Europe though it was attended with as much danger as the first. We met indeed no British Men of War, which in my Estimation were the Worst of all Evils. We had but one very violent Gale of Wind, and that was so much inferiour to those I had encountered the Year before in the Bay of Biscay, in the English Channel and above all in the Gulph Stream, that it appeared to me to have no terror in it. It was nevertheless furious enough to allarm the Officers and People, and their Apprehensions were increased by the foundering or at least by the sudden and final disappearance of a Chasse Maree, that had hitherto sailed under our Convoy from L'Orient. Their Fears as well as mine were increased by another Circumstance, which very seriously threatened destruction to Us all. We had not been two days at Sea before I perceived that the Pumps were going and that a Leak in the Ship was constantly admitting a great deal of Water. At first it was said to be a steady Leak, and not attended with much danger, but it constantly increased from day to day, till our Arrival in Spain. During all the latter part of the Voyage, a large Stream of Water was constantly pouring over each Side into the Sea, from the Pumps which were worked by day and by Night, till all the People on board, Passengers and Officers as well as Seamen were almost exhausted with fatigue. The Sensible was an old Frigate, and her Planks and timbers were so decayed, that one half the Violence of Winds and Waves which had so nearly wrecked the new and strong Ship the Boston the Year before, would have torn her to pieces. Or had We been chased by a superiour British Force, and obliged to spread all our Sails, it is highly probable that the Leak would have been increased and the Ship foundered.

November 25. 1779. The Wind was fair and the Weather pleasant. We had passed the Grand Bank, and found ourselves on the Eastermost Edge of it. On sounding We found Bottom in thirty fathoms of Water.

The Captain and all his Officers and Passengers were so much alarmed at the increasing danger of the Leak and at the fatiguing Labour of all hands in keeping the Pumps in play, that it was concluded to make for one of the Western Islands as the first Friendly Land We could possibly reach: but We missed them and some day in the beginning of December 1779 We found ourselves, as was supposed within one hundred Leagues of Ferrol or at least of Corunna, to one or the other of which places We determined to direct our Course with all the Sail, the Ship could prudently bare. The Leak which kept two Pumps constantly going, having determined the Captain to put into Spain. This Resolution was a great Embarrassment to me. Whether I should travel by Land to Paris a Journey of twelve or thirteen hundred miles, or Wait for the Frigate to be examined and repaired, which might require a long time? Whether I could get Carriages, Horses, Mules or any other Animals to convey Us? What Accommodations We could get upon the Road? How I could convey the Children, and what the Expences would be? were all questions which I could not answer: nor could I find any Person on board, who was able to give me any satisfactory Information. It was said however by some that the Passage of the Pyranees was very difficult: that there was no regular Stage or Post: that We must purchase Carriages and Horses &c. . . . I could not help reflecting how much greater these inconveniences had been rendered, and how much more our perplexity if the rest of my Family had been with me. With Ladies and young Children and Additional Servants Male and Female We should have been in more distress on Land than at Sea.

We dined one day with the Comte De Sade on Board the Triomphant, with all the principal Officers of the Fleet in all the Luxury of the French Navy.

A very fine Turkey was brought upon Table, among every Thing else that Land, Sea or Air could furnish. One of the Captains, as soon as he saw it, observed that he never saw one of those Birds on a Table but it excited in him a deep regret for the Abolition of that order of Ecclesiasticks the Jesuits to whom We were he said, indebted for so many Excellent Things, and among the Rest for Turkeys. These Birds he said were never seen or known in Europe till the Jesuits imported them from India. This occasioned much Conversation and some Controversy: but the majority of the Officers appeared to join in this regrett. The Jesuits were represented as the greatest Masters of Science and Litterature: as practising the best System of Education, and as having made the greatest improvements, the happiest Inventions and the greatest discoveries for the Comfort of Life and the Amelioration of Man and Society. Till this time I had thought that although millions of Jesuits, Pharisees and Machiavilians still existed in the World, yet that the Word Jesuit as well as that of Pharisee and Machiavilian, had become so odious in Courts and unpopular with Nations that neither was ever advocated in good Company. I now found my Error, and I afterwards perceived that even the Philosophers were the principal Friends left to the Jesuits.

The French Names Dindon and Poulet D'Inde, indicate that the Fowl was imported from India: But the English Name Turkey and Turkey fowl, seems to imply that the Bird was brought from the Levant. But if I am not mistaken, the English pretend that Sir Walter Raleigh first imported this Luxury from America. These important Questions of Natural History I shall leave to the Investigation and Discussion of those who have nothing else to do, nor any thing of more Taste and Consequence to contemplate.

I was highly entertained however with this Conversation and not a little delighted to find that I could so well understand a Conversation so rapid and lively in French.

As the Count De Sade placed me next to himself at Table, his chief and indeed his whole Conversation was with me. He was very inquisitive about every Thing in America, but the Subject which most engaged his Attention was the Commerce and especially the Naval Power of America. This Subject I always found most prevalent in the Minds of all the Naval Gentlemen both of France and Spain. The Count said that no Nation in Europe had such Advantages for Naval Power as America. We had Timber of the best Kinds in the World, our Oaks and Cedars especially the Live Oaks and Red Cædars, which America Possessed in such Abundance, were an Advantage that no Nation ever enjoyed before in such Perfection. That We had inexhaustible Mines of Iron Oar and all the Skill and Apparatus necessary to prepare it, work it and refine it. That our Soil produced Flax and Hemp of good quality, and our Agriculturalists knew how to raise it and preserve it. We have a Maxim among Us in the Marine, said the Count, That with Wood, Hemp and Iron, a Nation may do what it will. And you may do what you will, and you will do what you will. For No Nation has, and No Nation that ever existed ever had such Advantages for raising a formidable Navy in a short time as you have. For to all the Materials you add all the Skill and Art. You have already learned of the English, all the Skill in Naval Architecture and all the Art and Enterprise of Navigation, which was ever possessed by the most commercial and most maritime People that ever existed. In fine his Conversation was in the same Strain with that of Monsieur De Thevenot at L'Orient, in the Spring of the same Year, but more in detail. As the Count de Sade understood no English and my organs were not very flexible to the French, my part of the Conversation could not be very fluent. I made him however to understand, that I thought our People had so much Employment at home upon their Lands, which would be more comfortable and less hazardous if not more profitable that it would be a long time before they would turn their Attention to a Naval military Power. I must however now confess that I did not then believe that French, Spanish, Dutch and English Emissaries, would obtain so much influence in America as to cast a mist before the Eyes of the People and prevent them from seeing their own Interest and feeling their own Power for seven and twenty Years, to such a degree as to suffer their own Coasts and harbours to be insulted and their Commerce plundered even in the West Indies by Pirates, which a few Frigates might send to their [   ] place. The Count presented to me The Chevalier De Grasse, as his Captaine De Pavillon and as the Brother of the Count de Grasse, the Commander in America, and as a Gentleman of large and independent Fortune, who had no Occasion to go to Sea but chose to expose himself to the rough Life of a Sea Officer, from pure Zeal for the Kings Service.

The Chief Magistrate of the Town of Ferrol, is The Corregidor. For the Province or Kingdom of Gallicia, there is a Souvereign Court of Justice, which has both civil and criminal Jurisdiction. In all criminal Cases it is without Appeal, but in some civil Cases an Appeal lies to the Council at Madrid. There is no time allowed in criminal Cases for an Application for Pardon, for they execute forthwith. Hanging is the Capital Punishment. They burn sometimes but it is after death. There was lately a Sentence for Parricide. The Law required that the Criminal should be headed up in a hogshead, with an Adder, a Toad, a Dog and a Cat and cast into the Sea. But I was much pleased to hear that Spanish humanity had suggested and

Spanish Ingenuity invented a Device to avoid some part of the Cruelty and horror of this punishment. They had painted those Animals on the Cask, and the dead body was put into it, without any living Animals to attend it to its watery Grave. The ancient Laws of the Visigoths are still in Use, and these, with the Institutes, Codes, Novelles &c. of Justinian, the Cannon Law and the Ordinances of the King, constitute the Laws of the Kingdom of Gallicia.

The Bread, the Colliflowers, the Cabbages, Apples, Pears, Beef, Pork and Poultry were good. The Fish of several Sorts were good, excellent Eels, Sardines, and other Species, and the Oysters were tolerable, but not equal to ours in America.

I had not seen a Chariot, Coach, Phaeton, Chaise or Sulky, since I had been in the Place, very few Horses and those very small and miserably poor; Mules and Asses were numerous but small. There was no Hay in the Country: The Horses, Mules &c. eat Wheat Straw.

There had been no frost. The Verdure in the Gardens and Fields was fresh. The Weather was so warm that the Inhabitants had no Fires, nor Fire Places, but in their Kitchens. We were told We should have no colder Weather before May which is the coldest Month in the Year. We found however, when We travelled in the Month of January in the Mountains, Frost and Snow and Ice enough. But at this time and in this Neighbourhood of the Sea, Men, Women and Children were seen in the Streets, with naked Legs and feet, standing on the cold Stones in the mud, by the hour together. The Inhabitants of both Sexes have black hair and dark Complexions, with fine black Eyes. Men and Women had long hair ramilied down to their Waists and sometimes down to their Knees.

Though there was little Appearance of Commerce or Industry, except about the Kings Docks and Yards and Works, yet the Town had some Symptoms of Growth and Prosperity. Many new Houses were building of a Stone which comes from the rocky Mountains round about, of which there are many. There were few goods in the Shops, little Show in their Marketts, or on their Exchange. There was a pleasant Walk a little out of Town, between the Exchange and the Barracks.

There were but two Taverns in the Town. Captain Chavagne and his Officers lodged at one, at six Livres each a day.

The other was kept by a Native of America, who spoke English and French as well as Spanish, and was an obliging Man. Here We could have lodged at a dollar a day each: but where We were We were obliged to give an hundred and twenty nine dollars for six days besides a multitude of other Expences, and besides being kept constantly unhappy by an uneasy Landlady.

Finding that I must reside some Weeks in Spain, either waiting for the Frigate or travelling through the Kingdom, I determined to look a little into the Language. For which purpose I went to a Bookseller and purchased Sobrino's Dictionary in three Volumes in Quarto, The Grammatica Castillana an excellent Spanish Grammar in their own Tongue, and a Lattin Grammar in Spanish. My Friend Captain De Grasse made me a present of a very handsome Grammar of the Spanish Tongue by Sobrino. . . . By the help of these Books, the Children as well as the Gentlemen of our little Company were soon employed in learning the Language. To one who understood the Latin it seemed to be easy and some of Us flatter'd ourselves, that in a Month We might be able to read it, and understand the Spaniards as well as be understood by them. But experience taught Us our Error and that a Language is very difficult to acquire especially by Persons in middle Life.

Mr. Linde an Irish Gentleman, and Master of a Mathematical Accademy here, as well as Mr. De Tournelle, says, that the Spanish Nation in general have been of Opinion that the Revolution in America is a bad example to the Spanish Colonies, and dangerous to the Interests of Spain, as the United States if they should become ambitious and be seized with the Spirit of Conquest, might aim at Mexico and Peru. The Consul mentioned the Opinion of Raynalle, that it was not for the Interest of the Powers of Europe, that America should be independent.

To the Irish Gentleman I observed, that Americans hated War: that Agriculture and Commerce were their Objects, and it would be their Interest, as much as that of the Dutch to keep peace with all the World, untill their Country should be filled with People, which could not be for Centuries. That War and the Spirit of Conquest were the most diametrically opposite to their Interests, as they would divert their Attention, Wealth, Industry, Activity, from a certain Source of Prosperity and even Grandeur and Glory, to an uncertain one; nay to one, that it was certain never could be to their Advantage. That the Government of Spain over her Colonies had always been such, that she never could attempt to introduce such fundamental Innovations, as those by which England had provoked and compelled Us to revolt. And the Spanish Constitution was such, as could extinguish the first Sparks of discontent, and quell the first risings of the People. That it was amazing to me, that a Writer so well informed as Raynalle, could ever give an Opinion that it was not for the Interest of the Powers of Europe, that America should be independent, when it was so easy to demonstrate, that it was for the Interest of every one of them except England. That they could loose nothing by it, but certainly every one of them would gain something, and many of them a great deal.

Wee can see but a little Way into Futurity. . . . If, in 1807, We look back for seven and twenty Years, and consider what would have been the Consequence to Mexico and Peru and all South America, and all the French and Spanish West India Islands, had the United States remained subject to Great Britain, Mr. Linde and the Consul and the whole Spanish Nation might be convinced, that they owe much to the American Revolution. The English love War as much as We abhor it, and if they had now the American Cities for Places of Arms, the American Harbours for Shelter, American Provisions for Supplies and American Seamen and Soldiers for Reinforcements, by what tenure would France and Spain hold their American Dominions?

December 16. 1779. Thursday. This Morning the Governor of the Province of Gallicia and the Governor of the Town of Corunna came to my Quarters at the Hotel du grand Amiral, to return the Visits I made them the last Evening. His Excellency repeated his Invitation to me to dine with him the next day with all my Family. He insisted on seeing my Sons. Said I ran a great risque in taking my Children with me: He had once passed very near my Country in an Expedition in a former War, which he had made against the Portuguese; that himself and every Thing in his Power, were at my Service; that he did not speak English. . . . I knew not how to answer all this politeness, better than by saying that I was engaged in the Study of the Spanish, and hoped that the next time I should have the Honour of seeing his Excellency, I should be able to speak to him in his own Language. At this he smiled and made a low bow, made some further Enquiries concerning American Affairs and took Leave. Mr. Dana and I took a Walk about the Town, to see the Fortifications, the Shipping, the Marketts, Barracks &c.

1779 December 24. Fryday. Dined on board the Bellepoule with the Officers of that Ship and those of the Galatea.

We had now been about sixteen days in Spain at Ferrol and Corunna and had received Every Politeness We could desire from all the Officers civil and military both of the Army and Navy, and from the French Officers as well as the Spanish; the Climate was warm and salubrious, and the Provisions were plentifull, wholesome and agreable. But the Circumstance which destroyed all my Comfort and materially injured my health was the Want of rest. For the first Eight nights I know not that I slept at all and for the other eight very little. The Universal Sloth and Lazyness of the Inhabitants suffered not only all their Beds but all their Appartments to be infested with innumerable Swarms of Ennemies of all repose. And this torment did not cease at Corunna but persecuted me through the whole Kingdom of Spain to such a degree that I sometimes apprehended I should never live to see France.

1779 December 27. Monday. We travelled from Betanzos to Castillano. The roads still mountainous and rocky. Neither the Horses nor the Mules could be trusted, in ascending or descending the rocky Steeps of the Mountains in the Carriges without two Men on foot to hold them by their bridles and their heads, and with all our precautions, We broke one of our Axle Trees, early in the day which prevented Us from going more than four Leagues in the whole. The House in Castillano where We lodged was of Stone, two Stories in height. We entered into the Kitchen, where was no floor but the Ground and no Carpet but Straw trodden into mire by Men, Hogs, horses and Mules. In the middle of the Kitchen was a Mound raised a little above the Level of the Ground with Stones and Earth, on which was a fire, with Potts, Kettles, Skillets &c. of the fashion of the Country, over it, and round about it. There was no Chimney filled the room and if any of it ascended, it found no other passage to the open Air, but through two holes drilled through the Tyles of the roof, not perpendicularly over the fire, but at Angles of about forty five degrees. On one Side was a flew Oven, very large, black, smoaky and sooty. On the opposite Side of the fire was a Cabbin filled with Straw where I suppose the Patron del Casa, that is, the Master of the House, his Wife and four Chilldren, all lodged and slept together. On the same floor or rather on the same level of Ground, with the Kitchen was the Stable. There was indeed a Door which might have parted the Kitchen from the Stable: but this was always open, and indeed it would have been impossible to see or breath with it shut: and the floor or ground of the Stable, was covered with miry Straw like the Kitchen. I went into the Stable and saw it filled on all Sides with Mules belonging to Us and several other Travellers who were obliged to put up, by the Rain. The Smoke filled every part of the Kitchen, Stable, and all other parts of the House, and was so thick that it was very difficult to see or breath. There was a flight of Steps of Stone covered with Mud and Straw, from the Kitchen floor up into a Chamber. On the left hand as you ascended the Stairs, was a Stage, built up about half Way from the Kitchen floor to the Chamber floor. On this Stage was a bed of Straw and on the Straw lay, a fatting hog. Around the Kitchen fire were arranged the Man and Woman of the House, four Children, all the Travellers, Servants, Mulateers &c. Over the Fire was a very large Kettle, like a Pot Ash Kettle, full of Turnips and Onions, very large and very fine boiling for the Food of all the Family of Men and Beasts inhabiting both the Kitchen and the Stable, and the Stage.

The Chamber in which We lodged, had a large quantity, perhaps an hundred Bushells of Indian Corn in Ears, very small however, not half so large as our Corn in America. These

Ears were hanging over head upon Poles and pieces of Joist. In one Corner was a large Binn, full of Rape Seed, on the other Side, another full of Oats. In another part of the Chamber lay a few Bushells of Chesnuts. There were two frames for Beds with Straw beds upon them, and a Table in the middle. The Floor I believe had never been washed or swept for an hundred Years. Smoke, Soot and dirt, every where, and in every Thing. There were in the Chamber two Windows or rather Port holes without any glass. There were wooden dors to open and shut before the Windows. If these were shut there was no light and no Ventilator to draw off the unwholesome Air of the Chamber or let in any pure Air from abroad; if they were open We were exposed to all the cold and Vapours, from the external Air. My Inclination and Advice was to keep the Ports open, choosing to encounter the worst Air from abroad rather than be suffocated or poisoned with the Smoke and contaminated Air within. In addition to all these Comforts in such a Tavern it was not to be expected that We should escape the Bosom Companions and nocturnal Ennemies, which We had found every where else. Nevertheless, amidst all these horrors I slept better, than I had done before since my Arrival in Spain.

1779 December 28. Tuesday. We went from Castilliana to Baamonde, and found the first part of the Road very bad, but the latter part tolerable. The whole Country We had passed hitherto had been very mountainous and rocky. There was here and there a Valley, and now and then a farm that appeared handsomely cultivated. But in general the Mountains were covered with Furze, and not much cultivated. We were astonished to see so few Trees. There was scarce an Oak, Elm, or any other Tree to be seen, except a very few Madeira Nuts and a very few fruit Trees. At Baamonde we were obliged to rest for the day, to procure a new Axle Tree to one of our Calashes. The House where We were, was better than our last nights lodgings. We had a Chamber for seven of Us to lodge in. We laid our beds upon all the Tables and Chairs in the room and the rest on the floor as last night. We had no Smoke and less dirt than last night, though the floor had never been washed I believe since it was laid. The Kitchen and Stable were below as usual but in better order. The Fire was in the middle of the

Kitchen: but the Air-holes pierced thro the Tiles of the Roof, drew up the Smoke, so that one might sit at the Fire, without much inconvenience. The Mules, Hogs, fowls and human Inhabitants, however, all lived together below and Cleanliness seemed never to be regarded.

We went from Lugo to Galliego and arrived in good Season, having made six Leagues and an half from Lugo. The Road was mountainous but not rocky as it had been almost all the Way heretofore. We passed over a large Bridge over a River called Carasedo, which empties itself into the Minho not far from Lugo. I saw nothing but Signs of Poverty and misery among the People: a fertile Country not half cultivated: People ragged and dirty: the Houses universally nothing but mire, Smoke, Soot, fleas and Lice: nothing appeared rich but the Churches, nobody fat but the Clergy. Many of the Villages We passed, were built with Mud filled in between Joists, Nine tenths of them uninhabited and mouldering to dust. Yet in every one of these Scenes of desolation, you would see a splendid Church, and here and there a rosy faced Priest in his proud Canonicals rambling among the rubbish of the Village. The Roads the worst, without exception the worst that were ever travelled, in a Country where it would be easy to make them very good: No Simptoms of Commerce, or even of internal Trafick: No Appearance of Manufactures or Industry.

1780. January 4. Tuesday. At Astorga, We found clean Beds and no fleas for the first time since We had been in Spain. Walked twice round the Walls of the City, which are very ancient. We saw the Road to Leon and Bayonne and the road to Madrid. There is a pleasant Prospect of the Country from the Walls. Saw the Market of Vegetables. The Onions and Turnips were the largest and finest I ever saw. The Cabbages, Carrots &c. appeared very good. Saw the Markett of Fuel, which consisted of Wood, Coal, Turf and Brush. Numbers of the Marragatto Women attended the Market with their Vendibles. These were as fine as any of our American Indian Squaws and a great deal more filthy. Their Ornaments consisted of Crucifixes,

Beads, Chains, Earrings and Finger Rings, in Silver, brass or glass, about their Necks and Arms.

1780 January 6. Thursday. We went to see the Cathedral Church at Leon which though magnificent, is not equal to that at Astorga, if it is to that at Lugo. It was the day of the Feast of the King and We happened to be at the celebration of High Mass. We saw the Procession of the Bishop and of all the Canons, in rich habits of Silk, Velvet, Silver and gold. The Bishop as he turned the Corners of the Church spred out his hand to the People, in token of his Apostolical Benediction; and those, in token of their profound gratitude for the heavenly Blessing prostrated themselves on their Knees as he passed. Our Guide told Us We must do the same. But I contented myself with a Bow. The Eagle Eye of the Bishop did not fail to observe an Upright figure amidst the Crowd of prostrate Adorers: but no doubt perceiving in my Countenance and Air, but especially in my dress something that was not Spanish, he concluded I was some travelling Heretick and did not think it worth while to exert his Authority to bend my stiff Knees. His Eyes followed me so long that I thought I saw in his Countenance a reproof like this "You are not only a Heretick but you are not a Gentleman, for a Gentleman would have respected the Religion of the Country and its Usages so far as to have conformed externally to a Ceremony that cost so little."

We were conducted to see the Council Chamber of the Bishop and Chapter, hung round with Crimson Damask. The Seats all round the Chamber of crimson Velvet. This room and another, smaller one, where the Bishop sometimes took aside some of the Cannons, were very elegant.

We went to see the Casa del Cieudad: and the Castle of King Alphonsus which We were informed was Nineteen hundred and thirty six years old. It is of Stone and the Workmanship of it, very neat.

But there is in this City no Appearance of Commerce, Manufactures or Industry. The Houses are low, built of Brick and Mud and Pebble Stones from the neighbouring Fields. There was no Market worth notice. Nothing looked either rich or chearfull but the Churches and Churchmen. There was a

Statue of Charles the fifth in the Cathedral Church, but very badly done, as were all the Statues and Paintings I had seen in all the Churches, for which reason among others I have taken no notice of them. Indeed it would be endless to describe all the Images of Angells and Statues of Saints who have been canonized not so much for their moral and social Virtues or their Christian Graces as for their Superstition and Enthusiasm, or what is worse for their pious frauds in the Service of the Sovereign Pontiffs. Besides I saw among them no Sculpture or Painting that was worthy of Observation or Remembrance.

1780 January 8 Saturday. We rode from San Juan Segun to Paredise de Nava. At the distance of every League, We had passed through a Village built altogether of Mud and Straw. They have no timber nor Wood nor brick nor Stone. These Villages all appear going to decay and crumbling to dust. Can this be the ancient Kingdom of Leon? Nevertheless every Village has Churches and Convents enough in it, to ruin it, and the whole Country round about it; even if they had nothing to pay to the King, or the Landlords. But all three together Church, State and Nobility exhaust the Labour and Spirits of the People to such a degree, that I had no Idea of the Possibility of deeper Wretchedness. Ignorance more than Wickedness has produced this deplorable State of Things, Ignorance of the true Policy which encourages Agriculture, Manufactures and Commerce. The Selfishness and Lazyness of Courtiers and Nobles, have no doubt been the Cause of this Ignorance: and the blind Superstition of the Church has cooperated with all the other causes and increased them. There were in this little Village four Parish Churches and two Convents one of Monks and one of Nuns, both of the order of St. Francis.

The Parish Churches and their Curates are supported here, by the Tythes paid by the People. They pay every tenth pound of Wool; every tenth part of Wine, Grain, Honey; in short, every tenth part of every thing. The good Curates sometimes aleviate the Severity of this, by Compositions or Modus's. The Convents are supported by the Incomes of their Estates and foundations. But one would think this would require the Produce of the whole Country.

Nothing seems to be considered as the good of the People but their Religion. The Archbishop is said to have power to do every Thing for the good of the People. But when you enquire what he does or what he has power to do for the happiness of the People? to alleviate their burdens? or increase their Enjoyments? You are told he does nothing of all this, nor has power to do any thing. All his Power, to do every thing for the good of the People, consists in that of making new Parishes, and altering old ones at his Pleasure. We were told there were but four Archbishopricks in Spain. The Splendor of these Establishments may be conceived from that of Saint Iago whose Archbishop has one hundred and Eighty thousand Ducats a Year, in Rent. The War which then prevailed between France and Spain on one Side and England on the other, was said to be popular in Spain. The Clergy, the Religious Houses and other Communities had offered to grant large Sums of Money to the King for the Support of it. The English had become terrible to them, partly perhaps because English Sentiments of Liberty and Tolleration, had begun to creep in among the People and might threaten to become dangerous to the Wealth and Domination of the Clergy; and partly because their South American Dominions were too much in danger from the English and North America united.

From Astorga to this place Paredise de Nava, the Face of the Country was a great plain, and a striking Contrast to all the rest of the Country We had passed from Ferrol. But there was little Appearance of Improvement, Industry or Cultivation. Scarcely any Trees. No Forrest, Timber or fruit Trees. No Fences except a few Mud Walls for Sheep folds. This night We reached Sellada el Camino.

1780 January 11. Tuesday. We arrived at Burgos, from Sellada el Caminos, four Leagues. We had fog, rain, and Snow all the Way, very chilly and raw. When We arrived at the Tavern, We found no Chimney, though my Servant who went out to examine all the other public houses reported this to be the best. A Brazier, or Pan of Coals in a Chamber, without a Chimney and without Windows except Port holes, was all the heat We could procure. Uncomfortable however as We were, We went out to see the Cathedral which was ancient and very large. The whole Building was supported by four grand Pillars the largest

I ever had seen. Round the great Altar were represented our Saviour, from the Scene of his Agony in the Garden, when an Angel presents to him the Cup, to his Crucifixion between two Thieves, his descent from the Cross, and his Ascension into Heaven. The Chappells round the great Altar were the largest I had ever seen. Round the Altar these several Stages were represented. 1. The Agony in the Garden. 2. Carrying the Cross. 3. The Crucifixion between two Thieves. 4. The Descent from the Cross. 5. The Ascension into Heaven.

There was no Archbishop at Burgos, there had been one, who made the fifth in the Kingdom: but the King had abolished this Archbishoprick and there remained but four. There was also a Chappell of Saint Iago.

We went into three Booksellers Shops to search for a Map or Chart of Spain, but could find none, except a very small and erroneous one in a Compendio of History of Spain.

For more than twenty Years I had been almost continually engaged in Journeys and Voyages and had often undergone severe Tryals, as I thought; great hardships, cold, rain, Snow, heat, fatigue, bad rest, indifferent nourishment, want of Sleep &c. &c. &c. But I had never experienced any Thing like this Journey. If it were now left to my Choice to perform my first Voyage to Europe with all its horrors, or this Journey through Spain, I should prefer the former. Every Individual Person in Company had a violent Cold, and were all of Us in danger of fevers. We went along the Road, sneezing and coughing, in all that uncomfortable Weather, and with our uncomfortable Cavalry and Carriages, in very bad roads, and indeed were all of Us fitter for an Hospital than for Travellers with the best Accommodations on the most pleasant Roads. All the Servants in Company, were dull, discouraged and inactive, besides the total Ignorance of any Language in which they could converse with the People. The Children were sick. Mr. Thaxter was not much better, and as he understood neither Spanish nor French, he had enough to do to take care of himself. In short I was in a deplorable Situation. I knew not what to do nor where to go. In my whole Life my Patience was never so near being totally exhausted.

APPENDIX

DEFINITIVE TREATY OF PEACE BETWEEN GREAT BRITAIN AND THE UNITED STATES

Definitive Treaty of Peace between Great Britain and the United States

In the Name of the most Holy & undivided Trinity.

It having pleased the divine Providence to dispose the Hearts of the most Serene & most Potent Prince George the third, by the Grace of God, King of Great Britain, France & Ireland Defender of the Faith, Duke of Brunswick & Lunebourg, Arch-Treasurer, and Prince Elector of the holy Roman Empire &^ca: and of the United States of America to forget all past Misunderstandings and Differences that have unhappily interrupted the good Correspondence and Friendship which they mutually wish to restore; and to establish such a beneficial and satisfactory Intercourse between the two Countries upon the Ground of reciprocal Advantages and mutual Convenience as may promote and secure to both perpetual Peace & Harmony; and having for this desirable End already laid the Foundation of Peace & Reconciliation by the Provisional Articles signed at Paris on the 30th: of Nov^r: 1782 by the Commissioners empower'd on each Part, which Articles were agreed to be inserted in and to constitute the Treaty of Peace proposed to be concluded between the Crown of Great Britain and the said United States, but which Treaty was not to be concluded until Terms of Peace should be agreed upon between Great Britain & France, and his Britannic Majesty should be ready to conclude such Treaty accordingly: and the Treaty between Great Britain and France having since been concluded, His Britannic Majesty & the United States of America, in order to carry into full Effect the Provisional Articles above mentioned, according to the Tenor thereof, have constituted & appointed, that is to say His Britannic Majesty on his Part, David Hartley Esqre: Member of the Parliament of Great Britain; and the said United States on their Part John Adams Esqre: late a Commissioner of the United States of America at the Court of Versailles, late Delegate in Congress from the State of Massachusetts and Chief Justice of the said State; and Minister Plenipotentiary of the said United States to their High Mightinesses the States General of the United Netherlands; Benjamin

Franklin Esqre: late Delegate in Congress from the State of Pennsylvania, President of the Convention of the said State & Minister Plenipotentiary from the United States of America at the Court of Versailles; John Jay Esqre: late President of Congress, and Chief Justice of the State of New-York & Minister Plenipotentiary from the said United States at the Court of Madrid; to be the Plenipotentiaries for the concluding and signing the present Definitive Treaty; who after having reciprocally communicated their respective full Powers have agreed upon & confirmed the following Articles.

Article 1st:

His Britannic Majesty acknowledges the said United States, viz. New-Hampshire Massachusetts Bay, Rhode-Island & Providence Plantations, Connecticut, New-York, New Jersey, Pennsylvania Delaware, Maryland, Virginia, North Carolina, South Carolina & Georgia, to be free sovereign & Independent States; that he Treats with them as such, and for himself his Heirs & Successors relinquishes all Claims to the Government Propriety and Territorial Rights of the same & every Part thereof.

Article 2^d:

And that all Disputes which might arise in future on the Subject of the Boundaries of the said United States may be prevented, it is hereby agreed and declared, that the following are and shall be their Boundaries Viz: From the North West Angle of Nova Scotia, viz: that Angle which is formed by a Line drawn due North from the Source of St Croix River to the Highlands along the said High lands which divide those Rivers that empty themselves into the River S^t: Lawrence from those which fall into the Atlantic Ocean, to the Northwestern most Head of Connecticut River; Thence down along the Middle of that River to the forty fifth Degree of North Latitude; From thence by a Line due West on said Latitude until it strikes the River Iroquois or Cataraquy; Thence along the middle of said River into Lake Ontario; through the Middle of said Lake until it strikes the Communication by Water between that Lake & Lake Erie; Thence along the middle of said Communication into Lake Erie; through the middle of said Lake, untill it arrives at the Water Communication between that Lake & Lake Huron; Thence along the middle of said Water Communication into the Lake Huron, thence through the middle of said Lake to the Water-Communication between that Lake and Lake Superior thence through Lake Superior Northward of the Isles Royal & Phelipeaux to the Long Lake; Thence through the Middle of said Long Lake, and the Water Communication between it and the Lake of the Woods, to the said Lake of the Woods, Thence through the said Lake to the most Northwestern Point thereof, & from thence on a due West Course to the River Mississippi, Thence by a Line to be drawn along the middle of the said River Mississippi until it shall intersect the Northernmost Part of the thirty first Degree of North Latitude. South, by a Line to be drawn due East from the Determination of the Line last mentioned, in the Latitude of thirty one Degrees North of the Equator to the Middle of the River Apalachicola or Catahouchi: Thence along the middle thereof to its Junction with the Flint River; Thence strait to the Head of St Mary's River, and thence down along the Middle of St Mary's River to the Atlantic Ocean. East by a Line to be drawn along the Middle of the River St Croix, from its Mouth in the Bay of Funday to its Source, and from its Source directly North to the aforesaid Highlands, which divide the Rivers that fall into the Atlantic Ocean from those which fall into the River S^t· Lawrence; comprehending all Islands within twenty Leagues of any Part of the Shores of the United States, & lying between Lines to be drawn due East from the Points where the aforesaid Boundaries between Nova Scotia one the one Part and East Florida on the other, shall respectively touch the Bay of Fundy and the Atlantic Ocean, excepting such Islands as now are or heretofore have been within the Limits of the said Province of Nova Scotia.

Article. 3$^{d:}$

It is agreed that the People of the United States shall continue to enjoy unmolested the Right to take Fish of every kind on the Grand Bank and on all the other Banks of Newfoundland, also in the Gulph of S^t· Lawrence and at all other Places in the Sea where the Inhabitants of both Countries used at any time heretofore to fish. And also that the Inhabitants of the United States shall have Liberty to take Fish of every kind on such Part of the Coast of Newfoundland as British Fishermen shall use, (but not to dry or cure the same on that Island) and also on the Coasts Bays & Creeks of all other of his Britannic Majestys Dominions in America, and that the American Fishermen shall have Liberty to dry & cure Fish in any of the unsettled Bays Harbours and Creeks of Nova-Scotia, Magdalen Islands, and Labrador, so long as the same shall remain unsettled, but so soon as the same or either of them shall be settled, it shall not be lawful for the s$^{d:}$ Fishermen to dry or cure Fish at such Settlement, without a previous Agreement for that purpose with the Inhabitants, Proprietors or Possessors of the Ground.

Article 4$^{th:}$

It is agreed that Creditors on either Side shall meet with no Lawful Impediment to the Recovery of the full Value in Sterling Money of all bona fide Debts heretofore contracted.

Article 5$^{th:}$

It is agreed that the Congress shall earnestly recommend it to the Legislatures of the respective States to provide for the Restitution of all Estates, Rights and Properties which have been confiscated belonging to real British Subjects; and also of the Estates Rights & Properties of Persons resident in Districts in the Possession of his Majesty's Arms, and who have not borne Arms against the said United States. And that Persons of any other Description shall have free Liberty to go to any Part or Parts of any of the thirteen United States and therein to remain twelve Months unmolested in their Endeavours to obtain the Restitution of such of their Estates, Rights, and Properties as may have been confiscated. And that Congress shall also earnestly recommend to the several States, a Reconsideration and Revision of all Acts or Laws regarding the Premises, so as to render the said Laws or Acts perfectly consistent not only with Justice and Equity but with that Spirit of Conciliation which on the Return of the Blessings of Peace should universally prevail. And that Congress shall also earnestly recommend to the several States, that the Estates Rights & Property's of such last mentioned Persons shall be restored to them, they refunding to any Persons who may be now in Possession the bona fide Price (where any has been given) which such Persons may have Paid on purchasing any of the said Lands, Rights or Properties, since the Confiscation.

And it is agreed that all Persons who have any Interest in confiscated Lands either by Debts, Marriage Settlements or otherwise, shall meet with no lawful Impediment in the Prosecution of their just Rights.

Article 6[th:]

That there shall be no future Confiscations made, nor any Prosecutions commenced against any Person or Persons for or by Reason of the Part which he or they may have taken in the present War and that no Person shall on that Account suffer any future Loss or Damage either in his Person Liberty or Property; and that those who may be in Confinement on such Charges at the Time of the Ratification of the Treaty in America shall be immediately set at Liberty, and the Prosecutions so commenc'd be discontinued.

Article 7[th:]

There shall be a firm & perpetual Peace between his Britannic Majesty and the said States & between the Subjects of the one, and the Citizens of the other, wherefore all Hostilities both by Sea & Land shall from hence forth cease: All Prisoners on both sides shall be set at Liberty, and his Britannic Majesty shall with all convenient Speed, and without causing any Destruction, or carrying away any Negroes or other Property of the American Inhabitants, withdraw all his Armies, Garrisons and Fleets from the said United States, and from every Port, Place and Harbour within the same; leaving in all Fortifications the American Artillery that may be therein. And shall also order & cause all Archives, Records, Deeds & Papers belonging to any of the said States or their Citizens, which in the Course of the War may have fallen into the Hands of his Officers, to be forthwith restored and deliver'd to the proper States & Persons to whom they belong.

Article 8th:

The Navigation of the River Mississippi, from its Source to the Ocean shall forever remain free and open to the Subjects of Great Britain and the Citizens of the United States.

Article 9th:

In Case it should so happen that any Place or Territory belonging to Great Britain or to the United States should have been conquer'd by the Arms of either from the other before the Arrival of the said Provisional Articles in America it is agreed that the same shall be restored without Difficulty and without requiring any Compensation.

Article 10th:

The Solemn Ratifications of the present Treaty expedited in good and due Form shall be exchanged between the contracting Parties in the Space of Six Months or sooner if possible to be computed from the Day of the Signature of the present Treaty. In witness whereof we the undersigned their Ministers Plenipotentiary have in their Name & in Virtue of our full Powers signed with our Hands the present Definitive Treaty, and caused the Seals of our Arms to be affixed thereto.—

Done at Paris, this third Day of September, In the Year of our Lord, one thousand seven hundred & Eighty three.

D Hartley

John Adams.
B Franklin
John Jay

Chronology

1735   Born October 30 (October 19, Old Style) in the North Precinct of Braintree, Massachusetts, the first child of John Adams, a farmer, deacon, and shoemaker, and Susanna Boylston Adams. (Father, born 1691, is a great-grandson of Henry Adams, who immigrated to Massachusetts from Somerset in 1638. Mother, born 1709 in Brookline, is a granddaughter of Thomas Boylston, who immigrated to Massachusetts from London in 1656. Parents married in October 1734.)

1738   Brother Peter Boylston born October 16.

1741–49   Brother Elihu born May 29, 1741. After learning to read at home, Adams attends schools kept in Braintree by Mrs. Belcher and by Joseph Cleverly. Later describes himself as an indifferent student who wished to be a farmer like his father, despite his father's intention that he attend Harvard and become a minister.

1750–51   Complaining of the dullness of Cleverly's teaching, Adams is sent to Joseph Marsh's school in Braintree, where he thrives and dedicates himself to studying Latin, in keeping with traditional preparation for college. Begins personal library with an edition of Cicero's orations.

1751   Enrolls in Harvard College. Listed fourteenth out of the twenty-five entering students in class placement based on "dignity of family." Tutored in Latin by the Rev. Joseph Mayhew and studies mathematics and natural philosophy, including astronomy and meteorology, with Professor John Winthrop.

1753   Begins diary on June 8, with detailed records of the weather among the earliest entries (will intermittently keep diary for the remainder of his life).

1755   Graduates with B.A., and begins to keep school in Worcester, Massachusetts, in order to support himself while deciding whether to "study Divinity, Law or Physick." Lodges at the town's expense (6 shillings a week), with Dr. Nathum Willard and avails himself of his medical library. Writes to his classmate and cousin Nathan Webb: "At Colledge gay, gorgeous, prospects, danc'd before my Eyes, and Hope, sanguine Hope, invigorated my Body, and exhilerated my soul. But now hope has left me, my organ's rust and my Faculty's decay." Decries the "Frigid performances" of local ministers, the disciples of "Frigid John Calvin." Reads Milton, Virgil, Voltaire, and Bolingbroke.

1756   Signs contract on August 21 to read law for two years with Worcester's only attorney, James Putnam, who charges a fee of $100, payable when Adams could "find it convenient." Moves in with Putnam and pursues his studies at night, while continuing to keep school by day.

1758   Attends Harvard commencement July 19 and, after arguing the affirmative side of the question, "An Imperium civile, Hominibus prorsus necessarium, sit" ("Whether civil authority is absolutely necessary for mankind"), receives M.A. Moves back home to Braintree in October despite having received an offer from two of Worcester's leading residents to help establish him as the town's second attorney and its registrar of deeds. Meets on October 25 with prominent Boston lawyer Jeremiah Gridley, who advises him to prepare for admission to the bar of Suffolk County, which at that time includes both Boston and Braintree. (Gridley also advises against early marriage, company keeping, and the study of Greek, "a mere curiosity.") Adams is admitted to the Suffolk bar on November 6, with Gridley serving as his sponsor, and begins practice in the county court of common pleas and before local justices of the peace. Appears for the plaintiff in *Field v. Lambert* seeking damages for trespass, but loses his first case when he submits an improperly worded writ.

1759   In the spring, becomes increasingly attracted to Hannah Quincy, daughter of Colonel Josiah Quincy, a justice of the peace and leading citizen in Braintree, and nearly proposes to her on one occasion when they are alone, before being interrupted by his friend Jonathan Sewall and Quincy's cousin Esther. During the summer visits the Weymouth home of the Rev. William Smith and Elizabeth Quincy Smith, where he meets Abigail Smith (born 1744) and her sisters, but does not come away with a positive first impression, finding them neither "fond, nor frank, nor candid."

1760   Drafts several essays on the appointment of the colony's new chief justice and the evils of licensed houses in his diary, though none of them are known to have been published.

1761   Records argument made by James Otis Jr. on February 24 in the Superior Court of Judicature on writs of assistance, the general search warrants issued to royal customs officials. (In 1817 Adams describes Otis as a "flame of fire" during his argument and asserts: "then and there the child Independence was born.") Father dies on May 25. Adams inherits Braintree property (including the house now known as the John Quincy Adams Birthplace) and, as a freeholder, gains a place in the Braintree town meeting. Admitted to practice in the Superior Court of Judicature, the highest trial and appellate court in Massachusetts.

1762   Begins serving on town committees and traveling circuit of county courts of common pleas. Admitted as barrister in the Superior Court of Judicature. In November his close friend Richard Cranch marries Mary Smith, older sister of Abigail, whom Adams now begins to court.

1763   Publishes first known newspaper contribution in the *Boston Evening Post* on March 3. Signed "Humphrey Ploughjogger," the piece satirizes the political dispute between supporters of the Otis family and the faction led by Governor Francis Bernard and Lieutenant Governor Thomas Hutchinson. Publishes several more "Humphrey Ploughjogger" letters in the *Evening Post* throughout the summer, and responds as "U" in the *Boston Gazette* to his friend Jonathan Sewall, who is writing as "J" in defense of the Bernard-Hutchinson faction. Leaves off regular diary-keeping.

1764   Amid a smallpox outbreak in Boston, Adams is successfully inoculated for the disease on April 13 under the care of Dr. Joseph Warren, who becomes a close friend. Marries Abigail Smith in Weymouth on October 25, then returns with her to the house he had inherited from his father in Braintree.

1765   Joins Sodalitas, a small group of barristers in Boston formed by Jeremiah Gridley to study and discuss the law.

(At the group's February 21 meeting, Adams propounds Rousseau's *Du contrat social* [1762]; he owns both an edition in French and the first English translation, *A Treatise on the Social Compact, or the Principles of Politic Law* [1764].) The Stamp Act, which imposes tax on the paper used in the colonies for newspapers, almanacs, pamphlets, broadsides, and legal and commercial documents, is passed by the House of Commons on February 27, receives royal assent March 22, and is scheduled to take effect on November 1. Adams is elected surveyor of highways in Braintree in March. Attends sessions of the Plymouth and Bristol courts of common pleas, April–May and July–August, and travels court circuit in Maine, July. Daughter Abigail ("Nabby") born July 14. Adams publishes "A Dissertation on the Canon and the Feudal Law" in four installments in the *Boston Gazette*, August 12–October 21 (later reprinted in the *London Chronicle* and published in book form in London in 1768). Protests against the Stamp Act occur throughout the colonies during the summer. In Boston, mobs loot the homes of Andrew Oliver, a prominent merchant who had been appointed stamp distributor for Massachusetts, on August 14, and of Lieutenant Governor Thomas Hutchinson (Oliver's brother-in-law) on August 26. (Active opponents of the Stamp Act in Boston will adopt the name "Sons of Liberty" by the end of the year; among their leaders is Samuel Adams, a second cousin of John Adams.) Adams's instructions for the Braintree representatives to the Massachusetts General Court (legislature) denouncing the Stamp Act are adopted by the town meeting on September 24; the Braintree instructions are printed in the *Massachusetts Gazette* on October 10 and adopted by some forty other towns in the colony. Refusal of lawyers to use stamped legal paper results in closing of Massachusetts courts. On behalf of the Boston town meeting, Adams, Jeremiah Gridley, and James Otis Jr. appear before Governor Bernard on December 20 and argue unsuccessfully for the reopening of the courts. Renews regular diary-keeping on December 18, observing that "the Year 1765 has been the most remarkable Year of my Life."

1766   Publishes three letters signed "Clarendon" in the *Boston Gazette*, January 13, 20, and 27, defending the rights of the American colonists under the English constitution.

House of Commons repeals the Stamp Act on February 24. Adams is elected as a selectman in Braintree on March 3. Seeks to improve the practice of the law through his active involvement in the Suffolk County bar association.

1767 Publishes five pseudonymous essays in the *Boston Gazette*, January 5–February 16, in response to series of "Philanthrop" essays written by Jonathan Sewall in defense of Governor Bernard. Son John Quincy born March 4. Chancellor of the Exchequer Charles Townshend proposes imposing duties on lead, glass, paper, tea, and other goods imported into America. Passed by the House of Commons on July 2, the Townshend Acts renew tensions in the colonies; to enforce the acts, Parliament establishes board of custom commissioners headquartered in Boston. Jeremiah Gridley, recently appointed Massachusetts Attorney General, dies on September 10 after having referred many of his clients to Adams, whose law practice flourishes.

1768 Massachusetts House of Representatives (lower chamber of the General Court) adopts petition, written by Samuel Adams, protesting the Townshend Acts. After the protest is circulated to other colonial assemblies, Governor Bernard dissolves the General Court, prompting further popular unrest. Adams declines re-election as Braintree selectman and moves family in April to a rented house in Boston. Writing as "Sui Juris," publishes letter in the *Boston Gazette* on May 23 decrying the creation of an Anglican episcopacy in America. Writes instructions, dated June 17, for the Boston representatives to the General Court protesting the seizure of John Hancock's sloop *Liberty*, and later defends Hancock in admiralty court against smuggling charges (the charges are eventually dropped). Jonathan Sewall, now attorney general of Massachusetts, offers Adams the position of advocate general in the admiralty court; Adams declines, citing his "political Principles" and "Connections and Friendships." The first of five British regiments lands at Boston on October 1 after regular troops are requested by the increasingly harassed customs commissioners. Daughter Susanna born December 28.

1769 Writes instructions, dated May 8, for the Boston representatives to the General Court, protesting the presence of

British troops and the growing power of the admiralty court. Hires Jonathan Williams Austin and William Tudor as clerks to help with his expanding Boston legal practice. After James Otis Jr. is assaulted in a coffee house in September, Adams is engaged as co-counsel in civil case brought by Otis against his assailant, customs commissioner John Robinson.

1770   Begins serving as clerk of the Suffolk bar association on January 3. Daughter Susanna dies on February 4. British soldiers under the command of Captain Thomas Preston open fire on an angry, taunting crowd on March 5, killing five Boston residents. Preston and eight soldiers are indicted for murder, March 13. Parliament repeals most of the Townshend duties in April, retaining only the duty on tea. Adams agrees to lead the defense of Preston and the soldiers charged in the "Boston Massacre." Son Charles born May 29. Elected as a representative to the General Court from Boston on June 7 (serves until April 1771). Defends Captain Preston at trial, October 24–30, by disputing testimony that he had ordered his men to open fire; Preston is acquitted. Argues at the trial of the eight soldiers, November 27–December 5, that the accused had either not fired or had acted in self-defense. The jury convicts two of the defendants of manslaughter and acquits the remaining six (as first-time offenders, each of the convicted men is branded on his hand with a letter "M").

1771   Falls ill in February, suffering from "great anxiety and distress." Moves family back to Braintree in April. Takes mineral springs at Stafford, Connecticut, in late spring in an effort to restore his health. Helps try Otis-Robinson assault case; jury awards his client £2,000 in damages (Otis eventually settles for an apology from Robinson and £112 in costs.) Receives letter, dated July 19, from the English Whig historian Catherine Macaulay praising his essays on the canon and feudal law.

1772   At request of the Braintree town meeting, delivers election-day oration on May 18 on "the civil & religious rights & Priviledges of the People." Moves family back to Boston and maintains a law office there until the outbreak of hostilities. Son Thomas Boylston born September 15.

1773   Publishes articles under his own name in the *Boston Gazette*, January 11–February 22, opposing crown salaries for Superior Court judges, which he believes will compromise judicial independence in the colony and is contrary to the English constitution. Assists the House of Representatives in preparing its replies (January 26 and March 6) to addresses (January 6 and February 16) by Governor Thomas Hutchinson asserting parliamentary supremacy over the colonies. Parliament passes Tea Act on May 10, giving the East India Company a monopoly over the colonial tea trade. On the first day of the new General Court, May 26, Adams is elected by the House of Representatives to the Governor's Council (the upper chamber of the General Court), but his appointment is vetoed by Governor Hutchinson. On June 2 Samuel Adams reads to the House from letters sent by Hutchinson and Andrew Oliver (now lieutenant governor) to a British treasury official in 1767–69; in one letter, Hutchinson wrote that "Abridgement of what are called English Liberties" would be necessary to maintain order in the colony. (The letters were clandestinely obtained in England by Benjamin Franklin, at the time the colonial agent for Pennsylvania, Georgia, New Jersey, and Massachusetts.) Political tensions in the province increase when the House of Representatives adopts resolution charging Hutchinson and Oliver with seeking to subvert the 1691 Massachusetts Charter, petitions the crown for their removal, and makes the letters public. First of three ships carrying East India Company tea arrives in Boston on November 28. Duty is payable upon off-loading, which must by law be accomplished within twenty days of docking, but which Boston mobs prevent. Abigail Adams writes to her friend Mercy Otis Warren, December 5: "The Tea that bainfull weed is arrived. Great and I hope Effectual opposition has been made to the landing of it. . . . The proceedings of our Citizens have been United, Spirited and firm. The Flame is kindled and like Lightening it catches from Soul to Soul." Governor Hutchinson refuses entreaties to allow the ships to depart with their cargo, as happens at several other colonial ports. As the deadline approaches, on December 16, a large crowd boards the ships and dumps 342 chests of tea, worth an estimated £10,000, into the harbor.

1774   In February Adams purchases his father's homestead (now known as the John Adams Birthplace) from his brother Peter and moves his family to Braintree. Helps prepare articles of impeachment against Chief Justice Peter Oliver (brother of Lieutenant Governor Andrew Oliver, who dies March 3) for accepting a crown salary; the articles are adopted by the House before proceedings are stopped by Governor Hutchinson. Drafts report for General Court on Massachusetts's boundary disputes with New Hampshire and New York. Parliament responds to the Boston Tea Party by passing four Coercive Acts. The Boston Port Bill, which receives royal assent on March 31, closes port until the East India Company is compensated for the tea and order is restored. Massachusetts Government Act, signed May 20, abrogates the 1691 royal charter by removing the power to appoint the Governor's Council from the House of Representatives, limits town meetings to one annual session for elections, and gives the governor power to appoint all provincial judges and sheriffs. Administration of Justice Act, signed May 20, allows trials of persons accused of committing capital crimes while enforcing the law or collecting revenue to be removed to Nova Scotia or Britain. Quartering Act, signed June 2, allows the housing of soldiers in occupied dwellings throughout the colonies. General Thomas Gage, commander of the British army in North America, arrives in Boston and replaces Hutchinson as royal governor. Adams is again elected by the House to the Governor's Council, but his appointment is vetoed by Gage on May 25. (Hutchinson sails for London, and what will be permanent exile, on June 1, the day the Boston Port Act goes into effect.) On June 7, Gage moves the legislature to Salem, hoping to reduce the influence of Boston radicals; the House of Representatives adopts measure on June 20 calling for a "Meeting of Committees from the several Colonies on this Continent," and elects as delegates Adams, Samuel Adams, Robert Treat Paine, Thomas Cushing, and James Bowdoin (who does not attend). Gage dissolves the General Court on June 25. During July Adams attends circuit courts in Maine for the last time. Leaves for Philadelphia on August 10 and travels by way of New York. Widespread mob action and disobedience in Massachusetts prevents Gage from enforcing laws outside of Boston, and on September 5 he begins to fortify the town. Congress (later known as the First Continental Congress) opens in Philadelphia on September 5, attended by delegates from every colony except Georgia; it adopts rule giving each colony a single vote and makes its proceedings secret. Adams signs Declarations and Resolves, adopted on October 14, denouncing the Coercive Acts and enumerating colonial rights. Congress calls for a boycott of British imports after December 1 and for the election of delegates to a second Congress in May 1775. Adams leaves Philadelphia when Congress adjourns on October 28 and returns to Braintree in early November. Attends the first Massachusetts Provincial Congress, held in Cambridge December 5–10, as a member from Braintree. Elected as a delegate to Second Continental Congress along with Samuel Adams, Robert Treat Paine, Thomas Cushing, and John Hancock. First of seventeen "Massachusettensis" essays defending parliamentary rule appears in the *Massachusetts Gazette* on December 12 (series ends on April 3, 1775).

1775   Adams publishes twelve essays signed "Novanglus" in the *Boston Gazette*, January 23–April 17, written in response to "Massachusettensis." (Adams believes "Massachusettensis" is Jonathan Sewall, but will learn late in his life that the essays were written by Daniel Leonard, a former supporter of the colonial cause who had become disaffected by the lawlessness of the Tea Party.) Parliament declares Massachusetts to be in a state of rebellion on February 9. Adams is elected a selectman of Braintree on March 6. Attempt by Gage on April 19 to destroy military supplies stored at Concord leads to fighting at Lexington, Concord, and along the road to Boston in which seventy-three British soldiers and forty-nine Americans are killed. Massachusetts militia begin siege of Boston, and on April 23 the Provincial Congress votes to raise an army of 13,600 men. Adams travels to Philadelphia, where Second Continental Congress meets on May 10. Congress votes on June 14 to form a Continental army. Adams nominates George Washington, a Virginia delegate and colonel in the Virginia militia, to be its commander in chief, and Washington is appointed by a unanimous vote on June 15. Abigail and John Quincy watch Battle of Bunker Hill from Penn's Hill in Braintree, June 17; Adams's friend Dr. Joseph Warren is killed in the fighting while serving with the Massachusetts militia. Adams signs conciliatory Olive Branch Petition to George III, adopted by Congress July 5.

Writes letter to his friend James Warren, a member of the
Massachusetts Provincial Congress, on July 24 expressing
frustration with John Dickinson of Pennsylvania, the leading advocate in Congress of reconciliation with Britain
(letter is intercepted by the British and published in the
Massachusetts Gazette on August 17). Serves on nine committees during session, which adjourns August 1. Travels
to Watertown, Massachusetts, where he begins serving on
the Provincial Council, which functions as both the upper
chamber of the Provincial Congress and as the provincial
executive (will continue as member of the Council until
April 1776). Brother Elihu dies of dysentery on August 11
while serving as an officer in the Massachusetts militia.
Jonathan Sewall sails with his family from Boston for England. George III proclaims colonies in rebellion on August 23. Adams returns to Philadelphia for new session of
Congress, which meets on September 12. Serves on thirteen committees and plays a principal role in establishing
an American navy. Appointed Chief Justice of Massachusetts on October 28, but never serves (resigns in February
1777). Congress adjourns December 9. Adams travels to
Braintree and then to Watertown, where he resumes his
service on the Provincial Council.

1776   *Common Sense*, pamphlet by Thomas Paine denouncing
monarchical rule and advocating an independent American republic, is published anonymously in Philadelphia on
January 10, and sells tens of thousands of copies throughout the colonies. Adams, who is presumed by some to be
the pamphlet's author, praises its "Strength and Brevity,"
but expresses misgivings about its "feeble" understanding
of constitutional government. Returns to Philadelphia on
February 8 for the new session of Congress, during which
he will serve on more than thirty committees. British garrison evacuates Boston on March 17 and sails to Nova
Scotia. Abigail writes to her husband on March 31, asking
him to "Remember the Ladies" in "the new Code of Laws
which I suppose it will be necessary for you to make."
Adams writes essay "Thoughts on Government" in March
and April; circulated first in letters and then as a published
pamphlet, it is widely consulted in the making of new
state constitutions. Introduces resolution, adopted by Congress on May 10, recommending that each of the "United
Colonies" form a government, and drafts preamble,

adopted May 15, calling for royal authority in the colonies
to be "totally suppressed." Supports resolution introduced
on June 7 by Richard Henry Lee of Virginia declaring
that "these United Colonies are, and of right ought to
be, free and independent States." Resolution is referred
on June 11 to committee composed of Adams, Benjamin
Franklin (Pennsylvania), Robert R. Livingston (New
York), Thomas Jefferson (Virginia), and Roger Sherman
(Connecticut). Jefferson begins drafting declaration of independence. Adams becomes president of the Board of
War and Ordnance, created by Congress on June 12 and
responsible for raising troops and supplies for the Continental Army. John Dickinson and Adams debate independence resolution on July 1 (Jefferson later describes Adams
as "our Colossus on the floor"). Congress votes 12–0 in
favor of independence on July 2, with New York abstain-
ing. Declaration of Independence is adopted on July 4.
Adams participates in debates in August over proposed
Articles of Confederation, drafts model treaty with foreign
powers, and drafts instructions for Benjamin Franklin and
Silas Deane, the first American commissioners to France
(they will later be joined by Arthur Lee). Continental
Army suffers major defeat at the Battle of Long Island,
August 27. Congress sends Adams, Franklin, and Edward
Rutledge to meet with Admiral Lord Richard Howe, the
British naval commander in North America, and deter-
mine whether Howe is authorized to negotiate peace.
Howe refuses to recognize Congress or American inde-
pendence during conference held on Staten Island on
September 11, and Congress does not attempt further ne-
gotiations. Adams obtains leave of absence from Congress
in October and returns to Braintree in early November.

1777   Leaves Braintree in early January and arrives on February 1
            in Baltimore, where Congress had relocated in December
            1776. Resumes presidency of the Board of War while serv-
            ing on twenty-six committees. Congress returns to
            Philadelphia in March. Adams begins correspondence in
            May with Thomas Jefferson, who has returned to Virginia.
            Daughter Elizabeth is stillborn on July 11. Congress leaves
            Philadelphia and reconvenes in York, Pennsylvania, as
            British army under General William Howe, brother of
            Admiral Howe, occupies the city on September 26. After
            a series of defeats, General John Burgoyne surrenders

army of 5,000 men to Americans at Saratoga, New York, on October 17, a victory that bolsters American efforts to secure French aid. Adams obtains leave from Congress on November 7 and returns to Braintree on November 27, intending to resume his law practice. Learns that he has been chosen by Congress to replace Silas Deane and serve as commissioner to France along with Franklin and Arthur Lee. "After much Agitation of mind and a thousand reveries," Adams writes to Henry Laurens, the president of Congress, on December 23 and accepts the commission.

1778   France and the United States sign treaties of alliance and commerce in Paris on February 6; under their terms, France recognizes the independence of the United States and pledges to fight until American independence is won if the treaties lead to war between Britain and France. Adams sails for France with John Quincy on February 15 onboard the American frigate *Boston* and lands in Bordeaux on April 1, after an eventful passage that includes a March 10 encounter with a hostile privateer. Joins Franklin's household in Passy, a suburb of Paris, on April 9, and has his first audience with Louis XVI at Versailles on May 8. War begins between Britain and France on June 14. Congress abolishes three-member diplomatic commission and appoints Franklin as sole minister plenipotentiary to France on September 14.

1779   Adams becomes increasingly concerned with the impact of the bitter controversy involving his predecessor in France, Silas Deane, who had charged fellow commissioner Arthur Lee with disloyalty after Lee had accused him of profiting from French arms shipments to the United States. Sympathetic to Lee, Adams drafts a letter on February 10 and 11 to French foreign minister the Comte de Vergennes, addressing the Deane affair and seeking a private interview without Franklin, who supports Deane. Receives from the Marquis de Lafayette official notice from Congress on February 12 of the revocation of his commission and of Franklin's appointment as sole minister to France, and therefore withholds letter to Vergennes. The notification from Congress neither recalls him nor offers new instructions, simply stating that "In the mean Time we hope you will exercise your whole extensive Abilities on the Subject of our Finances."

Adams writes to Abigail on February 20 of his intention to return home and retire from politics: "I will draw Writs and Deeds, and harangue Jurys and be happy." Leaves Passy with John Quincy on March 8 and travels to Nantes and Lorient. While waiting for passage to the United States, spends time with John Paul Jones and becomes increasingly resentful and suspicious of Franklin. Sails with John Quincy from Lorient on June 17 onboard the French frigate *La Sensible* and arrives in Boston on August 3. Elected as Braintree delegate to the state constitutional convention, August 9. Attends convention in Cambridge in early September, and is appointed to prepare a draft constitution. Congress appoints Adams minister plenipotentiary to negotiate treaties of peace and commerce with Great Britain, September 27. Adams submits his *Report of a Constitution* to the state convention on November 1. (The convention approves his draft with some amendments and after ratification by the voters, the Massachusetts constitution goes into effect on October 25, 1780; it remains today the oldest functioning written constitution in the world.) Adams sails for France on November 15 on *La Sensible* with sons John Quincy and Charles and legation secretary Francis Dana. A series of leaks forces the ship to land on December 8 at El Ferrol, on the northwest coast of Spain. Adams begins overland trip to Paris with his sons and Dana.

1780   Arrives in Paris on February 8. Encounters resistance to his mission from Vergennes, who seeks to control any future peace negotiations. Sends detailed reports to Congress on European affairs and publishes anonymous articles in the weekly *Mercure de France*. Writes to Abigail on May 12: "I must study Politicks and War that my sons may have liberty to study Mathematicks and Philosophy. My sons ought to study Mathematicks and Philosophy, Geography, natural History, Naval Architecture, navigation, Commerce and Agriculture, in order to give their Children a right to study Painting, Poetry, Musick, Architecture, Statuary, Tapestry and Porcelaine." Prepares *Translation of the Memorial to the Sovereigns of Europe*, a condensed and rewritten version of pamphlet by Thomas Pownall, a former royal governor of Massachusetts, on Anglo-American commercial relations; Adams's version is published in French in November 1780 and in English in

January 1781. Writes twelve "Letters from a Distinguished American" in response to essays by the American Loyalist Joseph Galloway (letters are published in London, August–October 1782.) Adams resolves to go to Amsterdam "to try," as Franklin will later report to Congress, "whether something might not be done to render us less dependent on France." Leaves Paris on July 27 and arrives in Amsterdam with John Quincy and Charles on August 10. At the request of Vergennes, Franklin forwards to Congress letters Adams had written to Vergennes criticizing French policy, covering them with a letter, dated August 9, in which he asserts that Adams "has given extreme offense to the court here." Adams learns on September 16 that Congress has commissioned him to raise a loan in the Netherlands. Writes twenty-six letters in response to queries from Hendrik Calkoen, an influential Amsterdam lawyer sympathetic to the American cause (the letters are published in London in 1786 and in the United States in 1789). Seeking to cut off Dutch trade with the United States, Britain declares war on the Netherlands on December 20. Congress appoints Adams to negotiate a treaty of amity and commerce with the Netherlands, December 29.

1781   Arranges for John Quincy, age thirteen, and Charles, ten, to attend lectures at the University of Leyden in addition to their tutorial lessons. Without waiting to be formally received as an envoy, Adams drafts and submits memorial to the States General urging Dutch recognition of American independence and arranges for its publication in Dutch, French, and English. Congress appoints Franklin, Jefferson, John Jay, and Henry Laurens as additional peace negotiators on June 15 and instructs the negotiators to take no action without the "knowledge and concurrence" of the French. (Jefferson declines appointment, while Laurens, having been captured at sea in September 1780, is imprisoned in the Tower of London until December 1781.) Adams visits Paris in July to discuss with Vergennes proposals for Austro-Russian mediation of the American war, and advises against American participation unless all parties recognize the independence of the United States. John Quincy travels to St. Petersburg with Francis Dana, the American minister to Russia (though Catherine the Great withholds official recognition), where he will serve as Dana's secretary and French interpreter from August 1781 to October 1782. Charles leaves the Netherlands for the United States on August 12. Adams is seriously ill with a fever, possibly malarial, in Amsterdam from August to October. General Charles Cornwallis surrenders his army of 7,000 men to Washington at Yorktown, Virginia, on October 19.

1782   Defeat at Yorktown results in the resignation on March 20 of prime minister Lord North and the formation of a new ministry under Lord Rockingham that opens peace negotiations with Franklin in Paris on April 12. States General of the Netherlands recognizes American independence on April 19, and on April 22 Adams presents his diplomatic credentials to Stadholder William V of the Netherlands. Establishes residence at the Hôtel des Etats-Unis at The Hague, the first American legation building in Europe. Contracts with a syndicate of Amsterdam bankers for a loan to the United States of five million guilders on June 11. Signs treaty of amity and commerce with the Netherlands, October 8. Arrives in Paris on October 26 to join Franklin and Jay in negotiations with the British, and agrees with their decision to proceed without consulting the French. Takes leading role in securing recognition of American fishing rights off Canada in preliminary peace treaty, signed on November 30 by Richard Oswald and by Adams, Franklin, Jay, and Henry Laurens.

1783   Attends signing of preliminary Anglo-French and Anglo-Spanish peace treaties at Versailles on January 20. Helps negotiate final peace treaty, resisting British attempts to significantly modify the terms of the preliminary agreement. Travels to the Hague, July–August, and returns with John Quincy. Signs Definitive Treaty of Peace with Franklin, Jay, and British negotiator David Hartley in Paris on September 3. Falls ill with fever, September–October, and recovers in Auteuil outside of Paris. Travels to England in October with John Quincy and spends two months in London before going to Bath in late December.

1784   Learns that American bills of exchange are in danger of default in the Dutch financial markets. Crosses the North Sea with John Quincy during a three-day storm and lands in Zeeland, then travels by foot, iceboat, and farm cart to The Hague, arriving on January 12. Negotiates new loan of two million guilders, March 9, that preserves American credit. Appointed by Congress to serve with Franklin and Jefferson as commissioner to negotiate treaties of amity and commerce with twenty-three European and North African states. Abigail and Nabby sail from Boston, June 20, and arrive in London, July 21, where they are joined by John Quincy on July 30. (Charles and Thomas remain in Massachusetts with Abigail's sister Elizabeth and her husband, the Reverend John Shaw.) Adams returns from the Netherlands on August 7, and the reunited family travels to Paris and settles in Auteuil. Forms closer friendship with Jefferson, who had arrived in Paris with his daughter Martha in early August.

1785   Appointed by Congress on February 24 as the first American minister to Great Britain (continues to serve as minister to the Netherlands and as treaty commissioner). John Quincy leaves France to return to the United States, May 12. Jefferson succeeds Franklin as U.S. minister to France. Adams, Abigail, and Nabby arrive in London, May 26, and Adams has audience with George III, June 1, during which he expresses his desire to restore "the good old nature and the good old humor between people who, though separated by an ocean and under different governments, have the same language, a similar religion, and kindred blood." Latter writes that he "felt more than I did or could express," and describes George III as having listened "with dignity but with apparent emotion." Abigail and Nabby are presented to the King and Queen Charlotte on June 23. Family moves into house on Grosvenor Square that becomes the first American legation in London. Adams signs treaty of amity and commerce with Prussia in London on August 5. Has cordial meeting with Jonathan Sewall, who is living in exile in London. Becomes frustrated by the unwillingness of the British to enter into negotiations for a commercial treaty.

1786   Jefferson arrives in London on March 11 and joins Adams in negotiations with Tripoli; attempt to conclude treaty protecting American shipping from piracy fails because of the inability of the United States to pay the tribute demanded by the sultan's envoy. John Quincy admitted to Harvard College as a junior. Adams and Jefferson make progress in negotiating a commercial treaty with Portugal (agreement is finally concluded in 1791) and spend six days touring English country gardens before Jefferson returns to Paris on April 26. Nabby marries Colonel William Stephens Smith, secretary of the American legation and a former Continental Army officer, on June 12. Visits Braintree in Essex with his family in August, then travels to the Netherlands with Abigail to exchange ratifications of the treaty with Prussia. Witnesses political success of the Dutch Patriot party. Returns to London in September and begins writing treatise on ancient and modern governments.

1787   Somewhat hurriedly (he will later concede), Adams completes a partial manuscript of his historical analysis and publishes it in London in January as the first volume of *A Defence of the Constitutions of Government of the United States of America*. Signs treaty of peace and friendship with Morocco, January 25, that includes payment of tribute as protection against piracy. Grandson William Steuben Smith born in London on April 2. John Quincy graduates from Harvard College. Adams travels to the Netherlands, May–June, and negotiates a third Dutch loan to the United States. Returns to London, where Jefferson's daughter Mary (Polly), and his slave, Sally Hemings, age fourteen, stay with the Adamses, June–July, en route to live with Jefferson in Paris. Adams arranges for the purchase of the Vassall-Borland house in Braintree, Massachusetts, which he will call "Peacefield" and which will later be known as the "Old House," in preparation for his return from Europe. Publishes second volume of *A Defence of the Constitutions of Government of the United States of America* in September. Constitutional Convention ends in Philadelphia on September 17. In October Congress approves Adams's request that he be recalled from his diplomatic missions. Completes third and final volume of *A Defence of the Constitutions of Government of the United States of America* (published in early 1788).

1788   Has farewell audience with George III on February 20. Makes final visit to the Netherlands, where he arranges for a fourth Dutch loan. Sails from Portsmouth with Abigail in late April and arrives in Boston on June 17. After eleven of the thirteen states ratify the Constitution, Congress passes election ordinance on September 13 setting dates for choosing presidential electors and electing a president and vice president. Grandson John Adams

Smith born in New York in early November. Adams is elected to the House of Representatives in the First Federal Congress, but never serves.

1789   Presidential electors meet in their states on February 4 and vote for two candidates in balloting for president. George Washington receives the votes of all sixty-nine electors and is elected president, while Adams receives thrity-four votes and is elected vice president (John Jay receives nine votes, and twenty-six votes are divided among nine other candidates). Travels to New York City, the federal capital, and presides over the Senate for the first time on April 21. Attends Washington's inaugural at Federal Hall on April 30. Takes active role in prolonged Senate debate over the proper title for the president and unsuccessfully advocates variations on "His Highness." Refuses request from Mercy Otis Warren to help her husband James obtain a federal appointment. Abigail arrives in New York on June 24 and moves with Adams to Richmond Hill, a country estate overlooking the Hudson River in lower Manhattan (the house was located near present-day Varick and Charlton Streets). Charles graduates from Harvard College and begins studying law in the New York offices of Alexander Hamilton (later moves to the office of John Laurance). Adams casts first tie-breaking vote in the Senate on July 18, determining that the president does not need the consent of the Senate to remove executive officers who had been confirmed by the Senate. (During his two terms as vice president Adams will cast at least twenty-nine tie-breaking votes.) First session of the First Federal Congress adjourns on September 29.

1790   Presides over the second session of the Senate, January–August; takes less active role in debates while continuing to rule on questions of procedure. Jefferson arrives in New York in March to take up his duties as secretary of state. Adams begins publishing "Discourses on Davila," series of thirty-two essays criticizing unbalanced democracy and the French Revolution that appear in the *Gazette of the United States*, April 28, 1790–April 27, 1791 (although the essays are attributed to "an American Citizen," their authorship is widely known). Son Thomas Boylston graduates from Harvard College. Grandson Thomas Hollis Smith born August 7 in New York. Moves with Abigail to Philadelphia, where the federal capital has been relocated until 1800, and take up residence at Bush Hill, an estate west of the city. Presides over third session of the Senate, December 1790–March 1791.

1791   Elected president of the American Academy of Arts and Sciences in May (serves until 1813). An American edition of Thomas Paine's *Rights of Man* is published in May with an endorsement by Jefferson alluding to "the political heresies which have sprung up among us," a remark widely understood to be a reference to "Discourses of Davila." John Quincy responds by criticizing Paine and Jefferson in series of "Publicola" essays in the Boston *Columbian Centinel,* while other newspapers accuse Adams of supporting monarchy and aristocracy. Grandson Thomas Hollis Smith dies July 8. Jefferson writes to Adams on July 17 and explains that his private note to the printer's brother had been published without his permission. Adams replies on July 29, accepting Jefferson's explanation while denying that he favors "the Introduction of hereditary Monarchy and Aristocracy into this Country." Presides over the Senate during the first session of the Second Congress, October 1791–May 1792. Moves with Abigail from Bush Hill to a smaller house at Fourth and Arch Streets in Philadelphia.

1792   North Precinct of Braintree is incorporated as the town of Quincy in February. Returns to Philadelphia in the fall while Abigail remains in Quincy for health reasons (she will stay in Massachusetts for the remainder of Adams's vice presidency). Presides over the second session of the Senate, November 1792–March 1793. In the electoral balloting on December 5, Washington is reelected with the votes of all 132 electors, and Adams is reelected as vice president with seventy-seven votes, while George Clinton receives fifty electoral votes, Jefferson four, and Aaron Burr one.

1793   Supports Washington's decision to issue proclamation of neutrality, April 22, in the war between the revolutionary French republic and Great Britain. Controversy over relations with France contribute to the emergence of two political parties, with supporters of Jefferson and James Madison, who are sympathetic to France and oppose the financial policies of Secretary of the Treasury Alexander

Hamilton, calling themselves Republicans, and supporters of Hamilton, who favor closer relations with Britain, calling themselves Federalists. Adams presides over the Senate during first session of Third Congress, December 1793–June 1794. Son Thomas Boylston is admitted to the Philadelphia bar. Jefferson resigns as secretary of state, effective December 31.

1794   Washington appoints John Quincy minister resident to the Netherlands, May 30. John Quincy sails for Europe in September with Thomas Boylston as his secretary. Adams presides over the Senate during second session of Third Congress, November 1794–March 1795. John Jay signs treaty in London on November 19 that provides for evacuation of British garrisons from frontier posts in the Northwest (an unfulfilled provision of the 1783 peace treaty) and the establishment of a commission to resolve British claims against American debtors, but which contains few British concessions regarding Anglo-American commerce or neutral maritime rights.

1795   Granddaughter Caroline Amelia Smith born in New York in late January. Adams presides over a special session of the Senate called on June 8 to consider Jay's Treaty. Senate votes 20–10 on June 24 to ratify the treaty after a secret debate. Published on July 1, the treaty is widely attacked for failing to secure American rights, and the controversy further divides Republicans and Federalists. Charles marries Sarah Smith, sister of William Stephens Smith, in New York on August 29. Adams presides over the Senate during the first session of the Fourth Congress, December 1795–May 1796.

1796   Granddaughter Susanna Boylston Adams, first child of Charles and Sarah, born August 8 in New York. Washington makes public his decision not to seek a third term when his farewell address is published on September 19. In the presidential election, Federalists support Adams while Republicans support Jefferson; neither candidate makes any public statements. Adams is embittered by the support for Jefferson given by former friends, including James and Mercy Otis Warren, Benjamin Rush, and Samuel Adams. Returns to Philadelphia for the second session of the Fourth Congress, which begins on December 5. Presidential electors meet on December 7 (the 138 electors are chosen by the voters in seven states, by the legislature in seven states, by the voters and the legislature in one state, and by county delegates appointed by the legislature in one state). Adams receives seventy-one electoral votes and is elected president, Jefferson receives sixty-eight votes and becomes vice president, while Federalist Thomas Pinckney receives fifty-nine votes, Republican Aaron Burr thirty, and forty electoral votes are divided among nine other candidates.

1797   Inaugurated as president on March 4. Retains Washington's cabinet, consisting of Secretary of State Timothy Pickering, Secretary of the Treasury Oliver Wolcott Jr., Secretary of War James McHenry, and Attorney General Charles Lee. Learns that the French Directory has ordered Charles Cotesworth Pinckney, who had been appointed minister to France by Washington in 1796, to leave the country, and that the French navy has increased its seizures of American ships trading with Britain. Moves into the President's House at Sixth and Market Streets. Mother Susanna Boylston Adams dies in Quincy on April 17. Joined in Philadelphia by Abigail on May 10. Addresses special session of Congress on May 16, calling for the strengthening of the navy while announcing that a new diplomatic mission will be sent to France. Nominates Charles Cotesworth Pinckney, John Marshall, and Elbridge Gerry to serve as commissioners to France. Appoints John Quincy minister plenipotentiary to Prussia. Adams and Abigail leave Philadelphia for Quincy on July 19. John Quincy marries Louisa Catherine Johnson in London, July 26. American envoys to France have a brief informal meeting with Talleyrand, the French foreign minister, on October 8, and are then approached by three of Talleyrand's agents, who solicit $240,000 bribe as precondition for further negotiations; the agents also demand that the Americans agree to loan France $12 million and repudiate critical remarks about French policy made by Adams in his address to Congress on May 16. The American commissioners refuse to pay, and describe their reception in dispatches sent to Pickering on October 22 and November 8. Adams delivers his first annual message to Congress on November 22.

1798   Pickering receives coded dispatches from the envoys on March 4, along with an uncoded letter reporting that the

Directory has closed French ports to neutral shipping and made all ships carrying British products subject to capture. After the dispatches are decoded, Adams consults with his cabinet, which divides over whether to seek a declaration of war. Adams sends message to Congress on March 19 announcing failure of the peace mission and requesting the adoption of defensive measures. In response to request from the House of Representatives, Adams submits the dispatches to Congress on April 3, and they are quickly published, with Talleyrand's agents referred to as X, Y, and Z. Revelation of the "XYZ" affair causes popular furor against France. Congress establishes Department of the Navy on May 3, and Adams appoints Benjamin Stoddert as secretary of the navy on May 21. Appoints George Washington as commander of an expanded army on July 2 and, at Washington's request, names Alexander Hamilton as inspector general. Congress passes direct property tax on July 2 and adopts measure on July 9 authorizing the navy and armed merchant vessels to capture armed French ships. Adams signs into law the Alien and Sedition Acts, which extend the period required for naturalization from five to fourteen years; give the president the power to expel or, in time of declared war, to imprison dangerous aliens (no one is expelled under the law, though many French nationals leave voluntarily); and make the publication of "false, scandalous, and malicious writing" attacking the federal government, the president, or the Congress a crime punishable by up to two years in prison. (Ten Republican editors and printers are convicted under the Sedition Act during the Adams administration.) Adams and Abigail leave Philadelphia for Quincy on July 25. *A Selection of the Patriotic Addresses to the President of the United States, together with The President's Answers*, a volume collecting Adams's responses to numerous resolutions and memorials submitted in support of the administration, is published in Boston. Granddaughter Abigail Louisa Smith Adams, second child of Charles and Sarah, born September 8. Adams reluctantly appoints Hamilton as second in command of the army on October 15. Jefferson and Madison secretly draft resolutions attacking the Alien and Sedition Acts as unconstitutional and calling upon the states to resist them. (The Kentucky legislature adopts the Jefferson resolutions in modified form on November 10, and the Virginia legislature adopts the Madison resolutions on December 24). Adams departs for Philadelphia on November 12, while Abigail remains in Quincy. Limited naval war with France begins in the Caribbean. Adams delivers his second annual message to Congress December 8, in which he suggests the possibility of appointing a new peace mission to France. Appoints Bushrod Washington, nephew of George Washington, to the Supreme Court.

1799   Nominates William Vans Murray as special envoy to France on February 18 and declares that Murray will be sent only after Talleyrand gives assurances that he will be properly received; Adams later names Chief Justice Oliver Ellsworth and William Davie as additional negotiators. Peace overture splits Federalists into pro- and anti-Adams factions. Adams returns to Quincy in March and remains there until September 30. Learns that Charles, who has been drinking heavily for years, has deserted his family and is bankrupt. Arrives on October 10 in Trenton, where the government has relocated during a yellow fever outbreak in Philadelphia. Meets with cabinet to review instructions for the new peace commission, and orders its departure on October 16 despite the opposition of Pickering, McHenry, and Wolcott. (Adams will later write that his decision to send the mission was "the most disinterested, prudent, and successful conduct in my whole life.") Returns to Philadelphia in November and is joined by Abigail. Delivers third annual message to Congress on December 3. Federalist caucus in Congress endorses his reelection. Adams appoints Alfred Moore to the Supreme Court. George Washington dies on December 14.

1800   Adams refuses to promote Hamilton to commander in chief of the army, leaving the post unfilled. Demands the resignation of Secretary of War McHenry on May 5 and dismisses Secretary of State Pickering on May 12, accusing them of being subservient to Hamilton. Appoints Samuel Dexter as secretary of war, John Marshall as secretary of state, and orders the demobilization of the expanded "Additional" army created in 1798. Against the advice of his cabinet, on May 21 Adams pardons John Fries and two other men sentenced to hang for treason. (Fries had led a band of armed protestors who forced a federal marshal in March 1799 to release a group of prisoners jailed for resisting the 1798 federal property tax.) Federalist caucus again endorses Adams's reelection. Adams visits Washington, D.C., in June, then returns to Quincy. Hamilton meets with leading New England Federalists in June and urges them to support Charles Cotesworth Pinckney, the Federalist vice-presidential candidate, for the presidency over Adams. American envoys in France sign Convention of 1800 on September 30; treaty ends undeclared naval war and suspends 1778 treaty of alliance. Hamilton publishes pamphlet on October 24 describing Adams as unfit for the presidency. Adams arrives in Washington on November 1 and becomes the first occupant of the still unfinished President's House. Delivers fourth annual message to Congress on November 11. Charles dies of liver failure in East Chester, New York, November 30. Presidential electors meet on December 3 (the 138 electors are chosen by the voters in five states, by the legislature in ten states, and by county delegates appointed by the legislature in one state). Jefferson and Aaron Burr each receive seventy-three electoral votes, while Adams receives sixty-five, Charles Cotesworth Pinckney sixty-four, and John Jay one. Official copy of the treaty with France arrives in Washington on December 11. Secretary of the Treasury Wolcott resigns and is replaced by Samuel Dexter, who continues to serve as secretary of war.

1801   Adams appoints John Marshall chief justice of the Supreme Court on January 20 (Marshall continues to serve as secretary of state through the end of the administration). Senate ratifies the treaty with France in amended form on February 3. Adams signs on February 13 a new judiciary act that creates sixteen new circuit court judgeships. House of Representatives elects Jefferson president on February 17 after thirty-six ballots; Burr becomes vice president. Adams nominates, and the Federalist Senate confirms, Federalist circuit court judges. ("Midnight appointments" anger Jefferson and the Republicans, and in 1802 a Republican Congress repeals the judiciary act of 1801 and abolishes the new judgeships.) Adams recalls John Quincy from his position in Prussia. Leaves Washington for Quincy early on the morning of Jefferson's inauguration, March 4. Grandson George Washington Adams, the first child of John Quincy and Louisa Catherine, born April 12 in Berlin.

1802   In April, John Quincy is elected to Massachusetts State Senate. Adams begins writing the first part of his autobiography, "John Adams," on October 5 (completed in June 1805). In November, John Quincy is defeated in a close election as Federalist candidate for Congress.

1803   John Quincy is elected as a U.S. senator from Massachusetts (serves until 1808). Adams loses $13,000 in the failure of the London bank of Bird, Savage, & Bird. To compensate against the losses, John Quincy arranges to buy the Old House and surrounding property in stages. Grandson John Adams 2nd, second child of John Quincy and Louisa Catherine, born July 4 in Boston.

1805   Thomas Boylston marries Ann Harrod of Haverhill, Massachusetts, May 16. Adams resumes his correspondence with Benjamin Rush, which had lapsed amid the partisan contests of the 1790s. Publishes collected edition of *Discourses on Davila*. John Quincy becomes first Boylston Professor of Rhetoric and Oratory at Harvard.

1806   Begins second part of his autobiography, "Travels, and Negotiations" (completed early in 1807.) Granddaughter Abigail Smith Adams, first child of Thomas Boylston and Ann, born July 29 in Quincy.

1807   Commences writing the third part of his autobiography, "Peace," but breaks it off when he begins his controversy with Mercy Otis Warren over her *History of the Rise, Progress and Termination of the American Revolution*, a work highly critical of Adams. Between July 28 and August 19, he writes ten long, angry letters to Warren, who, after six letters of her own, finally ends the exchange by responding that as "an old friend, I pity you, as a Christian I forgive you." Grandson Charles Francis Adams, third child of John Quincy and Louisa Catherine, born August 18 in Boston.

1808   Granddaughter Elizabeth Coombs Adams, second child of Thomas Boylston and Ann, born June 9.

1809   Begins publishing letters of reminiscence in the *Boston Patriot* (his "second autobiography" continues until May 1812.) Publishes four letters in the *Patriot* on British impressment of American seamen that are collected in pamphlet *The Inadmissible Principles, of the King of England's*

Proclamation, of October 16, 1807—Considered. John Quincy appointed minister plenipotentiary to Russia by President James Madison, June 27. Grandson Thomas Boylston Adams Jr., born August 4. John Quincy and his family depart for Russia in August, accompanied by Adams's grandson William Steuben Smith, who serves as John Quincy's secretary.

1811   John Quincy is appointed to the Supreme Court by Madison on February 22; he declines the position. In June, Thomas Boylston is appointed chief justice of the Massachusetts court of common pleas for the Southern Circuit. Granddaughter Frances Foster Adams, fourth child of Thomas Boylston and Ann, born June 22. Granddaughter Louisa Catherine Adams, fourth child of John Quincy and Louisa Catherine, born August 12 in St. Petersburg, Russia. Nabby undergoes mastectomy at the Old House on October 8.

1812   On January 1, through the intercession of Benjamin Rush, Adams resumes his correspondence with Thomas Jefferson; over the next fourteen years he writes 109 letters to Jefferson, who responds with forty-nine. Frances Foster Adams dies March 4. Congress declares war with Great Britain, June 17. Louisa Catherine Adams dies September 15.

1813   Grandson Isaac Hull Adams, fifth child of Thomas Boylston and Ann, born May 26. Nabby dies of cancer at the Old House on August 15.

1814   John Quincy is appointed in January to five-member commission charged with negotiating an Anglo-American peace treaty. Adams begins correspondence with John Taylor of Virginia, whose work *Inquiry into the Principles and Policy of the Government of the United States* is largely a critique of Adams's *Defence.* John Quincy signs peace treaty with Great Britain at Ghent in December.

1815   Madison appoints John Quincy minister plenipotentiary to Great Britain (serves until 1817). Grandson John Quincy Adams, sixth child of Thomas Boylston and Ann, born December 16.

1817   President James Monroe appoints John Quincy secretary of state (serves until 1825). Grandson Joseph Harrod

Adams, seventh child of Thomas Boylston and Ann, born December 16.

1818   Abigail dies of typhoid fever on October 28.

1819   Adams publishes collected edition of *Novanglus and Massachusettensis.*

1820   Attends sessions of the convention called to revise the state constitution as Quincy delegate, and proposes that the Massachusetts bill of rights be changed so as to remove all restrictions on religious freedom.

1822   Gives to the town of Quincy several tracts of granite-bearing land, the profits from which are to be used to build a church and an academy that will eventually house his library.

1823   Brother Peter Boylston dies on June 2 in Braintree. Adams has a granite column erected in the Quincy burial ground with the inscription: "In memory of Henry Adams, who took his flight from the Dragon of persecution in Devonshire, England, and alighted with 8 sons near Mount Wollaston. One of the sons returned to England, and after taking some time to explore the country, four removed to Medfield and the neighboring towns; two to Chelmsford. One only, Joseph, who lies here at his left hand, remained here, who was an original proprietor in the township of Braintree, 1639. This stone and several others have been placed in their yard by a great-grandson from a veneration of the piety, humility, sympathy, prudence, patience, temperance, frugality, industry, and perseverance of his ancestors, in hope of recommending an emulation of their virtues to their posterity."

1824   John Quincy becomes candidate for president. In the election Andrew Jackson receives ninety-nine electoral votes, John Quincy eighty-four, William H. Crawford forty-one, and Henry Clay thirty-seven, forcing the contest into the House of Representatives.

1825   John Quincy is elected President of the United States by the House of Representatives on February 9, receiving the votes of thirteen out of twenty-four state delegations. Adams writes to the president-elect: "this is not an event to excite vanity." Grandson Charles Francis Adams graduates from Harvard in August.

1826   Adams dies at the Old House on the evening of July 4, several hours after Jefferson's death at Monticello; among his last words are "Thomas Jefferson survives." After service held at the First Congregational Church in Quincy on July 7, Adams is buried next to Abigail.

Note on the Texts

This volume prints the texts of 191 letters, essays, reports, resolutions, and memoranda written by John Adams between 1775 and 1783; seventeen selections from his diary for this period; and selected passages from his unfinished autobiography, drafted in 1804–5 and 1807, recalling his service in the Continental Congress and in Europe during the American Revolution, as well as notes made by Thomas Jefferson recording remarks Adams made in Congress in 1776. In addition, the text of the Anglo-American peace treaty of 1783, which Adams helped negotiate, is printed in an appendix to this volume. Although the majority of these documents existed only in autograph manuscript at the time of Adams's death in 1826, many of them were printed during his lifetime. Adams published newspaper essays both under his own name and under a variety of pseudonyms, and some of these essays were then published in pamphlet or book form.

During his service in the Continental Congress in 1776 Adams began making copies of his outgoing correspondence in letterbooks, a practice he followed for the remainder of his life. Always keenly aware of his reputation and his place in history, Adams took great care in safeguarding and transporting his papers throughout his many travels, regarding them "as a Sacred Deposit." On December 24, 1818, an eighty-three-year-old Adams wrote to his son John Quincy that he was hard at work searching "after old Papers. Trunks, Boxes, Desks, Drawers, locked up for thirty Years have been broken open because the keys are lost. Nothing stands in my Way. Every Scrap shall be found and preserved for your Affliction or for your good. . . . I shall leave you an inheritance sufficiently tormenting, for example, The huge Pile of family Letters, will make you Alternatly laugh and cry, fret and fume, stamp and scold as they do me." John Quincy Adams eventually entrusted his family's papers to his son, Charles Francis Adams, who edited and published two collections of correspondence, *Letters of Mrs. Adams, the Wife of John Adams* (1840) and *Letters of John Adams, Addressed to His Wife* (2 volumes, 1841), followed by *The Works of John Adams, Second President of the United States: with a Life of the Author, Notes and Illustrations, by his Grandson Charles Francis Adams* (10 volumes, 1850–56), which primarily presented Adams's public writings and official correspondence.

Charles Francis Adams later had a separate fireproof building, the

Stone Library, built on the grounds of the family estate in Quincy, Massachusetts, to house the family archive. On his death in 1886 he left his papers, and those of John Adams and Abigail Adams, and of John Quincy Adams and his wife, Louisa Catherine Adams, to his four sons, one of whom, Charles Francis Adams Jr., later became president of the Massachusetts Historical Society. In 1902 Charles Francis Adams Jr. had the family papers moved from the Stone Library to the Massachusetts Historical Society building in Boston, and in 1905 he created the Adams Manuscript Trust to ensure continued family ownership and control of the papers for the next fifty years. In 1954 the Adams Manuscript Trust entered into an agreement with the Massachusetts Historical Society and Harvard University Press to publish the papers of John Adams, John Quincy Adams, Charles Francis Adams Sr., and their families through the year 1889. The Adams Manuscript Trust was dissolved in 1956 after it transferred ownership of its papers to the Massachusetts Historical Society, which began to identify and photocopy Adams documents in repositories outside of the family archive. Publication of the Adams Family Papers began in 1961 and has proceeded in three series, two of which are still ongoing in respect to John Adams: *Diary and Autobiography of John Adams* (4 volumes; Cambridge: The Belknap Press of Harvard University Press, 1961), supplemented by *The Earliest Diary of John Adams* (Cambridge: The Belknap Press of Harvard University Press, 1966); *Adams Family Correspondence* (9 volumes to date; Cambridge: The Belknap Press of Harvard University Press, 1963–2009); and *Papers of John Adams* (15 volumes to date; Cambridge: The Belknap Press of Harvard University Press, 1977–2010). Documents are transcribed and printed without alteration in their spelling and paragraphing, and with minimal alterations in their capitalization and punctuation, mostly in the substitution of periods for dashes used to end sentences and the omission of dashes in instances where a dash appears following another punctuation mark.

The texts of the selections from the diary printed in this volume are taken from *Diary and Autobiography of John Adams*, volumes 1–3 (1961), edited by L. H. Butterfield. The texts of selections from the autobiography, as well as the text of John Adams's letter to Samuel Adams of May 21, 1778, are taken from *Diary and Autobiography of John Adams*, volume 3–4 (1961), edited by L. H. Butterfield. The texts of letters to Abigail Adams, John Quincy Adams, and Abigail Adams 2nd, are taken from *Adams Family Correspondence*, volumes 1–2 (1963), edited by L. H. Butterfield; volumes 3–4 (1973), edited by L. H. Butterfield and Marc Friedlaender; and volume 5 (1993), edited by Richard Alan Ryerson. The texts of the essays, reports, resolutions, memoranda, and other letters by John Adams included in this volume, as well as the text of the 1783 peace treaty, are taken from *Papers of John Adams*, volumes 3–4 (1979), edited by Robert J. Taylor; volumes 5–6 (1983), edited by Robert J. Taylor; volumes 7–8 (1989), edited by Gregg L. Lint, Robert J. Taylor, Richard Alan Ryerson, Celeste Walker, and Joanna M. Revelas; volumes 9–10 (1996), edited by Gregg L. Lint and Richard Alan Ryerson; volume 11 (2003), edited by Gregg L. Lint, Richard Alan Ryerson, Anne Decker Cecere, Celeste Walker, Jennifer Shea, and C. James Taylor; volume 12 (2004), edited by Gregg L. Lint, Richard Alan Ryerson, Anne Decker Cecere, C. James Taylor, Jennifer Shea, Celeste Walker, and Margaret A. Hogan; volume 13 (2006), edited by Gregg L. Lint, C. James Taylor, Margaret A. Hogan, Jessie May Rodrique, Mary T. Claffey, and Hobson Woodward; volume 14 (2008), edited by Gregg L. Lint, C. James Taylor, Hobson Woodward, Margaret A. Hogan, Mary T. Claffey, Sara B. Sikes, and Judith S. Graham; and volume 15 (2010), edited by Gregg L. Lint, C. James Taylor, Robert F. Karachuk, Hobson Woodward, Margaret A. Hogan, Sara B. Sikes, Mary T. Claffey, and Karen N. Barzilay. In volumes 14 and 15 of *Papers of John Adams*, the previous textual policy of the series has been revised, so that documents are now transcribed and printed without alteration in their capitalization and punctuation; in addition, superscript letters used in abbreviations and contractions are no longer brought down to the line. The text of Adams's remarks of July 30, 1788 in the Continental Congress on the Articles of Confederation are taken from *The Papers of Thomas Jefferson*, volume 1, edited by Julian P. Boyd (Princeton: Princeton University Press, 1950), pp. 321–22 and 325–26.

The present volume prints texts as they appeared in *The Adams Papers* and *The Papers of Thomas Jefferson*, but with a few alterations in editorial procedure. The bracketed conjectural readings of the editors of *The Adams Papers*, in cases where original manuscripts or printed texts were damaged or difficult to read, are accepted without brackets in this volume when those readings seem to be the only possible ones; but when they do not, or when the editors made no conjecture, the missing word or words are indicated by a bracketed two-em space, i.e., [   ]. In cases where *The Adams Papers* supplied in brackets punctuation, letters, or words that were omitted from the source text by an obvious slip of the pen or printer's error, this volume removes the brackets and accepts the editorial emendation. Similarly, in cases where an obvious slip of the pen or printing error is corrected in *The Adams Papers* by having the correction appear in brackets following the error, this volume removes the brackets and accepts the correction while deleting the error, e.g., at 223.15 "1768 [i.e. 1778]" becomes "1778." Bracketed editorial insertions used in *The Adams Papers* to expand abbreviations and contractions or to correct errors of dating in diary entries have been deleted in this volume. In some cases where Adams made changes in a document, the canceled text, if decipherable, was presented in *The Adams Papers* in italic within single angle brackets; this volume omits the canceled material.

This volume presents the texts of the editions chosen as sources here but does not attempt to reproduce features of their typographic design. The texts are printed without alteration except for the changes previously discussed, some changes in headings, and the correction of typographical errors. Spelling, punctuation, and capitalization are often expressive features, and they are not altered, even when inconsistent or irregular. The following is a list of typographical errors corrected, cited by page and line number: 313.35, The are; 549.28, whee; 576.10–11, ambitions.

Notes

In the notes below, the reference numbers denote page and line of this volume (the line count includes headings). No note is made for material included in the eleventh edition of *Merriam-Webster's Collegiate Dictionary*. In 1822 John Adams donated most of his library to the town of Quincy. In 1893 his books were transferred to the Boston Public Library, where they still reside. A note is provided when reference is made to a title found in the *Catalogue of the John Adams Library in the Public Library of the City of Boston* (Boston, 1917), hereafter cited as the *CJAL*. For further biographical background, references to other studies, and more detailed notes, see *Papers of John Adams*, edited by Robert J. Taylor, et al. (15 vols. to date, Cambridge: Harvard University Press, 1977–2010); *Diary and Autobiography of John Adams*, edited by L. H. Butterfield, et al. (4 vols., Cambridge: Harvard University Press, 1961); *The Earliest Diary of John Adams*, edited by L. H. Butterfield, et al. (Cambridge: Harvard University Press, 1966); *Adams Family Correspondence*, edited by L. H. Butterfield, et al. (9 vols. to date, Cambridge: Harvard University Press, 1963–2009); *Legal Papers of John Adams*, L. Kinvin Wroth and Hiller B. Zobel, editors (3 vols., Cambridge: Harvard University Press, 1965); James H. Hutson, *John Adams and the Diplomacy of the American Revolution* (Lexington: University Press of Kentucky, 1980); David McCollough, *John Adams* (New York: Simon & Schuster, 2001).

THE CONTINENTAL CONGRESS, 1775–1777

3.4   Mr. Eliot of Fairfield] The younger Andrew Eliot, Harvard 1762, minister at Fairfield, Connecticut, and the son of the distinguished minister of the New North Church in Boston, Dr. Andrew Eliot, Harvard 1737, who remained in Boston throughout the siege of the town.

3.31   our Children] Abigail ("Nabby"), age 9; John Quincy, age 8; Charles, age 4; and Thomas Boylston, age 2.

4.4   Our amiable Friend Hancock] Boston merchant John Hancock (1737–1793), Harvard 1754, was, like Adams, born in Braintree. He served as president of the first and second Massachusetts Provincial Congresses (1774–75) and as president of the Continental Congress from May 1775 to October 1777.

4.9   My Friend Joseph Bass] A Braintree shoemaker who was Adams's servant during his stay in Philadelphia.

4.17   Coll. Warren.] James Warren (1726–1808), Harvard 1745, president of the Provincial Congress in 1775 and Adams's close friend and confidant.

4.20   Dr. Young] Thomas Young (1732–1777), a self-educated Scots-Irish immigrant involved in radical politics in at least five colonies. He was associated with the Sons of Liberty in Boston in the 1760s and delivered the first oration commemorating the Boston Massacre in 1771. By 1775 he was in Philadelphia and helped write the radical Pennsylvania constitution of 1776. In 1776 he was appointed senior surgeon to the Continental hospital in Philadelphia, but died of a fever in 1777.

4.21   quantum sufficit] Quite enough.

4.30–31   Mr. Dickinson . . . Mr. Reed . . . Mr. Mifflin] John Dickinson (1732–1808), delegate from Pennsylvania who urged conciliation with Britain and often contested Adams in Congressional debate; Joseph Reed (1745–1781), College of New Jersey 1757, served as president of the Provincial Congress of Pennsylvania in 1775; Thomas Mifflin (1744–1800), Philadelphia merchant and avid patriot, became aide-de-camp to Washington in 1775 and was disowned by the Quakers for engaging in military service.

5.5   *Moses Gill*] Moses Gill (1734–1800) was elected councilor when Massachusetts revived its charter in 1775 upon the advice of the Continental Congress. In 1795 he became lieutenant governor of the state.

5.17   Pari Passu.] On an equal footing.

6.8–9   The Gentleman to whom most Letters from our Province] Presumably John Hancock, the leader of the Massachusetts delegation.

6.14   Mrs. Gill and Mr. Boylstone are out of Prison.] Rebecca Boylston Gill, first cousin of Adams's mother, left Boston sometime before June 24, 1775; but her brother Thomas Boylston remained in the town throughout the siege and in 1779 went to England.

6.20   Congress have made Choice] Virginia delegate George Washington (1732–1799) was unanimously elected commander in chief on June 15.

7.7–8   Kent, Swift, Tudor, Dr. Cooper, Dr. Winthrop] Benjamin Kent (1708–1788), Harvard 1727, a leading lawyer in Massachusetts and later attorney general of the colony; Samuel Swift (1715–1775), Harvard 1735, one of the older generations of Boston lawyers; William Tudor (1750–1819), Harvard 1769, was one of Adams's law students who became a life-long friend and the first judge advocate of the Continental army. Rev. Samuel Cooper (1725–1783), Harvard 1743, minister at the liberal Congregationalist Brattle Street Church in Boston; known for his eloquent sermons, he was deeply involved in the popular politics leading up to the Revolution. John Winthrop (1714–1779), the Hollis Professor of Mathematics and Natural Philosophy at Harvard College, and one of Adams's undergraduate instructors.

7.34   Uncle Quincy] Norton Quincy (1716–1801), Harvard 1736, Abigail's uncle.

8.2   *Elbridge Gerry*] Elbridge Gerry (1744–1813), Harvard 1762, was a Marblehead merchant who entered the General Court in 1772 and, as a member of the Second Continental Congress, became a close friend of Adams.

8.21–22   General Ward] Artemas Ward (1727–1800), Harvard 1748, storekeeper, and military officer who commanded the troops outside Boston until Washington assumed command in the summer of 1775.

8.22   General Lee] Charles Lee (1731–1782), British officer who had served in America 1755–1761, and later as a soldier of fortune in Poland. He returned to America in 1773 and became an ardent patriot. He hesitated to accept his commission until the Congress assured him that it would indemnify him if he lost his Irish estates for supporting the American cause.

8.23   Major Gates] Horatio Gates (1729–1806), British officer who had served in America in the Seven Years War and returned in 1772. He was drawn to the American cause by his hatred of the English caste system.

9.5–6   Mr. Adams, Mr. Paine] Fellow Massachusetts delegates Samuel Adams (1722–1803), Adams's famous cousin and the leader of the popular party in Boston, and Robert Treat Paine (1731–1814), a lawyer and professional rival.

9.32   Schuyler] Philip John Schuyler (1733–1804), a New York landowner who had military experience during the Seven Years War, was appointed major general in the Continental army in June 1775.

9.35   Major Mifflin] Thomas Mifflin (1744–1800), a Pennsylvania delegate to Congress who was commissioned as a major, becoming first Washington's aide-de-camp and then, on August 14, 1775, the army's first quartermaster general.

10.13–14   Gardiner mortally.] Thomas Gardiner, who had been elected colonel of the 1st Middlesex Regiment in Cambridge after the Loyalist Gen. William Brattle fled from the town to Boston in September 1774.

10.34   Governor Hopkins and Ward of Rhode Island] Stephen Hopkins (1707–1785) of Providence, and Samuel Ward (1725–1776) of Newport, were rivals for the governorship of Rhode Island in the years leading up to the Revolution. Hopkins, who was a signer of the Declaration of Independence, was a more fervent patriot than Ward. Their shared esteem for Warren was a rare point of agreement.

11.11   Since I heard of this Error] Referring to the difficulty of sorting out the precedence of the generals in Massachusetts. Many believed the John Thomas was the most able military officer in Massachusetts, but he had been placed below Artemas Ward, Seth Pomerory, and William Heath. Adams and Washington saw that Thomas was placed first.

11.17   Alass poor Warren! Dulce et decorum est pro Patria mori.]   Adams's
friend Dr. Joseph Warren (1741–1775), Harvard 1759, physician, ardent Whig,
and president of the provincial Congress, was killed at the Battle of Bunker
Hill on June 17, prompting Adams to quote from Horace, *Odes*, III.ii.13: "It
is sweet and becoming to die for one's country."

12.31   a Spirited Manifesto.]   "The Declaration of the Causes and Necessities of Taking Up Arms," July 6, 1775, drafted by Thomas Jefferson but then
revised by John Dickinson to be more moderate in tone.

12.36–37   your Friend has aimed at promoting from first to last]   Presumably Mercy Otis Warren, wife of James Warren, who was herself an ardent
patriot.

13.4–5   Dr. Franklin]   Benjamin Franklin (1706–1790) returned from London in May 1775 and was immediately appointed to the Congress from Pennsylvania. Since Franklin had been abroad almost continuously since 1757,
some delegates were suspicious of his patriotism; and thus he became especially eager to demonstrate his devotion to the cause.

13.30   particularly one]   John Dickinson, whose famous *Letters from a
Farmer in Pennsylvania* (Philadelphia, 1768) had placed him in the vanguard
of opposition to the Townshend duties, now took a conciliatory posture that
infuriated Adams.

13.32–33   whose Name is Wilson]   James Wilson (1742–1798), Scottish
graduate of St. Andrews and one of the most intellectually gifted of the
Revolutionaries; he would take a leading role in the 1787 Constitutional
Convention.

13.34   Mr. Biddle]   Edward Biddle (1738–1779).

13.35–36   Mr. Morton]   John Morton (1724–1777), Pennsylvania delegate
to the Continental Congress.

13.36–37   the Timidity of two overgrown Fortunes.]   Referring to Pennsylvania delegates Thomas Willing and John Dickinson.

14.9   piddling Genius]   Referring to John Dickinson. The British seized
this letter in transit and subsequently published it in the *Massachusetts
Gazette*, causing Adams some embarrassment but no serious harm.

15.3   the Oddity of a great Man]   Having read the published letter, General Charles Lee professed to find this reference to his eccentricity "extremely
flattering."

15.10   *Josiah Quincy*]   Col. Josiah Quincy, Sr. (1710–1784), prominent
Boston merchant and father of Josiah Quincy, Jr. who died at sea of tubercu-
losis in the spring of 1775 while returning from intelligence-gathering in
London.

16.8–9   Why should I grieve . . . I might share?]   Lines from Lord Bolingbroke's translation of the ancient Greek stoic philosopher Cleanthes in Bolingbroke's *Letters on the Study and Use of History* (London, 1752), 2: 285. Some of Bolingbroke's works are in the *CJAL*.

17.6–7   to two of them, . . . the American army]   Both John and Samuel Adams were influential in having Lee appointed a major general despite opposition from other members of the Massachusetts delegation.

17.17–18   in his Answer to the City.]   On July 16, 1775, King George III rejected the petition of the City of London calling upon him to dismiss his ministers and end the conflict with America.

17.19   wiseacre Gage]   Gen. Thomas Gage (1721–1787), commander of the British forces in Massachusetts and last royal governor of the colony.

17.24–25   suden Marriage of our President]   John Hancock, president of the Congress, married Dorothy Quincy at Fairfield, Connecticut, on August 28, 1775.

17.29   your Secretary]   Samuel Adams, who explained to Elbridge Gerry on September 26, 1775, that he had ridden a hundred miles on horseback for the first time in many years; he thought the riding had "contributed to the establishment of my health, for which I am obliged to my friend Mr. John Adams, who kindly offered one of his horses."

18.11–12   Taylor riding to Brentford]   The title of a well-known puppet show.

18.24   Mr. Dexters]   Samuel Dexter, formerly of Massachusetts, had moved to Woodstock Hill, Connecticut, in 1775.

19.14   Sully and Cecil]   Editions in French and English of the *Mémoires* of the staunch Huguenot statesman Maximilien de Béthune, duc de Sully (1560–1641) are in the *CJAL*. English statesman William Cecil, 1st Baron Burghley (1520–1598), was a principle advisor to Queen Elizabeth I and a fervent anti-Catholic.

19.21   Dyer]   Eliphalet Dyer (1721–1807), Connecticut delegate to the Continental Congress, and later chief justice of Connecticut.

19.24   Harrison]   Benjamin Harrison (1726–1791), prominent member of the Virginia delegation to the Continental Congress and later governor of the state. His son, William Henry Harrison, became the ninth President of the United States.

19.27   Ld. North]   Frederick North (1732–1792), prime minister of Great Britain, 1770–82, was known by the courtesy title Lord North from 1752 until 1790, when he succeeded his father as Earl of Guilford.

20.2   Carlton]   Sir Guy Carlton (1724–1808), governor of the Province of Canada, 1775–77; he led the defense of Quebec during the American invasion of 1775.

20.4   Coll. Roberdeau]   Daniel Roberdeau (1727–1795), Philadelphia merchant with whom Adams later stayed in York, Pennsylvania.

20.7   our Mr. Gordon]   William Gordon (1728–1807), Congregation clergymen who came to the colonies in 1770 and became pastor of the Roxbury, Massachusetts church. He served as chaplain to the Massachusetts Provincial Congress.

20.9   Stephen Collins]   A friend and sometimes courier. Adams called him "the most hospitable benevolent man alive," in a July 6 letter to James Warren.

20.20   Dr. Rush]   Benjamin Rush (1745–1813), a physician and member of the faculty of the College of Philadelphia who was elected to the Continental Congress in 1776.

20.22   Sawbridge, McCaulay, Burgh]   John Sawbridge (1732–1795), Catherine Macaulay (1731–1791), and James Burgh (1714–1775), well-known British radical Whigs who supported the American cause. Sawbridge was Catherine Macaulay's brother; together they helped organize the Society of Supporters of the Bill of Rights in 1769.

20.25   complains of D.]   That is, of John Dickinson.

20.34   Henry]   Patrick Henry (1736–1799), Virginia patriot and one of the most outspoken opponents of Great Britain; in March 1775 in Richmond he made his famous "Give me liberty, or give me death" speech.

20.37   Mr. Bullock and Mr. Houstoun]   Archibald Bulloch (1730–1777), first president of the Provincial Congress of Georgia, 1775–1777; John Houstoun (1744–1796), Revolutionary leader in Georgia and later governor of the state.

21.23   Dr. Coombe]   Rev. Thomas Coombe (1747–1822), of Philadelphia. Though sympathetic to the American cause, he had sworn allegiance to the crown in his Anglican ordination oath making it impossible for him to approve of the Declaration of Independence. In 1778 he moved to New York City, and the following year went to England.

21.24   Henry 4., Sully, Buckingham]   Henry IV of France (1553–1610) issued the Edict of Nantes in 1598 that granted toleration to Protestants and was assassinated in 1610; Maximilien de Béthune, duc de Sully, was his prime minister (see also the note 19.14); George Villiers, Duke of Buckingham (1592–1628), favorite of James I and Charles I, was assassinated in 1628.

21.30   excellent Marcia]   Mercy Otis Warren, James Warren's wife.

22.8   Portia]   A name which Adams often called Abigail.

22.12   *Unum Necessarium*]   The one necessity, that is, gunpowder.

22.26   Intelligence from Canada]   On August 28 an American force of

1,200 men led by General Richard Montgomery (1738–1775) left Fort Ticonderoga and invaded Canada by way of Lake Champlain. A second invasion force of 1,100 men, under Benedict Arnold (1741–1801), began its advance up the Kennebec River in Maine on September 25.

24.32 the Trade of America.] These discussions of trade would become central to American thinking over the next generation. The apparent effectiveness of the American non-importation agreements in the 1760s convinced many Americans that they had the power to affect European, especially British, policy by closing off American markets.

27.25 Vesseaux de Frize] Vaisseaux de frises, timber framed vessels filled with stone and sunk to obstruct passage in rivers or harbors.

30.3 Mr. Duane] James Duane (1733–1797), jurist and conservative delegate to the Congress from New York.

30.3–4 our late virtuous and able President] Peyton Randolph of Virginia, president of the Congress, died on October 22, 1775.

30.5 Mr. De Lancey] James De Lancey (1703–1760), member of the family that dominated New York politics in the years leading up the Revolution, had served as chief justice of the colony during the Zenger seditious libel trial in 1735. His nephew, James De Lancey (1747–1804), refused to support the patriot cause and recruited Loyalist militia in Westchester County.

30.10 Jefferson] Thomas Jefferson (1743–1826). Although this is the first mention of Jefferson in Adams's Diary, the two men had served together in the Congress for six weeks in the summer of 1775.

30.18 Mr. Hewes] Joseph Hewes (1730–1779), member of Congress from North Carolina.

30.19 Mr. Hog] Scottish-born James Hogg (1730–1804) was agent of the Transylvania Company, which was appealing to Congress to establish a fourteenth colony in what is now Kentucky and Tennessee.

30.21 Henderson] Richard Henderson (1735–1785) organized a land company to settle Kentucky with Daniel Boone as agent.

32.26–27 a Quarrell with Massachusetts.] A delegation of Baptists from Massachusetts and some Philadelphia Quakers confronted the Massachusetts delegates to Congress in Carpenters' Hall on October 14, 1774, to protest the Congregational church establishment in Massachusetts. The four-hour exchange was heated and embarrassing to Adams and the other members of the Massachusetts delegation. Some observers thought the Baptists were allied with the Anglicans and hostile to the patriot cause.

32.28 a Quarrell with Connecticut] After the Susquehannah Company settled people from Connecticut in the Wyoming Valley of Pennsylvania in the 1760s, the government of Connecticut in 1774 made the area part of one of its counties, which in turn led to armed conflict between Pennsylvania militia and Connecticut settlers in 1775.

32.33   *William Tudor*]   See note 7.7–8.

33.16   the Doctors Defence]   Dr. Benjamin Church (1734–1778), a Boston physician closely associated with the patriots whose miscarried cipher letter led to his arrest on September 29, 1775, for being a British spy. Following a trial before a military commission, Church was turned over to the Massachusetts House of Representatives, of which he was still a member. He was expelled from the House and eventually confined in a Boston jail. In 1778 he was placed on board a ship headed for Martinique; shortly after leaving port the ship sank in a storm with no survivors.

33.28   who Bellidore is.]   Probably a reference to Bernard Forest de Belidor (1698–1761), French military engineer and writer on fortification.

34.2   *Samuel Osgood*]   Samuel Osgood (1748–1813) served as aide-decamp to Gen. Artemas Ward in 1775 and later was a member of the Provincial Congress of Massachusetts.

34.5   General Frie]   Joseph Frye (1712–1794), of Massachusetts, was commissioned a major general on June 23, 1775.

34.15   Coll. Armstrong]   John Armstrong (1717–1795) had military experience in the French and Indian War and was commissioned a major general in 1777; he was the father of John Armstrong, later involved in the Newburgh conspiracy of 1783.

36.2   *Joseph Hawley*]   Joseph Hawley (1723–1788), Yale 1742, was a passionate patriot from Northampton, Massachusetts, and the central figure promoting Revolution in the Connecticut River Valley.

37.22–23   I wrote a letter . . . from their President]   On November 11, 1775, James Otis Sr., president of the Massachusetts Council, wrote to the Massachusetts delegates to Congress. Otis asked the delegation, and possibly Congress as a whole, to resolve a dispute between the Council and the Massachusetts House of Representatives as to whether a resolution adopted by Congress in July gave the House a role along with the Council in the appointment of militia officers. Adams replied to Otis on November 23, recommending that the Council accommodate the House on the militia question and strongly advising against having the matter brought before Congress.

37.24   which Letter Revere carried]   Boston silversmith Paul Revere (1735–1818) acted as courier between the Massachusetts Provincial Congress and its delegation in Philadelphia.

37.34   Mr. Cushing]   Thomas Cushing (1725–1788), member of the Massachusetts delegation to the Congress, whose caution and moderate positions irritated Adams and other more ardent patriots; he was replaced in December 1775.

38.5   *Mercy Otis Warren*]   Poet, dramatist, wife of James Warren, and sister of James Otis Jr., Mercy Otis Warren (1728–1814) was Adams's close friend and correspondent until she published her history of the American Revolution in 1805. (See chronology for the year 1807.)

38.15   Copeleys]   Painter John Singleton Copley (1738–1823). Disgusted with a provincial clientele that thought painting was "no more than any other useful trade, as they sometimes term it, like that of a Carpenter tailor or shoemaker," Copley had left Boston in June 1774 to further his artistic career in the presumably more receptive atmosphere of London.

40.6–7   occasioned by Burning Buildings I suppose.]   Patriot forces destroyed houses that had survived the burning of Charlestown during the battle of Bunker Hill in order to prevent the British besieged up in Boston from having access to firewood.

40.28–29   Cocknowaga]   The Caughnawagas had come to offer their services to the Americans.

41.3   *Memorandum on Agenda for Congress*]   Apparently composed after consultation with those delegates favoring independence, this list includes many measures proposed by Adams and other radicals in subsequent weeks and months.

41.22   Treaties of Commerce with F. S. H. D. &c.]   France, Spain, Holland, Denmark.

42.4–5   a Pamphlet intituled Common Sense]   Thomas Paine's *Common Sense* (Philadelphia, 1776) was published anonymously in mid-January, and immediately became a best seller. Some thought Adams was the author.

42.27–28   Dr. Franklin, . . . to go into Canada.]   Benjamin Franklin, Samuel Chase (1741–1811), a delegate from Maryland who strongly supported independence and later became an associate justice of the Supreme Court, and Charles Carroll of Carollton (1736–1832), a wealthy Maryland planter and Roman Catholic, were dispatched by Congress to convince the French in Quebec to join the other colonies against the British. Their mission was unsuccessful.

42.37   Mr. John Carroll of Maryland]   John Carroll (1735–1815), cousin of Charles Carroll of Carrollton; in 1790 he became the first Roman Catholic bishop in the United States.

44.35   The Lye]   In a letter of March 2 Abigail reported that a rumor was spreading that "you and your President [John Hancock] had gone on board a Man of War from N-y and sail'd for England."

45.37   certain Letters I dont lament]   Adams is referring to portions of his Novanglus Letters that the radical English bookseller, John Almon, published, without Adams's knowledge, in London in 1775 under the title *History of the Dispute with America, from its Origins in 1754.*

45.39   Mr. Dana]   Francis Dana (1743–1811), Harvard 1762, a Cambridge lawyer who was in England when war broke in Massachusetts. He returned to America convinced that reconciliation with Britain was hopeless.

49.1   *Thoughts on Government*]   This influential pamphlet began as letters to two North Carolina delegates in the Continental Congress who in March 1776 asked Adams for advice on drafting a form of government for their colony. When George Wythe of Virginia saw Adams's letter, he wanted a similar plan of government for himself. Then John Dickinson Sergeant of New Jersey asked for a copy, and Adams responded with a much enlarged version. Finally when Richard Henry Lee requested a copy, Adams decided in April to put the ideas of his various letters together in an anonymous pamphlet first advertised for sale in Philadelphia on April 22.

49.13–14   "For forms of government . . . administered is best."] Alexander Pope, *An Essay on Man* (1733), Epistle III, lines 303–04.

50.18–20   Sidney, Harrington, Locke, Milton, Nedham, Neville, Burnet, and Hoadley.]   English Whig writers especially admired by American patriots: Algernon Sidney (1623–1683), James Harrington (1611–1677), John Locke (1632–1704), John Milton (1608–1674), Marchamont Needham (1620–1678), Henry Neville (1620–1694), Gilbert Burnet (1643–1715), and Bishop Hoadly (1676–1761).

50. 26–27   "an Empire of Laws, and not of men."]   Used by Adams in the seventh Novanglus letter, this phrase can be traced back to James Harrington's *Oceana* (1656).

51.21–22   a people cannot . . . government is in one Assembly]   Nearly all the new states that framed constitutions in 1776–77 adopted bicameral legislatures, following the example of both the American colonial experience and of Great Britain. The great exception was Pennsylvania; its adoption of a unicameral legislature was considered highly radical, and remained a contentious issue in Pennsylvania politics until a new state constitution in 1790 created a bicameral legislature. (Georgia also adopted a unicameral assembly; in 1789 a new constitution created a bicameral legislature.)

53.19–20   "Where annual elections end, there slavery begins."]   A radical Whig maxim. Of the colonies only those in New England and Pennsylvania annually elected their assemblies; in Rhode Island elections were held every six months.

53.22–23   "Like bubbles on the sea . . . to that sea return."]   Pope, *An Essay on Man*, Epistle III, lines 19–20.

56.34–37   "I did but teach . . . assess, apes and dogs."]   Milton, "On the Detraction Which Followed upon My Writing Certain Treatises" (second part, "On the Same"), lines 1–4, adapted.

57.2   "Remember the Ladies"] This letter responds to the oft-quoted
letter from Abigail, which, written in two parts, reads as follows:

Braintree March 31 1776

I wish you would ever write me a Letter half as long as I write you;
and tell me if you may where your Fleet are gone? What sort of Defence Virginia can make against our common Enemy? Whether it is so
situated as to make an able Defence? Are not the Gentery Lords and
the common people vassals, are they not like the uncivilized Natives
Brittain represents us to be? I hope their Riffel Men who have shewen
themselves very savage and even Blood thirsty; are not a specimen of
the Generality of the people.

I am willing to allow the Colony great merrit for having produced
a Washington but they have been shamefully duped by a Dunmore.

I have sometimes been ready to think that the passion for Liberty
cannot be Eaquelly Strong in the Breasts of those who have been accustomed to deprive their fellow Creatures of theirs. Of this I am certain that it is not founded upon that generous and christian principal
of doing to others as we would that others should do unto us.

Do not you want to see Boston; I am fearfull of the small pox, or I
should have been in before this time. I got Mr. Crane to go to our
House and see what state it was in. I find it has been occupied by one
of the Doctors of a Regiment, very dirty, but no other damage has
been done to it. The few things which were left in it are all gone.
Cranch has the key which he never deliverd up. I have wrote to him
for it and am determined to get it cleand as soon as possible and shut
it up. I look upon it a new acquisition of property, a property which
one month ago I did not value at a single Shilling, and could with
pleasure have seen it in flames.

The Town in General is left in a better state than we expected,
more oweing to a percipitate flight than any Regard to the inhabitants, tho some individuals discoverd a sense of honour and justice
and have left the rent of the Houses in which they were, for the owners and the furniture unhurt, or if damaged sufficent to make it good.

Others have committed abominable Ravages. The Mansion House
of your President is safe and the furniture unhurt whilst both the
House and Furniture of the Solisiter General have fallen a prey to their
own merciless party. Surely the very Fiends feel a Reverential awe for
Virtue and patriotism, whilst they Detest the paricide and traitor.

I feel very differently at the approach of spring to what I did a
month ago. We knew not then whether we could plant or sow with
safety, whether when we had toild we could reap the fruits of our own
industery, whether we could rest in our own Cottages, or whether we
should not be driven from the sea coasts to seek shelter in the wilderness, but now we feel as if we might sit under our own vine and eat
the good of the land.

I feel a gaieti de Coar to which before I was a stranger. I think the Sun looks brighter, the Birds sing more melodiously, and Nature puts on a more chearfull countanance. We feel a temporary peace, and the poor fugitives are returning to their deserted habitations.

Tho we felicitate ourselves, we sympathize with those who are trembling least the Lot of Boston should be theirs. But they cannot be in similar circumstances unless pusilanimity and cowardise should take possession of them. They have time and warning given them to see the Evil and shun it.—I long to hear that you have declared an independancy—and by the way in the new Code of Laws which I suppose it will be necessary for you to make I desire you would Remember the Ladies, and be more generous and favourable to them than your ancestors. Do not put such unlimited power into the hands of the Husbands. Remember all Men would be tyrants if they could. If perticuliar care and attention is not paid to the Laidies we are determined to foment a Rebelion, and will not hold ourselves bound by any Laws in which we have no voice, or Representation.

That your Sex are Naturally Tyrannical is a Truth so thoroughly established as to admit of no dispute, but such of you as wish to be happy willingly give up the harsh title of Master for the more tender and endearing one of Friend. Why then, not put it out of the power of the vicious and the Lawless to use us with cruelty and indignity with impunity. Men of Sense in all Ages abhor those customs which treat us only as the vassals of your Sex. Regard us then as Beings placed by providence under your protection and in immitation of the Supreem Being make use of that power only for our happiness.

April 5

Not having an opportunity of sending this I shall add a few lines more; tho not with a heart so gay. I have been attending the sick chamber of our Neighbor Trot whose affliction I most sensibly feel but cannot discribe, striped of two lovely children in one week. Gorge the Eldest died on wedensday and Billy the youngest on fryday, with the Canker fever, a terible disorder so much like the throat distemper, that it differs but little from it. Betsy Cranch has been very bad, but upon the recovery. Becky Peck they do not expect will live out the day. Many grown persons are now sick with it, in this Street 5. It rages much in other Towns. The Mumps too are very frequent. Isaac is now confined with it. Our own little flock are yet well. My Heart trembles with anxiety for them. God preserve them.

I want to hear much oftener from you than I do. March 8 was the last date of any that I have yet had. —You inquire of whether I am making Salt peter. I have not yet attempted it, but after Soap making believe I shall make the experiment. I find as much as I can do to manufacture cloathing for my family which would else be Naked. I know of but one person in this part of the Town who has made any, that is Mr. Tertias Bass as he is calld who has got very near an hundred weight which has been found to be very good. I have heard of some others in the other parishes. Mr. Reed of Weymouth has been applied to, to go to Andover to the mills which are now at work, and has gone. I have lately seen a small Manuscrip describing the proportions for the various sorts of powder, fit for cannon, small arms and pistols. If it would be of any Service your way I will get it transcribed and send it to you.—Every one of your Friends send their Regards, and all the little ones. Your Brothers youngest child lies bad with convulsion fitts. Adieu. I need not say how much I am Your ever faithfull Friend.

57.24   Common Sense.] That is, Thomas Paine's pamphlet.

57.27   Dunmore.] John Murray, Earl of Dunmore (1732–1809), royal governor of Virginia who resisted patriot efforts in his colony with force.

58.3   Solicitor General?] Samuel Quincy (1735–1789), Harvard 1754, son of Col. Josiah Quincy; he became a Loyalist.

59.14   We are Waiting it is said for Commissioners] Reports that the British were sending a peace commissioner to the colonies proved correct. In the spring of 1776 Admiral Lord Richard Howe, British naval commander in North America, and his brother, General William Howe, the commander of land forces, were named peace commissioners. After the American defeat at the Battle of Long Island moderates in Congress sought to discover what terms the Howes might offer, and on September 11, 1776, Adams, Benjamin Franklin, and Edward Rutledge met with Admiral Howe for three hours at the Billop House on Staten Island. The conference revealed that the Howes were authorized only to issue pardons in return for submission to royal authority, and that their instructions prohibited any negotiations with Congress or recognition of American independence.

63.25   The News from South Carolina] On March 26, 1776, South Carolina had drawn up a preliminary constitution in place of the royal government.

63.29   The Royal Proclamation, and the late Act of Parliament] The king's proclamation of August 23, 1775, calling for the suppression of rebellion, and Parliament's American Prohibitory Act of December 22, 1775, closing off commerce with the colonies and making American ships subject to seizures.

63.31   The two Proprietary Colonies] Maryland and Pennsylvania.

64.19   Coll. Whipples] William Whipple (1730–1785), delegate to the Congress from New Hampshire.

65.15   your Election in May] Referring to the election of councilors, the first for Massachusetts under the revised form of its 1692 charter.

65.30   taken [ ] into pay]   The manuscript is blank, but in an April 11 letter Abigail had informed Adams that "I have taken Belcher into pay" as a farm hand.

67.31   your Unkle]   Isaac Smith Sr. (1719–1787), a Boston merchant and ship owner, now removed to Salem.

67.38–39   James Cannon]   James Cannon, a mathematics instructor at the College of Philadelphia and one of the radical leaders who drafted the Pennsylvania constitution in 1776.

67.39–40   Cato is reported here to be Dr. Smith]   William Smith (1727–1803), provost of the College of Philadelphia, who was unsympathetic to the move toward independence.

67.40   a Match for Brattle.]   In early 1773 Adams had engaged in a newspaper debate about judicial independence with William Brattle, Harvard 1722, a wealthy landowner, military officer, and senior member of the Governor's Council. A selection of Adams's contributions to the debate can be found in the companion to this volume, *John Adams: Revolutionary Writings 1755–1775*.

68.12   The late Act of Parliament]   The American Prohibitory Act. See note 63.29.

68.31–69.16   Whereas his Britannic Majesty . . . depredations of their enemies]   As Adams rightly understood but few have remembered, this preamble was one of the most important contributions he made to the drive toward independence.

69.29   Mr. Duffil]   Rev. George Duffield (1732–1790), minister to the Third Presbyterian Church in Philadelphia.

71.4   a Relation of yours, a Mr. Smith]   Benjamin Smith (1757–1826), a distant cousin of Abigail; he later became governor of North Carolina.

71.7–8   Coll. Reberdeau and Major Bayard]   Daniel Roberdeau (1727–1795) and John Bayard (1738–1807), Philadelphia merchants and patriots.

71.16   *James Sullivan*]   James Sullivan (1744–1808), lawyer and brother of John Sullivan, who served as a delegate from New Hampshire to the Continental Congress and as a general; James Sullivan later became Democratic-Republican governor of Massachusetts in 1807–08.

71.25   Mr. Gerry]   Elbridge Gerry (1744–1814), Harvard 1762, merchant, patriot, and close confidant of Adams. In his letter to Gerry, Sullivan had called for abolishing property qualifications for voting for the legislature and for government appropriations to be determined by property owners.

73.7   Harrington has Shewn]   James Harrington (1611–1677), English republican political philosopher. A copy of his *Oceana* (1656) is in the *CJAL*.

75.2   *Henry Knox*]   Henry Knox (1750–1806), Boston bookseller who made a special study of military science and engineering and became Washington's commander of artillery.

75.13 those who think . . . Lord Drummond] Thomas Lundin (1742–1780), a Scotsman who used the courtesy title Lord Drummond, had moved to New York City in 1768. He sailed to England in late 1774 and met with Lord North and Lord Dartmouth, the secretary of state for the colonies, before returning to North America in the fall of 1775. Claiming to be an unofficial envoy from Lord North, Drummond met in Philadelphia with several members of Congress from New York, New Jersey, and Pennsylvania in January 1776 and negotiated the framework of a peace agreement. His attempts to arrange further negotiations soon failed, in part because of uncertainty as to whether his mission was authorized by the British government. In a letter of February 5, 1776, to British General James Robertson, Drummond used the phrase "those gentleman whose province it now is to think for the publick."

76.32–33 Warren or Montgomery] Joseph Warren, killed at the Battle of Bunker Hill on June 18, 1775, and Richard Montgomery, killed during the failed American attempt to capture Quebec City on December 31, 1775.

77.5 nullius Filius] An unacknowledged child, in this case referring to *Thoughts on Government*, which Adams had sent to Henry.

78.10–11 We all look up to Virginia for Examples] Virginia was by far the most populous, richest, and largest colony of the original thirteen, and without its vigorous involvement there could have been no Revolution.

78.18 The little Pamphlet, you mention] Carter Braxton's *Address to the Convention of the Colony and Ancient Dominion of Virginia* (Philadelphia, 1776), which had called for a governor to serve during good behavior and members of an upper house to serve for life.

79.4 *William Cushing*] Jurist William Cushing (1732–1810), Harvard 1751, was in 1777 appointed chief justice of the superior court of Massachusetts as Adams's replacement.

79.10–11 my Appointment to the Bench] In October 1775 Massachusetts appointed Adams chief justice of the superior court of judicature. Adams initially thought he would assume the office, but finally resigned in February 1777 when he realized that congressional business would prevent him from serving.

79.22 Sargeant] Nathaniel Peaslee Sargeant (1731–1791) refused appointment to the Massachusetts superior court.

79.24 Paine] Longtime professional rival Robert Treat Paine (1731–1814) turned down appointment to the Massachusetts superior court apparently because he had been ranked below Adams.

79.34 Lowell] John Lowell (1743–1802), Newburyport lawyer and grandfather of critic and poet James Russell Lowell.

80.1   Mr. Winthrop] Samuel Winthrop (1716–1779), brother of Professor John Winthrop and clerk of the superior court.

80.7   the Jus Gladii] The right of the sword.

80.15   this Eastern Circuit] From 1765 to 1774 Adams tried cases in Massachusetts's Eastern Circuit, now the state of Maine.

80. 34   my Nunc Dimittes] The first phrase, in Latin, of a traditional nightly prayer drawn from the story of Simeon in the temple (Luke 2:29–32).

81.27   *Nathanael Greene*] Rhode Islander Nathanael Greene (1742–1786) was commissioned brigadier general in the Continental army in June 1775; in June 1776 he proposed to Adams that Congress grant higher pay and pensions for officers and soldiers.

83.33–84.4   "Without attempting to judge . . . other Circumstances."] A quotation from Sully's *Mémoires* which Adams copied from a May 27, 1776, letter from Abigail. See note 19.14.

84.20   *Benjamin Kent*] Benjamin Kent (1708–1788), Harvard 1727, attorney general of Massachusetts.

84.33   Vinculo] A legal term for complete divorce.

85.12–13   ordered Church . . . to be let out upon Bail] Benjamin Church, the alleged traitor. See note 33.16.

85.20   Samuel Holden Parsons] Connecticut legislator Samuel Holden Parsons (1737–1789), Harvard 1769, was commissioned a brigadier general in the Continental army in June 1775; he complained to Adams of the problems of promotion among officers in the army.

87.16–17   New York must continue to embarrass the Continent?] Without clear instructions from the New York Provincial Congress, the New York delegation to Congress repeatedly abstained from voting on issues related to independence, to Adams's considerable frustration. On June 30, the Provincial Congress fled New York City in advance of the anticipated British invasion, not convening again until July 10; this prevented the New York delegation from participating even in the crucial July 2 vote for independence.

87.29   *John Winthrop*] Winthrop (1714–1779), Harvard 1732, professor of mathematics and natural philosophy at Harvard and an ardent patriot.

90.1   Mrs. Polly Palmer] Mary Palmer (1746–1791), niece of Mr. and Mrs. Richard Cranch (see note 104.12); Adams often used "Mrs." to refer to unmarried as well as married women.

90.12   Dr. Bulfinches Petition] Dr. Thomas Bulfinch (1728–1802), Harvard 1746, who inoculated Abigail and the children for smallpox in July 1776.

90.16–17   Mr. Whitney and Mrs. Katy Quincy] Massachusetts citizens who traveled to Philadelphia for inoculation. Katherine Quincy (1733–1804) was the sister of Dorothy (Quincy) Hancock, the wife of John Hancock.

90.22–23   our Friends refusing his Appointment] James Warren had declined appointment as associate justice of the Massachusetts superior court. Abigail had said that his wife, Mercy Otis Warren, was against his accepting the appointment.

93.6   The Second Day of July 1776] While the crucial vote for independence occurred on July 2, the celebrations Adams predicted of course occur on July 4, the day the final text of the declaration was approved and sent to the printer.

94.10–11   the Leaves of the Præceptor] Robert Dodsley, *The Preceptor: Containing a General Course of Education*, 5th ed., 2 vols. (London, 1769); in the *CJAL*.

94.31   Gays Letter] Adams may have come across this letter, presumably by the English writer John Gay, either in Dodsley's *Preceptor*, or in an edition of Pope's works; it is not clear whether the letter was written by Gay or Pope.

94.35   Rollins Belles Letters] Charles Rollin, *The Method of Teaching and Studying the Belles Lettres, or, an Introduction to the Languages, Poetry, Rhetoric, History, Moral Philosophy, Physics, &c.*, 6th ed., 3 vols. (London, 1769); in the *CJAL*. Rector of the University of Paris, Rollin (1661–1741) was a classical historian whose writings were read in England and America well into the nineteenth century. Both John and Abigail Adams were enthusiasts of his works.

96.8   *Dr. Witherspoon.*] Jonathan Witherspoon (1723–1794), Presbyterian president of the College of New Jersey (Princeton), elected a New Jersey delegate to the Continental Congress in June 1776.

96.16   *Clark.*] Abraham Clark (1726–1794), radical member of the Congress from New Jersey.

96.18   *Wilson.*] See note 13.32–33.

96.21   *Chase.*] Samuel Chase (1741–1811), member of the Congress from Maryland; an enthusiast for independence, he later was a Federalist associate justice of the Supreme Court.

97.6   *Lynch.*] Thomas Lynch (1749–1779), educated in England, a member of the South Carolina delegation to the Congress and a signer of the Declaration of Independence.

97.16   *Rutledge.*] Edward Rutledge (1749–1800), member of Congress from South Carolina, originally opposed to independence but then influenced his delegation toward it.

97.23   *Hooper.*] William Hooper (1742–1790), member of Congress from North Carolina and signer of the Declaration of Independence.

97.36   *Mr. Middleton*]   Arthur Middleton (1742–1787), member of Congress from South Carolina and signer of the Declaration of Independence.

97.38   *Sherman*]   Roger Sherman (1721–1793), a member of the committee appointed to draft the Declaration of Independence. Adams described him as "an old Puritan, as honest as an angel and as firm in the cause of American Independence as Mount Atlas."

98.39   *G Hopkins.*]   Governor Stephen Hopkins, delegate from Rhode Island. See note 10.34.

99.37   *Harrison.*]   See note 19.24.

100.3   *Huntington.*]   Samuel Huntington (1731–1796), delegate from Connecticut and a signer of the Declaration of Independence; he later served as president of the Congress and as third governor of his state.

100.14   *Stone.*]   Thomas Stone (1743–1787), delegate from Maryland and a signer of the Declaration of Independence; he did important work on framing the Articles of Confederation.

102.3   Mr. John Adams observed . . .]   This debate in the Congress was over how much each state would pay to support the Confederation that the delegates were trying to create and how many representatives each state would have in that government. Delegates from Virginia, Massachusetts, including Adams, and other populous states preferred representation in proportion to population for voting in the Congress. Most states objected and held out for the equal representation of each state, which was what carried. When it came to assessments of monetary contributions to the common treasury, the Northern delegates thought they ought to be based on each state's total population, including slaves. The Southern states objected, and suggested that each state's quota of contributions ought to be based on the value of land. The delegates from the New England states, where land values were high, objected, Adams being especially vocal in opposition. Although the Congress decided in favor of assessing each state's quota on the basis of land, that method of assessment eventually proved to be so difficult and impractical that in 1783 the Congress was forced to adopt requisitions based on population, with slaves, however, counting as three-fifths of a free person, creating the three-fifths proportion later incorporated in the federal Constitution.

103.25   Mr. Stillman]   Rev. Samuel Stillman (1737–1807), formerly of the First Baptist Church in Boston. An ardent patriot, he was a member of the American Philosophical Society.

104.10   A philosophical society shall be established at Boston]   Adams eventually made good on his promise by helping to establish the American Academy of Arts and Sciences in Massachusetts in 1780; he served as its president from 1791 to 1813.

104.12 Brother Cranch's] Richard Cranch (1726–1811) migrated from England to Massachusetts in 1746 and married Mary Smith, elder sister of Abigail, in 1762; he became Adams's "brother" when John and Abigail wed in 1764. He was a lifelong friend and correspondent.

105.4–5 the Anniversary . . . History of America] Adams is referring to August 14, 1765, when a Boston mob prevented the implementation of the Stamp Act in Massachusetts by intimidating, and destroying the property of, Andrew Oliver, the prominent merchant who was to be commissioned distributor of stamps. Confronted by his effigy hanging from what would become known as the Liberty Tree, Oliver resigned his commission—before it had even arrived from England—as would appointees in other colonies in the face of similar coercion.

105.8–9 the two *gratefull* Brothers] General William Howe, commander of the British army in North America, and Admiral Lord Richard Howe, commander of the British navy in North America. In a conversation with Benjamin Franklin in 1775, Lord Howe had expressed his family's gratitude for the memorial tablet placed by the Massachusetts legislature in Westminster Abbey in honor of his brother, George Augustus Howe, who had been killed in 1758 near Fort Ticonderoga during the French and Indian War. General Howe began landing his troops on Long Island on August 22, 1776.

105.27 Du simitiere] Pierre Eugène Du Simitière (1736–1784), Swissborn artist and antiquary.

107.3 The whole Force is arrived at Staten Island.] A massive British fleet, consisting of 30 warships with 1200 cannon, 30,000 soldiers, 10,000 sailors, and 300 supply ships, had been gathering off Staten Island since early July.

107.11 Austin] Maj. Jonathan Williams Austin, one of Adams's former law clerks.

108.4–5 Lt. Coll. Shepherd and Major Brooks.] In August 1776, Samuel Holden Parsons described Lt. Col. William Shepard as "a Man of great Spirit" who resented the individual appointed to command his regiment; Tudor had referred to Major John Brooks, not Adams's friend Edward Brooks, as Adams mistakenly thought. Few things was more frustrating to Adams and the other members of Congress than the squabbling that took place among the officers over rank and precedence. Adams was especially upset by the quality of those being appointed officers in Massachusetts.

109.33–34 Mr. Hazard] Ebenezer Hazard (1744–1817), bookseller and postmaster of New York City.

111.12 Knox and Porter] Henry Knox (see note 75.2) and Elisha Porter, a colonel in the Massachusetts militia.

113.1 Plan of Treaties] The Plan of Treaties, or the Model Treaty, was one of the most important documents of the Revolutionary era. In June 1776 Adams was appointed to a committee to draw up a model treaty that would govern the new nation's relationships with the other states in the world. Adams became its principal drafter, framing it as a treaty with France, the most obvious choice, and as a commercial agreement. The principle behind the treaty was the enlightened hope of the age that traditional military and political alliances might be supplanted by more liberal and peace-loving relations in which commerce would become the most important link connecting nations with one another. By emphasizing equality and absolute reciprocity of trade between nations, a limited list of contraband during wartime, and the principle of free ships making free goods in wartime (that is, the ships of neutral nations carrying non-contraband goods to a belligerent power would be free from seizure by other belligerents), the United States hoped to transform international relations while also promoting its own interests as a neutral trading power without a large navy.

Although the Model Treaty was initially designed for France, the United States was compelled by circumstance in February 1778 to sign a military alliance with Louis XVI, along with a commercial treaty. With the resumption of war between Britain and France in 1793, the challenge of maintaining the principles of maritime rights set forth in the Model Treaty would become the central question in American foreign policy for the next two decades, and dominate the presidential administrations of George Washington, John Adams, Thomas Jefferson, and James Madison.

116.34–35   exempt from the Droit d'Aubeine.]   The ancient right of the French kings to claim the property of foreigners who died within the country without being naturalized subjects.

125.11–12   They have abolished the oath]   The radicals who wrote the Pennsylvania constitution of 1776 required all voters to swear an oath to uphold the constitution. Not only did this disfranchise Quakers who did not swear oaths, but it angered those who were opposed to the constitution and wanted to change it.

125.22   Mr. Caswell]   Richard Caswell (1729–1789).

125.25–26   compleat Liberty of Conscience to Dissenters]   Virginia's declaration of rights provided for liberty of conscience, but final disestablishment of the Church of England in the state had to await Jefferson's famous bill for religious freedom enacted in 1786.

126.23   Loan Office]   On January 14 Congress established loan offices in the several states to sell government securities and to disburse and receive public moneys.

130.16–17   Mr. Carroll Barrister.]   The reference to Charles Carroll, Barrister (1723–1783), was to distinguish him from his more well-known relative

Charles Carroll of Carrollton (1736–1832). Both men served in the Continental Congress from Maryland, although not at the same time.

130.26   William Smith]   William Smith (1728–1814), Maryland delegate to the Continental Congress.

130.27   Dr. Lyon, Mr. Merriman]   Dr. William Lyon and John Merryman.

131.25   Philanthrop]   In the winter of 1766–67 Adams's friend Jonathan Sewall published a series of defenses of the administration of Massachusetts Governor Francis Bernard under this pseudonym. Adams replied with a series of twelve letters of his own, deprecating the superior tone of Philanthrop's calls for order; two of these letters can be found in the companion to this volume, *John Adams: Revolutionary Writings 1755–1775*.

132.25   his Business to this Place]   Rhode Island had dispatched Jacob Greene to Congress to seek remittance for expenditures on behalf of the United States.

133.32   Epaminondas]   Greek statesman and general Epaminondas (c. 418–362 B.C.E.) led the Theban forces that defeated a much larger Spartan army at Leuctra in 371 B.C.E.; he was said to possess a pure and noble character.

135.4   The Words of the Count La Tour]   At the outset of the Thirty Years War, Count La Tour led an insurrection in Bohemia against the Hapsburg prince Ferdinand II. He is quoted from Pierre Bayle, *The Dictionary Historical and Critical of Mr. Peter Bayle*, 2nd ed., 5 vols. (London, 1734–38), 5: 673, 675.

135.21–31   "The Princes of the Union . . . unfortunate."]   A quotation from "An Historical Discourse on the Life of Gustavus Adolphus, King of Sweden" in Pierre Bayle, *The Dictionary Historical and Critical*, 5: 651–682.

136.1   the Proclamations.]   The King's proclamation of August 23, 1775, declaring the colonies in rebellion, and his speeches to Parliament on October 26 and October 31, 1775, which referred to the Americans as traitors and to their rejection of conciliation as an insult.

137.2   Lurry]   Jumble.

137.29   Thou art the Man]   The prophet Nathan's accusation of David, from 2 Samuel 12:7.

138.25   The inclosed Evening Post]   The April 24 edition of the *Pennsylvania Evening Post* devoted its entire front page to a report from Congress detailing atrocities committed by British and Hessian forces.

139.25–26   the Alberts . . . the Grislers]   A typology of oppressors: Albrecht I, the first Hapsburg king; Philip II, Hapsburg king of Spain; King George III; the Duke of Alva, the Spanish officer who suppressed the Dutch revolt in the Low Countries in the sixteenth century; Herman Gessler, the

Hapsburg tyrant, probably legendary, who famously persecuted the Swiss patriot William Tell.

141.10   General Arnold, on Horseback] Recently returned to Connecticut from Canada, Benedict Arnold led American efforts to harass a British expedition after its successful April 26 raid of an American depot at Danbury. Arnold had his horse shot out from under him, and was promoted to major general for his bravery.

141.26   600 Men, Surprizes me, much] The action stemming from the Danbury raid resulted in American casualties of 20 killed and 80 wounded, while the British suffered a total of 154 casualties. Rumors quickly circulated of much larger British losses, however, including the following cited in Greene's May 7 letter to Adams: "The Spy sais our friends in Brunswick have receivd letters from their friends at N York giving an account of the Danbury affair. They write the Enemy lost Nine hundred kild wounded and missing."

141.36   Congress were too anxious for Ti.] Having sailed up the Hudson River from the British garrison at New York, about 500 British troops raided Peekskill, New York on March 23, 1777, destroying the small American depot there. Washington feared that this action was the start of a full-scale British effort to seize the Hudson Valley and directed several newly formed Continental army regiments to Peekskill and Fort Ticonderoga. The latter position fell on July 6 to a British army advancing from the north.

142.6   Strechy] Henry Strachey, secretary to the Howe peace commission. See note 59.14.

145.16–19   Mr. Dunlap has moved or packed up his Types.] John Dunlap (1747–1812) was the publisher of *The Pennsylvania Packet* as well as the printer to Congress.

145.17   G. Dickinson] Gen. Philemon Dickinson, brother of John Dickinson.

145.26   McDougal] Alexander McDougall (1732–1786), merchant and New York radical.

145.31–32   How has marked his Course] General William Howe had sailed with his army from New York on July 23, 1777, in a fleet commanded by his brother, Admiral Richard Howe. When the fleet reached Delaware Bay, the Howes were told by a British frigate captain that the Delaware River below Philadelphia was difficult to navigate and strongly defended. They decided to sail for Chesapeake Bay, and began landing troops at Head of Elk, Maryland, on August 25, 1777.

145.37–38   the Battle of the Brandywine] The British lost nearly 600 men killed and wounded in their victory in the Battle of Brandywine on September 11, 1777. Americans casualties were about twice those of the British.

147.22–23   our Flight from Philadelphia.] Howe occupied Philadelphia six days after this letter was written, on September 27, 1777.

147.34   Burgoine] General John Burgoyne (1722–1792) led the large invasion force from Canada which, having taken Ticonderoga, was to continue its march south in an effort to isolate New England from the rest of the colonies. He would ultimately surrender nearly 6,000 troops to the Americans at Saratoga on October 17, 1777.

148.13   by a blissfull Fireside] Fatigued by lengthy service in Congress, Adams had obtained leave and returned to Braintree on November 27, 1777 to reunite with his family and resume his law practice.

148.15–16   York Town] After adjourning in Philadelphia on September 18, 1777 in order to flee from Howe's army, Congress reconvened for one day, September 27, at Lancaster before reconvening on September 30 at York, Pennsylvania, where they met until June 1778.

148.18   half Jo's] Short for Johannes, the Portuguese gold coin worth £1.80 sterling.

148.32–33   Fiat Justitia ruat Cœlum.] Let justice be done though the heavens should fall.

149.29   *James Lovell*] James Lovell (1737–1814), Harvard 1756, Massachusetts delegate to the Continental Congress, where he served on the Committee of Foreign Correspondence.

149.34   a certain Commission] On November 28, 1777, Adams was elected by Congress a joint commissioner to France along with Benjamin Franklin and Arthur Lee, replacing Silas Deane, who was to be recalled. The commission sought French aid and diplomatic recognition of the United States.

COMMISSIONER TO FRANCE AND FRAMER OF THE MASSACHUSETTS CONSTITUTION, 1778–1779

153.4   Beneaters] Most likely Atlantic bonitos (*Sarda sarda*), a type of mackerel.

154.14   Captn. Tucker] Capt. Samuel Tucker, captain of the *Boston*, the twenty-four-gun Continental frigate that took Adams to France.

154.38   thought he should die] Lt. Barron died eleven or twelve days after his leg was amputated. Evidently Adams kept his promise to write the Congress on behalf of Barron's family.

156.25   Mrs Jesse and Johnny] That is, Masters Jesse and Johnny: Jesse Deane, the son of Silas Deane, who was going to Europe to be educated; and John Quincy Adams, Adams's eleven-year-old son.

157.2   Dr. Noel] Dr. Nicholas Noel, a French army physician.

157.13   C. Palmes]   Richard Palmes, captain of the marines on board the *Boston*.

157.28   Mr. Lee]   Arthur Lee (1740–1792) was one of the American commissioners in Paris who negotiated the agreement that brought France into the Revolutionary War on the side of the Americans.

157.29   Count De Vergennes]   Charles Gravier, Comte de Vergennes (1717–1787), foreign minister of Louis XVI's government and the official with whom the American commissioners most had to deal.

157.36–37   Suspension of Burgoines Embarkation]   The convention governing Burgoyne's surrender of his army of nearly 6,000 men in October 1777 provided that the British troops could embark for England on condition that they not serve again in North America during the war. Congress, fearing that these troops would simply release others to fight in America, refused to honor the convention, citing a series of alleged British violations of its terms. Most of Burgoyne's army remained in the United States as prisoners until the end of the war.

158.1   Count Maurepas]   Jean Frédéric Phélypeaux, Comte de Maurepas, King Louis XVI's elderly mentor, recalled to office after having been dismissed by Louis XV in 1748.

158.11   Count De Noailles]   Louis Marie, Vicount de Noailles (1756–1804), younger son of the Duc de Mouchy, served under Gen. Rochambeau (see note 415.32) in America.

158.19   Mm. Brillons]   Mme. d'Hardancourt Brillon, whom Adams in his Autobiography called "one of the most beautiful Women in France."

158.19–20   Voyage picturesque de Paris]   Antoine Nicolas Dezallier d'Argenville, *Voyage pittoresque de Paris* . . . (Paris, 1778); a copy of the 6th edition is in the *CJAL*.

160.7   Sir John Pringle]   Sir John Pringle (1707–1782), Scottish physician and friend of Benjamin Franklin; appointed physician to George III in 1774.

160.11   Mr. La Freté's.]   French family friendly to the American commissioners with a countryseat near Mount Calvarie.

160.17   Mr. Chaumonts]   Jacque Donatien Le Ray de Chaumont (1725–1803), wealthy French merchant and enthusiast for the American cause, deeply involved in war contracts. He offered accommodations to Franklin in Passy, to which Adams eventually removed.

160.18–19   Marquis D Argenson]   René Louis de Voyer, Marquis d' Argenson, author of *Considérations sur le government ancien et présent de la France* (Amsterdam, 1765), which Adams purchased in 1778; it is in the *CJAL*.

160.19   Marshall de Maillebois]   Yves Marie Desmarets, Comte de Maillebois (1715–1790), French military official from a distinguished family.

160.21   Mr. Foucault]   Jean Simon David de Foucault, the wealthy husband of Chaumont's daughter, whose house much impressed Adams.

160.24   Mr. Sartine.]   Antoine Raymond Jean Gualbert Gabriel de Sartine, Comte d'Alby (1729–1801), French minister of marine.

160.27   Mr. D]   Silas Deane (1737–1789), Yale 1758, agent whom Congress authorized in March 1776 to buy supplies in France for the American cause. Later he, Franklin (Dr. F), and Arthur Lee (Mr. L) negotiated the commercial and military treaties of February 1778 with France. Lee charged Deane with embezzling funds, and Congress recalled him later in 1778.

160.28   Mr. Iz]   Ralph Izard (1742–1804), wealthy South Carolina planter; when Tuscany refused to recognize his credential as minister, he joined the American commissioners in Paris and made life difficult for Franklin.

160.29   Dr. B . . . Mr. C.]   Edward Bancroft (1744–1821), Massachusetts-born secretary of the American legation in Paris; he was secretly in the pay of the British government. William Carmichael, a Marylander who acted informally as secretary to the American commission in 1777–1778 and later became chargé d'affaires at Madrid.

161.1   Sir J J]   Sir James Jay, physician and brother of John Jay.

161.5–6   Mr. McC]   William McClary, merchant from Baltimore.

161.11   Ld. Shel]   William Petty-Fitzmaurice, Earl of Shelbourne (1737–1805), later prime minister of the British government that recognized the independence of the United States.

161.26   Mr. Gerard]   Conrad-Alexandre Gérard (1729–1790), the first French minister to the United States.

161.31   Mr. Adams]   Referring to himself.

162.24   Mr. Garnier]   Charles Jean Garnier (1738–1783?), who seems to have had influence in the French foreign office and ties to Englishmen sympathetic to the American cause; Adams thought Garnier would eventually replace Gérard.

163.22   Chatham the great is no more]   William Pitt, Lord Chatham, died on May 11, 1778.

163.28   The Commissioners from England, who sailed]   The treaty with France caused the British government to attempt to negotiate a settlement with the former colonies. In April 1778 a commission headed by the Earl of Carlisle, and composed of William Eden, a member of the board of trade, and George Johnstone, former governor of West Florida, sailed for America with the authority to grant American demands short of independence.

165.31   Mr. Austin]   Jonathan Loring Austin, Adams's law clerk.

166.3–4   Dr. Holten] Dr. Samuel Holten (1738–1816), physician and Massachusetts delegate to the Continental Congress.

166.4–5   Mr. Paine.] Robert Treat Paine, serving as attorney general of Massachusetts, did not attend the Congress in 1778.

166.7   Dana] Francis Dana (1743–1811), Harvard 1762, member of Congress, in 1780 became secretary of the American legation in Paris.

167.26–27   The Resolutions of Congress . . . the Address to the people] The Resolutions apparently were the congressional report of April 22, 1778, dismissing British efforts at conciliation; the Address was the congressional statement of May 8, 1778, regarding the ratification of the Franco-American treaties that had taken place on May 4.

167.28   the Presidents Letter] The letter of June 17, 1778, written to the Carlisle Commission by Henry Laurens, president of the Congress, defended the France-American alliance and demanded British recognition of American independence.

167.28–29   the Message of G Livingston] William Livingston (1723–1790), governor of New Jersey; his message dealing with the ratification of the Franco-American treaties and the treachery of the Tories was published on May 29, 1778, and widely circulated.

167.29   the Letter of Mr. Drayton] William Henry Drayton (1742–1779), delegate from South Carolina, issued letters on June 17, 1778, dealing with the British peace commission.

168.8   Engagement between D'Orvielliers and Keppell] The indecisive battle between the fleets of the Comte de Orvielliers and British Admiral Augustus Keppel that took place on July 27, 1778, seventy miles off the coast of Brittany; it was the first fleet action of the war.

168.10   D'Estaing's Success] Charles Henri Théodat, Comte d'Estaing (1729–1794), the commander of the French navy in America from 1778 to 1780; he scarcely fulfilled Adams's hope for success.

171.23   unfortunate Events at Rhode Island] A combined American land and French naval assault on Newport in August 1778 was unsuccessful. With this failure, Admiral d'Estaing sailed for the West Indies in November 1778.

173.3–4   not much less I believe than fifty Letters] Only eighteen of these letters are known to be extant.

174.10   Fabricius] Gaius Fabricius Luscinus, Roman statesman of the third century B.C.E., famous for his austerity and incorruptibility.

174.11   Aristides] Aristides (530 B.C.E.–468 B.C.E.), Athenian statesman known for his impartiality and sense of justice.

174.22   Chesterfield] Philip Stanhope, Lord Chesterfield (1694–1773),

English statesman whose *Letters to His Son* became a popular manual for genteel education in manners on both sides of the Atlantic.

175.17   Modesty is a Virtue] The lengthy and impassioned criticism of the pursuit of fame in this letter was provoked by Warren telling Adams of John Hancock's efforts to build a faction around himself in Massachusetts.

176.35   Mr. Vernon] William Vernon Sr. (1719–1806), a Rhode Island merchant and leading member of Newport's Committee of Correspondence; he became chairman of the navy board for New England in 1777.

178.3   the Weathersfield Family] The family of Silas Deane in Weathersfield, Connecticut, where Deane lived and had his law practice.

178.15–16   to refuse a certain elevated Office.] The office of chief justice of Massachusetts, to which Adams had been appointed in 1775, but which he declined early in 1777 without ever serving.

180.5   But it is exactly equal and alike to all three.] Actually Vergennes was not withholding information from Franklin; he may have withheld news of Spanish policy from the other two commissioners because he did not trust Arthur Lee and was not sure where Adams stood.

180.23   Mr. D's Letters] Silas Deane and his letters to the press attacking the Lees and Congress.

181.20   Your old Friend] Arthur Lee, whom Samuel Adams fervently defended against Silas Deane in the Congress.

181.26   The other you know personally] Benjamin Franklin.

182.17   the other Colleague] Silas Deane.

183.1   The other Gentleman] Silas Deane.

183.12–13   An intimate Friend of his] Probably Edward Bancroft, secretary of the legation and a British spy, was the person who recommended Major Elias Wrixton, a former British Army officer; Wrixton sought employment in the Continental Army, but ultimately declined the appointment that Samuel Adams and others had secured for him.

183.33–34   the Minister and Consul] Conrad Alexandre Gérard, the French minister to the United States, and John Holker, the French consul in Boston.

183.35–36   your old Correspondent.] Arthur Lee.

183.39   The other Gentleman] Silas Deane.

184.32   Mr. Le Maire] Captain Jacques Le Maire, who carried goods and letters to America from France.

185.10   Clinton and Byron] Sir Henry Clinton (1738–1795), who early in 1778 had replaced General William Howe as commander in chief of the British army in North America, and Admiral John Byron (1723–1786), who in the summer of 1778 was ordered to reinforce Admiral Howe in America with thirteen ships of the line.

186.31   Mr. Wyth]   George Wythe (1726–1806), Virginia jurist who served in the Congress in 1776.

187.29–30   the Comte D'Estaing . . . their Politeness to you]   On October 21, 1778, Abigail told Adams that the Count d'Estaing had recently visited her and invited her and her friends to dine with him and his officers aboard his ship. She later reported that the evening was "An entertainment fit for a princess."

188.16–17   the unshaken Patriot you mention]   Mercy Otis Warren's husband, James Warren, who was always thinking of retiring from public office.

189.6   Mrs. Holker]   Wife of John Holker, the French consul.

189.13   Tacitus]   Gaius Cornelius Tacitus (56 C.E.–117 C.E.), Roman senator and historian who wrote of the luxury and corruption of the Roman Empire; his works had a profound effect on subsequent Western thinking about the health and sickness of states.

190.5–6   a little Friend of hers is the Clerk]   Eleven-year-old John Quincy Adams transcribed the letter.

190.11–12   Mr. Deanes Address to the People of America]   In 1778 Congress had recalled Silas Deane from Paris to answer charges of corruption leveled by his fellow commissioner Arthur Lee. Deane felt he was unable to get a satisfactory hearing from a Congress bitterly divided between his supporters and those of Lee, and in December 1778 he published an address "To the Free and Virtuous Citizens of America," in which he denounced his enemies and the Congress. Since Franklin enthusiastically supported Deane, and Samuel Adams supported Lee, Adams became even more suspicious of Franklin's character.

191.18   *Abbe C.*]   Abbé Chalut, elderly cleric; he and his inseparable companion Abbé Arnoux were enthusiasts for the American cause and taught Adams French.

191.19–22   Terruit Hispanos . . . vivito sicut ibi.]   Punning verses based on the life of the famous seventeenth-century Dutch admiral, M. A. Ruyter, who threatened the English in 1667 and died fighting the French in 1676. The verses, presumably written by Chalut, may be translated as follows: "Ruyter, who terrified the Spaniards, who terrified the English, and thrice fell upon the French, himself has fallen, terrified himself."

191.27–28   There are two Men in the World]   Arthur Lee and Ralph Izard.

191.30–31   there is another]   Benjamin Franklin.

191.36   G] God.

192.1   Mr. Grands.] Originally a Swiss family who had become bankers in Paris and Amsterdam; they had a country seat near Passy and were hospitable to Adams.

192.2   bien faché.] Very angry.

192.8–9   il est soupsonneux . . . le Monde est—] he is suspicious—he trusts no one. He thinks that everyone is—.

193.20–21   Cette un homme . . . bien connu ici.] "He is a famous man. Your name is well known here." The switch from the third to the second person may be indicative of the play of memory or of Adams's faulty French.

194.27–28   the Pieces signed Senex and Common Sense] A series of articles for and against Deane, published, beginning on December 15, 1778, in the *Pennsylvania Packet*; the articles attacking Deane were written by Thomas Paine.

195.3   Dr. Winship] Amos Windship, Harvard 1771, physician on the *Alliance*.

195.5–6   Dr. Franklin is sole Plenipotentiary] On September 14, 1778, Congress dissolved the American Commission in France and appointed Franklin the sole plenipotentiary.

195.29   Dr. J.] Mistake for Dr. F, that is, Franklin.

196.26   The Commissioners Proclamation] The Carlisle Commission issued a proclamation on October 3, 1778, warning that the war would become more severe if the Americans continued their alliance with France.

197.4   The Marquiss de la Fayette] Marie Joseph Paul Yves Boch Gilbert du Motier, Marquis de Lafayette (1757–1834), French aristocrat commissioned a major general in the Continental army by Congress in 1777; he became Washington's surrogate son and the most famous foreigner to fight on behalf of the American cause.

197.24   The Removal of Mr. Lee] Arthur Lee was acting as an unofficial agent in Spain trying to induce Spain to declare war on Britain.

198.7   Brother Lovel] James Lovell, Massachusetts member of the Congress and ally of Samuel Adams in the Lee-Adams opposition to Deane and his supporters. See note 149.29.

198.39–40   my Love to Mr. P.] Thomas Paine, who in the sixth number of his "American Crisis," dated October 20, 1779, had denied the claim of the Carlisle Commission that France was the natural enemy of the English-speaking peoples.

199.32   Their Proclamations are all alike] Referring to the proclamation of Gen. Burgoyne on June 22, 1777, a bombastic effort to instill fear in the inhabitants of the upper Hudson Valley in advance of his army's march, and that of the Carlisle Commission of October 3, 1778.

200.25   Our old incidental Agent]   Arthur Lee.

200.34   There is another Character here]   Ralph Izard.

201.12–13   the Dr. and Mr. D.]   Benjamin Franklin and Silas Deane.

201.38   the whole Alley]   The London stock market, or 'Change Alley.

202.20   especially my Wife.]   Abigail did continually protest that Adams was not writing her enough, with some justification, since he sometimes went weeks and even months without writing her.

202.21   The Address you mention]   Deane's address to the people of America, published in December 1778, attacking the Lees and the Congress.

203.2   that he will succeed]   Silas Deane, that is.

203.29   C.]   Congress.

204.29   I have the Honour to be reduced to a private Citizen]   In February 1779 Adams learned that the three-man American commission was dissolved and that Franklin had been named sole minister plenipotentiary to the court of Louis XVI. See note 195.5–6.

205.2   *John Jay*]   Prominent New Yorker John Jay (1745–1829) served as chief justice of his state, president of the Continental Congress, and, beginning in 1780, minister to Spain.

206.36   that Event.]   Jay had been chosen to replace Henry Laurens as Congress's president on December 10, 1778, after Laurens had resigned to protest what he felt was Congress's ineffectual response to Silas Deane's attack upon it.

207.26–27   Carmen Seculare]   A choral hymn written by Horace in 17 B.C.E. at the command of the emperor Augustus.

208.16   *Ingraham.*]   Matthew Ingram.

208.22   *Ford.*]   Hezekiah Ford, an Anglican clergyman in Virginia before the war. Although he claimed to have become an army chaplain, he seems to have left America under British protection. After many adventures and stories of being captured by the British, he made his way to Paris where he became Arthur Lee's secretary.

209.13   L]   Pierre Landais, captain of the *Alliance*; he had accompanied Bougainville in his voyage of 1766–1769.

209.29–30   Intrigue of Jones's.]   Adams thought that the famous American seaman John Paul Jones (1747–1792), Franklin, and Chaumont had schemed to delay his return to America, forcing him to sail in July instead of in May, when he had expected to depart.

211.25   Mr. Gimaet]   Jean Joseph Sourbader de Gimat, aide-de-camp of Lafayette in America.

211.28   I see C.J.Q. or C.B.]   The former refers probably to Col. Josiah Quincy; it is not known to whom the latter initials refer.

212.18   *Edmund Jennings*]   Born in Annapolis, Maryland, but educated at Eton and the Middle Temple in London, Edmund Jennings (1731–1819) had in 1778 moved to the continent and stayed there for five years, during which time he met Adams. He became an important contact, supplying information and news articles from London and planting pro-American pieces for Adams in British newspapers and journals.

213.6   Governor Johnstone.]   George Johnstone (1730–1787), British naval officer and former governor of West Florida; as a member of the Carlisle Commission he created a scandal by trying to bribe members of Congress.

214.28   Marbois]   François Barbé-Marbois (1745–1837), secretary to the Chevalier Anne César de La Luzerne, the new French minister to America sailing to his new post aboard *La Sensible.*

217.34–35   Mr. De Thevenards Table]   Antoine Jean Marie, Comte de Thevenard, commandant of the port of Lorient.

217.36–37   M. Franklin parle Francais . . . mieux que lui.]   Mr. Franklin speaks French well.—Oh, but, no, said the Chevalier, very bad. Mr. Adams speaks better than he.

218.2–7   Vous connoissez . . . possible de l'entendre.]   You know well the foundations of our language. You speak slowly and with difficulty, like a man who is searching for words, but you don't commit sins against the pronunciation. You pronounce well. You pronounce much better than Mr. Franklin. It is impossible to understand him.

218.38   Governeur Morris]   Gouverneur Morris (1752–1816), conservative New York member of Congress, who supported Deane in the Lee-Deane affair; when he lost election to Congress in 1779, he moved to Philadelphia. In 1781 he became assistant superintendent of finance for the United States.

219.16   M.M.]   Monsieur Barbé-Marbois. See note 214.28.

222.37   Russia and the Port]   France in March 1779 mediated a conflict between Russia and the Porte, that is, the government of the Ottoman Empire.

223.11   on the one Part the Emperor]   Joseph II (1741–1790), Emperor of the Holy Roman Empire, was the son of Maria Theresa and ruled with her over the Hapsburgs' Austrian-Hungarian Empire.

223.26–27   the Work begun . . . Cabinet of Versailles.]   On January 15, 1778, the Elector of Palatine signed an agreement with the Hapsburgs ceding Bavaria to the Austrian-Hungarian Empire. This provoked a confrontation between Prussia, supporting the heir to the Palatine Electorate, and Emperor Joseph. Mediation by France and Russia prevented war.

224.9–10   the late Family Connection]   In 1770 Marie Antoinette, a daughter of Maria Theresa, had married Louis XVI.

227.21   the Treaty]   Of San Ildefonso, signed on October 1, 1777. It paved the way for a defensive alliance between the kingdoms that would figure in Spain's decision to go to war with Britain.

229.38   the Compte De Schulemberg, to Mr. A. Lee.]   Probably referring to the letter of January 16, 1778, from Baron von Schulenberg, the Prussian minister of war, to Arthur Lee, in which he seemed to promise that Prussia would recognize American independence as soon as France did. In fact, Prussia did not acknowledge American independence until Britain did in 1783.

230.17   a shamefull Treaty]   Referring to the First Partition of Poland, February 1772, when Russia, Prussia, and Austria each annexed portions of Poland.

230.27–28   their late Declarations . . . interrupt their Navigation]   In March 1779 Sweden declared that it would provide convoys for its merchant vessels; in April the Netherlands made a similar commitment to protect its ships against British seizure. These actions prepared the way for the formation of the League of Armed Neutrality in 1780.

233.8   In a late Letter of yours to W. You quote a Letter to H.]   Referring to Warren and John Holker, the French consul in Boston. The letter that Holker received from an unspecified French correspondent suggested that Adams had failed in France because he "appears to be intirely devoted to Mr. Lee, who, as you know, is a sort of mad-man."

236.3   Mr. Genet]   Edmé Jacques Genet, editor of *Affaires de l'Angleterre et de l'Amérique* and "the first Comis," that is, clerk, of the foreign ministry's translators bureau. Genet often acted as a conduit between Adams and the French ministry, especially on naval matters.

237.5   Compte De Grass]   François Joseph Paul, Comte de Grasse (1722–1788), French admiral who made possible the Franco-American victory at Yorktown.

237.7   Mr. De la Motte Piquet]   Toussaint Guillaume, Comte Picquet de Motte (1720–1791), French naval officer who served under Admiral D'Estaing.

239.24–25   the Conduct of those . . . my Friends]   In April 1779 Congress adopted a report on the conduct of the American commissioners in France that referred to the "suspicions and animosities" among Benjamin Franklin, Silas Deane, Arthur Lee, William Lee, and Ralph Izard. The vote to include Adams's name among the commissioners cited failed to gain a majority of states, with Maryland, New Hampshire, Connecticut, and Virginia voting to include Adams, and New York, Pennsylvania, North Carolina, and South Carolina opposed; the Massachusetts delegation was divided. To Adams's amazement, both Samuel Adams and James Lovell had voted to cite him by name.

240.2   *Thomas McKean*]   Thomas McKean (1734–1817), Congressional delegate from Delaware and later chief justice of Pennsylvania, 1777–99.

242.6   Mr. D.]   John Dickinson.

242.29–30   Mr. B. Deane, wrote something by me to Dr. B]   Referring to Barnabas Deane, brother of Silas, and Edward Bancroft.

244.30–31   under the Auspices of Mr. Dunning.]   John Dunning (1731–1783), one of England's most distinguished lawyers and a supporter of John Wilkes's right to free speech.

246.26–27   Shakespeares Idea of Ariel]   Referring to *The Tempest*, I.ii.274–79.

247.2   certain Appeal to the People]   Silas Deane's address of December 5, 1778. See notes 190.11–12 and 206.36.

247.4   a Picture]   Almost certainly "Collapse of a Wooden Bridge," (c. 1770, 227 x 283 cm), a painting by the Italian artist Francesco Casanova (1727–1803). The painting hung in the apartments of the foreign minister at Versailles from 1775 to 1787. It is now in the Musée des Beaux-Arts in Rennes.

249.1   *The Report of a Constitution*]   The Massachusetts constitution was the last Revolutionary state constitution to be established. The General Court had drafted a constitution in 1778, but the towns had rejected it for a number of reasons, including its lack of a bill of rights and the failure to have it drawn up by a body distinct from the legislature. By calling for a special convention followed by ratification by the people in 1779, the Massachusetts framers set the pattern for subsequent American constitution-making.

The drafting committee of the convention turned over their task to Adams, and between mid-September and mid-October 1779 he created the draft that became the longest and most detailed of the Revolutionary state constitutions, and the only one still largely in effect today. Although he borrowed heavily from the previously produced constitutions, especially in drawing up the Massachusetts Declaration of Rights, the overall conception of the constitution was his. It expressed principles he had long espoused, including checks and balances, an independent judiciary, and a strong popularly elected executive with veto power over legislation—something that no other state constitution contained. He also placed limits on the legislature, changed the basis of representation in the lower house, and organized the written document into chapters, sections, and articles, which made the constitution much easier to read and refer to. He was especially proud of the section that declared that since "wisdom, and knowledge, as well as virtue" needed to be spread generally among the people, the government had the duty to cherish "the interests of literature and the sciences" and to encourage education and the inculcation of the principles of humanity and benevolence in every conceivable way.

The convention made some significant changes in Adams's draft. Instead of the governor possessing an absolute veto, his veto could be overridden by a two-thirds vote of each house of the General Court. Where Adams wanted the governor to appoint militia officers, the convention preferred the traditional method of election by the militiamen. The convention also rejected Adams's proposal that the governor serve no more than five one-year terms out of seven, and it broadened Adams's proposed property qualifications for legislators to include personal property as well as freeholds. More sensitive than Adams to the widespread notions of town autonomy, the convention rejected as well his suggestion that small towns join with larger ones in electing representatives. Some of the most important changes are noted, but the copy that went to the convention printed here should be compared with the final adopted constitution of 1780 in Francis N. Thorpe, ed., *The Federal and State Constitutions, Colonial Charters, and Other Organic Laws of the States, Territories, and Colonies Now or Hereafter Forming the United States of America*, 7 vols. (Washington, 1909).

249.20   Commonwealth]   A term borrowed from the Virginia constitution that better expressed the republicanism of the American polities than the more generic "state."

250.24   ALL men are born equally free and independent]   The convention changed this to "born free and equal."

250.38   GOOD Morals being necessary]   Adams later claimed that he did not write Chapter I, Article III.

256.3–4   AND the first magistrate . . . all the laws]   The most important article changed by the convention. It replaced Adams's absolute veto with a limited one.

260.15–16   of the christian religion, and]   The convention eliminated these words.

261.16   And forever hereafter . . . rateable polls . . .]   The convention eliminated the rest of this article.

262.25–26   unless he be of the christian religion]   The convention deleted this phrase.

266.6   THE Governor of this Commonwealth . . .] The convention made a number of changes to this article, in particular in regard to the governor's power to appoint militia officers.

268.17–19   no man shall be eligible . . . in any seven years.] The convention eliminated this provision.

272.21–24   Provided nevertheless, . . . both Houses of the legislature] In other words, the judges, like those in eighteenth-century England, were independent of the executive, but not independent of a majority of the legislature.

277.5   ERRATA.] Printing of the Report began even as the Massachusetts constitutional convention was still meeting. This list of "errors" records changes made by the convention in the Preamble and Articles I and II of the Declaration of Rights. (Line and page number are for this volume.)

277.23   equally and] The printer omitted "free" here. Cf. 250.24.

279.3   You think my Appointment ought not to be divulged] In September 1779 the Congress appointed Adams to be minister plenipotentiary to negotiate treaties of peace and commerce with Great Britain.

279.29   a Pamphlet] *The Report of a Constitution.*

279.34–35   unhappy affair, at Coll Wilsons.] On October 4, 1779, a group of Pennsylvania militiamen attacked the Philadelphia house of James Wilson (see note 13.32–33), a leading opponent of extralegal price controls and the radical 1776 state constitution, and a prominent legal defender of Tories accused of treason. Wilson had gathered about twenty friends and political allies inside his house, and in the exchange of fire between the two groups five attackers and one defender were killed. The fighting ended when Joseph Reed, president of the Pennsylvania executive council, arrived with a mounted militia unit and dispersed the crowd. In March 1780 the executive council pardoned all persons involved in the "Fort Wilson Riot."

280.9   Leonidas] The pen name of a writer in the *Pennsylvania Packet,* August 14, 1779.

280.36   The Appointment of Mr. Dana] Francis Dana was appointed to be Adams's secretary on his peace mission. See notes 45.39 and 166.7.

280.38–39   the Complaints against the Director.] John Morgan had been director of the hospital of the army, but opposition from William Shippen and others led to his dismissal in 1777. Morgan spent the next two years seeking vindication.

PEACE NEGOTIATOR WITH BRITAIN AND MINISTER TO THE NETHERLANDS, 1779–1783

285.8   in the Latitude of 43] Adams wrote to his daughter from El Ferrol, on the northwest coast of Spain, where *La Sensible,* the leaky vessel he and his sons had crossed the Atlantic aboard, had made an emergency landing. Adams's party traveled overland to Paris, arriving February 9, 1780.

286.32–33   Ireland . . . Use of this Machine]   The threat of French invasion in 1778 led to more than 40,000 men volunteering for militia service in Ireland. In 1779 many of the volunteers joined a mass movement against British restrictions on Irish trade that adopted a successful nonimportation agreement. Concerned about the possibility of armed unrest, in December 1779 the North ministry began removing restrictions against Irish trade both within and outside the empire.

287.3   Mr. Dalton's Vessel]   The *Fair Play*, owned by Tristram Dalton, was sunk in January 1779 by French batteries on the island of Guadeloupe. Dalton wanted compensation from France.

287.16   Mr. Lee, Mr. Wharton, Mr. Brown]   Arthur Lee, Samuel Wharton of Philadelphia, and Joseph Brown Jr. of Charleston.

288.25   I have received your Letter]   In a letter written the day before at Passy, John Quincy had outlined "my Work for a day." "Make Latin, Explain Cicero Erasmus Appendix [Supplement on the Pagan Gods and Heroes] Peirce [parse] Phaedrus. Learn greek Racines [roots] greek Grammar Geography geometry fractions Writing Drawing." But since "a young boy can not apply himself to all those Things and keep a remembrance of them all," John Quincy asked his father to tell him which he should "begin upon at first."

290.21   *Samuel Huntington*]   See note 100.3.

290.35   to produce a Congress in Fact]   Adams is referring to the extra-parliamentary county association movement in England in 1780 led by Christopher Wyvil that threatened the entire antiquated representational structure of the House of Commons.

291.26   the Sucesses of Admiral Rodney's Fleet]   On January 8, 1780, Admiral George Rodney (1719–1792) captured a Spanish convoy off Cape Finisterre, and on January 16 he defeated a Spanish fleet at the battle of Cape St. Vincent, capturing or destroying seven ships.

292.20   Sir George Saville threw out in the House]   George Saville and David Hartley were Whig members of the House of Commons sympathetic to America; Hartley, a friend of Franklin, was later appointed as a minister plenipotentiary to negotiate peace with the Americans.

294.26–27   "a Dissertation on the Cannon and the feudal Law."]   Reprinted in the companion to this volume, *John Adams: Revolutionary Writings 1755–1775*.

295.16   I have Reasons]   Adams was provoked by his reading of Thomas Pownall, *A Memorial, Most Humbly Addressed to the Sovereigns of Europe* (London, 1780).

296.2   *Elkanah Watson Jr.*]   An ambitious merchant, Elkanah Watson (1758–1842) came to Europe in 1779 looking for commercial opportunities, but eventually returned to the United States in 1783.

297.16–17   Mr. Williams and Mr. Schweighauser]   Jonathan Williams and John Daniel Schweighauser were U.S. commercial agents in Nantes.

298.6–7   Buffon, . . . whose Works you have]   George Louis Leclerc, Comte de Buffon (1707–1788), whose works concluded that the climate of the New World was deleterious to all living creatures. This pessimistic conclusion provoked Jefferson's spirited response in his *Notes on the State of Virginia* (1784). Two multi-volume editions of Buffon are in the *CJAL*.

298.12   Gov. Tryon]   William Tryon, royal governor of North Carolina.

298.29   Mr. D]   Francis Dana. Young Charles was approaching his tenth birthday when this letter was written.

299.14   The inclosed Dialogue in the Shades]   A political piece not found but described by Adams elsewhere as a dialogue "between the Duke of Devonshire, the Earl of Chatham and Mr. Charles York."

299.20   Mr. T's]   John Thaxter Jr., Abigail's cousin and Adams's private secretary on this second mission to Europe, served as tutor to John Quincy and Charles.

299.21   Mr. L. is coming here.]   Probably Henry Laurens.

300.27   *Thomas Digges*]   A merchant and member of a prominent Maryland family who became involved in clandestine trade through Portugal and Spain during the Revolution, Thomas Digges corresponded with Adams under a number of aliases and sent him English newspapers and pamphlets; he may have been a British spy.

300.33   upon Cs motion.]   Apparently Adams read in the papers that David Hartley and General Henry Seymour Conway intended to introduce motions in the House of Commons to end the American war.

300.33–34   It is the scene of the Goddess in the Dunciad]   An allusion to Alexander Pope's *Dunciad* (1728–44), probably to book 2, lines 368–370, where the goddess of Dullness stresses the heaviness of debate that soothes the soul in slumbers.

301.4   F. and S.]   France and Spain.

301.38   to the Leeks of Egypt.]   An allusion to Numbers 11:5.

302.17   F. R. S.]   Adams's first use of the pseudonym Ferdinando Raymond San as a signature.

306.5   *William Gordon*]   See note 20.7.

306.14   Mr. Jackson] Jonathan Jackson, Newbury merchant and member of the committee that drafted the Massachusetts constitution.

306.23–24   the first Essay] Referring to the proposed constitution of 1778 that the Massachusetts towns rejected.

307.30   Mr. Historiographer] Gordon was preparing his *History of the Rise, Progress, and Establishment of the Independence of the United States of America*, 4 vols. (London, 1788).

310.4   Lord Mansfield's Words] Adams is referring to the speech of William Murray, 1st Earl of Mansfield, in the House of Lords on December 20, 1775, in which he called for quick and harsh repression of the American rebels, saying that "if you do not kill them, they will kill you."

310.5–6   fas and nefas] Fair means and foul.

310.6   Delenda est Carthago] Carthage must be destroyed: a Roman rallying cry before and during the Third Punic War.

311.14   Mr. Johonnot] Gabriel Johonnot, Boston merchant, whose son Samuel Cooper Johonnot was being schooled in France under Adams's care.

311.24–25   Hutchinson fell down dead] Adams old adversary, former Massachusetts governor Thomas Hutchinson (b. 1711), died suddenly in London on June 3, 1780, the day after major rioting began in London. On June 2 Lord George Gordon (1751–1793), a leading anti-Catholic agitator, led a crowd of about 50,000 people to the Houses of Parliament, where he presented a petition calling for repeal of the Catholic Relief Act of 1778, which granted limited civil rights to Catholics who swore allegiance to the king. Although the crowd dispersed peacefully, rioting broke out in London later that night and continued for a week as mobs destroyed Catholic chapels, ransacked Catholic neighborhoods, burned Newgate and several other prisons, and attacked the Inns of Court, the Bank of England, and the homes of prominent persons, including magistrate Sir John Fielding and Lord Chief Justice Mansfield. At least 285 and possibly as many as 850 people were killed during the riots, and twenty-one persons were later hanged.

312.6   Govr. Bernard] Sir Francis Bernard (1712–1779) was Massachusetts governor from 1760–1769.

313.1   *Translation of Thomas Pownall's "Memorial to the Sovereigns of Europe"*] Thomas Pownall (1722–1805) was a former governor of colonial New Jersey and colonial Massachusetts who maintained a continuing interest in America. In 1780 Pownall published a pamphlet, *A Memorial, Most Humbly Addressed to the Sovereigns of Europe, on the Present State of Affairs, Between the Old and New World*. Adams's reading of the pamphlet prompted him to bring together ideas about America's relationship to the world that went back to his "Dissertation on the Canon and Feudal Law" of 1765 and the Model Treaty of 1776. Condensing and rewriting Pownall's *Memorial* helped Adams formulate a coherent and integrated vision of the extraordinary and bustling nature of the United States and its proper role in the world as the center of international commerce—a vision of a new liberal world order dominated by the free and natural exchange of goods and the end of the artificial dynastic rivalries and wars of the monarchical past. Indeed, there is probably no document in Adams's writings more revealing of his thinking about the unprecedented rise of the United States as a political and commercial power in the world than his *Translation of Thomas Pownall's Memorial*.

315.9–10   Foedere inaquali.]   A party to an unequal alliance.

316.27   Lord Bacon calls]   Francis Bacon (1561–1626), in "Of the True Greatness of the Kingdom of Britain" (1607–08).

327.31–32   Civitas incredibie . . . brevi creverit.]   It is amazing to relate how quickly the state grew once it had acquired liberty. Salust, *Conspiracy of Cataline*, 7.3.

332.17   Magni Nominis Umbra]   Shadow of a great name.

340.1–2   *"Letters from a Distinguished American"*]   These "Letters" were Adams's response in 1780 to Joseph Galloway's *Cool Thoughts on the Consequences of American Independence* (London, 1780 [i.e., 1779]), in which the former Pennsylvanian argued that recognizing the independence of the United States would be a disaster for Great Britain. More and more Britons, including Thomas Pownall, in his *Memorial*, and Josiah Tucker, the Dean of Gloucester, in his *Dispassionate Thoughts on the American War Addressed to Moderates of All Parties* (1780), were contending that Britain could profit from American independence since it could reap the rewards of American trade without the burdens of defending an empire. Galloway wrote in opposition to this kind of thinking, actually contending that the loss of America would so weaken Britain as to make it vulnerable to foreign conquest. Adams thought Galloway's pamphlet was ridiculous, but at the same time dangerous because it fed the delusions of those British leaders who believed that the war could be settled without complete American independence. Ultimately, however, he came to see Galloway's pamphlet as an opportunity to develop his emerging view that Britain and a fully independent America could prosper together in a commercially free world.

Adams was fortunate that the "Letters" were not published in 1780 when they were written, for they contained statements about the presumably temporary character of the Franco-American alliance that would have been embarrassing if his authorship had become known. Adams's correspondent Edmund Jennings published the "Letters" in London between August and October (with one in December) 1782, but Jennings curiously noted that they had been written in Paris in January–February 1782. Furthermore, he entitled them as written by "a Distinguished American" when in fact, as Adams noted in a letter to Jennings of September 16, 1782, Adams had written them

"with the Design of being printed as written by a Briton." The retention of
Adams's "We's, Us's &C." to indicate British authorship would thus seem
"very Odd," and would likely lead readers to conclude, as Adams lamented,
that the "Letters" were the work of "a Penitent Refugee" rather than a fervent American partisan. He also asked Jennings why the dates were altered.
"They ought to have more Weight for having been written two Years and a
half ago." But, he generously told Jennings, "No matter again. They will
serve to keep up the Ball."

345.17–18   Germain] Lord George Germain (1716–1785) replaced Dartmouth as secretary of state for the colonies in November 1775; he remained
in the post until February 1782, often quarreling with his American field commanders.

346.3–4   Sir Henry Clinton and Earl Cornwallis] For Clinton see note
185.10. Charles Cornwallis, 2nd Earl Cornwallis (1738–1805), British soldier
and statesman, later served as British governor-general of India (1786–93,
1805) and viceroy of Ireland (1798–1801).

346.16   their. . . .] Adams probably intended to use the word "King"
here (the ellipses appear in the original publication).

356.20–21   This treaty lasts no longer than this war.] This statement contradicted numerous statements by the Congress and the language of the
treaty itself.

358.36–37   "How sharper than a serpent's tooth it is to have thirteen
thankless children!"] This and the following quotations are variations on
King Lear, I.iv.310–11 and III.ii.14–15.

359.18–19   that "with wood, iron, hemp, mankind may do what they
please."] Popular sailor's maxim.

368.4   *cæteris paribus.*] Other things being equal.

372.39–373.1   sunk as we are in dissipation, avarice, and pleasure.] Lines
like these would certainly confuse readers about the character of the author
who, according to the title inserted by Edmund Jennings or the publisher,
was a "Distinguished American." Of course, Adams had intended the letters
to appear to be written by a Briton. See note 340.1–2.

379.33   De Mably] Gabriel Bonnot, Abbé de Mably (1709–1785). The
quote is from *Des principes des négociations, pour server d'introduction au
droit public de l'Europe, fondé sur les traités* (The Hague, 1767).

384.29–30   Lord Clarendon] Edward Hyde, Earl of Clarendon (1609–
1674), distinguished statesman who tried to reconcile the king and the
Parliament; when that effort failed, he moved to the king's side during the
Civil War. He returned to England with the Restoration of Charles II, but in

1667 was impeached and went into exile, where he wrote his classic account of the Civil War. Adams had adopted the pseudonym of "Clarendon" in a newspaper contest with "William Pym" in 1766; his side of the exchange can be found in the companion to this volume, *John Adams: Revolutionary Writings 1755–1775*.

386.10–11   Britain changefull . . . then drove away] Alexander Pope, *Imitations of Horace*, Epistle II.i, lines 155–56.

387.13–14   could obtain only 210 Names] After Charleston, South Carolina, surrendered to the British in May 1780, only 210 inhabitants petitioned General Clinton to swear allegiance as British subjects.

392.1   *Hendrik Calkoen*]   Hendrik Calkoen (1742–1818) was a member of the Patriot party in the Netherlands and very sympathetic to the American cause. Adams later described him as "the giant of the law in Amsterdam." Thinking of the Dutch revolt against Spain in the sixteenth century, Calkoen was curious about the prospects of the American Revolution. After meeting Adams at a dinner party, he wrote him on August 31, 1780, with a list of twenty-nine questions to which Adams replied with twenty-six letters written in October 1780. Since Adams was in the Netherlands seeking a Dutch loan, Calkoen's questions gave him an opportunity to address directly an influential member of the Dutch community. Calkoen did not publish the letters but instead used them to compose a talk he presented to an influential group of forty gentlemen in Amsterdam. Although Adams was unsuccessful in retrieving his original letters from Calkoen, he was eventually able to draw upon his drafts to see the letters into publication in London. They were published privately in 1786, first under the title, *Letters*, and later, presumably that same year, as *Twenty-six Letters, Upon Interesting Subjects, Respecting the Revolution of America. Written in Holland in the Year 1780. By His Excellency John Adams, while He was Sole Minister Plenipotentiary from the United States of America, for Negotiating a Peace, and Treaty of Commerce, with Great Britain*. The letters were first published in the United States in 1789.

394.17–18   where it finally perished.]   Actually, the tea in Charleston was ultimately sold to finance the war effort.

396.20   Boston to Savanna.]   This letter continues below with what Adams suggests are lengthy excerpts from Sir William Howe's *The Narrative of Lieut. Gen. Sir William Howe, in a Committee of the House of Commons, on the 29th of April 1779, Relative to His Conduct during His Late Command of the King's Troops in North America: To which are added, Some Observations upon a Pamphlet, Entitled Letters to a Nobleman* (London, 1780); however Adams actually quoted not from this narrative but from Howe's observations on Joseph Galloway's *Letters to a Nobleman, On the Conduct of the War in the Middle Colonies* (London, 1779). Amid the excerpt Adams injects a parenthetical correction—"(He should have Said Regulators)"—referring to a group of Scots-Irish vigilantes in the backcountry of North Carolina that rose in rebellion against fee-gouging officials and the underrepresentation of the western counties in the assembly. They were defeated by Governor William Tryon and eastern militia in the Battle of Alamance in 1771. Within the quoted material Howe refers to the following: Governor Josiah Martin (1737–1786), who replaced William Tryon as royal governor of North Carolina in 1771; Oliver de Lancey, a member of the royal governor's council and a prominent military figure in colonial New York who was, with his appointment as brigadier general in 1776, the highest ranking Loyalist officer in America; and Courtland Skinner, who was the last royal attorney general of New Jersey.

2. Your second Proposition is to shew that this is general, at least so general that the Tories are in so small a Number, and of such little Force, that they are counted as Nothing.

If Mr. Calkoen would believe me, I could testify as a Witness. I could describe all the sources; all the Grounds, Springs, Principles and Motives to Toryism through the Continent. This would lead me into great length: and the Result of all would be my Sincere opinion that the Tories through out the whole Continent do not amount to the twentyeth Part of the People. I will not however obtrude my Testimony, nor my opinion. I will appeal to Witnesses who cannot be Suspected. General Burgoine and General How. Burgoine has published a Narrative of his Proceedings in which he Speaks of the Tories. I left the Pamphlet at Paris, but it may easily be had from London.

General How has also published a Narrative relative to his Conduct in America. Page 49 General How says "The only attempt by Bodies of Men to form themselves in Arms, and to assist in Suppressing the Rebellion, happened in North Carolina, in the Spring of 1776, when it was absolutely impossible for me to give Assistance to the Insurrection. The Plan was concerted between a Settlement of highland Emigrants, and a Body of Americans in that Province, distinguished by the name of Royalists. (He should have Said Regulators). They engaged to obey the orders of Governor Martin, who proposed they Should operate in favour of the Troops from Europe, under Earl Cornwallis. The Loyalists promised 5000, the Highlanders 700, Men. The former insisted upon their assembling immediately; the latter urged the Expediency of waiting the Arrival of the British Troops, but yeilded to the Importunity of the Royalists, and repaired in Arms to the Rendezvous, Stronger than the stipulated Compliment. The Loyalists, instead of 5000, did not assemble a Twentyeth Part of that Number, and two Companies of these deserted, upon the near Approach of the Rebells. The Highlanders Stood their ground, and fought bravely, but being overpowered, were defeated with considerable Loss, and forced to disperse.

"My Letter of 20 Dec. 1776 was written before the Affair of Trenton, and I could have no reason to Suspect the Fidelity of those who came in, to Us from Monmouth; but I was Soon undeceived. Many, very many, of these Loyalists, were a Short time afterwards taken in Arms against Us, and others killed with my Protections in their Pocketts. In the Pocketts of the Killed, and Prisoners, were also found Certificates of those very Men having Subscribed a declaration of Allegiance, in Consequence of the Proclamation of the Kings Commissioners for a general Indemnity. These are notorious Facts.

"Various offers of raising Men were made to me, nor did I decline any of those offers that brought with them the least Prospect of Success; but I must add, that very few of them were fulfilled in the Extent proposed.

"Mr. Oliver Delancey, who was reputed to be the most likely man in New York, to induce the Loyalists of that Province to join the Kings Troops was appointed a Brigadier General, and authorized to raise three Battalions, to consist of 1500 privates, placing at the Head of each the most respectable Characters, recommended as Such by himself, and by Governor Tryon. Every possible Effort was used by those Gentlemen, not only in the districts possessed by the Kings Troops but by employing persons to go through the country, and invite the well affected to come in. Several of the officers (as I have Since been informed) anxious to complete their Corps, sought for Recruits, even among the Prisoners, who were then very numerous, and ventured to hold out to them the Temptations of pay, Liberty, and Pardon. Notwithstanding all these Efforts and Encouragements, Brigadier-General Delancey, at the opening of the Campain in 1777, instead of 1500, had raised only 597.

"Mr. Courtland Skinner, who was acknowledged to possess considerable Influence in the Jersies, where he had Served the office of Attorney General with great Integrity and Reputation, was also appointed a Brigadier General, and authorized to raise five Battalions, to consist of 2500 privates, under the command of Gentlemen of the Country, nominated by himself. The Same Efforts were made as for the raising of Delanceys Corps; but at the opening of the Campaign of 1777, Brigadier General Skinners numbers amounted only to 517, towards his expected Battalions of 2500.

"In November 1777 Brigadier General Delanceys Corps encreased to 693 and Brigadier General Skinners to 859—In May 1778 their progress was so slow, that the first had only advanced to 707, the latter to 1101.

"Several other Corps were offered to be raised, and were accepted, in the Winter of 1776, making in the whole thirteen, to consist of 6,500 men, including the Brigades of Delancey and Skinner. But in May, 1778, the whole Number in all these thirteen Corps amounted only to 3,609, little more than half the proposed complement, and of these, only a small Proportion were Americans.

"Upon our taking Possession of Philadelphia, the Same, and indeed, greater Encouragements were held out to the People of Pensylvania.

Mr. William Allen, a Gentleman who was Supposed to have great Family Influence in that Province—Mr. Chalmers, much respected in the three lower Counties on Delaware, and in Maryland—and Mr. Clifton, the Chief of the Roman Catholic Perswasion, of whom there were Said to be many in Philadelphia, as well as in the Rebel Army, serving against their Inclinations: These Gentleman were appointed Commandants of Corps, to receive, and form for Service, all the well affected that could be obtained. And what was the Success of these Efforts? In May 1778, when I left America, Colonel Allen had raised only 152 rank and File—Colonel Chalmers 336—and Coll. Clifton 180, which, together with three Troops of light Dragoons, consisting of 132 Troopers, and 174 real volunteers from Jersey, under Coll. Vandyke amounting in the whole to 974 men, constituted all the Force that could be collected in Pensylvania, after the most indefatigable Exertions, during Eight months.

"To make the Conclusion as easy as possible, I shall state a very Strong Fact, to shew how far the Inhabitants were anxious to promote the Kings service, even without carrying Arms.

"As soon as we were in Possession of Philadelphia, my Intention was to fortify it in Such a manner, as that it might be tenable by a small Number of Men, whilst the main Army should keep the Field, and Act against General Washington. To effectuate this Purpose, I sent orders from Germantown to the Chief Engineer, to construct Redoubts and to form the necessary Lines of Communication. That the Work might be expedited and the Labour of the Soldiers Spared, I, at the Same time directed him to employ the Inhabitants, and pay them 8d a day besides a Ration of Salt Provisions each, without which I was convinced they could not have been persuaded to have worked at all.

"Mr. Galloway, whom I had previously talked with upon the Subject had assured me there would be no difficulty in finding 500 men for this Business; and I presume he exerted himself to fulfil the Expectations he had given me. But with all the Assiduity of that Gentleman, and all the means made use of by the Chief Engineer, the whole Number that could be prevailed on to handle the Pick axe, and Spade, for the Construction of the Redoubts and Abbatis, amounted, each day, upon an average to no more than between Seventy and Eighty Men."

I have quoted to you General Hows Words, and one would think this was Sufficient to shew how much, or how little Zeal there is for the British Cause in North America. When We consider, that in the Period, here mentioned the English Army had been in Possession of the Cities of Boston, Newport, New York and Philadelphia, and that they had marched through the Jersies, Part of Maryland and Pensilvania, and with all their Arts, Bribes, Threats and Flatteries, which General How calls their Efforts and Exertions they were able to obtain so few

Recruits and very few of these Americans, I think that any impartial Man must be convinced that the Aversion and Antipathy to the British Cause is very general, So general that the Tories are to be accounted but a very little Thing.

The Addresses, which they have obtained to the King and his Generals when their Army was in Boston, Newport, New York, Philadelphia, Savanna and Charlestown shew the same Thing. It is well known that every Art of Flattery, and of Terror was always used to obtain subscribers to these Addresses. Yet the miserable Numbers they have obtained and the still more despicable Character of most of these small Numbers shew that the British Cause is held in very low Esteem. Even in Charlestown, the Capital of a Province which contains two hundred thousand Whites, they were able to obtain only 210 subscribers, and among these there is not one Name that I ever remember to have heard before.

I am Sorry I have not Burgoines Narrative, which shews in the same Point of Light, the Resources the English are likely to find in the Tories, to be nothing more than a sure Means of getting rid of a great Number of their Guineas.

I have the Honour to be, Sir, your humble sert John Adams

To learn the present state of America, it is sufficient to read the public Papers. The present State of Great Britain and its Dependencies may be learned the Same Way. The omnipotence of the British Parliament and the omnipotence of the British Navy, are like to go the Same Way.

405.7   Lycurgus's Hay cocks.]   See Plutarch, *Lives,* vol. 1.

406.36–37   are but Bubbles . . . to that Sea return.]   Alexander Pope, *An Essay on Man,* Epistle III, lines 19–20 adapted.

409.7   The People of that Country often rose in large Bodies]   Referring to the North Carolina Regulators. See note 396.20.

411.7–8   the Armies of Semiramis]   According to Greek legend Semiramis, the daughter of the Syrian goddess Derceto, was famous for her military feats.

415.32   Comte De Rochambeau.]   Jean-Baptiste-Donatien de Vimeur, Comte de Rochambeau (1725–1807), the French general who combined with Washington to defeat Cornwallis at Yorktown in October 1781.

415.33   General Gates]   Gen. Horatio Gates, the victor at Saratoga in October 1777, was given command of American forces in the southern theater in May 1780.

419.15   a Member of Congress]   Elbridge Gerry.

421.31   Chevalier de Ternay]   Charles-Henri-Louis Arsac Ternay (1723–

1780), French naval commander who transported General Rochambeau and his troops to America.

437.4 General Monk] Though commander of the parliamentary forces in 1659, George Monck (1608–1670), 1st Duke of Albemarle, facilitated the restoration of Charles II in 1660.

443.11 boxing the Children, upon every Turn.] Evidently this is as much as Adams told Abigail, at least at this time, of the reasons he withdrew their sons, John Quincy and Charles, from the Latin School in Amsterdam.

444.8 *Baron Van der Cappellen*] An important spokesman for the Patriot party challenging the quasi-monarchical Stadtholder regime of the House of Orange, Joan Derk, Baron Van der Capellen tot den Pol (1741–1784) was a firm supporter of the American cause. Adams's letter was a response to the anxiety expressed by the Baron about the Americans' ability to sustain their revolution.

445.6 The Capture of Charlestown] The British captured Charleston, South Carolina, on May 12, 1780.

445.28 The Defeat of Gates.] General Horatio Gates was routed by Lord Cornwallis at Camden, South Carolina, on August 16, 1780.

445.34–35 The inaction . . . De Guichen and Solano] Comte de Guichen, French naval commander, and Admiral José Solano y Bote of the Spanish navy.

446.13 The Defection of Arnold] Gen. Benedict Arnold fled to the British on September 25, 1780, when his attempt to turn over West Point to the enemy was discovered.

446.28 The Discontent of the Army.] The severe cold and hunger suffered by the troops of the Continental army at Morristown, New Jersey, in the winter of 1779–1780 led to mounting discontent, eventually resulting in outbreaks of mutiny.

447.1 Mr. Neckar] French finance minister Jacques Necker (1732–1804) borrowed heavily to finance support for the American Revolution.

447.10 The Depreciation of the Paper Money] The extraordinary inflation of America's paper currency by 1780 was, as Adams correctly pointed out, an unequal form of taxation that hurt mostly creditors and those on fixed incomes; those who moved goods rapidly were much less harmed.

447.17 G. Livingston] Presumably Gov. William Livingston of New Jersey.

450.7 Calkoens, Pamphlet] Calkoens had written pamphlets on behalf of the Patriot party against the pro-English Stadtholder party.

451.33 Will your Friend insert my Plan in his Leaf] Apparently Adams wanted Jennings to convince Dérival de Gomicourt to include Adams's plan for a Dutch loan in his *Lettres hollandoises, ou correspondence politique sur l'étate present de l'europe, notamment de la République des Sept Provinces-Unis*, 8 vols. (Amsterdam, 1779–1781). Vols. 3 and 4 are in the *CJAL*.

453.19 Mr. Tracy] Nathaniel Tracy, merchant of Newburyport.

455.1–2 *Memorial to the States General of the Netherlands*] Adams deliberately dated the Memorial April 19, the date of the battles of Lexington and Concord in 1775, though it was not published until May 4, 1781. Although the Dutch government had not yet received Adams as an envoy, and thus Adams had no legitimate diplomatic standing, he nonetheless went ahead with his *Memorial to the States General*, published in English and French as well as Dutch, with the aim of influencing public opinion. It may have been the most widely published piece Adams ever wrote.

465.27 *Robert R. Livingston*] A member of a distinguished New York family, Robert R. Livingston (1746–1813) served as the first secretary of the Confederation Congress's newly created department of foreign affairs.

466.23 the Treaty.] The Anglo-Dutch alliance of 1648.

466.24 Burgomaster Temmink] Egbert de Virj Temminck, burgomaster of Amsterdam.

466.25 Mr. Van Berkel] Pieter Johan van Berckel (1725–1800), first Dutch minister to the United States.

466.28 Sir Joseph York] British minister in the Netherlands.

466.34 Sir G. Rodney] Sir George Rodney (1719–1792), British admiral who defeated a larger Spanish fleet off Cape St. Vincent on January 16, 1781.

467.20–21 on fait tout . . . aux Anglomanes.] They were doing everything they could to sacrifice me to the English Party. See note 468.30–31.

467.22 Capture of St. Eustatia] On February 3, 1781, Admiral Rodney captured the Dutch island of St. Eustatius, which had been an important center of contraband trade during the war.

468.13–14 Six or seven months . . . appeared in Dutch] Rijklof Michaël van Goens, *Consideratien op de Memorie aan H.H.M.M. geaddesseerd door John Adams, en geteekend Leiden, den* 19 April 1781 (Amsterdam, 1781); this pamphlet advocated Dutch recognition of the United States only after the latter had reached a final settlement with Great Britain.

468.30–31 as there was in the Year 1748.] Since the death of William of Orange in 1702, the Netherlands had been governed by the States General, the representative body of the seven provinces. By 1747 the country was threatened by France and divided by factions with no clear leadership. This led to a call for English aid and to a resurgence of popular support for the House of Orange. With English backing, William IV was restored in 1748 as the hereditary stadtholder over all seven of the United Provinces and hailed the savior of the Republic. His supporters were known as the Anglomanes or the English party.

469.2   Battle of Doggersbank]   On August 5, 1781 a British squadron under the command of Vice-Admiral Sir Hyde Parker fought an indecisive battle with a Dutch convoy under the protection of Rutger Bucking at Dogger Bank in the North Sea.

469.18–19   the Emperor of Germany]   See note 223.11. Following the death of his mother and co-regent Maria Theresa in 1780, Joseph II was free to carry out a number of enlightened reforms within his domains, including issuing a patent of religious toleration in 1781. Apparently he sought to communicate with Adams under the guise of Count Falkenstein.

470.1–2   il abonde trop . . . il ne voit que lui]   He is too taken with himself—he is vain and conceited—he is full of himself—he is self-absorbed.

470.11   Duke de la Vauguyon]   Paul François de Quelende La Vauguyon (1746–1828), French minister to the Estates General of the Dutch Republic, and in 1784 minister to Spain.

471.9   Senior del Campo]   Bernardo del Campo, secretary to the Spanish foreign minister.

471.10   Colo. Laurens]   Lt. Colonel John Laurens (1754–1782), son of Henry Laurens, served as an aide-de-camp to General Washington and as a special envoy to France. He was killed in one of the final skirmishes of the war.

472.12   Mr. D'Alembert and Mr. Raynal]   Jean le Rond d'Albert (1717–1783), mathematician and co-editor of the *Encyclopédie*, and Abbé Guillaume Thomas Raynal (1711–1796), author of *L'Histoire philosophique et politque des établissements et du commerce des Européens dans les deux Indes*, 4 vols. (Amsterdam, 1770).

474.28   Mr Peter Paulus]   Dutch immigrant to the United States who carried a letter of introduction by Adams to Robert Morris. In September Morris complained to Adams that Paulus had requested money "to set up his Trade."

475. 21   Yours of March 20/31]   John Quincy had written to his father from St. Petersburg. When Francis Dana was sent to St. Petersburg in 1781 to induce Catherine the Great to recognize the United States, he needed a secretary who knew French, and he suggested John Quincy; the fourteen-year-old John Quincy found Russia was "not a very good place for learning the Latin and Greek languages."

476.6   Mr. Ridley]   Matthew Ridley, English-born merchant who had settled in Baltimore. He came to France in late 1781, bringing news of

Cornwallis's surrender at Yorktown in October. He moved on to the Netherlands in May 1782.

477.4–5   Lord Shelburne, Dunning and others of his Connections]   In May 1782 Shelburne was home secretary in the ministry of Lord Rockingham; upon Rockingham's death in July 1782, Shelburne became the prime minister. Like Shelburne, John Dunning was a Whig politician sympathetic to the American cause.

478.33–34   I wont go to Vermont.]   A reference to Abigail's plan to purchase land in Vermont as a country retreat.

479.4   *Philip Mazzei*]   An Italian physician and a vocal supporter of the American cause, Philip Mazzei (1730–1816) came to Virginia in 1773 and became a close friend of Jefferson. He returned to Italy in 1779 and became a secret arms dealer for Virginia during the remainder of the Revolutionary War.

479.27   confederated Neutral Powers]   Under the leadership of Catherine the Great, Russia, Denmark, and Sweden in March 1780 joined in an League of Armed Neutrality, claiming the right to trade with belligerents without fear of their goods being seized (except for a limited list of contraband), adopting a principle, similar to that expressed in the Model Treaty of 1776, that free ships make free goods. Its members threatened armed retaliation if any of their ships were seized. By 1783 Prussia, the Holy Roman Empire, the Netherlands, Portugal, the Kingdom of the Two Sicilies, and the Ottoman Empire had joined the League as well. Although the British fleet outnumbered all the ships of the League, Great Britain was diplomatically isolated for the first time in the eighteenth century and sought to avoid conflict with the League. Adams was suggesting in July 1782 that by accepting the United States as a member of the League, the states of Europe would be effectively recognizing the independence of the new nation.

480.35   Lady Macbeth uttered a Sentiment]   The following lines are from Shakespeare's *Macbeth*, I.vii.55–58.

483.2–3   the Spanish Ambassador expressed but the litteral Truth]   The Spanish minister at The Hague was Sebastián de Llano y de la Quadra, Conde de Sanafé and Vizcande. Adams loved the Spaniard's praise that follows so much that he conveyed it to others as well as to Abigail, always in imperfect French. It may be translated as: "The gentleman has struck the best deal in all of Europe. This recognition brings infinite honor to the gentleman. It is he who has frightened and confounded the English Party. It is he who has filled the nation with enthusiasm."

483.14–15   *Draft of the Memorial to the Sovereigns of Europe*]   This Memorial was probably initially intended for the Duc de La Vasuguyon, the French ambassador to the Netherlands. Adams decided not to send it but instead to remove the salutation, date, and personal pronouns and have it translated and published in various European newspapers and journals; it was eventually published in the *Boston Evening Post* of November 2, 1782.

484.26–27   the Mediation . . . proposed last Year.]   At the suggestion of Great Britain, Russia and Austria early in 1781 had offered to mediate the Anglo-French war. Adams was partly responsible for the French decision to decline the offer of mediation.

485.30–31   the Principles of the marine Treaty of Neutrality]   That is, the Treaty of Armed Neutrality. See note 479.26–27.

486.28–29   the late Revolution in the British Ministry]   Lord North had resigned in March 1782 and was replaced by Lord Rockingham, with Charles James Fox (1749–1806) as foreign secretary. But when Rockingham suddenly died on July 1, Fox, largely for personal reasons, refused to serve in the ministry of Rockingham's successor, Lord Shelburne. Fox's resignation split the Whig party.

487.37   Mr Alexander]   William Alexander went to London in winter of 1781–82 as an agent for Franklin.

488.1–2   commit an assassination of my Character at Philadelphia]   Adams blamed Franklin's letter to Congress of August 9, 1780, for two congressional decisions at his expense: the first, in June 1781, when Congress elected to create a joint peace commission in place of the commission of 1779 that had made Adams the sole minister responsible for negotiating an Anglo-American peace treaty, and the second, in July 1781, when it revoked his authority to conclude an Anglo-American treaty of commerce.

488.10–11   The anonimous scribbler . . . hurting Franklin.]   On June 6, 1782, Jennings had reported that he had received word of an anonymous letter that was supposed to be passed on to Henry Laurens, cautioning him about Adams's views of Franklin.

488.21–22   all that Burke says of shelburne.]   In a July 9, 1782, speech Edmund Burke had compared Shelburne to the wolf impersonating Little Red Riding Hood's grandmother.

489.17–18   I have planted the American Standard at the Hague.]   Referring to the agreements negotiated by Adams by which the Dutch contracted to lend money to the United States and to sign a Treaty of Amity and Commerce with the new nation; the treaty was formally signed on October 8, 1782.

489.35   Mrs. Rogers.]   Mrs. Daniel Denison Rogers, wife of a Boston merchant, who was traveling to Europe with her husband for her health.

490.11   Bell's British Poets.]   *The Poets of Great Britain Complete from Chaucer to Churchill*, issued in London by John Bell, beginning in 1777 and eventually running to 109 pocket-sized volumes.

491.29 Ridley] Matthew Ridley, merchant and agent for the state of Maryland in Europe.

491.34 D'Aranda] Pedro Pablo Abarca y Bolea, Conde de Aranda, the Spanish minister to France.

492.2 Oswald] Richard Oswald, British representative in Paris. John Jay ("J") wanted Oswald to recognize the independence of the United States before negotiating the terms of the peace treaty.

492.7 De Fleury has attacked De Castries] Two French officials: Jean François, Joly de Fleury (1718–1802), director general of finances, and Charles Eugène Gabriel de La Croix, Marquis de Castries (1727–1801), secretary of state of the navy.

492.9–10 De Choiseul] Étienne-François de Choiseul, duke de Choiseul (1719–1785), had been, as foreign secretary, the dominant figure in the government of Louis XV.

492.13 W.] William Temple Franklin (1762–1823), Franklin's grandson and longtime secretary, had been appointed secretary to the American peace commission on October 1, 1782. Adams was vexed that he had not been consulted in advance.

492.27 C de V] Vergennes. See note 157.29.

492.32 O] Oswald.

493.35 Mr. Fitzherbert] Alleyne Fitzherbert (1753–1839), British diplomat commissioned to negotiate peace with France and Spain.

494.13 Mr. Rayneval] Joseph Mathias Gérard de Rayneval (1746–1812), secretary in the French foreign office and younger brother of Conrad Alexandre Gérard, the first French minister to the United States.

494.17 Stratchey] Henry Strachey, British under secretary of state, was sent to Paris to harden what the government thought was the overly lenient attitude of Richard Oswald toward the Americans.

494.33 Mr. Morris's] Robert Morris (1734–1806), wealthy merchant and the Confederation Congress's newly created superintendant of finance.

495.15 Madame de Montmorin] Madame de Montmorin, wife of the French ambassador to Spain.

495.30–39 Je vous félicite . . . le Washington de la Negotiation.] I congratulate you on your Success, is common to all. One adds, Sir, my word, you have succeeded marvelously. You have gained recognition of your independence. You have made a treaty, and you have procured funds. You are a perfect success.—Another says, you have performed wonders in Holland. You have upset the Stadtholder and the English Party. You have advanced the cause. You have awakened the world.—Another said, Sir, you are the Washington of negotiation.

498.17–18   The Farmer General]   M. Chalut de Vérin, brother of the
Abbé Chalut, with whom Adams was very friendly.

498.25–29   "Monsieur   vous   etes   le   Washington . . . l'avez   bien
merité.]   "Sir you are the Washington of negotiation" was repeated to me,
by more than one person. I answered Sir you give me the greatest honor and
the most sublime compliment possible. —And Sir, in truth, you truly have
earned it.

498.32   Baron de Linden]   Dirk Wolter Lynden van Blitterswyck, former
Dutch minister to Sweden, was eager to be minister to the United States.

498.33   Messrs. Vaughans]   Benjamin Vaughan and probably his brother
Samuel. Benjamin Vaughan served as Lord Shelburne's observer at the peace
negotiations and helped the Americans secure British concessions; he later
settled in Maine.

499.18   Mr. Paines Answer]   Thomas Paine, *Letter Addressed to the Abbé
Raynal on the Affaires of North-America* (Philadelphia, 1782).

500.8   Mr. S.A.]   Samuel Adams. Barbé-Marbois, secretary to the French
minister to the United States, wrote a letter on March 13, 1782, to Vergennes
reporting that Samuel Adams was the leader of an anti-French faction in the
United States and opposed any peace agreement that excluded New En-
glanders from the North Atlantic fisheries. The British intercepted the letter
and turned it over to the American peace negotiators.

501.30   Mr. Fox and Mr. Burke]   Charles James Fox and Edmund Burke,
Whig political leaders who had been the most scathing critics of the North
government. Although Lord Shelburne was a Whig, his elevation to prime
minister in July 1782 split the Whigs. Fox left the government and formed,
with his old adversary Lord North, a coalition that gained power in April 1783.

502.5   Ld. Townsend]   Thomas Townshend (1733–1800), home secretary
in Shelburne's ministry.

503.13   Mr. Allen]   Jeremiah Allen, Boston merchant who had sailed with
Adams aboard the *Sensible*.

503.15   Capt. Barney]   Joshua Barney, of the packet *Washington*.

504.27–28   You will certainly have the Picture.]   A miniature of King
Louis XVI, that is.

508.12   Mr. Laurens]   Henry Laurens (1724–1792), South Carolina mer-
chant-planter who had become president of the Congress in 1777–1778; appointed minister to the Netherlands in 1779, he was captured by the British
at sea and imprisoned in the Tower of London for over a year. In 1781 he was
named to be one of the commissioners to negotiate peace with Britain. See
note 206.36.

511.36–37   "Thank God, I had a Son, who dared to die for his Country!"]
Statement Laurens made in a November 12, 1782, letter to Adams; his bright
and promising son, Col. John Laurens, had been killed in an obscure action
in South Carolina in August 1782. See note 471.10.

519.19   Mr. Williams of Nantes]   Jonathan Williams (1750–1815), Franklin's
grand nephew and the American commercial agent at Nantes.

519.25   Mr. Sam White]   Samuel White of Marblehead, Massachusetts.

522.14   C. Sarsfield]   Guy Claude, Comte de Sarsfield (1718–1789), a
French military officer with an Irish background who knew Franklin for many
years and had a special sympathy for America.

525.35   Mr. Brantzen.]   Gerad Brantzen, Dutch diplomat.

526.12   Mr. Harris]   Sir James Harris, British minister to Russia.

526.13–14   Prince Potempkin or the C. D'osterman]   Grégoire Alexan-
drovitch, Prince Potemkin (1739–1791), Catherine the Great's chief minister
and Ivan Andreyevitch, Count de Ostermann (1725–1811), the Russian vice-
chancellor.

527.32–33   England has been wise . . . to acknowledge Us]   England
recognized the independence of the United States after France and the
United Provinces had.

528.24   Mr. W. T. Franklin]   See note 492.13. Adams had wanted his private secretary John Thaxter Jr. to be named secretary of the commission.

530.38   were revoked.]   Congress's revoking of his commission was
one of the most humiliating blows in Adams's public career. He attributed
Congress's action to the influence of Vergennes.

531.33–34   and four other Gentlemen who could not attend.]   That is,
Franklin, plus Adams, Jay, Laurens, and Jefferson were named as peace commissioners. Only Jefferson did not accept.

538.27   Demerary and Essquibo]   Dutch colonies in Dutch Guiana.

538.28   Trincamale]   Trincomale, Dutch colony in Ceylon.

538.29   Negapatnam.]   Negapatam, Dutch colony in India.

539.20   yours of 23 decr.]   In this letter Abigail informed Adams that a
young lawyer named Royall Tyler (1757–1826) was courting seventeen-year-
old Nabby, as the Adamses called their daughter Abigail. Abigail wrote that
Tyler had led a life of "dissipation" for several years after graduating from
Harvard in 1776, but had now settled down. She sang his praises to Adams,
declaring that "he cannot fail of making a distinguished figure in his profession if he steadily pursues it." Moreover, she said, she was "not acquainted
with any young Gentleman whose attainments in literature are equal to his."
No one, she claimed, "judges with greater accuracy or discovers with a more

delicate and refined taste" than he. After failing in his suit of Nabby, Tyler went on to write *The Contrast* (1787) and other plays, and eventually became chief justice of the Vermont supreme court.

540.21   This Youth has had a Brother in Europe] Adams had met John Steele Tyler in Europe in June 1780.

548.30   Baron Van der Capellen de Poll] See note 444.8.

554.3–4   I could go home with the Dutch Ambassador] Pieter Johan van Berckel, who sailed for America on June 23, 1783.

554.40–555.1   Mr. Adams the President of the senate.] Samuel Adams had been elected president of the Massachusetts senate in 1781.

560.10–11   Mais Je ne Scais . . . Convenances et Bienseances.] But I don't know how to give in to such conventions and proprieties.

560.13–14   who "dares to love his Country and be poor."] Alexander Pope, "On His Grotto at Twickenham" (1741) last line, slightly altered.

560.26   Cato will never be Consull] Marcus Porcius Cato Uticensis (95 B.C.E.–46 B.C.E.), known as Cato the Younger, famous for his moral integrity; rather than succumb to Caesar's tyranny he committed suicide. Joseph Addison in his play *Cato* (1712) made the character familiar to the English-speaking world.

562.33   Storer.] Charles Storer (1761–1829), Harvard 1779, who had served without pay for several years as Adams's secretary in Europe.

563.5–6   Ld. G. Germaine] Lord George Germain, the British colonial secretary. See note 345.17–18.

564.32   a Fennings Algebra.] Daniel Fenning, *The Young Algebraist's Companion, or, a New and Easy Guide to Algebra*, 2d. ed. (London, 1751), in the *CJAL*.

565.8   Mr. Dumas's.] Charles William Frederic Dumas, American agent at The Hague.

566.28   Mr. Markoff] Arcadius Markow, Russian minister at The Hague.

567.18   Herreria . . . and the Duke of Berwick.] Don Ignacio, Conde de Heredia, Spanish minister at The Hague; James Fitz-James Stuart, 3rd Duke of Berwick, who married a Spanish women and owned estates in Spain.

568.8   Mr. Marbois Letter] See note 500.8.

568.23   Mr. Rayneval's Correspondence] Joseph Mathias Gérard de Rayneval, secretary to Vergennes.

569. 5–6   Duke de la Vauguyon] Paul François de Quelende La Vauguyon (1746–1828), French minister to the Estates General of the Dutch Republic, and in 1784 minister to Spain.

571.19   an Application] Adams is referring to the Dutch loan to the United States.

572.17   Spung] Sponge, that is, to expunge or default on the debt.

573.11   Mr. Smith] Isaac Smith Sr., Abigail's uncle.

579.1   Chaumiere.] Thatched cottage.

579.3   You Speak of a high Office.] Some opponents of John Hancock were apparently talking about Adams becoming governor of Massachusetts when he returned.

581.28–29   the battle of Naseby . . . Oliver Cromwell.] Oliver Cromwell defeated Charles II at Worcester on September 3, 1651, and died on September 3, 1658. The Battle of Naseby was fought on June 15, 1645; Adams may have confused it with the Battle of Dunbar, where Cromwell defeated the Scots on September 3, 1650.

585.35   Comte de Mercy] Florimond Claude, Comte Mercy d'Argenteau, Austrian minister to France.

586.32   Du Coudrai] Philippe Charles Jean Baptiste Tronson Du Condray, French officer who had a promise from Silas Deane of a retroactive commission of major general in the Continental Army.

587.2   Marshall M.] Yves Maris Desmaretz, Comte Maillebois, French officer who suggested the possibility of raising a corps for service in America.

587.4–5   hæc olim meminisse juvabit.] Maybe someday you will rejoice to recall even this. Virgil, *The Aeneid*, Bk. I, line 239.

587.10   Deane has at last let out the Cat.] In a series of letters written in the spring of 1781 and published in the fall of 1782, Deane claimed that France had refrained from fully supporting the American cause and had prolonged hostilities in order to weaken Britain at the expense of the United States.

589.8–9   the Duke of Manchester and the Comte D'Adhemar] The British minister to France and the French minister to Great Britain.

592.16   if the Ballon, Should be carried] Joseph Michael and Jacques Etienne Montgolfier had made the first public launching of their balloon in June 1783, capturing the imagination of the French.

593.2–3   which a former Proceeding had taken away.] That is, the revocation in July 1781 of his commission to negotiate a commercial treaty with Great Britain. See note 530.38.

595.1   Timeo Danaos, et dona ferentes.] I fear the Greeks especially when they bear gifts. Virgil, *The Aeneid*, Bk. II, line 62.

595.1–2   to send Ambassadors] Because ambassadors represented the ruler of a country and not its government, they were considered monarchial by many Amercans, and the United States did not appoint diplomats with that rank until the second Cleveland administration in 1893.

596.25   Mr. West the Painter] Benjamin West (1738–1820), American-born artist, who went to Italy in 1760, and then to Britain in 1763, where he eventually became history painter to the king.

597.25–26   innumerable Lyes about Jay and me.] Presumably Adams was worried about rumors that he disagreed with both Jay and Franklin over the treaty negotiations.

598.3   In order to drive out Shelburne] When Shelburne took over as prime minster in July 1782 upon the death of the Duke of Rockingham, Charles James Fox left the cabinet and joined his old enemy Lord North in opposition. In April 1783 the Fox-North coalition compelled the king to dismiss Shelburne and accept their ministry, nominally headed by the Duke of Portland (1738–1809). Despite Adams's opinion that this coalition ministry stood on very strong ground, it lasted only until December 1783.

SELECTIONS FROM THE AUTOBIOGRAPHY

603.1   Congress assembled] Adams began writing the first part of his autobiography on October 5, 1802. He advanced the story only to his admittance to Harvard in 1751 before abandoning the task. He took it up again on November 6, 1804, and over the next seven months he completed Part One, which carries the story to October 1776.

605.15–16   Mr. Bowdoins] James Bowdoin (1727–1790), Massachusetts statesman who presided over the state's constitutional convention in 1780; he was later the third governor of the state.

610.11–12   Mr. Matlock, Mr. Cannon, and Dr. Young.] Timothy Matlack, James Cannon, and Thomas Young: radical leaders who wrote the controversial Pennsylvania constitution of 1776.

610.29   Mr. Wythe] George Wythe (1726–1806), speaker of the Virginia House of Delegates in 1777 and one of the three judges on the high court of chancery in 1778; he was appointed to the chair of law at William and Mary, the first such chair in the nation. See note 186.31.

615.30   Marshall in his Life of Washington] John Marshall, *Life of George Washington* (Philadelphia, 1804–1807), 2: 402–03, 409–10. Adams mixed up the May resolve with the resolution of independence of June 7, 1776.

616.8   Essex Juntoes] The Essex Junto was a group of Federalists of Essex County, Massachusetts, who had been disappointed by Adams's presidency.

616.36   Edward Church] Brother of Benjamin Church (see note 33.16); Edward Church's "political Libel" against Adams was an anonymous satire,

The Dangerous Vice———, A Fragment Addressed to All Whom It May Concern. By a Gentleman formerly of Boston (Columbia [i.e., New York], 1789).

617.19–20   his Cousin Dr. Jarvis's Virulence] Charles Jarvis, Harvard 1766, Boston physician and supporter of Jefferson.

620.16   Mr. Morton] See note 13.35–36.

626.1–2   Lord Drummonds Letters] Lord Drummond (see note 75.13), sent letters to Washington and others in February 1776 proposing reconciliation. They angered Adams, for, as he described them in his autobiography, they were "a fine Engine to play cold Water on the fire of Independence."

627.36   When I asked Leave of Congress] This passage begins Part Two of Adams's Autobiography, which he started writing in December 1806.

628.22   Coll. Elisha Doane] Captain Elisha Doane, a Cape Cod merchant.

628.27   Mr. Langdon] John Langdon, delegate to Congress from New Hampshire.

630.33   Mr. Hooper and Mr. Lee of Marblehead] Robert Hooper and Jeremiah Lee.

631.35   Captain McIntosh] Capt. Peter McIntosh, captured master of the British merchant ship *Martha* (with its valuable cargo), was taken by the *Boston* in March 1778.

633.23   Mr. Bondfield] John Bondfield, commercial agent for the United States in Bordeaux.

634.1   Major Fraser.] John Gizzard Frazier of Massachusetts served as assistant to the quartermaster general in 1775.

636.24   Kamshatska] The Kamchatka peninsula in the Russian Far East.

638.10   Monsieur Le Vailliant] Possibly Louis Guillaume Le Veillard, who ran the mineral baths at Passy; he was an intimate of Franklin's.

639.3   Madam Helvetius] Anne Catherine de Ligniville, Mme. Helvétius, widow of the famous philosopher, Claude Adrien Helvétius, noted for her salon; Franklin proposed to her.

639.14–17   Toi dont l'ame . . . jouer de ma douleur.] You whose soul sublime and tender / Was my glory and my happiness, / I have lost you: near your ashes / I come to indulge my sorrow.

640.13   Sallust] Sallust (86 B.C.E.–34 B.C.E.), Roman historian best known for his account of the conspiracy of Cataline and the Jugurthine War.

640.31   Mr. Amiel . . . Mr. Austin] Peter Amiel; John Loring Austin, Harvard 1766, who acted as Adams's secretary in the summer of 1778.

640.31–32   Mr. Alexander &c.]   William Alexander Jr. and family, from Scotland.

641.30   the palace of Bellvue.]   Bellevue, the luxurious place built for Mme. De Pompadour on the Seine near Meudon.

644.21   Mr. Beaumarchais, Mr. Monthieu]   Pierre Augustin Caron de Beaumarchais (1732–1799), French playwright, most famous for *Le Barbier de Séville*, a merchant and a secret supplier of arms to the Americans on behalf of the French government; John Joseph Monthieu, French merchant of military supplies with whom Deane dealt.

648.19–20   Mr. Turgot or the Duke de la Rochefaucault]   Anne Robert Jacques Turgot, Baron de Laume (1727–1781), French minister of the navy in 1774–1776; a laissez-faire economist and author of Enlightenment works, he was opposed to financial support of the Americans. Louis Alexandre de La Rochefoucauld d'Enville, great-great-grandson of the aphorist, a close friend of Franklin, and a warm advocate of the American cause; he was stoned to death in 1792 by a Revolutionary mob.

652.27–28   Marshall Brolie]   Victor François Duc and Maréchal de Broglie, who apparently had aspirations to assume supreme command in America.

653.34–35   "Il faut s'embrasser, a la francoise."]   "They have to embrace each other in the French manner."

654.4–5   Mr. Jurieu . . . Mr. Duhamel]   Both of the French Academy of Sciences.

654.33–34   the Brother of the Duke]   A mistake of memory for "Nephew."

655.9–10   Mr. Malesherbes]   Guillaume-Chrétien de Lamoignon de Malesherbes (1721–1794), enlightened French statesman, who wrote on behalf of Protestants in France.

659.7   Dr. Watts]   Isaac Watts (1674–1748), popular English hymn-writer who also wrote many books, including *Logic* (1724), which was a popular guide against error in affairs of religion and human life.

663.5   Marli.]   Marly, ten miles west of Paris.

666.35–36   I leave this Enterprize to Mr. Burke.]   Edmund Burke, *Reflections on the Revolution in France* (London, 1790), contained a famous description of Queen Marie Antoinette of France.

667.33   the Tryal of Mr. Hastings]   Warren Hastings (1732–1818), governor-general of India, impeached by the House of Commons in 1787 for extortion and tried before the House of Lords; the trial ended with his acquittal in 1795.

672.2–3   appeared to me to have a personal Animosity . . . against the King.] Franklin did indeed have grounds for a personal animosity towards King George III. Unlike the other Revolutionary leaders, he had been personally humiliated by the King's Solicitor General in front of the elite of London at Whitehall on January 29, 1774. At the signing of the treaty with France in February 1778, Franklin deliberately wore the same old blue coat he had worn on that day in 1774, as he said, "to give it a little revenge."

672.7–8   Judge Fosters discourse . . . Seamen] The classic common law defense of impressment was given by Sir Michael Foster (1689–1763), judge of the King's Bench, in his *Report of Some Proceedings of Oyer and Terminer . . . and of other Crown Cases* (Oxford, 1762). *A Discourse on the Impressing of Mariners: Wherein Judge Foster's Argument is Considered and Answered* (London, 1777) was a tract put together by Granville Sharp (1735–1813), the radical English reformer, and Thomas Green (1722–1794), a political writer from Ipswich, in opposition to Foster's legal argument.

672.28   I mention this merely as conjecture] Adams's conjecture was not wrong. Franklin was indeed an intimate of Lord Bute, George III's former tutor and chief minister following George's accession to the throne. That intimacy probably led to the appointment of William Franklin, his thirty-one-year-old son, as governor of New Jersey in 1762.

673.18   On the Thirteenth day] Adams began "Peace," Part Three of his autobiography, in 1807; it picks up the thread of his narrative in September 1779.

677.3–4   Monsieur De Thevenot] Antoine Jean Marie Thevenard, commandant of the port of Lorient.

678.39–40   Captain Chavagne] Bidé de Chavagnes, captain of the *Sensible*, the French frigate that took Adams to Europe in 1779.

679.10   Sobrino's Dictionary] Francisco Sobrino was an eighteenth-century compiler of Spanish and French dictionaries.

679.24   Mr. De Tournelle] French consul at La Coruña, Spain.

688.33   The Children were sick.] Adams had with him his sons, twelve-year-old John Quincy and nine-year-old Charles. The other members of the party included Francis Dana, secretary to the Commission, John Thaxter, Adams's own private secretary and tutor for the boys, and two servants.

Index

THE LIBRARY OF AMERICA SERIES

The Library of America fosters appreciation and pride in America's literary heritage by publishing, and keeping permanently in print, authoritative editions of America's best and most significant writing. An independent nonprofit organization, it was founded in 1979 with seed money from the National Endowment for the Humanities and the Ford Foundation.

To subscribe to the series or to order individual copies, please visit www.loa.org or call (800) 964.5778.

This book is set in 10 point Linotron Galliard,
a face designed for photocomposition by Matthew Carter
and based on the sixteenth-century face Granjon. The paper
is acid-free lightweight opaque and meets the requirements
for permanence of the American National Standards Institute.
The binding material is Brillianta, a woven rayon cloth made
by Van Heek-Scholco Textielfabrieken, Holland. Composition by Dedicated Business Services. Printing by
Malloy Incorporated. Binding by Dekker Bookbinding. Designed by Bruce Campbell.

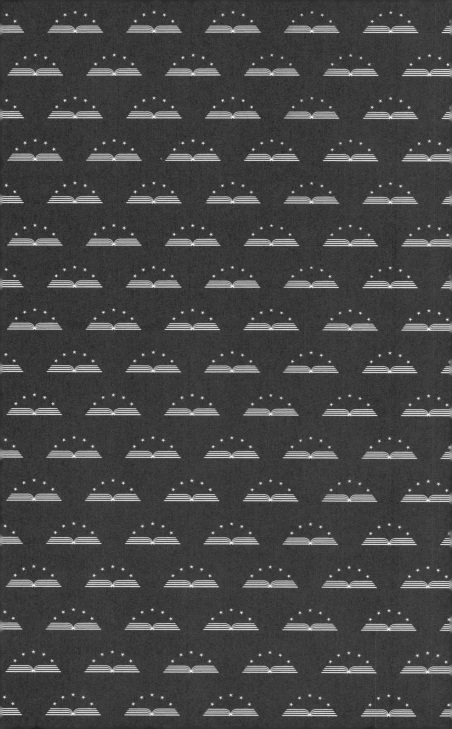